Palestine and the Palestinians

PALESTINE AND THE PALESTINIANS

A Social and Political History

SECOND EDITION

Samih K. Farsoun
Naseer H. Aruri

Westview
PRESS

A Member of the Perseus Books Group

Copyright © 2006 by Westview Press, a Member of the Perseus Books Group.

Published in the United States of America by Westview Press, A Member of the Perseus Books Group, 5500 Central Avenue, Boulder, Colorado 80301-2877.

Find us on the world wide web at www.westviewpress.com.

Westview Press books are available at special discounts for bulk purchases in the United States by corporations, institutions, and other organizations. For more information, please contact the Special Markets Department at the Perseus Books Group, 11 Cambridge Center, Cambridge, MA 02142, or call (617) 252-5298 or (800) 255-1514, or email special.markets@perseusbooks.com.

Library of Congress Cataloging-in-Publication data

Farsoun, Samih K.
    Palestine and the Palestinians / Samih K. Farsoun, Naseer H. Aruri.—2nd ed.
        p. cm.
    Includes bibliographical references and index.
    ISBN-13: 978-0-8133-4336-5
    ISBN-10: 0-8133-4336-4 (pbk.)
    1. Palestinian Arabs—Economic conditions. 2. Palestinian Arabs—Social conditions. 3. Palestinian Arabs—Politics and government. 4. Arab-Israeli conflict.
I. Aruri, Naseer Hasan, 1934- . II. Title.

DS119.7.F336 2006
956.9405'4—dc22
                                                                    2006000041

The paper used in this publication meets the requirements of the American National Standard for Permanence of Paper for Printed Library Materials Z39.48-1984.

10   9   8   7   6   5   4   3   2   1

For Katha and Joyce

Contents

List of Tables and Maps

Tables

Maps

Preface and Acknowledgments: Second Edition

Professor Samih K. Farsoun, who was born in Haifa, Palestine, in 1937, died unexpectedly on June 9, 2005, at the age of sixty-eight, in New Buffalo, Michigan, while beginning to update this book. The first edition of *Palestine and the Palestinians* (1997), written by Dr. Farsoun with Dr. Christina Zaccharia, immediately stood out as a shining star in the literature about the social history of Palestine. It dealt with Palestine as a society and Palestinians as a people during the past two centuries. The need for that general and comprehensive study stemmed from the fact that there was hardly one volume that incorporated all the important components of Palestinian economic and political history, the internal and external dynamics of the Palestine question, the Palestinian resistance to foreign occupations, and the ongoing diplomatic pretense called the peace process. It brought together significant developments affecting the people, their institutions, and society, historically and in the present. Some of the existing studies have dealt with the social consequences of the changed economic structure of Palestine in the nineteenth century. Other studies have concentrated on the land tenure system and the socioeconomic impact of European penetration. But the nature, structure, and dynamics of Palestinian society and the impact of Europe and the West throughout the eighteenth and nineteenth centuries had not been fully analyzed before this work.

Among the unique features of the first edition of this book, and its major concern, is the political economy of Palestine prior to the 1948 al-Nakbah (the Catastrophe). After 1948, the focus shifts to the implications and consequences of the Nakbah: rebuilding institutions; coping with dispersal, dispossession, and de-development; organizing a national liberation movement; and waging a diplomatic struggle. The ending of the book, which makes an assessment and critique of the Oslo process and its impact on the future directions of change for Palestine and the Palestinians, is both brilliant and courageous. It reveals meticulous scholarship and rigorous scrutiny.

Nine years after the publication of the first edition, Farsoun's words about the future remain eloquent and, unfortunately for the Palestinians, prophetic. He described the peace process as an absence of peace, as one that produced a veritable carbon copy of the Transkei (Bantustan) Republic of Apartheid South Africa constitution. He saw the road to Oslo as an Israeli project with Palestinian collaboration, to set up a legitimized structure of Israeli domination over the Palestinian territories based on both economic and political means.

I am deeply honored, though extremely sad, that I have been asked to assume the task of updating what Dr. Farsoun was cruelly prevented from doing. My dearest friend and colleague had just embarked on the process of chronicling the salient features of the past eight years when he was suddenly taken from us. I resolved to do my very best to complete the unfinished task, but I doubt that I will ever accomplish what he had set out to do.

The second edition involves not only updating but also the shortening of earlier chapters in order to make space for a considerable amount of essential new material. The original eight chapters of the first edition have been condensed to almost half their size, without, I think, undue impingement on the value of their historical summary and analysis. As a result, the second edition is able to include detailed and updated coverage of Arafat's legacy, the Road Map to Peace, and the Gaza disengagement, among many other recent and current issues and concerns. In addition, the second edition presents entirely new chapters devoted to:

- The Palestinians in Israel
- The structural flaws of the Oslo Accords, and the Second Intifada
- Jerusalem
- The right of refugees to return to their homes and property

Specifically, the new organization of the second edition reflects the following considerations:

- Chapter 5, which covers the Palestinians in Israel, appears here much condensed from the form in which it was originally written in Arabic by Dr. Farsoun before he could finish incorporating it into the present edition.

- Chapter 8, dealing with the structure and dynamics of the Oslo Accords, has been thoroughly revised.
- Chapter 9, analyzing the structural flaws of Oslo and their contributions to the Second Intifada, has been thoroughly revised, restructured, and updated.
- Chapter 10, on the Palestinian refugees and their right of return, is a new chapter that, with the new Chapter 5, now completes the book's coverage of the three fragmented components of the Palestinians: those under occupation in the West Bank and Gaza, the Palestinian community in Israel proper, and the more than five million refugees in exile.
- The new Chapter 11 on Jerusalem and its transformation covers Jerusalem's unique role for Palestine and the Palestinians. Both Chapters 10 and 11 follow Chapter 9 in the book's principally chronological organization because the refugees and Jerusalem were both designated as final status issues by the Oslo agreements, and in fact both reflect the structural flaws of Oslo (which constitute the subject of Chapter 9).
- Like Chapters 10 and 11, Chapter 12 is new to the second edition. It brings the diplomatic dimensions up-to-date, treating the salient issues that span the period between Camp David (2000) and the Gaza disengagement (2005). It analyzes the Road Map and the policies of the George W. Bush administration, which seem to have embraced the worldview of Ariel Sharon by setting aside the entire Oslo process, and by acquiescing in Sharon's unilateralism and his strategy of removing bilateral negotiations from the "peace process."
- The last chapter, Chapter 13, is also a new addition that considers the future of Palestine and the Palestinians, particularly after the demise of Yasser Arafat in November 2004. It examines alternatives to the two-state solution, which seems to have run its course under the impact of a US policy that has dealt a crippling blow to the idea of a viable Palestinian state. The chapter raises the question of whether the architects of Oslo have unwittingly paved the way to a binational solution and a single pluralistic state for Arabs and Jews in what the former call historic Palestine and the latter call Eretz Israel.

I wish to acknowledge my deep gratitude to certain individuals whose assistance was indeed very crucial. The task of condensation was nothing less than prodigious. The greatest contribution in that area belonged incontestably to Karl Yambert, senior editor at Westview Press, who handled that task with great proficiency, momentum, and effectiveness. Margaret Ritchie has done superb work copyediting the entire manuscript. Katha Kissman, the widow of Professor Farsoun, maintained a strong interest in this edition and provided various types of assistance, particularly in utilizing her computer skills, which kept me organized. Her support and substantive help gave me encouragement in the midst of shared grief and bewilderment. Sincere gratitude goes to the Jerusalem-based Palestinian Academic Society for the Study of International Affairs (Passia) and its board chairman, Dr. Mahdi Abdul Hadi, as well as the webmaster, Mr. Mahmoud Abu Rmeileh, for their kind permission to use many of the maps that appear in this book. Thanks also to Ruth Cardona, a senior majoring in international affairs and Middle Eastern studies at George Washington University. Samar Asad, Director of the Jerusalem Fund/Palestine Center in Washington, D.C., was kind enough to share the time and skills of student interns, who worked on new tables and maps. My wife Joyce's unremitting support during a difficult period and painful times helped make the sudden and unexpected undertaking of this project not only satisfying, but a powerful testimony to our dear friend, Samih Farsoun.

Naseer H. Aruri

Preface and Acknowledgments:
First Edition

The Palestine question and the Arab-Israeli conflict have generated an enormous amount of literature over the years. Most of it, often partisan and polemical, has been concerned with political history, international relations, and current developments in the conflict. More recent studies deal with the Palestinians themselves, especially the politics and internal dynamics of the Palestine Liberation Organization (PLO). The Palestinian uprising (intifada) against the Israeli occupation of the West Bank and the Gaza Strip also generated many worthwhile analyses, and there have been numerous studies on the social organization, political economy, and varied social aspects of different periods of Palestine's history and of the occupied territories. Far fewer studies have focused on the varied diaspora Palestinian communities. Together, the extensive published and unpublished works (in the form of reports, doctoral dissertations, and master's theses) provide us with a relatively comprehensive if not a truly complete overview of Palestine and the Palestinians.

Nevertheless, we believed that a single volume that tied together the various strands of knowledge about Palestine and the Palestinians historically and in the present was still missing. This book is a political economy of Palestine prior to the Catastrophe (al-Nakbah in Arabic) of the destruction of Palestinian society in 1948 and, since then, of the Palestinian communities, their institutions, and their national liberation movement and the intifada of those under occupation. It also offers an assessment of the Israel-PLO accords and their consequences for the Palestinian future.

However, an important caveat must be noted at the outset. In the post-1948 era, the Palestinian people and their patrimony were dismembered, and three Palestinian population groupings, vastly unequal in size and varied in structure, emerged. The largest is the diaspora, or refugee communities; the second is made up of the Palestinians in the Israeli-occupied areas of Palestine called the West Bank and the Gaza Strip; the third and smallest is the Palestinian community that remained on its land inside Israel after Israel emerged. These Palestinians with Israeli citizenship are what Israel and many Western scholars call the Israeli Arabs. More than 0.75 million people (out of a total Palestinian population of 6.8 million in 1996), about 17 percent of the population of Israel, these Palestinians came to play an increasingly important role both inside 1948–1967 Israel and with regard to their Palestinian compatriots outside its borders. Because of space considerations, we do not analyze the structure, dynamics, and influence of the Palestinian community in Israel.

In writing this overview of the political economy of Palestine and the Palestinians, we have relied on a large number of historical and contemporary source materials. Christina Zacharia researched and wrote Chapter 7, "Palestinian Resistance to Israeli Occupation: The First Intifada." In addition, she helped in revising and editing much of the manuscript and in preparing tables. She has been a keen critic and an untiring coworker.

This work would not have been possible without the help of many institutions and individuals, including the American University in Washington, D.C.; the School of Oriental and African Studies (SOAS) in London; and the Institute for Palestine Studies (IPS) and the Center for Policy Analysis on Palestine (now the Palestine Center), which are both in Washington, D.C., and both of which offered invaluable research facilities and sources. We wish to thank Naomi Baron and the Mellon Grant Program of the College of Arts and Sciences of the American University and especially Ramzi A. Dalloul of London for research funds.

We are also grateful to the numerous individuals who assisted with or contributed to this project in one way or another, in particular Anita DePree, Heidi Shoup, Georgina Copty, Michael F. Brown, Helen Koustenis, Michael Webb, Greg Welsh, Kyu Bum Lee, Katherine Zacharia, Philip Mattar, Heather Henyon, George Abed, and Bill Vornberger; Barbara Ellington and Laura Parsons of Westview Press; and copyeditor Alice Colwell. Naseer Aruri of the University of Massachusetts at Dartmouth provided us with many important materials, commented on a number of chapters, and has offered much encouragement and support over the years of our friendship. Naji 'Allush kindly allowed us to use two of his tables. Special thanks also go to Katha Kissman for her extensive help.

We wish to thank the following publishers and institutions for permission to reprint or reproduce tables and maps: Addison-Wesley, Longman, Harlow, UK; Americans for Middle East Understanding, Inc., New York; Cambridge University Press, New York; the Center for Policy Analysis on

Palestine, Washington, D.C.; Foundation for Middle East Peace, Washington, D.C.; Indiana University Press, Bloomington; Institute for Palestine Studies, Washington, D.C.; International and Area Studies, University of California, Berkeley; Magnes Press, Jerusalem; Princeton University Press, Princeton, New Jersey; Routledge, London; United Nations Educational, Scientific, and Cultural Organization (UNESCO), Paris; United Nations Relief and Works Agency (UNRWA), New York; World Bank, New York; Yale University Press, New Haven, Connecticut; and Zed Books, London.

Finally, to many others we cannot name here, we extend our gratitude. Named or unnamed, of course, those who helped us bear no blame for any errors, omissions, interpretations, or conclusions of this book. Those remain our responsibility.

Samih K. Farsoun
Christina E. Zacharia

Acronyms

ADP	Arab Democratic Party
AHC	Arab Higher Committee
AIPAC	American Israel Public Affairs Committee
ALNL	Arab League for National Liberation
CA	Civil Administration
CIVITAS	Civic Structures for the Palestinian Refugee Camps and Exile Communities
COHRE	Centre on Housing Rights and Evictions
CPI	Communist Party of Israel
DFLP	Democratic Front for the Liberation of Palestine
DOP	Declaration of Principles (the first Oslo Accord)
EU	European Union
FATU	Federation of Arab Trade Unions
GDP	gross domestic product
GNP	gross national product
ICA	Jewish Colonization Association
ICJ	International Court of Justice
IMF	International Monetary Fund
IPC	Iraq Petroleum Company
JNF	Jewish National Fund
LNM	Lebanese National Movement
MAN	Movement of Arab Nationalists (also called Arab Nationalist Movement, ANM)
MOF	Ministry of Finance
MOSA	Ministry of Social Affairs
NDA	National Democratic Assembly
NGC	National Guidance Committee
NGO	nongovernmental organization
OETA	Occupied Enemy Territory Administration

PA	Palestinian Authority
PANU	Palestine Arab National Union
PAWS	Palestine Arab Workers Society
PCBS	Palestinian Central Bureau of Statistics
PCP	Palestine Communist Party
PDC	Palestinian Democratic Coalition
PDP	Palestinian Development Programme
PECDAR	Palestine Economic Council for Development and Reconstruction
PFLP	Popular Front for the Liberation of Palestine
PICA	Palestine Jewish Colonization Association
PISGA	Palestinian Interim Self-Governing Authority
PLA	Palestine Liberation Army
PLC	Palestinian Legislative Council
PLDC	Palestine Land Development Company
PLO	Palestine Liberation Organization
PLP	Progressive List for Peace
PNA	Palestinian National Authority
PNC	Palestine National Council
PNF	Palestine National Front
PPP	Palestine People's Party
PRM	Palestinian Resistance Movement; the Resistance
UN	United Nations
UNCCP	United Nations Conciliation Commission on Palestine
UNCTAD	United Nations Conference on Trade and Development
UNGA	United Nations General Assembly
UNLU	Unified National Leadership of the Uprising
UNRWA	United Nations Relief and Works Agency
WZO	World Zionist Organization

1

The Question of Palestine and the Palestinians

Palestine is a small territory, and the Palestinians—the indigenous Arab people of Palestine—are a relatively small population, numbering nine million in 2005. Yet the Palestinian problem has loomed large on the international scene for nearly sixty years, with tangled roots over a century old. Since 1948, the Arab-Israeli conflict has been punctuated by a major war nearly every decade and countless invasions, incursions, clashes, and skirmishes, producing regional and global tensions and even threatening world peace during the cold war. Indeed, since the advent of the nuclear age, the only known nuclear war alert was issued by the United States during the fourth major Israeli-Arab war, the October War of 1973.

The question of Palestine and the Palestinians continues to be central in international affairs, as the United States, China and the Pacific Rim, and the European Union (EU) compete for economic domination in the emerging new world order. The hegemony of industrial and postindustrial societies depends upon oil, a commodity entangled in the volatile conflict over Palestine. The 1973 Arab oil embargo, a result of the Arab-Israeli war of that year, is a potent reminder of the political and economic linkages of the issue, as is the 1991 Gulf War and the invasion of Iraq in 2003. Reportedly, debates inside the George W. Bush administration in the United States concerning the invasion of Iraq centered importantly on resolution of the Palestine conflict before the invasion of Iraq or on whether the invasion of Iraq and regime change there would facilitate solving the Palestine question. Those who argued the latter, the pro-Israel neocons especially inside the Pentagon and the White House, won the day. Middle Eastern oil, which consists of the largest reserves and productive capacity on earth, and the derivative "military hardware" market are a lucrative prize for contemporary rival economic powers. As Simon Bromley argued, control of world oil has been pivotal in the US post–World War II global hegemony.[1] Thus the problem of Palestine has been a hidden side of the global political economy.

Palestine Within the Arab Context

Significant as it is in the international context, the question of Palestine is far more critical in the Middle East and Arab regions. In their history, culture, politics, and religion, Palestine and the Palestinians have long been an integral part of the Arab and Islamic worlds. For centuries, the country and the people have been the geographical and social bridge connecting the Mashreq (the Arab east) to Egypt and the Maghreb (the Arab west, or North Africa). Palestinians are related by kinship, economic, religious, and political ties to the people of Lebanon and Syria to the north, Jordan and Iraq to the east, Saudi Arabia to the southeast, and Egypt to the southwest. Since the destruction of Palestine in 1948 and the forceful dispossession and dispersal of most of its people into the surrounding Arab states, the Palestinian question has influenced the political and economic dynamics of the eastern Arab world, including, of course, matters involving oil. It has been a formative issue not only in relation to conflicts between states in the region but also between contending political groups and between regimes and the people within many states. The cause of Palestine became central to both the secular (nationalist, radical) and the religious political and ideological movements buffeting the region.

One of the most powerful ideological concerns regarding Palestine involves religion. Islam holds Palestine sacred; the Qur'an refers to the country as al-Ard al-Muqaddasah (the Holy Land). al-Khalil (Hebron) and al-Quds (Jerusalem) are sacred cities. The Ibrahimi Mosque in al-Khalil is the site of the grave of the prophet Abraham (Ibrahim, in Arabic). al-Quds is the site of al-Haram al-Sharif (the Noble Sanctuary) upon the high plateau inside the Old City of Jerusalem, called Temple Mount in the Jewish tradition, the third holiest shrine of Islam, after Mecca and Medina. The Noble Sanctuary includes al-Masjed al-Aqsa and the Qubbat al-Sakhra (Dome of the Rock) mosques. It is from the Dome of the Rock during the night of al-Isra' and al-Mi'raj that the prophet Muhammad miraculously ascended to heaven upon the winged stallion al-Buraq. al-Quds and al-Ard al-Muqaddasah of Filastin (Palestine) are powerful symbols of identity for Muslim individuals and the entire Islamic *umma,* the nation or community of believers. al-Ard al-Muqaddasah is part of the Muslim *umma* lands as much as it is part of Arab patrimony. Islamic fundamentalists, traditionalists, and modernizers do not waver from this perception.

The significance of al-Quds and Palestine to Muslim Arabs should not be construed as less important than its importance to Christian Arabs, who are an integral part of the Arab and Islamic worlds. For Christian Arabs, no less than for Christians the world over, Jerusalem, Bethlehem, Nazareth, and the rest of Palestine are holy and central to their belief system. In the modern history of the region, Christian Arabs were leaders in the Arab cultural renaissance, the struggle for Palestine, and the movement to free the Arab world from European domination.[2] The founders of two of the most important pan-Arab political movements in the post–World War II period—George Habash, a Palestinian who launched the Movement of Arab Nationalists, and Michel 'Aflaq, a Syrian who established the Ba'ath Party—are Christians, as are many leaders and activists of several other influential political groups throughout the Arab Mashreq. In short, Palestine and its people, both Muslims and Christians, are interwoven into the complex human social, cultural, and political network of the region.

In modern times, until the 1980s, Arab nationalism mobilized the Arab peoples. Developed among the elites in the Mashreq, Arab nationalism became the rallying ideology in the effort to win independence, which began in the latter period of Ottoman Turkish rule, in the second half of the nineteenth century. At war with the Ottomans during World War I, the British, and to a lesser extent the French, encouraged Arab nationalists to launch a revolt against the Ottoman Turks, to help defeat their armies, and to liberate Arab lands from four hundred years of Ottoman dominion. Through deception and collusion, however, the British and French undermined efforts to establish an independent Arab kingdom in the Mashreq areas liberated from the Turks. After the Allied victory, the British and the French, with the approval of the League of Nations (the organization they founded and controlled), divided the Arab Mashreq into a group of small states according to their own interests, without any indigenous economic or political rationale. The French created modern Syria and Lebanon, and the British created modern Iraq, Jordan, and Palestine as separate independent states.

Most threatening for Palestine and the Palestinians and other Arabs was the 1917 Balfour Declaration by the British government, which promised the European Zionists a Jewish homeland in Palestine (see Appendix 2).[3] Zionism was from the start a Western colonialist project, and Arab nationalists opposed both Zionism and Western imperialism. Arab nationalists of the 1950s and 1960s viewed the emergence of Israel as a direct threat and a tool of Western, by then principally US, imperialism to divide, dominate, and exploit the Arabs. Similarly, the politically renascent Muslim revivalists of the last three decades of the twentieth century considered Zionism, Israel, and Western (especially US) hegemony in the region as a threat to Islam and the Islamic community. Many politically active Muslims believe that Western and Israeli hegemony in the region must be resisted resolutely.

Since World War I, especially after 1948, Palestine stood as the emotional and ideological symbol of both secular Arab nationalism and political Islam, embodying concern for kin people and fellow believers as well as resentment against foreign domination. The threats of Zionism and Israel and the struggle against them have historically resonated among all sectors of the Palestinian and Arab populations: Muslim and Christian; religious and secular; modern and traditional; rural and urban; elite and mass; bourgeois, worker, and peasant. Thus the Palestine question has been a powerful domestic issue in Mashreq Arab states and among the pan-Arab and Islamic movements since the turn of the twentieth century.

Before 1948 the peoples and governments of the Mashreq strongly supported the beleaguered Palestinians in conflict with the British mandate authorities and European Zionist Jewish settlers. The Palestinian revolt of 1936–1939 against the British mandate profoundly affected the opinions of Arab intellectuals, politicians, activists, and youths in surrounding countries. Local military officers in Syria, Egypt, and later Iraq justified the takeovers of the established civil governments in part because of the 1948 defeat of the Palestinians at the hands of Israel. These officers argued that the loss of Palestine was due to the negligence, corruption, and treachery of the monarchical governments.[4] The Palestine question and the threat of Israel provided these new, modernizing military rulers of the 1950s and 1960s with the ideological legitimacy to acquire and exercise full control over their nascent states, under the banner of *ma'arakat al-massir* (the battle of destiny)—the confrontation with both Israel and its European and US supporters. For these regimes, the Palestine question was the focus of national solidarity and consensus, the liberation of Palestine justifying the dramatic changes in the traditional social, economic, and political order.[5]

The defeat of the Arab nationalist states by Israel in six days in the June 1967 War discredited these regimes and ushered in another period of internal change. Palestine and Palestinian rights were reduced to secondary (if not rhetorical) status as Arab states redefined the Arab-Israeli conflict as the struggle to regain only the territories that Israel began to occupy in 1967. This redefinition was codified in the Arab states' acceptance of UN Security Council Resolution 242, which confirmed the inadmissibility of the acquisition of territory by force and the withdrawal of Israel from Arab territory in return for peace but referred to Palestine and the Palestinians only indirectly as refugees. By 1973, regional Arab political leadership had shifted to the more conservative oil-exporting states (particularly Saudi Arabia), as did the national Arab responsibility for Palestine.[6] The cause of Palestine served the rulers of the oil states by appeasing popular sentiment.

The oil-exporting states of the Arabian Peninsula supported the Palestinian cause (and the PLO) financially and diplomatically in all international forums, including the United Nations. During the 1970s, the level of Arab support grew as Arab control of oil and financial power increased. By 1981, at the high point of Arab oil power, King Fahd of Saudi Arabia spearheaded an Arab League plan for the political settlement of the Palestine question and the Arab-Israeli conflict: recognition of Israel in return for establishment of a Palestinian state in the West Bank and Gaza. This plan was ignored by both Israel and the United States.

After the June 1967 War, however, Palestinian guerrilla organizations emerged and engaged in armed struggle against Israel; under the umbrella of the PLO, they linked together the exiled Palestinian communities and, to an extent, those under Israeli occupation. Through the PLO, Palestinians regained control of their cause from the guardianship of the other Arab states. But the growth and power of the guerrilla organizations politically destabilized the countries in which the Palestinian refugees had significant presence, particularly Jordan and Lebanon. The reason was, in part, the disruption of the domestic balance of political power and, in part, the punitive Israeli attacks, which the host governments tried to avoid by controlling Palestinian activity.[7]

Nonetheless, until the 1991 Gulf War, the Palestinian cause continued to provide legitimacy for Arab leaders (and ongoing strong sentiment among the varied Arab populations). The authenticity of their regimes was measured by their lip service or active commitment to Palestine and the Palestinians. President Anwar Sadat of Egypt, for example, justified his stunning trip to Jerusalem in 1977 and the 1979 Israeli-Egyptian peace treaty by claiming that they would not only bring peace between Arabs and Israelis but also solve the problem of Palestine. Similarly, in the name of serving the cause of Palestine, the Syrian government in 1976 sent troops to Lebanon to contain the militarily ascendant Palestinian guerrillas and their secular nationalist and leftist Lebanese allies. In 1986 King Hussein of Jordan said his involvement in the "peace process" initiated by the United States was intended only to help achieve a political settlement of the question of Palestine. In 1986 King Hassan of Morocco, in an extraordinary move, met with the Israeli prime minister, Shimon Peres, to explore, as the king stated, advancing Arab (League) demands regarding Palestinian rights. Similarly, negotiating and signing a peace treaty with Israel was partly justified by Jordan under the late King Hussein as a step in the process of solving the Palestine question.

Except among oppositional movements of political Islam and secular Arab nationalists and leftists, the ideological importance of the Palestinian cause in domestic Arab politics receded sharply as a result of the PLO's affiliation with Iraq during the 1991 Gulf War. Even popular support for Palestine and the Palestinians among the Arab host populations declined. The expulsion of over 350,000 Palestinian civilians from Kuwait after it was liberated from Iraqi occupation did not create a political crisis for that regime or major reverberations in pan-Arab politics. In short, the political capital and goodwill afforded to the PLO within most official Arab circles was largely spent by 1991. The oil-exporting states ostracized and ceased providing funds to the PLO. The 1991 Gulf War therefore left the organization politically and diplomatically isolated and financially weakened.

Although Israelis and the Western media, intellectuals, and politicians may charge Arab politicians and their opponents with opportunism, these politicians do not use the Palestine cause merely for partisan purposes.[8] The Palestinian cause has always retained popular support among the mainstream Mashreq Arab public and has remained crucial for domestic legitimacy (even stability) of the regimes; its importance is rarely underestimated by Arab political leaders. Already by 1993, Arab financial support for the PLO and Palestinian institutions under occupation had resumed, although not at the same level as before.

> And yet, it is hard to exaggerate the importance [that] Palestine . . . had acquired in the politics and psyche of the Arabs and Muslim worlds. By the eve of 9/11, with the *Intifada* about to enter its second year, a survey revealed that some 60 per cent of the people in four rather disparate Arab countries—Saudi Arabia, Kuwait, the United Arab Emirates and Lebanon—regarded it as the "single most important issue to them personally"; in Egypt, the most powerful and populous Arab country, that figure rose to a remarkable 79 per cent. "The Palestinian issue remains an identity concern for most Arabs; most Arabs are ashamed by their inability to help the Palestinians."[9]

The strong and emotional sentiment of identification and support for Palestine and the Palestinians is expressed as well in popular culture all over the Arab world. Songs, operettas, and musicals have been written, sung, and performed all over the Arab world. The content and subject of the songs have expressed the tragedy of Palestine and the changing fortunes and character of the struggles of the Palestinians since 1948.

> While Palestinians and other Arabs expressed their sense of loss in a number of literary and artistic genres (including poetry, novels, painting, film, and plays), song, by its very nature the most popular of forms, probably reached the largest number of people.[10]

Written by Lebanese, Egyptians, Palestinians, and others, songs have expressed a strong sentiment and helped mobilize popular support for the Palestinian cause.

> The songs have shifted from songs of a united Arab front fighting for liberation and the return of refugees in the context of Arab unity, to songs celebrating the Palestinian guerrillas' fight for their people's independence, to songs that describe the oppression under which all Palestinians, whether under Israeli rule or in exile, languish, to songs again of rejuvenated Arab solidarity with resisting civilians being murdered on television screens nightly.[11]

Perhaps some of the most enduring songs that "stirred the masses" after the Arab defeat of 1967 and the hope raised by the rise of the Palestinian guerrilla movement are those of the Lebanese Rahbani brothers, sung by the premier Arab singer, Fairuz. "It is their paean to [fallen] Jerusalem, 'Zahrat al-Mada'in' (the flower of [all] cities), which stands out as the most popular song of the period."[12]

For Palestinians and other Arabs, the 1991 Gulf War underscored the US government's double standard: The United States would not tolerate the Iraqi invasion and occupation of Kuwait but turned a blind eye to Israeli occupation of Palestinian and other Arab territories.

The incongruity in US foreign policy aggravated the political predicament of Arab rulers allied with the United States or dependent on US protection. Since 1948, Arab political leaders, particularly government officials, have been faced with a persistent dilemma: the discrepancy between their strong public rhetorical posture in support of Palestine and their political pragmatism regarding the conflict. Since the 1970s, this dilemma has become more intense and complex because of three factors. The first is the increasing integration into and dependence of the Mashreq states, especially oil exporters, on the West (in particular the United States), which does not share the Arab view of Palestine and actively works against it. The second is the rise of Palestinians who recaptured their cause in the 1960s, mobilized their dispersed people, and influenced both domestic and inter-Arab politics. The third is the spread of politicized Islam, which also militantly adopted the cause of Palestine, accenting its domestic and foreign policy differences with the pro-Western regimes of the Arab countries.

The interpenetration of the domestic, pan-Arab foreign policy and Palestinian issues had long propelled the PLO into regional interstate Arab politics, popular pan-Arab and Islamic movements, and domestic oppositional and factional politics. Conversely, this interpenetration encouraged the countervailing intervention of Arab states, parties, and political movements in Palestinian politics. In the context of growing Arab economic and political interdependence with the West, the interlocking of Palestinian and Arab issues heightened the Arab leaders' political dilemma, emphasizing the gap between the image and the reality of their support of Palestine and the Palestinians. As this issue became entangled in political and economic relations with the United States, Israel's superpower patron, Arab governments were all the more eager to contain the destabilizing contradiction, if not eliminate it altogether, by solving the Palestine problem.

The contradictions facing Arab governments have become even further intensified since the American-led invasion and occupation of Iraq in 2003 and the American policy of forcing "democracy" and a neoliberal economic structure on Arab states by military power. Aggressive American military and diplomatic policy in the region is now widely perceived in the Arab world as a means to rearrange the domestic and regional political landscape for a hegemonic political-economic Pax Americana, allied with and supportive of an expansionist colonialist Israel. As a result, David Hirst argued correctly:

> It is hard to exaggerate . . . the level of resentment to which American purblindness and partisanship had by now given rise. Throughout the nineties—ever since the 1991 Gulf war and the subsequent "containment" of Iraq which, in Arab minds, became a secondary source of grievance inextricably linked with, and reinforcing, the primary one (Palestine)—anti-Americanism had steadily, remorselessly grown.[13]

Indeed, Arab governments increasingly fear that the Palestinian-Arab-Israeli conflict, especially after the 2003 Iraq war, is being superseded by a "broader and more dangerous Arab-American conflict"[14] that is placing

Arab regimes, especially pro-American ones, in an untenable quandary about their survival.

The Question of Palestine and the Palestinians

In the West the most misunderstood element within the question of Palestine is the Palestinian people. It is their unceasing, persistent activism that keeps the cause of Palestine at the fore. Despite dispersal and the absence of a stable territorial base, Palestinians have been the founders, leaders, and untiring activists not only of Palestinian but also of pan-Arab political movements. They have been the engineers, designers, teachers, professionals, consultants, advisers, and diplomats to the peoples and governments of the oil-exporting states. They intermarry with and are the colleagues, comrades, friends, and business partners of other Arabs. After their diasporas, the Palestinians entered the social, economic, and political fabric of Mashreq Arab societies. In many respects, they have become the political conscience of the Arab world.

In general, neither Palestinians' life in exile since 1948, nor Palestinians' life under occupation since 1967, nor their life as second-class citizens inside Israel has been secure. Yet from being a nation largely of rural peasants, the Palestinians have become urban, skilled, educated, and cosmopolitan. Nearly two generations after the destruction of their society in 1948, the exiles had achieved the highest education rates in the Middle East.[15] Despite the trauma of dispossession and dispersal, many have flourished economically. A nation of demoralized, leaderless refugees turned into a nation of revolutionaries.[16] Palestinians under occupation in the West Bank and the Gaza Strip tenaciously resisted Israeli domination and eventually launched a spectacular intifada in 1987 and a second and a more lethal one in 2001.

The experience of the Palestinians is unique and remarkable: After dispossession, destitution, and dispersal, and during a national struggle that has spanned more than eight decades, they have become a productive people politically and economically as well as in academe, science and engineering, medicine, journalism, literature, poetry, art, and music.[17] Although Palestine was a diverse society prior to 1948, the catastrophe that divided the people physically kept them united culturally, socially, and politically. Since 1948, they have articulated common aspirations for the restitution of their political rights and a vision for building a humane and democratic society in a liberated, independent Palestine. This book therefore concentrates on the Palestinian people, society, and politics; their communal structures and economic roles; their political culture and dynamics; and their future.

Perceptions of Palestinians

Palestinians and the West

The Palestinian image in western Europe and the United States metamorphosed considerably over the twentieth century. Western cultural and ideological views of Palestinians are remarkably deep-rooted and persistent. Edward Said documented in great and compelling detail the development and evolution of European anti-Islamic and anti-Arab sentiment since medieval times.[18] The medieval Crusades intensified the hostile European attitude toward Muslims and Arabs, reinforced in later centuries by the Christian reconquest of Spain from the Muslim Arab rulers (commonly called Moors in the West). Such attitudes were further consolidated by the rise of the Muslim Ottoman Empire and its conquests in Europe and the Mediterranean. Such imagery was inspired as well by the political culture of nineteenth-century European imperialism.[19] Imperialism was premised on the right of conquest, on the right of the "superior" white Europeans to rule over "inferior" nonwhites in Africa and Asia. British and Continental attitudes toward the colonized world of Asia and Africa were characterized at best by noblesse oblige and at worst by arrogance, racism, and disregard for indigenous peoples.

Indigenous Palestinians were presumed to be unworthy, nonexistent, or dispensable. In a compelling and comprehensive study of American perceptions of Palestine and the Palestinians, Kathleen Christison documented such remarkably persistent negative views among both the politicians and the public, simultaneous with sympathetic attitudes toward Jewish views of, claims to, and plans for Palestine. These views of the Holy Land and its destiny have been predicated on a Christian (Protestant) biblical tradition among American policymakers and the public and reinforced since the start of the twentieth century by a determined and active Jewish, Zionist, and Christian American lobby and pressure groups. They underline a policy frame of reference that was Jewish-centered and Zionist-centered before the creation of the state of Israel; since then, it has been Israel-centered. The indigenous Palestinians have been, at best, absent from this frame of reference and these policy actions and, at worst, have been seen as an irrational, hostile, almost genocidal group of Arabs bent on denying Jews and Israelis their God-given right to Palestine.

Christison traced these perceptions of Palestine and the development of the Jewish-centered, later Israeli-centered, frame of reference in American popular and political culture and the derivative policy toward the country and its people. She analyzed the evolution and consolidation of these perceptions and of the Zionist-centered frame of reference of the Holy Land from the nineteenth century through the administration of Woodrow Wilson, who supported the Balfour Declaration, to US policy in the administrations of American presidents from Franklin D. Roosevelt to George H. W. Bush.[20] For example,

a frame of mind in which (Palestinian) Arabs essentially played no part, in which they were politically invisible, patronized, disdained, or ignored altogether—this is the mind-set with which the policymakers who made the first official decisions on Palestine for the United States after World War I grew up. . . . Like most U.S. Christians of his day, [President Woodrow Wilson] had grown up well tutored in the biblical history of Jews and Christians in Palestine. For Wilson, the notion of a Jewish return to Palestine seemed a natural fulfillment of biblical prophesies.[21]

In her analysis, Christison also factored in the US domestic political dimension of support for the Jewish claims in Palestine.

Everything militated against the Palestinians' obtaining a hearing:

The frame of reference that automatically assumed a Jewish place in Palestine and assumed the Arabs' claim to be inferior was so deeply rooted in a century of Orientalist literature and anti-Arab stereotyping that little could have fundamentally altered it; . . . U.S. Zionist activists were highly skilled, extremely well organized, and well connected at high levels of the policymaking establishment and the Congress, and they represented a segment of the U.S. population several times the size of the small Arab American population.[22]

In short, the Palestinians have been severely disadvantaged in American popular and political cultures because in the United States "the perception that the Palestinians have no rational basis for their hostility to Israel and no legitimate national claim to the land of Palestine is fundamental to the misconception (deliberately promoted by pro-Israel political forces) surrounding this conflict."[23] Worse yet, self-serving images of Palestine promoted by the Zionists internationally gained almost unquestioned acceptance in the United States.

Among these is a powerful image created by European Jewish Zionists and reflected in a slogan that declared Palestine a "land without people for a people without a land." Coined by Israel Zangwill in the early 1900s, it sought to generate popular support for the Zionist project in Palestine by denying the existence of the natives. On November 2, 1917, with its army at the gates of the southern Palestinian city of Gaza, imperial Britain issued the Balfour Declaration (named after Lord Arthur James Balfour, the foreign secretary), which promised the European Zionist movement support for "the establishment in Palestine of a national home for the Jewish people" (see Appendix 2). It ignored the indigenous Palestinians except as "the existing non-Jewish communities." The declaration provided that Britain would facilitate the achievement of the Zionist project so long as "nothing shall be done which may prejudice the civil and religious rights" of non-Jews. This backhanded provision failed to refer to the national or political rights of the Palestinian Arabs. Two years after the declaration, Lord Balfour explained:

> In Palestine we do not propose even to go through the form of consulting the wishes of the present inhabitants of the country. Zionism, be it right or wrong, good or bad, is rooted in age-old traditions, in present needs, in future hopes of far profounder import than the desires and prejudices of the 700,000 Arabs who now inhabit that ancient land.[24]

Once seen as insignificant, the Palestinians were perceived after 1948 as miserable, idle "Arab refugees" who irrationally begrudged Israelis their homeland. Following 1967 the Palestinians were portrayed as violent terrorists. With the eruption of the intifada in 1987, the image began to shift to that of youthful rebels resisting, under great odds, the Israeli military occupation of the West Bank and the Gaza Strip. Sensational television footage of Palestinian youths being beaten mercilessly by Israeli soldiers contributed to the change in image. For the first time, the long-cherished Western perception of a little, beleaguered Israel facing the Arab Goliath was reversed. Having been portrayed dramatically on television screens worldwide, Israel's harsh policies toward Palestinians elicited widespread criticism.

Long demonized by Israel and its supporters, Palestinians under occupation suddenly became humanized, and the intifada restructured the parameters of the Palestine question and the Arab-Israeli conflict. After the 1993 signing of the secretly negotiated Oslo Accords in Washington, D.C., the overall Palestinian and PLO images were transformed significantly to those of partners to Israel in the process of peacemaking in the Middle East.

Nonetheless, in the West and Israel and often even among officials of the Palestinian Authority (PA) in the West Bank and the Gaza Strip, Palestinian opponents of the terms of the so-called Oslo peace agreements continue to be labeled as terrorists, whether they commit acts of violence or not.

With the failure of the Camp David negotiations between Israel and the PLO/PA under the guardianship of US president Bill Clinton in 2000, the eruption of the al-Aqsa uprising (intifada) in 2001, and the rise of suicide bombings inside Israel in response to Israeli attacks and assassinations of Palestinians, the image of Palestinians seemed to suffer again in the United States and the rest of the West. Suicide bombings by the Palestinian Islamic political movements Hamas and Islamic Jihad played into a revived anti-Islamic and anti-Arab sentiment in the West in the wake of the September 11, 2001, attacks on the World Trade Center in New York City and the Pentagon in Washington. The terrorist image of Palestinians was resurrected with a vengeance, and any resistance or political activism in defense of Palestinian rights inside the occupied territories was labeled terrorist activity, especially by Israel and its supporters in the West. The official American and media postures in support of the brutal policies of Israel's prime minister, Ariel Sharon, and the global "war on terror" that the United States launched both directly and indirectly recolored the Palestinians as inveterate terrorists. Palestinian trauma, suffering, dispossession, and destitution and the depredations of the Israeli occupation were rarely portrayed in Western media or academic tomes and tended to be seen as inconsequential or, as Edward Said once put it, as an "offstage catastrophe."

The image of the Palestinians was dramatically transformed. The "terrorist" epithet is now used principally by Israel, its supporters in the West, and Western conservatives to describe Islamic Palestinian militants and others who object to the terms of the Oslo Accords. Yet even though the image of the PLO and the Palestinians has brightened in the international arena, in practice Israel and the United States continue to resist acceptance of their internationally codified political and civil rights. Both governments vigorously reject Palestinian national rights, including the right of return to their homes and property and establishment of an independent sovereign state in the West Bank and the Gaza Strip.[25]

Palestinian Self-Image

In contrast to Israel and the West, the third world views the Palestinians positively because the Palestinians have been able to promote their own image there. Although in some cases they have been relegated to awkward political and diplomatic status, they have rarely been degraded, as third-world governments, nongovernmental organizations, media, and intellectuals respect the Palestinian perspective. In most of the world—the non-Western world—the Palestinians are viewed as a dispossessed people who have struggled to regain their inalienable national rights. The PLO is recognized as a national liberation movement that solely and legitimately represents the Palestinian people and provides the organizational framework for mobilizing them and serving their needs.

This perspective is derived from the Palestinians' self-image.[26] They consider themselves the indigenous people of Palestine who have inalienable national rights. Pre-1948 Palestinians constitute al-Sha'ab al-Filastini (the Palestinian people), part of the greater Arab *umma* whose *watan* (homeland) is Filastin. They see themselves, however, as divided into two great segments: those in *al-dakhel* (literally, "inside" historic Palestine, both citizens of Israel and those under occupation in the West Bank and Gaza) and those in *al-manfa* (exile) or *al-ghourba* (estrangement) dispersed in the Arab states, Europe, the Americas, and elsewhere.[27]

In the Palestinian view, a child born of Palestinian parents, either in *al-dakhel* or *al-manfa,* is automatically a new member of al-Sha'ab al-Filastini and, by virtue of descent, never forfeits the political right to Palestine no matter what travel document or passport he or she carries. The person is both Palestinian and Arab, just as someone may be Syrian and Arab or Egyptian and Arab. Although similar to the Egyptian Arab or Syrian Arab in identity, the Palestinian Arab has lost his or her *watan.* He or she believes that the Palestinian people have been dispossessed of their homeland of Palestine, dispersed physically, and denied elemental political rights of return, self-determination, and statehood. Thus, in the consciousness of the Palestinians, they are a stateless nation struggling to regain their rights to statehood in Palestine.

A Stateless Nation

Ironically, not unlike the Diaspora Jews who perceived themselves as a nation, the Palestinians are in this sense the mirror image of those who dispossessed and dispersed them. The conditions that shaped the modern Palestinian identity are complex and deep; they began forming in the last years of Ottoman rule but have much earlier roots. The Greek, Roman, and Arab designation of Philistia, Palaestina, and Filastin, respectively, continued to exist until the Mongolian invasion of the thirteenth century. In the following two centuries, however, under Mameluke rule from Cairo, the territory was divided into districts named after the major cities from which they were administered. Similarly, during their four-hundred-year rule (1516–1917), the Ottomans divided that same territory into three *sanjaks* (subdistricts) under the *wilaya* (governorate) of Damascus. During the late Ottoman period, the larger autonomous *sanjak* of al-Quds covered most of Palestine. Historically, the administrative integrity of Palestine has been continually reaffirmed.

With the defeat of the Ottomans in World War I, the victorious British, under the auspices of the League of Nations, established the Mandate of Palestine. Unlike the Ottoman rulers, the League of Nations meant its trusteeships to prepare the natives for self-rule. Thus came into formal being the modern country of Palestine and the legal identity of modern Palestinians. With the establishment of the British mandate over Palestine and its declared intent of fostering a "national home" for Jews, Zionism presented a clear and present threat. Palestinian response to both the Zionist-British action and its ideology furthered Palestinians' identity and consciousness of their historical rights to the land.

Overall, Palestinian Arabs perceived Zionism as a new European crusade. Palestinian Arab rights that had been challenged nearly a millennium before were challenged again. This unique sense of Arab Palestinianism was strengthened during the mandate period in the struggles—ideological, political, and armed—against both the British colonial authorities and the Jewish Zionist settlers. By the time in 1948 that Palestine was shattered as a society, partitioned as a country, and destroyed as a nation, modern Palestinian identity was consolidated.

The trauma of the destruction of their society and of dispossession and dispersal—al-Nakbah (the Catastrophe), as they call it—solidified Palestinians' self-consciousness, creating among them a psychological bond and a strong feeling of identity and unity, of mutual care and responsibility. Palestinians after 1948, inside historic Palestine and as refugees outside, clung to their identity as Palestinians and their self-conception as rightfully belonging to the country. Numerous formal Western missions that proposed solutions to the Middle East conflict assumed that with sufficient material inducements, Palestinian refugees would accept resettlement and relinquish claims to their homes, villages, and homeland. Western analysts and politicians also assumed that the new generation of Palestinians born in exile would have no attachment to Palestine.[28] They were wrong.

The rise of the PLO in 1967 gave Palestinians an institutional framework, a stronger sense of resolve, and greater unity around the announced goals of the movement. These were the liberation of Palestine and the return of the refugees to their homes. Palestinian political consensus and commitment escalated even higher with the intifada.

On Studying Palestine and the Palestinians

The question of Palestine has generated a jungle of literature, heavily polemical, but there are few studies of Palestine as a society and Palestinians as a people. Recent studies of the social and economic history of the nineteenth century and mandatory Palestine, many of which are excellent, more point out the gaps in our knowledge than they provide us with a comprehensive overview of the country's and the diaspora communities' structure and dynamics. These historical studies have generated different paradigms, each of which yields insights, but the implications of which have not been fully developed or resolved. To begin with, Palestine was subjected to abrupt changes of regime: In 1917 with the British invasion, in 1948 with the destruction of the country and the creation of Israel, and in 1967 with the Israeli occupation of the rest of historic Palestine, the West Bank, and the Gaza Strip. Each wrenching event had consequences for the socioeconomic structure and political dynamics of the society that need to be examined as a whole, not as separate processes. Although the problem of reliable data is acute, the frame of reference of the data also poses sticky questions. Three competing paradigms can be discerned: twentieth-century Palestine as a typical European colony; Palestine as two separate, coexisting communities, Arab and Jewish, each with its own social, economic, and political arrangements; and Palestine as two sectors, the capitalist sector (principally Jewish) progressively dominating the precapitalist (primarily Arab) sector.[29]

Difficult as it is to mentally reconstruct mandatory Palestine, conceptualizing Palestinian society after 1948 is even more challenging. Since 1948 the Palestinians as a people have been divided into three broad segments: those in Israel, who remained on the land after the formation of the state of Israel (the smallest segment); those in the West Bank and the Gaza Strip who came under Israeli military occupation after the June 1967 War (a larger segment); and those dispersed communities in exile from 1948 until the present (the largest segment). Yet they have developed one nuanced collective identity as Palestinians. A study of the post-1948 Palestinian people, then, would of necessity have to contain these three segments, the different conditions and factors that shaped their varied communal structures and histories, those that drew them closer or pushed them apart, and the interlocking and overarching dynamics that sustained this unique, postdismemberment syncretic society.

There are enormous gaps in our knowledge of the three segments of post-1948 Palestinian social structure. Above all, there is no general or comprehensive social history of the Palestinian people. What exist for the post-1948 period are disparate studies of isolated aspects of the Palestinian people. And many, although not all, of these studies are framed by narrowly or pseudo-objective theoretical frameworks derived from adversarial or unsympathetic political concerns.[30] Studies of the Palestinian Arabs in Israel are a prime example. Khalil Nakhleh noted:

> The questions most of these studies raised . . . often related to undefined sociological processes which Western social science has generated (e.g., modernization), rather than to the basic ideological underpinnings of the State of Israel which created the minority status of the [Palestinian] Arab population. . . . Such a persistent avoidance is purposeful, and it can be understood mainly in terms of an a priori adherence on the part of these researchers to the major ideological construct of political Zionism.[31]

The thrust of Nakhleh's critique is (1) that (Zionist) ideology supersedes evidence and influences the direction of interpretation of the research on the Palestinian "Arabs of Israel"; (2) that these Arabs are conceptualized as isolated fragments, their nationalism as an aberration, not a natural response to their oppressed collective status; (3) that Israeli Arabs' social structure is stagnant, locked into traditional relationships as if the Arabs were still living in Ottoman times; and (4) that the methodological dichotomy, comparing traditional and modern social structure, masks contradictory ideologies and moral judgments. Nakhleh therefore called for an examination of the presuppositions of such research in order to understand the status and contradictions of the life of the Palestinian minority inside Israel.

Furthermore, the socioeconomic transformations of Palestinian communities in exile do not take place in isolation from the dynamics of change in the specific countries in which they reside or the political economy of the region as a whole. Since 1948, the region has become far more integrated, although differentially, into the world market. Thus the transformations of the region, including Palestine and the post-1948 Palestinian communities, are directly related to the changes of the global political economy. A more comprehensive formulation that ties Palestine, the Palestinian communities, and the region to the world's political economy is needed. This will allow the identification of both the general and the specific structural factors and conditions responsible for shaping Palestinian society in the nineteenth century, during the mandate period, in the post-1948 era, and in the post-Oslo era, as well as the probable future direction of change. The purpose of this book is to provide a general and comprehensive formulation of Palestine and the post-1948 Palestinian communities that links their social transformation to regional and global restructuring.

Notes

1. S. Bromley, *American Hegemony and World Oil* (University Park: Pennsylvania State University Press, 1991).

2. G. Antonius, *The Arab Awakening: The Story of the Arab National Movement* (New York: Capricorn Books, 1965). See also H. Sharabi, *Arab Intellectuals and the West: The Formative Years, 1875–1914* (Baltimore: Johns Hopkins University Press, 1970).

3. See the text of the Balfour Declaration and many other important documents in United Nations, *The Origins and Evolution of the Palestine Problem, 1917–1988* (New York: United Nations, 1990).

4. Ibid., 302; see also H. Sharabi, *Nationalism and Revolution in the Arab World* (Princeton, NJ: Van Nostrand, 1966).

5. The manner and degree of support for the Palestine cause emerged as one of the key issues in the Arab cold war between the Egypt of Gamal Abdul-Nasser (leader of the nationalist camp) and Saudi Arabia (leader of the conservative camp). See M. H. Kerr, *The Arab Cold War* (New York: Oxford University Press, 1971).

6. W. Kazziha, "The Impact of Palestine on Arab Politics," in G. Luciani, ed., *The Arab State* (Berkeley: University of California Press, 1990): 306–309.

7. N. Chomsky, "Middle East Terrorism and the American Ideological System," in E. W. Said and C. Hitchens, eds., *Blaming the Victims* (London: Verso, 1988): 97–147, especially 106; see also N. Chomsky, *The Fateful Triangle: The United States, Israel and the Palestinians* (Boston: South End Press, 1983).

8. E. W. Said, *The Question of Palestine* (New York: Vintage Books, 1980), 6.

9. D. Hirst, *The Gun and the Olive Branch*, 3rd ed. (New York: Nations Books, 2003): 100.

10. J Massad, "Liberating Songs: Palestine Put to Music," *Journal of Palestine Studies* 32 (Spring 2003): 22.

11. Ibid., 37.

12. Ibid., 25.

13. Hirst, *Gun and the Olive Branch,* 101

14. Cited in Ibid., 101.

15. A. Zahlan and R. S. Zahlan, "The Palestinian Future: Education and Manpower," *Journal of Palestine Studies* 6 (Summer 1977): 103–112. See also I. Abu-Lughod, "Educating a Community in Exile: The Palestinian Experience," *Journal of Palestine Studies* 2 (Spring 1973): 94–111; N. Badran, "The Means of Survival: Education and the Palestinian Community, 1948–67," *Journal of Palestine Studies* 10 (Summer 1980): 44–74. A comprehensive study of the educational experiences and attainments of the varied Palestinian population segments was produced by

S. Graham-Brown, *Education, Repression and Liberation: Palestinians* (London: World University Service UK, 1984).

16. R. Sayigh, *Palestinians: From Peasants to Revolutionaries* (London: Zed Press, 1979).

17. S. K. Farsoun, *Culture and Customs of the Palestinians* (Westport, CT: Greenwood Press, 2004).

18. E. W. Said, *Orientalism* (New York, Pantheon, 1978).

19. Said, *Question of Palestine,* 73–82.

20. K. Christison, *Perceptions of Palestine: Their Influence on U.S. Middle East Policy* (Berkeley: University of California Press, 1999).

21. Ibid., 26.

22. Ibid., 59.

23. Ibid., 1.

24. Quoted in L. Jenkins, "Palestine Exiled," *Rolling Stone* 9 (June 1983): 32.

25. For some time, public opinion polls in the United States have shown that official government policy toward the Middle East is at variance with public attitudes. Public opinion favors a Palestinian state as a solution to the Middle East conflict. See F. Moughrabi, "American Public Opinion and the Palestine Question," Occasional Paper 4 (Washington, DC: International Center for Research and Public Policy, 1986).

26. See N. H. Aruri, "Dialectics of Dispossession," in N. H. Aruri, ed., *Occupation: Israel over Palestine,* 2nd ed. (Belmont, MA: Association of Arab-American University Graduates, 1989): 3–28, and E. W. Said, *The Politics of Dispossession: The Struggle for Palestinian Self-Determination, 1969–1994* (New York: Pantheon, 1994).

27. Sayigh, *Palestinians,* 8.

28. Hirst, *Gun and the Olive Branch,* 1st ed. (London: Futura), 264–266.

29. Ibid., 4.

30. B. Kimmerling, "Sociology, Ideology and Nation Building: The Palestinians in Israeli Sociology," *American Sociological Review* 57 (August 1992): 446–460.

31. K. Nakhleh, "Anthropological and Sociological Studies on the Arabs in Israel: A Critique," *Journal of Palestine Studies* 6 (Summer 1977): 61–62.

2

Before al-Nakbah

The Modern Social History of Palestine

The modern history of Palestine before al-Nakbah—Palestine's catastrophic destruction—begins around 1800 and ends in 1948. It is divided into two main historical periods: The first covers the nineteenth century and World War I (1914–1917), and the second begins after World War I with the establishment of the British mandate over Palestine under the auspices of the League of Nations. Together, these powerful forces may be summarized in one phrase: European interventionism. This chapter concentrates on the structure and transformation of Palestinian society during the first period. It identifies the major social, economic, and political factors and trends that transformed Palestine *and* that, we believe, continue to shape attitudes and events in the region, in Israel, in the occupied territories of the West Bank and the Gaza Strip, and among the Palestinians in exile.

European intervention in Palestine encouraged the process of European settlement in the country, transformed the economy, created new social classes, and rearranged power relations among the existing social groups, including the recent Jewish immigrant settlers. This process of intervention started slowly in the early nineteenth century but intensified and accelerated in the second half of the century after the conclusion of the Crimean War (1853–1856), which hastened the opening of the Ottoman Empire, especially Palestine. From 1800 to 1848, economic activity and productivity in trade, agriculture, industry, and services expanded substantially but became more closely linked to and dependent on Europe, especially Britain, the hegemonic colonial power. European interventionism propelled Palestine from a largely subsistence and semifeudal, tribute-paying mode of existence into a market economy and finally, before its destruction, into dependent capitalist underdevelopment. Most significant, it created the conditions for the destruction of Palestine and the dispossession of its people in 1948, the year of al-Nakbah.

The nineteenth century thus saw not only a new emphasis on monetary relations over the whole of Palestine with the expansion of the market but also the initiation of capitalist social relationships of production and exchange.[1] Accompanying these shifts were structural changes in the land tenure and ownership systems, the development of industrial-artisanal and service activity, labor force transformation, population redistribution, and commensurate urban growth. The Ottoman authorities had introduced administrative, legal, and governmental reform and centralization, which also contributed to the process of transformation. No less significant was the new "peaceful crusade"[2] of religiously inspired European immigration, investment, and institutional development. Just as important, modern education expanded and increased in scope, and social values, norms, and lifestyles changed. Arab and Palestinian nationalism and Islamist consciousness awoke. And all of this occurred in the context of a rapidly increasing population, both because of natural increase and (to a lesser extent) because of the immigration of European Christians and Jews, which restructured the demographic composition of the country. This latter aspect, which began in earnest only in the 1880s, had become a critical factor in Palestine by the mid twentieth century.

Social and Economic Organization

In the eighteenth century, Palestinians raised cotton in the western plains and some of the flat areas of higher elevation, but most of the terraced hills of central Palestine were planted with olive trees, which are well suited to the climate and soil. Other agricultural products—wheat, corn, barley, and sesame in particular—were grown in the valleys and nearby plains. Oil extracted from olives was and continues to be a primary material in cooking and soap making, and prior to the twentieth century it was also used for paying taxes and as fuel for lamps. Olive oil, soap, textiles, grain, and sesame seeds were important export commodities to the regional market.

Although the plains were accessible to the military arms of the central authorities (Ottoman or Egyptian) and vulnerable to the periodic raids of nomadic bedouins, the central hills of Palestine provided natural barriers. Because of its ruggedness and the difficulty of conquering and holding it, the hill country afforded the Palestinian people—peasants, town dwellers, and local political lords—a measure of autonomy that allowed the development of an indigenous political economy and unique social formations. This occurred not only in the hills of Palestine but also on Mount Lebanon and in the Nusayriyyah hills of northwestern Syria.

In one sense, the four hill regions of Palestine—al-Jaleel (Galilee), Jabal Nablus, Jabal al-Quds (Jerusalem), and Jabal al-Khalil (Hebron)—had more or less distinct socioeconomic forms, although they were in many ways interconnected to each other and to the surrounding regions. For example, the city of Nablus, the administrative, commercial, manufacturing, and cultural center of the Jabal Nablus district, was connected by trade, especially in textiles, olive oil, and soap, to the rest of Palestine, to the hajj caravans east of the Jordan River, to Damascus, and to Cairo and Damietta in Egypt.[3]

The hill regions, which always had the highest population densities and autonomy in Palestine, shared a number of important social organizational features. All the hill country in Palestine and other mountainous regions of the eastern Mediterranean were, up to the nineteenth century, characterized by a highly autonomous peasantry, resistant to externally imposed authority, organized in patrilineal clans, surviving by farming small plots of land, and living by norms, customs, and values anchored in their Islamic civilization (except, of course, for the native Christian communities). Peasants were typically armed, and the Ottoman authorities did not have a direct military presence in or control over the hill regions. They relied on indigenous leaders, often rural *shaykh*s, for control, administration, and taxation until the centralization drive of the mid nineteenth century. Thus the hilly regions of Palestine collectively developed a unique and distinctive political economy and social formation: the *musha'a* land use system and the *hamula* structure of social organization.

The land-equalizing *musha'a* village had four basic features:

> The cultivated land was divided into several sections, each of which was fairly homogeneous with regard to soil type, terrain, access from the village and other advantages [in other words, equalization was according to quality, not value]. Each share was entitled to an equal portion of the common cultivated land as a whole, and of each of those sections. Finally, all of the common arable land was periodically redistributed, usually by lot in proportion to the number of shares held by each titleholder.[4]

Of course, each of these features was subject to variation. By the nineteenth century, however, redistribution gradually ceased. The *musha'a* system provided the peasantry with subsistence and a surplus with which to pay taxes. Its slow change in the modern era of exchange or market economy was due to the lack of cash, which became available only as the peasant earnings increased over the late nineteenth and early twentieth centuries. Of course, cash was available to the peasant patrons and protectors—the *shaykh*s and notables—who were in good positions to acquire such land.[5]

*Hamula*s varied in size, power, and influence. Over the years some *hamula*s grew and split into several segments. Others declined and disappeared or were incorporated into more powerful *hamula*s. *Hamula*s could extend over one or more villages, and villages typically had residents from more than one *hamula*. During much of the Ottoman period, groups of villages were organized into subdistricts called *nahiya*s, each under the control of a *shaykh*, who typically belonged to the strongest family of the most powerful *hamula* in the area. As long as the *hamula shaykh*s performed their tax-collecting function appropriately, they were confirmed as tax farmers and political leaders by the provincial Ottoman governors. When feuds and conflicts emerged within or among the *hamula*s or clans, district officials or urban notables (*wujaha* and *a'yan*) with tax-farming interests would exploit these divisions and manipulate the *hamula shaykh*s to their advantage. In such situations, *nahiya shaykh*s would often lose much of their autonomy.

The Palestinian rural political economy was not isolated. Rural surplus not only was appropriated as tax by the Ottomans and local leaders but also was part of a larger economic system of trade, exchange, or barter with the nearby city or commercial center. Besides being commercial centers, the cities of nineteenth-century Palestine were also the sites of manufacture, crafts and artisanal work, administrative offices, and religious and judicial activity. They were populated by Ottoman officials (Turkish and local Arab), local merchants, craftsmen, artisans, shopkeepers, innkeepers, laborers, *'ulama* (theologians), and *qadi*s (judges) of the shari'a courts.

In the city of Nablus, textiles, soap, and other manufactures gave the city a central role in Palestine as the Ottoman period progressed. Artisans and craftsmen were organized into guildlike groups that regulated the process of production, pricing, and standards. The political economy of Nablus included bedouins, who supplied it with an important resource, *qilli*, an alkaline powder made by burning certain desert plants and used in the production of soap. B. B. Doumani estimated that the population of Nablus increased from four thousand or five thousand in the late sixteenth century to twenty thousand by the mid nineteenth century.[6]

Peasant, pastoral nomadic, and urban social patterns coexisted and inter-locked in a complex political economy. It was not feudal as was Europe, nor even as was Mount Lebanon, with its autonomous emir and its authority structure characterized by parceled-out sovereignties held together by net-works of loyalties and obligations. Each Lebanese feudal lord, or *muqata'aji,* autonomously exercised economic, judicial, social, and political control over the peasantry, which depended on him for protection. In contrast, the *hamula* chiefs and *nahiya shaykh*s of Palestine were principally appointed or recognized as de facto Ottoman authorities (tax-collecting officials), not au-tonomous *muqata'aji*s. In short, rather than feudal lords, Palestine was ruled by what Alexander J. Schölch simply calls "local lords," *shaykh*s, who were Ottoman tax farmers, collecting the rural surplus as tribute to the Turkish overlords.[7]

During periods of Ottoman decentralization or of weakness of central authority, the local Palestinian lords gained a greater measure of autonomy, which perhaps enabled some feudalization. Ottoman-appointed or -con-firmed *nahiya shaykh*s ruled the Palestinian countryside next to urban no-tables, along with the Ottoman religious or administrative officials. The families of some of these rural *shaykh*s and urban notables remained influ-ential into the twentieth century, not because their official positions sus-tained them but (as discussed in the next chapter) because they were able to accommodate and adapt their positions and material bases of power to the changing economic situation. The drive for reform (the Tanzimat), adminis-trative reorganization, and centralization by the Ottoman authorities in the middle of the nineteenth century disempowered the rural *nahiya shaykh*s. The whole of Palestine came under direct Ottoman control based in the major cities, which privileged the urban notables over the rural *shaykh*s.

European Penetration: The Prelude

While the economic conditions of Palestine during the first three centuries of Ottoman rule vacillated between the extremes of depression and prosperity, the social and political structures remained essentially unchanged. Ottoman functionaries came and went as officials, but no Turkish colonization or Turkification took place. Palestine's Arab character remained intact, and many of the ethnic minorities and remnants of invaders became Arabized over the years. The Ottoman Turkish administrators themselves were al-ways a tiny numerical minority who relied heavily in their bureaucratic ap-paratuses on local Arabs, who typically were their coreligionists. With respect to the Christian and the tiny Jewish minorities in Palestine, the Ottomans abided by the old covenant of the caliph 'Umar, the second successor after the Prophet Muhammad, and formalized it into the *millet* (sectarian) system. The social (including family) and religious affairs and courts of the "People of the Book," the Christians and Jews, were completely autonomous, though they had to pay a poll tax. A chief cleric of each sect *(millet)* was assigned to represent the sect before the Sublime Porte in Istanbul.

Of greater significance to the future of Palestine and the Arab Mashreq was Ottoman encouragement of the export-import trade with Europe. The Ottomans allowed European merchants, missionaries, and consuls to reside in the territory. As a result, the value of British and French trade with the Arab coastal cities rose during most of the nineteenth century. The primary agricultural commodities of the Palestinian and Arab Mashreq were exchanged for manufactured European goods—a pattern of trade that became the hallmark of underdevelopment in the twentieth century.

European missionary and cultural activity in Palestine and the region resumed after its long absence since the Crusades. Through concessions by the Sublime Porte to France, French (and Italian) Catholic missionary activity intensified but came into conflict with local Christian churches—the Orthodox, Coptic, Armenian, and Abyssinian. The Ottomans treated European merchants and other European residents in their domains, including Palestine, as another Christian *millet* and allowed them extraterritorial judicial, religious, cultural, and social autonomy. Contrary to the Arab *millet*s, which were subject to the sultan's authority, the European Christian *millet*s had the backing of the powerful and rising European states.

As the central Ottoman authorities weakened in the nineteenth century, European states extended their protection to the local Arab Christians and other minorities. France claimed protection over all the Catholics—Eastern and Western—of the Ottoman domains. Eastern Catholic ranks had swelled as the Maronite church of Mount Lebanon united with Rome and as Orthodox churches splintered, with some of these factions uniting with Rome as well. These sects became known as the Uniate churches. Not to be outdone, imperial Russia claimed protection over all the Orthodox churches. The British joined the trend by claiming protection over the tiny minorities of Jews, the Druze (a unique, independent splinter sect from Shi'a Islam), and the newly recruited local Protestants. The European claims of protection emerged as one of the most powerful forms of leverage on the weakened Ottoman Empire. European economic, political, and cultural intervention in Ottoman Palestine and the Arab Mashreq became the overwhelming force that has shaped the economic, social, cultural, and political history of Palestine and the region ever since.

Opening to the West:
Egyptian Occupation, Palestinian Revolt

Napoleon Bonaparte's invasion of Egypt and Palestine in 1798–1799 both symbolizes and signals intensive European intervention in the region. Napoleon's march into Palestine was unsuccessful. He was stopped at the gates of 'Akka by the allied forces of the Ottoman governor, Ahmad al-Jazzar, and local Arabs. In his retreat from Palestine, Napoleon unleashed a scorched-earth policy, his troops destroying and burning the coastal area of Palestine. His depredations followed upon the disasters of the plague, the locust, the tax farmer, and the heavy-handed repression of al-Jazzar in the last quarter of the eighteenth century. Palestine thus began its modern period in an inauspicious condition.

Within the region the Ottomans were challenged by Muhammad Ali, the ruler of Egypt, victor over Napoleon and nominally their subordinate. In a military campaign by Ibrahim Pasha, Muhammad Ali's son, Egypt wrested control of Palestine and Syria from central Ottoman authority. The Egyptian occupation (1831–1840) introduced reforms that led to the dismantling of the old order. The Egyptian policy of centralized control rapidly came into conflict with the system of local notables and rural *shaykh*s who had established themselves as autonomous tax farmers and political brokers during Ottoman rule. The Egyptian ruler attempted to disarm the population, institute military conscription and corvée labor, increase the rate of taxation, impose a capitation tax (*ferde,* Turkish for "individual," from the Arabic *fard*), and establish trade monopolies.

Egyptian policies became burdensome to the Palestinian population, which consequently rebelled in 1834.[8] The peasants resisted heavier taxes and conscription, while the notables resisted Egyptian centralization of tax collection, the basis of their long-standing power and autonomy.

Determined to quell the rebellion, Ibrahim Pasha ordered attacks on the cities and leaders of the revolt. Parts of several towns and many villages were destroyed; rape and mass killings were perpetrated. It is estimated that Ibrahim Pasha forcibly conscripted ten thousand men to serve in Egypt. The population was disarmed and an iron rule reimposed. In the six more years of Egyptian rule following the rebellion, until 1840, governmental control in local affairs increasingly tightened.

The Egyptian era initiated other important social developments that accelerated in pace and widened in scope during the Ottoman period that followed. For example, the Egyptians lifted economic and other restrictions on Christians (and the small minority of Jews), and European Christian missionaries flowed into the country. Egyptian rule thus opened Palestine to Western intervention on a larger scale and encouraged the emergence of local urban notables, who inserted themselves as intermediaries on behalf of the western European capitalist economies.

Ironically, Ibrahim's process of centralization facilitated the nearly nationwide revolt in 1834 against his rule and further integrated the country. From then on, but especially after the end of the Crimean War in 1856, varied processes and factors progressively gave the area of Palestine social, economic, administrative, and political coherence, which culminated in the twentieth-century (Mandate of) Palestine.[9] If a modern state is defined by its monopoly over the use of violence and the regulation of both national and local affairs, then the Egyptian administration of Palestine in the 1830s formed the first such entity in the region, and the resurgent Ottoman Empire, which reconquered Syria and Palestine in 1840, continued the process.

Egyptian rule in Palestine ended not because Palestinians managed to overthrow the occupiers. Rather, Ibrahim Pasha was defeated by the combined forces of the Ottoman sultan, the British navy, and troops raised locally (Syrian, Lebanese, and Palestinian). Europe, especially Britain, feared the end of the Ottoman Empire—the so-called sick man of Europe—as it was being challenged and replaced by the newly rising power of Muhammad Ali's Egypt. The British thus conspired against Muhammad Ali with his erstwhile French allies by agreeing to the French conquest of northern Africa, by helping to rearm and resupply the Ottoman army and some local forces, and by engaging directly in naval attacks against Egyptian forces. The Ottoman sultan reimposed his authority over Syria and Palestine, and Muhammad Ali was reduced to a mere weakened local monarch under the nominal sovereignty of the sultan.

The price the Ottomans paid for regaining Syria and Palestine was high; the British acquired strategic power in the whole Near East. Perhaps as an act of goodwill, or pressure, the Ottoman authorities agreed to the Anglo-Turkish commercial convention of 1838:[10] reduction of import duties, abolition of prohibitions and duties on exports, and in general the elimination of trade barriers. And in 1839 the Ottomans issued the famous Hatt-i Sherif of Gulhane. This was one of several generations of famous edicts of reform that the Ottoman authorities issued during the nineteenth century and that are collectively known as the Tanzimat (rationalization and reorganization). The commercial convention and reforms gave the British and the other Europeans much greater leverage in penetrating the Ottoman domains, including Palestine.

After the exit of the Egyptian army in 1840, Ottoman authority did not control the rivalry and power struggles of the local Palestinian notables. Palestine lapsed into some disorder as the notables and their factional allies, some of whom had profited by and emerged stronger from the Egyptian occupation, struggled for power. By the 1860s, however, the Ottomans had become determined to impose their policy of centralization, direct control, and reform. To this end, they launched a systematic military campaign to subjugate and break the power of the local lords. The rural *shaykh*s succumbed or were defeated militarily by Ottoman armies; some were sent into exile. A new order was emerging in the second half of the nineteenth century. The *shaykh*s and notables tried to protect their sociopolitical positions by integrating themselves into the new structures of the resurgent Ottoman administration, especially the urban political-administrative *majalis,* councils that supervised tax farming, the commercial boards, the courts of law, and so forth. Social, economic, and political power shifted from the rural *shaykh*s to the urban notables in these councils.

From Subsistence to Market Economy

Although the feuds of the notables during the 1840s and 1850s were at times economically destructive,[11] economic activity generally increased throughout the first half of the nineteenth century. As an example, and perhaps as a measure of improved economic conditions, trade between the Palestinian districts and the rest of the Middle Eastern region and Europe grew substantially. The available figures indicate that British exports to Syria and Palestine rose from an annual average of £119,753 between 1836 and 1839 to a high of £303,254 in 1850.[12] The majority of imports were cotton goods. Palestine exported cereals to Britain from Gaza and Jaffa.

During this period Palestine was also involved in trade with other parts of the eastern Ottoman domains. Syrian and Palestinian exports to Egypt and Turkey rose from £250,504 in 1836 to £359,732 in 1838, while imports rose from £197,272 to £296,996 for the same years. This process of increased commercialization (or, to be more correct, the transition from a subsistence to a market economy) in the course of the disintegration of quasi-feudal relations in Syria, Palestine, and Lebanon in the mid nineteenth century is detailed in the works of many scholars, especially I. M. Smilianskaya, Roger Owen, and Beshara Doumani.[13] However, whereas both Owen and Charles Issawi stressed the relative importance of the European over the regional trade sector, Doumani disputed that conclusion, arguing that the impetus for the development of a market economy in Palestine came as well from the indigenous regional dynamics of agricultural specialization.[14]

Indigenous Commercialization: The Case of Nablus

The major industrial regional centers and internationally linked commercial cities such as Aleppo and Damascus in Syria experienced a sharp decline as a result of the direct European economic onslaught, whereas the religiously significant city of al-Quds (Jerusalem) started its steep economic, demographic, and institutional ascendance. Nablus, however, a smaller, inland, and relatively autonomous urban center, underwent a process of commercialization and transformation that was a result more of indigenous investment activity than of foreign capital.

Nablus had long manufactured and traded, locally and regionally, in textiles and soap. Both industries relied on locally grown agricultural products: cotton and olive oil. Textile manufacturing and the expansion of soap production began in the 1820s—before the emergence of competition from machine-made European textiles. As Owen, Haim Gerber, and Doumani pointed out, European goods did not cut into the Nablus textile market until the 1850s, because Nablus supplied the poorer and more traditional peasants.[15] By the 1850s, the textile industry of Nablus had been put at a disadvantage by imports from Damascus and Cairo.

Not so, however, the soap industry. Olive oil was always in demand as a cash crop. As the regional and local demand for soap increased, the merchants of Nablus actively sought and encouraged olive oil production.[16]

The principal mechanism for the Nablus merchants' appropriation of the olive oil surplus of the countryside was the *salam* (futures purchase) contract and moneylending system, which was legitimate under the shari'a as interpreted by the Hanafi school of Islamic jurisprudence.[17] The *salam* system encouraged trade, provided liquid capital to the rural population, intensified the monetization of the economy, and increased the levels of investment and production. Without political positions or power (as tax farmers or large landowners), the Nablus merchants and financiers had only moneylending to access the rural surplus. By the mid nineteenth century, the Nablus merchants had replaced landlords and rural *shaykh*s as the prime agents of moneylending to the rural population. They also acted as mercantile middlemen in the supply of cash crops to European traders and entered into alliances with the existing elites: landowners, rural *shaykh*s, and religious and administrative officials.

Most important for the Palestinian peasantry, usurious moneylending (involving 15–35 percent interest rates) led to the massive indebtedness of the peasantry—who were increasingly forced to pay taxes in cash rather than kind—and the commercialization of the agricultural land and its loss as collateral. By the second half of the century, a growing number of peasants had lost their land and become sharecroppers and tenant farmers on land that their ancestors had tilled for centuries. As a result, usurious merchants transformed themselves into large landlords. Further, a growing differentiation among the peasantry led to new patterns of stratification: the emergence of both landless and rich peasants.[18]

Changes in class structure and relations were not limited to the Nablus countryside. The city itself also changed as a consequence of the capitalization and consolidation of the soap industry. Because soap production was a capital-intensive industry, it favored single merchants, partners, or joint owners with concentrated wealth, who came increasingly to finance every stage of production. Many individuals simultaneously became soap manufacturers, oil merchants, moneylenders, entrepreneurs, and landowners.[19]

In short, by mid century a new composite ruling class, based principally on the expropriation of the rural surplus (from peasants who had been disarmed, left indebted, and abandoned by their traditional rural leaders), was composed of merchants, tax-farming urban notables, religious functionaries, and urbanized landowners. In contrast to these powerful notables and families, the peasantry began a long process of dispossession and emergence as a proletarianized mass.

Palestine at Mid Nineteenth Century

Palestinian cities and their surrounding areas during the eighteenth century can be divided into two types: those directly impacted by the Western thrust into Palestine, which included Jerusalem, Bethlehem, Nazareth, Jaffa, and Haifa, and those that were less directly affected, such as Nablus, Gaza, al-Khalil, Safad, Tabariyya, and ʿAkka.

Except for the demographic decline of ʿAkka, the available data indicate that the latter cities and their districts generally experienced economic and sociopolitical developments similar to those of Nablus.[20] For example, by the 1850s the older tetrapolis of al-Khalil (Hebron) had merged into a single city as a consequence of its economic and demographic growth. Hebron was known for its glassware, colorful jewelry, leather tanning, and water bags. Although these were important, the city relied mostly on viticulture, sheep and goat herding, trade with the bedouins, and the sale of grapes, raisins, and *dibs* (molasses made from carob) within Palestine and for export to the region. Imported Bohemian and other European glassware did not have an immediate impact in the local market, as Hebron glass was sold to poorer peasants and nomads. In urban centers, such as Jerusalem, shops stocked both Hebron and European glassware.

The market for glassware was similar to that for pottery, soap, and fabrics produced in Gaza. Although the black pottery of Gaza was a conspicuous product, the city's weaving industry was no less significant. The Gazans turned wool from the bedouins and flax and cotton from Egypt into textiles. Gaza, however, relied less on handicrafts and industry than on agriculture and trade.

In the 1850s Gaza was an important trade entrepôt, a node in the regional trade routes between Egypt, Arabia, and the Fertile Crescent and also with Europe. During the boom years of international grain demand (especially around the time of the Crimean War), Gaza and Jaffa were vital grain-exporting centers. Similar to Nablus and Hebron, Gaza was also directly linked to the annual hajj caravan from Damascus and the north. Gaza began to decline as a regional trade center only after the opening of the Suez Canal in 1869. The secondary cities of Palestine did not undergo a fundamental economic restructuring during this period, although they shared in the general economic upswing.

The experience of Nablus, Gaza, and Hebron—substantially different from that of the major cities of Jerusalem, Jaffa, and Haifa—indicates that the development of capitalism in the mid nineteenth century was slow and uneven. It was also based largely on the production and manufacture of goods from agricultural crops. However, capital accumulation increasingly shifted from a base of regional trade to export-oriented agriculture and import trade in manufactured goods, which placed Palestine at a disadvantage in relation to industrializing Europe. The development of capitalism in Palestine was slow despite the presence of a money-commodity nexus. Nevertheless, wage labor appeared in the form of farmworkers and urban artisan-industrial labor, construction labor, and service workers.

As in Jabal Nablus, rural wage labor, although on a small scale, signified labor and social differentiation of the peasantry throughout Palestine at mid century. Most significant, however, was the dispossession of the peasantry and its "transformation from owners of allotments and small proprietors to *metayer*s (tenant farmers)."[21] Large-scale farming had not yet appeared, and the peasant-*metayer* was economically exploited by semifeudal conditions imposed by the usurer merchants and landlords. This class of landlords and merchants reinvested not in agriculture but in trade, usury, real estate in the urban areas, and to a much less extent in manufactures such as spinning mills. The Palestine-wide composite class of interlocked urbanized notables, together with the emergent coastal comprador bourgeoisie (agents of foreign firms), commanded an important role in the second half of the nineteenth century and the first half of the twentieth century. The comprador bourgeoisie in particular and the merchants and landed gentry connected to it by trade and money operations were the indigenous social classes that facilitated the European penetration of Palestine and the rest of the Mashreq.

In short, the development of a market economy and the advancement of capitalism in mid-nineteenth-century Palestine were based primarily on agricultural specialization in the context of increasing population and trade. As a result, villages sprang up on the plains, and the population shifted westward. Coastal urban centers began their rapid growth, and Christian merchants profited most from the European connection. Most important, the old subsistence and semifeudal order died, and the new market economy based on money and commodities triggered deep and qualitative social structural change that set the stage for greater transformation in the second half of the nineteenth century.

Integration of Palestine into the World Economy: 1856–1914

After the Crimean War, Palestine became more intensively and extensively integrated into the world economy, laying the foundations for its capitalist peripheralization. This period advanced the destruction of the old subsistence, pastoral, semifeudal, and commercial society, as agrarian production, agrarian landownership, agricultural export trade, urbanization, and urban economic development expanded. In addition to the penetration of foreign capital, the combined and mutually reinforcing factors of Ottoman reform and the growing link between indigenous commercial and finance capital and European markets impelled the change.

Ottoman Reform

Administrative and legal reforms were part of a general Ottoman policy of modernizing and centralizing the state against the European threat. The Ottomans also renewed their interest in the Arab provinces as they lost their eastern European territories. With respect to Palestine, the administrative reorganization linked the territory directly to Istanbul. Nevertheless, the Ottomans popularly and often formally referred to the country as Arz-i Filistin ("land of Palestine"), not unlike the Arabic name its indigenous inhabitants used.[22] Ottoman reform and reorganization began, as we noted in an earlier section, in 1839 with the Hatt-i Sherif of Gulhane (the Noble Rescript).[23] The Hatt guaranteed the security of life, honor, and fortune for Ottoman subjects regardless of their religion. It called for the establishment of systems of assessing, fixing, and levying taxes, of raising troops by conscription, and of the creation of a salaried government bureaucracy. The assurance of free possession, utilization, and inheritance of property and guarantees against arbitrary confiscation was noteworthy. In effect, this decree created the minimal conditions for the development of private property, a market, and bourgeois social relations and culture.[24]

The weakness of central Ottoman authorities and their involvement in major border wars, however, discouraged full implementation of the Hatt-i Sherif Tanzimat. Social and political upheavals of the 1850s and 1860s led both the Ottomans and the leading Europeans powers to formulate new political and administrative structures that would produce a more secure framework for the expansion of commercial agriculture and the growth of trade.[25] Accordingly, in 1856 the Ottoman sultan 'Abdul-Majid issued a new decree, the Hatt-i Humayun (the Imperial Rescript).

The new edict reaffirmed the principles of the Hatt-i Sherif of Gulhane, including equal rights for non-Muslims. It also specified the rationalization of administration, taxation, and justice. Most important for the economy of the empire, the Tanzimat produced new land and penal codes in 1858, a reorganization of the legal system in 1860, and new maritime and commercial codes in 1861. Perhaps most relevant were the 1861 *tapu* (Arabic *tabu*), or land registration laws, which formally allowed state *miri* land to be sold as *mulk,* or private property, and which gave foreigners the right to own landed property. As a consequence, Christian and Jewish Europeans bought land, and the process of colonization commenced.

The expenditures for the Crimean War and the corruption and extravagance of the ruling class contributed to an Ottoman financial crisis, forcing the government to obtain loans from European banks and eventually leading to Ottoman bankruptcy. In 1881 the Muharram Decree (named after the Muslim month in which it was issued) consolidated European financial control over the empire. In a parallel development, the Egyptian government also went bankrupt, and Britain occupied Egypt and took control of its finances in 1882. Overall, these events intensified European influence in the Ottoman Empire and Egypt and accelerated the development of distorted and dependent capitalism in the whole region, including Palestine.

The Expansion and Consolidation of Private Property

The consequences of the Ottoman reforms on landownership in Palestine were complex and in some instances contradictory. Schölch believes that in spite of the privatization of much communal land *(miri* and *musha'a),* the *musha'a* system may have actually increased with the expansion of cultivation in the coastal and inland plains.[26] Yet the profitability of cash crop agriculture and the tax revenues accrued may have encouraged the Ottoman authorities to codify informal private landownership patterns in the land law of 1858 and the *tabu* land registration law of 1861. These changes in the land law led to the rise of extensive landed estates privately owned by urban notables from Palestine and Lebanon. For the peasantry, the ownership of private property was more of a short-term liability than an asset. Because peasants feared that the *tabu* law would increase taxation and extortion and the conscription of the owner and family members into the military, many registered their land in the names of their clan chiefs or urban *a'yan.* Often the *tabu* law confirmed the de jure right of rural and urban tax farmers to lands they had managed to appropriate de facto. Over the years, a great number of peasants lost the legal rights to their land and became mere sharecroppers, tenant farmers, and rural wage laborers. Furthermore, in the late 1860s the Ottoman authorities carried out land sale campaigns, especially in northern Palestine.[27]

Privatization of landholding in Palestine thus contributed to the decline of small and medium-sized properties, the rise of huge landed estates, and the increase in land prices. The arable land of Palestine amounts to 8.76 million *dunum*s (4 *dunum*s to 1 acre), that is, 33 percent of the total land area. "According to official data for 1909, 16,910 families worked 785,000 dunums in the sanjaks of Jerusalem, Nablus and Acre, or an average of 46 dunums each. A register from the second decade of this century listed 144 large landed proprietors in Palestine owning 3,130,000 dunums, or an average of 22,000 dunums each."[28] Naji 'Allush noted that 250 large landlords owned 4.143 million *dunums,* representing nearly half the agricultural land of Palestine.[29] Table 2.1 provides a breakdown of such large landholding.

Schölch identified three principal groups that acquired the land: the urban *a'yan,* members of the coastal commercial and financial bourgeoisie (most of them Europeans and European protégés, including those of

TABLE 2.1 Large Landholdings in Palestine by District, Early Twentieth Century

	Number of Landlords	Area[a] (in thousands of dunums)
Jerusalem and Hebron	26	240
Jaffa	45	162
Nablus and Tulkaren	5	121
Jenin	6	114
Haifa	15	141
Nazareth	8	123
'Akka	5	157
Tabariyya	6	73

[a]1 *dunum* = 919 square meters, or roughly 0.25 acre.

SOURCE: N. 'Allush, *Arab Resistance in Palestine (1917–1948)* (in Arabic) (Berirut: Dar al-Tali'a, 1975), 15.

Beirut), and European colonists (German Christian Templars and Jews). *Awqaf* lands (untaxable religious properties) were also extensive, estimated at 100,000 *dunums*. The German Pietistic Protestant colonizing by the Templars started somewhat ahead of that of the European Jews; however, Jewish colonization, which began after 1882, surpassed that of the Templars quickly as Jews acquired large land areas by World War I. Of the European Jews, the most notable was Melville Bergheim, a German merchant, banker, industrialist, and landowner who acquired 20,000 *dunum*s near the village of Abu-Gush.[30]

Trade and Agriculture

From mid century until World War I, Palestine tremendously increased agricultural production and exports. The growing trade volume also reflected the extension of cultivation to nearly all land previously used for pasturage. Schölch provided figures for land used for grain production in northern Palestine; his data show that 49 percent of the land was devoted to wheat and barley, 13 percent to sesame, and the rest to other grains and olives.[31]

During this same period, agricultural production and export shifted. Starting in the early 1850s, demand for sesame (by France, which used the oil in the manufacture of soap and perfume) increased production sharply. While sesame replaced cotton and grains in the more hilly regions of Palestine, the production of oranges in western coastal areas leaped significantly, especially around Jaffa. Between 1850 and 1880 alone, the orange grove

TABLE 2.2 Average Yearly Exports of the Main Goods from Jaffa, Haifa, and
'Akka, 1872–1882 (in millions of *kiles, oqqas,* and units)

Export Goods	Jaffa (1873–1877 and 1879–1882)	Haifa (1872–1880)	'Akka
Wheat (*kiles*)[a]	0.279	0.429	1.2911
Barley (*kiles*)	0.102	0.111	0.203
Dura (*kiles*)	0.062	0.233	0.625
Sesame (*oqqas*)[b]	2.059	0.800	1.000
Olive oil (*oqqas*)	1.027	0.053	0.260
Soap (*oqqas*)	0.904	–	–
Wool (*oqqas*)	0.115	–	–
Oranges (*units*)	19.650	–	–

[a]1 *kile* = 36 liters.
[b]1 *oqqa* = 1.28 kilograms.
SOURCE: A. Schölch, *Palestine in Transformation, 1856–1882: Studies in Social, Economic and Political Development,* translated by W. C. Young and M. C. Gerrity (Washington, DC: Institute for Palestine Studies, 1993), 82.

areas of Jaffa quadrupled in size,[32] and the orange harvest increased from 20 million units in the mid-1850s to 36 million in 1880. Orange groves were the most profitable form of capital investment of the period.

Beside grains, sesame, and oranges, Palestine exported olive oil and *durra* (maize) as well as soap and other minor products. Table 2.2 provides data on the average yearly export values between 1872 and 1882. The table shows that oranges and sesame, and secondarily wheat, became the principal exports of Palestine.

The prosperity of Palestine continued to grow in the first decade of the twentieth century. The value of production and export had fluctuated throughout the nineteenth century, however, as a result of weather, market demands, and the political and security conditions in Palestine, the region, Europe, and the United States. As examples, a boom in cotton prices occurred during the first half of the 1860s as a result of the American Civil War, and grain prices surged in the mid-1850s as a result of the Crimean War. In contrast, in 1877–1879 Palestine was hit by drought and locusts in addition to heavy Ottoman conscription, factors that led to depressed levels of production and the importation of grain and flour.[33] Table 2.3 gives the total values of exports from Jaffa from 1885 to the early twentieth century.

During most of the second half of the nineteenth century, Palestine showed an export surplus that helped offset the larger Syrian-Ottoman balance-of-trade deficits.[34] This pattern reversed in the early years of the

TABLE 2.3 Total Value of Exports from Jaffa, 1885–1905 (in thousands of pounds sterling)

	Wheat	Maize	Olive Oil	Sesame	Soap	Wool	Oranges	Colocynth	Hides	Wines and Spirits	Water-melon	Handi-crafts	Other Articles
1885	3.60	7.87	5.26	32.00	13.72	2.40	26.50	0.80	0.64	–	–	–	19.77
1886	3.32	9.00	–	45.53	8.96	3.70	22.40	2.15	0.54	–	–	–	18.93
1887	15.00	21.00	7.55	42.50	38.40	3.60	36.00	1.60	1.00	–	–	–	19.72
1888	7.80	16.96	20.62	28.12	45.00	2.00	55.00	2.00	0.75	–	–	–	26.06
1889	16.95	18.20	26.43	62.66	33.60	2.30	51.20	1.80	–	–	–	–	30.40
1890	19.92	111.24	75.08	109.32	44.70	4.56	83.12	2.20	7.62	–	–	–	89.62
1891	3.30	17.30	20.70	30.80	124.00	4.30	108.40	3.80	8.60	–	–	–	79.33
1892	–	0.42	1.35	69.35	46.80	5.55	62.00	2.58	7.10	–	–	–	63.30
1893	–	2.58	13.84	54.94	112.00	2.40	69.50	0.95	4.07	–	–	–	73.34
1894	–	2.00	9.05	42.15	114.00	0.40	51.00	0.8.	1.20	–	–	–	65.00
1895	3.56	3.20	2.60	42.75	93.24	2.70	65.00	1.40	3.80	–	–	–	65.37
1896	1.92	14.17	6.05	59.80	113.11	5.32	72.60	2.50	14.27	–	–	–	83.69
1897	–	8.45	3.50	40.00	81.90	4.00	75.80	1.00	9.80	–	26.00	–	58.93
1898	14.00	3.00	4.50	28.00	62.00	3.36	82.50	1.40	8.10	–	24.85	–	75.07
1899	–	1.22	11.35	21.00	125.75	1.75	77.00	1.30	10.25	2.90	26.10	–	47.52
1900	–	2.95	9.11	30.56	44.55	1.36	74.21	1.88	1.16	21.84	24.50	–	52.37
1901	–	0.12	11.50	25.20	57.00	2.15	86.52	2.19	3.45	35.35	21.75	–	42.40
1902	–	1.45	–	29.26	18.76	1.32	86.50	1.45	2.98	18.40	17.65	4.85	20.77
1903	–	–	5.33	30.04	77.56	4.50	93.43	3.70	4.00	30.35	19.00	7.10	47.23
1904	–	–	0.95	23.35	62.00	7.93	103.95	3.65	6.00	37.86	11.00	9.00	29.61
1905	11.0	–	–	13.82	56.91	4.54	114.65	3.37	8.11	47.02	18.80	12.58	77.01
Total	100.37	141.13	234.77	861.15	1374.05	70.51	1504.28	42.52	102.81	193.72	189.65	33.53	1085.44

SOURCE: M. Buheiry, "The Agricultural Exports of Southern Palestine, 1885–1914," *Journal of Palestine Studies* 10, 4 (Summer 1981): 70.

twentieth century, during which the value of imports exceeded that of exports. Still, Palestine did not develop a deficit, because of the flow of capital into the country from varied sources: immigrant Palestinians in the Americas who sent remittances; European interests that sought to build up and support the increasing number of Christian settlers and institutions in the country; Jewish settlers and institutions; and European companies and entrepreneurs who invested especially in infrastructure and railways. This "invisible" capital inflow helped to redress the early-twentieth-century balance-of-trade deficit and stimulated steady economic growth, uneven prosperity, and expansion of the market economy.

Jerusalem and Coastal Urban Development

Beginning with the end of the Crimean War, commercial activity in Jerusalem and the coastal urban centers of Jaffa and Haifa increased rapidly. This increase, in turn, triggered growth in the size of the urban population, the spatial area of the cities, productivity, monetization and capitalization of the economy, and social differentiation. In general, the development of commercial exchange and growth in the market were greater in the coastal area than inland. There were, however, two exceptions: Jerusalem, an interior city, was much more integrated into the European economy, and Nablus, also a city in the interior, was more integrated into the local and regional markets.

Jerusalem became an important center of religious activity for European Christians and Jews. Europeans built and maintained Christian schools, hospitals, convents, monasteries, churches, and charitable institutions, which may have stimulated local Arab Christians to do the same. Similarly, Jewish immigration and charitable activity grew, although settler colonies were not established until 1882. During the 1870s Jerusalem supported an average of ten thousand to twenty thousand pilgrims a year during the pilgrimage seasons.[35] Jerusalem's growth,[36] like that of Jaffa and Haifa, triggered a construction boom that both signified and furthered the general economic expansion.

Nablus, in contrast, grew as a regional manufacturing and trade center unconnected to European pilgrimage. Its main industries, as we noted earlier in the chapter, were the manufacture of soap, olive oil, and cotton textiles. Between 1860 and 1882, the number of soap factories increased from fifteen to thirty.[37] Nablus textiles supplied the local and regional markets, and Nablus trade was connected to the hajj caravans to Mecca. Although not directly linked to European trade and pilgrimage, Nablus shared in the general market expansion and economic growth of the period.

Of the coastal cities, 'Akka declined as nearby Haifa, because of the deepness of its port and its metropolitan atmosphere, acquired a favored position for European steamship trade.[38] Haifa and Jaffa grew in economic activity, population, and social heterogeneity. Between 1841 and 1917, the built-up areas of Haifa and Jaffa expanded dramatically—from 123 *dunum*s to 1,201 and from 98 to 1,280, respectively, although population densities actually declined.[39] Haifa and Jaffa also benefited from the construction of roads and a railway connecting them to the interior in the late Ottoman era.

The most important port city during the last days of the Ottoman control of Palestine was Jaffa. It was the principal port for the export of agricultural products and the nearest seaport to Jerusalem.[40] Although Jaffa had no harbor for large seagoing vessels, it processed eighty thousand passengers annually during the 1890s.[41] A road connecting Jaffa and Jerusalem opened in 1868, a railway in 1892; both furthered commercial activity along the coast. Jaffa was also a center of manufacture (soap, olive oil, and sesame oil), although orange production was the most important source of a need for seasonal wage labor. In short, Jaffa, like all Palestinian towns, grew rapidly, engaging in economic exchange with the surrounding areas, relying less on subsistence farming and production for use, and creating more wage labor.

Handicrafts and Industry.   Urban centers were the sites of relatively vigorous industrial and handicraft production. Overall figures for soap production in Palestine are unavailable. However, one index of its significance is the figures for export from the seaport of Jaffa. Jaffa alone exported 43,000 tons (at £1.4 million) in 1885, which rose to 525,000 tons (at £12.6 million) in 1899 and then declined to 227,500 tons (at £5.7 million) in 1905.[42]

Similar to that of olive oil, sesame oil extraction was vital to trade and to local consumption. It is estimated that toward the end of the nineteenth century, between thirty and forty presses existed in the Ramleh, Jaffa, and Jerusalem triangle. Moreover, spinning and weaving were important to cities such as Safad, Nazareth, Nablus, Beit Jala, al-Khalil, and Gaza and continued to expand despite the increase in imported manufactured cotton goods throughout most of the nineteenth century.[43] Reports from around the turn of the twentieth century, however, indicate a decline in those activities. Nevertheless, the production of Christian devotional artifacts and souvenirs in Bethlehem, Jerusalem, and Nazareth, destined for pilgrims and for export, rose sharply. Except for soap and souvenirs, the major share of manufactured products was destined for the local and regional markets, another index of the expanding integrative capitalist market of Palestine. Regular weekly market *(souq)* days—Fridays in al-Quds, Jaffa, al-Khalil, Majdal, Gaza, and elsewhere—were important in furthering rural-urban exchange.

In general, industrial and craft production in Palestine during this period was labor-intensive and technologically primitive. For example, soap was produced in huge brass cooking vats, surrounded by containers for storing oil and trays for pouring out, leveling, and cutting the soap into cakes. Skilled soap workers were organized into guilds, supervised by a *shaykh* who maintained standards, regulated trade, and appropriated the taxes due to the authorities.[44] The master and the workers had always been paid in kind, but by the turn of the century, some were paid a wage.

Banking and Credit Systems.   Perhaps one of the most important mechanisms of the penetration by European capital, the growth of a market economy, and the integration of Palestine into the world economy was banking and other systems of credit, necessitated by the rise of the export-import trade. The first bank, the Imperial Ottoman Bank, a joint British-French venture, opened in 1885 in Jerusalem and Jaffa. Other banks followed shortly thereafter: Crédit Lyonnais in Jaffa and Jerusalem; the Anglo-Palestine Company (a Jewish bank) and the Deutsche Palästina Bank in Haifa, Jaffa, and Jerusalem; and the Palestinian Commercial Bank.[45] These banks were pivotal in the financing of infrastructure late in the Ottoman era; projects included the port facilities in Jaffa and Haifa, highways and railways, and telegraph and other facilities. The banks were also crucial in processing the capital flows from Europe and the Americas and in the building of factories just prior to World War I.

Transportation and Communication.   Besides banking and credit systems, another factor in facilitating the development of an internal market in Palestine and of integration of the country into the European markets was the newly developed communications and transport network. Prior to the building of the Jaffa-Jerusalem carriageway in 1868, all transport depended on animal power: horses, mules, donkeys, and camels. With the paving of roads, the volume of traffic in goods and people rose considerably. By 1913 Palestine had the highest ratio of length of railways to population in the region: more than six hundred kilometers per million people.[46] The material, fuel, and skills necessary for railway construction and maintenance came from outside Palestine and thus did not have a strong effect on the economy except to increase export, import, and to some degree internal trade.[47]

The Ottomans established a postal service and allowed the foreign powers—Austria, Germany, France, and Russia—to do the same in Palestinian cities. In addition, a telegraph network, established in 1865, connected Palestinian towns with the region. Although humble, these facilities and services laid the foundations for the expansion of the market in Palestine and the country's greater integration into the European economies.

European Immigration and Colonial Settlement: The Beginnings

European colonists settled in Palestine, accelerating the integration of the country into Europe. Initially, however, immigrants in small numbers were Muslims from formerly held Ottoman territories: Maghrebis who had been pushed out by the French colonization of North Africa, Bosnians fleeing Austrian repression in Yugoslavia, and Circassian refugees from the Russian Caucasus.[48] They arrived in relatively small numbers and assimilated quickly into the culture and society of Arab Palestine.

Unlike the Muslim immigrants, who were refugees, the Christian and Jewish settlers were religiously and ideologically motivated. European Christian settlement began in 1868. The most successful settlers belonged to the Tempelgesellschaft (Association of Templars), an offshoot of a Protestant pietistic religious movement in the German kingdom of Württemberg. By World War I, the German Templars had established seven urban and agricultural settlements in Haifa, Jaffa, Sarouna, Jerusalem, Wilhelma, Galilean Bethlehem, and Waldheim. In addition to their agricultural, trade, and tourist activities, the German colonists organized a carriage service between Jaffa and Jerusalem and Haifa and Nazareth.

Templar numbers and impact on Palestine remained minimal compared to the influence of the Jewish immigrants. Small numbers of Jews lived in Palestine prior to 1882. They were Sephardic, originating from Spain, North Africa, and other parts of the Ottoman domains, and spoke Turkish or Arabic and often Ladino (a mixture of Spanish and Hebrew). Over the years they became acculturated and similar to the local Palestinian Arabs in most aspects of their life except religion. Following the pogroms in eastern Europe and Russia, however, Jewish immigration gained momentum: Approximately fifty thousand European Jews migrated to Palestine between 1882 and the beginning of World War I. Although the majority of Jewish migrants clustered in Palestinian cities, some attempted to establish themselves in agricultural settlements. "By 1908 there were twenty-six such colonies with 10,000 members and 400,000 dunums (100,000 acres) of land."[49] Most of this land had been purchased from one of two sources: the Ottoman government or large estate owners. Few Palestinian peasants sold their land, which they had long cultivated under the traditional land tenure system. Instead, they had found themselves either evicted or employed as laborers. Thus began a process of dispossession and peasant disaffection that would culminate in violent conflicts late in the nineteenth century and the early twentieth century.[50]

European Jewish agricultural settlements at first produced specialized cash crops, such as grapes for wine and spirits. Later, using poorly paid Palestinian labor, the settlements entered into citrus fruit production and established marketing cooperatives. By 1913, Jewish orange production was 15 percent of the total Palestinian export for that year.[51] Shortly after the new century began, Jewish settlements stopped employing Palestinian Arab workers, instead relying exclusively on Jewish labor. In 1909, at Degania, the first kibbutz, an agricultural cooperative based on mixed farming with limited or no use of Arab labor, established an effective instrument for Jewish colonization of Palestine.[52]

Transformation of the Social Structure

Western intervention, the development of the market, and the initiation of European settlement in Palestine triggered profound changes in social structure during the last years of Ottoman rule. We analyze these social changes in terms of three broad areas: (1) population structure, distribution, and change; (2) reorganization in rural and urban class structure and commensurate changes in ethnic ties, religion, values, and social consciousness; and (3) the development of political consciousness and movements. The Ottoman capitulation agreements (accords that privileged the European merchants), the Tanzimat reforms, and the intrusive European presence combined to wrest Palestine from Ottoman authority in all but a nominal sense. Thus the economic and commensurate demographic, social, and political transformation occurred spontaneously, without central control, planning, or direction.

Population Change: Size and Distribution

Using the Ottoman census of 1849, Schölch estimated that 365,224 people lived in the Jerusalem province that included the central and southern districts of Palestine.[53] Two-thirds of the population lived in 657 villages and one-third in 13 major cities and towns.[54] Roughly 85 percent of the population was Muslim, 11 percent Christian (who lived principally in the major cities and villages around Jerusalem), and less than 4 percent Jewish (who lived primarily in the cities of Jerusalem, Hebron, Safad, and Tabariyya). From 1865 to 1866, a cholera epidemic struck the population, and the massive Ottoman conscription levies of Palestinian men for the Ottoman wars of 1876–1878 in the Balkans further depopulated the country. After the epidemics, the country grew rapidly: from roughly 0.5 million to over 700,000 between 1880 and 1913.[55]

This high rate of natural increase was accompanied by two other demographic processes. The first was the immigration of European Jews and Christians. As noted in the previous section, fifty thousand Jews immigrated to Palestine during this period. On the eve of World War I, the ratio of Jews in the total population had risen to nearly 10 percent, the majority of them European (Ashkenazi) rather than Sephardic. The influx of European Christians had raised the total Christian population from 11 to 16 percent by 1914.[56] Most European immigrants settled in the cities, especially Haifa, Jaffa, and Jerusalem.

The process of Palestinian urbanization, the second demographic process, escalated throughout the century but received a significant push three decades before 1914. The settlement of European Jews and Christians in the coastal cities and Jerusalem coincided with the migration of Palestinians from the rural areas, from the smaller outlying villages to the economically vigorous urban centers located along the principal arteries of transportation.

The urbanization process, instead of integrating the rural migrants into the urban community, seemed to increase the cultural divide between the *madaniyyin* (urbanites) and *fallahin* (peasants). A polarization in terms of income, education, and Westernization (in dress, use of consumer goods, taste, and behavior patterns) was superimposed on the already-existing attitude of superiority of the urban-based rulers, religious clerics, administrators, merchants, and landlords toward the peasant producers and taxpayers. The Palestinian *madani-fallah* dichotomy at the end of the Ottoman era represented the opposing social processes of creating a bourgeoisie and a proletariat.

Social Class Changes: The Rural Structure

Private property and capitalist relations of production in the context of an expanding market economy transformed class structure. In the rural areas, a complex process of social differentiation and stratification occurred, characterized by inequalities in landholding and new social relationships of production and distribution.[57] Toward the end of the Ottoman period, traditional rural institutions underwent important change as the autonomous *hamula* elders and *shaykh*s gave way to officially appointed village selectmen, *mukhtars*, the Ottoman state's representatives in the villages. All matters of personal and economic affairs came to require the written confirmation of the *mukhtar,* who was at first paid in kind and later salaried. With the decline of the corporate village socioeconomic institutions, social relations became increasingly between individuals rather than families or clans, and village solidarity began to disintegrate.

Earlier in the chapter there occurred a discussion of the rise of huge private estates owned by rural notables and (even more likely) by absentee urban landlords. This process of large- and medium-scale privatization of agricultural land inevitably led to the eviction of some peasants, who composed a stratum of landless peasants or "free" laborers. They, along with the hired plowmen, formed the bottom rural social class. Often seasonal workers, they sought wage employment in the unskilled construction jobs in neighboring towns and cities. By 1914 the class of unskilled workers had expanded considerably. Pamela Smith cited the diary of a Jewish Zionist immigrant-settler: "Hundreds of Arabs are gathering in the wide market square. . . . They are seasonal workers. Among them are a number of full time Arab workers, who live on the settler's farm and go straight to the orange grove. There are about 1,500 of them altogether, everyday."[58] Other peasants became sharecroppers, especially on the estates of absentee landlords. Their material condition was better than that of the wage laborers, as they combined sharecropping with rural wage labor.

Above the landless sharecroppers and wage laborers came the small landowners, who also worked as sharecroppers. Often the land they owned, small gardens *(hawakir),* allowed them to live above the subsistence level. Between the stratified lower peasantry and the large landlords existed a middle class of peasants, especially in the highlands of Jabal al-Quds, Jabal Nablus, and the Galilee. Over the years these relatively independent farmers became differentiated into a new class of peasants, and even landowners. But peasant indebtedness also led to evictions from the land, as reported by European travelers.[59] The loss of land or its fragmentation shunted many peasants into a variety of economic activities. The market or money economy in the countryside forced Palestinians to pursue several sources of income, a practice that blurred class lines, inhibited the consolidation of social class consciousness, and both constrained and encouraged the rupture of traditional social relations. The increasing disaggregation of the village structure marked the demise of self-governing rural society.

The Urban Class Structure

By the start of the twentieth century, as we have seen, Palestinian cities underwent some industrialization, escalating the expansion of commerce and tourist services. Beginning with the enlargement of the export and import trade, economic activities had an increasing effect on urban economic life that transformed the urban and ethnic social class structure. Five broad classes emerged: the *ashraf* (nobility), the merchants, the retail traders, the artisans, and the nucleus of an urban proletariat.[60]

The *ashraf* were descendants of Hijazi families, either from the Prophet or Muhammad's companions and the Arab Islamic military commanders who conquered Palestine in the seventh century. Among these families (who continue to play an important role in contemporary Palestinian affairs) were the Tamimis, who, like the Dajanis (Daoudis), were entrusted with *awqaf,* and the Nusseibehs, whom the second caliph, 'Umar, gave the keys to the city of al-Quds. Other families, such as the Husseinis, Khalidis, Alamis, and Nashashibis, were given similar trusts. *Waqf* trustees kept a share of the *waqf* revenue for their own use.

The *ashraf* were recognized as a corporate body with their own elected leader (the *naqib*), were exempted from paying taxes, and could be prosecuted only by their own council, not Ottoman authorities. Because they were literate, they often occupied Ottoman governmental posts and so were in an excellent position to take advantage of the changes made by the Ottoman administrative and economic reforms. Much peasant land was registered in their names, and they eventually converted it into private property. This property, in addition to the increase in their revenues, especially from management and control of religious *waqf*s, allowed them to accumulate capital rapidly and engage in other economic activities, sometimes competing with the non-*ashraf* urban merchants.

The emergent commercial bourgeoisie, especially the import-export merchants, tended to be Christian minorities, rather than the *ashraf,* because of the capitulations system that had begun centuries earlier. Favored by the European powers, the Palestinian and Lebanese Christian Arabs, and to a much smaller extent the Jewish minority, were able to take advantage of the expansion of the import-export trade. With the rapid increase in urban population and demand, these merchants accumulated vast wealth and diversified their economic activity into banking, credit services, real estate, some industry, and agricultural estates. Although the Christian Palestinian urban merchants became important economic movers in the country, the Muslim notables were politically more powerful in late Ottoman times. As educated Muslims, they were considered natural leaders of the Palestinian people, who were expressing a nascent patriotism, and they came to dominate the political life of Palestine.

Palestine's rapid and differentiated urbanization also brought forth a petite bourgeoisie of small (retail) merchants and shopkeepers and the beginnings of a new "middle class" of white-collar functionaries: civil servants, police, teachers, and clerks. Modern professionals such as journalists, lawyers, medical doctors, and engineers also began to appear in small numbers. Relative to their overall proportion in the population, Christians were overrepresented in the emerging intelligentsia and professional classes, largely because of the education they received from European missionaries. This overrepresentation of certain religious groups in different occupations gave Western observers the impression of ethnic specialization in economic activity. Although I believe that the thesis of ethnic division of labor in late Ottoman Palestine is overstated, Western sources note that Muslims dominated in the milling of wheat and other grains and the production of meat, sweets, glass, and wool; Orthodox Christians tended to be gold jewelers, makers of brass and copper utensils, and sellers of wines and spirits; Latins (local Roman Catholics) specialized in carpentry, blacksmithing, and barbering; and Jews were prominent in the production of wines and spirits, the repair of clocks and watches, the sale of perfumes, and banking and money changing. Other crafts and economic activity were common to all.[61]

Artisans were variously affected by market development in the cities. Many of the goods imported did not directly compete with locally produced crafts or products. They reflected the needs of the European settlers and the acquired tastes of the new Westernized, bourgeois Palestinians. Those artisans who produced for the bulk of the unmodernized population were not initially affected adversely. By World War I the demand structure for artisan goods had changed, as changing tastes, impoverishment of the peasantry, and price inflation decreased in some established crafts, such as textiles, but increased in new ones, such as roof tiles and metal and wood frames for construction purposes. Studies suggest that 10–15 percent of the labor force was involved in artisan production. Most artisans were in workshops, usually not exceeding five workers, or at home in cottage industries. Some worked as wage laborers for small merchants who supplied them with the raw materials and working capital; others worked for payment in kind.

Finally, although increasing numbers of people found themselves earning wages for their labor, a genuine, industrial proletariat had not yet appeared. The traditional patriarchal values and norms governing the social relations of production, including the urban guilds, were indeed decaying, but an absolute rupture with the past culture had not yet occurred. In an effort to further liberalize the economy, guilds were abolished outright by the Young Turks in control of the Ottoman Empire in 1912. More people were cast out of the corporate fold before new, more modern collective structures could smooth the transition. However, the restructuring of the modes of production and of sociopolitical relations, especially vis-à-vis the newly arriving foreign settlers and residents, triggered a process of indigenous political mobilization.

Political and Cultural Reactions

The structural transformations of Palestinian (as well as Syrian, Egyptian, and Iraqi) society during the nineteenth century encouraged the reemergence of an Arab rather than simply an Islamic consciousness and set the population on a collision course with the Turkish Ottoman overlords. For example, in the 1840s and 1850s, Western consuls reported that large segments of the Palestinian Arab population disliked or hated the Ottoman Turkish authorities. They "regarded the Turkish Caliphate as a fraud and distorted (as a political pun) the (honorific Turkish) title of *khan* into *kha'in* (traitor, in Arabic)."[62] The Ottoman Turks were also seen as responsible for the European economic and cultural assault on Palestine, especially during and after the Crimean War. In Palestine the reemergence and consolidation of Arab consciousness were accompanied by the emergence of Palestinian consciousness—the ideological side of the structural transformation of Palestinian society. These two identities, Arab and Palestinian, were mutually reinforcing.

Reflecting the Ottoman administrative divisions of Palestine into subdistricts of larger units based in Damascus and Sidon (later Beirut), the political economy of the country was also segmented in the latter half of the nineteenth century. Both the economy of the hills (traditionally semifeudal, provincial, and subsistence-based) and the economy of the plains (tribal, pastoral, and semisettled) were, as we have seen above, being transformed by monetization and capitalization. And yet the countrywide "parties" or factional alliances of Qays and Yaman[63] (ancient Arab names for a binary political division that existed as well in much of the rest of the Fertile Crescent) politically interlocked the Palestinians across religious, clan *(hamula),* and district divides. In short, although segments of Palestinian society were structurally (that is, physically and economically) isolated, they were nevertheless interconnected politically. The embryonic factors of capitalist development, such as the expansion of trade, the expansion and monetization of internal markets in both commodities and labor, and the extension of the communication infrastructure, overcame the structural isolation. Most visibly, subsistence farming and geographic isolation began to disappear as people increasingly came into contact with one another and with the more intrusive governmental authorities. The administrative reorganization, which elevated the *mutasariffiyya* (subdistrict) of Jerusalem into an independent unit directly linked to Istanbul and referred to the historic territory (including the northern districts of Nablus, 'Akka, and Galilee) as Arz-i Filistin, reflected Palestine's emergence as a single entity.

Religious Institutional Foundations

Palestine's status as a Christian Holy Land was upheld in the administrative institutions of three principal Christian denominations. The jurisdiction of the Greek Orthodox patriarchate of Jerusalem extended over the three ancient Roman districts of Palestine. So did the Latin (Roman Catholic) patriarchate and the Anglican (British Protestant) bishopric of Jerusalem. Each held authority throughout Palestine. It is therefore not surprising that Christians fostered the concept of "Filastin" as a country.[64] In general, local Arab Christian activism, including the establishment of social service institutions (schools, hospitals, orphanages, etc.), became all the more assertive as European and American missionary groups targeted them for proselytization. Rather than reinforcing their differences from their Muslim neighbors, then, Christians in Palestine tended to affirm their sense of belonging to a larger Arab and Palestinian community.

The informal or popular religion of the common and mostly illiterate people encouraged a "national" Palestinian consciousness. Two of the most important expressions of folk religion, those most "national" in character, were the *maqam*s and festivals of Nabi Saleh (the prophet Saleh) and Nabi Musa (the prophet Moses). Held after the spring harvests, these festivals drew thousands of people from villages all over Palestine, not only to celebrate the holiday but also to exchange information, commercial products, and political news; resolve feuds; and arrange marriages. In short, these festivals, attended by native Christians and Muslims alike, reasserted shared values and norms and encouraged a common Palestinian identity.

The Role of Modern Education and Values

Arab consciousness in Palestine was strengthened with the spread of literacy and formal education. Ottoman reforms included the establishment of schools for training modern cadres in administrative and military skills. The study of Arabic language and literature was secondary to the study of Turkish in these schools. The missionary and local private and religious schools, however, stressed Arabic; competing missionary educators thus distinguished their missions from the Ottoman authorities in order to ingratiate themselves with the indigenous Palestinian people.[65] At the same time, a growing intelligentsia was introduced to modern secular and scientific thought, which, in the context of an expansive market economy, stimulated new sociopolitical values, spurred an Arabic literary and language renaissance, encouraged wider intellectual horizons, and furthered Arab (as distinct from Ottoman or Islamic) consciousness.

The traditional sources of values in Palestinian society were the ideologies of Islam and Christianity, the semifeudal system, and tribal social organization. In sum, these fostered a sense of fatalism, dependency on a superior power, and social corporateness allied with the insignificance of the individual. The semifeudal order emphasized absoluteness in rule, social ascription, and status distinction, whereas the tribal organization taught strong corporate loyalty, independence of action, and egalitarianism. Though in many ways contradictory systems, both highlighted a narrowness of identity, of loyalty, and of sociopolitical consciousness. In addition, they were patriarchal, relegating women to an inferior status and circumscribed conditions. This narrowness, ascription, and absolutism conflicted with the values of secularism, liberalism, and new concepts regarding the value of the individual. The emergence of a modern, secular, and educated intelligentsia brought a new social division to the country (and the region): modernist versus traditionalist. The intelligentsia's debates inadvertently integrated the traditional tribal and semifeudal segments of society, as the elites from both competed for the leadership of "the people."

Palestinian Response to Pre–World War I Jewish Colonization

Unlike the Palestinian Jews (Sephardic and Oriental), who were culturally assimilated, the European Jews (Ashkenazim) tended to live in separate quarters in the cities of Jerusalem, al-Khalil, Tabariyya, and Safad. The new immigrant Ashkenazim rapidly became the majority of Jewish residents of Palestine: In 1845, 32 percent of Jews were Ashkenazim; by 1916 they made up 59 percent. Perhaps much more important for Palestine and the Palestinians was the rapid increase of the total Jewish population after 1882 and the establishment of agricultural colonies. Jewish population in agricultural colonies increased from 500 in 1882 to 11,990 in 1914, and in the urban areas it increased from 23,500 to 73,010 in the same period.[66]

Jewish agricultural land settlement in Ottoman Palestine went through two broad phases. The first (1870–1900) was unsystematic and dependent on the purchase of land and the direct financial support of wealthy European Jews. Most notably, the French Jewish banker Baron Edmund de Rothschild purchased land for seven settlements, the earliest of which were Migve Yisra'el (1870) and Petah Tiqva (1878) south and east of Jaffa, respectively. Unorganized settlements between 1876 and 1900 numbered twenty-two, with a land area of 167,073 *dunum*s. The second phase of organized settlements began when Rothschild turned over control and financing of the settlements to the Jewish Colonization Association (ICA), after the establishment of the World Zionist Organization (WZO) in Basel, Switzerland, in 1897. Between 1900 and 1914, twenty-five settlements were established with a land area of 163,984 *dunum*s.[67]

Spontaneous and intermittent Jewish settlement activity became systematic and expansive with the formal launching of the Zionist movement. Although early Palestinian reaction to Jewish settlement and land purchases was localized and impulsive, it became more conscious, political, and sustained with the second and later phases. The early responses were attacks by peasants and bedouins who were shut off from their communal or grazing land by Jewish settler-colonists.[68] For example, at the end of the century the ICA, with the forceful intervention of Ottoman troops, was able to expel the peasants from and take control of more than sixty thousand *dunum*s of land in the Tabariyya area. This and another case, in 'Afula, generated a great deal of newspaper coverage and agitation warning of the threat of dispossession by Zionism.

In general, urban Jewish immigration increased rapidly. Jerusalem's Jewish population nearly doubled between 1881 (13,920) and 1891 (25,322).[69] In Jaffa, Haifa, and other cities, it grew at an even faster pace, alarming urban Palestinians and creating some ill will among them, according to Jewish sources of the period. The first formally recorded act of Palestinian opposition and protest occurred in 1891. A telegram signed by a number of Palestinian notables, sent from Jerusalem to Istanbul, urged the Ottoman authorities to prohibit Russian Jews from entering Palestine and acquiring land.[70] Opposition by native Palestinian Arabs to foreign immigration thus preceded the foundation of the Zionist movement.

One of the earliest written documents in opposition to Zionism was a booklet by Najib 'Azoury. 'Azoury wrote prophetically,

> Two important phenomena, of identical character but nevertheless opposed, which till now have not attracted attention, are now making their appearance in Asian Turkey: these are the awakening of the Arab nation and the latent efforts of the Jews to re-establish, on an extremely large scale, the ancient kingdom of Israel. These two movements are destined to struggle continuously with one another, until one prevails over the other. The fate of the entire world depends on the result of this struggle between the two peoples, which represent two contradictory principles.[71]

With the appearance of Arabic newspapers, opposition to Zionism was articulated more frequently and popularly. With the introduction of parliamentary life in the Ottoman Empire (1908–1912), Istanbul became a platform for rhetoric against Zionism; leading the oratory were Palestinian representatives such as Rouhi al-Khalidi and Said al-Husseini, two Jerusalem notables. Another Jerusalem notable, Raghib al-Nashashibi, a candidate for the 1914 elections to the parliament, declared, "If I am elected as a representative I shall devote all my strength day and night to doing away with the damage and threat of the Zionists and Zionism."[72] He was elected by an overwhelming majority. In short, mainstream Palestinian public opinion sensed the threat of Zionism and coalesced against it.

Political events during that period moved swiftly in the region. In 1908 the Young Turks' revolution inside the Ottoman Empire effectively removed the sultan from power. Their attempt to centralize control of the empire more firmly and to emphasize Turkification (and their ideology of pan-Turanism) reawakened Arab consciousness and rekindled open Arab opposition to Turkish rule. The nascent Arab consciousness and its politicization into pan-Arabism reinforced Palestinian identity. On the eve of World War I, the Palestinian Arabs were on the verge of coalescing as a nation. But Palestinian consciousness had not yet transformed itself into an all-Palestinian, nationalist movement or developed an independent, centralized political organization. The Palestine Arabs were thus unable to act decisively on their own behalf either against the Ottoman Turks before World War I or, as discussed in Chapter 3, against the British authorities during the mandate period between the two world wars.

Notes

1. R. Owen, *The Middle East in the World Economy: 1800–1914* (London: Methuen, 1981); see also B. B. Doumani, "Merchants, Socioeconomic Change and the State in Ottoman Palestine: The Nablus Region, 1800–1869," Ph.D. dissertation, Georgetown University, 1990, subsequently published as *Rediscovering Palestine: Merchants and Peasants in Jabal Nablus, 1700–1900* (Berkeley: University of California Press, 1995).

2. A. Schölch, "European Penetration and the Economic Development of Palestine, 1856–1882," in R. Owen, ed., *Studies in the Economic and Social History of Palestine in the Nineteenth and Twentieth Centuries* (Carbondale: Southern Illinois University Press, 1982): 11. See also A. Schölch, "Britain in Palestine, 1838–1882: The Roots of the Balfour Policy," *Journal of Palestine Studies* 22 (Autumn 1992): 39–56, and A. Schölch, *Palestine in Transformation, 1856–1882: Studies in Social, Economic and Political Development*, translated by W. C. Young and M. C. Gerrity (Washington, DC: Institute for Palestine Studies, 1993): 48–75.

3. Doumani, "Merchants, Socioeconomic Change," 33.

4. Y. Firestone, "The Land-Equalizing *Musha'* Village: A Reassessment," in G. G. Gilbar, ed., *Ottoman Palestine, 1800–1914: Studies in Economic and Social History* (Leiden: E. J. Brill, 1990): 92.

5. Ibid., 96–101; see also Y. Firestone, "Production and Trade in an Islamic Context: Sharika Contracts in the Transitional Economy of Northern Samaria, 1853–1943," *International Journal of Middle East Studies* 4 (April 1975): 308–324.

6. B. B. Doumani, "The Political Economy of Population Counts in Ottoman Palestine: Nablus Circa 1850," *International Journal of Middle East Studies* 26 (February 1994): 1–17.

7. Schölch, *Palestine in Transformation*, 181–190.

8. A. J. Rustum, *The Royal Archives of Egypt and the Disturbances in Palestine, 1834* (Beirut: American University of Beirut, 1938); O. Barghouthi and K. Tawtah, *History of Palestine* (in Arabic) (Jerusalem, 1923); and Kimmerling and Migdal, *Palestinians*, 6–12.

9. Schölch, "Britain in Palestine," 39–56, and Schölch, *Palestine in Transformation*, 9–17.

10. "Anglo-Turkish Commercial Convention of 1838," in C. Issawi, ed., *The Economic History of the Middle East, 1800–1914* (Chicago: University of Chicago Press, 1966): 38–40.

11. Just as significant, rural security, especially in the plains, declined. N. Badran cited an English traveler, W. M. Thomson, on the condition of two villages, Al-'Afula and Fula, which were prosperous until 1859, then became ruins; see N. Badran, "The Palestinian Countryside Before World War I" (in Arabic), *Palestine Affairs* 7 (March 1972): 118.

12. Owen, *Middle East,* 85. Figures are given in either British pounds sterling (£) or Palestinian pounds (£P), depending both on our sources and on the period we are discussing. The Palestinian pound, in use during the mandate period, was tied to British currency; its value, of course, fluctuated.

13. I. M. Smilianskaya, "From Subsistence to Market Economy," in Issawi, *Economic History,* 226–247; Owen, *Studies in the Economic;* and B. Doumani, "Merchants, Socioeconomic Change."

14. See Doumani's critique of this thesis in "Merchants, Socioeconomic Change."

15. Owen, *The Middle East;* H. Gerber, "Modernization in Nineteenth Century Palestine: The Role of Foreign Trade," *Middle Eastern Studies* 18 (July 1982): 250–264.

16. Doumani detailed the structure, dynamics, mechanics, and consequences of the olive oil and soap industries as an example of the role of local mercantile and finance capital in commercializing and transforming the Palestinian countryside prior to the penetration of European capital. See Doumani, "Merchants, Socioeconomic Change," 389–390.

17. This section is based on Chapter 7, "The Political Economy of Olive Oil," and Chapter 8, "Soap, Class and the State," in ibid., 252–382.

18. Doumani provided evidence for the emergence of an alliance between the rural elite (including the newly rich peasants) and the urban elite against the peasantry. The peasantry, aware of the disadvantages in such an alliance, took a position against it. See Doumani, "Merchants, Socioeconomic Change," 275–285.

19. Ibid., 381. The economic and legal mechanisms of capital accumulation and concentration, which involved the use of Islamic *waqf*s, need not be detailed here.

20. See the description of the economic bases and social trends in Palestinian cities from early in the nineteenth century until 1882 in Schölch, *Palestine in Transformation,* 110–117, 118–168.

21. Ibid., 236.

22. Even European Jews and the organized Zionist movement referred to this land as Palestine. N. Mandel, *The Arabs and Zionism Before World War I* (Berkeley: University of California Press, 1976).

23. M. Ma'oz, ed., *Studies in Palestine During the Ottoman Period* (Jerusalem: Magness Press, 1975): 21–29.

24. V. Lutsky, *Modern History of the Arab Countries* (Moscow: Progress House, 1971).

25. Owen, *Middle East,* 153.

26. Schölch, "European Penetration," 22.

27. Schölch, *Palestine in Transformation,* 111.

28. Schölch, "European Penetration," 24. See also A. Granott, *The Land System in Palestine,* translated by M. Sinion (London: Eyre and Spottiswoode, 1952): 38.

29. Granott, *Land System,* 38–39; N. 'Allush, *Arab Resistance in Palestine (1917–1948)* (in Arabic) (Beirut: Dar al-Tali'a, 1975): 15.

30. P. A. Smith, *Palestine and the Palestinians, 1876–1983* (New York: St. Martin's Press, 1984): 13, and Schölch, "European Penetration," 25.

31. Schölch, "European Penetration," 61.

32. Schölch, *Palestine in Transformation,* 92.

33. Ibid., 90.

34. See the table in ibid., 93, 106–109.

35. Schölch, "European Penetration," 27.

36. Y. Ben-Arieh, "The Growth of Jerusalem in the Nineteenth Century," *Annals of the Association of American Geographers* 65 (1975); see also Y. Ben-Arieh, "The Population of the Large Towns in Palestine During the First Eighty Years of the Nineteenth Century, According to Western Sources," in Ma'oz, *Studies on Pales-*

tine, 49–69. Additionally, see R. Kark, "The Contribution of the Ottoman Regime to the Development of Jerusalem and Jaffa, 1840–1917," in D. Kushner, ed., *Palestine in the Late Ottoman Period: Political, Social and Economic Transformation* (Jerusalem: Yad Izhak Ben Zvi, 1986): 30–45.

37. A. Rabay'ah, "Palestine Industry in Modern Times," paper presented at the third international conference on Levantine history, Amman, 1980.

38. R. Kark, "The Rise and Decline of Coastal Towns in Palestine," in Gilbar, *Ottoman Palestine*, 69–90.

39. Ibid., 84.

40. Schölch, "European Penetration," 34; see also Kark, "Rise and Decline."

41. Schölch, *Palestine in Transformation*, 38.

42. Buheiry, "The Agricultural Exports of Southern Palestine, 1885–1914," *Journal of Palestine Studies* 10 (Summer 1981): 69–70.

43. Owen, *Middle East*, 93–94, 266.

44. A. al-Ramini, *Nablus in the Nineteenth Century* (in Arabic) (Amman: Dar al-Sha'ab, 1979): 110–114.

45. E. Weakley, "Report on the Conditions and Prospects of British Trade in Syria," 279, and N. T. Gross, "The Anglo-Palestine Company: The Formative Years, 1903–1914," both in Gilbar, *Ottoman Palestine*, 219–253.

46. G. Baer, "The Impact of Economic Change on Traditional Society in Nineteenth Century Palestine," in Ma'oz, *Studies on Palestine*, 497.

47. Ibid.

48. Smith, *Palestine and the Palestinians*, 15.

49. Owen, *Middle East*, 446, and Schölch, "European Penetration," 45.

50. R. Khalidi, "Palestinian Peasant Resistance to Zionism Before World War I," in E. W. Said and C. Hitchens, eds., *Blaming the Victims* (London: Verso, 1988): 207–233.

51. Owen, *Middle East*, 271.

52. Ibid., 272.

53. Schölch, *Palestine in Transformation*, 29, 31, 42.

54. Ibid., 284.

55. J. B. Barron, *Palestine: Report and General Abstracts of the Census of 1922* (Jerusalem: Government of Palestine, 1923): 3.

56. Smith, *Palestine and the Palestinians*, 21, citing Mandel, *Arabs and Zionism*, xxi.

57. See Badran, "Palestinian Countryside," 118ff.

58. P. A. Smith, *Palestine and the Palestinians*, 35.

59. Granott, *Land System*, 294.

60. The following is based on I. al-Nimr, *History of Jabal Nablus and al-Balqa*, Vol. 1 (in Arabic) (Nablus: N.p., 1936); Barghouthi and Tawtah, *History of Palestine*; M. al-Sharif and N. Badran, "Emergence and Evolution," 34–48; M. al-Sharif, "A Contribution to the Study of the Process of the Emergence of the Arab Labor Movement in Palestine" (in Arabic), *Samed al-Iqtisadi* 18 (July 1980): 50–77; N. Badran, *Education and Modernization in Palestinian Arab Society* (in Arabic) (Beirut: PLO Research Center, 1978): 18–58; and P. A. Smith, *Palestine and the Palestinians*, 18–31.

61. A. Awad, *Introduction to the Modern History of Palestine, 1831–1914* (in Arabic) (Beirut: Arab Institution for Studies and Publishing, 1983): 104.

62. Y. Porath, "The Political Awakening of the Palestinian Arabs and Their Leadership Toward the End of the Ottoman Period," in Ma'oz, *Ottoman Reform,* 371, citing J. Finn, *Stirring Times,* 2 vols. (London: Kegan Paul, 1978).

63. Ibid., 191–196; see also M. Hoexter, "The Role of Qays and Yaman Factions in Local Political Divisions: Jabal Nablus Compared with the Judean Hills in the First Half of the Nineteenth Century," *Asian and African Studies* 9 (Fall 1973): 249–311.

64. Porath, "Political Awakening," 359.

65. G. Antonius, *The Arab Awakening: The Story of the Arab National Movement* (New York: Capricorn Books, 1965), and A. Hourani, *Arabic Thought in the Liberal Age: 1798–1939* (Oxford: Oxford University Press, 1970).

66. Jewish Agency, *Statistical Abstract of Palestine, 1944–1945* (Jerusalem: Jewish Agency, 1946): 234.

67. Data are from N. Sokolow, *History of Zionism,* Vol. 2 (London: Longmans, 1919): 329–331.

68. Khalidi, "Palestinian Peasant Resistance," 207–233.

69. Mandel, *Arabs and Zionism,* 38.

70. Awad, *Introduction to the Modern History,* 132; Mandel, *Arabs and Zionism,* 39–40; Porath, "Political Awakening," 376.

71. N. 'Azoury, "Le Réveil de la nation arabe," cited in Hourani, *Arabic Thought,* 279; and Mandel, *Arabs and Zionism,* 52.

72. Porath, "Political Awakening," 377.

3

The Road to al-Nakbah

The Palestine Mandate, 1917–1948

In the mid nineteenth century, the traditional subsistence, semifeudal, and tribute-paying economy of Palestine was eroding under a regime of clan-based local notables subject to Ottoman suzerainty. The old order gave way to a new order of commercial agriculture, a monetized economy, and the beginnings of an indigenous market linked by trade to the region and to Europe under a more centralized Ottoman control. Social change accompanied this new political-economic order: increased population, urbanization and westward (to the coast) migration, the domination of urban over rural notables, the rise of Palestinian Christian and Muslim merchants, and the beginnings of new forms of social organization and consciousness. In the second half of the nineteenth century and the early twentieth century before World War I, however, this new order was itself restructured and reoriented toward dependent peripheral market capitalism as a result of both European intervention and the active participation of native landed and comprador classes. This transformation was similar to that of the surrounding Arab region except in one major respect: the arrival in the country of European colonial settlers and immigrants, principally Jewish, which eventually led to the dispossession of Palestine's native people.

The process of settler colonialism in Palestine was similar to the earlier such processes in Algeria, South Africa, and the Western Hemisphere.[1] Gershon Shafir, an Israeli sociologist, identified three broad types of settler colonies: mixed colonies, which incorporate natives; plantation or extractive colonies, which incorporate slaves and indentured labor (such as the Caribbean colonies and the New World colonies in general); and pure settler colonies, which reject native labor in favor of poor white settler-workers.[2]

According to Shafir, Jewish settlement in Palestine was of the pure settler colony variety, although populated Palestine was ill suited to such colonies. Palestine was relatively heavily populated, with a thriving agrarian-based society. It did not have "free territory"; that is, it had little or no unpopulated land available to immigrant-settlers, as Baruch Kimmerling, another Israeli sociologist, pointed out.[3] Accordingly, European (Jewish Zionist and some Christian) settlers had to purchase land from indigenous owners. But as Shafir argued, "In the first stage of Zionist settlement, the only way open for the acquisition of land was ownership—the exchange of capital for land. When the Jewish collectivity achieved sovereignty and became militarily powerful, the *conquest* of land replaced buying it" (italics added).[4]

This chapter analyzes the impact on Palestine and the Palestinians of the process, under British auspices, of the creation of a European Jewish collectivity in the country, its achievement of sovereignty, and its conquest of the land, which together resulted in al-Nakbah. Two structural processes—rapid settler colonizing and colonial capitalist transformation—combined during the British mandate period to subjugate the Palestinian people and destroy Palestinian society. Although the emergent Palestinian bourgeoisie participated in a minor way in the process, it was the European Jewish settlers, with the help and protection of the British authorities, who were the principal agents of the dual processes.

World War I: Britain and Zionism

The Palestinian struggle had been part of the nationalist Arab resistance, first to Turkish rule in the late nineteenth century and second to British and French colonialism over the region in the wake of World War I.[5] In the Middle East, World War I was a watershed that, along with the collapse of the Ottoman Empire, directed the twentieth-century destiny of the Arab Mashreq, including Palestine.

Starting in 1915, within two years Britain entered into three pivotal and contradictory agreements with three different parties: the French government; the leader of the Arab revolt against the Ottoman Turks, Sharif Hussein of Mecca; and the leader of the Zionist movement in Britain, the aforementioned Lord Rothschild. These were, respectively, the secret Sykes-Picot agreement, the McMahon-Hussein agreements (Appendix 3), and the Balfour Declaration (Appendix 2). Together these agreements transformed the Arab Mashreq and Palestine forever.

The Sykes-Picot agreement of May 16, 1916, divided the former Ottoman dominions in the Arab east between Britain and France as administered territories and zones of influence: what emerged as Syria and Lebanon under the French, Transjordan and Iraq under the British. Palestine was to be internationalized.[6] This British-French compact contradicted the British agreement with Sharif Hussein of October 24, 1915. According to this agreement, in return for an Arab revolt launched against the Ottoman Turks, "Great Britain [was] prepared to recognize and support the independence of the Arabs in all the regions within the limits demanded by the Sharif of Mecca."[7] The Arab leaders and rebels viewed this agreement as the basis for a united Arab kingdom in the former domains of the Ottoman Empire in the Arab east, including Palestine.[8] The Balfour Declaration of November 2, 1917, a letter from the British foreign minister, Lord Balfour, to the Zionist leader Lord Rothschild, stated that "His Majesty's Government view with favour the establishment in Palestine of a national home for the Jewish people . . . it being clearly understood that nothing shall be done which may prejudice the civil and religious rights of existing non-Jewish communities in Palestine."[9] These contradictory commitments were complicated further by the Anglo-French declaration of November 7, 1918, which called for "the complete and definite emancipation of the [Arab] peoples so long oppressed by the Turks and the establishment of national governments and administrations deriving their authority from the initiative and free choice of the indigenous populations."[10]

Zionism, a modern Jewish political movement, dates from the nineteenth century.[11] Prior to that the theology and mystique of the Holy Land of the Old Testament had been kept alive among Jews since their Diaspora. However, in the context of the European age of imperialism, secular nationalism, and anti-Semitism, especially in Russia and eastern Europe, Zionism, a movement of secular Jewish nationalism rather than Jewish religious identity, took hold among key segments of European Jewry. A principal cause was the sharp rise in anti-Semitism, leading to pogroms and the flight of Jews from Russia and eastern Europe; these Jews by and large were assimilated into western Europe. In Russia the escalation of anti-Jewish prejudice and pogroms led to Jewish flight not only to western Europe but also to other countries, including Palestine, where Jews established agricultural settlements on land purchased and supported by the Jewish philanthropists Baron Rothschild and, to a lesser extent, Sir Moses Montefiore. This organized movement—especially Hovevei Zion (Lovers of Zion)—inspired Y. L. Pinsker to write a book calling on Jewish autoemancipation as a solution to

Russian and east European anti-Semitism. This movement envisioned the restoration of Eretz Israel (the land of Israel) in Palestine.[12]

In western Europe, despite the Enlightenment-inspired processes of liberalization and Jewish assimilation, the arrival of Jewish refugees in increasing numbers forced the reemergence of the "Jewish question." Theodor Herzl, a Viennese journalist who had lived in Paris in the 1890s, proposed a solution to the European Jewish question in a book entitled *Der Judenstaat* ("The Jewish State"). Herzl's solution, like that of Pinsker earlier, was the creation of a separate Jewish state—not in Europe but in some colonial domain. The colonial Jewish state would absorb all of European Jewry and end anti-Semitism on the Continent. This was a precise formulation of the idea of restoration of the Jewish nation long espoused by British religious and secular writers.[13] In 1897 in a meeting in Basel, Switzerland, Herzl organized and became head of the World Zionist Organization (WZO), the political arm of the Zionist movement. The WZO declared that its mission was "the creation of a home for the Jewish people in Palestine"[14] and outlined a strategy for achieving this.[15] It was the WZO's British leaders who received the 1917 Balfour Declaration.

Zionism was a colonial project of European settlers much like those of Algeria, South Africa, Rhodesia, Uganda, Kenya, and elsewhere. The Zionist movement, however, differed in several respects: its religious-ideological justification for the project; the recruitment of Jewish settlers from all, not just one, European countries; and perhaps most important, the absence of imperial backing. Eventually, however, the WZO did acquire the support of Great Britain, the imperial European power necessary for its colonial enterprise in Palestine. At the insistence of the British government, the Balfour Declaration, vague as to the meaning of a "national home" for the Jews (always defined as an independent state by the Zionists) and contradictory as to the rights of Palestinians, was incorporated into the articles of the Mandate of Palestine by the League of Nations, itself a creation of the victorious allies of World War I. The disposition of the former Arab domains of the Ottoman Empire followed the outlines of the Sykes-Picot agreement and the Balfour Declaration far more than it did the McMahon-Hussein understanding.

Palestine Under British Military Administration

Palestine first came under British control in December 1917 in the course of the war against Ottoman Turkey, which had joined World War I on the side of Germany against the Allies. Invading from the Egyptian Sinai, British troops under General Edmund Allenby conquered Palestine and established a military administration that was called the Occupied Enemy Territory Administration (OETA). The British OETA lasted for thirty months, until 1920, when it was replaced by a civilian administration. The administration was bound by and attempted to rule Palestine in accordance with international law, which obligated conquering armies to maintain the status quo in conquered territories until their future had been determined. Thus none of the senior British military administrators of Palestine was sympathetic to the idea of a "national home" for the Jews. Consequently, the military administration of Palestine quickly clashed with Zionist efforts to change the conditions and privilege the immigrant-settler Jews in Palestine.

The Zionist-OETA dispute started within the first month of the occupation when Chaim Weizmann, at the head of the Zionist Commission, requested permission personally to survey Palestine. Major General Gilbert Clayton, political officer of the OETA, objected, in large part because of international law and the rising discontent of the Palestinians with Zionism. This discontent was perhaps best stated by chief military administrator General A. W. Money shortly before his departure in 1919: "The Palestinians desire their country for themselves and will resist any general immigration of Jews, however gradual, by every means in their power including active hostilities."[16] In August 1919 Money's successor, Major General H. D. Watson, elaborated further: "The antagonism to Zionism of the majority of the population is deep-rooted—it is fast leading to hatred of the British—and will result, if the Zionist programme is forced upon them, in an outbreak of serious character."[17]

Both Money and Watson were right, as was the report of the King-Crane Commission (see Appendix 4), an unbiased U.S. commission known by the names of its two members, Henry C. King, president of Oberlin College, and Charles Crane, a businessman. At the suggestion of U.S. president Woodrow Wilson, the Allies in 1919 empowered the King-Crane Commission to inform them of the wishes of the Palestinian and Arab peoples for their future. The commission reported that Arab wishes "were nationalistic, that is to say, they called for a united Syria [including Lebanon and Palestine] under a democratic constitution, making no distinction on the basis of religion."[18] The commission recommended independence for Syria, including Palestine or, failing that, a mandate under the United States (not Britain), in accordance with the wishes of the Arab people. In regard to the Zionist project, the commission recommended "serious modification of the extreme Zionist Program."[19] Because the King-Crane report was unfavorable to Zionism and Anglo-French plans for the area, it was not published until 1922, three years after it was written—after the mandate system had been established. The suppression of the King-Crane report and the impending Allied conference in San Remo, Italy, to decide the destiny of the eastern Arab world did not reassure the Palestinians or the other Arabs of the Mashreq.

The Arab and Palestinian people's fears were well founded. The San Remo conference—in direct contradiction of President Wilson's declaration in January 1918 of the principle of self-determination, which had raised Arab hopes—confirmed the Sykes-Picot agreement. Continued foreign rule (now, of course, British and French) of Arab lands reasserted the British intention to pursue the provisions of the Balfour Declaration. Arab and Palestinian discontent increased as the Damascus Congress of March 1920 came to naught. A gathering of leading Arab nationalists, this congress had created hope and excitement when it declared Arab lands independent and named Amir Faisal bin Hussein (son of Sharif Hussein of Mecca) king of Syria and Palestine and his brother, Amir Abdullah bin Hussein, king of Mesopotamia (Iraq). In Palestine, escalating Palestinian–Zionist Jewish tension exploded in political demonstrations, rioting, and violence that peaked in early April 1920 during a holiday celebrated by all three religions.

The British Commission of Inquiry, appointed to investigate the riots, submitted its report on July 1, 1920, a day after the military administration ended. It "listed as the causes of unrest in the country: British promises to Arabs during the war; the conflict between these promises and the Balfour Declaration; fear of Jewish domination; Zionist over-aggressiveness; and foreign propaganda."[20] The commission added that the "Zionists' attitude justifies the description . . . as arrogant, insolent and provocative. . . . If not carefully checked they may easily precipitate a catastrophe, the end of which it is difficult to forecast."[21] Nevertheless, the British political leadership, headed by Prime Minister David Lloyd George, pushed the Jewish national home provision of the Balfour Declaration. By the end of the military administration, on June 30, 1920, Lloyd George had appointed Herbert Samuel, who was a Zionist Jew from Britain, as first civilian high commissioner of Palestine. He was, of course, much more favorable to the building of the Jewish national home than was the OETA of the previous period.

The Palestine Mandate, 1920–1948

Under the direct and powerful influence of Britain and France, the victorious Allies of World War I, the League of Nations created the mandate system and granted Britain mandatory power over Palestine. Map 3.1 shows mandate Palestine and other countries of the region. Formally in place by

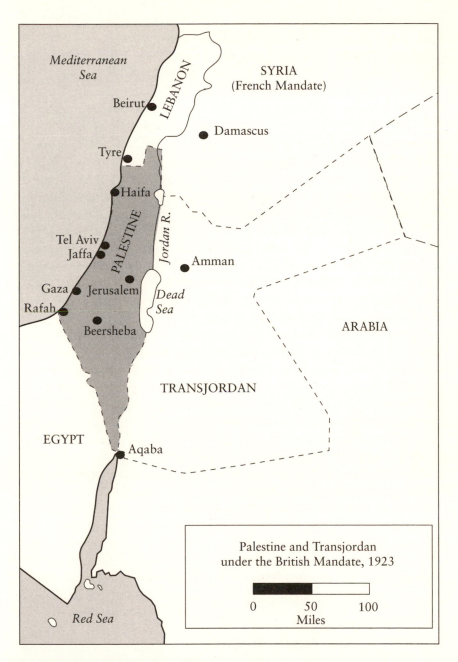

MAP 3.1   The Palestine Mandate

SOURCE: M. Tessler, *A History of the Israeli-Palestinian Conflict* (Bloomington: Indiana University Press, 1994): 166.

1922, the Palestine mandate came to a close in May 1948, when Britain gave up its authority to the United Nations Organization.

The official purpose of the mandate system was to maintain an international trusteeship to prepare former enemy territories for self-rule. However, the terms of the British mandate over Palestine included provisions for implementing the Balfour Declaration: It set up irreconcilable and contradictory goals of self-rule for the native Palestinians and a national home (still not specifically defined by Britain) for European Jews. For the Zionists, the national home meant quite simply a "Palestine . . . as Jewish as England is English, or as Canada is Canadian."[22] In addition to incorporating the whole of the Balfour Declaration, Britain provided for the establishment of a Jewish Agency, to be, in its official language, "recognized as a public body for the purpose of advising and cooperating with the Administration of Palestine in such economic, social and other matters as may affect the establishment of the Jewish population in Palestine," the facilitation of the immigration of Jews to Palestine, and "the close settlement by Jews on the Land." The mandate agreement was thus framed largely with clauses that favored the Zionist cause over Palestinian self-determination.

The Zionists were pleased with the mandate provisions, but "the [Palestinian] Arabs were especially aroused because, whereas numerous articles of the mandatory agreement referred to the Jewish community by name, the Arabs, 90 per cent of the population, were referred to merely as 'the other sections' of the population."[23] The British mandate government in Palestine undertook to provide the underpinnings of any successful settler movement; to ensure that settlers could numerically expand their base through the right to immigration; to make land available for the new settlers; and to grant the Zionists various forms of preferential treatment or economic concessions in the country.[24]

Under the mandate system, the political and economic frameworks for the colonization of Palestine and the disfranchisement of its people were put into place. Thus the colonial state (the Palestine mandate government) and the actions of the Jewish settler-colonial community created the historical conditions for the development of classic patterns of capitalism in Palestine: expropriation of the land and proletarianization of the peasantry.

Uniqueness of the Palestine Mandate

Palestine's was unique among the mandates created by the League of Nations in that the mandatory power encouraged (European Jewish) immigrants to settle in the country (in accordance with the Balfour Declaration). Otherwise the British treated Palestine as an ordinary colony with the typical links to the mother country—Britain in this case—in trade, finance, currency, administrative, and defensive policies. Palestine, like other colonies, was supposed to pay the costs of its own internal and external security and, in this instance, to guarantee the safety of Jewish colonial settlers against the native Palestinians.

Palestine was a poor country lacking in resources and in investment and growth potential. Britain's main interest in Palestine was strategic, despite the Balfour Declaration's religious and cultural justifications. The country was the key buffer state in the British imperial defense of India, Egypt, and the Suez Canal (the shortest sea route to India); part of the air routes also to India and Iraq; and the principal terminus of the oil pipelines from the Iraqi oil fields (of the British-owned Iraq Petroleum Company, or IPC). However, British and Zionist ideology saw the potential for the economic growth of Palestine in the "yeast" of Jewish immigrants with superior education, technological know-how, and capital that would produce an economic "cake" that would be shared with the poor and backward Palestinian Arabs.[25] Indeed, through this Jewish-based development, both the British and the Zionists believed that Palestine would be capable of sustaining a much larger population (including, of course, the Jewish immigrant-settlers). In this potential the British also saw the resolution of the dual and contradictory obligations they had made to the Palestinians (self-determination) and the Zionist Jews (a national home) in the mandate agreement.

Implementation of the Zionist Project in Palestine

The Zionist project was fraught with discontinuities with, contradictions to, and conflicts with the Palestinian natives and occasionally the British mandate administration, but in the final analysis its implementation was quite successful. By 1948 it had achieved an independent Jewish state. This section analyzes the process in terms of the size, character, and timing of the waves of Jewish settler-immigrants; their land purchases and settlements; their enclave economy; their policies for separate labor; their segregated and exclusivist social institutions; their political organization; and the supportive, preferential, and protectionist British policies.

In-Migration and Demographic Transformation

Palestine in 1882 had a small, native migrant religious Jewish community (or *yishuv,* as Israeli and Western Jewish historians call it) of roughly

TABLE 3.1 Population Distribution in Palestine, 1880–1947

	Arabs		Jews	
	Numbers	%	Numbers	%
1880	300,000	94	24,000	6
1917[a]	504,000	90	56,000	10
1922	666,000	89	84,000	11
1931	850,000	83	174,096	17
1936	916,000	72	384,078	28
1945–1946	1,242,000	69	608,000	31
1947[b]	1,300,000	67	640,298	33

[a]Balfour Declaration.

[b]UN partition.

SOURCE: *Facts and Figures About the Palestinians* (Washington, DC: Center for Policy Analysis on Palestine, 1992), 7.

24,000 among a population of nearly 500,000 Palestinians.[26] The size of the Jewish settler community in Palestine increased, over the period after 1882, through several major waves (called *aliyah*s by Israeli and Jewish historians) of in-migration. The first wave, between 1882 and 1903, totaled about 25,000 Jews, most of Russian origin, and the second, between 1904 and 1914, brought in around 35,000 Jews, most of them eastern Europeans. In the 1922 census conducted by the mandate government, the country had a population of 757,182 (perhaps an undercount, as many observers note), with 89 percent Palestinian Arab and 11 percent Jewish. Most Jews lived in the urban areas of new western Jerusalem and the exclusively Jewish Tel Aviv suburb of Jaffa.[27] (See Table 3.1.)

The number of Jewish settlers increased with the third and subsequent sporadic waves. The third wave, between 1919 and 1923, brought in 35,000 (again, most of them Russian), and the fourth, between 1924 and 1931, added another 85,000 immigrants (most of middle-class Polish[28] background). The fifth wave of Jewish immigration, between 1932 and 1938, may have numbered close to 200,000. Indeed because of the rise of Nazism, 174,000 Jews immigrated to Palestine between 1932 and 1936, suddenly raising the Jewish population to an estimated 370,000 in 1936, that is, 28 percent of the total population of Palestine, a dramatic increase from the 16 percent reported in the 1931 census. "It was therefore not surprising that the Arab population should have become alarmed at the rapid rate at which the demographic composition of their country was being altered, without their consent and against their will. . . . This radical change, occurring in the brief span of only five years, must certainly be recognized as an important cause of the [Palestinian] Arab rebellion of 1936."[29]

Map 3.2 shows the distribution of population by subdistricts, with percentages of Jews and Palestinians. By the end of 1947, Palestine mandate government estimates indicate that of a total population of 1.9 million, Jews made up only 31 percent of the population and the rest was Arab (except for the small numbers of British and other Europeans).[30] Thus only a year before "the state of Israel was unilaterally declared and its effective control expanded by force to most of the area contained in the former country of Palestine, the Jewish population still constituted a minority of less than one-third."[31] Eighty-five percent of the Jewish population remained centered in three major urban centers and their surrounding areas: Jaffa–Tel Aviv, Jerusalem, and Haifa.

Land Acquisition

Despite their view that Palestine was a land without people, the Zionists, as early as 1882, discovered that Palestinian land was not uninhabited or readily available.[32] Except for certain swampy areas, Palestine was densely populated and intensively cultivated. Moreover, the land tenure and ownership system was complex and encumbered by varied forms of private and public usufruct rights, despite nineteenth-century Ottoman reforms and liberalization. Available land was expensive and became more so with the rising demand of a population growing as a result of both natural increase and in-migration. With the establishment of the Palestine mandate, Zionist hopes that state land—perceived as vast and potentially accessible—would serve as a basis for land acquisition also turned out to be largely unrealistic.[33] Nevertheless, by 1947 approximately 195,000 *dunum*s of state land had been granted or leased to Jewish settlers by the British mandate authorities.

The Zionist policy of land acquisition had a political logic: The Zionists looked for quantity and quality, location, and contiguity. Accordingly, they tended to purchase land in large, contiguous areas of the inland and coastal plains. These acquisitions were made not by private individuals but by political agencies of the Zionist movement, such as the Jewish National Fund (JNF,[34] also called Keren Kayemeth Leisrael), the Keren Hayesod (or the Palestine Foundation Fund, established in 1920), the Palestine Land Development Company (PLDC), the Palestine Jewish Colonization Association (PICA), and the Jewish Colonization Association.[35] Around 70 percent of all Palestinian land that the Zionists acquired was purchased by the PLDC

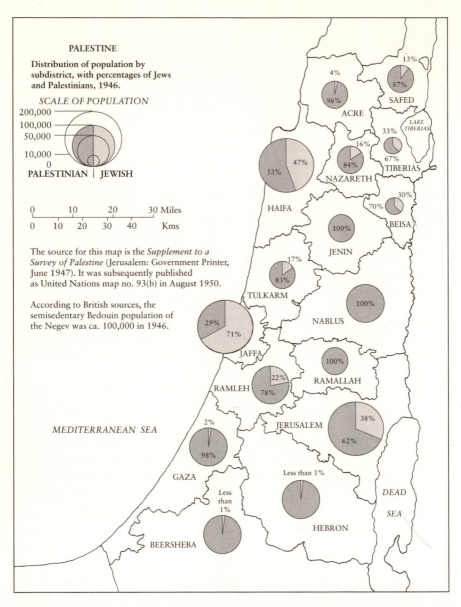

PALESTINE

Distribution of population by
subdistrict, with percentages of Jews
and Palestinians, 1946.

SCALE OF POPULATION

200,000
100,000
50,000

10,000
0
PALESTINIAN | JEWISH

0   10   20   30 Miles

0   10   20   30   40   Kms

The source for this map is the *Supplement to a
Survey of Palestine* (Jerusalem: Government Printer,
June 1947). It was subsequently published
as United Nations map no. 93(b) in August 1950.

According to British sources, the
semisedentary Bedouin population of
the Negev was ca. 100,000 in 1946.

MEDITERRANEAN SEA

13%
87%
SAFED

4%
96%
ACRE

*LAKE
TIBERIAS*

33%
16%
84%
67%
NAZARETH
TIBERIAS

47%
53%
HAIFA

30%
70%
BEISA

100%
JENIN

17%
83%
TULKARM

100%
NABLUS

29%
71%
JAFFA

22%
78%
RAMLEH

100%
RAMALLAH

2%
98%
GAZA

38%
62%
JERUSALEM

Less than 1%

Less
than
1%

DEAD

SEA

HEBRON

BEERSHEBA

MAP 3.2   Distribution of Population by Subdistrict, with Percentages of Jews and
Palestinian Arabs, 1946

SOURCE: W. Khalidi, *Before Their Diaspora* (Washington, DC: Institute for Palestine Studies,
1984): 239.

TABLE 3.2 Estimated Jewish Land Purchases in Palestine, 1882–1947
(in thousands of *dunum*s)

	Total Area Owned by Jews	Area Owned by JNF	Total Land Purchased
Until 1882	22	–	22
1883–1890	104	–	82
1891–1900	218	–	114
1901–1914	418	16	200
1914–1919	–	25	–
1920–1922	557	72	139
1923–1927	865	197	307
1928–1931	994	298	130
1932–1935	1,232	371	238
1936–1939	1,358	478	126
1940–1941	1,431	566	73
1942–1945	1,606	813	75
1946–1947	1,734	933	22

SOURCE: B. Kimmerling, *Zionism and Territory* (Berkeley: Institute of International Studies, University of California, 1983), 43.

on behalf of the JNF. Collectively owned land was purchased in the name of the Jewish people and reserved exclusively for Jewish use.[36]

The formal establishment of the Palestine mandate under Britain, and to the north the Lebanon mandate under the French, created a strong impetus for the sale of vast estates by absentee Lebanese landlords to the Zionist organizations, which were well endowed with capital. Granott noted that between 1920 and 1927, 82 percent of all land acquired by the Zionist organizations was purchased from absentee landlords.[37] Table 3.2 summarizes data on all Jewish land acquisition in Palestine between 1882 and 1947.

From the data it is possible to discern three periods of intensive land acquisition in Palestine by Jews and Zionist organizations. These were 1923–1927, with an average annual 61,400 *dunum*s of land purchased; 1932–1935, with 59,500 *dunum*s; and 1942–1947, with 61,200 *dunum*s. Most Jews in Palestine, however, lived in cities, as previously discussed. At no time did the percentage of Jews living on the land—that is, on farms—exceed 19.3 percent.[38] Map 3.3 indicates Jewish and Palestinian landownership in percentages by subdistrict in 1945.

The withdrawal of so much arable land from access or use by Palestinian peasants led not only to their landlessness and proletarianization but also to economic hardship.[39] Thus Palestinian peasant discontent, political activism,

70

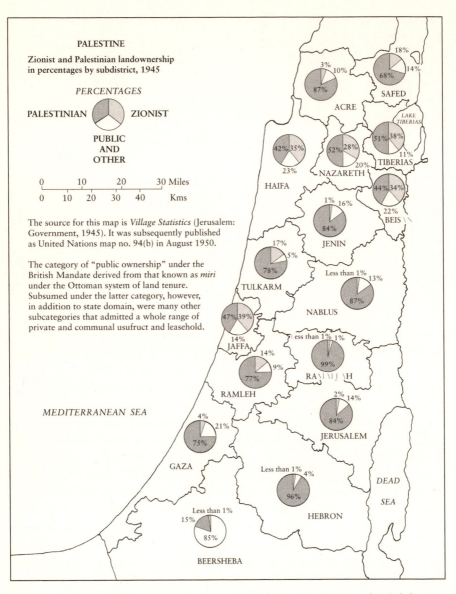

MAP 3.3 Zionist and Palestinian Landownership in Percentages by Subdistrict,
1945

SOURCE: W. Khalidi, *Before Their Diaspora* (Washington, DC: Institute for Palestine Studies,
1984): 237.

and hostility to and violence against the Zionists and the British authorities were highest after periods of high transfer of land, accounting for the 1929 upheaval, the 1936–1939 revolt, and the 1947–1948 internal war. These periods also coincided with heavy waves of Jewish immigration.

A Separate Jewish Economy

The British policy of economic development in Palestine and, specifically, of granting Jewish settlers monopolistic concessions and industrial protectionism facilitated the building of an exclusively Jewish economy, for what the Zionists called the "conquest of land and of labor." In her excellent study of British policy in the 1920s, Barbara Smith shows that even though a part of the British Empire, Palestine was a weak link because of its lack of resources and because the British sought to establish, strengthen, and consolidate a Jewish settler community with wider international links. Economically, Britain facilitated Jewish land acquisition and provided for Jewish enterprises in an "incoherent but clearly recognizable" protectionist policy and preferential tariffs that included "the free importation of raw materials already produced in Palestine" by Palestinians.[40] According to Article 6 of the mandate charter, Britain promised to facilitate Jewish settlement on state lands and land not required for public purposes.

Besides land for colonies in Atlit, Caesarea, Kabbara, and Beisan, three main national monopolistic concessions were granted to Jewish entrepreneurs in the first decade: the Rutenberg concession, the Dead Sea salt, and the Atlit Salt Company. The Rutenberg concession was ambitious and controversial:

> Rutenberg was granted exclusive rights to use the waters of the Auja basin and to provide power, electric light, and irrigation using any type of energy in the district of Jaffa . . . and exclusive rights . . . to carry out a grand hydroelectric and irrigation scheme [based in the Jordan and Yarmouk River basins]. The concession also gave Rutenberg monopolistic rights over the supply of electric power throughout Palestine (excluding Jerusalem) and Trans-Jordan and the possibility of the electrification of the entire railway system.[41]

Opposition to the Rutenberg concession emerged both in Palestine among the Palestinian Arabs, who viewed it as economically privileging Jews, and in Britain among conservative politicians, who detested seeing economic benefits going to a German Jew and to Germany. The Palestine mandate and the British government ignored these objections, and the Jaffa

Electric Company and the Palestine Electric Corporation were formed with a majority of Jewish capital in 1921 and 1923. These companies helped electrify a new settlement, Tel Aviv, providing a service crucial to its rapid rise from being a suburb of Jaffa to being a modern, European-style Jewish city in Palestine.

The Dead Sea salt concession went to a team headed by Moses Novomeysky, a Russian Zionist. The Palestine Potash Company, as the concession was called, was clearly a Zionist industrial venture. One final major concession—in addition to several smaller ones—was the Atlit Salt Company, a Jewish enterprise licensed to produce salt. The artificially high price placed on salt hurt the Palestinian Arabs in all walks of life.[42] Salt was not just a basic daily food necessity for all, it was a crucial element in the manufacture of soap and leather goods, long established as industries of Palestine.

Jewish settlers had laid the foundation for an industrial sector[43] that was more capital-intensive and efficient than the Palestinian. This transplanted, rationally organized Jewish industrial sector experienced a new and significant advance during the mandate. Although British authorities did not generally support industrialization in the colonies, they encouraged Jewish industry in Palestine. Industrialization took off in the mid-1920s after an urban boom following the wave of migration of middle-class Polish Jews, who were sophisticated in industry and business and who settled in cities rather than rural agricultural settlements. This trend was further bolstered and consolidated in the 1930s after the German Jewish immigrants arrived in great numbers in urban centers with even larger capital and technical skills. These developments firmly established Jewish industry in Palestine.[44] By 1939 the *Survey of Palestine* indicated that while Jews composed only 31 percent of the total population, Jewish capital investment in industry was 88 percent of total industrial investment, 90 percent of installed horsepower, and 89 percent of total net industrial output, and Jewish workers represented 79 percent of all industrial workers in Palestine.[45] In short, by 1939 British and Zionist policy had brought forth a Jewish industrial sector that had little connection to the Palestinian Arab economy or population.

The Jewish Manufacturers' Association energized the Zionist establishment to push the Palestine mandate government for more favorable industrial policies. By the mid- to late 1920s, customs regulations had been changed and a clear protectionist policy had been instituted that included reduced (and sometimes exempted) import duties on raw materials and often on machinery needed for production, as well as the abolition of the 1 percent ad valorem export duty. The Rutenberg concession, the Nesher Ce-

TABLE 3.3 Source of Food for the Jewish Community in Palestine, 1939 and 1944

	1939	*1944*
Jewish agriculture	26	47
Imports	67	47
Arab agriculture	7	6

SOURCE: Esco Foundation for Palestine, *A Study of Jewish, Arab, and British Policies,* vol. 2 (New Haven, CT: Yale University Press, 1947), 1052.

ment Company, Shemen (Palestine Oil Industry), and a long list of other Jewish industrial enterprises (in silk, textiles, tanning, confectionery, false teeth, umbrellas, etc.) received *specific* customs concessions despite the meager finances of the Palestine government.[46] Most directly deleterious to Palestinian industry and agriculture was the exemption of import duties on the importation of olive oil and sesame seeds from neighboring countries and Europe to benefit Shemen. At the same time, import duties on cement were constantly *raised* in order to protect the Jewish-owned Nesher Cement Company.

Such preferential treatment for Jewish industry extended into the World War II period. As in the previous era, British mandate government policy during the war advantaged Jewish industry at the expense of Palestinian industry, placing orders for military goods with Jewish firms (by 1945 these orders were valued at 28 million Palestine pounds) and nurturing the expansion of nondutiable raw and semifinished goods. Jewish industry was also guaranteed access to Arab consumers in Palestine and the Arab world, a circumstance further aggravating the Palestinians' predicament.[47] "The result of this situation for Arab industrial development was that Jewish-owned industry grew in those light industries in which Arabs were trying to make headway. Thus, the Jewish sector came into direct competition with [Palestinian] Arab industry."[48] The separate development of the Jewish economy in Palestine is illustrated in Table 3.3, which shows that although Palestine had a primarily agricultural economy, especially in the Palestinian Arab sector, the Jewish community acquired only 7 percent of its food from the Arab sector in 1939 and 6 percent in 1944.

Jewish Labor

As in the development of exclusively Jewish institutions, economy, and land base, the British colonial government of Palestine contributed to the creation, protection, and unemployment relief of exclusively Jewish labor; that is, the British did not extend this policy to the Palestinian Arab labor force. Further, the British facilitated the creation of a two-tier wage structure for Palestinian Arabs and Jews in both the private and the public sectors.[49] These discriminatory labor policies handicapped Palestinian labor in wage levels and working conditions, contributing to Palestinian unemployment and indebtedness, and to severe Palestinian discontent. These factors were important determinants of the sociopolitical upheavals of the Palestinians in 1929, 1936–1939, and 1947–1948.

British colonial economic development policy in Palestine had three basic tenets. The first was a conservative fiscal policy (common to other colonies) by which the colonized people had to pay internal and external security and public expenditures, no matter how narrow the colony's revenue base. The second was a development theory of the Jewish inputs in an undeveloped, resource-poor Palestine that would lead to a structural rise of the whole economy. This idea was predicated on the potential importation into the country of vast Jewish capital and skilled Jewish capitalists. This theory, however, belied the Zionist organizations' labor policies, which encouraged Jewish employers to hire more expensive Jewish workers over the much cheaper Palestinian Arab labor and thus hurt the general growth of all sectors of the Palestinian economy.[50]

According to the third tenet, Britain regulated Jewish migration into Palestine in accordance with the "absorptive capacity" of the country.[51] Early in the mandate period this concept was redefined to mean the absorptive capacity of the Jewish economy only. The Palestine mandate government was reluctant to address labor issues, refusing to arbitrate or attempt to resolve labor-management conflicts between Jewish workers and Jewish owners. It left the resolution of such controversies to the Zionist organizations.

The principal means through which the Zionists succeeded in building a separate and privileged Jewish labor force was the Histadrut,[52] the General Federation of Jewish Labor, established in 1920. The Histadrut was like no other union. It owned a construction cooperative (called Solel Boneh), consumer and marketing cooperatives, and a bank (Bank Hapoelim), as well as credit, insurance, and publishing institutions. The great majority of Jewish workers belonged to the Histadrut, and it became one of the largest employers after the establishment of Israel. In contrast to the poorly organized Palestinian workers, organized Jewish labor exerted strong pressure on the executive of the Jewish Agency (a sort of government within the British mandate government) and the British government in Palestine. As a result, the Histadrut was able through the executive of the Jewish Agency to gain many concessions from the mandate government.

Separate Social and Political Institutions

As in other practices of the Zionists, the social service institutions were exclusive to Jews. The most important of these were the health and educational sectors. Health services were provided principally by the Hadassah Medical Organization, which established a number of hospitals with clinics, laboratories, and pharmacies in most of the cities of Palestine with heavy Jewish populations (e.g., Jerusalem, Tel Aviv, Haifa, Tabariyya, Safad). Haddassah also established a nurses' training school, the Straus Health Center for All Races and Creeds, infant welfare stations, school hygiene and school lunch programs, and playgrounds, and it developed public health programs for reducing trachoma and malaria among Jews. As a consequence of these raised health standards, the death rate among Jews was less than half that among the majority of the Palestinians.

One of the most important efforts in re-creating a Jewish national identity was the educational system. In the mandate agreement in the early 1920s, the Zionists won from the British and the League of Nations the recognition of Hebrew as an official language, along with Arabic and English, although Jews represented no more than about 10 percent of the population in Palestine. They also acquired British consent and financial support for a separate and exclusive private Jewish school system. Zionist authorities, furthermore, gained autonomy over the curriculum, which was imbued with Zionist-inspired Jewish nationalism. This educational system eventually covered kindergarten through secondary schools, vocational schools to technical institutes (e.g., the Technion in Haifa) and major universities (e.g., the Hebrew University in Jerusalem).

Whereas the British authorities allowed the Zionists great autonomy in setting up an educational system, they denied such freedom—and financial support—to the Palestinian Arabs.[53] Palestinian Arabs were disadvantaged relative to the settler-immigrant Jews. Mandate government figures indicate that in 1944 only 32.5 percent of Palestinian Arab children between five and fourteen years old were enrolled in schools; the figure was 97 percent for Jewish children in the same age group.[54] The private and governmental Palestinian Arab school system helped reduce illiteracy substantially, yet failed to provide the technical or higher education that the Jewish community provided. Secondary education for urban Palestinians was limited, and unless they attended a teachers' college in Jerusalem, Palestinians had to leave the country to go to a university.

Palestine's educational system for the two communities under the mandate was separate and unequal in terms of quality, financing, levels, and delivery, especially in the rural areas. As the assistant director of education in the mandate government, Jerome Farrell, noted concerning the economizing educational policy: "The natural result of the disparity between the educational facilities offered to Arabs and Jews is to widen the cultural gap between the two races, to prevent social intermixture on equal terms and to tend to reduce the Arabs to a position of permanent inferiority."[55] In order to suppress the rising Palestinian Arab consciousness, British authorities denied the Palestinian Arabs the right to teach nationalism.[56] Nationalist sentiment and activity nonetheless surged in the schools, which became the site of political mobilization during the mandate, as they were later for Arab Palestinians in exile and during the occupation of the West Bank and the Gaza Strip.[57]

A Jewish State-Within-a-State

The British authorized the establishment of the Jewish Agency to represent, lead, and negotiate on behalf of the Jewish settler community in Palestine on all aspects of British policy. In turn, the Jewish Agency established various social, economic, and political agencies, institutions, and organizations, including military and intelligence units. Together, these organizations were the nucleus of an emerging autonomous Jewish political authority within the Palestine mandate government. It was this well-organized, well-financed, and efficient state-within-a-state that mobilized the Jewish population; conducted an effective internal war against the less-well-organized, mobilized, and financed Palestinians in 1947–1948; defeated the Arab armies in the first Arab-Israeli war of 1948; and became the institutional foundation for the state of Israel.

The Palestinian Arabs had no such centralized political agency, nor did the political leaders have the capacity to mobilize the population effectively on a national level. Although the British made numerous proposals for the formation of a parallel Arab Agency, Palestinian Arab leaders flatly rejected the notion because it would have placed the Arab and Jewish agencies on an equal political and moral level at a time when the indigenous people and their leaders were refusing to negotiate their stand on the Zionist settler-colonial project and were demanding independence from British rule.

The Economic Transformation of the Palestine Mandate

Palestine was unique compared to other British colonial possessions. As discussed above, this uniqueness lay in the British encouragement of Jewish settler colonialism and in facilitating a modern, industrial economic enclave even at the expense of the economic (but not strategic) interests of the British Empire. Accordingly, the Jewish settlers created in Palestine an enclave society with a European organization and standard of living and a demand for European goods and services.

These socioeconomic developments vastly escalated the pace of change and reoriented the structure of the Palestinian economy and society. To begin with, the population increased rapidly. As two British censuses (in 1922 and 1931) and subsequent governmental estimates suggest, Palestine's population more than doubled between 1922 and 1946, from 750,000 to 1.8 million (see Table 3.1). The change resulted principally from a natural increase among the Palestinians and from the waves of migration of Jews into the country. The rate of increase of the migrant Jewish population, however, was higher than that of the natural increment among Palestinian Arabs, and therefore the Jewish ratio to the total population grew larger: from roughly 11 percent to 31 percent in twenty-four years. While the Palestinian Arab population doubled in size, the Jewish population nearly tripled. Nevertheless, the Palestinian Arab population was still greater by a ratio of two to one.

The population shifted toward urban centers, although the distribution between Jews and Arab Palestinians was uneven. The Arab Palestinian population was still largely rural in the mid-1930s, less so in the 1940s, with roughly 25–35 percent urban; the opposite held for the Jewish population, with roughly 75 percent urban in the same period. Palestinian Arab urbanization between the intercensus years (1922–1931) was highest in Haifa (87 percent), Jaffa (63 percent), Ramleh (43 percent), and Jerusalem (37 percent).[58] Commensurate with this difference in geographic distribution of the population was the occupational distribution. Estimates in 1936 indicate that 21 percent of the Jewish labor force worked in agriculture, 20 percent in industry, and 50 percent in services. In contrast, 62 percent of the Palestinian Arab labor force was occupied in agriculture, 8 percent in manufacturing, and 14 percent in services.[59] Owen asserted that although Palestinians outnumbered Jews two to one, both labor forces were roughly the same size as a result of the age distribution (50 percent were below the age of fifteen) and low female participation in wage labor among the Arab Palestinians and because most Jewish migrant-settlers were of the productive age (fifteen to twenty-nine years old). Furthermore, well over 90 percent of the Jews were literate, in contrast to 30 percent of the Arab Palestinians.[60] And the two-tier wage system instituted by the British provided Jewish workers with a wage rate up to three times higher than that of the Arab Palestinians. Accordingly, the per capita income of Jews was also nearly three times as high as that of Arab Palestinians.

The First Economic Phase, 1920–1939

The structure and dynamics of Palestine's economy during the mandate went through two distinct phases. The first extended from the beginning of the mandate until 1939, and the second, a wartime economy, lasted until 1945, its consequences reaching into 1948, the year of al-Nakbah. In both periods the Jewish and Arab Palestinian communities developed differently, but during the war the Arab Palestinian economy experienced much greater rates of change and transformation.

Overall, there are two noteworthy features of Palestine's economy during the mandate period. First, unlike other British colonies, Palestine had high growth rates, which were due in large measure to the immense scale of Jewish migration and to the large amount of Jewish capital transfers.[61] Adding further to these growth rates was the comparatively high economic demand of the Jewish settlers, who had a Western-style standard of living much higher than that of most indigenous Palestinians.

The second feature, which also derives from the scale and timing of Jewish migration into Palestine, was that the Palestine economy did *not* follow the world cycle of economic depression except in the early 1930s. In fact, it was countercyclical and grew more rapidly because Jewish migration and capital transfers into Palestine came at the height of the world cycles of depression, when prejudice, anti-Semitism, and repression were greatest in Europe. The sharp worldwide decline in cereal prices in the early 1930s and simultaneous bad harvests, however, devastated Palestinian agriculturalists, especially the Palestinian peasantry, and associated businesses. In general, then, apart from the impact of the cereal crisis, the Palestinian economic cycle coincided with that of the Jewish settler immigration.

The Palestinian Arab economy remained overwhelmingly agrarian. In the plains large tracts of land were devoted to irrigated, export-oriented citrus fruits, while in the hill country cereal, olives, and olive oil were produced for self-consumption, the local market, and, if there was a surplus, for export.

The whole Palestinian economy, however, turned more capitalistic as land became alienable, peasants more proletarianized, and wage labor more prevalent. Loss of land to Jewish purchases in the context of population pressure and agricultural stagnation created surplus labor and high unemployment in the countryside. Rural-to-town migration gained momentum, and more Arab Palestinians entered the wage labor market. The Palestinian Arab urban population rose by 85 percent between 1931 and 1944, whereas the rural population increased by 40 percent in the same period.[62] Shantytowns sprang up around the coastal cities of Haifa and Jaffa, where displaced peasant poverty and lack of security were evident.

Substantial growth in manufacturing also occurred during the first phase. The number of industrial enterprises rose from 1,240 in 1913 to 3,505 in 1927 and about 6,000 in 1936. Industrial workers also grew in number (from 17,955 in 1927 to 48,000 in 1939), and industrial output jumped from 3.89 million Palestinian pounds (£P) in 1927 to £P9.1 million in 1936.[63] Industrial enterprises, however, remained largely small handicraft workshops. Very few factories employed one hundred workers or more, and only a fraction ran on motor power. By European standards, Arab Palestine's industry was backward. Jewish immigrant-settlers owned the majority of Palestine's industry. The 1939 government census of industry found 13,678 Jewish workers engaged in industry in contrast to only 4,117 "non-Jewish" (Palestinian Arab) workers.[64] Nevertheless, the number of Palestinian wage laborers increased steadily throughout the 1930s as opportunities in public works and private enterprises, including some Jewish ventures, increased (e.g., in citrus groves, the Nesher Cement Company, and the Palestine Potash Company). However, much of Palestinian Arab wage labor remained seasonal and itinerant, and a reserve army of labor grew in size and destitution by the end of the 1930s, contributing to the violent explosion of the 1936 revolt.

Following the colonial and postcolonial model, both Jews and Arab Palestinians produced more substitutions for imports and less for export. However, unlike the Arab Palestinians, who followed the colonial model of producing textiles, processed foodstuff, cigarettes, and leather goods, the Jewish immigrant-settlers entered as well into the production of metalwork, chemicals, and electrical products along with other, more technically advanced goods. Although the impact of Jewish industrial activity on Palestinian Arab industrial development is difficult to assess, it is possible to argue that it worked to the Arab Palestinians' detriment, especially as the two communities engaged, at different times during the mandate, in one-sided or mutual economic boycotts.

The consequences of the first two decades of the Palestine mandate's economic growth and development varied widely between the two communities, the native Palestinians and the Jewish immigrant-settlers, and they were increasingly confronting each other politically and violently. Whereas economic growth strengthened and consolidated the Jewish immigrant-settler community and its political leadership, the uneven and rapid capitalist economic change polarized the Arab Palestinians; dispossessed and substantially decreased the well-being of growing numbers of the peasantry; atomized, displaced, and proletarianized much of it; and fractionalized Palestinian Arab social and political leadership. Community-based social relations, which had long been on the decline, continued a sharp decrease. The increasing impoverishment and declining conditions of the peasantry seemed to generate among them a shared sense not only of dispossession and deprivation but also of oppression. As traditional solidarities based on the *hamula,* kin, religion, and the Arab notables waned and were not replaced successfully by more modern, effective, associational ones, the Arab Palestinian nationalist movement resisting Zionist dispossession and seeking independence from Britain faced significant challenges.

The Palestinian War Economy, 1939–1945

During World War II, Palestine became a strategic outpost for the British in the Middle East and the eastern Mediterranean. Palestine became the fortified base of large land, air, and naval military forces; the terminus of oil pipelines from Iraq; and the location of a key oil refinery. The British devised an economic plan—through the Middle East Supply Center (in Cairo), the War Supplies Board, and the Directorate of War Production—to mobilize local and regional agricultural and industrial production for both military and civilian needs in order to reduce dependence on external (European and US) sources of supply. This successful strategy resulted in rapid economic development of nearly all sectors of Palestine's economy, though it was uneven between the Jewish and Arab Palestinian parts. The economy rebounded from the recession and dislocations of the late 1930s, and income levels and standards of living rose. As significant, this effort accelerated the process of social change. In a short period of five years, Palestine underwent a profound structural transformation.

British mobilization in the agricultural sector produced mixed results, especially as cereal and primarily citrus markets suffered. Tremendous increases in potato, olive, and poultry production occurred. However, the export of citrus fruit dropped precipitously during the war, from 15.3 million cases valued at £P4.35 million between 1938 and 1939 to 4,594 cases valued at £P3.51 million between 1942 and 1943.[65] Banks made cash/credit advances, some guaranteed by the Palestine mandate government, to maintain citrus groves. By the end of the war in 1945, citrus production recovered.

Industry also underwent a major expansion. There was a phenomenal increase in industrial capacity, output, and the types of products supplied to the military, Palestine's internal market, and the region. By 1946 the number of industrial enterprises had risen to well above six thousand, the majority Jewish-owned and only several hundred owned by Arab Palestinians. The percentage of increase of workers in industry, most of them Jewish, was 145 percent between 1939 and 1942.[66] Besides the rise in output and labor, there were sharp increases in capital investment (e.g., from £P11.1 million in 1937 to £P20.5 million in 1943),[67] power use, and wages.

Most remarkable was the production of military and other sophisticated hardware (antitank mines, steel containers, hydraulic jacks, and bodies for military vehicles), especially in the peak years of the Allied North African campaign against German general Erwin Rommel's Afrika Korps. In a report dated April 23, 1943, Sir Douglas Harris, chairman of the Palestine War Supply Board, stated that "the share of the Jewish population in both capital investment and value of production in industry is about 85 percent. The Jewish share in industrial production for the Army, however, exceeds 95 percent of the total."[68] By 1944, after the victory over Rommel, these Jewish factories shifted to the production of civilian goods already in short supply (industrial machinery, diesel engines, fishing trawlers, tools, spare parts for automobiles, electrical and medical equipment, textiles and clothing, home utensils, and pharmaceuticals).[69] Also during this period the Jewish-owned diamond-cutting and -polishing industry (thirty factories employing three thousand workers) expanded. The net national product of the Jewish economy in Palestine nearly doubled during the war, from £P16.7 million to £P29.9 million valued at 1936 prices.[70]

Production on small farms and large estates owned by Arab Palestinians increased sharply and was accompanied by the decline, from 180,000 in 1939 to 100,000 in 1944, of rural male laborers who derived a livelihood from agriculture.[71] Delayed British efforts to introduce modern production techniques proved ineffective. Without a comprehensive road network, production in Palestinian Arab agriculture remained largely traditional, especially on the smaller and more remote farms. In industry only a tiny fraction of the Arab Palestinian enterprises were large, powered by electricity or oil (Arab Palestinian industry in 1942 had a total horsepower of 3,812; Jewish industry 57,410), or employed more than one hundred workers.

The majority of the enterprises were small workshops using human and animal power, employing small amounts of capital and small numbers of workers, and organized along traditional lines. The cultural and technological divide between Arab Palestinians and European settler Jews could not have been more stark.

Accompanying the growth and diversification of the Palestinian manufacturing and productive bourgeoisie was the rise of a commercial and professional stratum. The Jerusalem Chamber of Commerce membership list included 118 manufacturing enterprises in 1947 as contrasted with 85 in 1938. In addition, it listed 260 businesses ranging from commission agents to wholesalers of cereals, textiles, and so on. There were also 150 retail and service businesses registered. Jaffa's Chamber of Commerce listed 670 businesses, of which 64 were light-manufacturing establishments, 41 small enterprises such as contractors and printers, and nearly 500 retailers and merchants of a vast array of goods and services, including banks, hotels, and bus and taxi companies. Jaffa also had the Palestine Brass Foundry and the Palestine Building and Construction Company.[72] Liberal professionals such as doctors, teachers, and lawyers sharply increased in numbers as well.

The heated economic expansion of the war period generated in Palestine large labor demands; labor shortages developed as early as 1942. Arab workers from Egypt, Transjordan, Syria, and Lebanon were imported by the British but could not ease the strong demand. Rachel Taqqu estimated that "by the 1940's, when labor mobilization reached a wartime peak, the total Arab wage force had expanded to include nearly one third of the entire male [Palestinian] Arab population of working age."[73]

As a consequence of the demand for labor, average industrial wage earnings rose by 200 percent for Arab Palestinians and 258 percent for Jews; those for unskilled construction workers advanced by 405 percent and 329 percent, respectively. Similarly, in the rural areas agricultural wages rose; however, the prices of agricultural products shot up sevenfold by 1943. According to one estimate, the index of farm prices rose steadily from 100 in 1938–1939 to 560 in 1943–1944.[74] This dramatic rural economic development quadrupled agricultural income between 1939 and 1944–1945 and provided some segments of the Arab Palestinian peasantry with a "large measure of prosperity," the largest in a very long time.[75] Nevertheless, socioeconomic differentiation and polarization in the population swelled the ranks of both the middle and landless peasantry and also the urban middle class and the city poor. Nearly one-third of Palestine's Arab peasantry was landless by the end of the war, and urban misery increased tremendously.

By the end of 1944, 70 percent of Jaffa's Palestinian Arab population lived in slums; the figure for Haifa was 41 percent.[76]

With the rapid formation of the Palestinian wage-earning labor force in the 1940s, working-class organizations sprang up throughout the urban centers.[77] Established in 1925, the Palestine Arab Workers Society (PAWS) grew rapidly during the war. Unions were especially active in the coastal industrial cities of Haifa and Jaffa and in Jerusalem. Another major union, the Federation of Arab Trade Unions (FATU), emerged in 1942 in a split with PAWS. PAWS' political orientation was social democratic, while FATU was communist-influenced. FATU concentrated on organizing skilled workers and affiliated worker associations in such large establishments as the British-owned Iraq Petroleum Company, Shell Oil, Consolidated Refineries, the Haifa Harbor, the Royal Depot at Haifa Bay, and the Haifa Public Works Department. Although originally syndicalist, both PAWS and FATU had become increasingly politicized by the end of the war. Branches and individuals from both trade union organizations were connected to and influenced by a small leftist Palestinian party, the Arab League for National Liberation (ALNL), founded in 1944 and led by a communist, Emile Tuma. They also were closely linked to the radical and nationalist Arab Intellectuals League, led by Musa Dajani and Mukhlis 'Amr, which boasted two thousand members.

Arab Palestinian wage labor by the end of the mandate had "scored impressive gains, as witnessed by its growth, activism, and independence. There is no doubt that it had succeeded in forging a relatively strong class consciousness and a working-class culture."[78] The labor movement achieved such accomplishments in the absence of progressive labor laws. Although early in the war the British encouraged unionization as part of their labor recruitment policy, by the end of the war the authorities were hostile to the increasingly politicized movement. But neither the labor movement nor the political organizations were sufficiently strong to enable them, along with the more traditional leadership and parties, to succeed in the national political struggle against dispossession in the postwar era.

The Palestinian Struggle Against Dispossession

During the last years of the Ottoman era, Palestinian and other Arab leaders lobbied the Ottoman authorities against the Zionist project. Arab intellectuals' criticisms of Zionism and peasant resistance to evictions from land purchased by Zionist Jewish agencies indicated concern about the threat of Zionism and presaged the character of the forthcoming resistance. Concern turned into alarm, anger, and hostility when the League of Nations incorporated the Balfour Declaration into the Mandate of Palestine. Discontent spread wider and deeper in Palestinian society as the implementation of the Palestine mandate's pro-Zionist provisions, especially those of Jewish immigration and land purchases, proceeded. In short, Palestinian actions against both Zionism and the British mandate of Palestine became highly politicized. Small, seemingly unimportant social and religious incidents quickly erupted into major political confrontations between Arab Palestinians and Jewish immigrant-settlers. Capitalist economic changes that had a negative impact on the peasantry and the urban poor also triggered political uprisings. By the 1930s the clashes and riots were targeting the British authorities of the Palestine mandate government as well.

The process of Jewish empowerment and the commensurate inverse process of Palestinian disenfranchisement, both highly politicized under British auspices, developed through three stages that coincided roughly with the three decades of British colonial rule. The period from 1920 to 1929 culminated in serious rioting, political conflict and violence, and critical British government investigative and policy reports: the Shaw Commission report, the Hope Simpson report, and the Passfield white paper. The period from 1930 to 1939 witnessed a general Palestinian Arab revolt between 1936 and 1939 and forced the British government to issue the 1937 Peel Commission report and the 1939 white paper. The period from 1940 to 1948, a time of dramatic economic transformation and political conflict, saw the establishment of a United Nations partition plan in 1947, an internal Jewish-Arab war, the destruction of Palestine, and the rise of Israel as a Jewish state.

The 1920–1929 Decade

In Palestine mass Jewish immigration commenced in accordance with the British policy of establishing a Jewish national home. Arab Palestinians perceived the arrival of ten thousand Jewish immigrants between December 1920 and April 1921 as a harbinger of the future. A riot that started in Jaffa between radical leftist and centrist Zionist groups quickly involved the Arab Palestinians, who also attacked the immigration hostel, a symbolic target of their hostility. In this riot, 48 Arab Palestinians and 47 Jews were killed, and 219 people were wounded. From Jaffa, Arab Palestinian rioting spread to rural areas, fueled by wild rumors of Jews killing

Arabs. Several Palestinians were killed by British soldiers defending Jewish settlements.

The British appointed a committee to investigate the incident. The Haycraft Commission, led by Sir Thomas Haycraft, chief justice of Palestine, found that the riots were spontaneous and that Palestinian Arabs felt "discontent with and hostility toward" the Jews from "political and economic causes, especially the issue of Jewish immigration into Palestine."[79] To underscore this point, the commission cited the testimony of David Eder, acting chair of the Zionist Commission, who commented that "there can only be one National Home in Palestine, and that a Jewish one, and no equality in the partnership between Jews and Arabs, but a Jewish predominance as soon as the numbers of that race are sufficiently increased."[80]

While peasants and the urban poor rioted and used violence against Jewish settlers (but not yet against the British authorities), the Palestinian Arabs in the towns and villages organized themselves into Muslim-Christian associations, Arab literary clubs, the Higher Islamic Council, and other groups in a national effort to resist Zionist designs. The elite launched a movement to unite their political efforts to influence British policy. In December 1920 a Palestine Arab Congress representing, it claimed, "all classes and creeds of the Arab people of Palestine,"[81] was held in Haifa and elected a twenty-four-member leadership called the Palestine Arab Executive. It joined the top leaders of the two competing notable families of Jerusalem who had national stature, the Husseinis and the Nashashibis. The political platform of the congress included condemnation of the Balfour Declaration, the idea of a Jewish national home, and the mandate's support of it; rejection of the principle of mass Jewish immigration into Palestine; and advocacy of the establishment of a national government in Palestine.[82]

The last point was especially significant because Palestine, like Syria and Iraq, was designated by the League of Nations as a Class A mandate, which required the mandatory to establish a national government with legislative and administrative structures. Yet Palestine was treated more like a Class B mandate, in which all legislative and administrative powers were vested in the mandatory. However, diplomatic pressure by the Palestine Arab delegation that lobbied in London and Geneva (at the League of Nations) led the British colonial secretary, Winston Churchill, to clarify the Balfour Declaration. In 1922 the Churchill white paper reasserted British pro-Zionist policy but proposed to allow Jewish immigration only in accordance with the economic "absorptive capacity" of Palestine and to establish a legislative council. Once again the Palestine Arab Congress countered by proposing the creation of an elected representative legislative council like those in the neighboring Class A mandates of Syria and Lebanon, but the British refused.

In October 1923 the British once again offered to create an Arab Agency analogous to the Jewish Agency already established under the provisions of the mandate. The Palestinian leadership again turned down the proposal because they believed that an analogy was unfair, given the demographic and historical conditions. Further, the Jewish Agency was elected by the whole Jewish community, whereas the proposed Arab Agency would be appointed by the British authorities. Accordingly, the British blocked the Arab Palestinian leadership's request for an elected parliament for self-rule, leaving the Palestine Arab Executive merely a mouthpiece; unlike the Jewish Agency, the Palestine Arab Executive was not officially recognized by the British Palestine mandate government[83] and therefore had no official advisory or consultative status. The Palestine Arab Congress, which met regularly, remained the principal Palestinian representative, despite the deep fissures in the nationalist ranks, until it was replaced by the Arab Higher Committee (AHC) in 1936.

Although the Palestine Arab Executive included the rival political clans of the Husseinis and the Nashashibis in an organization that spoke for all Arab Palestinians, these clans' rivalry actually intensified and undermined the unity of the struggle against the settler Zionists and the British. What had exacerbated the rivalry was the successful campaign of al-Hajj Amin al-Husseini against the Nashashibi candidate to be appointed mufti in 1921 by Herbert Samuel, first civilian high commissioner of Palestine, as well as elected president of the Supreme Muslim Council, which controlled the Islamic *awqaf* and the financial resources involved; the shari'a courts and their officialdom; and mosques, schools, orphanages, and other institutions, to which he could appoint or from which he could dismiss many employees. The mandatory government (Britain) legitimized and recognized the religious leadership of al-Hajj Amin al-Husseini. He expanded welfare and health clinics, built an orphanage, renovated and supported schools, and organized a tree-planting program on *waqf* lands. Most symbolic, however, was his project of restoring the two mosques—Al-Aqsa and the Dome of the Rock—on the al-Haram al-Sharif in Jerusalem through an international Muslim fund-raising campaign.

To counter the influence of al-Hajj Amin and the ascendant Husseinis' control of the Palestine Arab Executive, the Nashashibis attempted to form an opposing power base. Raghib al-Nashashibi formed national Muslim societies and the National Party (1923) and encouraged the creation of peasant parties (1924). These latter moves were supported by the Zionists as an effort to split Palestinian ranks along social class lines. The National Party countered the Arab Executive by arguing that it had failed to change British policy through opposition and thus it would be more productive to work, as it were, in cooperation with the British authorities. These political developments both reflected and fueled the bitter rivalry between the two nationalist factions and, in turn, kept the Palestinians from achieving their larger political goals.

The peasant parties or groups were in the vanguard of the violent struggle against the Zionists in the 1920s and the British authorities in the 1930s. The leaders of the peasantry, perhaps more than the elite politicians, demanded immediate social and economic protection against the peasants' worsening situation. The platforms of the rural political groups were noteworthy for their attention to economic matters. They called on the government to adopt specific policies: reduction of taxes; extension of the maturity of debts; provision of long-term loans; building of roads, schools, and the educational system; and the encouragement of agricultural cooperation.

The land purchases and immigration of Jews, along with the infrastructural buildup of the Jewish community under British auspices, created general alarm, but Palestinian diplomacy and political tactics failed to change British policy. Concurrently, during the 1920s a sudden downturn in the economy caused a sharp decline in the well-being of all Arab Palestinians, especially the peasantry. Arab Palestinian concern was reflected in the reunification of the Palestinian nationalist factions in the seventh Palestine Arab Congress, held in 1928. Its resolutions stressed the economic dilemma, calling for tax reform, social welfare for the workers, and increased public expenditure on education. In addition it repeated its abiding political concerns and demands: "The people of Palestine cannot and will not tolerate the present absolute colonial system of government, and urgently insist upon and demand the establishment of a representative body to lay its own Constitution and guarantee the formation of a democratic parliamentary Government."[84]

Although violence had largely subsided by 1921, a combination of factors created a highly charged political situation. As was often the case, a minor religious incident in 1929 at the Western (Wailing) Wall of the ancient Jewish Temple triggered a crisis over rights to the wall and an explosion of violence.[85] Stoked by wild rumor, demonstrations and riots started in Jerusalem and spread to cities such as Haifa, Jaffa, Safad, and Hebron, where Palestinian Arab and Jewish mobs murdered 133 Jews and 116 Arabs before the violence was suppressed by the British authorities.

The British government response was predictable. It set up a commission, the Shaw Commission, to study the causes of the disturbances; sent another, the Hope Simpson Commission, to conduct a thorough study of the socioeconomic conditions in the country; and issued a policy statement, the Passfield white paper.

The Shaw Commission determined that contributing factors to the disturbances were Arab Palestinian apprehension over Jewish immigration, which it found excessive in 1925–1926, and indiscriminate land sales to Jewish organizations that was leading to the creation of "a landless and discontented class."[86] In short, the Shaw Commission concluded that the basic cause of the disturbances was the Palestinian Arabs' feeling "of disappointment of their political and national aspirations and fear for their economic future."

In his report Sir John Hope Simpson analyzed the land problem and the social and economic conditions of the peasantry in Palestine. He found that the area of arable land was far less than had been assumed. Substantial growth of the Palestinian Arab population during the decade, combined with increased land sales to the Jews, had created landless Arab Palestinians. For example, in a survey of 104 representative villages, 29.4 percent of the families were landless.[87] Furthermore, after centuries of use and abuse of the land, the yield was low. Thus the majority of the Palestinian Arab population already lived on farms that did not provide a subsistence minimum.[88] As Hope Simpson described the situation: "Evidence from every possible source tends to support the conclusion that the Arab fellah [peasant] cultivator is in a desperate position. He has no capital for his farm. He is, on the contrary, heavily in debt. His rent is rising, he has to pay very heavy taxes, and the rate of interest on his loans is incredibly high."[89]

Hope Simpson concluded his report with a number of specific and general policy proposals. For immediate relief, he recommended ending imprisonment for debt, exemption from taxation for any peasant making less than £P30 per annum, credit and education for the peasantry, and for the longer term, extensive agricultural development programs. He strongly argued, as did the Shaw Commission, that "there is at the present time and with the present methods of Arab cultivation no margin of land available for agricultural settlement by new immigrants, with the exception of such undeveloped land as the various Jewish Agencies hold in reserve."[90] He urged the regulation of land transfer and tight restrictions on immigration. Although he said that Palestinian Arab unemployment was not directly linked to Jewish immigration, he nevertheless stated that the policy of the British mandate government in regard to immigration must be determined by unemployment in Palestine overall, not just in the Jewish community. He recognized that "it is wrong that a Jew from Poland, Lithuania or the Yemen, should be admitted to fill an existing vacancy, while in Palestine there are already workmen capable of filling that vacancy, who are unable to find employment."[91]

The recommendations of Hope Simpson and the Shaw Commission were largely reflected in the Passfield white paper, a policy paper the British government issued in 1930 in an effort to address the causes of the 1929 disturbances. In addition, the Passfield white paper proposed that it was time to develop self-rule institutions in Palestine, although the legislative council it proposed was patterned after that in the 1922 Churchill white paper.[92]

Lord Passfield was Sidney Webb, the famous Fabian socialist; he and his white paper came under vigorous attack by the Zionists and pro-Zionists in Britain and Palestine. This political pressure overwhelmed the minority government of Prime Minister Ramsay MacDonald. In a letter that the Palestinian Arabs dubbed the "black letter," MacDonald in effect repudiated and reversed the policy changes of the Passfield white paper. This policy reversal kept in place the very social, economic, and institutional processes that the British authorities had determined to be the causes of the disturbances in Palestine. Indeed these processes picked up momentum in the first five years of the 1930s, leading to a greater Palestinian revolt not only against the Jewish settlers but also directly against British rule.

The 1930s and the 1936–1939 "Arab Revolt"

Through the moderate political-diplomatic tactics of petitions, testimonies, delegations, public meetings, congresses, and resolutions with the Palestine mandate government, elite Arab Palestinian leaders achieved little.[93] According to Philip Mattar, by 1929 the Palestinian people "had become frustrated, more militant, and anti-British."[94] The MacDonald "black letter" added proof of the ineffectiveness of moderate politics. A new tone of militancy characterized newspaper articles, reports, and public speeches, which challenged the traditional notables' leadership and unsuccessful methods, and there emerged a new generation of leaders.[95] An all-out revolt was in the making.

The root causes of the revolt remained unchanged: the Arab Palestinians' antipathy toward pro-Zionist British policies and their inability to advance toward self-rule. The new British high commissioner, Sir Arthur Wauchope, pushed his superiors in the Colonial Office in London for the establishment of a Palestinian Arab legislative council. Pro-Zionist politicians defeated this proposal in the British Parliament. The rejection frustrated Palestinian Arabs because neighboring Arab mandates, especially Syria, Iraq, and (earlier) Egypt, had made strides toward sovereignty.

Exacerbating the situation for the peasantry was a land tax, introduced by the British authorities in 1928. These "crippling tax rates" and a sharp drop in income may have led some peasants and landlords to sell their land.[96] Arab Palestinian land brokers, usurers, and middlemen were especially active in land sales to the Jewish organizations, despite being pilloried and on occasion threatened with physical harm. The difficult economic situation led the mandate government to remit the taxes of the poorest peasants, as recommended by Hope Simpson. Beyond doubt, it was also this economic situation that spurred the peasants to revolt against the British authorities, who in the peasants' view had created the conditions that continued to jeopardize their place in their homeland.

More alarming for the Arab Palestinians in this economic context was the sudden and spectacular rise of Jewish immigration into the country in the first half of the 1930s. In spite of governmental decisions to regulate and reduce the number of Jewish immigrants into the country in accordance with the vague concept of "absorptive capacity," tens of thousands of Jews poured into Palestine when the rise of Nazism in Germany pushed them out of central Europe. Only 4,075 immigrated into Palestine in 1931, but the numbers soared to 30,327 in 1933, 42,359 in 1934, and 61,854 in 1935. As noted above, the ratio of Jews within the total population of Palestine jumped from 16 percent in 1931 to 28 percent in 1936.

These contextual factors coincided with the death in 1934 of the head of the Palestine Arab Executive, the organization's demise, and the emergence of more militant groupings, especially the Istiqlal (Independence) Party. The leaders of these new organizations were pan-Arabist and critical of the moderate Palestinian Arab leadership and its diplomatic methods. They included such articulate and modern men as Awni 'Abdul-Hadi, Akram Zu'ayter, Izzat Darwaza, and Ahmad al-Shuqayri (who became the first chairman of the PLO in 1964). These leaders advocated strong active opposition to the Zionists and, significantly, to the British and the mandate governments; they called for the dismantling of the mandate and its replacement by a parliamentary Palestinian Arab government. Such views captured the imagination and support of a frustrated and combative public. By 1936 a number of Palestinian political parties reflecting varied socioeconomic and ideological interests had formed.[97] These included the Youth Congress, the National Defense Party (dominated by the Nashashibis), the Palestine Arab Party (dominated by al-Hajj Amin and the Husseinis), the Reform Party, and the National Bloc Party. A Palestine Communist Party had existed since the early 1920s but had little direct influence.[98] It called for an independent Palestine for both Palestinian Arabs and Jews free from British imperialism. Unable to overcome the intercommunal conflict, it split into separate Arab and Jewish parties by the late 1930s.

The activism that produced the new political groupings found a stronger and more militant echo in an underground religious organization led by Shaykh 'Izz ed-Din al-Qassam. Like the Istiqlalis, pan-Arabists, and nationalists, he became convinced that the diplomatic and political tactics of the elite leadership had not only been ineffective in securing Arab Palestinian rights but had also brought the country to the edge of disaster.

Al-Qassam and his followers took up arms in the countryside as the renewed urban violence and Jewish counterviolence intensified. In November 1935 he and his band of guerrillas were ambushed and killed by British troops. His martyrdom, self-sacrifice, and commitment to the national cause offered the Palestinian Arabs a more honorable and popular model of struggle than that of the elite leadership. A large number of youths throughout Palestine formed guerrilla bands, called themselves Ikhwan al-Qassam (Brothers of al-Qassam), and launched an armed struggle against both the Jewish settlers and the British authorities.

On April 19, 1936, Istiqlal leaders and other nationalists announced a general strike that spread throughout the country and involved middle-class businessmen and professionals in local leadership roles.[99] Organizations of the emergent Arab Palestinian civil society (unions, chambers of commerce, the All-Palestine Conference of Arab Students, etc.) and traditional bedouin and clan leaders supported the strike. To lead the strike, the elite leadership quickly reorganized into the Arab Higher Committee, made up of representatives of the new parties under the chairmanship of the mufti, al-Hajj Amin al-Husseini, who although appointed by and beholden to the British authorities, had no alternative but to join the militants. The AHC represented all political factions and social sectors of Arab Palestinian society and announced its goals to be the complete cessation of Jewish immigration, the prohibition of land transfer to Jews, and the establishment of a national government responsible to a representative council.

The strike lasted six months, and before it ended, civil disobedience turned into armed insurrection. In the countryside the revolt was to a considerable extent spontaneously organized, autonomous, and anchored in peasant norms.[100] There was wide variation in the recruitment, organization, leadership, and command structures. Recruitment ranged from voluntary enrollment to selection by the *hamula* or family to selection by the village elders to compulsion.

The rebels organized themselves into guerrilla bands *(fasa'il)* of a few men with a leader *(qa'id)*, on either a temporary or a permanent basis. Guerrilla *fasa'il* often used hit-and-run tactics, at night and principally in their local areas. When called upon, they operated under a regional or national command structure, especially after the arrival of Fawzi al-Qawuqji, a military man of Syrian heritage who also served in the 1947–1948 conflict. The local guerrilla bands had the advantage of their small size and knowledge of the terrain to escape the British and hide among their kinspeople and fellow villagers.

In the course of the revolt, the rebels gained control of much of the countryside. They then were faced with administering it. They developed systems of taxation, supply, and armaments. Rebel courts were created to adjudicate village civil conflicts and criminal cases. These replaced traditional institutions; elders and their role in social mediation, conflict resolution, and adjudication; and the British courts. Some rebel leaders codified new regulations in written form and appointed *qadi*s (judges) and other officials.

Both the strike and the armed insurrection were thus a direct challenge to British authority. In an early attempt to end the unrest, the British appointed a new commission, the Peel Commission, to investigate Palestinian grievances. Its report lucidly stated that the causes of this revolt were the same as those that had triggered the "disturbances" of 1920, 1921, 1929, and 1933: "the desire of the Arabs for national independence" and "their hatred and fear of the establishment of the Jewish National Home." The commission's recommendations were therefore to end the mandate and to partition Palestine into a Jewish state, an Arab state, and a British zone in and around Jerusalem.

This proposal outraged the Arab Palestinians, who viewed it as a means to dismember their homeland. The revolt intensified and reached its climax in the summer of 1938. Major Arab Palestinian cities, including Jerusalem, joined the rebellion. With rumors that the threat of war was easing in Europe (because of the 1938 British appeasement pact with Germany), the British launched an all-out campaign to crush the revolt. But they could not defeat the estimated two thousand Arab Palestinian rebels until 1939, when the Palestinian Arabs became exhausted and wearied. Its political leaders in exile, its military commands contained and segmented, the revolt dwindled. The British government issued a white paper that, for the first time during the mandate, *reversed* its previous policy and responded to Arab Palestinian concerns.

The 1939 white paper capped Jewish immigration at seventy-five thousand over five years, restricted land transfers to limited areas, and proposed to make Palestine independent within ten years if Arab-Jewish relations improved. The rebels rejected the white paper, as did, finally, the Zionist Jewish leadership. Despite its rejection by both sides, the British implemented the new policy unilaterally. Although it gained important concessions from a British government faced with a new world war, the revolt failed to achieve its principal goal of immediate Palestinian independence.

1940–1948: Arab Palestinian Political and Military Collapse, al-Nakbah

The war in Europe, the Holocaust, the increased Jewish immigration (legal and illegal) to Palestine, sympathy for European Jewry, the rising international influence of the Zionist movement (especially in the United States), the weakening of the British Empire, the emergence of the United Nations, the dramatic structural transformation within Palestine, and the defeat of the Arab Palestinian revolt all combined to overwhelm Palestine and the Palestinians during the decade of the 1940s.

The Palestinian Community.   The harsh British suppression of the Palestinian revolt and the reconquest of the country by 1939 decimated Arab Palestinian political and military institutions. Palestinian parties and political activity were made illegal by the British, Palestinian leaders were either in detention camps or in exile, Palestinian political activists and fighters in the thousands were in prison or concentration camps, and the community was largely disarmed. Palestinian society was economically devastated, politically and militarily defeated, and psychologically crushed. The collective will to struggle had been broken. The forceful spirit that had animated political activism and revolt in the 1930s did not return in full force in the 1940s to resist the ferocious Zionist onslaught of 1947–1948 that resulted in the Palestinian Nakbah.

The Jewish Community.   In contrast, the Jewish community in the 1940s grew economically strong, became tightly organized politically, and mobilized militarily. With the aid of British training, the Haganah (the mainstream Zionist militia), the forces controlled by the Jewish Agency, and other defense militias grew in numbers, skill level, and sophistication during the 1936–1939 Arab Palestinian revolt. In addition, underground extremist and terrorist Jewish groups, the Irgun Z'vai Leumi and the Lohamei Herut Yisrael (Lehi, or the Stern Gang, as the British called it), also proliferated. Jewish military power was further augmented by the experience and technical skill acquired by the thirty-seven thousand volunteers in the Jewish Brigade and other units who served in the British army during World War II. From dependency on British protection since the start of the mandate, the Jewish community by the end of World War II had become militarily strong enough to launch a revolt against the British in 1945 and the conquest of Palestine in 1948. There was a decisive shift in the balance of power on the ground between the immigrant-settler Jewish community and the indigenous Palestinians.

Breakdown of the Zionist-British Entente.   The Zionists, both extremists and centrists, were especially alarmed and antagonized by the 1939 white paper and its unilateral implementation. Frustrated by Britain, whose regional political calculations in the context of World War II necessitated placating Arab public opinion and the Arab states, the Zionists turned for support to the United States, the emerging world power.

In 1942, at a Zionist conference at the Biltmore Hotel in New York City, a new Zionist program was announced. In opposition to the white paper, it demanded open immigration into Palestine and settlement of unoccupied land in the country; for the first time, it declared *publicly* the Zionist intention to establish a Jewish commonwealth in Palestine. Zionist policy goals had evolved since 1917 from a Jewish national home to a state in part of Palestine (the 1937 Peel partition proposal) to the whole of Palestine as the Jewish state. Shortly after the Biltmore convention, a number of US senators and members of Congress signed a letter to President Franklin Roosevelt supporting Jewish rights to Palestine. And in January 1944, within less than two years, the US Congress passed a joint resolution endorsing the Biltmore program.

The Zionist Revolt.   The Palestine quandary after World War II led the British and US governments in 1946 to form an investigative commission jointly headed by a Britisher and an American. The Anglo-American Commission (also called the Morrison-Grady Commission) recommended the conversion of the Palestine mandate into a trusteeship divided into two autonomous provinces, Jewish (Jerusalem) and Arab (the Naqab Desert), to remain under British control. The Zionists, the US government, and the Arab Palestinians rejected the plan; the British accepted it. Further, the

British resisted US and Zionist pressure to open the gates of Palestine for another 100,000 Jewish immigrants before consideration of the trusteeship proposal in a London roundtable conference planned for September 1946.

Perhaps as a result, the Jewish forces of the Haganah and the Irgun launched a terror campaign and revolt against the British in Palestine. In July 1946, Jewish terrorists blew up the King David Hotel, headquarters of the British mandate authorities in Jerusalem, killing ninety-one British, Jewish, and Arab Palestinian individuals. The Zionist revolt against the British and attacks against Arab Palestinians by Jewish forces created a tense civil-war-like situation. British control over Palestine began to erode rapidly. It was clear that the British were in retreat and under siege.[101]

United Nations Partition Plan and Descent into War. The British government decided to withdraw its troops, relinquish control of Palestine, and turn over responsibility for the mandate to the United Nations. On November 29, 1947, the UN General Assembly voted Resolution 181 on the Future Government of Palestine (see Appendix 5), which partitioned Palestine into an Arab and a Jewish state. Map 3.4 shows how Palestine was purposely gerrymandered by the United Nations to create a Jewish majority in the proposed Jewish state.

The United Nations partition plan was based on the Zionists' own plan endorsed by the United States in August 1946.[102] At a time when the Jewish population of Palestine was around 31 percent of the total, the size of the proposed Jewish state was roughly 55 percent of historic Palestine and included a sizable Palestinian minority of 45 percent. The proposed Palestinian Arab state, in contrast, was awarded 45 percent of the land of Palestine and a negligible Jewish minority. Jerusalem and Bethlehem were supposed to be separate territories, under international auspices. Palestinians and other Arabs were outraged and rejected the United Nations resolution.

The British set July 31, 1948, for their final withdrawal and secretly informed the Zionist leadership but not the Arab Palestinians. In the event, they pulled out by the end of May and left Palestine in disarray. Instead of designing a rational process for transferring the central institutions and functions of government to the majority Arab Palestinians or to the respective Zionist and Palestinian authorities in accordance with the United Nations partition plan, the British in effect simply abandoned everything. This disorderly process added confusion to the rapidly developing internal war between the Jewish forces and the Arab Palestinians.

The self-contained, well-organized, and tightly controlled Jewish community, on the one hand, was well positioned to assume the functions and

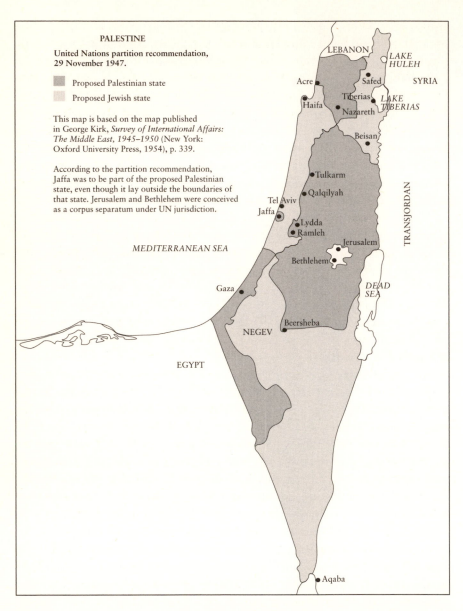

PALESTINE

United Nations partition recommendation,
29 November 1947.

Proposed Palestinian state

Proposed Jewish state

This map is based on the map published
in George Kirk, *Survey of International Affairs:
The Middle East, 1945–1950* (New York:
Oxford University Press, 1954), p. 339.

According to the partition recommendation,
Jaffa was to be part of the proposed Palestinian
state, even though it lay outside the boundaries of
that state. Jerusalem and Bethlehem were conceived
as a corpus separatum under UN jurisdiction.

LEBANON
*LAKE
HULEH*
Acre
Safed
SYRIA
Tiberias
*LAKE
TIBERIAS*
Haifa
Nazareth
Beisan
TRANSJORDAN
Tulkarm
Qalqilyah
Tel Aviv
Jaffa
Lydda
Ramleh
Jerusalem
Bethlehem
*DEAD
SEA*
MEDITERRANEAN SEA
Gaza
Beersheba
NEGEV
EGYPT
Aqaba

MAP 3.4   United Nations Partition Plan of Palestine
SOURCE: W. Khalidi, *Before Their Diaspora* (Washington, DC: Institute for Palestine Studies,
1984): 307.

institutions of government. With the support of the British authorities, they, after all, had built parallel autonomous institutions of governance and control in the course of the mandate. After their 1939 defeat, the Arab Palestinians, on the other hand, were unable to rebuild central leadership institutions or the mediating and local civil structures in order to mobilize the exhausted people. When the British abandoned the Arab areas, they left to the unprepared municipal and village authorities the immense responsibility of providing security; policing; defense; electric power; water; and sanitation, medical, educational, and other services. The resulting confusion was at the same time a product and a reflection of the disunity and disorganization of the Palestinian political leadership.

Efforts in the postwar period by the titular Arab Palestinian leader, al-Hajj Amin al-Husseini, to unite the weakened political groups and mobilize the fractured polity into a new national movement failed. With Arabs' public concern for their compatriots in Palestine, the nominally independent Arab states joined to help the beleaguered Palestinians. The League of Arab States was founded in part as a mechanism to create a united Arab policy on Palestine and to coordinate aid to the Palestinian people against dispossession by the increasingly evident Zionist threat. The Arab states and public opinion viewed Zionism as a threat not only to Palestine but also to the rest of the Arab world. Thus by 1945–1946 diplomatic policy and decisions regarding the question of Palestine were progressively appropriated from the Palestinian leadership by the Arab states in the framework of the Arab League.

Further compromising the Palestinian cause internationally and its leadership regionally were the machinations of the ambitious Amir Abdullah (son of Sharif Hussein of Mecca), ruler of Transjordan. After World War II, he had set his sights on reuniting and ruling greater Syria (which had been under the control of Vichy France) with the backing of the British. In return, he supported British policy (especially the Peel Commission's recommendation of partition) on Palestine and secretly colluded across the Jordan River with the Zionist leadership for the partition of Palestine.[103] As a participant in Arab League deliberations and decisions on the Palestine question, the Transjordanian government of Amir Abdullah was able to undermine both Palestinian and Arab efforts to save the country.

The Zionists had planned and organized a Jewish army, not just defensive guards, since 1942—one of the two key decisions of the Biltmore Zionist program—while the Arab Palestinians were being disarmed by the British authorities.[104] Jewish forces numbered roughly fifteen thousand in early 1948 but had swelled to over sixty thousand by May 1948. The majority of them were part of Haganah (with World War II experience), and the rest belonged to the terrorist groups, the Irgun and the Stern Gang. For the 1947–1948 hostilities, they recruited a large number of professional military volunteers from all over the world.

The Palestinian leader, al-Hajj Amin al-Husseini, waited to form a volunteer force, al-Jihad al-Muqaddas (the Holy Struggle), until December 1947, after the United Nations partition decision and after hostilities began. By March the irregular force, under two commanders, numbered around sixteen hundred. The Arab League organized and financially supported a volunteer Arab force, Jaysh al-Inqath (Army of Salvation), under the command of Fawzi al-Qawuqji. With a promised 10,000 rifles, 3,830 Arab men, including 500–1,000 Palestinians, were organized into eight battalions that operated in north-central Palestine. Palestinian and Arab fighters were outnumbered and outarmed by the Jewish regulars and their allied international volunteers. The Palestinians were unprepared politically or militarily to defend the integrity and unity of their country.

The Zionist Conquest of Palestine and al-Nakbah. The intercommunal Jewish-Palestinian fighting unleashed after the United Nations partition decision was terroristic and defensive. By March 1948 it appeared as if the Palestinians and their volunteer Arab supporters had the upper hand. This was a false impression, as the Zionists had yet to implement their offensive plan.

In April 1948 the Haganah and its international volunteers launched major operations throughout Palestine. Beginning in the second half of April, Jewish military assaults led to the fall of Tabariyya (April 18), Haifa (April 23), Jaffa (April 25), West Jerusalem (April 26), eastern Galilee (April 28), the central plain between Latrun and Ramleh (May 8–9), Safad (May 11–12), Beisan (May 12), and the Naqab villages (May 12). The attacks were brutal. Through terror, psychological warfare, and direct conquests, Palestine was dismembered, many of its villages were purposely destroyed, and many of its people were expelled as refugees.

As hundreds of thousands of refugees poured into safer areas of Palestine and into neighboring Arab countries, the members of the Arab League could not ignore the tragedy. They ordered their regular armies into battle for Palestine. The numbers, equipment, and firepower of those regular armies were less than half of what the Arab League's own Military Technical Committee had recommended. As important was the collusion of Abdullah (now king) with the Zionists: He ordered his British-commanded

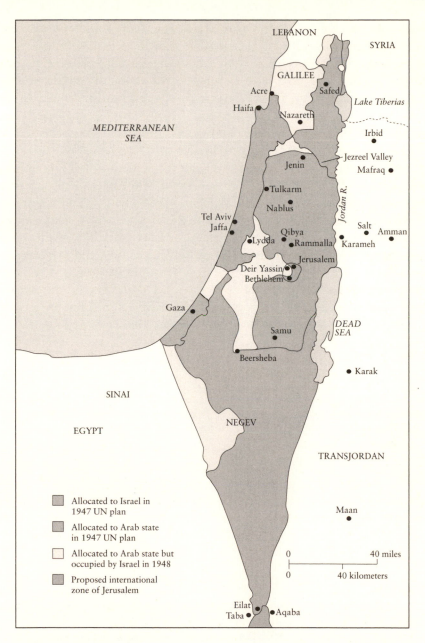

MAP 3.5   Areas of Palestine Conquered by Zionist-Israeli Forces Beyond
the Partition Plan

SOURCE: R. Ovendale, *The Longman Companion to the Middle East Since 1914*
(London: Longman Group, 1992): 355.

Arab Legion to secure only the part of Palestine allotted to the Arab state, which he had planned, with the agreement of the Zionists, to annex to Transjordan. The armies of the Arab states (Egypt, Iraq, Syria, and Jordan) arrived too late, and their intervention was not enough to save Palestine. Map 3.5 shows the areas of Palestine conquered by the Zionist-Israeli forces in 1948–1949, areas allocated to the Jewish state by the United Nations partition plan, and territories allocated to the Arab state. These areas form the state of Israel according to the armistice lines of 1949.

On May 14, 1948, the Zionists declared the State of Israel. Eleven minutes later, the United States recognized Israel. While an expanded Jewish state was forcibly created beyond the area allotted to the Jewish community in the United Nations partition plan, a Palestinian Arab state was not created within the UN-defined boundaries of the Palestinian Arab state. East-central Palestine came under Transjordanian control and was later annexed as the West Bank of the expanded kingdom of Jordan. The Gaza Strip came under Egyptian military control. Hundreds of thousands of Arab Palestinians became refugees in the parts of Palestine under Arab control and in neighboring Arab countries. Palestine thus ceased to exist.

Notes

1. B. Kimmerling, *Zionism and Territory* (Berkeley: Institute of International Studies, University of California, 1983): 1–30. See also G. Shafir, *Land, Labor and the Origins of Israeli-Palestinian Conflict, 1882–1914* (Cambridge: Cambridge University Press, 1989).

2. Shafir, *Land, Labor,* 14–17.

3. Kimmerling, *Zionism and Territory,* 3.

4. Shafir, *Land, Labor,* 21.

5. M. Y. Muslih, *The Origins of Palestinian Nationalism* (New York: Columbia University Press, 1988). See also W. Abboushi, *The Unmaking of Palestine* (Middle East Press, Boulder, CO, 1985); Y. Porath, *The Emergence of the Palestinian Arab National Movement, 1918–1929* (London: Frank Cass, 1974); and N. Mandel, *The Arabs and Zionism Before World War I* (Berkeley: University of California Press, 1976).

6. F. J. Khouri, *The Arab-Israeli Dilemma,* 3rd ed. (Syracuse: Syracuse University Press, 1985): 8.

7. Second note from Sir Henry McMahon to Sharif Hussein of the Hijaz, October 24, 1915. The note is reprinted in Appendix 3.

8. There was, however, some dispute and lack of clarity in this agreement over the eastern Mediterranean coastal regions of the area. The McMahon note—and it is unclear if Sharif Hussein agreed to this—excluded from the agreement the districts of Mersina and Alexandretta and "portions of Syria lying west of Damascus, Homs, Hama and Aleppo" (see Appendix 3), all regions to the north of Palestine.

9. The Balfour Declaration, November 2, 1917, reprinted in Appendix 2.

10. Anglo-French Declaration, November 7, 1918, cited in Appendix A, 6, in Khouri, *Arab-Israeli Dilemma, 527*.

11. See a sympathetic and concise account in Esco Foundation for Palestine, *Palestine: A Study of Jewish, Arab, and British Policies,* Vol. 1, (New Haven: Yale University Press, 1947): Part 1, Ch. 1, 1–56.

12. See N. G. Finkelstein, *Image and Reality of the Israel-Palestine Conflict* (London: Verso, 1995): Ch. 1: "Zionist Orientations," 7–20.

13. A. M. Hyamson, *Palestine Under the Mandate, 1920–1948* (Westport, CT: Greenwood Press, 1950): 1–25.

14. D. Vital, *The Origins of Zionism* (Oxford: Oxford University Press, 1975): 214.

15. Hyamson, *Palestine Under the Mandate,* 29.

16. Clayton to Foreign Office (enclosure), May 2, 1919, F.O. 371/2117/68848, cited in ibid., 58.

17. Watson to Allenby, August 16, 1919, F.O. 371/1051/124482, cited in ibid.

18. Quoted in Abboushi, *Unmaking of Palestine,* 10.

19. Ibid.

20. J. J. McTague, Jr., "The British Military Administration in Palestine, 1917–1920" *Journal of Palestine Studies* 7 (Spring 1978): 70.

21. Quoted in ibid.

22. Quoted from *Jewish Chronicle* of May 20, 1921, in Porath, *Emergence of the Palestinian,* 56.

23. Khouri, *Arab-Israeli Dilemma,* 17.

24. B. J. Smith, *The Roots of Separatism in Palestine, British Economic Policy, 1920–1929* (Syracuse: Syracuse University Press, 1993): 6.

25. Ibid., 7.

26. *A Survey of Palestine*, Vol. 1 (Washington, DC: Institute for Palestine Studies, 1991), Ch. 6, unnumbered table, 144.

27. J. L. Abu-Lughod, "The Demographic Transformation of Palestine," in I. Abu-Lughod, ed., *The Transformation of Palestine* (Evanston, IL: Northwestern University Press, 1971): 142.

28. *Survey of Palestine,* Ch. 7, Tables 2–11, pp. 187–203.

29. Ibid., 150, 151.

30. See the official British estimate for the end of 1944 in *Survey of Palestine*, Ch. 6, Table 5, p. 143: Of an estimated total population of 1.76 million, there were 1.18 million Palestinian Arabs, 554,000 Jews, and 32,000 others.

31. Abu-Lughod, "Demographic Transformation," 152.

32. See J. Ruedy, "Dynamics of Land Alienation," in Abu-Lughod, *Transformation of Palestine,* 119–138.

33. Kimmerling, *Zionism and Territory,* 37–38.

34. See W. Lehn and U. Davis, *The Jewish National Fund* (London: Kegan Paul International, 1988).

35. Esco Foundation, *Palestine: A Study,* 331–349.

36. See K. W. Stein, *The Land Question in Palestine* (Chapel Hill: University of North Carolina Press, 1984): 19ff. See also Kimmerling, *Zionism and Territory;* Shafir, *Land, Labor.*

37. A. Granott, *The Land System of Palestine,* translated by M. Sinion (London: Eyre and Spottiswoode, 1952). See also Stein, *Land Question,* 226–227, for a list of Jewish land purchases up to 1945 totaling 1.39 million *dunums.*

38. Ibid., 127.

39. John Hope Simpson, *Palestine, Report on Immigration, Land Settlement and Development* [the Hope Simpson report] (London: His Majesty's Stationery Office, 1930): 141–143.

40. B. Smith, *Roots of Separatism,* 9.

41. Ibid., 119.

42. Ibid., 131.

43. Esco Foundation, *Palestine: A Study,* 381–388.

44. Ibid., 696.

45. *A Survey of Palestine,* quoted in B. Smith, *Roots of Separatism,* 178. See also M. Seikaly, *Haifa: Transformation of an Arab Society, 1918–1939* (London: I. B. Tauris, 1995).

46. B. Smith, *Roots of Separatism,* 164–167.

47. I. Khalaf, *Politics in Palestine* (Albany: State University of New York Press, 1991): 48.

48. Ibid.

49. The actual wage structure in 1928 in the public sector was Arab rural, 120–150 mils per day (a Palestine pound, £P, equals 1,000 mils); Arab urban, 140–170; Jewish nonunion, 150–300; and Jewish union, 280–300. Cited in B. Smith, *Roots of Separatism,* 156.

50. See the point of view of J. Metzer and O. Kaplan, "Jointly and Severally: Arab-Jewish Dualism and Economic Growth in Palestine," *Journal of Economic History* 65 (June 1985): 327–345.

51. N. Halevi, "The Political Economy of Absorptive Capacity: Growth and Cycles in Jewish Palestine Under the British Mandate," *Middle Eastern Studies* 19 (October 1983): 456–469. See official regulations and figures on Jewish immigration in *Survey of Palestine,* Ch. 7, 165–224.

52. See Esco Foundation, *Palestine: A Study,* 366–369.

53. A. L. Tibawi, *Arab Education in Mandatory Palestine: A Study of Three Decades of British Administration* (London: Luzac, 1956): 205ff.

54. *Survey of Palestine,* Vol. 2, 638.

55. Cited in Y. N. Miller, *Government and Society in Rural Palestine, 1920–1948* (Austin: University of Texas Press, 1985): 95.

56. See A. Abu-Ghazaleh, *Arab Cultural Nationalism in Palestine* (Beirut: Institute for Palestine Studies, 1973), for a different viewpoint. See also Miller, *Government and Society,* 95–97.

57. Abu-Ghazaleh, *Arab Cultural Nationalism,* 19.

58. See the tables of absolute numbers in *Survey of Palestine,* Vol. 1, 147–149.

59. R. Szerezewski, *Essays on the Structure of the Jewish Economy in Palestine and Israel* (Jerusalem: Maurice Falk Institute, 1968): Table 5; Owen, "Economic Development in Mandatory Palestine," 16.

60. Owen, "Economic Development," 16.

61. The Esco Foundation study claims that "including both public and private sources, it is probable that the Jews brought into Palestine a sum of over

£125,000,000 during the last generation. Money was also sent to Palestine through the post office, of which there is no estimate." *Palestine: A Study,* Vol. 1, 384–385.

62. See Tables 8a and 8b in *Survey of Palestine,* Vol. 1, Ch. 6, 150–151.

63. Owen, "Economic Development," 20–27. See also *Survey of Palestine,* Vol. 1, Ch. 13, Section 4, "A Survey of Industry," 497–534.

64. *Survey of Palestine,* Vol. 1, 499.

65. Esco Foundation, *Palestine: A Study,* Vol. 2, 1056.

66. *Survey of Palestine,* Vol. 1, Ch. 13, 507.

67. *Survey of Palestine,* Vol. 2, Ch. 13, 502.

68. Cited in Esco Foundation, *Palestine: A Study*, Vol. 2, 1053.

69. Ibid., 1054–1055.

70. Owen, "Economic Development," 30.

71. *First Interim Report of Employment Committee,* October 27, 1944, cited in Khalaf, *Politics in Palestine,* 36–37.

72. Ibid., 52–53.

73. R. Taqqu, "Peasants into Workmen: Internal Labor Migration and the Arab Village Community under the Mandate," in J. S. Migdal, ed., *Palestinian Society and Politics* (Princeton: Princeton University Press, 1980): 261.

74. R. A. Nathan, O. Gass, and D. Creamer, *Palestine: Problem and Promise* (Washington, DC: Middle East Institute, 1946): 213.

75. Citing many sources, Owen, "Economic Development," 30.

76. *Survey of Palestine,* Vol. 2, 694, 696.

77. Data in this part come from Khalaf, *Politics in Palestine*, 38–44.

78. Ibid., 41–42.

79. R. N. Verdery, "Arab 'Disturbances' and the Commissions of Inquiry," in Abu-Lughod, *Transformation of Palestine,* 281.

80. Ibid., 282.

81. M. E. T. Mogannam, *The Arab Woman and the Palestine Problem* (London, 1937): 125, cited in D. Waines, "The Failure of the Nationalist Resistance," in Abu-Lughod, *Transformation of Palestine,* 220.

82. See the text of the resolution in Esco Foundation, *Palestine: A Study,* Vol. 1, 475.

83. A. M. Lesch, "The Palestine Arab Nationalist Movement Under the Mandate," in W. B. Quandt, F. Jabber, and A. M. Lesch, *The Politics of Palestinian Nationalism* (Berkeley: University of California Press, 1973): 20–21.

84. League of Nations, Permanent Mandates Commission, *Minutes of the 14th Session,* October-November 1928, Annex 9, 246. Cited in Waines, "The Failure of the Nationalist Resistance," 226.

85. See the details in P. Mattar, *The Mufti of Jerusalem* (New York: Columbia University Press, 1992): Ch. 3, 33–49.

86. Cited in Verdery, "Arab 'Disturbances,'" 290.

87. John Hope Simpson, *Palestine, Report on Immigration, Land Settlement and Development,* 26. According to the 1931 census, 22 percent of the total number of families dependent on agriculture were landless. Cited in D. Warriner, *Land and Poverty in the Middle East* (London: Royal Institute of International Affairs, 1948): 63.

88. Warriner, *Land and Poverty,* 57.

89. Hope Simpson, *Palestine, Report,* 64.

90. Ibid., 141.

91. Ibid., 136.

92. See *Palestine, Statement of Policy by His Majesty's Government in the United Kingdom,* presented by the Secretary of State for the Colonies, London, October 1930, 1–24; known as the Passfield white paper.

93. See P. Mattar, "Politics of Moderation and the General Islamic Congress," in P. Mattar, *The Mufti of Jerusalem* (New York: Columbia University Press, 1992): 50–64.

94. Ibid., 63.

95. Ibid., 64.

96. See the discussion in T. R. Swedenburg, *Memories of Revolt: The 1936–1939 Rebellion and the Palestinian National Past* (Minneapolis: University of Minnesota Press, 1995): 199.

97. See B. N. al-Hout, "The Palestinian Political Elite During the Mandate Period," *Journal of Palestine Studies* 9 (Autumn 1979): 85–111.

98. M. Budeiri, *The Palestine Communist Party, 1919–1948* (London: Ithaca Press, 1979).

99. B. Kalkas, "The Revolt of 1936: A Chronicle of Events," in Abu-Lughod, *Transformation of Palestine,* 241–242.

100. This section depends largely on Swedenburg, *Memories of Revolt,* 122–133.

101. This is not the place to analyze the factors responsible for British behavior at this point. See W. Khalidi, *From Haven to Conquest: Readings in Zionism and the Palestine Problem Until 1948* (Beirut: Institute for Palestine Studies, 1971), and W. Khalidi, *Before Their Diaspora: A Photographic History of the Palestinians, 1876–1948* (Washington, DC: Institute for Palestine Studies, 1984). See also J. C. Hurewitz, *The Struggle for Palestine* (New York: Norton, 1950), and Khouri, *Arab-Israeli Dilemma.*

102. Khalidi, *Before Their Diaspora,* 305.

103. A. Shlaim, *Collusion Across the Jordan: King Abdullah, the Zionist Movement, and the Partition of Palestine* (New York: Columbia University Press, 1988).

104. On the numbers and types of arms confiscated from the Palestinians between 1936 and 1945, see Khalidi, *From Haven to Conquest,* 845.

4

After al-Nakbah

The Palestinian Diaspora, 1948–1993

Al-Nakbah meant the destruction of Arab Palestinian society and patrimony and Palestinians' dispossession, dispersal, and destitution. This destruction was largely the result of Zionist policy and the tactics of expulsion in order to secure as much as possible of the land of Palestine for a Jewish state without indigenous Arab Palestinians. Of the total land of Palestine, the Israelis captured over 76 percent; the UN partition plan allotted them 55 percent. Map 4.1 shows Israel's 1949 cease-fire "borders," officially recognized as Israel by most governments, before further conquest and expansion during the 1967 Arab-Israeli war. From an estimated total population of 900,000 Palestinians in the areas occupied by Israel in 1947–1948, 750,000 to 800,000 became refugees.[1] In a matter of a few weeks in the spring of 1948, Palestine, a complex, developing, and differentiated society, was abruptly and haphazardly segmented, most of its people were dispossessed, and their lives were completely disrupted.

The Arabs of Palestine became divided into three widely dispersed and numerically unequal segments. First, 100,000 to 180,000 Palestinians remained in their homes and lands in what became Israel. Second, around 500,000 people remained behind Arab military lines in east-central Palestine and the Gaza Strip. Third, more than 750,000 of the total 1948 Palestinian population of 1.4 million became refugees in east-central Palestine (later known as the West Bank), the Gaza Strip, and neighboring Arab countries.[2] Table 4.1 provides numerical estimates of the Palestinian refugees and their destinations from varied sources.

Although the largest area of Palestine became Israel, two other parts, east-central Palestine (annexed in 1950 as the West Bank of the kingdom

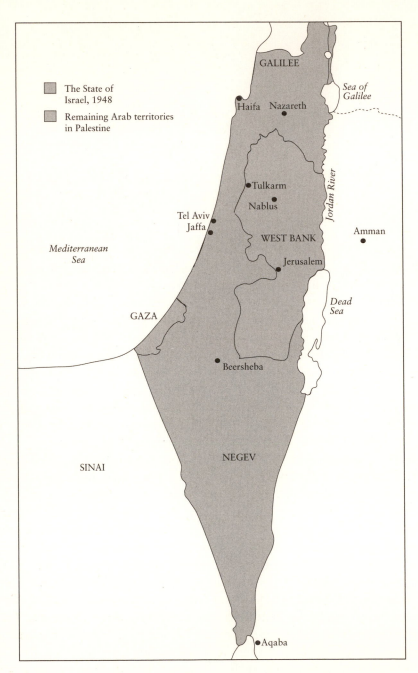

MAP 4.1   Israel and the West Bank and Gaza Strip, 1949 Armistice
Frontiers
SOURCE: Adapted from Simha Flapan, *The Birth of Israel: Myths and Realities*
(New York: Pantheon Books, 1987): 51.

TABLE 4.1 Estimates of Palestinian Refugees and Their Destinations, 1948–1949

Destination	British Government	U.S. Estimates	United Nations	Private Israeli Estimates	Israeli Government	Palestinian Sources
Gaza	210,000	208,000	280,000	200,000	–	201,173
West Bank	320,000	–	190,000	200,000	–	363,689
Jordan, Syria, Lebanon, etc.	280,000	667,000	256,000	250,000	–	284,324
Total	810,000 (Feb. 1949)	875,000 (1953)	726,000 (Sept. 1949) 957,000 (May 1950)	650,000 (end 1949) 600,000–760,000 (1948–1950)	520,000 (1948) 590,000 (1952)	850,276 (Nov. 1952) 770,100–780,000 (end 1948) 714,150–744,150 (mid-1948)

SOURCE: *Facts and Figures About Palestinians* (Washington, DC: Center for Policy Analysis on Palestine, 1992), 13.

of Jordan) and the Gaza Strip, came under control of the Jordanian and Egyptian military authorities, respectively. Although the Arab Higher Committee, the national Palestinian political organization, was finally allowed by the Arab League to declare a government in Gaza, Hukoumat 'Umoum Filastin (the All-Palestine Government), in effect it was a symbolic and futile act. Both segments of Jewish- and Arab-occupied Palestine passed from under the political control of the Palestinian Arabs. Palestine as a unitary state was no more. It lived on only in the imaginings, struggles, and plans of the Palestinian people.

Unable to return to their homeland after the cessation of hostilities, Palestinian refugees forged livelihoods in the areas and countries where they took initial refuge. Over the next two generations, however, voluntary Palestinian migrations took them in large numbers to the oil-exporting states of the Arabian Peninsula, Europe, and the Americas. The flow of Palestinian dispersal between 1948 and 2005 is provided in Table 4.2. Shortly after al-Nakbah nearly 80 percent of the Palestinian population lived in dismembered historic Palestine (Israel, the West Bank, and Gaza Strip), but by 1991 only a little over 40 percent remained there.[3] The majority composes the diaspora.

Although stateless (except for those in Jordan), everywhere in their diaspora the Palestinians built vibrant communities—at times under inhospitable conditions—that preserved their identity, social and cultural life, and political aspirations. In this chapter we analyze the structure and dynamics of these diaspora communities.

The well-documented political history of the region since al-Nakbah is framed largely by the Arab-Israeli state-to-state conflict in the context of the cold war. The social history of the Palestinians since 1948 and their struggle to regain their political right of self-determination have been portrayed by Western and Israeli scholars and media principally as a sideshow to the "larger" and "more significant" Arab-Israeli conflict, itself viewed as proxy Soviet–US confrontations in the region. The Arab-Israeli wars of 1956, 1967, and 1973 (the Suez War, the Six-Day War, and the Yom Kippur War, as these wars were called in Israel and the West) and the innumerable attacks, counterattacks, skirmishes, invasions, and short wars that often involved the superpowers diplomatically and otherwise captured the attention of most Western and many Middle Eastern journalists and scholars confirmed the conflict's principal focus as that between states. Nonetheless, the civil wars in Jordan (1970–1971) and Lebanon (1975–1982) forced the Palestine question to the fore. The 1978 and the more massive 1982 Israeli invasions of Lebanon, both in reality Israeli-Palestinian wars on Lebanese territory, and the 1987 Palestinian intifada more directly re-confirmed the question of Palestine as the underlying cause of the Arab-Israeli conflict and reasserted the fundamental centrality of the Palestinian-Zionist struggle over Palestine. Western politicians and experts alike also viewed the signing of an Israeli-PLO agreement in 1993 as the key to open-ing Arab doors in the current Middle East "peace process."

In short, Middle Eastern conflicts or peace processes and their interna-tional extensions have been invariably intertwined with the Palestine ques-tion and almost as often directly with the Palestinian national liberation movement, internal Palestinian politics, and the Palestinian people. In this chapter, then, we specifically analyze the causes, magnitude, distribution, and destination of the forced exodus of the Palestinian refugees. We also examine the demography, structure, transformation, and dynamics of Palestinian diaspora communities in the context of change in the host coun-tries and the transformation of the Middle East region. And finally, we ap-praise the metamorphosis of these communities from aggregations of refugee populations into a Palestinian political community. Chapter 6 is saved for a discussion of the significant role of the PLO in that change, in the development of economic and social service institutions among the di-aspora Palestinians, and in the evolution of Palestinian political identity, ideology, and strategy.

Palestinian Refugees: The Dynamics of Dispossession

One profound consequence of al-Nakbah of 1948 and the Arab-Israeli war of 1967 was the displacement of more than half the Palestinian Arab popu-lation. The bulk of the 1948 Palestinians fled their homes, villages, and land primarily because of mortal fear created by systematic terror campaigns conducted by the Israeli state forces. Even as they took flight, however, the question was always when and how, not whether, they would return. As time went on and the tragedies accumulated, the mystique of "the return" became even stronger. In many a Palestinian home in the diaspora, families display olive wood carvings or framed needlework pictures with the words "Innana raji'oun" or "Innana 'ai'doun" ("We shall return").

The irony deeply embedded in the refugee question is that as the Pales-tinians were expelled or fled in 1948, they were quickly replaced by hun-dreds of thousands of European and Asian (Arab) Jews, displaced persons, and immigrants. Throughout the urban and rural areas, movable and im-movable Palestinian property—homes, businesses, factories, orchards, and

TABLE 4.2 Summary of the Flow of Palestinian Dispersal from 1948–2005

Country or Region of Residence					Percentages of Total in Region				
	1948	1952	1961	1967 (prewar)	1967 (postwar)	1970	1975	1980	1985
Total Population	100	100	100	100	100	100	100	100	100
Palestinians in Palestine	100	76	65	63	50	46	45	43	41
Israel		11	11	12	15	15	16	16	16
West Bank		47	37	34	22	20	19	17	16
Gaza		18	17	18	13	11	11	10	9
Palestinians Outside of Palestine	0	24	35	37	50	54	55	57	59
Lebanon	0	7	8	8	8	8	8	8	8
East Bank of Jordan	0	9	17	18	27	30	28	25	23
Syria	0	5	5	5	5	5	5	5	5
Outside Core	0	5	(4.5)	(6)	(10)	(11)	(13)	(19)	(23)
Kuwait	—	(2)	2	3	4	5	6	6.3	6.5
Gulf states	—	—	2.5	1	3	0.6	1	1.5	2.0
Saudi Arabia	—	—		2		1.3	2.5	4.5	5.1
Libya	—	—				0.3	0.3	0.5	0.5
Iraq	—	—				0.8	0.9	0.9	0.9
Egypt	—	—			1	1.0	1	1	1
Rest of the world	—	—		2	2	2	2	4	7

(continues)

TABLE 4.2 (continued)

	1990–1991	1995	2001	2005
Total Population	5,780,422	6,692,153	8,807,518	10,100,000
Palestinians in Palestine				
Israel	12.6	12.0	11.5	11.2
West Bank	18.6	18.3	37.4	23.8
Gaza	10.8	10.9	–	13.9
Palestinians Outside Palestine				
Lebanon	5.7	5.9	5.2	4.2
East Bank of Jordan	31.6	32.4	28.1	29.4
Syria	5.2	5.3	5.6	4.6
Outside Core				
Rest of the Arab World	7.7	7.7	6.6	7.3
Rest of the World	7.8	7.5	5.6	5.6

SOURCES: For 1948–1980 figures, J. Abu-Lughod, "Demographic Charecteristics of Palestinian Population: Relevance for Planning Palestine Open University," *Palestine Open University: Feasibility Study*, part 2 (Paris: UNESCO, 1980) 39; for 1985–2000 figures, *Facts and Figures About the Palestinians* (Washington, DC: Center for Policy Analysis on Palestine, 1992), 4–5; for the 2001 figures, http://www.Jewishvirtuallibrary.org/Jsource/Arabs/Palpoptotal.html; for the 2005 figures, http://www.pcbs.org/portals/_pcbs/pressrelease/endyrrelseo5e.pdf.

fields filled with produce—was seized, and the ownership was transferred to Jewish occupants by the newly formed Israeli state. Close to four hundred villages and towns that the Israeli authorities could not or would not populate with immigrant Jews were plundered and razed.[4] Among the Palestinians who remained in what became Israel, village "populations were ejected forcibly in order to make room for Jewish settlements, . . . a form of compulsory *internal* migration" (italics added).[5] Official committees, formed by the Haganah before and the Knesset (Israeli parliament) after the declaration of the establishment of Israel, handled the "absorption" (e.g., appropriation) of Palestinian property under the guise of "custodianship." Given that the Jews owned only 10 percent of the land within the gerrymandered borders allotted to them in the 1947 United Nations partition plan and composed only 55 percent of the total population there, the dispossession and transfer of the Palestinians became crucial to the realization of an exclusively Jewish Israel. So was preventing the Palestinians' return and, alternatively, denying their claims for compensation and reparations.

The long-standing controversy over the flight/expulsion of the Palestinians revolves around a set of fundamental questions: Was the exodus deliberate, intended, forced, anticipated, planned? Or was it devoid of volition, a result of mass panic, uncontrolled crowd behavior? Contained in both Israeli and Palestinian accounts of the precipitant events are the elements of intention and panic alike, though each side places the burden of responsibility on the other. Essential to Israel's national definition are several recurrent themes in what it labels its "war of independence," the 1948 Palestinian Arab-Israeli war. These themes include, first, that the Palestinians and the wider Arab peoples and armies represented a potentially overwhelming military threat to the much smaller but better-trained and -armed Jewish forces. Second, Israel's role in creating the refugee problem was an unintended, although desirable, outcome of a series of life-or-death battles. To Palestinians and sympathizers, the birth of Israel was their Nakbah, their catastrophe. In a sense, al-Nakbah put an abrupt halt to the Palestinian prospects of modern nation-statehood, because that implies territorial grounding and economic and cultural cohesion. Instead, they became a fractured people, scattered in diaspora in several neighboring and more distant Arab states and throughout the world. In the Palestinians' own recollection of the events of 1948—that is, in their histories and collective memories—the picture that surfaces is antithetical to that of the Israelis in one major respect: Palestinians have long believed that the Zionist project, since its early conception, was built on the eradication of Palestine and with it the Palestinian people. Benny Morris closely examined an archival report entitled "The Emigration of Arabs of Palestine in the Period 1/12/1947–1/6/1948," which assesses the causes of the Palestinian exodus.[6] Culled from Israel's intelligence agency archives, the report quite bluntly admits that "without doubt, hostile [Haganah and Israeli military] operations were the main cause of the movement of population."[7] Reports from other sources confirm Jewish Zionist culpability. Sir John Bagot Glubb, the British commander of the Arab Legion, the Transjordanian army that fought in the 1948 war, disclosed in his autobiography that he had asked a Jewish official of the Palestine mandate government "whether the new Jewish state would have many internal troubles in view of the fact that the Arab inhabitants of the Jewish state would be equal in number to the Jews." Glubb reported that the official had replied, "Oh no! That will be fixed. A few calculated massacres will soon get rid of them."[8]

Through extensive and intensive interviews in refugee camps in southern Lebanon, Rosemary Sayigh was able to reconstruct the processes of expulsion and dispersal of this group of peasants. Based on the recollections of the 1948 refugees who had gone to Lebanon, these recorded stories and oral histories could probably be generalized beyond this particular population. She found the primary causes of the flight "so obvious only deliberate mystification could have obscured them . . . : direct military attack on the villages; terrorism; lack of leadership; lack of arms; in short, chaos and fear."[9] A secondary but still significant motive was the fear, generated by personal experience and rumor, of rape and other atrocities Israeli soldiers had perpetrated on defenseless Palestinian civilians. As a man of peasant origins intimated to Sayigh:

> My village, Sa'sa, didn't leave because of a battle. There was fighting around, there were air-raids and bombardments. But the reason we left was the news of the massacre of Safsaf, where fifty young men were killed. There were other massacres—Jish, Deir Yasseen—and there were stories of attacks on women's honour. Our villagers were especially concerned to protect their women, and because of this fear, many of the northern villages evacuated even before the war reached them.[10]

Crimes against *al-'ard* (the honor of the women of the family) tore at the sturdy fabric of village life, woven as it was from kinship ties, familial obligations, and communal duties. The conquering Israeli troops were not bound to such tradition, nor did they respect its sanctity. As Israeli agriculture minister, Aharon Cizling, stated at a July 21, 1948, cabinet meeting,

"It has been said that there were cases of rape in Ramle. I can forgive acts of rape but I won't forgive other deeds which appear to me graver."[11] The threat against or actual violation of family honor, an integral component of the Palestinians' culture and community, and the slim possibility of retaliation in order to redeem al-'ard brought home the necessity of flight, at least temporarily, in order to protect the traditional way of life.

The reasons for the flight of approximately 400,000 Palestinians during the June 1967 War (small numbers of whom the Israeli government eventually allowed to return) are not as politically controversial as those for the 1948 exodus, but they are similar. In the folklore of the Palestinians in diaspora, the exodus of 1967 from the West Bank and Gaza was far less extensive than that of 1948 from Palestine because they had learned an important lesson: While the protection of al-'ard (family honor) may have come before the protection of al-Ard (the land) in 1948, priorities were reversed in 1967: Al-Ard came before al-'ard. Thus, unlike in 1948, most Palestinians in the 1967 war stayed put on their land in the West Bank and Gaza. Yet the events of 1948 and 1967 left an indelible imprint on the collective memory of Palestinians. They were experiences that still echo and create debate and division within the varied Palestinian communities.

The Expulsion: Magnitude, Patterns, and Destinations

The expulsion of Palestinians in 1948 occurred with little warning or preparation. Usually, whole villages, towns, and urban centers were quickly evacuated or expelled as the Haganah and Israeli forces approached or attacked an area. Map 4.2 shows the distribution and destinations of the 846,000 dispossessed Palestinians. Although the causes of their flight varied by region, social class, and time period, several (forced) flight patterns can be discerned from statistical data as well as subsequent qualitative investigations. Overall, these patterns share a common characteristic: The bulk of the 1948 refugees resisted crossing the borders of Palestine. The majority of Palestinians who lived within the territory of what is now Israel left their homes as danger seemed imminent, as the fighting caught them defenseless, or as they were expelled. Most first found refuge in a nearby village where they may have had kin, on the outskirts of an urban center, or even in an unpopulated area (a field, forest, or mountainous area).

Contrary to the image of masses of Palestinians steadily streaming across the nearest border, then, most refugees made multiple internal migrations before reaching an end point. Furthermore, that end point, for the majority

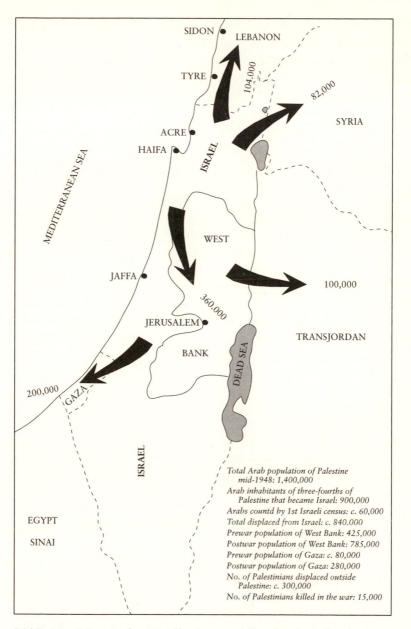

Total Arab population of Palestine
   mid-1948: 1,400,000
Arab inhabitants of three-fourths of
   Palestine that became Israel: 900,000
Arabs countd by 1st Israeli census: c. 60,000
Total displaced from Israel: c. 840.000
Prewar population of West Bank: 425,000
Postwar population of West Bank: 785,000
Prewar population of Gaza: c. 80,000
Postwar population of Gaza: 280,000
No. of Palestinians displaced outside
   Palestine: c. 300,000
No. of Palestinians killed in the war: 15,000

MAP 4.2   Magnitude, Distribution, and Destination of Palestinian
Refugees, 1948
SOURCE: R. Sayigh, *Palestinians: From Peasants to Revolutionaries* (London: Zed
Press, 1979): 65.

of Palestinians, became east-central Palestine (the West Bank) or the Gaza Strip. And those who crossed into Arab countries such as Lebanon tended to remain at first near the border of Palestine, to wait for the repatriation they believed was imminent, and to resist transfer to other areas.[12] As time went on and material resources were exhausted, refugees accepted transfer to camps in the interior of the host country.

Palestinian Population: Demographic and Geographic Transition

As we noted previously, in 1995 only around 40 percent of the total population of Palestinians continued to live in historic Palestine (Israel, the West Bank, and the Gaza Strip). The factors that impelled this demographic transformation between 1948 and 1995 were both economic and political. To start with, the greater economic investment favoring the East Bank encouraged many Palestinians from the West Bank to emigrate there throughout the 1950s and 1960s. Others, because of West Bank and Gaza Strip economic stagnation, migrated to the oil-exporting states of the Arabian Peninsula and Libya, which were in desperate need of unskilled, skilled, and educated labor forces. Others emigrated to Lebanon, which also experienced an economic boom linked in part to the early oil bonanza of the 1960s.[13] As a result of this wave of voluntary migration, the percentage of Palestinians living inside historic Palestine dropped from roughly 80 percent after al-Nakbah in 1948 to 63 percent just before the June 1967 War.

The 1967 war also had a profound impact on Palestinian population movements. Israel's conquest of the rest of Palestine led, as noted already, to a second major exodus, estimated at around 400,000 Palestinians.[14] Out of a total Palestinian population of approximately 2.65 million in 1967, the ratio of the Palestinians residing inside historic Palestine dropped sharply, from 63 to 50 percent after the war. Specifically, the West Bank population decreased by 12 percent as a result of the war (from a total of 34 percent of all Palestinians) and the Gaza population declined by 5 percent (from 18 to 13 percent). Simultaneously, the ratio of Palestinians in the East Bank of Jordan jumped substantially from 17.5 percent of all Palestinians to 27 percent.[15]

After the second displacement, in the June 1967 War, migrations to the oil-exporting states of the Arabian Peninsula picked up momentum, especially in the oil-boom period of the 1970s and early 1980s. Additionally, Palestinian migrations from (rather than to) Lebanon increased further during the Lebanese civil war (1975 onward) and jumped greatly as a result of the Israeli invasion of Lebanon of 1982. Palestinian emigration to Europe and the Americas, too, increased substantially during the 1980s. It is estimated that in 1995 about 200,000 Palestinians resided in the United States and Canada and a similar number in the rest of the Western Hemisphere. The percentage of Palestinians outside historic Palestine *and* the neighboring Arab countries rose from 6 percent of all Palestinians before the June 1967 War to 23 percent (1.13 million out of 4.9 million) by 1985.[16]

The diaspora Palestinians and those under occupation have remarkably high fertility and low mortality rates and thus a high rate of population increase. Already high during the mandate period,[17] the birth rate continued to rise, in large part because of better health conditions. However, the dispersed Palestinian society after al-Nakbah became occupationally differentiated, urbanized, educated, and socially mobile, factors typically associated with declining fertility rates. As a result, among the middle and upper social classes the rate of population increase declined. But the rate of increase among the Palestinians in Israel, those under occupation in Gaza and in most refugee camps—the proletarianized classes—continued to rise and peaked at 4 percent per annum, canceling out the decline among the bourgeois Palestinians.[18] Thus the overall rate of Palestinian population increase has been phenomenally high, more than doubling the size of the population every generation since 1948.

The high rate of population increase among Palestinians also means a young population, the second key feature of the Palestinian population. Generally, Palestinians below the age of eighteen years have rarely represented less than 50 percent of the total population.[19] Indeed in the camps, such as those of Lebanon, Jordan, and the West Bank, and in Palestinian communities in Kuwait and Saudi Arabia, the ratio of those below fifteen years reached much above the 50 percent level during the 1970s and 1980s. In the mid-1990s that ratio was estimated to be close to 60 percent in Gaza, especially in the camps. The range of median ages of between fifteen and eighteen years in various communities of Palestinians is dramatic if compared to the current median age of thirty-two years in an aging population like that of the United States.

Such a young population has immense social, economic, and political implications. For example, the ratio of those of productive age is low compared to that in most Western countries: In Lebanon the Palestinian labor force was 17 percent of the population in 1951 but increased steadily to 30 percent by 1976.[20] And providing education and jobs for the Palestinians is

TABLE 4.3 Global Distribution of the Palestinian People

	1986	1990–1991	1995	2000	2005
Jordan	1,398,050	1,824,179	2,170,101	2,596,986	2,753,012
West Bank/East Jerusalem	951,520	1,075,531	1,227,545	1,383,415	1,651,000
Gaza	545,100	622,016	726,832	837,699	961,643
Israel	608,200	730,000	800,755	919,453	1,112,000
Lebanon	271,434	331,757	392,315	463,067	400,582
Syria	242,474	301,744	357,881	410,599	424,650
Remaining Arab states	582,894	445,195	516,724	599,389	623,000
Rest of world	280,846	450,000	500,000	550,000	681,000
Total	4,880,518	5,780,422	6,692,153	7,760,608	7,645,354

SOURCES: *Facts and Figures About the Palestinians* (Washington, DC: Center for Policy Analysis on Palestine, 1992), 4; www.un.org/unrwa/publications/pdf/unif-June05.pdf (figures from UNRWA do not include unregistered refugees).

always an important consideration for whichever authority is in control of their lives. Further, the young Palestinian population has always provided a large supply of youthful activists who carried out the task of political and military mobilization. Also significant, labor migrations to the Arabian Peninsula and the West often involved young men and thus created skewed population structures in both the home and work communities. In short, the characteristics of the Palestinian population, including especially the high ratios of population increase, will add to the dilemmas of resolving the Palestine problem. Overall, the Palestinian population increased from roughly 1.4 million people in 1948 to an estimated 10.1 million in 2005 (see Table 4.3).[21]

Communities in Diaspora

From the onset of al-Nakbah, there were two kinds of refugees. The middle- and upper-class Palestinians, many of whom left the areas of armed conflict and potential war zones just before the Zionist onslaught, took refuge, as some had earlier in the 1936 revolt, in nearby Arab cities such as Amman, Beirut, Cairo, and Damascus. They rented apartments short-term with the hope of returning to their homeland after the conclusion of the hostilities. The second and by far the largest group of refugees was the mass of poor and peasant Palestinians, who were destitute and desperate. They became the refugee camp dwellers.

Refugee Camps and the Role of UNRWA

The United Nations qualified "a needy person, who as a result of the war in Palestine, has lost his home and his means of livelihood" as a refugee. Later the definition was expanded to include "direct descendants." In September 1949, 726,000 Palestinians were classified as refugees (see Table 4.1). Initially, the Arab host countries helped the Palestinians, but their meager resources were quickly overwhelmed. Also in 1948 the United Nations passed General Assembly Resolution 194 (see Appendix 6) affirming the Palestinian refugees' right to repatriation and/or compensation and urged Israel to accept the return of the refugees. Israel refused. It stonewalled despite international, including some US, pressure to allow the return or compensation of the refugees. Nearly two years after al-Nakbah, the United Nations Relief and Works Agency (UNRWA) assumed relief operations (provision of tents, food staples, and health care) in Gaza, the West Bank, Transjordan, Lebanon, and Syria where Palestinians had clustered. Although UNRWA was conceived as a temporary agency, by 1955, as the refugee problem became more intractable, UNRWA reoriented its services toward integrating Palestinians into their surroundings. Education, housing, training, and employment within the camps were offered as a means toward that end. By 1992 UNRWA had become one of the largest international agencies, employing close to 19,000 people who served more than 2.7 million camp refugees (including those of 1967).

A large number of refugee camps were established by mutual agreement of the host country and the United Nations. As Table 4.4 shows, in the mid-1990s there were twelve camps in Lebanon, ten each in Syria and Jordan, nineteen in the West Bank, and eight in the Gaza Strip. In 1993 UNRWA listed 2.73 million officially registered refugees. Over nearly five decades, as their economic well-being improved, Palestinians sought residence outside the camps in the host countries or elsewhere.

Accordingly, after two generations, as Table 4.5 indicates, camp-dwellers constituted 52.2 percent of all registered refugees in Lebanon, 29.1 percent in Syria, 22.8 percent in Jordan, 26.3 percent in the West Bank, and 55.0 percent in the Gaza Strip.

The sites of camps were determined by the host country in accordance with internal economic and political considerations. In Lebanon the bulk of the refugees were herded into rural camps in the south and north of the country and in the eastern Beqa'a Valley, which provided Lebanese landlords with cheap agricultural labor. Yet Shatila camp, near the city of Beirut, was founded spontaneously, as few other camps were, through the

TABLE 4.4 UNRWA General Information Concerning Refugees

	Lebanon	Syria	Jordan	Gaza	West Bank	Total
Demographic characteristics						
Country area (sq km)	10,452	185,180	91,860	360	5,500	293,352
Country population (CP)	3,400,000	14,618,390	4,139,458	963,000	1,571,575	24,692,426
Registered refugees (RR)	352,668	347,391	1,358,706	716,930	532,438	3,308,133
RR growth (%) (1995–1996)	1.9	3	5.5	4.9	2.9	4.3
RR as % of CP	10.4	2.4	32.8	74.4	33.9	13.4
Existing camps	12	10	10	8	19	59
RR in camps (RRCs)	192,052	101,027	258,204	395,987	148,105	1,095,375
Education training						
Schools	74	110	198	155	100	637
Pupils (1995–1996) enrollment	36,498	62,046	148,004	129,494	45,812	421,854
Female pupils (%)	50.3	48.4	49.1	49.4	55.5	49.6
Cost per preparatory pupil ($)	386	178	292	271	372	300
Cost per preparatory pupil ($)	512	256	348	484	501	420
Vocational & technical training centers	1	1	2	1	3	8
Vocational & technical training places	608	800	1,224	732	1,260	4,624
Educational sciences faculty training places	N.A.	N.A.	855	N.A.	N.A.	1,455
In-service teacher trainees	98	108	175	164	106	651
University scholarships awarded	77	240	246	231	149	943
Total education posts	1,538	2,063	4,965	4,133	2,093	14,863
Infrastructure/services (as of 1993)						
Health center/units & dental clinics	40	29	36	25	49	179
Indoor water supply in camps (%)	89	75	92	100	98	92
Sewered shelters in camps (%)	56	85	45	27	31	47
Unemployment % (estimate)	40	10	20	30–40	30–40	28
Total 1993 budget ($ thousands)	31,540	36,537	61,183	63,896	47,846	297,185

SOURCE: United Nations Relief and Works Agency, *Annual Report* (New York: UNRWA, 1993 and 1996).

TABLE 4.5 Occupational Distribution of Palestinian Males in Selected Countries and Regions (in percentages)

Country or Region of Residence	Professional, Technical	Administrative Manager	Clerical	Sales and Commerce	Industrial, Transport, Utilities	Services (personal)	Agriculture, Fishing, Mining
Saudi Arabia	51.5	2.9	6.0	3.2	28.9	3.3	4.3
Jordanians	63.0	3.1	6.1	3.1	20.1	1.9	2.1
Palestinians	36.9	2.6	5.7	3.3	39.3	5.0	7.1
Kuwait	20.8	1.3	17.8	8.6	41.1	8.4	2.1
Jordan East Bank	9.7		7.0	11.8	45.4	11.2	14.5
Syria	10.8	0.7	8.2	8.9	57.0	6.6	7.9
Israel	6.6	3.9		8.2	51.4	10.0	19.9
(1972 census)							
(1976 census)	6.2	0.4	3.9	7.3	57.3	9.7	15.2
West Bank	6.2	0.9	3.0	12.5	50.1	7.8	19.5
Gaza	5.1	0.6	3.1	11.9	47.4	8.7	23.2
Lebanon camps	3.7		1.4	15.3	46.1	8.9	24.7

SOURCE: J. Abu-Lughod, "Demographic Characteristics of the Palestinian Population: Relevance for Planning Palestine Open University," *Palestine Open University Feasibility Study*, part 3 (Paris: UNESCO, 1980), 61. ©UNESCO 1980. Reproduced by permission of UNESCO.

effort of a former Palestinian rebel leader who was seeking immediate, temporary shelter for his family and kin. Shatila, like other small suburban camps and settlements in Lebanon, Jordan, and elsewhere, grew fast in subsequent years as it attracted people from rural camps who sought jobs in the booming construction industry of Arab capital cities. Migration from rural to urban camps was extensive during the urban boom years and was further increased by the presence of the Palestine Liberation Organization (PLO), first in Amman (1968–1970) and later in Beirut (1970–1982). The host governmental authorities ignored the urban-oriented movement of camp refugees, especially as the urban construction labor market demanded a vast pool of cheap labor.

At first the International Red Cross and then the UNRWA provided the refugees with tents and supplied them with trucked-in water, some food staples, and medical service. Prevented from building more permanent housing, Palestinians in Lebanon over the years erected dwellings *(barrakiyat)* of corrugated iron, tin, wood, and other materials. Not until 1969, with the emergence of Harakat al-Muqawama al-Filastiniyya (the Palestinian Resistance Movement, PRM)—as the national liberation movement in general and its leadership, the newly radicalized PLO, were called—did the camp-dwellers begin to build concrete and cinder block housing, to pipe in running water, and to install some sewerage and electricity. In part this happened because the PRM took control of most camps (principally in Lebanon, Syria, and earlier in Jordan, but not in the West Bank and the Gaza Strip, which were under Israeli occupation) and in part because the new generation of skilled Palestinians built such amenities for themselves.

Thus, in a little over one generation, refugee camps developed from precarious, wind-swept tent cities with hardly any services into highly congested minicities or shantytowns of concrete, asphalt, and some infrastructure. Although running water eventually was piped into most residences in the camps, in 1992 only 56 percent of all shelters were sewered in Lebanon, 85 percent in Syria, 45 percent in Jordan, 31 percent in the West Bank, and 27 percent in Gaza. Otherwise, the camps had open sewers. Of course by then the population congestion was immense, and the land area of the camps was strictly circumscribed by the respective Arab and Israeli authorities. The physical infrastructure, the social and medical services, and the quality of life became totally inadequate, perhaps miserable, in the majority of the camps—worst in those under Israeli control.

Social and Economic Integration

The different Palestinian communities in the diaspora have had diverse and unique social, economic, and political histories since 1948 and therefore have developed distinctive occupational and social structures. As is clear from Table 4.5, the refugee communities in the occupied West Bank and the Gaza Strip and the indigenous Palestinian community in Israel were completely proletarianized (lumpenproletarianized in Gaza) by Israel and turned into cheap sources of unskilled labor. So were most of the Palestinian camp-dwellers of Lebanon and Jordan (fewer of them in Syria). Those of the Arabian Peninsula were socially more diverse. As a result, the communities have shown differing levels of political and economic involvement and contributions in support of the Palestinian national liberation movement. For example, the PLO was anchored in Jordan during its early period, 1968–1970, and the Palestinians of Jordan were its principal social base. After its expulsion from Jordan, the PLO's social and economic base shifted to the Palestinians of Lebanon; this lasted from 1970 until the exodus from Beirut in 1982. Recruits for its political cadres and fighters nevertheless came from all the far-flung communities, including the Palestinians of Israel (the so-called Israeli Arabs). The most prominent of the Palestinians from Israel is the celebrated Palestinian poet laureate Mahmoud Darwish, who emerged as the voice of the movement and the interpreter of its struggles. Certain communities, like those of the Arabian Peninsula, especially Saudi Arabia and Kuwait (before the 1991 Iraqi invasion), contributed financially more than others. As the diaspora communities have become more differentiated from each other and experienced divergent social histories and political legacies, the future integration of Palestinian society becomes more problematic.[22]

The Camp-Dwellers.   The pattern of proletarianization and indeed lumpenproletarianization is especially manifest among camp-dwellers, as shown in Table 4.5. The Shatila camp (with 75,000 residents in the early 1980s) near Beirut, the ‘Ayn al-Hilweh camp (100,000 in the mid-1990s) near Sidon, Lebanon, and the Baqa‘a camp (about 65,000) on the outskirts of Amman, Jordan, are tremendously overcrowded minicities whose labor force has been engaged in unskilled and skilled labor, tertiary occupations, low-level clerical work, and part-time or temporary work in the nearby urban center and surrounding agricultural areas. Although to a much smaller extent than men, women, too, sought paid work, although mostly inside the camp.

A study by Samir Ayyoub of the class structure of the Palestinians in Lebanon found that only 15.6 percent of the grandfathers were employed in *wage* labor in Palestine, as were 39.6 percent of the parents and 63.3 percent of the respondents in the sample. Put differently, the source of income of 76.1 percent of the sample derived from wage labor, a high degree of proletarianization in one generation. In the 1950s in Shatila camp, unskilled workers earned the equivalent of sixty-five cents per day, grossly insufficient wages for the survival of their families.

By the 1960s camp-dwellers had developed into specialists in the building trades: plumbers, tilers, plasterers, electricians, and so on.[23] What allowed many to escape the camp was what the Palestinians themselves call the "education revolution," which in one generation turned many of the children of proletarianized Palestinian refugees into professionals. Shatila and other urban camps have often served as way stations for upgrading skills and emigrating to the Arabian Peninsula oil-exporting economies and to the West.

Based on ties of kinship, locality (villages or city quarters), patronage, and patrimonial political factions, traditional Palestinian social structure was reconstituted in the newly formed refugee camps.[24] Early in this process, the traditional patterns of kinship obligations and, to a lesser extent, patronage served the traumatized refugees well. Over the years, however, both began to undergo change as their functions in the context of dispersal, landlessness, wage labor, and increased social differentiation undermined their ability to serve the people's needs. In their stead, beginning in the late 1960s, factions of the PLO and their modern, secular organizing practices provided both social services and social safety nets for the camp-dwellers. Yet village customs that were expressive and symbolic of the traditional values and culture[25] and therefore of identity did remain relatively strong within the camps.

As more modern sociopolitical organizations (student unions, workers' unions, and women's organizations) began to be reconstituted or emerge with a modern, secular pan-Arabist ideology, however, they modified those traditional social relations and values. Thus, with the rise of Arab nationalism, the emergence of the PLO in 1964, and the surfacing of the PRM in 1968, social change, political consciousness, and activism significantly increased in the camps. One generation after al-Nakbah, an indigenous, more modern leadership emerged and attempted to establish among the dispersed communities and fractured society quasi state institutions as a framework for the restoration of Palestinian political rights, repatriation, self-determination, and nationhood. This revolutionary transformation of the Palestinian people and the birth of the PLO are discussed in the next chapter.

Religion, typically a conservative social force, was embedded in the traditional popular culture of the camps, but it became irrelevant to the emergent secular nationalist discourse. New secular nationalist symbols proliferated, as did literature, songs, and gatherings: rallies, celebrations, funerals of martyrs. The secular, nationalist discourse and organization remained dominant until the 1980s, when the influence of religion among the camp-dwellers and the poor Palestinian masses resurfaced in a politicized, radicalized, activist, even militant form, especially in the Gaza Strip. Many factors contributed to this phenomenon in Palestinian politics. Not least was the rise of political Islam throughout the Middle East. Most important in the Gaza Strip, however, were the unrelenting pressure of Israel's occupying army, the severe degradation of the people's economic well-being, and the ineffectiveness or failure of the secular PLO and PRM to end the occupation and relieve the misery.[26] Although political Islam has not yet developed significantly in the diaspora Palestinian camps in the Arab host countries, it has nonetheless become an important factor in Palestinian, regional, and international political calculations. Its influence on the people is contradictory: It is politically radical, militant, and activist yet socially conservative and regressive, especially in relation to women's status and role in public life. However, it has also provided economic relief and social services for the needy and destitute.

The Middle Class. A minority of the Palestinian non-camp-dwellers in Lebanon, a small and strongly Christian fraction of the Palestinians there, became highly educated, Westernized, and rapidly integrated into the expanding service economy of the country and the region.[27] Larger Palestinian middle and upper classes also evolved in Jordan on the East and West Banks, both because of the size of the community and because of the underdeveloped Transjordanian counterparts. Because they were new citizens of Jordan,[28] economic life in the private, public, and governmental sectors was open to them. Some even became prime ministers, cabinet members, ambassadors, and heads of major governmental agencies in the 1950s and early 1960s before tension, a power struggle, and conflict between the PLO and the Jordanian monarchy and between the two communities (Transjordanian and Palestinian) developed in the late 1960s. In Jordan, Lebanon, Kuwait (before 1991), Saudi Arabia, and elsewhere, an entrepreneurial, professional, and commercial Palestinian bourgeoisie emerged and became quite distinguished and socially disconnected from its compatriot proletarian camp-dwellers.

The Palestinian middle and bourgeois classes in Lebanon, Jordan, and the Arabian Peninsula played pivotal roles in the economic development of those countries. The Palestinian bourgeoisie was prominent in building the Lebanese, Jordanian, and peninsular banking institutions (e.g., Intra Bank and Arab Bank); airlines (Middle East Airlines and Trans Mediterranean Airways); design, auditing, marketing, consulting, construction, and other technical firms; the hotel and tourist industry; and other service industries. The Palestinian middle and upper classes in both countries expanded and flourished all the more during the regionwide oil boom of the 1970s and early 1980s. In the oil-exporting states of the Arabian Peninsula, the Palestinian professional elite contributed considerably as well to the planning, design, and construction of the physical infrastructure (from sewers to hospitals and from roads to airports); the creation of the social and economic infrastructure (schools, universities, hospitals, factories, businesses, and banks); and the development of the public sector, the governmental bureaucracy, the diplomatic corps, and the economy in general. This role was most pronounced in Kuwait. A 1975 survey conducted in Kuwait by the United Nations Economic and Social Commission for West Asia (ESCWA) found that Palestinians "constituted 28 percent of all engineers, 34 percent of surveyors and draftsmen, 37 percent of all doctors and pharmacists, 25 percent of the nursing staff, 38 percent of all economists and accountants, [and] 30 percent of the teaching staff."[29]

The Palestinian community in Saudi Arabia was also highly skilled: Over 50 percent of the labor force of the Palestinians (and Jordanians, many if not most of whom are Palestinians with Jordanian citizenship) occupied high technical, professional, and managerial positions. Here, as in Lebanon and Jordan, the rapid economic development of the oil-exporting countries afforded the Palestinians an opportunity for socioeconomic mobility. A new and larger class of nouveaux riches emerged and became even more removed from the diaspora camp-dwellers and the proletarianized masses in the occupied territories of the West Bank and the Gaza Strip. Yet, for a time, most remained close to and supportive of the PLO and its leadership.

Social Mobility and Political Influence: Expansion and Contraction. The expansion and increased influence of the Palestinian middle class and bourgeoisie, as has been pointed out, occurred especially in the context of the oil-based economic boom that raised sharply the growth rates of individual Arab economies and the income levels and standards of living of most people in the Arab east. The new Palestinian multimillionaires, however, had internationalized their investments, interests, and residences by the early 1980s.[30] This dispersed elite developed as the most important philanthropic force (organizing itself in 1982 in the [Palestine] Welfare Association based in Geneva) and as a pivotal player in the politics of the Palestinian national liberation movement, especially within the PLO.

Making the most of the opportunity for acquiring individual fortunes and political influence, Palestinians were able to ride the tide of pan-Arab nationalism (whose ideology included the liberation of Palestine as a central tenet) during the 1950s, 1960s, and in particular the oil decade of the 1970s and early 1980s. Even when they were uncomfortable with it, regimes such as the Saudi Arabian monarchy nevertheless supported pan-Arabism, perhaps even favored Arab nationalists and Palestinians in some governmental and diplomatic positions. Although disenfranchised politically (except formally in Jordan), Palestinians nonetheless were a political factor in the support and spread of liberationist pan-Arab ideologies and movements (e.g., Nasserism, the Ba'ath Party, and the Movement of Arab Nationalists [MAN]) and specifically the Palestinian resistance movement throughout the region. These political movements strongly supported the cause of Palestine and the Palestinians under the leadership of the PLO. In short, the popular pan-Arabist sentiment had opened many regional doors for the Palestinians.

By the early 1980s, however, this pan-Arabist tide ebbed for a number of reasons, including repeated political and military defeats and the rise of individual state nationalism, as each local state consolidated its power and ideology and privileged its citizens over other Arabs. Worse yet for the Palestinians, the successive defeats of its guerrilla factions at the hands of both other Arabs and Israel, especially the forced exit of the PLO from Beirut in 1982, coupled with charges and practices of corruption and malfeasance by its political cadres, reduced the luster and élan of the Palestine cause and the credibility of its leadership. With the general and severe downturn in oil revenue in the second half of the 1980s, pan-Arab nationalist politics gave way to the more immediate, persistent bread-and-butter or social class issues and to the cultural threats from the West as perceived by activist Islamists. Thus the growth and influence of the Palestinian elite in the Arab world in general had peaked by the early to mid-1980s and then waned.

The economic downturn of the 1980s was a consequence of the coincidence of two factors: First, oil-exporting countries, as noted above, experienced a sharp drop in oil-based revenues; second, oil states began to employ their own newly trained citizens, who gradually replaced the Palestinians and other Arabs in governmental and public agencies. As private and public economic, financial, commercial, technical, and political advisers, consultants, and planners, Palestinians lost out not only to citizens of the oil states but also to competition from other Arabs and increasingly from individual entrepreneurs, firms, and agencies from other parts of the world (especially the United States). The 1980s thus witnessed not only the waning of Palestinian influence in the Arabian oil-exporting states but also the beginnings of a reverse Palestinian migration (back to Jordan, the West Bank and Gaza, and Lebanon) and dispersal (to western Europe and the Americas) from the oil economies of the Arabian Peninsula.

In the post–Gulf War period, as economic stagnation in the oil-exporting states and economic decline and structural crisis in the nonoil states of the region have became critical, socioeconomic issues dominated over political issues.[31] These issues and the commensurate ideological concerns over Western cultural penetration into the Arab Islamic region have been championed vigorously by a resurgent, vigorous, and militant movement, political Islam. And although more recently political Islam has come to advocate the Palestine cause more vocally, the ebb of secular pan-Arab nationalism also brought about the ebb of Palestinian political and economic influence in and commensurate support from the Arab world. The coup de grâce in the demise of official and informal Palestinian influence both in the oil-exporting Arabian Peninsula states and elsewhere took place in 1991 during the Gulf War. The position of PLO leader Yasser Arafat on the Gulf War had angered the oil monarchs, who stopped the previously generous aid to the organization and expelled and circumscribed many of the activists. Worse yet, around 350,000 Palestinians who had long been resident in the Gulf and the Arabian Peninsula were forced to flee or were expelled from Iraq, Kuwait, Saudi Arabia, and other Gulf countries during and after the 1991 Gulf War. Most expellees returned to Jordan, a few to the West Bank and the Gaza Strip, and some middle- and upper-middle-class families emigrated to the West.

Palestinians as Minorities
in Arab Host Countries

In nearly all the Arab host countries, as we noted earlier, Palestinians live in refugee camps or city districts and neighborhoods that are often overwhelmingly Palestinian. Successive waves of migration brought kin, clanspeople, and covillagers to the same locations. As a result, the social relations, employment opportunities, and political involvements of Palestinians in Arab host countries have been principally with other Palestinians.

Their relatively segregated existence enabled the exiled Palestinian communities to reproduce much of their prediaspora social and cultural traits: distinctive Arabic dialects, social customs, folklore, and, to a certain degree, dress. It also enabled them to memorialize their shared loss of country, property, and livelihood and reinforced their collective consciousness. Thus, despite the potential for assimilation and acculturation within the Arab economies (uneven though it has been from country to country), the Palestinians' experience of social segregation in and political repression by the Arab host states has strengthened their social and cultural identity as well as their solidarity and political consciousness. This circumstance is best expressed by a passage from Fawaz Turki's passionate and powerful book *The Disinherited: Journal of a Palestinian Exile:*

> If I was not a Palestinian when I left Haifa as a child, I am one now. Living in Beirut as a stateless person for most of my growing up years, many of them in a refugee camp, I did not feel I was living among my "Arab brothers." I did not feel I was an Arab, a Lebanese, or as some wretchedly pious writer claimed, a "southern Syrian." I was a Palestinian. And that meant I was an outsider, an alien, a refugee, a burden. To be that, for us, for my generation, meant to look inward, to draw closer, to be part of a minority that had its own way of doing and seeing and feeling and reacting.[32]

Exile, the traumatic experience of being expelled from one's homeland or of being born stateless, without rights, or with a stigmatized identity, is common to almost all Palestinians. For the majority, insecure, second-class status and repression by their fellow Arabs has reinforced their self-consciousness. Palestinian diaspora communities may thus be usefully conceptualized as minority groups in the Arab host countries.[33] Minorities are defined by the society of which they are a part. They are collectivities viewed and treated as different by the majority in that society and by its established institutions. The Palestinians are culturally, linguistically, religiously, and racially similar to the Arabs of the host countries. Yet they have been defined as different and treated accordingly because of their legal and political status: They have been circumscribed socially, economically, and politically. But the Palestinians also have viewed themselves as different; they have rejected *tawtin*—mass naturalization and settlement—and have sought freedom of economic and political action within their own (especially camp) communities.

A key factor in the lives of Palestinians in diaspora communities has been their uncertain legal status. Different states have granted them different rights. Although Jordan granted most Palestinians citizenship and the right to work within its new expanded borders after 1948, the other Palestinian diaspora communities had no legal identity and thus no psychological, social, economic, or political security. In Lebanon, for example, Palestinians were treated as foreigners in relation to the right-to-work laws and were subject to quotas in private companies and agencies; work in the public sector and enrollment in the state university were closed to them. In 1951 Lebanon's labor minister "attempted to illegalize all employment of Palestinians."[34] When the number of Palestinians was estimated at 225,000 in 1969, only 1 percent held official work permits.[35] Although labor shortages in Kuwait opened the job market for Palestinians, their schooling was separate from that of the native Kuwaitis.[36] In Syria, however, all institutions, including the governmental bureaucracies, the public sector, the universities, and the military, were open to Palestinians, who were allowed to fully participate in private and public life without full citizenship. However, their political and guerrilla organizations and their freedom of military action were tightly controlled.

In the Arabian Peninsula, all the oil-exporting states treated Palestinians as foreign guest workers, allowed to live there only if officially employed or married to a native. And although many were born there to Palestinian parents, they had no rights to citizenship, residence, or work upon achieving adulthood, as the parents had no rights to retirement in the country: After thirty to forty years of life and work in oil-exporting states, most Palestinians have been forced to leave to retire elsewhere. Like all foreigners, they have been legally prohibited from owning productive or profitable property, such as businesses, land, or factories, except as minority holders. They have also been prohibited from participating in political life, although through agreements with the PLO, they could participate in organized celebrations, fund-raising, and the like in support of the Palestinian political movement. Nowhere have the Palestinians been allowed to participate in the host country's public life except in Jordan, where this privilege has been limited and controlled.

Nonetheless, Palestinians were always a political presence or factor by virtue of their participation in and support from the pan-Arabist movements and ideology of the time. But the pan-Arab nationalist movements and ideologies were themselves perceived as threats to most established regimes. In short, nearly everywhere the Palestinians have lived in the diaspora, they have been viewed with suspicion and distrust and treated as less than full members of the societies—even where they have full citizen-ship, as in Jordan (and, for that matter, Israel)—by the authorities who have jurisdiction over them. Such exclusion and distrust have reinforced their unique identity, bonded them together, and politicized their existence. The dispossessed and stateless Palestinians have had powerful incentives to struggle for the restoration of their political right of self-determination and statehood; these incentives magnify the dilemma of their existence in exile.

Power Struggles and Violence: Palestinians Versus Arab Host States

Although official policy has varied in Arab host countries, common to all of them has been rhetorical support for the Palestinian cause and simultane-ous denial of freedom of action (especially political and military) to pursue that cause. The principal reason for this paradox is not only the oft-stated fear of military retaliation by Israel but also the perceived challenge to the established regime and elites. It is this contradiction that explains the expe-rience of violence in some of the diaspora communities.

Even before the rise of political Islam, typically pan-Arabist movements, or parties, Palestinians' political organizing to pursue the cause of national liberation not only challenged Israel but also threatened the host regimes where the Palestinians were a sizable minority, where they were economi-cally significant, and especially where they were organized and allied politi-cally with regime opposition. Thus the Palestinians in Arab host countries have always been problematic minorities insofar as, through domestic and regional pan-Arab nationalist allies, they have resisted subordination to and restriction by the host majorities. In two instances, Jordan and Lebanon, this friction led to armed conflict and civil war between the orga-nized and politicized Palestinian diaspora communities and the Arab host.

At different but extended times in Jordan, Lebanon, Kuwait, and else-where and in the West Bank and Gaza, where the Palestinians resisted Is-raeli occupation forces, violence has been an integral part of Palestinian life ever since the mandate period. The extent and persistence of violence in the lives of the Palestinians over at least the last half century has been as awe-some, shattering, and traumatic for the Palestinian people as it is incompre-hensible to others. The violence began with the uprooting and continues in daily violence and humiliation by the police, intelligence and security appa-ratuses, and military forces in the Arab host countries, in Israel proper, and in the occupied territories.

As will be clear in Chapter 7 on the occupation and the intifada, violence since Israel's occupation of the West Bank and the Gaza Strip has been extraordinarily intense, common, and extensive. Between December 1987 and 1993, over 1,283 Palestinians were killed in the West Bank and the Gaza Strip; an estimated 130,472 sustained injuries requiring hospitalization; 2,533 homes were demolished or sealed; 481 Palestinians were deported; and 22,088 have been administratively detained (never brought before a court of law), many of them beaten and tortured. Occupation authorities have confiscated 116,918 acres and uprooted 184,257 trees ("for security reasons"). One of the most egregious acts by Israel has been collective punishments of all sorts, especially the twenty-four-hour curfews. Such violence has not abated since the 1993 Oslo Accords, as is discussed in Chapter 8. Indeed, as is shown later, the most draconian curfews occurred after the accords were signed.

In the Arab host countries, violence against the Palestinians has peaked and ebbed continually. In Jordan it culminated during September 1970, labeled Black September by the Palestinians because of the high death toll they suffered, when King Hussein ordered his regular troops to launch an all-out assault on the refugee camps to suppress the guerrillas of the PRM in and around Amman.[37] Innocent thousands were killed as the Jordanian army, supported by heavy armor, reconquered and occupied the Palestinian camps that were in guerrilla hands.

In Lebanon the Palestinians sustained horrific assaults and casualties during Lebanon's civil war (1975–1982), the two Israeli invasions of Lebanon, the massacres in the Lebanese Sabra-Shatila and Tal al-Za'atar camps by right-wing Christian Maronite militias (the area around the Sabra-Shatila camp was under Israeli control), and several bloody and devastating sieges by Shi'a militias (with Syrian support) in 1985–1986 (after the exit of the PLO from Beirut). During the civil war, the Palestinians and their Lebanese allies also fought against the Syrian army (in 1975–1976), which intervened in Lebanon on the side of the rightist Lebanese militias.

From 1970 onward in Lebanon, the Palestinians and their Lebanese allies have also suffered constant and immensely costly attacks, bombings, shelling, incursions, and assassinations at the hands of Israel. This unrelenting and escalating Israeli warfare on the Palestinians and their Lebanese allies peaked in two major Israeli invasions (1978 and 1982) of the country, which caused tens of thousands of deaths, a much greater number of wounded, and tremendous physical and economic destruction. After the departure from Beirut of the PLO bureaucracy, regular Palestine Liberation Army (PLA) troops, and the factional guerrillas in 1982, the Palestinian population there succumbed to severe political repression and commensurate economic degradation imposed by the rightist Lebanese government. In the mid-1990s, the UNRWA reported that the condition of Palestinians in Lebanon was desperate.[38]

The large (400,000 strong) and long-standing (94 percent of the "returnees" in a sample survey had lived there more than fifteen years)[39] Palestinian community in Kuwait was suddenly attacked and most of it expelled in 1991 in the context of the invasion of Kuwait by Iraq. Collectively accused of collaborating with the Iraqi occupiers, the Palestinians were savaged by Kuwaiti vigilantes, militias, and the regular army upon its return to the country behind the allied forces of liberation. A large number of Palestinians were stripped of their private property and valuables; many were killed, maimed, or tortured; and most were expelled from Kuwait—a form of ethnic cleansing. The economic disaster that befell the Palestinian community of Kuwait is incalculable, not only because the Palestinians had thrived there (reportedly 30 percent of Kuwait's private business was Palestinian-owned or -controlled) but also because a large group of other Palestinians in both Jordan and the occupied territories depended on the financial remittances from that community (estimated during the peak oil-boom years at between $1.0 and $1.5 billion per year). The anti-Palestinian hysteria that has led to the collective accusations, punishments, and pogroms is only the current manifestation of phenomena that originated with the Zionists, especially during the 1947–1948 wars in Palestine. Attitudes and actions not unlike those typical of the Kuwaitis were evident in certain East Jordanians and right-wing Lebanese militias during the civil conflicts in these Arab host countries in the 1970s.

Finally, and perhaps most tragic, is the violence Palestinians have perpetrated against one another. Conflicts over strategy and policy have led to schisms, armed conflict, and assassinations within the ranks of the PRM and the PLO. Certain defectors, such as Abu Nidal and his group, became notorious terrorists who assassinated Palestinian diplomats because of their political views. The worst of all inter-Palestinian violence, however, was the small-scale Palestinian civil war in 1983 in and around the Nahr al-Bared refugee camp in north Lebanon. Anti-Arafat dissidents (with the aid of the Syrian army) and loyalists of the PLO chairman's faction shelled each other, in the process killing many of their own civilian people caught in the crossfire.

The 1991 expulsion or flight of Palestinians from Kuwait points to another feature of the precarious Palestinian existence since al-Nakbah: transience and impermanence. Transience and the associated social and psychological insecurity were noted above with respect to the 1967 refugees, many of whom were displaced for a second or third time in their lives. Not only were Palestinians forced across state borders, as from Palestine (1948, 1967), the occupied territories (1967–1993), Jordan (1970–1971), Lebanon (1975–present), and Kuwait (1990–1991), but they were also often forced to move inside a given country. In many instances in Lebanon (and also in Jordan as a consequence of the 1967 war and Black September, and in Syria as a result of the 1973 Arab-Israeli war), the displaced Palestinians, the *muhajjarin* of the civil war, have had to move several times within twenty years, as a result losing not only kinspeople and friends but also homes, possessions, and jobs. This militarily, politically, and economically forced transience has been the lot of a large number (and percentage) of the Palestinian population. Even the relatively secure and assimilated Palestinian middle class in Lebanon was forced (as was much of the Lebanese middle and upper classes) to emigrate (flee) from the country to Europe and North America during and after the Israeli invasion of 1982.

This uncertain and vulnerable existence, characterized by all-too-frequent dislocation, has long generated tremendous psychological anxiety and insecurity and constant angst among diaspora Palestinians. Stateless, without a legal identity or a passport with which to travel, and without a territorial homeland, one Palestinian worker, expelled from Kuwait and refused entry back into Lebanon, was forced to fly back and forth between the airports of the two countries nearly twelve times—he was labeled "the Flying Palestinian" by the journalists who covered his saga—before his case was finally resolved. In 1995, when the government of Libya expelled a large number of Palestinians, neither the Arab host countries from which these refugees had originally emigrated nor Israel, which continues to control the autonomous Palestinian areas (nominally under the Palestinian Authority, or PA, of Arafat), allowed them to reenter their territories. Thus they were stuck for weeks in legal and physical limbo in tents on the Libyan-Egyptian border and on ferryboats in the harbors of Cyprus before Syria accepted those on the ferryboats on humanitarian grounds and Libya consented to the return of others from the border. In early 1997 some still remained in the border area.

The Oslo and Cairo Accords between the PLO and Israel have allowed the return to the autonomous areas of the West Bank and the Gaza Strip of some Palestinians who had been deported from the occupied territories, and of others who were entering for the first time in their young lives, as members of the PLO/Palestinian Authority police force and bureaucratic personnel—the nucleus of the Palestinian Authority that took control of the

Israeli-evacuated areas. Although the Palestinian Authority is not a state and the right of return is still subject to Israeli approval, the direction of Palestinian dispersal has been reversed for the first time since 1948. It is a symbolic step that may give hope to the millions of dispossessed and dispersed Palestinians. However, whether this will be the beginning of a more extensive process of repatriation remains to be seen. For those who returned, a measure of psychological security may have been achieved, but statelessness and insecurity continue to be the lot of the millions still in exile and the hundreds of thousands in legal limbo.

To further comprehend their plight and psychological paradox, we must identify the impact on the individual Palestinian. Diaspora Palestinians since 1948 have had no state to provide them legitimacy or shield them effectively from harm or difficulty. Except for those in Jordan, they carry identity cards issued by host governments that identify them as refugees. Nevertheless, these identity cards or laissez-passer travel documents typically deny them legitimate legal standing or recognition. These Palestinians see it as intensely ironic that they who are without legal identity have to prove their "identity" at every turn. Stopped at borders and denied entry, reentry, or residence, they nonetheless try to make an acceptable, "official," stable, and secure place for themselves in an international order that gives them no legitimacy.

Two Cases: Palestinians in Jordan and Lebanon

A review of the communal political history of Palestinians in Jordan (briefly) and Lebanon (in greater detail) will better depict the lives, sentiments, aspirations, and political and military actions of Palestinians in the diaspora. The Palestinian communities in Jordan and Lebanon are appropriate examples because the former, always a large and important community, gave early support to the PRM/PLO, and the latter became the movement's anchor during its pivotal and influential years and its greatest political independence. (Although the Palestinian community in East Jordan is the largest diaspora community, it has not been as directly nor as intimately involved in the struggles of the PRM/PLO since the PLO and all its factions were expelled from Jordan in 1970 in a brutal civil war.)

Jordan. Shortly after the 1949 armistice agreement between Transjordan and Israel, King Abdullah annexed east-central Palestine and created the kingdom of Jordan. Jordan granted citizenship to all Palestinians under its jurisdiction, the only Arab country to do so. But only a fraction were politically enfranchised, as the right to vote was tied to landownership. Palestinians emerged as the numerical majority (roughly 60–70 percent of the population, including the West Bank before the 1967 war, and about 55 percent, without the West Bank after that) of the new country. When the PRM first surfaced in 1968, a power struggle quickly ensued between the Jordanian regime of King Hussein and the PRM guerrillas and the PLO anchored in the camps in and around Amman and in the Jordanian hills facing Israel. Spectacularly popular throughout the Arab world for resisting Israel after the devastating Arab defeat in six days in the June 1967 War, Hussein's regime could not at first move against the Palestinian guerrillas.

However, by 1970 the regime had succeeded in orchestrating an anti-guerrilla propaganda campaign and unleashed against the guerrillas a savage military attack in September (Black September), which drove them out of the camps and the city of Amman at a horrendous cost in lives of innocent camp civilians, estimated in the tens of thousands. In 1971 the mountain-based Palestinian guerrillas were driven out of the western hills of Jordan; they took refuge in southwestern Lebanon. After their departure, the Palestinian camps and other population concentrations in Jordan lived under a police state until the 1990s, when Jordan instituted some political liberalization and some democratic reforms.

Lebanon.   Palestinian communal history in Lebanon is divided into three broad eras: 1948–1969, including the rule of the Deuxième Bureau; 1969–1982, "the days of the revolution" (as a respondent in Sayigh's study termed them) and of civil war; and 1982 to the present, the era of camp sieges, political suppression, and economic degradation.[40] Although the liberal economic and political conditions in Lebanon allowed a small Palestinian middle class (professionals, small-business people, etc.) and bourgeoisie (wealthy entrepreneurs and investors) to flourish until the start of the civil war—many, especially Palestinian Christians, were encouraged by the Lebanese government to purchase Lebanese citizenship—the majority did not fare as well. And indeed, although these conditions also allowed the PLO to prosper, the camp-dwellers bore the brunt of civil conflict, Israeli attacks and invasions, and economic exploitation.

The Palestinian camps were controlled through the first decade after al-Nakbah by the Lebanese police and security agents, the cooperative remnants of the Arab Higher Committee of al-Hajj Amin al-Husseini, and the UNRWA. But the first modern civil war in Lebanon in 1958, a harbinger of the more savage and longer civil conflict of 1975–1982, introduced far more repressive and direct state control of the camps through the army's

Deuxième Bureau. The camp Palestinians were bullied and cowed by agents of the Deuxième Bureau; they were exploited economically and forced to pay bribes and other gratuities for any legal or informal business transactions.

The rule of the Deuxième Bureau ended in 1969, when the surging PRM, with the considerable support of the leftist, progressive, and pan-Arabist parties of Lebanon (a coalition that called itself the Lebanese National Movement, or LNM), gained control of the camps and the right to conduct guerrilla warfare against Israel from Lebanese territory. The power struggle and military confrontation between the PRM and the Lebanese army was resolved in favor of the PRM in an agreement—the Cairo agreement—arbitrated by the still-popular Egyptian president Gamal Abdul-Nasser.

This agreement and the rising strength of the PRM ushered in the second era for the Palestinians in Lebanon. From 1969 until the exit of the PLO and its forces in 1982, the camps were under Palestinian jurisdiction as quasi-liberated zones of the new "Palestinian revolution." During this period, the PRM, formally in control of the PLO, developed its civil, economic, political, administrative, and military institutions. A veritable Palestinian economy evolved with the PLO not only because of expanding employment in its variegated bureaucracies but also because of its development of factories (producing clothing, furniture, leather goods, ironwork, some arms, and handicrafts), printing and publishing, filmmaking, and other industries. This development triggered the rapid expansion not only of the PLO's productive enterprises but also social service and social welfare institutions, all in an effort to provide jobs for unemployed *muhajjarin* and camp residents. One important consequence of this effort "was that, instead of emigrating to oil-producing countries, more highly educated Palestinian workers now stayed in Lebanon to work with the 'Revolution' in sha'abi (popular, low-income) areas."[41]

The PLO consolidated and strengthened its governing structures—a cabinet (the Executive Committee), a parliament in exile (the Palestine National Council, or PNC), and an army (the Palestine Liberation Army, or PLA)—all the outwardly formal institutions of a government-in-exile. And with the disintegration of the Lebanese government between 1975 and 1982, the PLO, with its LNM allies, exercised de facto sovereignty over large segments of Lebanese territory and emerged as a state-within-a-state until it was driven out by Israel.

Israel's invasion of Lebanon in June 1982, the three-month siege of Beirut, the massacre of hundreds of Palestinians in Shatila camp, and the United States–brokered exit of the PLO from the city signaled the end of the "days of the revolution" in Lebanon and the start of the current phase. Both the US and Lebanese governments promised to guarantee the safety of Palestinians left behind in the country. Neither government honored its commitment, nor could the powerless and distant (in Tunis) PLO provide much protection to the largely disarmed Palestinian community in Lebanon. Palestinians in and outside the camps came under intense political, military, and economic pressure.

Israel's invasion had devastated the already limping Lebanese economy, spurring emigration of both the Palestinian and Lebanese middle classes. Without resources and legitimate travel documents, camp-dwellers were trapped and bore the brunt again of hostile and alienated Lebanese. The civil war in Lebanon took its toll on the PRM/PLO–LNM alliance as well. The LNM lost its own solidarity and coherence, and some factions became alienated from the Palestinians. Worst of all, large segments of the previously supportive Lebanese Shi'a community, long outside the formal LNM alliance, was becoming increasingly anti-Palestinian by the time of the Shi'ite Iranian revolution of 1979. Facing the enmity of Israel, the newly installed rightist Lebanese government, the right-wing Christian coalition, and the rapidly politicizing and mobilizing Shi'a community, the Palestinians in Lebanon completely lost their long-established popular Lebanese base of support. Once party to the de facto sovereign PLO power over large sections of Lebanon during the civil war, the remaining Palestinians were reduced to a dazed, defeated, and unprotected minority in besieged camps.

Finally, as Sayigh wrote, the Palestinians in Lebanon after 1982 had become an "endangered species."[42] In the wake of the Oslo Accords, Lebanese politicians and government officials spoke out in strong terms against the *tawtin* (naturalization and settlement) of Palestinians in Lebanon. The destiny of the Palestinian community in that country now depends to a large extent on the agreements that will issue from the "final status" negotiations between Israel and the Palestinian Authority/PLO on the occupied territories, borders, settlements, Jerusalem, and the Palestinian refugees.

Conclusion

Beginning in 1948 the Palestinians lost their homeland and became dispossessed, dispersed, and destitute. The majority were herded into refugee camps, becoming dependent on the UNRWA dole, or into urban neighborhoods of the major cities in the Arab host countries. There they were suppressed politically and exploited economically. Within only ten years after al-Nakbah, they began a long struggle for economic well-being, social and psychological security, affirmation of identity, and restoration of political rights of self-determination and independent statehood. The Palestinian refugees have risen phoenixlike from the ashes of the destruction of their society to preserve their identity, flourish economically and socially, and build a political movement of national liberation. The year 1993 was a turning point in their history because their political representative, the PLO under Arafat, signed with Israel, the state that had dispossessed and dispersed them, the Oslo Accords, probably the key political event for the Palestinians since 1948. Stunning and significant as that event is in Palestinian political and social history, the signatories to that accord agreed to postpone consideration of the status of the refugees for three years. The structural dilemmas of the Palestinian diaspora communities is thus unchanged, as the Oslo Accords are now effectively defunct, and the Palestinians are perhaps far more vulnerable and anxiety-ridden. Arab host states (especially Lebanon) and Israel have expressed opposition to any *tawtin*, repatriation, or compensation. The destiny of a large segment of the nearly five million diaspora Palestinians, then, remains uncertain, insecure, and in legal limbo.

Notes

1. J. L. Abu-Lughod, "The Demographic Transformation of Palestine: Relevance for Planning Palestine Open University," in *Palestine Open University Feasibility Study*, part 2 (Paris: UNESCO, 1980), 160–161.

2. Ibid., 6.

3. Ibid., 16–46.

4. W. Khalidi, ed., *All That Remains: The Palestinian Villages Occupied and Depopulated by Israel in 1948* (Washington, DC: Institute for Palestine Studies, 1992); see also W. Khalidi, *Before Their Diaspora: A Photographic History of the Palestinians, 1876–1948* (Washington, DC: Institute for Palestine Studies, 1984).

5. G. Kossaifi, "Demographic Characteristics of the Arab Palestinian People," in G. Nakhleh and E. Zureik, eds., *The Sociology of the Palestinians* (London: Croom Helm, 1980): 21.

6. B. Morris, *1948 and After* (New York: Oxford University Press, 1990): 69–88. See also M. Palumbo, *The Palestinian Catastrophe: The 1948 Expulsion of a People from Their Homeland* (London: Quartet Books, 1987), and N. Nazzal, *The Palestinian Exodus from Galilee* (Beirut: Institute for Palestine Studies, 1978).

7. Ibid., 74.

8. J. B. Glubb, *A Soldier with the Arabs* (London: Hodder and Stoughton, 1957): 81. See also the report of A. Yitzhaqi in *Yediot Aharonot*, April 14, 1972. Reproduced in *Journal of Palestine Studies* 1 (Summer 1972): 142–146.

9. R. Sayigh, *Palestinians: From Peasants to Revolutionaries* (London: Zed Press, 1979): 64.

10. Ibid., 92.

11. Quotation cited by M. Palumbo, *Palestinian Catastrophe,* 133.

12. R. Sayigh, *Too Many Enemies: The Palestinian Experience in Lebanon* (London: Zed Press, 1994): 36.

13. S. M. Ayyoub, *The Class Structure of Palestinians in Lebanon* (in Arabic) (Beirut: Beirut Arab University, 1978): 173–174.

14. J. Abu-Lughod, "Demographic Characteristics," Part 2, Table 5, 23.

15. Ibid.

16. Ibid., Table 8, 39.

17. Ibid., 6.

18. A. L. Adlakha, K. G. Kinsella, and Marwan Khawaja estimated that Gaza's natural growth rate in 1995 was 4.6 percent, in "Demography of the Palestinian Population with Special Emphasis on the Occupied Territories," *Population Bulletin of ESCWA* 43 (1995): 11, Table 3.

19. The estimates in Abu-Lughod's "Demographic Characteristics" are carefully argued and internally consistent and differ substantially from those of the US government and the UNRWA cited in D. Peretz, *Palestinians, Refugees and the Middle East Peace Process* (Washington, DC: United States Institute of Peace Press, 1993). We believe Abu-Lughod's estimates are more correct.

20. Ayyoub, *Class Structure,* 240.

21. Ibid., Table 2, 15. See also Adlakha et al., "Demography of the Palestinian Population," 5–27. This study by the International Division of the US Census Bureau estimates total Palestinian population in Middle Eastern countries in 1995 at only 6.45 million. However, it excludes Palestinians outside the Middle East, a number that would easily bring the total number to 6.8 million. See also G. F. Kossaifi, *The Palestinian Refugees and the Right of Return* (Washington, DC: Center for Policy Analysis on Palestine, 1996). The total of 7.6 million in Table 4.3 does not include unregistered refugees, hence the 10.1 million.

22. Abu-Lughod, "Demographic Characteristics," 58.

23. Sayigh, *Too Many Enemies,* 42.

24. Ibid., 59–64.

25. Ibid.

26. See Z. Abu-Amr, *Islamic Fundamentalism in the West Bank and Gaza* (Bloomington: Indiana University Press, 1994).

27. Ayyoub, *Class Structure,* 231.

28. Transjordan was renamed the kingdom of Jordan in 1950, when it annexed east-central Palestine and labeled it the West Bank, in contrast to Transjordan proper, which was then called the East Bank.

29. Cited in Peretz, *Palestinians, Refugees,* 22.

30. The biggest shareholder and owner of the largest private Arab bank (also one of the larger banks in the world) is a Palestinian, as are the shareholders and managers of the largest and most successful Arab (now international) construction companies.

31. S. K. Farsoun, "Oil, State and Social Structure in the Middle East," *Arab Studies Quarterly* 10 (Spring 1988): 156–175.

32. F. Turki, *The Disinherited: Journal of a Palestinian Exile* (New York: Monthly Review Press, 1972): 8.

33. This part is taken largely from N. H. Aruri and S. Farsoun, "Palestinian Communities and Arab Host Countries," in Nakhleh and Zureik, *Sociology of the Palestinians,* 112–146. See also L. A. Brand, "Palestinians in Syria: The Politics of Integration," *Middle East Journal* 42 (Autumn 1988): 621–637.

34. Sayigh, *Too Many Enemies,* 23.

35. S. Hijjawi, "The Palestinians in Lebanon" (in Arabic), *Journal of the Center for Palestinian Studies* (Baghdad) 22 (May-June 1977): 44.

36. See S. Ghabra, *The Palestinians in Kuwait: The Family and Politics of Survival* (Boulder, CO: Westview Press, 1987).

37. Black September later became the name of a secret Palestinian organization that attacked the Israeli athletes at the Olympic Games in Munich in 1972.

38. *Report of the Commissioner-General of the UNRWA in the Near East, 1 July 1992–30 June 1993* (New York: United Nations, 1994).

39. Y. J. El-Uteibi and M. Amous, "Jordanian Returnees Profile" (Photocopy, Returnees Compensation Center, the Hashemite Charity Organization, Geneva, 1993), 20.

40. See Sayigh, *Too Many Enemies;* see also R. Brynen, *Sanctuary and Survival: The PLO in Lebanon* (Boulder, CO: Westview Press, 1990), and H. Cobban, *The Palestinian Liberation Organization: People, Power and Politics* (Cambridge: Cambridge University Press, 1984).

41. Ibid.

42. Sayigh, *Palestinians.*

5

After al-Nakbah

The Palestinians in Israel, 1948–2000

The last chapter discussed the Jewish Zionist warfare in 1948 that led to the conquest of two-thirds of Palestine and the expulsion (and flight) of the great majority of its people from their homeland. Israel nearly succeeded in creating what the Zionists had long claimed in their ideological mantra: Palestine as a land without people (the Palestinian Arabs) for a people (European Jews) without a land. Nonetheless, despite all their plans and efforts to empty the Palestinians from Palestine, an estimated 150,000 to 180,000 Palestinians, comprising approximately 18 percent of the population of the newly declared state of Israel, remained on their land after the cease-fire agreements between the Arab states and Israel were signed. Israel thus gained control of the majority of Palestinian land but also found itself in control of a Palestinian population, now a minority among a majority of Jews, principally concentrated in the Galilean hills, especially the central and western parts, with another segment, principally bedouins, in the south. This chapter analyzes the structure, transformation, and dynamics of the Palestinian minority in Israel from 1948 to the present.

The Palestinians Who Became a Minority in Israel

The vast majority of the approximately 850,000 Palestinian population in 1948 that had lived in the 78 percent of Palestine that became the state of Israel became refugees in east-central Palestine, behind the Jordanian military lines; in the Gaza Strip, behind Egyptian military lines; in the neighboring Arab countries of Transjordan, Lebanon, and Syria; and to a much smaller extent in other Arab countries. Although the Palestinian exodus from the Galilee, and from the city of Haifa and its coastal areas, was extensive, the majority of the Palestinians who remained in what became Israel was and continues to be in the Galilee. However, the Palestinians that remained in Israel were not sociologically representative of the Palestinian people as a whole.[1] They were principally rural farmers and peasants, subsisting on agriculture that was traditional in methods, products, consumption, and marketing. They lived mostly in villages and very small towns, the more remote of which were often unconnected to the larger towns by paved roadways.

The massive Palestinian exodus included extensively the urban middle class that had comprised the leadership of the Palestinian people during the mandate period and the struggle for independence. Thus the Palestinian minority in Israel was left largely without a national social, economic, or political leadership. This political collapse was disastrous as organized political parties (except for the Palestine Communist Party, or PCP), unions, syndicates, associations, and social and cultural organizations disappeared practically overnight.[2]

Internal Refugees

The Palestinian community that remained was further disoriented and demoralized because one-fifth to one-fourth of its members were "internal refugees"[3] because their own villages and towns had been destroyed by the Zionist forces and they had been moved by force to other villages and towns in the country. Perhaps more significant, these internal refugees lost their lands and their property and were classified by the Israeli government as "absentees." In addition, many of the villages and small localities in which Palestinians lived were not recognized by the state of Israel as legal entities entitled to municipal rights. In short, the Palestinians who remained in Israel were themselves dispossessed and leaderless, with hardly any functioning institutions or organizations and with undeveloped infrastructure, intimidated by Israeli military power and collectively traumatized no less than their compatriot refugees who had been dispersed, dispossessed, traumatized, and made destitute.

The "unrecognized villages" cannot be found on any official map. They receive no municipal services, even though their inhabitants are Israeli citizens who pay the same taxes as all other Israelis. They are not entitled to water, electricity, schools, health facilities, or paved roads. Palestinian citizens of Israel who are internally displaced from their homes and villages—politically recognized, but legally denied their rights—number between 150,000 and 200,000. For example, the residents and home owners of two border villages, Iqrit and Kufr bar'am, are not allowed to return to their homes or work their agricultural lands and have been forced to live elsewhere in Israel since 1948. The villagers and their descendants have attempted to pressure the Israeli government to permit their return, but to no avail.

The internal refugees constitute a significant sector of the Palestinian community who carry Israeli citizenship in the Galilee, in Negev, and in what are known as the "mixed" cities (i.e., cities where there is no Jewish hegemony, such as the Haifa and Lydda areas). About half of Nazareth's Arab residents are internal refugees and their descendants; more than half of Umm al Fahem's residents belong to this group.

The dilemma for the internal refugees is which is worse: incorporating their legal, public, and political struggle for basic rights within the diplomatic negotiations of the PA, which may make further concessions that would not ensure their basic rights, *or* to wage their own struggle within the framework of the state of Israel?

It must also be kept in mind that new refugees continue to be created by Israel's campaign of territorial domination in and around Jerusalem, under way since 1967, which continues to escalate. Residency cards are confiscated at will, and building permits are all but denied to Palestinians in all parts of the West Bank. This territory includes "greater Jerusalem," a concept that has no juridical meaning and would appear to be a euphemism for Jewish land expansion and ownership via expropriation, eminent domain policies, and other methods of land domination. Palestinian homes are being demolished wholesale. The bulldozer is the most lethal instrument of war against the Palestinian people (as it was in 1948).

Mechanisms of Erecting an Internal Colonial Regime

This section analyzes the mechanics of Jewish state intrusion into the Palestinian Arab community and the structure of its suppression, exploitation, and control of and discrimination against that minority, which it created. As Israel was intent on building a Jewish state comprising Jews (only), its first task after consolidating control of the conquered part of Palestine was to block the return of the Palestinian refugees and to populate this new country with immigrant Jews. The events associated with the forceful establishment of Israel allowed the attainment of that goal. First, Israel refused to repatriate the 1948 Palestinian refugees, allowing in only a token few under a UN program of family reunification. On the other hand, it opened the new country's gates to immigrant Jews.

Between May 15, 1948 (when Israel was declared a state), and December 1950, 511,960 new Jewish immigrants settled in the country. By 1950, the Jewish population in Israel numbered 1,203,000, and the Palestinian Arabs, who had represented approximately 92 percent of the Palestinian population at the turn of the twentieth century, became 12 percent of the population of Israel in 1950. The Jewish population in Israel increased largely through immigration after May 1948. Between 1951 and 1980 the increase in the Jewish population due to immigration declined as the Israeli population became denser. The decline in the 1980s was sharp and was compounded by a process of Jewish migration *out* of Israel, principally to Europe, the Americas, and South Africa. This declining rate of immigration was dramatically reversed in the 1990s as the Soviet Union collapsed and about one million Russian immigrants entered Israel.

The Emergence of the Palestinian Minority

The Palestinian Arab minority that remained in Israel not only did not decline in number but actually increased dramatically in both absolute numbers and percentages after 1948, from 12.2 percent of the total population of Israel in 1950 to 18.6 percent in 1998 to nearly 20 percent now. Palestinian Arab population growth was entirely due to a high natural increase, contrasted with the Jewish rate of increase, which, as noted above, was largely due to immigration. Nevertheless, the Jewish rate of population growth has been declining since the 1980s, even including immigrants (except in the 1990s because of the massive Russian influx).

The Palestinian rate of population growth, on the other hand, has remained high. As a result, the Palestinian Arab population in Israel increased from roughly 175,000 in 1950 to about 1,105,400 in 1998 to nearly 20 percent. The prospects for a continuing increase in the size (and proportion) of this population are clearly indicated by a comparison of the age distribution between Arab Palestinians and Jews. Whereas the average age of Israeli Jews increased from 27.6 to 30.6 years between 1955 and 1980, that of the Palestinians decreased from 23.0 to 20.9. In 1998 the median age of Jews was 29.6; among the Palestinians it was 19.5. The demographic consequences of this difference in age distribution are accentuated by the greater fertility of Palestinians over Jews in Israel. According to the

2000 Statistical Abstract of Israel, total fertility (the average number of children a woman bears during her lifetime) of Jews was 2.67, compared to 4.76 for Arab Muslims. Thus, although the difference in fertility between Jews and Arab Palestinians has been falling over the years, the continuing large difference and the relative youth of the Palestinian Arab population is likely to produce a major increase in the absolute number and proportion of Palestinian Arabs in Israel.

Early in the life of the state of Israel, to encourage immigration and larger Jewish families, the Zionist authorities enacted laws such as the Law of Return, enacted in 1950, and the Israeli Nationality Act, enacted in 1952. Together these laws effectively meant that any Jew from any country in the world was entitled to Israeli citizenship practically upon arrival. Of course, these laws defined citizenship in religious terms and thus denied any others, especially the Palestinian refugees, of that right. In short, the Jewish colonial settlers had an automatic right that is denied to the indigenous Arab people.

Geographic Concentration of the Palestinian Population

Compounding the total population question in the eyes of the Israeli state is the concentration of the Palestinian Arab population in northern Israel. In 1998 the Northern District, which includes western Galilee, had 46.8 percent of the Palestinian Arab population, and Haifa, farther to the west, had an additional 14.9 percent. No region or district in Israel had an Arab majority until 1998, when the Arab population in the Northern District increased to a slight majority. Arabs do predominate in certain subdistricts: Eastern Lower Galilee, the Nazareth area, Shefa 'Amr, the Karmel region, the Yehi'am region, and the Alexander Mountain region. Although the concentration of the Palestinian population in Israel is part of an effective Israeli system of social-residential segregation, it has also given the Palestinian minority a critical population mass in one area, the Galilee and much of the rest of the northern region. Such a concentrated population mass has had the unintended consequence of facilitating social, cultural, and political mobilization.

However, much more striking than the regional population shifts is the significant change in the distribution of the Palestinian Arabs between rural and urban areas. The Palestinian population that remained in Israel was overwhelmingly rural, as is clear in Table 5.1. However, the urbanization of Palestinian Arabs has been very dramatic since 1948. Since the mid-1970s,

TABLE 5.1 Rural/Urban Population by Population Group (in thousands)

	Palestinian Arab				Jews & Others			
	Urban	%	Rural	%	Urban	%	Rural	%
1998	1,028.0	93.0	77.8	7.0	4,491.2	91.0	444.8	9.0
1980	419.2	67.9	198.6	32.1	2,967.9	90.4	314.8	9.6
1970	188.4	42.8	251.6	57.8	2,288.6	89.3	271.9	10.7
1961	63.4	26.0	183.7	74.0	1,634.5	84.6	297.9	15.4
1955	52.1	26.0	146.5	74.0	1,215.6	76.7	371.2	23.3

SOURCES: Statistical Abstract (SA), 1955–1956, Table 6; SA, 1973, Table 11.9; SA, 1981, Table 11.9; SA, 1999, Table 2.12. Urban is defined as a population center of 2,000 or more.

the proportion of the Palestinians residing in rural areas declined sharply, and those in urban areas jumped from 42.8 percent to 93 percent, superseding even the Jewish population ratio. This spectacular process of urbanization of the Palestinian Arab population in Israel reflects the proletarianization of the Palestinian peasantry.

However, the villages and small towns that grew into Arab "cities" were cities in name only. Arab cities in Israel lack a cultural base, having no university, public library, publishing house, theater or musical or other auditorium, nor even a genuine middle class that infuses them with a dynamic social, cultural, and political life. Perhaps most important, Palestinian Arab "cities" have not been and still are not centers of economic production but are largely of commerce. They are principally "bedroom cities" for the commuting proletariat that works in the Jewish sector. The three processes of economic peripheralization, proletarianization, and urbanization of the Palestinian community in Israel since the mid-1950s are directly related to the question of Arab Palestinian land and agriculture.

Palestinian Land and Its Expropriation

Creating a Jewish state in Palestine, like creating any settler colonial project, necessitated first and foremost the acquisition of land from the indigenous Palestinians. Israel's expropriation and confiscation of Palestinian land and properties in the 1948 war did not end with the conclusion of that war. One of the most important laws enacted by the Israeli state to expropriate Palestinian property of both refugees and the Palestinian minority in Israel was the Absentee Property Law of 1950. According to this law, the properties of the refugees were transferred to a so-called Custodian of Absentee Property, who would manage and negotiate with the government the disposition of these properties.

Israeli authorities called state land and the private land and properties left behind by the Palestinian refugees "abandoned properties" and (as Palestinian refugees were denied repatriation, so their properties were indeed "abandoned") expropriated these properties without paying any compensation for them. This is an issue that is still pending in the political resolution of the Palestine question.

In 1953, the absentee properties were turned over to a Development Authority, which in turn sold them to the state for absorption of and use by new Jewish immigrants.

The primary resource of the Palestinian farmers and peasants has always been land. Israel expropriated their land, thus denying them any economic independence and forcing them to "hew the wood and carry the water" for the Israeli economy, as had been urged by the early Zionist theoreticians. Using the Absentee Property Law, the Israeli authorities seized an estimated 40 percent of the land owned by Arab residents of Israel by classifying legal Palestinian residents of Israel as "present absentees," a bizarre oxymoronic legal category that allowed the Jewish state to dispossess its own putative citizens of their property. "Present absentees" were principally Arab Palestinians, especially in the Galilee and in mixed Jewish-Arab cities elsewhere, who for whatever reason (for example, because they were traveling abroad) were absent from "their usual place of residence," according to the law, when Jewish forces gained control of these areas. According to Lustick, 81,000 out of the estimated 160,000 Palestinians who remained in Israel were classified as "present absentees": In other words, half of the Arab inhabitants of Israel could, at the discretion of the custodian, be declared absentees and their property thereby made subject to confiscation.

The Land Acquisition Law, enacted in 1953, legalized seizure of Palestinian land by the state and legitimized its redistribution to Jews and Jewish organizations. Through this law and the use of certain provisions of the Defense (Emergency) Regulations, the Israeli government expropriated a large amount of the land of the Palestinians. Typically, the process worked as follows:

An area encompassing Arab-owned agricultural lands is declared a "closed area." The owners of the lands are then denied permission by the security authorities to enter the area for any purpose whatsoever, including cultivation. After three years pass, the Ministry of Agriculture issues certificates, which classify the lands as uncultivated. The owners are notified that unless cultivation is renewed immediately, the lands will be subject to expropriation. The owners, still barred by the security authorities from entering the "closed area" within which their lands are located, cannot resume cultivation. The lands are then expropriated. Eventually permission to enter the "closed area" is granted to Jewish farmers.

When expropriating Palestinian land that had clear private title, Israel made the gesture of compensating the owners. However, as all analysts of that process indicate, the amount offered or paid was grossly below market value, and/or the offered alternative, less desirable land, forced many Palestinian citizens of Israel to refuse the payment even though they lost the property. For only one-quarter of the expropriated land did the owners receive even so much as the unfair compensation. As important, the Palestinians could not buy alternative agricultural land from Jewish-owned tracts, as Jewish land is legally inalienable. Thus, in most instances, former farmers and peasants became exploitable wage laborers in Jewish enterprises or economic projects.

Palestinian Agriculture, the Peasantry, and Proletarianization

The history and fate of Palestinian agriculture and the livelihood it provided Palestinian Arabs in Israel cannot be understood on its own terms. It can be comprehended only in terms of the Israeli government policy of subjecting Arab-owned land to Jewish agricultural interests. In other words, the domination of one system (the Palestinian) by the other (Jewish) in the competition for the agricultural resources of land, water, and government subsidy and in marketing was a direct result of the systematic policies of the Israeli state.

To begin with, the possibility of regaining lost lands or of expanding Palestinian Arab ownership was practically nonexistent in Israel. The only possibilities lay in cultivating some marginal lands that continued to be in Arab hands. Thus the land area under cultivation by Palestinian Arabs rose from 690,000 *dunum*s in 1949–1950 to only 855,000 *dunum*s in 1975–1976, whereas in the Jewish sector it rose from 1,790,000 *dunum*s to 3,445,000 *dunum*s in the same period. Ninety percent of the increase in land cultivation, then, occurred in the Jewish sector.

The lack of development of Arab agriculture in the first three decades after 1948 is bleaker if we factor in irrigation. By 1976 nearly 52 percent of all Jewish cultivated land was under irrigation, compared to only 8 percent of Palestinian cultivated land. As of 1999, Palestinians cultivated about 15 percent of the land but continued to receive less than 3 percent of the water allocated for agriculture.

Just as discriminatory were the marketing arrangements. Marketing of Palestinian Arab agricultural products was monopolized by Jewish firms. In the early 1970s, Palestinian Arab farmers contributed the overwhelming majority or Israel's olive and tobacco production but were disadvantaged by the monopoly that Jewish marketing concerns had over the selling of these products and by the grants (by the Jewish Agency) of subsidies to Jewish tobacco farmers. The products produced by Palestinian farmers were not protected against the price of imported goods, as were the products of Jewish farmers under the same law.

Palestinian agricultural production remained largely based on family farms and was probably largely uncapitalized and unmechanized. Excess farm or rural population could not find employment in agriculture but sought employment in the nonagricultural sectors that are principally owned by Israeli Jews. Although the Palestinian population has grown enormously since 1948, the agricultural base it depends on has not; indeed, it has shrunk as a result of expropriation. Thus, not only has Palestinian agriculture failed to provide a relatively independent (from the Jewish sectors) base of productive economic activity, but it has also been unable to absorb the progeny of the farmers and villagers living in the rural areas. Instead, the Arab rural areas have emerged in the Israeli economic system as the producers of cheap labor for the Jewish economy.

Palestinians in Israel's Economic System

In 1955, 50.5 percent of economically active Palestinians were employed in the agricultural sector. By 1990, this proportion had fallen to 6.3 percent. For over two generations the Palestinian community in Israel experienced a fundamental economic transformation, from a society based on independent agricultural production to one providing labor for an economic system owned and controlled by the Jews who had usurped the Arab society. Beginning in 1948 as agricultural workers producing on their own lands, by 1980, and even more by 1990, Palestinians had been transformed into nonagricultural wage laborers, from a majority of self-employed workers into a mass of employees.

Although Jews also shifted out of agriculture over the same period (from 15.3 percent in 1955–1956 to 3.9 percent in 1990), they moved into different economic branches and superior occupations in a system that advantages them and discriminates against the Palestinians. The Israeli economy itself shifted from an agricultural focus to an industrial-service economy. Historical trends indicate that while Palestinians have moved from the agricultural to the nonagricultural productive sectors of the Israeli economy (and the white-collar public sector in their own economy), Jews have moved out of the same branches into the white-collar service sectors that dominate and control Israel's economy, and also into the high-tech sectors that are connected to the global economy. This shift is a clear indication of an ethnic-based system of occupational stratification. The economic role of Palestinian labor is at the bottom (typically low-skilled) of the Israeli system of production. It is mostly employed by Jewish capital. Most Arab "employers" are owners of family farms or are small contractors in construction and industry.

In two generations the great majority of Palestinian labor has been proletarianized. Indeed, it is a commuting working class, not a suburbanite commuting white-collar class, of rural residents forced by the lack of development of the Arab economy in Israel to seek employment in Jewish-owned enterprises in the larger cities. In 1980 nearly half of Palestinian workers worked outside their residential locality. Beginning shortly after the June war of 1967, Palestinian workers also commuted from the West Bank and the Gaza Strip to jobs in Israel. The Israeli occupation also opened for Arab Palestinians new economic opportunities as middlemen (they speak Hebrew and know the Israeli system better) between Israeli entrepreneurs and the state, on the one hand, and the Palestinians in the occupied territories, on the other. This middleman activity has become especially pronounced in agriculture and construction. In addition, these middlemen do labor contracting for Palestinians from the occupied territories and contracting for capital investment by Israeli Jewish entrepreneurs in those territories. The number and percentage of Palestinian citizens of Israel in the lowest occupational categories would have been even larger had Palestinians from the occupied territories (and other imported immigrant labor) not been allowed to work in Israel as even cheaper labor.

The manner of integration of Palestinian labor into the Israeli economic system—as exploited and disadvantaged workers at the bottom of the Israeli occupational structure—is further evidenced in data on white-collar occupations. In 1999 only 9.9 percent of Palestinian Arabs were in clerical and managerial occupations, compared to 27.4 percent of Jews. The figures for clerical and managerial positions for Palestinians actually increased over the years, from 1.4 percent in 1960–1961 to the 9.9 percent of 1999. But even though the increase in the number of Palestinian white-collar workers is noteworthy, these workers are not integrated into the Jewish economic system. They serve largely their own separate communities. Nevertheless, their increase and development are important because from these white-collar middle-class strata emerged the intellectual leaders who challenged the traditional kin-based (*hamula*-based) and sectarian-based leadership and contributed significantly, as will be seen, to the development of new political discourses and to the evolution of several pivotal political trends, movements, and parties.

Palestinian Women Workers

The overall pattern of discrimination and exploitation of the Palestinian minority in Israel includes the Palestinian women in the labor force. In 1999 about 17.2 percent of the Palestinian labor force in Israel was women. This proportion had been increasing over the years, and in 1999 it corresponded to the enormous social transformation, especially in education, that the Arab minority had experienced in the decades since the establishment of the state of Israel. By contrast, in 1999 the ratio of employment of Jewish women was triple that of Palestinian women. Although Palestinian women workers in Israel "suffer from two fold exploitation and discrimination"[4] because they reside in rural communities that restrict their movement and because they are part of a national minority itself suffering discrimination, they nevertheless are somewhat protected from Jewish competition in opportunities in their own Palestinian Arab employment market.

The Palestinian women working in Israel fall into two groups: They work primarily in professional, semiprofessional, and clerical positions and in unskilled manual jobs. They have almost no managerial positions, and there are very few in skilled manual occupations. They are even less integrated into the Jewish sectors than the men are, the majority of them working within the Palestinian Arab market and constituting a very small portion of the Jewish labor market. Although initially Palestinian women replaced the men in agricultural work, by 1983 those between the ages of twenty-five and sixty-five were concentrated in professional and semiprofessional occupations (as teachers, nurses, social workers, and so on). Indeed, Palestinian women suffer less discrimination in pay rates in the Palestinian labor market than in the Jewish labor market.

However, in the mid-1980s new developments began to change significantly the patterns of labor participation of Palestinian women in Israel. Increasing numbers of Palestinian women have been entering unskilled jobs, especially in the textile and clothing workshops and factories that have been located by Israelis in Palestinian areas, an internal colonial development not unlike the emergence of American maquiladoras across the border in Mexico. These factories require Palestinian women to take part in "organized commuting": All women from one population center are transported together to and from work, and most of the women work in "women only" factories. As these maquiladoras increase the number of Palestinian women in the labor force, they also, as is usual in third-world countries, increase the rate of exploitation of Palestinian women, as they are paid less in the Jewish economy than in the Palestinian economy.

Income Discrimination Against Palestinians

The skewed occupational distribution of Palestinian labor in Israel involves not only a concentration in manual labor and a relative absence from managerial and supervisory roles but also low income. To begin with, the income of workers in certain branches of production (especially agriculture, construction, and industry) in Israel tends to be lower than the income of workers in public service, finance, and even transport. Of course Palestinian labor, as was seen above, is concentrated in the low-paying branches. A 1998 survey of monthly income and expenditure by the Central Bureau of Statistics of Israel indicates that 85 percent of the Palestinians were in the bottom five deciles of the income distribution while half of Jews were in the upper five deciles, at the better end of the income distribution. A Palestinian family earns, on the average, less than 65 percent of the average income of a Jewish family. Furthermore, the income levels of Palestinian families did not improve over the last three decades of the twentieth century relative to the income level of Jewish families. Indeed, according to the December 2000 National Insurance Report, 50 percent of the Palestinian Arab children in Israel live in poverty.

Finally, it should be pointed out that the structure of exploitation and discrimination against the Palestinian labor force in Israel is not even. The Palestinian labor force in Israel can be divided into three groupings: those who commute to work in Jewish sectors outside their communities (the commuters), those who live and work in mixed Jewish and Arab towns and cities (the residents), and those who live and work in the Palestinian enclave (the segregated). Lewin-Epstein and Semyonov found that the Palestinian residents in mixed communities who work in what these authors call a binational labor market suffer the most discrimination, including in income levels. The Palestinians who live and work in what the authors describe as the mononational labor market (the Palestinian enclave that is protected from Jewish competition) suffer the least discrimination; the commuters tend to fall in the middle. Of course, the status of the migrant Palestinian labor force from the occupied territories is even worse.

These results point to a bleak future for Palestinians in Israel as they are increasingly integrated into a binational labor market. Such "integration" is less integration in the positive sense and more "mal-integration" into Israel's economy, similar to what Michael Hechter argued in his classic study *Internal Colonialism.*[5] Continuing mal-integration of the Palestinian minority in Israel along with the mal-integration of Palestinian labor from the occupied territories appears to be proceeding, perhaps more rapidly now with the high-tech transformation of Israel's economy, and may create the conditions for greater discontent among the two segments of the Palestinian population in historic Palestine.

Education of the Palestinians

The previous two sections have analyzed the process of property dispossession and the corresponding processes of proletarianization and peripheralization of the Palestinians. These conditions have produced in the Palestinian community a huge class of low-skilled employees instead of self-employed and employers. In employment, occupational status is determined by the character and requirements of the labor itself, particularly the educational level. In the context of the industrial-service, and more recently high-tech, economy in Israel, education is a critical factor.

To begin with, the rate of literacy in the Jewish population is significantly higher than among Palestinians. By 1972 the percentage of literacy of Jewish males and females above the age of fourteen was already high—94.1 percent and 87.1 percent, respectively—whereas the corresponding figures for Palestinian males and females was only 77.8 percent and 48.8 percent, respectively. Although the overall Palestinian literacy rate has increased considerably since then, a large, although diminished, gap remains between Jews and Palestinians in Israel. For example, although illiteracy among Palestinians was reduced from 50 percent in 1961 to 7 percent in 1999, it remained almost three times higher than among Jews (2.5 percent). Despite compulsory schooling in Israel, the rate of zero years of schooling was still three times higher for Palestinian Arabs than for Jews in 1999.

Clear, consistent, and significant differences existed and continue to exist at the higher end of the educational spectrum. The percentage of Palestinians with nine years or more of schooling rose from 9.1 percent in 1961 to 66.7 percent in 1999, whereas the corresponding figures for Jews rose from

44.5 percent in 1961 to 87.8 percent in 1999. Also, in 1999, 87.8 percent of the Jews in Israel had nine or more years of schooling, whereas 33.4 percent of the Palestinians had eight years or fewer of schooling.

Although most of the education of the Palestinians through high school is in Arabic, there is not a single Arabic-language university in Israel. A number of requests in the 1980s to establish an Arab university in Nazareth, the largest Palestinian Arab city in Israel, were rejected by the state's Council on Higher Education.[6] At the same time, at least six universities were established by Palestinians in the West Bank and the Gaza Strip. Most Palestinians lack the opportunity to be admitted into Hebrew-language universities as their command of the Hebrew language may not be sufficient for university-level training. Many, therefore, have been studying in universities in the occupied territories.

Low levels of education among the Palestinians compared to Jews have other derivative, structural sources besides the deliberate discrimination practiced by the Israeli state. Palestinian poverty levels and large families encourage young Palestinians to stop their education and seek early employment in order to reduce the ratio of dependents to earners in those families. Furthermore, higher education for Palestinians guarantees neither a better position nor a higher income in the Jewish economy. Jews are favored over Palestinian Arabs, who are typically hired last and fired first, a pattern typical of biased dual-ethnic markets. Consequently, a strong sentiment seems to exist among secondary school students that job opportunities are fairly minimal for educated Arabs, except in the already crowded Palestinian enclave economy, a rational disincentive to further education.

In conclusion, the low levels of education of Palestinians relative to Jews in Israel guarantee an inferior status in the social and economic system of the country. The policies of the state shortchange Arab education financially and thus guarantee an inadequate and inferior educational system. Therefore, one must come to the conclusion that the Israeli state continues deliberately to produce a lower-educated and lower-skilled Palestinian workforce to occupy the most menial occupations in the Jewish economic system while allowing a small segment to pursue higher education in order to serve the evolving health, education, and welfare needs of the Palestinian minority.

Health of the Palestinians

The system of health care in Israel is very complex, consisting of government, municipal, nonprofit, missionary, and private suppliers with overlapping constituencies. A number of indicators show conclusively the different levels of health care provided for Palestinians and Jews. For example, data on live births indicate the rapid growth in parity between the two populations: By 1978 the percentage of live births in hospitals differed by only 1.5 percent between Jews and Palestinians. However, this apparent near equality in treatment is belied by the rates of infant mortality, which is nearly twice as great among Palestinians as among Jews. One explanation may be that health care after delivery is not provided for Palestinians as it is for Jews. Palestinian rates of infant mortality are lowest in rural areas and highest in "mixed" Jewish-Arab cities. This fact suggests that social conditions impact on the health of the Palestinians in Israel and that the health care system does little to compensate.

Another measure of overall health is life expectancy. Life expectancy for both population groups in Israel has been rising over the years. In 1980 it was 72.1 years for Jewish males and 75.7 for Jewish females, compared to 70.0 for Palestinian Arab males and 73.4 for females. In 1997 the figures were 76.4 for Jewish males and 80.5 for Jewish females; the Palestinian figures were 73.9 and 77.3, respectively. Although the figures for life expectancy among Jews and Palestinians are close, the *quality* of healthful life, including in old age, is nowhere near equal. Although the health of the Palestinian community in Israel has improved over the years, as did that of the Jewish population, disparities continue to exist.

The Political System of Control

What are the structures, processes, and practices of the system of political control that created and continues the internal colonialism over the Palestinian minority in Israel? And how has this system changed over the years? An answer to these questions must begin by identifying the self-definition by the Zionist leadership of the nature of the Jewish state.

Israel in Its Own Eyes

In the Declaration of Independence of Israel, the terms *Jewish state* and the *state of the Jewish people* are used interchangeably. These terms have quite distinct meanings and therefore important implications for the Palestinian Arab minority in the country. Indeed, as Rouhana pointed out, the term *Jewish state* has several meanings, all with different implications for the Palestinian minority in Israel (as of course they do for the Palestinian refugees). He therefore noted that in the minds and hearts of the Zionists and Israeli officials:

Israel is a Jewish state in the sense that it is the exclusive state of the Jewish people in Israel and worldwide and not the state of its citizens who are not Jewish. According to this meaning, Israel is the political tool of the Jewish people regardless of citizenship. So it is membership in the Jewish people, not citizenship in Israel that is the sole criterion for the claim of state ownership.[7]

The set of basic laws that have been enacted by the Jewish state over the years define Israel as the "state of the Jewish people rather than the more limited interpretation that Israel is a state with a Jewish majority whose cultural, religious, and national character is by definition determined by the majority or that Israel is the state of its Jewish citizens."[8] As many analysts have pointed out, the national flag, the state emblem, the stamps, and the national anthem, which are specified by law, are not only those of the pre-state Zionist movement but also are strictly Jewish, admitting no recognition of minorities, especially the non-Jewish Arab minority. Especially significant is that Independence Day celebrations, which celebrate the 1948 victory of Zionism over the Palestinians and other Arabs, simultaneously symbolize for the Palestinians—those who are citizens of Israel, those under occupation, and those in the diaspora—the destruction of Palestine and its dismemberment, as well as the dispossession, dispersal, and the destitution of the largest segment of its population. It is thus clear that the laws and the practices (official and popular) not only stress the Jewish character and identity of the state but also provide a basis for biased and preferential treatment of the Jewish citizens over the Arab citizens. Israel, therefore, in the ideology and practice of Zionism and of the officials of the government, is not a civil state of all its citizens; it belongs only to Jews. Such an ideology and derivative and commensurate legislation are the legal basis for institutional discrimination against the Palestinian Arab minority.

The ideology and practice in the self-definition and identity of Israel have three pillars, according to Rouhana: Israel as a Jewish state, Israel as a democracy, and the security of Israel. Besides identifying Israel as a Jewish state, Israel's Declaration of Independence also proclaims that the state "will maintain complete equality of social and political rights for all citizens, without distinction of creed, race or sex. It will guarantee freedom of religion and conscience, of language, education and culture."[9] We have seen that the guarantees have been violated by the very state that promised them to the Palestinian minority in the country.

Democracy is a complex phenomenon involving procedural, legal, and other dimensions related to individual and collective rights. It is typically conceptualized as having two aspects: the formal procedural aspect (including universal free suffrage, an electoral system based on transparent regulations for competition, and independent legislative and judicial bodies) and the civil rights aspect (including the human and civil rights of the individual, the rule of law, equal treatment under the law, and freedom of association). But Israeli democracy is fraught with contradictions. Not the least of them is the role of religion in public life and generally in the relationship between state, society, and religion. Whereas in Western secular democracies these three domains are typically separated (as in the separation of church and state), in Israel they are intimately intertwined, and laws, policies, practices, and procedures are often derived from and based on religious Jewish law and biblical justification. For example, the justifications for establishing a Jewish homeland in Palestine and for the occupation and settlement building in the West Bank and Gaza are given in religious (biblical) terms. Indeed, the political discourse in Israel is deeply infused with religious references, terms, symbolism, ideology, and legitimizations.

Although most Jews are secular in their private and public life and do not observe religious practice, the Israeli state imposes religious laws, such as marriage laws and food-preparation regulations, on all its citizens. Yet Palestinians in Israel typically frame their rights and their demands on the government in terms of an image of Israel as a democratic society. The individual and collective rights articulated by Palestinian Arabs are appeals to the universal principles of democracy and do not include the special nature of Israel as a Jewish state. Thus, Palestinians are seen as a threat to the concept of the Jewish character of the state and its basis as the state of all the Jewish people.

The third pillar of Israeli policy and ideology is the "security" of the Israeli state and individual. The Israeli sense of threat and insecurity is promoted and heightened by the state, the media, and public discourse because of the numerous wars and armed clashes in which Israel has been engaged since its establishment as well as the experience of the Jewish Holocaust in Europe.

Two things are remarkable about this ideology of felt threat and insecurity in Israel. The first is that the Zionist colonial project of Judaizing Palestine was achieved through brutal force that terrorized, expelled, and killed the indigenous Palestinians. Second, in the name of security, Israel has built itself (with the help of the United States) into the regional military superpower. Over the years, it has used its overwhelming power to kill tens of thousands of Palestinians and other Arabs in wars, invasions, attacks, aerial bombardment, and a very long occupation, yet it believes it is and has managed to successfully portray itself in the West as the victim of Arab and Palestinian violence and threats.

Suppression of Palestinian Political Action

Calls for autonomy and self-rule by Palestinian Arabs have begun to appear more persistently in the past decade (1990s). The head of the Progressive List for Peace (PLP) and Knesset member Mohammad Miari stated, "I am not the only one among my people who has despaired of the chance to achieve equality. We have despaired of Arab-Jewish cooperation. . . . Today I and many others have reached the conclusion that we must give up the demand for the unattained equality and call instead for self-rule."[10]

Of course, the Israeli state refuses to extend to the Palestinian minority in Israel the status of a national minority with full collective rights because "Jews fear Arab national autonomy might turn into a firm power base for challenging Jewish dominance, might erode Israel's Jewish character and transform it into a bi-national state, and might become a prelude to a separatist movement."[11]

As in the formal and official institutions of the state, the Jewish political parties have also isolated the Palestinian Arabs. Early in the history of Israel, Arabs were discouraged from any political action except as local leaders (whose power base was the *hamula* or the kinship-based clans) who were affiliated with the Zionist Jewish parties. Beginning in the 1950s the Jewish political parties decided to seek the "Arab vote." The governments that they formed (especially Labor) showered the Arab political affiliates and their *hamula*s with some services and occasional material benefits. Significantly, the government agencies and Jewish party activists converted many of these leaders into collaborators and informers on other *hamula*s, other *hamula* leaders, and especially political activists who articulated Arab nationalist rhetoric. The Palestinian social, *hamula,* and village leaders willing to cooperate or collaborate with the Jewish parties and authorities provided votes in return for small favors to them personally or to the village and local area they lived in. Often, these returns were services and infrastructural development projects that were due those locales or villages anyway, according to Israeli law.

The only party that sought to represent and integrate the Palestinian community was the Communist Party of Israel (CPI), especially a faction attuned to Arab concerns that became known as Rakah. CPI became popular with the Palestinian community as the Arab states, especially Egypt under President Gamal Abdul-Nasser, established international alliances with the Soviet Union and third-world powers against US, British, and French imperialism in the area. But precisely because it championed the Palestinian cause in Israel and supported Soviet foreign policy, it was ostracized by the Israeli political establishment and thus served to keep the Palestinian Arabs out of the mainstream of Israeli politics. Nevertheless, it was able to get three to five of its candidate list elected to the Knesset, the Israeli legislature.

The traditional Palestinian community in the first decades of its life in the Jewish state was structurally fragmented and therefore susceptible to manipulation and control by the Israeli authorities. Although the *hamula* as a political organization or grouping in pre-1948 Palestine was declining during the mandate, the *hamula* was deliberately revived by the Israeli authorities. The conscious establishment of proportional representation in local councils increased the fragmentation and political rivalry of *hamula*s and played into Israeli hands.[12] The reason is that the function of the local council, especially the chairman, became crucial in almost all village and community social, economic, and political affairs. The councils not only oversaw the collection of taxes but also appointed school administrators, approved teachers, and oversaw infrastructural issues such as electrical transmission lines and roads. *Hamula* rivalry was deliberately enhanced to block any redevelopment of communitywide Palestinian Arab consciousness, mobilization, and political action. Although this maneuver succeeded for a long period in blocking communitywide political action, the following discussion shows that the Palestinians in Israel overcame much of this fragmentation as they struggled for their rights starting in the mid-1970s.

The Dynamics of Palestinian Political Action

The history of Palestinian politics can be divided into several distinct and recognizable periods. The first extended from 1948 to 1967, when the June war led to the Israeli occupation of the West Bank and the Gaza Strip. The second period began in 1967 and ended with the signing of the Oslo Accords in 1993. Long and eventful, this period witnessed significant political change among the Palestinians in Israel. The third period lasted from the Oslo period up to the Al-Aqsa Intifada of the year 2000. Since then, a new political situation, perhaps pivotal, has emerged.

The Formative Years and the
Politics of Survival: 1948–1967

In general, the key dilemmas facing the Palestinians from 1948 to 1967 can be summarized as basic survival in the context of an oppressive military rule, the loss of land and the livelihood tied to it, the loss of kinspeople who became refugees, the exile of the political leadership, and cultural and economic isolation from the rest of the Arab world. The military rule that Israel imposed on the Palestinian population in the country and the treatment it accorded the Palestinians as a fifth column, an extension of Israel's Arab enemies, and especially Israel's vast and extensive land expropriation generated enormous fear and discontent. In the beginning, fear for personal security and for one's property, along with the struggle to earn a living, seems to have generated quiescence and muted anger.

In the first two decades of Israel's establishment, there were three distinct political tendencies among the Palestinians in Israel. The first was the collaborators and cooperators with and beneficiaries of the authorities and the Mapai (later Labor) Party. The traditional *hamula* and sectarian leaders, who anchored this tendency, wanted no political activism except to show the Israeli authorities how loyal they were. The Palestinian electorate voted overwhelmingly for Mapai, Mapam (a more leftist party), and, to a much smaller extent, other Zionist parties. In 1951, Mapai received 66.9 of the Palestinian vote, a ratio that gradually declined to just over half in 1958. This collaborationist tendency resisted any political agitation to protest land confiscation and the severe repression of the military governors or to demand equal rights for the Palestinian minority. Instead, leaders in this period often attempted to convince the Palestinians whose lands had been confiscated to accept the nominal compensation offered by the Israeli state. Indeed, when opposition to maintaining military rule over the Palestinian Arab areas was strong even in the Jewish community and polity, two Palestinian Arab members of the Knesset voted to retain military rule.[13]

The second tendency was the support of the Communist Party, which gained greater credibility and backing when it championed Palestinian rights on all the issues of discontent, especially land. This support also coincided with the regional development that led to a political and diplomatic alliance of the nationalist Arab states with the Soviet Union while Israel allied itself with Western imperialists: Britain, France, and the United States. This rise in support occurred after the party had lost significantly within Arab circles when it sided with the United Nation's 1947 partition of Palestine. However, with the rise of the cold war in the region, the Communist Party of Israel became suspect by the Israeli government. It was monitored and harassed by the authorities, but it was not declared illegal, nor were its leaders imprisoned, probably because many of them were Jews. The CPI never became part of the ruling Zionist establishment but remained active nationally (as a loyal opposition) and on the local level.

The third tendency, which began to form in the 1950s, was an Arab nationalist movement led by both older intellectuals and activists and the new ones who had come of age in Israel. The Palestinian Arabs were not allowed to form independent parties or even publish a newspaper. An attempt to form an Arab writers' union was harassed and eventually disrupted and eliminated by suspicious Israeli authorities, on the grounds that it was a front for anti-Israeli activities. Israel saw Arab nationalism as a threatening and dangerous ideology and its proponents as treacherous and disloyal individuals.

A number of factors coalesced to promote Arab nationalist feelings in Israel. In addition to the internal disaffection already noted, the regional developments were very significant. The most important was the rise of popular Arab nationalism under the leadership of President Gamal Abdul-Nasser of Egypt. Egypt's confrontation with Britain and France over the nationalization of the Suez Canal, the tripartite war launched against Egypt in 1956 (the Suez War), and the political victory of Abdul-Nasser despite Egypt's military defeat led the Palestinians in Israel to a heightened consciousness of their Arab heritage, to pride in being Arab, and to the hope that progressive Arab nationalism would deliver the region from Western imperialism and unite and launch the Arab world into socioeconomic development and independence from foreign domination. The struggles and drama of Arab nationalism led by Abdul-Nasser strongly excited and inspired the Palestinians in Israel. Like all Arabs in the Mashreq, the Palestinians were glued to their radio sets listening to the speeches of Abdul-Nasser and the Cairo-based Voice of the Arabs.

The most significant Palestinian effort in Israel in the late 1950s to organize and mobilize involved the Al-Ard Movement. A movement of Arab nationalists, it sought to politically mobilize the Palestinians to fight for an end to military rule, to achieve their socioeconomic rights, and to support their refugee compatriots' right of return. In addition, the movement was allied to the anti-imperialist struggle of the Arab states. In the view of the Al-Ard activists, the split between the Arab nationalists and the Communist Party in nearly all the Arab states—despite the strategic alliance with the Soviet Union—necessitated organizing a separate Arab nationalist movement in Israel as well. This movement found strong resonance among the Palestinians, especially as there was also a robust desire to have an independent Arab organization. Many who joined that movement were students and the young. Its ideology and demands were quite straightforward: In addition to the call to end the military rule of and to gain equal rights for the Palestinians in Israel, it also called for the right of the Palestinian refugees to return and for positive neutrality in the cold war.

The signal political event for this movement, for the Communist Party, and for the Palestinians in general, however, was the 1958 May Day demonstration. The conflict and violence that accompanied the demonstration quickly developed into a Palestinian Arab confrontation with Jewish authorities. Palestinian Arab ferment in Israel had been fed by the regional developments of that year: the union of Egypt and Syria into the United Arab Republic and later the Iraqi coup that led to the end of the dependent pro-Western monarchy and the establishment of a republic in that country. Shortly after the demonstrations in Nazareth and Umm al-Fahem, the leaders of the Palestinian opposition announced the formation of the Arab Popular Front, a coalition incorporating the political trends and ideologies of all of the leaders.

The Israeli authorities swiftly moved to crush the front and the movement in its infancy. It declared the Al-Ard Movement illegal; arrested, detained administratively, and harassed its leaders; and exiled some of them to different parts of Israel. Within about three years, Al-Ard and its newspaper, also titled *Al-Ard*, disappeared.[14] Nevertheless, the movement gave momentum to protesting the increasingly unpopular military rule. As some leftist Jews and others joined the call for ending military rule, the mainstream Zionist parties other than Mapai and Mapam recognized that the military rule—and through it the Palestinian Arab vote—had served the narrow political electoral interests of the ruling Labor coalition. Thus, an internal Israeli struggle for "Arab votes," along with Palestinian Arab agitation, led to the abolition of the military rule over the Arab minority in Israel by 1966.

Political Assertion and Political Differentiation, from Marginality to Influence: 1967–1993

With the repeal of military rule, the struggle for the Palestinians in Israel shifted to the protection of their land from continuing expropriation. Also, the occupation of the rest of Palestine in the course of the June 5, 1967, Arab-Israeli war introduced political demands to end the occupation. In addition, the emergence of the revolutionary Palestinian guerrilla movement and the concept of armed struggle to liberate Palestine inspired not only the diaspora Palestinians (and other Arabs) but also those under occupation and inside Israel. These regional developments strengthened the Arab nationalist current inside Israel, and some individuals from the Palestinian community in Israel even joined the guerrilla movement and participated in guerrilla raids inside Israel. But as the PLO accepted the idea of a diplomatic struggle after the 1973 Arab-Israeli war and redefined its goal away from the liberation of all of Palestine and toward the idea of an independent state in the West Bank and the Gaza Strip, the Palestinians in Israel were left with a small or no role in the Palestinian movement. At best, they became an electoral pressure group of sorts to ensure the election into power of Zionist parties more interested in a peaceful or political settlement (supposedly Labor over Likud).

Whereas up to 1967 the peasants' proletarianization in the service of the Jewish economy was the key to transforming the class structure of the Palestinian community, the period after 1967 was characterized by a rapid increase in the white-collar stratum. Perhaps as relevant was the emergence of a small Palestinian bourgeoisie. These developments reinforced further the Arab nationalist tendency as an articulate intelligentsia asserted its role and its nationalist credentials.

The land question increased in significance as all political trends, including the traditional *hamula* and sectarian leaders, who were mostly organized in the Committee of Heads of Local Authorities, rallied to it. By 1976, the land issue had galvanized the Palestinians in Israel. On March 30, a Committee to Defend the Land, formed from many political groups, called for a general strike and massive demonstrations to protest land confiscation. The traditional leadership, organized in the Committee of Heads of Local Authorities, objected to and did not endorse the political action.

What is significant about the movement of the Land Day is the fact that it merged the nationalist demands with the civil rights demands and thus was able to mobilize a large part of the Palestinian Arab population. On the day of the demonstration, Israeli authorities attempted to clamp down on the demonstrators, and clashes between the police and the Palestinians led to several casualties. Israel moved to create a Ministry of Arab Affairs in place of the Advisor to the Prime Minister for Arab Affairs, and to alter and modify some of the heavy-handed practices of control over the Palestinian community.

Unfortunately, the organizations that emerged from this eventful action quickly became ends in their own right instead of the means to mobilize the populace further. The popular committee that had led the struggle became institutionalized into a committee that principally commemorated Land Day. With the demise of the Land Day Committee there was no other communitywide organization or structure that could bring the national and local Palestinian leadership together. The political vacuum allowed the old Committee of the Heads of Local Authorities to emerge as an important organizational framework, especially as its membership began to change to reflect the increasing presence of a new and younger generation of leaders and others who represented the more nationalist Palestinian Arab parties. This change led to the formation of the Committee to Follow Up on the Concerns of Arab Citizens, which included, besides the heads of local councils and authorities, Palestinian members of the Knesset and of the executive of the Histadrut. Although the Follow-up Committee, as it was popularly known, emerged as the de facto leadership of the Palestinian Arab community, its concerns were largely local in character and did not help in developing a national vision for the Palestinian community.

Politics in the 1980s

During the 1980s the hold of Rakah, the Communist Party, over the Palestinian community was broken because of the rising tide of the nationalist movement and also because it had never articulated a coherent or comprehensive platform regarding the Palestinian community. Its position on the national Palestinian question (the two-state solution to the Arab-Israeli conflict) was consonant with the goals of the PLO and identical to that of the Soviet Union, which supported the establishment of an independent Palestinian state in the West Bank and the Gaza Strip. Perhaps most important, until 1984 (when the Progressive List for Peace was able to establish itself and run for Knesset elections), Rakah, a Jewish-Arab party, was the only party in Israel that was an alternative to the purely Zionist Jewish parties. The emergence of Palestinian Arab parties after 1984 ended Rakah's unique political role. Furthermore, the rise of Arab nationalism in the political culture of the Palestinians in Israel accompanied the reemergence or reaffirmation of Palestinian identity among the Arab population in Israel.

The convergence of the regional and the domestic Israeli conditions during this period enhanced or accentuated the Palestinian identity in Israel. There is no doubt that the conflict with and attacks on Palestinian communities in the neighboring Arab countries—Jordan and Lebanon—increased the Israeli Palestinians' sense of solidarity with their compatriots and heightened Palestinian identity in Israel.

The de-Arabization and the re-Palestinization of the conflict with Israel during this period also contributed to heightened Palestinian identity in Israel and elsewhere. The sense of victimization, shared by all Palestinians, accentuated the unique identity of the Palestinians in Israel. A major leap in that direction took place as the First Intifada erupted in December 1987. Palestinians in Israel sent material help—money, food, and clothing—in support of the intifada and held strikes and demonstrations (for example, on December 21, 1987) to show support of and solidarity with the uprising and to protest the savage repression practiced by the Israeli occupation army. Indeed, one of the largest national Palestinian Arab demonstrations in Israel took place on January 23, 1988, and it was also followed by a national strike on Land Day 1989. And yet, the intifada, the PLO goal of statehood in the West Bank and the Gaza Strip, brought home to the Palestinians in Israel that their own future was separate from the rest of the Palestinians and lies instead in Israel. It was in part a consequence of this recognition that led the Palestinians in Israel to articulate early in the 1990s the political notion of the transformation of Israel from a "Jewish state" into a democratic state of all of its citizens: Jews and Arabs.

As the PLO redefined its goals and strategy—abandoning liberation as the cause of all Palestinians in favor of a sovereign state in the occupied territories—the Palestinians in Israel were left out of this strategic political change. They were left to fend for themselves in regard to civil rights in the context of Israel and to act as a support group within Israel for the diplomatic effort, later the peace process, of the PLO. The urgings of the PLO to vote in Israeli elections—and to vote, first, for the Democratic Front for Peace and Equality and, later, in 1992, indirectly for the "peace party" (Labor)—did play a role in Palestinian political action in Israel, although it may not have been the decisive factor in the restructuring of Palestinian political activity.

Arab nationalist parties or electoral lists emerged beginning in 1984. The PLP defined itself as a Palestinian grouping in ideological terms and quickly won 18 percent of the Arab Palestinian vote and two seats in the Knesset at a point when Palestinian nationalism among the Palestinian Arabs in Israel was very high. However, just as quickly, it lost the support of the Palestinian electorate as it was ostracized by the Jewish establishment (as a mouthpiece for the PLO inside Israel) and could not deliver the needed resources and services to its constituency. In the 1988 elections it won one seat and then none in 1992. Besides its ineffectiveness in providing services for its constituency, its demise came at the hands of the PLO.

The Arab Democratic Party (ADP), founded by a former Labor Party af-filiate and Knesset member, emerged as an opportunistic party, after the image of its leader, stressing no ideology, even playing down Palestinian identity in favor of Arab identity. It prefers instead to work within the sys-tem of Israeli coalition politics with the hope of becoming a coalition part-ner with Labor. It thus accepts the marginal status of Palestinians in the Israeli system and wishes to play politics by the Israeli Jewish rules. In the 1988 election the ADP received 11 percent of the Arab vote and one seat in the Knesset; it won 15 percent of the vote and two seats in the 1992 elections.

The Islamic political movement among the Palestinians in Israel also started to form in the early 1980s. Like its counterparts in many Arab coun-tries, it began as a social service movement, helping people in need at the lo-cal level. Thus its appeal may be similar to that of other such movements in the Arab world in the contexts of ideological fragmentation, loss of group cohesion, socioeconomic need, and frustration. In the 1992 national elec-tions, the Islamist movement could not inspire its adherents to maintain a united position. The distribution of the votes of the Islamists seems to have been similar to that of the rest of the Arab votes. The Islamic movement in Israel does not call for the establishment of an Islamic state in the country but hopes to create local ordinances that are Islamic in character.

Politics in the Wake of the Oslo Accords: 1993–Present

The 1992 Israeli election that just predated the Oslo agreements may be considered another political watershed in the eventful political history of the Palestinian community in Israel. This judgment is based on the relegit-imization of the Zionist Jewish political parties amid the Palestinian Arabs in Israel. With the installation of a system of primaries in the election process, 16,000 Palestinian Arabs rushed to participate in the process by registering in Zionist parties. The Zionist parties in this election gained over 50 percent of the Palestinian Arab vote. Ironically, this seemingly quantum leap in the process of the political Israelization of the Palestinian minority in Israel was taking place at the very moment that the Israeli Jews were reaffirming their rejection of Palestinians among them. In 1992 the Is-raeli Knesset passed two basic laws that reaffirmed the principles of the Declaration of Independence and reasserted that Israel is the state of the Jewish people only.[15]

The new phenomenon of participation in Zionist parties differed from the old and condemned pattern of collaboration in that these participants see themselves as pragmatic actors, concerned to achieve a thorough engagement with the Zionist establishment. This participation therefore is part of the Israelization of the Palestinian minority in the country, and of accepting second-class citizenship, sociopolitical and economic marginalization, and legitimization of collaboration with the Israeli authorities and institutions. The most that such a crucial Palestinian vote was able to accomplish after it was successful in helping bring to power the Labor Party was a demand for an Arab minister in the coalition government. No Arab minister was appointed until the government of Prime Minister Ariel Sharon, who was elected in February 2001, but the "Arab minister," Salah Tarif, has little or no legitimacy in the eyes of the Palestinian community.

The social, economic, and political processes that transformed the Palestinian community in the 1980s have continued unchanged. Palestinian Arab political leaders—many of the nationalists, the Islamists, the leftists, and even the collaborationists—seem to have reached a consensus on a basic two-point ideological position: support for an independent Palestinian state in the West Bank and the Gaza Strip and advocacy of the right of Palestinians to equality in Israel—though within the context of Israeli law (which favors Jews) and of the unchanged Israeli institutions, which define the state as belonging to Jews and not to all its citizens.

Ideological Dilemma and Ideological Contradictions

All the parties representing or concerned with the Palestinian minority in Israel face an ideological dilemma and a basic contradiction in their practice: how to overcome marginality and discrimination and secure the needed and legitimate resources and services from a state that excludes them from its own self-definition as a state for all Jews, not of its citizens. There are many factors that contribute to this dilemma, not the least of which is the power of the Jewish state and its determination to serve the Jews only and to exclude the Palestinian minority from meaningful participation in decisionmaking and the Jewish power structure. But perhaps the absence of a mobilizing Palestinian ideology and leadership that are socially inclusive also contributes to this dilemma. What has existed in the way of ideology or political discourse since the mid-1990s—support for an independent Palestinian state in the West Bank and the Gaza Strip, on the one hand, and the struggle for civil rights inside Israel, on the other—and a leadership committed to it led to the abandonment of the "national question." Its redefinition as an independent Palestinian state in the occupied territories meant its "export" beyond the Green Line (the West Bank and the Gaza Strip). It also led to the increasing acceptance of cooperators and collaborators with the Israeli institutions and authorities as legitimate political actors in the eyes of the Palestinian community. For example, a former Palestinian Arab member of the Zionist Labor Party formed the Arab Democratic Party and has become, with other elected members of his party, a respected and influential politician. Although they have changed their rhetoric and political discourse to suit the times, they have continued in their old ways of cooperating and collaborating with the Israeli authorities. As disturbing is the apparent depoliticization of some important members of the socially transformed Palestinian community in Israel. A new social profile has emerged within the Palestinian community: the entrepreneur who is content with the possibility of individual economic success and commensurate social mobility at the expense of collective community rights. Yet the goal of fully integrating as individuals into Israeli society cannot be attained as long as Israel continues to define itself as a Jewish state and not a state of all its citizens. By joining the political process of Israel on Jewish Zionist terms, the Palestinians are increasingly accepting their Israelization, which means acceptance of the status of second-class citizens and a marginal presence in the political system in return for receiving small benefits that do not alter the structural basis of internal colonialism or the basic character of the Jewish state.

Yet Palestinians in Israel have a strong emotional identification with the Palestinian people everywhere and have little sense of belonging to Jewish-centered Israel, even as they nonetheless accept citizenship in the state of Israel and conform to its laws. These attitudes are in part behind the rise to prominence of two important political movements in the 1990s. The first is the strengthening of the Islamists, and the second is the emergence of al-Balad (not the Arab nationalist organization Abnaa al-Balad, which no longer exists), formally known as the National Democratic Assembly (NDA), a democratic, progressive national party. It was founded in 1996 under the leadership of Azmi Bishara, a dynamic and charismatic leader among the Palestinians. Its political platform is nothing less than revolutionary in the context of Jewish-Zionist Israel. It states, "The NDA seeks to transform Israel from a Jewish state into a democratic state, a state with equality for all its citizens, Jews and Arabs alike, and to eliminate all state institutions and laws which discriminate against Arabs in Israel."[16]

In line with the United Nations charter, the NDA demands that Israel officially recognize the Palestinian Arab citizens as a national minority entitled to the rights granted to all national minorities, including self-rule and autonomy in education and the media. It pledges itself to struggle against land confiscation and for government recognition of "unrecognized Arab villages" (over fifty villages comprising 8 percent of the Palestinian population). It also supports full equality between men and women and the elimination of sectarianism and clan favoritism (long promoted, as has been seen, by the government of Israel to divide the Palestinian Arabs and rule over them). The NDA's political program is genuinely revolutionary not only in regard to the Jewish character of the state but also within the Palestinian Arab community.

The NDA joined forces in 1996 with the Front for Peace and Equality (Rakah-based) to run for elections. Bishara became a member of the Knesset then. However, in the 1999 elections the NDA headed its own electoral list with other groups and leaders of inactive or defunct organizations such as Abnaa al-Balad, the Progressive List for Peace, and other nationalist personalities and groups. Between them the NDA and the Islamists emerged as the strongest political currents among the Palestinians in Israel at the start of the twenty-first century.

Conclusion: A New Turning Point?

The Al-Aqsa Intifada has triggered events among Palestinian Arabs that seem to suggest another turning point in the political struggles of the Palestinian community in Israel. In the wake of the "internal intifada"—or "Black October," as many Palestinians in Israel call the solidarity demonstrations and civil disobedience they practiced in October 2000—a vicious Jewish backlash erupted. Jewish mobs attacked Palestinian citizens of Israel and burned down the home of the Palestinian member of the Knesset, Azmi Bishara, the leader of the National Democratic Assembly. Attacks on mosques in the "mixed Jewish-Arab cities" of Jaffa, Hadera, and Tabariyya and a Jewish boycott of Palestinian businesses and workers were launched. Perhaps as dangerous were the articles in the mainstream media that called for the "transfer" (expulsion) of the Palestinian minority to the West Bank and the Gaza Strip, a political view that has never disappeared from Israeli political discourse and that is reasserted periodically when the tension and conflict with Palestinians in Israel intensifies.

The significance of these events is that they may have changed dramatically the character of the relationship between the Palestinian minority and the Israeli state. Palestinian community alienation from Israel has increased in the wake of Black October. This apparent turnaround in Palestinian Arab attitudes toward Israel and the Israeli state is caused not only by the policies and practices of the state toward the Palestinian minority but also by the parallel rise of Islamic and Arab nationalist (the National Democratic Assembly) sentiment, as well as regional developments, especially Al-Aqsa Intifada. The events inside Israel and in the occupied territories have therefore brought about a new chapter in the history of the Palestinians in Israel.[17] There are two significant aspects to these events. The first is that they may have altered, if not ended, the long-term dependent and subordinate association of much of the Palestinian community with the Labor Party. The understanding that produced that relationship consisted of delivering Palestinian Arab votes for Labor in return for promises of programs, resources, and services that were needed by the community but that rarely materialized. The second and perhaps more important development is the "decline in the politics of equality" and the eruption of "politics of national identity," as indicated by the upheaval in October 2000 and confirmed by the extensive Palestinian boycott of the Israeli Independence Day celebrations. Instead, many Palestinians in Israel, like Palestinians everywhere, commemorated al-Nakbah Day on May 14.

The current struggle of the Palestinian people is three-pronged: full equality for the Palestinians in Israel, self-determination for the Palestinians in the West Bank and the Gaza Strip, and the right of return and compensation for the Palestinian refugees. Israel is unlikely to yield to any of these Palestinian goals. But if these goals remain unfulfilled, especially inside Israel, separatist tendencies may emerge among the Palestinians in Israel, and they may try to join forces with the Palestinians in the occupied territories in a struggle for a binational Arab-Jewish democratic state or even a single democratic state in historic Palestine, as some intellectuals and activists have begun to argue.[18] Feeling an identity as Palestinians, rather than as Israel's Arab minority, may be necessary for a political discourse, ideology, and action that will permit the Palestinian people in Israel to organize themselves nationally and make their own history not only by and for themselves but also as part of the whole people of Palestine.

Notes

1. Nadim N. Rouhana, *Palestinian Citizens in an Ethnic Jewish State: Identities in Conflict* (New Haven: Yale University Press, 1997). This section is largely based on Rouhana's chapter titled "Controlled Internal Developments: Demography, Education, Socio-Economics, and Politics," 79–82.

2. Ibid., 81, citing B. N. Al-Hout, *Leadership and Political Institutions in Palestine, 1917–1948* (in Arabic) (Beirut: Institute for Palestine Studies, 1981).

3. Sammy Smooha, *The Orientation and Politicization of the Arab Minority in Israel* (Haifa: Haifa University Press, 1980).

4. A. Haidar, *The Arab Population in the Israeli Economy* (Tel Aviv: International Center for Peace in the Middle East, 1990).

5. M. Hechter, *Internal Colonialism* (London: Routledge & Kegan Paul, 1975).

6. Smooha, *Orientation,* 102.

7. Rouhana, *Palestinian Citizens,* 31.

8. Ibid., 32.

9. See Israel's Declaration of Independence at www.Israel.gov.

10. Y. Algazi, "The Arabs in Israel Request Autonomy," *Ha'aretz* (July 27, 1990), cited in Smooha, *Orientation,* 98.

11. Ibid., 99.

12. A. Cohen, *Arab Border Villages in Israel* (Manchester: Manchester University Press, 1965), and S. Abu-Ghosh, "The Politics of an Arab Village in Israel," Ph.D. dissertation, Princeton University, 1965.

13. Rouhana, *Palestinian Citizens,* 97.

14. See H. Qahwaji, *The Complete Story of Al-Ard Movement* (Jerusalem: Al-Arabi, 1978).

15. Rouhana, *Palestinian Citizens,* 35.

16. "Principles and Aims," at www.balad.org.

17. A. Bishara, "A New Chapter in the History of the Arab Masses Inside" (in Arabic), *Journal of Palestinian Studies* 44 (Autumn 2000): 3–25.

18. See Rouhana, *Palestinian Citizens,* 201–217. Naseer Aruri argued for a single democratic state that provides for Palestinian rights and lives by the rule of law: N. Aruri, "Towards Convening a Congress of Return and Self Determination," in N. Aruri, ed., *Palestinian Refugees: The Right of Return* (London: Pluto Press, 2001).

6

The Rise and Fall of the Palestinian National Liberation Movement, 1948–1993

Palestine and the Palestinians have had a long and eventful history. At the crossroads of the Old World and of three continents, Palestine was often the destination of conquerors and the center of conflict, for it is as well a Holy Land for three major monotheistic religions: Judaism, Christianity, and Islam. Palestine was Arabized and Islamized beginning in the seventh century but experienced severely disruptive European interventions in three important periods of its history: the Crusades in the early medieval period, imperialism in the nineteenth century, and Zionism in the twentieth century. After nearly two centuries of rule by feudal European Christian kings, Palestine was restored to its Islamic and Arab heritage by the victory of Saladin over the Crusaders in Hittin in northern Palestine in 1187. And despite the four centuries (1517–1917) of Ottoman Turkish dominion over the country, it remained Arab and, of course, Islamic in its culture, but with a unique and important Christian Arab presence.

Nineteenth-century European imperialism, however, resulted in a different sort of conquest. Western imperialism launched the Arab Mashreq, including Palestine, into an economic process of capitalist underdevelopment and dependency. As part of that process, the Arab Mashreq was economically and politically balkanized. World War I and the great Arab revolt against the Ottoman Turkish overlords promised to end this slide. But instead of a new era of independence, socioeconomic advancement, and modernization in a united Arab kingdom, that the leaders of the revolt hoped for and expected, the Arab Mashreq was jurisdictionally fragmented, and it succumbed to direct British and French colonialism.

Britain and France created and assumed control of the balkanized Arab Mashreq—the states of Syria, Lebanon, Palestine, Transjordan, and Iraq—under the auspices of the League of Nations. Palestine was unique among all the other new states in the region in that it became not merely a mandate of Britain but also a "promised homeland" for European Jews. During the mandate period (1917–1948), the powerful mix of forces unleashed on Palestine—British imperialism, Jewish settlement-colonialism, uneven capitalist development, and modernization—wrought profound and dramatic change in Palestinian society and overwhelmed the Palestinian people.

Unlike the neighboring Arab countries (Syria, Lebanon, Transjordan, Iraq, and Egypt), which achieved political independence after World War II, Palestine was de-Arabized and de-Islamized. In 1948 it became a Jewish state (Israel).

Those Palestinians who remained in what became the state of Israel survived not only as alienated strangers in their own country but also as a suppressed and exploited second-class minority. Other Palestinians were incorporated into Jordan (as the West Bank) or were administered by Egypt (in the Gaza Strip). All others became refugees in the newly independent Arab states. Thus, Palestine's people were in 1948 scattered into separate and disconnected communities residing in what had historically been Palestine and in neighboring Arab countries.

Despite the repeated traumas, losses, setbacks, dispossession, and dispersals, and despite the social, political, and ideological differences among the dispersed communities, the Palestinians in the diaspora nevertheless forged a national liberation movement (under the umbrella of a single organization, the PLO) that mobilized and politically united the communities, internationalized their cause, and gained them strong support and legitimacy—except, of course, from Israel and the United States. How the Palestinians forged their national liberation movement in the context of dispersal and occupation, how the PLO was born, how and why this movement and the PLO became transformed, and how the intifada affected their cause, modified their goals, and revised their strategy are the subjects of this chapter.

Palestinian National Liberation and the Palestinian Liberation Organization

In the immediate wake of their dispossession and expulsion from Palestine in 1948, the Palestinian refugees were so traumatized and consumed with mere physical survival (most became wards of the international community, the United Nations) that they were politically paralyzed. However, this paralysis did not last long; by 1957 it had given way to a new political activism anchored in a new and younger generation of Palestinians and in new ideologies. One current of the new activism was formal and bureaucratic, organized by Arab nationalist states through the Arab League, and led from above by a Palestinian professional elite. The other was varied, spontaneous, underground, and populist and emerged independently and almost simultaneously within most concentrations of the diaspora Palestinians.

Renewed Palestinian Activism in the Arab Political Context

The 1950s were a period of feverish political activism throughout the Arab Mashreq. Political parties or movements ranged ideologically from communist parties on the left to conservative movements such as al-Ikhwan al-Muslimin (the Muslim Brotherhood) on the right. The dominant and ascendant current, however, was secular pan-Arab nationalism. Parties and movements such as the Ba'ath Party, the Movement of Arab Nationalists (MAN, also called the Arab Nationalist Movement, or ANM), and the Nasserists (after the populist pan-Arab appeals of Egyptian president Gamal Abdul-Nasser) were active and competitive throughout all Mashreq Arab countries.[1] They vied with one another for influence in the Arab world and in support of Arab unity, Arab independence from European control, and especially the cause of Palestine. Pan-Arab parties called not only for the liberation (decolonization) of all Arab countries, including Palestine, from Western and Israeli political domination but also for Arab-controlled economic self-sufficiency and independent social and cultural transformation.

Through pan-Arab political movements, Palestinians thus found a window of opportunity for political expression and activism despite the repression of some of the insecure and suspicious Arab regimes. In responding to such pan-Arabist appeals, especially those of the Nasserists and the Ba'athists, which in political opposition to established Western-dependent, conservative, or liberal regimes (as in Jordan, Lebanon, Iraq, and even Syria at the time), Palestinians more readily earned the enmity of the Arab regimes under which they lived and that earlier had intervened on their behalf and lost the 1948 war with Israel.

Palestinians were swept up by the tide of pan-Arab nationalism in the 1950s and thus became politically active despite the lack of independent

Palestinian organizations. This pan-Arabist tide crested as a result of the 1956 Suez War (the second Arab-Israeli war), in which Israel, in collusion with Britain and France, invaded the Sinai Desert and the Suez Canal zone of Egypt through the Gaza Strip. That war rapidly transformed the political order of many Mashreq Arab states away from conservative or liberal Western-dependent regimes to regimes that were radically nationalist and internationally nonaligned. The war also gave a strong impetus to Palestinian activism. Besides Egypt, which in 1952 had experienced a coup d'état by pan-Arabist army officers led by Colonel Gamal Abdul-Nasser, Syria and Iraq also succumbed to such nationalist military regimes (eventually, in those instances, stabilized under wings of the Ba'ath Party). Although they did not give way to pan-Arabist regimes, Jordan and Lebanon nevertheless came under tremendous indigenous and regional nationalist pressure that forced the two states to align their domestic and foreign policies with those of the Arab nationalists;[2] many of the emergent oil-exporting states of the Arabian Peninsula did the same.

For the Palestinians, the new collective experience of defending themselves against Israel in Gaza in 1956 so soon after the 1948 Nakbah was an early stimulus for the reemergence of independent Palestinian political-military activism. Popular resistance erupted in the Gaza Strip against Israel's conquest and occupation of the territory during the Suez War. This resistance was aided by the training some Palestinians had received from the Egyptian army in the Gaza Strip between 1948 and 1956.[3] Israel was forced to withdraw from Sinai and the Gaza Strip under strong (especially US) international pressure. Soon after, Palestinians in the Gaza Strip and elsewhere began independent, clandestine campaigns of political organizing and military training.

The founders, organizers, and leaders of this movement were Gaza Strip university student activists studying in Egypt, who had surfaced after the Arab defeat in 1967 as the leaders of Fateh.[4] The name Fateh is the inverse Arabic acronym for Harakat al-Tahrir al-Watani al-Filastini (the Palestine National Liberation Movement). Fateh was led by a collective leadership of a few close comrades, including especially Salah Khalaf, whose nom de guerre was Abu Iyad; Khalil al-Wazir, or Abu Jihad; Farouk al-Qaddoumi, or Abu Lutuf; Khalid al-Hassan, or Abu Said; and Yasser Arafat, or Abu Ammar, who emerged as the spokesman (and leader) of Fateh and, in 1969, chairman of the PLO.[5]

What distinguished Fateh from the start was that its ideology went against the grain of the pan-Arabism of the times. The group believed that the cause of Palestine would be advanced and won only by Palestinians, not by the Arab states; thus it reversed the conventional view of pan-Arabism. Fateh remained the largest, most populist, and most influential of the new political and guerrilla organizations (to be identified and analyzed below) that have been established among the diaspora Palestinians and that together have defined Palestinian politics and the character of the struggle for the liberation of Palestine since 1968.

Arafat's Early Career

Palestinian leader Muhammad Yasser Arafat, whose career spanned four decades, died in Paris on Thursday, November 11, 2004, at the age of seventy-five. He was one of seven children born to Palestinian parents, Abdul-Raouf Arafat (from the al-Qudwah family of Gaza and Khan Younis), and mother, Zahwa (from the Abu al-Saoud family of Jerusalem). Born in Cairo on August 24, 1929, he spent his youth going back and forth between Cairo and Jerusalem. He acquired interest in the Palestine question at an early age, and by 1946, at the age of seventeen, he was smuggling weapons to Palestine from Cairo. He participated in some of the battles of the 1948 war and preached the idea that the Palestinians should do their own fighting to protect their country from the Zionists, and that Arab governments should confine their role to supplying military and material help. When he enrolled at King Fuad University (now Cairo University) in 1950, he was highly politicized, leading a number of demonstrations trying to persuade the Egyptian authorities to allow him to set up a military training camp in preparation for a future struggle inside Palestine. It was in student politics in the early 1950s that he met most of his future colleagues in the Palestine Liberation Organization, including Salah Khalaf (Abu Iyad) and Salim Zanoun (Abu Adeeb). In 1952, he was elected president of the Union of Palestinian Students, a position from which he addressed the new Egyptian revolutionary leaders, focusing on the need to create an independent Palestinian movement. He succeeded in gaining permission to publish a student newspaper, *The Voice of Palestine,* but he also succeeded in landing himself in an Egyptian jail because of his perceived cooperation with the Muslim Brotherhood, which had been outlawed.

According to his biographer, Alan Hart, Arafat's first major act that turned a regional conflict into a potential global confrontation was the sabotaging of a huge Israeli water supply near Faluja, which is adjacent to the Gaza Strip.[6] It provoked the February 28, 1955, Israeli attack on Gaza, bringing Nasser's Egypt into an eventually effective alliance with the Soviet Union. The resultant change in Egyptian policy and the subsequent Israeli invasion and occupation of Gaza and Sinai brought Arafat closer to Nasser's government, which had offered him a job in the Egyptian Army. However, by 1957, he had made his decision to leave Cairo for Kuwait in order to pursue his long-standing goal of organizing the Palestinians. There, together with Khalil al-Wazir (later known as Abu Jihad), Khalid al-Hasan, and other activists, he established the first underground cell of what became known as Fateh (Movement for the National Liberation of Palestine)-Harakat al-Tahrir al-Watani al-Filastini. It remained a nationalist movement, devoid of a real ideology and a clear vision.

Origins of the PLO and the PRM

Although the activities of the women's, workers', and teachers' unions and the charitable organizations in different diaspora communities were important in reaffirming Palestinian identity, developing political consciousness, creating representative institutions, establishing welfare institutions,[7] and restarting the process of building a (diasporawide) movement of national solidarity and mobilization, the student organizations gave this effort political content, direction, and method. As a group they constituted the first purely Palestinian diaspora organizations to call for an independent Palestine, mandatory conscription of Palestinians, and freedom of political action. The Palestinian student movement, independently in Egypt and Lebanon, created organizational structures that allowed the students to pursue clandestine political and military activism after their student days.[8] Others in the Gaza Strip, after Israel's withdrawal, established a legislative council there and set up the Palestine Arab National Union (PANU) as a framework for aboveground Palestinian political organizing. The Gaza-based efforts had the blessing and patronage of the nationalist Egyptian government of Abdul-Nasser.

Almost simultaneously, from his Beirut exile, al-Hajj Amin al-Husseini, the Mufti of Palestine, was pressuring the League of Arabs to form an independent Palestinian state. The league, which had increasingly come under the influence of the Arab nationalist regimes, decided to reconstitute the political organization of the dispersed Palestinians and give them a political voice. An early decision was to establish a Palestinian army, the Palestine Liberation Army (PLA), units of which would be under the command of the various Arab states' armies. A new Palestine National Council (PNC, a legislative congress) met in Jerusalem in 1964 and founded the PLO as its executive arm.

The PLO attempted to organize the diaspora Palestinians on a regional, not corporate, basis, opening offices in many Arab cities where they were concentrated. However, the bureaucratic and appointive character of the PLO and the PLA commanding officers were elitist, organized from the top, and did not succeed in inspiring or mobilizing the Palestinian people. From the beginning, there was no agreement as to the nature and goals of the proposed PLO, either among the Arab leaders or between those leaders and the grassroots Palestinian activists. But in the view of many of the Arab leaders, the organization was a means not only to pursue and influence the cause of Palestine but also to control Palestinian political and military activity on their borders, especially as they feared Israel's aggressive retaliation against them. Ironically, it was for those very reasons and because of their disappointment in the Arab states' inaction on the Palestine question that the new underground activists were at the time opposed to the elitist, bureaucratic PLO of the Arab League.

Two separate political efforts were evident among the Palestinians by the 1960s: The first was by the PLO—aboveground, elitist, toeing the line of the Arab states (especially Egypt), and legitimized by the Arab League; the second was by Fateh and other groups—underground, secretive, populist, activist, and radical. They competed with each other and to a lesser extent with the notables of the West Bank and the Gaza Strip for the support of the Palestinian people. Early in that period, several Palestinian unions and other sociopolitical organizations formally declared their support for the PLO. Thus, despite the absence of support from the underground political movement, the PLO was gaining legitimacy in the eyes of many Palestinians. The radical underground current that came to be collectively called Harakat al-Muqawama al-Filastiniyya (the Palestinian Resistance Movement), or simply al-Muqawama (the Resistance), and its guerrillas, the *feda'iyyin* ("self-sacrificers"), were independent of the PLO and anchored among the people and the dispersed but interconnected Palestinian civil institutions then emerging.

The ideology and strategy of the clandestine Palestinian groups were significantly influenced by the revolutions in Algeria, Cuba, and China and by the Vietnam War and the general radicalization of third-world peoples in the 1950s and 1960s. The PRM viewed these as revolutions and national liberation movements that had succeeded through guerrilla tactics and people's war in the face of overwhelming military power. Hence the populist Palestinian organizations came to see armed struggle as the key to redeeming the lost homeland.

Unlike the Arab nationalist states, these organizations believed that the liberation of Palestine would take place not in a conventional war against Israel but through a long-drawn-out struggle of guerrilla warfare and people's war. Fateh specified four stages of guerrilla warfare: hit-and-run operations, limited confrontations, temporary occupation of liberated zones, and, finally, permanent occupation of liberated areas. Fateh accordingly launched its first *feda'iyyin* guerrilla attack against Israel on January 1, 1965, a date the PLO now regularly celebrates as the start of the contemporary "Palestinian revolution." Another important political and guerrilla group, the Popular Front for the Liberation of Palestine (PFLP), also began both guerrilla warfare and underground political organizing in order to prepare the people for a long-term struggle and to gain pan-Arab support.[9]

Although most organizations agreed on the form of struggle, they disagreed on the role of the Arab states in that struggle and on Palestinian relations with those states. The growth of Arab nationalism in the two decades after World War II led some Palestinian activists to theorize that common Arab action—that is, Arab unity—was the road to the liberation of Palestine. This was the view not only of the PFLP but of many other organizations that were influenced by one or another variation of pan-Arab ideology (Nasserist, Syrian Ba'athist, or Iraqi Ba'athist). Fateh leaders adopted the inverse view: They were convinced that the liberation of Palestine was the road to Arab unity.[10] Fateh believed Arab armies should defend their borders against Israel and support and protect the Palestinian guerrillas returning from military operations inside Israel. The PFLP and other more radical groups, however, believed this approach was not possible unless Arab revolutionary regimes gave the Palestinian guerrillas genuine, active backing. Thus the PFLP called for revolution in the entire Arab world as the context and prelude to the liberation of Palestine. This strategy threatened established Arab regimes.

These conflicting views not only derived from but also contributed to the fundamental contradiction that marked the entire history of relations between the militant and populist Palestinian guerrilla movement and the Arab states. Both sides of the Palestinian liberation movement (the pan-Arabists and the Palestine-first theoreticians) believed that they could not win against Israel without the support of the Arab states, and yet the movement's autonomous growth and development always led to disputes with the host countries over either sovereignty or foreign policy.[11] In Jordan and Lebanon, it was the former; in Egypt, Syria, and Iraq, it was the latter. These contradictions also generated different policies and practices by the Palestinian organizations toward the respective Arab regimes. For example, in the gathering conflict between the Palestinian guerrillas and the Jordanian regime, the radical pan-Arabist groups called for elimination of the regime whereas Fateh advocated coexistence and mutual noninterference in internal affairs but support for the guerrillas. In the end, neither practice was viable, nor were the Palestinian guerrillas savaged by the regular Jordanian armed forces during Black September 1970. With regard to Egypt and Syria, the PRM opposed their policy of accepting in 1970 the plan of US secretary of state William Rogers for a negotiated settlement based on UN Security Council Resolution 242: the land-for-peace formula. Peace with and recognition of Israel on the basis of this UN resolution by these leading Arab states would have undermined Palestinian rights and the PRM's ideological consensus and political-military momentum. In short, Palestinians feared that they would be sold out by the Arab states.

Although united in their overall goal, then, Palestinian politics and activity in the diaspora were diverse, complex, dynamic, and often contradictory. Accordingly, a central concern and goal of the leaders of the PRM was always (except when Arafat unilaterally signed the Oslo Accords) political consensus and unity among the different groups. Consensus and unity were also important in securing wide support not only among the Palestinian people but also among the Arab countries. Nevertheless, all efforts at genuine organizational unity among the groups at various times failed because of a number of complex internal and external factors, and the PLO remained the umbrella organization for the groups until the Oslo process, as will be seen later, tore it apart.

A Turning Point: The 1967 War and the Rise of the Palestinian Resistance Movement

The official PLO and the organizations of the PRM were separate, unconnected, and competing movements for a brief period between 1964 and 1968. The 1967 Arab-Israeli war, however, changed that and the course of history in the Middle East. In six short days, the nationalist Arab republics of Egypt, Syria, and Iraq (all of which had promised the Arab peoples political independence, socioeconomic transformation, jobs, education, economic well-being, and the liberation of Palestine), in alliance with monarchic Jordan, were defeated by Israel. The war changed the balance of power not only between Israel and the surrounding Arab states but also among those Arab states, especially the nationalist republics and the conservative oil-exporting monarchies of the Arabian Peninsula. For the Palestinians, that war also tipped the balance of power to the *feda'iyyin* organizations of the PRM against the discredited elitist establishment of the PLO, which was associated with the defeated Arab states.

The Arab world was reeling from the defeat. A sense of doom and paralysis had set in, especially in the defeated countries. This created a regional political vacuum and gave the *feda'iyyin* guerrilla groups the opportunity to forge ahead autonomously. In short, they became, perhaps for the first time in recent history, independent actors in the Palestinian, Arab, and Middle Eastern arenas. Their revolutionary ideology was popular and was spreading widely within the diaspora Palestinian communities and the Arab world. But the conservative Arab monarchies, especially those of the Arabian Peninsula, who feared the "Arab revolution" as much as Israel, also emerged from under the shadow of the nationalist republics. Thus two opposing political tendencies appeared simultaneously in the Arab Mashreq: a revolutionary one led by the Palestinians and a conservative, accommodationist one led by Saudi Arabia and a defeated and chastened Arab nationalist Egypt of Abdul-Nasser.

Most significantly for Palestine and the Palestinians, Israel conquered and occupied the remaining Arab areas of Palestine—the West Bank (including the Old City and East Jerusalem) and the Gaza Strip. It also occupied the Golan Heights of Syria and all of the Sinai Peninsula up to the eastern bank of the Suez Canal in Egypt. Israel's conquests thus brought the rest of historical Palestine and all its resident Palestinians under Israeli rule. After the pivotal 1948 Palestine catastrophe, the 1967 war redefined and restructured the politics of the Middle East.

In the wake of the 1967 defeat, the discredited and militarily devastated nationalist Arab states were unable to mount any kind of resistance to the Israeli occupation. Only the Palestinian *feda'iyyin* had the temerity and will to launch guerrilla attacks on the overwhelming Israeli occupation forces. In 1967 the Palestinian *feda'iyyin* attempted to establish underground cells and bases in the occupied West Bank, in an effort to start guerrilla attacks from within the occupied territories. However, failure in the West Bank forced the retreat of the *feda'iyyin* militants to secure bases, principally across the Jordan River, and allowed attacks on Israeli occupation troops and installations from those bases in Jordan. In March 1968 Israel launched a punitive invasion of the East Bank of Jordan, whose objective was the small village and refugee camp of Al-Karameh, a base for the Palestinian guerrillas. Instead of fading and withdrawing from the onslaught of a powerful force, as guerrilla tactics prescribe, the Palestinian *feda'iyyin*, principally those of Fateh, stood their ground and fought a desperate but heroic battle against the superior Israeli force.[12] In so doing they inspired the regular Jordanian forces, deployed in the neighboring hills, which then joined the battle and, together with the *feda'iyyin,* bloodied the Israelis and forced them to retreat behind their cease-fire lines in the occupied West Bank.

Although the 1967 Arab-Israeli war was a turning point in the contemporary political history of the Arab-Israeli conflict, the inspiring battle of Al-Karameh was the pivotal counterpoint that allowed the radical, revolutionary guerrilla organizations to move aboveground, take off politically, and redefine the nature and tactics of the Palestinian-Israeli conflict. Tens of thousands of Palestinian and Arab volunteers joined the ranks of the *feda'iyyin* in the next few months.[13] The new ideology of national liberation—people's war and guerrilla tactics—spread like wildfire in the Arab Mashreq, and the Arab-Israeli conflict came to be refocused increasingly as the Palestinian-Israeli struggle.[14]

The battle of Al-Karameh had several meanings for both Palestinians and Arabs. In Arabic the noun *al-karameh* means "dignity," and the battle was seen as the beginning of the restoration of Arab dignity after the humiliating defeat of the Six-Day War. Further, it was fought by Palestinians who had been distrusted and hounded previously by the defeated states that had promised to liberate Palestine. Perhaps more significant, the revolutionary ideology of the *feda'iyyin,* an amalgam of third-world–style ideas of social, economic, and political-military revolution—and thus radical societal transformation—became a popular and widespread political stance throughout the eastern Arab world. The popularity of the *feda'iyyin* guerrillas and their organizations was reflected not only in the Arab media but also in the support and praise they received from ordinary people, intellectuals, political leaders, and states. For example, unable to contain their rapidly rising influence in his own kingdom in the wake of the 1967 defeat, King Hussein of Jordan declared in 1969 that "we are all *feda'iyyin.*"

One of the major consequences of the rise and popularity of the *feda'iyyin* was radicalization of the PLO. In the 1968 PNC meeting the *feda'iyyin* formally gained control of the PLO and, with it, inherited the formal legitimacy of the Arab League. An internal debate on whether the PLO should be one group among many existing ones or the representative for all was resolved in favor of the latter.[15] The radical militant groups of *feda'iyyin* thus turned the PLO into the revolutionary umbrella organization under the influence and leadership of Fateh and Fateh's leader, Arafat.[16] Understanding the following political history of the Mashreq, the Palestine question, the Arab-Israeli conflict, the cold war in the region, and the "peace process" of the 1990s depends on a knowledge of the role and actions of the revolutionary

PLO of the *feda'iyyin* and its long-term political transformation, deradicalization, and eventual demise.

The Arrival–and Departure–of the Revolutionary Moment

The *feda'iyyin*'s and their radical Arab allies' call for mobilizing, training, and arming all of the Arab people for a people's war against Israel was ignored by the fearful defeated rulers, including the charismatic and popular Abdul-Nasser of Egypt. The revolutionary moment had arrived in the Arab east, but it was to pass quickly. No general and popular mobilization was instituted by any Arab leader or regime. Instead, all the political leaders of the radical nationalist republics and the conservative monarchies closed ranks and pledged to support one another under the ideology of Arab solidarity, at the same time paying much lip service to the Palestinian movement. The Egyptian regime of Abdul-Nasser agreed to an accommodation with the conservative oil-exporting monarchies of the Arabian Peninsula (thus ending the Arab cold war),[17] launched a war of attrition against the Israeli army entrenched on the east bank of the Suez Canal, but also consented in 1970 to the special mission of mediation by Gunnar Jarring, envoy of the United Nations, for a political solution to the conflict between Israel and the Arab states on the basis of UN Security Council Resolution 242, which specified land for peace. By these actions, Abdul-Nasser in effect abandoned the liberation of Palestine as a firm goal of Arab nationalist ideology—and thus abandoned the cause of the Palestinians—and sought instead only "elimination of the consequences of the (1967 Israeli) aggression," a slogan that meant the restoration of the territorial status quo ante in return for an Arab-Israeli peace. The Palestinian people, the *feda'iyyin*, and the new leaders of the PLO felt betrayed.[18]

In Jordan, where the Palestinian *feda'iyyin* were based and where their influence was growing by leaps and bounds, a power struggle between them and the regime of King Hussein quickly erupted despite his rhetoric of support. Indeed the exaggerated rhetorical support by nearly all political leaders and Arab governments and the unprecedented popular political and financial support by all the Arab people may have lulled the *feda'iyyin* and masked an Arab state policy of retrenchment and accommodation (with one another; with the West, especially the United States; and indirectly with Israel) by all the discredited regimes. Thus, while declaring his support, King Hussein was maneuvering to contain, if not suppress, the *feda'iyyin*. The leftist *feda'iyyin* organizations, especially the PFLP and the Democratic Front for the Liberation of Palestine (DFLP), were suspicious and clashed with Hussein's army a number of times in the years right after the 1967 war. Unlike the reluctant Fateh leadership, they pushed for a confrontation with King Hussein's regime and expected (as did Fateh) his army (which had not only a large number of Palestinians but also some who were in important positions) to crack and join them. However, Hussein successfully prepared the army and the local political climate for a showdown with the increasingly arrogant and provocative *feda'iyyin*. His regime stoked the communal and ethnic rivalry between Palestinians and Transjordanians (especially between the *feda'iyyin* and Hussein's army, which was composed largely of Transjordanian bedouins). Also, to mobilize strong opposition to the *feda'iyyin*, Hussein played up, in a traditional and religiously conservative society, the threat of their secular social revolutionary (Marxist and Maoist) ideology.

In September 1970 King Hussein launched a vicious assault on the *feda'iyyin* bases in the urban Palestinian refugee camps in and around the capital of Amman. As the Jordanian army suffered minimal Palestinian desertions in the course of the fighting, the result was a bloody and costly defeat for the guerrillas at the hands of the more professional and heavily armed Jordanian units. The Arab world watched in horror and helplessness the high Palestinian civilian toll and the demise of its new heroes. The halfhearted intervention of the radical nationalist Ba'ath regime of Syria in support of the *feda'iyyin* came to naught. And despite their radical pan-Arabist ideology, the troops of Ba'athist Iraq, who had been stationed in Jordan since the 1967 war, also watched the unfolding bloody drama without intervening.

The fighting during that month of Black September in Amman ended only because of the active mediation of Abdul-Nasser. But the defeat of the *feda'iyyin* in Jordan (and the untimely death of Abdul-Nasser later that same year) was the end of the revolutionary moment in the Arab world. Because of the defeat in Jordan and local and regional changes, the *feda'iyyin* were forced to scale down their revolutionary political program sharply, although not their rhetoric. Nonetheless, although the revolutionary program was effectively abandoned, the goal of "liberating Palestine" by other (e.g., diplomatic) means was not. The revolutionary moment had passed, but popular momentum and determination propelled the PLO forward.[19]

The PLO of the *Feda'iyyin*: Structure, Function, and Dynamics

Once the *feda'iyyin* had taken control of the PLO, the PLO also became largely independent of direct control by any one Arab government. As the original elitist and traditional leadership was removed, the PLO came to be anchored in the principal autonomous political and guerrilla organizations: Fateh under the leadership of Arafat; the PFLP under the leadership of George Habash, a physician from Lydda; the DFLP (a splinter of the PFLP) under the leadership of Nayef Hawatmeh, a Jordanian, who still heads the DFLP; the PFLP–General Command (another split from the PFLP) under the leadership of Ahmad Jibril, a Palestinian officer in the Syrian army; other smaller organizations; and in 1987 the Palestine Communist Party (the Palestine People's Party, or PPP, after 1991) of the West Bank and the Gaza Strip. The only major political organization that has remained outside the framework of the PLO is the newest, Hamas (an acronym for Harakat al-Tahrir al-Islami, "Islamic Liberation Movement," and an Arabic word that means "zeal" or "enthusiasm"), which emerged in 1987 and is based primarily in the Gaza Strip, as is al-Jihad al-Islami (Islamic Jihad), a similar but smaller and more radical organization. As were the *feda'iyyin* of the 1950s and 1960s, Hamas and al-Jihad al-Islami have also been clandestine movements whose armed wings for the most part remained underground even after the establishment of the limited Palestinian Authority in the Gaza Strip and the West Bank in 1994–1995.

PLO Expansion and Development

The PLO under the *feda'iyyin* experienced two major spurts of expansion and development. In the first, in 1969, the PLO was reorganized and consolidated internally, and new functions were added; the second happened during the civil war in Lebanon (1975–1982), when the PLO's social and economic functions were dramatically enlarged.

Besides the PNC (the Palestinian legislature-in-exile) and the Executive Committee, the new leaders of the PLO established the Central Council (a consultative-legislative subgroup of the PNC), the Political Department (the agency for external relations), and the Military Department. The Palestine Liberation Army was composed of four units—the Yarmouk Brigade, the Hittin Division (based in Syria), the 'Ain Jalut Forces (based in Egypt), and the Qadisiyyah Division (based in Iraq)—all of which were named after historic victories that had preserved the Arab and Islamic character of Palestine and the region: The Yarmouk battle, on the border of Palestine, was a pivotal seventh-century victory of the Arab-Islamic forces over the Byzantine armies in the Near East that allowed the Islamization and Arabization of the Fertile Crescent. At Hittin in Palestine in the twelfth century, Saladin defeated the Crusader armies and re-Arabized and Islamized the region.

'Ain Jalut, also in Palestine, was the site of a battle in the thirteenth century in which the Mongol invaders were defeated by the rising Egyptian-based Mamluke dynasty. And the battle of Al-Qadisiyyah in Iraq in the seventh century completed the conquest of Iraq by the Arab-Islamic forces against the then non-Islamic Persians.

The new PLO also set up the Palestine National Fund (PNF); the Department of Education; the Red Crescent Society for health services; Departments of Information, Popular Mobilization, and the Occupied Homeland; a research center; a planning center; a social affairs institute; and the Samed (Economic) Institute (originally an organization for the support of the children of *feda'iyyin* martyrs who had fallen in battle or had been killed by Israeli bombing).[20] In effect, the PLO grew into an organization that provided needed services, protection, and leadership directly to the diaspora Palestinians, indirectly to those under occupation, and in a more veiled manner even to those who had remained inside Israel, the so-called Israeli Arabs. By the mid-1970s, the PLO had developed the structure of a de facto government-in-exile. It and its constituent groups raised funds from a number of sources: private contributions from Palestinians and other sympathetic Arabs and Muslims, taxes on Palestinians employed in the Arabian Peninsula (collected by state governments on behalf of the PLO), Arab governments, the PLO's own investments, and international sources. In its peak years before its exit from Beirut, the PLO budget reached several hundred million dollars a year.

The PLO had also achieved several important political goals by the mid-1970s. During the 1973 Arab summit in Algiers, the Arab states recognized the PLO as the "sole representative of the Palestinians." Again, at the 1974 Arab summit in Rabat, the PLO was recognized, despite the objections of King Hussein (who still hoped to regain the West Bank and whose kingdom had a Palestinian majority even among the East Bank residents), as "the sole legitimate representative of the Palestinian people."

In a series of resolutions starting in 1969 (especially Resolution 2535), the United Nations General Assembly recognized and reaffirmed the "inalienable rights of the people of Palestine." In 1974 the General Assembly also recognized the PLO as the sole legitimate representative of the Palestinian people; invited Arafat to address the assembly; voted Resolution 3236, the most comprehensive international affirmation of Palestinian rights of self-determination and national independence; and granted the PLO permanent observer status at the United Nations with rights of participation in most of its agencies. Recognition of Palestinian rights and PLO legitimacy had already been achieved in many important regional organizations: the Islamic Conference, the Nonaligned Countries, the Organization of African Unity, the Afro-Asian Peoples' Solidarity Organization, the Warsaw Pact members, the World Peace Council, and more than one hundred individual states, most of them in the third world and the Soviet bloc. Through these diplomatic achievements, the PLO internationalized the recognition of and support for Palestinian rights as never before.

The second period of expansion in the structure and function of the PLO was during the civil war in Lebanon. The PLO was faced with a social crisis among its people, who had been displaced in that civil war, losing their homes and jobs and becoming destitute. It rose to the occasion, established nearly fifty different industrial and business enterprises, expanded its social services and training institutes, enlarged its own bureaucracy, and, including its military units, employed close to 70 percent of the Palestinian labor force in Lebanon. These achievements gave the PLO structural solidity and strong legitimacy in the eyes of the Palestinian people and others.

The PLO: Ideology, Strategy, and Peace Plans

Internal Divisions

Ever since coming under the control of the *feda'iyyin* guerrilla organizations, the PLO has been dominated by Fateh and Fateh's strategy. One source of difference and division within the PLO has been the differences in ideology and practice of Fateh and of the internal loyal "opposition," the ideologically leftist PFLP, and to a lesser extent the DFLP and the other less autonomous groups. Fateh was populist and nationalist and actually opposed to formulating an ideological program of its own. Its only clear formulation, other than the goal of liberating Palestine, was the method by which it would be liberated: through revolutionary violence or a people's war of national liberation, including guerrilla tactics, a significant component of the overall political struggle against the Israeli enemy. This revolutionary armed struggle, Fateh believed, would also mobilize the people. Fateh's simple program and ideology appealed to all Palestinian social classes, from the proletarianized refugees to the high bourgeoisie. Thus Fateh's revolutionary rhetoric and strategy never achieved a fundamental or radical break with the Palestinian or Arab social or political past.

Fateh preached populist revolution to its Palestinian constituency but stability, support, and nonintervention in the deradicalized and conservative Arab regional environment. It effected no social or economic revolution among its refugee constituency, although it did provide extensive social services. Its leadership was pragmatic and retained strong and mutually supportive relations with both the deradicalized nationalist Arab states and the conservative, oil-exporting monarchies of the Arabian Peninsula.[21] The oil-exporting regimes therefore gave both Fateh and the PLO generous financial support until the 1991 Gulf War. Despite occasional internal splits, factors such as its extensive financial resources, its populist and traditional nationalist appeal, and perhaps its simple program and loose organization helped Fateh become and stay the most popular and important political organization in the diaspora communities and in the West Bank and the Gaza Strip territories under occupation. In contrast, the radical rhetoric, ideology, and practices of the leftist organizations, especially the PFLP and the DFLP, isolated them from broad financial support and kept them small in number, although not in influence.

Most crucial, these factors also allowed Fateh to transform its goal and strategy: from liberating all of Palestine through armed struggle to creating an independent state in the West Bank and the Gaza Strip through diplomacy. The loyal opposition to Fateh until the 1993 signing of the Oslo and Cairo Accords (a serious break occurred thereafter) was made up of the PFLP, DFLP, and other lesser organizations. Of course, the newer and more radical Hamas and al-Jihad al-Islami, as stated earlier, are outside the umbrella of the PLO and seem unalterably opposed to the PLO and the Oslo Accords.

Deriving from a strong pan-Arab nationalist background, the PFLP transformed itself into a Marxist-Leninist party in the late 1960s, becoming militant and revolutionary in its social and economic agendas. It viewed as enemies of the Palestinian people and its goal of liberating Palestine not only Israel (and internationally organized Zionism) and imperialism (represented after World War II by the United States) but also the reactionary Arabs (especially the conservative oil-exporting regimes and the other Arab comprador bourgeoisies). It defined the enemies and friends of the Palestinian revolution in terms of class. Thus, for the liberation of Palestine to succeed, revolution must take place among dispossessed Palestinians and, in the Arab world, among the disadvantaged classes of peasants, workers, and the petty bourgeoisie. The PFLP insisted on the need for revolution not only by the Palestinian people and society but also by the rest of the Arab world, and it even saw itself as part of the worldwide revolutionary forces. It thus rejected all "defeatist peace proposals" and sought alliances with revolutionary or progressive political groups in the Arab world, the third world, and Western Europe.

For the PFLP, liberated Palestine was to be not only secular and democratic but also a socialist country. In the context of the Arab world, the PFLP tended to work politically at the grassroots level and to build bridges with the opposition parties or movements, whereas Fateh (and the PLO it controlled) increasingly stressed working with the governments and formal institutions of the respective countries. In short, the PFLP and its cadres emerged as the hard-liners in the politics of the diaspora Palestinians, whereas Fateh and its leadership can be portrayed as, at best, flexible and pragmatic and, at worst, too accommodating to superior power and soft on principle. From the point of view of the PFLP, Fateh has, since the early 1970s, given up on the revolution in the Palestinian and Arab political environment necessary for the long-term struggle, has become contented and bureaucratized, is tired of armed struggle, has come under the influence of the Palestinian bourgeoisie and its Arab allies, has developed a stake in the Arab state system (the status quo), and has begun to seek a diplomatic solution from a weak and disadvantaged position.

We can summarize the PFLP-Fateh differences as ones over goals (until 1983, liberation of all of Palestine versus the creation of an independent state in the West Bank and the Gaza Strip), strategy (armed struggle, sociopolitical revolution, and diplomacy versus diplomacy alone), and tactics (until 1972, the use of external operations versus those only inside Israel). In general, it was a difference over the nature of the Palestinian national liberation movement itself: Was it a revolution or merely an independence movement? For the PFLP, it was the former; for Fateh, the latter. And what of the nature of liberated Palestine? Would it be a socialist Arab state with a Jewish minority, as the PFLP imagined it, or an independent ordinary Arab state in the West Bank and the Gaza Strip, as Fateh planned it? The PFLP is much smaller and has had far fewer resources than Fateh, but it has still always commanded a strong minority following and a stronger overall political influence. Because many Arab and Palestinian intellectuals, current and former activists and sympathizers in the Arab nationalist movements (especially MAN), and journalists supported it, the PFLP has developed greater influence than its size would suggest. In one sense, the PFLP and its leader, Habash, have been "the conscience" of the Palestinian national liberation movement. This difference in both approach and principle between mainstream Fateh and the PFLP is clear from the opposing stands the two organizations have taken on a number of issues over the years, the most significant of these being policy differences over the Oslo Accords and derivative accords. The PFLP denounced the accords and the defeatist leadership of the PLO and in 1996 formally withdrew from the Arafat-controlled PLO.

The second important group in the Palestinian political divide is the DFLP. Having split from the PFLP in 1969, the Democratic Front differed from the PFLP during the cold war in that its ideology was more orthodox Marxist and much more attuned to Soviet policy. In general, however, the DFLP has been more similar to than different from the PFLP. Its major contribution is a theoretical reconceptualization of the Palestine question and its formulation of a solution: Liberated Palestine, it says, cannot be Arab, Muslim, or Jewish but must be nonsectarian, a "secular democratic state" where Muslims, Jews, and Christians are equal citizens. For a while during the 1970s, this was the political platform and preferred position of the Palestine national liberation movement and many of its cadres and intellectuals. As discussed in the next section, this notion was not voted officially into any PNC resolution. Events and strategic realignments in the Middle East moved fast throughout the 1970s and 1980s and favored a new concept: the "two-state solution" (Israeli and Palestinian states side by side in historical Palestine), which became and continues to be the formal Palestinian position for solving the Palestine conflict.

The left wing of Fateh, a minority coalition of several political tendencies, played a critical role in keeping the organization and the loyal opposition (PFLP, DFLP, and others) unified during serious policy rifts. However, beginning with differences in policy in the Lebanon war in 1976, leaders of the leftist faction within Fateh drifted away from the mainstream and in 1983, after the disastrous siege of Beirut by Israel and the exit of the PLO from the city, organized an internal rebellion that led to a small-scale Palestinian civil war.

Although the 1983 internal Fateh rebellion failed, it had serious consequences, not the least of which was that it left little or no internal opposition to Arafat's policy and leadership. Arafat consolidated his hold and became dictatorial and autocratic. He tended to ignore the consultative, legislative, and executive institutions of the PLO and to make unilateral decisions with a group of dependent allies and clients. It was in this context that Arafat and three other secret collaborators agreed to the Oslo Accords.

The Palestine People's Party (formerly the Palestine Communist Party, founded in the West Bank during the Jordanian era, 1951–1967) became increasingly active and important during Israel's occupation and the eruption of the intifada. It developed a significant following, especially in the West Bank. Its political platform was far more moderate than that of the hard-line PFLP and thus was closer to that of the centrist Fateh, which sought a diplomatic resolution to the Palestine question. Some of the PPP's leaders were deported by Israel from the occupied territories, and one, Suleiman al-Najjab, officially joined the Executive Committee of the PLO as representative of the party in 1988. The PPP was central in organizing the unified underground leadership of the intifada. Although a strong supporter of Arafat, the "peace process" in general, the Madrid conference, and the Washington negotiations, the PPP broke with Arafat over the Oslo and Cairo Accords. Since the establishment of the Palestinian Authority, the leaders of the PPP have disagreed among themselves, and the party has lost popularity and influence. Nonetheless, its skilled and activist cadres continue to fill important leadership positions in the social service and cultural organizations that were so important in mobilizing people during the intifada. Some of these organizations are now central in the "third alternative," a movement that opposes both the "capitulationist" Arafat faction and the militant and socially conservative Hamas and Islamic Jihad.

Given the sharp differences in both ideology and method among the principal Palestinian organizations and also among the clients of Arab regimes, the PLO and the Palestine national liberation movement in general have been saddled with problems of unity and cohesion, finding shared goals and common strategy. The differences among the constituent organizations of the PLO over short- and long-term goals, tactics, and direction have called into question the legitimacy of the PLO leadership and its ability to act. This dilemma has become more complex with the rise of Hamas and al-Jihad al-Islami in the Gaza Strip and the West Bank, as their ideology and tactics are considerably at odds with those of the secular, Fateh-controlled PLO.

Whereas the PLO follows a secular nationalist political line, Islamic political ideology sees all of Palestine as holy Muslim land (indeed, *waqf* land): This land must be liberated, and an Islamic society and state must be established there. Muslim strategy for this liberation has always been jihad ("struggle"), but this was not practiced by the Islamist groups until after the intifada broke out. During the intifada the Islamic movement adopted more activist, militant, and violent tactics against the Israeli occupation army. Immediately upon the outbreak of the intifada in 1987, the clerical leadership of the Islamic movement in Gaza organized Hamas to pursue the intifada and actively resist Israel. Hamas declared its goal of the liberation of all of Palestine and its strategy of armed struggle at a time when mainstream Fateh and other constituent members of the PLO had abandoned this ideology and strategy. Hamas has refused to join the PLO except on its own terms, as the majority party, and has challenged the Palestinian Authority , which was established in 1994 in what were stated by the Oslo Declaration of Principles to be autonomous areas in Gaza and small parts of the West Bank. Hamas rejected the Israel-PLO Declaration of Principles (the Oslo Accords) and the derivative accords. Its suicidal operations and those of al-Jihad al-Islami since the signing of the declaration have complicated Palestinian-Israeli negotiations and have reinforced Israeli insistence on security issues. Hamas and the Islamic political movement are engaged not only in resisting the Israeli occupation but also in a power struggle with the PLO and the Palestinian Authority in both the "autonomous" and the occupied territories.

Political consensus sustained the legitimacy and relative coherence of the PLO despite its exile to Tunis and financial decline during the 1980s. This consensus also allowed the weakened PLO, a year after the start of the intifada, to pursue aggressive diplomatic initiatives that opened the door to dialogue with the United States but only partially broke the Palestinian-Israeli impasse. However, the consensus began to fray over the terms of the 1991 Madrid conference and was finally torn apart by Arafat's acceptance of the Oslo, Cairo, and Oslo II Accords. Arafat, according to the opposition, had gone much too far (that is, conceded much too much) beyond the formal Palestinian consensus codified in the PNC resolutions.

The key element in Palestinian political unity in the context of communal and institutional dispersal has long been agreement on goals and aspirations. But just as important to the PLO was basing decisions on a consensus of all the major factions. Although consensus over the ultimate goals was relatively easy to achieve and may have given the organization coherence and solidity, it often created paralysis in decisionmaking and in the interpretation and implementation of those decisions. When consensus was not reached, especially on pivotal issues of diplomacy (e.g., whether to accept a diplomatic route or the terms of a certain peace initiative advanced by others), the organization was politically immobilized, and Arafat often acted unilaterally, without clear authority. These problems were compounded by nepotism, corruption, and autocracy on the part of Arafat and the Fateh leadership of the PLO. Such divisiveness caused a breakdown in the functioning of PLO institutions and thus, at frequent and crucial times, not only paralyzed the PLO and allowed Arafat to act with impunity but also hurt the cause of Palestine and its people. The PLO's paralysis, for example, allowed Arafat to singlehandedly establish the Palestinian Authority in the West Bank and the Gaza Strip and to merge it with the PLO bureaucracy, without any formal or official authority.

The PLO, which had always represented the whole Palestinian people, became, in the immediate wake of the Oslo agreement, indistinguishable from the Palestinian administration of the autonomous territories. It effectively lost its national, all-Palestinian representative function and its policy-making authority. It left the diaspora communities—the largest segment of the total Palestinian population—without the needed social and economic services, disenfranchised politically, and bereft of any organization to pursue their neglected rights.

Evolution of Ideology and Strategy

In the regional and the international (especially third-world) context of decolonization and nationalism, the *feda'iyyin* guerrilla groups came to a basic consensus that Israel, a European settler colonial project in the era of decolonization, was anachronistic. Thus it was the right of the dispossessed Palestinian people to liberate their homeland from the colonial settlers, to return to their homes, and to rebuild their independent Arab country, itself an inseparable part of the larger Arab *umma*.

This early political consensus was enshrined in the national charter of the PLO (1968) and only peripherally addressed the status of the Israeli Jews: Those who had resided in the country before "the Zionist invasion" were welcome to stay and live as Palestinians (Article 6); by implication all others were not. And as the charter stated, "The partition of Palestine in 1947 and the creation of Israel are both null and void [as is the] Balfour Declaration" (Articles 19 and 20). In general, the substance of the charter affirmed the Arabness of Palestine and the right of its dispossessed people to struggle for its liberation. In any case, the radical political consensus of the high revolutionary moment (1968–1970), when the PLO was committed to an uncompromising revolutionary approach, was not to last long, as first the 1970 Black September attack on the guerrillas, then the October 1973 Arab-Israeli war, and then the diplomatic offensive of President Anwar Sadat of Egypt made dramatic changes in the political climate of the region. In the atmosphere of the Soviet-US détente of the time, the more orthodox Marxist DFLP's proposal for a "secular democratic" state in Palestine for all its people—Muslim, Jewish, and Christian—eventually emerged as the PLO's new consensus and was offered as the peace plan of the Palestinian militants.

As the solution for the Palestine problem, this view of a future secular democratic state in Palestine, where the Palestinian natives (Muslim and Christian) and the foreign Jewish settlers would live together in harmony and democracy, coexisted with the vision of the PLO charter, which stressed an Arab Palestine that in effect actually superseded the charter. What is important about the proposal of a democratic secular state in *all* of Palestine is that it went beyond the vague concept of coexistence and acknowledged the presence of two nationalities (ethnic groups), or nations, in the country. The recognition of two different nations in one country meant, from the PLO leftist factions' Marxist-Leninist perspective, a recognition of the right of each to self-determination and therefore to separation or independence and thus implicitly meant recognition of the state of Israel. A secular democratic state in Palestine was declared the PLO's just solution to the Palestinian-Israeli conundrum. Palestinian activists considered this a moral, revolutionary proposal by the victims of the conflict. Israel and its Western supporters, however, cynically dismissed or ignored the proposal. Nevertheless, the goal of establishing in Palestine a secular democratic state for all the people of Palestine, not excluding any one religious group or sect, also prepared the ground for a later debate on the two-state solution.

In the rapidly changing context of the Middle East of the 1970s—including Egypt's go-it-alone policy in search of peace with Israel and the rise of oil revenues and of Arab financial and diplomatic power—the prospects for diplomatic initiatives in the area increased. Under the combined external pressure of the Soviet Union and the Arab states and internal pressure of Fateh and the DFLP, the PLO reformulated its ideology and developed a new policy goal: Instead of a secular democratic state in a unified Palestine, it proposed a two-state solution to the Israel-Palestine dilemma. Israel and a Palestinian state would exist side by side in historical Palestine. The compromise language that passed as a resolution in the PNC, with the support of the PFLP, was the idea of establishing a "national authority" in any part of Palestine liberated from occupation.

For the PFLP, the DFLP, and other radicals, the projected "national authority" would be a revolutionary one, in control of liberated zones in Palestine, which would be bases for carrying on the armed struggle. However, for Fateh, and therefore the PLO, it meant simply a Palestinian authority (as a basis for an eventual state) in any part of Palestine liberated from or relinquished by Israel, an authority that would coexist with Israel. Although dramatically different, the two interpretations nonetheless coexisted within the movement, paved the way for acceptance of the Arab League's peace plan in 1983, and did not cause any serious or paralytic divisiveness within the PLO until the Oslo Accords. Of course, as will be seen in later chapters, limited autonomy over civilian matters in the Gaza Strip and the West Bank population centers as prescribed by the Declaration of

Principles and subsequent agreements was a far cry from the "national authority" envisioned by either mainstream Fateh or the radical PFLP. It was neither a liberated nor a sovereign zone.

The PLO and the rest of the world were stunned by Egyptian president Sadat's visit to Jerusalem and Egypt's acceptance of the Camp David Accords in 1978, as well as Egypt's signing of a bilateral peace treaty with Israel in 1979—developments agreed to by Israel and Egypt under the auspices of the United States and thrust in the disbelieving faces of the Palestinians and all other Arabs. As a face-saving mechanism for these accords, the Egyptian-Israeli agreement provided—without any consultation with the PLO—for a regime of Palestinian autonomy (over the people but not the land) in the West Bank and the Gaza Strip for five years. In the fourteenth PNC meeting in 1979, the PLO formally rejected this autonomy provision and the Israel-Egypt peace treaty itself; the rest of the Arab world did the same. The Arab League expelled Egypt, moved its headquarters from Cairo to Tunis, and ostracized the Egyptian government politically and financially.

Because of the bilateral peace treaty between Israel and Egypt, the eastern Arab world lost the most powerful armed forces and the principal military deterrent against Israel. The regional balance of power thus suddenly shifted significantly to Israel over all the Arab states of the Fertile Crescent and the PLO, and Israel, under the right-wing Likud coalition government, was led into military adventurism. The most important and dramatic example was the 1982 invasion of Lebanon, during which Israel expelled the PLO from Beirut and altered the strategic Palestinian-Israeli situation considerably, an event that set the PLO on a course of rapid decline. The newly expressed PLO goal of establishing a "national authority" in liberated Palestine came increasingly to be interpreted as a two-state solution by diplomats, the media, and much of the Palestinian leadership. Accordingly, with the active support of the PLO, the 1983 Arab summit in Fez developed a peace plan in which it clearly specified the establishment of an independent Palestinian state in the West Bank and the Gaza Strip as a condition for Middle East peace; confirmed the right of all states, including the proposed Palestinian state, to live in peace and security; but only indirectly recognized the state of Israel. The PNC ratified this plan that year at its sixteenth meeting.

The sixteenth PNC meeting was thus a landmark session, which moved the Palestinian national liberation movement and the PLO, officially and formally, from their former radical political agenda (liberation of all of Palestine and thus the dismantling of the Israeli state) to a more diplomatically acceptable formulation and a more strategically realizable goal (the coexistence of a Palestinian state with Israel in historical Palestine). Such a formulation was regarded internationally as necessary for a political (peaceful) solution of the Palestine problem. In short, the sixteenth PNC session resolutions formally confirmed the shift of the PLO's goal from national liberation of all of Palestine to the establishment of an independent Palestinian state in the West Bank and the Gaza Strip. The Palestinian national liberation movement was officially deradicalized and transformed into an independence movement.

Contrary to numerous reports in the Western and Israeli media and scholarship, the Arab states (since the 1967 UN Security Council Resolution 242) and the PLO (indirectly since 1974 and directly and officially since 1983) accepted the "existence" of the state of Israel and since 1983 have sought a peaceful solution to the Arab-Israeli conflict. As Naseer Aruri, Noam Chomsky, and Cheryl Rubenberg[22] have shown, it was in fact Israel and the United States that never accepted Palestinian national rights or the various peace plans offered and pursued by the Arab states and the PLO over the years.[23] Chomsky and Aruri have compellingly argued that Israel and the United States were the "rejectionists" of a just peace in the area.[24]

In retrospect, it seems that all the internal disagreements and divisiveness among the constituent parties or groups of the PLO were of little significance and reflected, after the exit from Beirut, a movement that had lost its consensus and an organization that had lost its bearings. This result came, in part, from its being forced out of its long-term and highly autonomous base in Lebanon, which was near its homeland and from which it could always exercise a military option.

During the second half of the 1980s, the oil-exporting states were in serious economic retrenchment. The regionwide oil-based Arab economy was in a deep recession that affected not only the Arab states' finances but also those of the PLO. Most directly relevant to the oil monarchies was the long (1980–1987) Iraq-Iran war, which threatened their security and drained their decreasing financial resources. In addition to being in economic trouble, the Arab world was in political disarray by the end of the 1980s. Egypt was ostracized, Iraq (and the oil monarchies) was consumed by its war with Iran, Lebanon was still paralyzed by the civil war and occupation, and Syria was at odds with the PLO of Arafat (and in strategic alliance with Iran against the rest of the Arab states). The PLO was isolated, and the Palestine question fell sharply in importance among the political priorities of the Arab world.

The best indication of this decline in significance is the set of resolutions adopted by the 1987 Arab summit in Amman, scarcely forty miles from the occupied West Bank. The lead item of the resolutions, and therefore the prime concern of the assembled Arab rulers, was the threat of the revolutionary Islamic Iran. The Palestine question was addressed in a perfunctory manner at the end of the resolutions, and at the meeting Arafat was treated as something less than a head of state. This event had a profound impact on the Palestinians, especially those under occupation. In this Arab climate of economic retreat, political retrenchment and insecurity, and gathering social discontent, the long-standing premier Arab cause of Palestine and the PLO was of distinctly less importance to the Arab states and rulers. It appeared that the cause of Palestine and the fortunes of the PLO were being rapidly eclipsed when suddenly, in December 1987, shortly after the Arab summit and the eighteenth meeting of the PNC, a dramatic uprising, an intifada, broke out among the Palestinians of the occupied territories.

The Political Impact of the Intifada

The Western media that covered the intifada, especially the confrontations between stone-throwing Palestinian youths and the heavily armed Israeli occupation soldiers, captured on film images that were far different from those long held of the Arab-Israeli or Palestinian-Israeli conflicts. The old myth of Israel's David facing the Arab Goliath was shattered and actually reversed: Israel now appeared before all the world as the vicious Goliath beating up on the Palestinian David. Thus the remarkable and sustained intifada had significant political consequences. Its simple ideological message exposed once and for all the brutal character of Israel's occupation and the Palestinian wish for an end to that occupation. As important, the intifada and its spokespeople tirelessly reaffirmed the oneness of the Palestinian people (under occupation and in the diaspora) and the legitimate leadership of the PLO.

The intifada unexpectedly and considerably reenergized the Palestinian national movement and brought back the Palestine question and the PLO to center stage not only in the region but also internationally—even during the time of other stunning international and regional political developments. The collapse of communism and the end of the Iraq-Iran war were important events that, with the intifada, triggered ideological and political changes within the PLO and advanced its diplomacy. In 1988, a little less than a year later, the intifada made its dramatic political impact and jogged the PLO out of its impasse; the PNC held what may be considered another landmark meeting, perhaps the most significant since its founding and its capture by the *feda'iyyin* guerrilla organizations. It recognized UN Security Council Resolutions 242 and 338 (see Appendix 1 and Appendix 8), which set the conditions for a Middle East political settlement (the land-for-peace formula), proclaiming the state of Palestine with the occupied territories as its patrimony and East Jerusalem (including the Old City) as its capital (see Appendix 9). It also authorized the Executive Committee and its chairman, Arafat, to pursue diplomatic initiatives. At a meeting in Stockholm, the PLO and a US Jewish delegation issued a joint statement (see Appendix 10) in which the PLO:

1. Agreed to enter into peace negotiations at an international conference under the auspices of the UN. . . .
2. Established the independent state of Palestine and accepted the existence of Israel as a state in the region;
3. Declared its rejection and condemnation of terrorism in all its forms, including state terrorism;
4. Called for a solution to the Palestinian refugee problem in accordance with international law and practices and relevant UN resolutions (including right of return or compensation).

In light of these developments, the United Nations invited Arafat to address the General Assembly. When the US government denied him a visa to enter New York, the General Assembly moved its meeting to Geneva, where Arafat offered what he called the Palestinian peace initiative (see Appendix 11). In his speech to the General Assembly, Arafat expressed the desire of the PLO to participate in an international peace conference under the auspices of the United Nations, in which the PLO would seek a comprehensive settlement among the parties concerned in the Arab-Israel conflict on the basis of UN Security Council Resolutions 242 and 338. Both the United States and Israel boycotted the United Nations session in Geneva, even as more than one hundred states formally recognized the state of Palestine.[25] Israeli prime minister Yitzhak Shamir described the Palestinian peace proposal as a "monumental act of deception," and the US government insisted on clarification of what it interpreted as ambiguous language. The United States specifically demanded that Arafat "renounce" violence and terrorism, not merely "denounce" those kinds of acts on both sides of the conflict. Arafat complied with US demands, as he, along with many others in the PNC, believed that only the United States could mount any kind of pressure on Israel to accept the offer. The day after the Geneva event, US president Ronald Reagan announced at a White House press conference that the United States would open a dialogue with the PLO. The US ambassador to Tunisia, Robert Pelletreau, was appointed to initiate the direct talks, the United States carefully avoiding the involvement of high-level State Department officials.

Finally, after a quarter of a century of struggle, the PLO, with the reluctant acquiescence of the United States, was able to enter both directly and indirectly into the deliberations of international diplomacy in the forums and venues concerned with the question of Palestine. Although Israel ignored its official recognition by the PLO and objected to the US-PLO dialogue, the PNC actions and Arafat's follow-up statements were nevertheless crucial first steps in the process of breaking the critical impasse that had long prevented, in the words of Western diplomats and media, Arab acceptance of Israel—although the Arab states and the PLO had in fact long sought a political solution to the conflict. Mutual Arab-Israeli recognition and normalization were now possible.

But it was not until the defeat of radical Arab nationalism (the Iraqi version) and the restructured strategic balance in the region in the wake of the 1991 Gulf War that a revived United States–led "peace process" started in earnest. The Gulf War and the collapse of the Soviet Union allowed the United States to emerge as the sole hegemonic power in the Middle East. Stung by charges of a double standard regarding its position on the occupation of Kuwait by Iraq and that of the West Bank and the Gaza Strip by Israel, the United States moved quickly to restart its Middle East "peace process." The United States officially ignored the PLO as it focused on bringing to the negotiating table only representatives of the Palestinians of the occupied West Bank and Gaza Strip and the government of Israel. Chosen were Palestinian leaders from the West Bank and the Gaza Strip who were approved by Israel, the United States, and (indirectly) the PLO and who were not officials of the PLO. However, as these Palestinian leaders insisted that they openly consult with and be led by the PLO, a diplomatic charade was conducted in which both Israel and the United States pretended that the PLO was not involved.

This was the diplomatic background of the Madrid peace conference of November 1991, attended by Israel; the surrounding Arab states of Syria and Lebanon and a joint Jordanian-Palestinian delegation from the West Bank and the Gaza Strip; and the two sponsors, the United States and Russia. The conference was the opening session of multilateral and bilateral peace negotiations between Israel and its Arab neighbors. Twelve bilateral sessions over two years were held in Washington and came to no agree-

ment. It was this new impasse that in part led to the secret back-room negotiations between Israel and the PLO that led to the 1993 Oslo Accords.

Conclusion

It should be clear that the PLO has come a long way and its accomplishments
are many. Not the least were preserving Palestinian identity; providing services to stateless, dispersed, dispossessed, and suppressed communities; developing representative institutions for its constituency; reaffirming its
national political rights; and internationalizing the Palestine cause. Through
the PLO, the Palestinians achieved these goals in spite of tremendous obstacles and savage warfare against them not only by Israel but also by fellow
Arabs.

The PLO went through three phases in its ideological, strategic, and organizational evolution before it signed the Oslo Accords in 1993.

The first, between 1964 and 1968, was a start-up period during which
the PLO was a creation of the Arab states, more of an organization to control Palestinian activism than it was to give Palestinians a political voice.

The second, from 1968 to 1982, was a time of social and political revolution during which it established and developed all its civil and service institutions, gave specificity and coherence to the Palestinian political cause,
effected most of its important political achievements and ideological transformations, and placed the Palestinians and the Palestine question on the
international political agenda. This phase ended in military defeat in 1982
in the Israeli siege of Beirut and the PLO exodus from the city. This second
phase was also the nadir of diaspora Palestinian political, economic, and
social development, an era during which the PLO failed to liberate any part
of Palestine.

The third phase began in 1982 and ended in 1993 with the signing of the
Oslo Accords. Eventful though this period was—especially because of the
outbreak of the intifada, the collapse of communism and the Soviet Union,
and the 1991 Gulf War—the PLO not only failed to advance the cause of
Palestine and the Palestinians but also blundered into making serious concessions of principle (e.g., recognition of the state of Israel without a reciprocal
Israeli recognition of the right of the Palestinian people to self-determination
and an independent state of their own) and degenerated into an isolated and
decrepit bureaucracy rendered ineffective by mismanagement, autocracy, corruption, nepotism, declining funds, and political bankruptcy.

During this period, the varied diaspora communities of the Palestinian
people were set adrift, and nearly all their PLO-funded institutions were in

disarray or stopped functioning. Economic and social disaster befell the large Palestinian community in Kuwait, which was expelled from the country because of Arafat's policy in the 1990–1991 Gulf crises. After the Gulf War, the PLO sank even further into financial bankruptcy and political irrelevance. Despite its earlier concessions, it thus was largely ignored in the new "peace process" initiated by the United States. Had it not been for the unwavering support for and recognition of the PLO as the political representative of all the Palestinians (under occupation and in the diaspora) by the West Bank and Gaza Strip Palestinians and their leaders and the emergence of a militant Islamic resistance movement, Hamas, the PLO might have vanished into oblivion.

To be sure, with the intifada, an uprising not of its own making, the PLO under Arafat revised formally and officially Palestinian ideology, goals, and strategy, and its position became internationally more acceptable diplomatically. But instead of taking advantage of the locally, regionally, and internationally changed political climate to bring about a just and honorable resolution of the Palestine conflict—an independent Palestinian state in the West Bank and the Gaza Strip, mutual recognition of and by Israel, and establishment of the rights of the refugees—the Arafat-controlled PLO stumbled into the Oslo Accords.

It has become clear to most Palestinians that Arafat's PLO regime sought to maintain itself in the diplomatic game and to retain international legitimacy. It held on to this recognition by ignoring the rights of its own constituency and offering unprincipled concessions to the enemy, first to the US government, in order to engage in a mere dialogue (without receiving formal US diplomatic recognition), and then to Israel by accepting Israel's choice of the Palestinian negotiating team, in order to participate indirectly in the Madrid peace conference and the fruitless twelve rounds of the Washington Arab-Israeli peace negotiations. And finally, in a move disastrous for the Palestinian people, the PLO accepted the Oslo Accords for limited autonomy in the Gaza Strip and the West Bank cities, areas that have remained under Israeli control and sovereignty, and for uncertainty about the occupied territories and the central issues of the conflict (the refugees, Jerusalem, borders, sovereignty, and settlements), which were to be determined in the "final status" negotiations, which have been effectively forgotten.

The PLO's signal achievement in the Oslo Accords was its recognition by Israel, for the first time, as representative of the Palestinian people. But the concessions the PLO made not only indicate its demise as a framework for serving the Palestinian people but also raise serious questions about the restoration of the Palestinians' historic rights, the reconstruction of an independent Palestinian society, and indeed the very existence of the Palestinian people's collective identity.

Notes

1. On Arab nationalism, see G. Antonius, *The Arab Awakening: The Story of the Arab National Movement*, 3rd ed. (New York: Capricorn Books, 1965); S. G. Haim, ed., *Arab Nationalism: An Anthology* (Berkeley: University of California Press, 1964); and H. Sharabi, *Governments and Politics of the Middle East in the Twentieth Century* (Princeton, NJ: Van Nostrand, 1962).

2. N. H. Aruri, *Jordan: A Study in Political Development, 1921–1965* (The Hague: Nijhoff, 1972); see also N. H. Aruri and S. Farsoun, "Palestinians in Arab Host Countries," in K. Nakhleh and E. Zureik, eds., *The Sociology of the Palestinians* (London: Croom Helm, 1980); and F. Qubain, *Crisis in Lebanon* (Washington, DC: Middle East Institute, 1961).

3. D. Hirst, *The Gun and the Olive Branch* (London: Futura, 1977); see also, W. B. Quandt, "Political and Military Dimensions of Contemporary Palestinian Nationalism," Part 2, in W. B. Quandt, F. Jabber, and A. M. Lesch, *The Politics of Palestinian Nationalism* (Berkeley: University of California Press, 1973): 55–56.

4. *Fateh* is often transliterated into English as *Fatah* or *Al-Fatah,* both of which are inaccurate. Occasionally it is also transliterated as *Fath,* a rendition of classical Arabic.

5. H. Cobban, *The Palestinian Liberation Organization: People, Power and Politics* (Cambridge: Cambridge University Press, 1984), Ch. 2: "The Phoenix Hatches (1948–67)," 21–35.

6. Alan Hart, *Arafat, Terrorist or Peacemaker?* (London: Sidgwick and Jackson, 1984).

7. L. A. Brand, *Palestinians in the Arab World* (New York: Columbia University Press, 1988): 39.

8. Cobban, *Palestinian Liberation,* 21–35.

9. There was an important difference between the two radical groupings. Fateh followed the Cuban model of the "foco theory," by which a guerrilla group triggers a revolution through direct armed attacks. PFLP theorized, in accordance with the Soviet and Chinese models, the importance of political organizing before and during the initiation of armed struggle. As we see later in this chapter, Fateh's popularity took off precisely because of its armed activism.

10. See Abu Iyad, with Eric Rouleau, *My Home, My Land* (New York: Times Books, 1981): 20–23. See also Khaled al-Hassan, one of the senior Fateh leaders, as quoted by Cobban, *Palestinian Liberation,* 24; and Quandt, "Political and Military Dimensions," 51, 55–58.

11. See F. Jabber, "The Palestinian Resistance and Inter-Arab Politics," Part 3, in Quandt et al., *Politics of Palestinian Nationalism,* 157–216. For a more critical perspective, see R. D. McLaurin, "The PLO and the Arab Fertile Crescent," in

A. R. Norton and M. H. Greenberg, eds., *The International Relations of the Palestine Liberation Organization* (Carbondale: Southern Illinois University Press, 1989): 12–58.

12. J. K. Cooley, *Green March, Black September: The Story of the Palestinian Arabs* (London: Frank Cass, 1973); see also Hirst, *Gun and the Olive Branch*, and Cobban, *Palestinian Liberation*, especially Ch. 3, "The Joy of Flying (1967–73)," 36–39.

13. M. Hudson, "The Palestinian Arab Resistance Movement: Its Significance in the Middle East Crisis," *Middle East Journal* 23 (Summer 1969): 300ff.

14. D. Hirst, *Gun and the Olive Branch*; Quandt et al., *Politics of Palestinian Nationalism*; Cobban, *Palestinian Liberation*.

15. A. Gresh, *The PLO: The Struggle Within* (London: Zed Press, 1985): 11

16. See Cobban, *Palestinian Liberation*, 42ff; and Hirst, *Gun and the Olive Branch*.

17. M. H. Kerr, *The Arab Cold War* (New York: Oxford University Press, 1971).

18. See F. Jabber, "The Arab Regimes and the Palestinian Revolution," *Journal of Palestine Studies* 2 (Winter 1973): 79–101; see also W. Kazziha, *Palestine in the Arab Dilemma* (New York: Barnes and Noble, 1979).

19. There are a number of books on the history and politics of the PLO. These include R. N. El-Rayyes and D. Nahhas, *Guerrillas for Palestine: A Study of the Palestinian Commando Organizations* (Beirut: An-Nahar Press, 1974); R. Brynen, *Sanctuary and Survival: The PLO in Lebanon* (Boulder, CO: Westview Press, 1990); R. Khalidi, *Under Siege: PLO Decision-Making in the 1982 War* (New York: Columbia University Press, 1986). See also J. R. Nassar, *The Palestine Liberation Organization* (New York: Praeger, 1991), and B. Rubin, *Revolution Until Victory? The Politics and History of the PLO* (Cambridge: Harvard University Press, 1994). Already cited are Cobban, *Palestinian Liberation*, and others.

20. C. Rubenberg, *The Palestine Liberation Organization: Its Institutional Infrastructure* (Belmont, MA: Institute for Arab Studies, 1983). See also Nassar, *Palestine Liberation*, and Brand, *Palestinians in the Arab World*.

21. Cobban, *Palestinian Liberation*, and Quandt et al., *Politics of Palestinian Nationalism*.

22. Cheryl A. Rubenberg, *Israel and the American National Interest: A Critical Examination* (Urbana and Chicago: University of Illinois Press, 1986), and Cheryl A. Rubenberg, *The Palestinians in Search of a Just Peace* (Boulder, CO: Lynne Rienner, 2003).

23. N. Chomsky, *The Fateful Triangle: The United States, Israel and the Palestinians* (Boston: South End Press, 1983); see also Chomsky's extensive writings on the same subject in numerous issues of *Zeta* magazine during the 1980s and 1990s. See also N. Chomsky, *Deterring Democracy* (New York: Vintage, 1992) and *World Orders: Old and New* (New York: Columbia University Press, 1994); and especially N. Aruri, *The Obstruction of Peace: The U.S., Israel and the Palestinians* (Boston: Common Courage Press, 1995).

24. See Chomsky, *Deterring Democracy*, and Aruri, *Obstruction of Peace*.

25. In mid-January 1989 the president of the United Nations Security Council accepted the PLO's request for the right to speak directly to the council as "Palestine" (on the same basis as all UN member nations).

7

Palestinian Resistance to Israeli Occupation

The First Intifada

Throughout Palestine's long history, international, regional, and local events have been linked: Trade, invasion, and pilgrimage routes often put this territory and its people at the center of international attention. Modern Palestinian history in particular stands out against the backdrop of world events. Forced into exile by the catastrophic wars of 1948 and 1967, Palestinians were dispersed throughout the globe or suspended in political limbo on the land they had inhabited for centuries.[1] In the mid-1990s, about 40 percent of the estimated 6.8 million Palestinians resided in historical Palestine; the rest were scattered throughout the Arab world (significant numbers living in Jordan, Syria, Lebanon, and the Arabian Peninsula) and abroad.[2] From their precarious position since 1948, Palestinians have engaged in various forms of resistance at critical historical periods and in everyday life.

After 1967, Palestinians in the West Bank and the Gaza Strip directly confronted the Israeli occupation with demonstrations, tax revolts, merchant and labor strikes, displays of the Palestinian flag or national colors, and clashes with soldiers. The Israelis considered proclaiming oneself a Palestinian who belonged in Palestine a security offense—punishable with a prison sentence under Israeli military law—against the illegitimate occupation and against the state of Israel itself. Opposition led to repression but did not silence the Palestinians' call for self-determination and statehood. The prickly cactus bush called the *sabr* became a national symbol because it dots Palestine, marking the areas of destroyed villages. In Palestinian folk-lore it is known as a symbol of patience and perseverance.

Toward the end of the 1980s, twenty years after Israel captured the West Bank from Jordanian rule and the Gaza Strip from Egyptian control, the Palestinians in these territories combined *sumoud* ("perseverance") with a more demonstrative form of resistance, intifada ("uprising"). The often-recounted incident that sparked the intifada on December 8, 1987, was sadly common in daily life under occupation. On a narrow and congested road, weary Palestinian men waited to cross a military checkpoint, the only entrance into Gaza, after a day of low-paid work in Israel. Unexpectedly, a military tank swerved into a line of cars: Four men died on impact, and seven sustained serious injuries. A rumor that the crash was deliberate, in retaliation for the death of the relative of an Israeli soldier, quickly spread throughout the densely populated towns and refugee camps. According to official reports, brake failure caused the crash. To Palestinians the rumor was more credible. More than six thousand people from all over Gaza joined the people of the Jabalya refugee camp, where three of the four killed had lived, to bury their dead. The funeral erupted into a massive spontaneous demonstration that continued the next day. The Israeli mili-tary, as usual, used live ammunition, beatings, arrests, and tear gas to try to disperse the angry protesters. In the clash scores were injured, and twenty-year-old Hatem al-Sisi became the first martyr in the intifada against the brutal Israeli occupation.

Demonstrations fanned into the West Bank, Jerusalem, and among Arabs inside Israel. On December 10 another youth was killed by the Israeli occu-pation forces at Balata refugee camp, near Nablus. Again, people poured into the streets to protest, and this demonstration prompted a violent re-sponse from the military. Few initially suspected that the increasingly orga-nized demonstrations would last beyond a few days or weeks. Men, women, and children armed with the most readily available materials—stones, slingshots, burning debris, and makeshift barricades—were facing one of the most advanced military forces in the world, one accustomed to dealing with more limited demonstrations.[3]

After its dramatic eruption, the intifada was never crushed. It did, how-ever, go through three stages, which coincided with pivotal regional events, the last of which effectively ended it. The initial phase, December 1987 to the 1991 Gulf War, was marked by a forceful unification and recognition by various organs of the UN system of the Palestinian people's right to self-determination. Palestinians asserted not only their *right to exist* but also their *right to resist Israel,* with resounding international support. In the second phase, from after the Gulf War to the 1993 Oslo Accords, the intifada waned because of relentless Israeli repression and the political and economic isolation of the Palestinians by the regional hegemonic states in the Gulf. The Arab-Israeli peace process, sponsored and initiated by the United States, first in the Madrid conference and subsequently in bilateral negotiations in Washington, shifted the focus and force from the grass roots, from which the intifada had sprung, to the higher-level leadership. In its current phase, which began after the Oslo Accords were announced and signed in September 1993, the intifada has largely ended but threatens to reemerge. A significant proportion of Palestinians were engaging in protest against the occupation *and* the leadership of the PLO. This chapter analyzes the political, economic, and social contours of the first two phases, leaving the third to be discussed in the following chapter.

The roots of the intifada can be traced to the formation of Israel as an exclusionary Jewish state on the land of Palestine. The conflict has become more complex because of the presence of intransigent Jewish settlers near populated Palestinian areas; the acute underdevelopment and de-development[4] of nearly all productive sectors and social institutions; a large, young population, born under occupation, reaching the age for employment; and so forth. The core of the problem, however, is that this contested space is intricately tied to the idea of self-determination, cultural integrity, and personal dignity for 6.8 million Palestinians.[5] To them, Palestine means their humanity. And the intifada was a means of reclaiming their humanity.

Israel, as it is now formed and was conceived by early Zionists, negates the rights of an entire people in order to justify its own existence and maintain its security. UN General Assembly Resolution 194 (see Appendix 6), passed no less than thirty-five times since 1948, calls upon Israel to repatriate hundreds of thousands of Palestinians into the Jewish state or to compensate them. Israel has ignored each of these calls and the legal basis on which they are founded. Moreover, it has continued to pursue a strategy of illegally dislocating Palestinians from their land. The Palestinians' legitimate struggle against dispossession and alienation from their homeland has been distorted by labeling them terrorists, Jordanians, refugees—anything other than Palestinians. Their basic human rights have been systematically denied by all but a minority of Israelis.

A Palestinian—no matter where, how old, or how bold—has been and still is a political-ideological threat to the state of Israel. The Palestinian-Israeli relationship cannot be described as a protracted war between two equipped armies. Nor can it be considered an ethnic conflict, like the conflicts of the Kurds in Turkey and Iraq. Rather, the relationship stems from and is a living remnant of the colonialist and racist European era of the eighteenth and nineteenth centuries. It is ironic that the Palestinians were rendered stateless just as the modern nation-state model of governance emerged throughout the once-colonized continents of Asia, Africa, and Latin America.

From its relative vantage position, in its colonialist effort, Israel has used the tactics and pursued the strategies of the classical colonial era: economic exploitation, mass expulsion from the land, extensive incarceration of resisters, killing. After 1967, these tactics were applied even more viciously in the occupied territories. Ironically, the Israeli strategies, in an illegitimate occupation enforced by a heavy military presence, did not divide the Palestinians but brought them together to form a state, though without a recognized country. These tactics and the response to them made the Palestinians in the occupied territories *seem* disjoined but in fact forced their political, social, and economic activities closer together.

Palestinians emerged throwing stones from the ground beneath them, from the land they firmly believed they had to liberate in order to liberate themselves. The process of shaking off the oppressive Israeli military rule and asserting a unified Palestinian identity in the larger Arab context became what is known internationally as the intifada.

Thwarted Expectations: New Problems and New Solutions (1967–1979)

The Israeli military occupation, on June 6, 1967, of the West Bank and the Gaza Strip signaled the beginning of the end of pan-Arabism and burdened the Palestinians themselves with the struggle for the national liberation of Palestine. This burden was made evident as the Israeli army moved across the 1949 armistice lines and began to restructure the legal, social, and economic conditions in Gaza and the West Bank in a manner tantamount to annexation. On June 27, 1967, the Israeli Knesset added to the existing Jordanian laws in the West Bank and the Egyptian laws in the Gaza Strip the Law and Administrative Ordinance, which enabled "the Government to extend Israeli law, jurisdiction and public administration over the entire area of Eretz Israel" (the former Palestine of the British mandate).[6] All Palestinians were issued a *hawiyya,* an identity card, registered with the Israeli military, written in Arabic and Hebrew, that made possible state control and surveillance. Gaza and the West Bank each had a different local civil administration, but they were unified in that both were under the authority of the Israeli minister of defense. At the same time, the newly conquered territories were to become economically integrated with each other yet subservient to Israel.

On June 28, 1967, the Knesset widened the borders of West Jerusalem to illegally incorporate the Palestinian capital in the east, including the Old City, with more than 100,000 Arab residents. It declared Jerusalem the nonnegotiable "eternal" capital of Israel; seized one thousand acres of privately owned Palestinian property in 1968 and another thirty-five hundred acres in 1970; and began building a belt of Jewish settlements around Jerusalem.[7] The annexation of Jerusalem has been one of the few belligerent Israeli acts repeatedly condemned by the UN General Assembly *and* the Security Council, the latter of which is dominated by the United States, which has protected Israel from international condemnation through its veto on dozens of occasions. On July 4, 1971, the General Assembly unanimously passed Resolution 2253 (ES-V), urging Israel to "rescind all measures taken [and] to desist forthwith, from taking any action which would alter the status of Jerusalem." On September 25, 1971, the UN Security Council passed Resolution 298 (Appendix 12) deploring Israel's actions on Jerusalem, labeling them totally invalid, and calling on Israel to rescind all its actions and measures to change the status of the city. Israel blatantly ignored international pressure.

Israel left the status of the West Bank, the Gaza Strip, and the Golan Heights open to direct negotiations with the concerned Arab states: Jordan, which had an interest in at least a partial recovery of its West Bank; Egypt regarding the Gaza Strip; and Syria with respect to the militarily strategic and fertile Golan Heights. At the same time, however, there were calls for de facto annexation of the territories by a new movement within the Knesset, the Greater Land of Israel, led by prominent military and political figures who later formed the Likud Party coalition in 1969. Minister Menachem Begin, supported by the minister of defense, General Moshe Dayan, argued for the creation of strategic Jewish settlements. These "facts on the ground" were intended to rule out the possibility of returning the land to Arab control.[8] At this point, Palestinian sovereignty was not a consideration. During the early 1970s, Jewish settlements were installed in the West Bank, the Gaza Strip, Egypt's Sinai Peninsula, and Syria's Golan Heights.

The document that became the key legal referent for control of the occupied territories, Resolution 242, was passed by the UN Security Council on November 22, 1967 (see Appendix 1 for the text). Resolution 242, based on the principles of recognition of states' "territorial integrity," "the inadmissibility of acquisition of territory by force," and *"withdrawal of Israel from territories occupied in the recent conflict,"* is commonly called the "land-for-peace formula." To Israel's advantage, the language of the last phrase is ambiguous. Purposely omitted from the resolution was the definite article *the* before *territories,* as originally intended by the United States and the Soviet Union in their July 1967 draft. The omission of this single word reinforced Israel's position that these borders were indefinite and therefore open to political interpretation and negotiation. The only mention of the Palestinians is in reference to "a just solution to the refugee problem"—an echo of the 1917 Balfour Declaration, which urged the early Zionists not to "prejudice the civil and religious rights of the non-Jewish communities in Palestine," which then composed over 90 percent of the population. Moreover, the reference to refugees in this context meant all Arab refugees, including Egyptians and Syrians from the territories taken by Israel.

Following the 1967 war, the territories newly occupied by Israel's military included an estimated 1.3 million Palestinians; the occupation created over 400,000 new refugees and added at least 20,000 to the camps. The rights of these people, as civilian inhabitants of territories acquired by war, are defined by numerous international treaties, conventions, and charters. The most essential of these are The Hague Regulation of 1907 and the fourth Geneva Convention of 1949, "Relative to the Protection of Civilian Persons in Times of War." Each is founded on a broad conception of human rights, under which the Palestinians involved would be regarded as "protected persons," safeguarded from the "forcible transfer" of the population.

Israel contests these conventions, even as a signatory of the UN Charter and a member of the United Nations, arguing that the Arab parties rejected the 1948 partition plan that would have granted independent statehood to Palestinians in 32 percent of British mandate Palestine. As this argument goes, Jordan and Egypt did not constitute "legitimate sovereigns" in the occupied territories, and therefore applicable international conventions did not apply. Israel overruled them with Military Order 144, which effectively barred international human rights observers from the territories (except by special Israeli high court permission). Naseer Aruri noted the irony that "this occupation is uniquely distinguished by the claim that it does not constitute an occupation,"[9] a claim repeatedly contradicted by Israel's preconditions to negotiate with Arab states (and later the PLO) only on the basis of UN Resolutions 242 and 338.

Regarding the conduct of the occupier in relation to administering the conquered territories, Regulation 43 of The Hague convention forbids the occupier to significantly alter existing legislation of the occupied territory, unless it is "absolutely impossible" to abide by the established law. Palestinian laws are drawn from four independent legal traditions: Ottoman, especially in regard to land appropriation and taxation; British mandate defense emergency regulations (passed in 1945), invoked primarily to justify curfews, censorship, and house demolitions; Jordanian and Egyptian civil laws, which regulate criminal and landlord-tenant disputes; and Israeli civil law, under the jurisdiction of the military courts, which is often derived from state security considerations. All combine to create a "complex web of legal traditions," of which only some are effectively enforced, legitimate, or even clear to Palestinians, who tend to practice customary law (*'urf*) to settle civil disputes outside the official civil or religious courts.[10] This tangle of laws applied through the military court system Israel erected in the occupied territories has the politicolegal function of maintaining control over the Palestinians living under occupation.[11]

Inside the Prison of Occupation: The Emergence of New Palestinian Leadership

The applicability of Antonio Gramsci's concept of hegemony,[12] even in its abstracted form, to the Palestinian case is limited in two major respects. First, as an occupier, Israel, especially after Likud rose to power in the late 1970s, relied most on coercive military power to secure its hegemony. Second, Israel had to contend with a fragmented Palestinian community with exogenous leadership (the PLO) that acted as a counterweight to Israeli leadership inside the occupied territories. Although Israel threatened the use of force against the people over which it maintained occupation, it could never legitimize its presence to the Palestinians.

The *process* of developing alternative civil institutions under occupation, however, closely resembles what Gramsci described as the "war of position."[13] Israel's ideological and material strength took the form of military infallibility—or its power, on the one hand, to resist international pressure to relinquish the occupied territories and, on the other hand, to forcefully assert its rule over the Palestinians. Its alignment with the United States explains Israel's regional military dominance throughout the cold war and after the collapse of the Soviet Union. Moreover, at some points in its history, Israel tried to gain ideological consent for its existence from certain sectors of Palestinian society by offering municipal "autonomy," a far cry from the explicit goal of statehood. Failing in these attempts, Israel resorted to draconian coercion.

Although many smaller organizations emerged during the early period of the occupation, a semiclandestine umbrella group, the Palestine National

Front (PNF, established August 15, 1973), took a leading role in resistance efforts. The leaders of the PNF represented various student, labor union, and women's organizations from a wide political spectrum—communist to nationalist. Through nonviolent strategies of civil disobedience, the organization played a leading role in organizing protests against Israeli land confiscation, deportation of political leaders, and the treatment of political prisoners.[14] One of its most successful efforts was the Palestinian boycott of municipal elections in Jerusalem that threatened to legitimize Israeli annexation.

The necessity for an ideological and tactical turn toward diplomacy became painfully obvious as Israel mounted its military forces against Palestinians inside the occupied territories and in Lebanon. As discussed in the previous chapter, two significant episodes weakened the PLO: the civil war in Lebanon (1975–1982) and the Israeli invasion of Lebanon (1982). Both assaults were designed to preempt the formation of a Palestinian government-in-exile and resulted in the massacre of tens of thousands of Palestinians, most of them civilians residing in refugee camps. Outside the occupied territories throughout the early 1970s, a series of events made a primarily political rather than military strategy feasible to Palestinian leadership. The PLO, at the June 12, 1974, Palestine National Council meeting, replaced the vision of a secular democratic state in all of Palestine with the goal of an "independent Palestinian state" in any part of Palestine liberated from occupation. Implicit in this revision was the recognition of Israel, as required by UN Resolution 242. This move was affirmed later that year, on October 28, at the seventh Arab summit meeting in Rabat, Morocco, where Arab leaders recognized "the right of the Palestinian people to establish an independent national authority under the command of the Palestinian Liberation Organization, the sole legitimate representative of the Palestinian people, in any Palestinian territory that is liberated." One month later PLO chairman Arafat addressed the international community at the United Nations, in New York, with this plan. UN General Assembly Resolution 3236 (Appendix 7) reaffirmed "the inalienable rights of the Palestinian people in Palestine" to self-determination and national independence and granted the PLO observer status.

In 1976 Israeli prime minister Yitzhak Rabin initiated municipal elections in the West Bank, and for the first time Palestinian women voted. Rabin expected a nationalist boycott, as in earlier Jerusalem elections, which would then "democratically" install Israeli collaborators. His strategy backfired, and openly pro-PLO PNF candidates swept eighteen of the twenty-four councils by an overwhelming majority.[15] Most of the other seats were won by conservative, traditional leaders who were independents or loyal to the Jordanian monarchy, not Israeli collaborators.

The victory of the PNF was dampened the next year by the Likud's rise to power in the Israeli parliamentary elections of 1977. In October 1978 the PNF (strongly influenced by homegrown communist activists) was somewhat opposed by more conservative Fateh leaders and declared illegal by Israel. But by then it had reorganized and expanded under the more mainstream, Fateh-dominated National Guidance Committee (NGC). The NGC's first major challenge was to counter plans to grant Palestinians autonomy but not statehood, embodied in the 1978 Camp David Accords signed as the Israeli-Egyptian peace treaty by Menachem Begin and Anwar Sadat and witnessed by President Jimmy Carter of the United States. Palestinians from the entire political spectrum (Islamists, nationalists, and communists) resoundingly rejected the plan on the basis that it "condemned the West Bank and Gaza to a permanent exile, with less real authority than a [South African] Bantustan."[16] The Palestinian activist Fayez Sayegh warned that it was "as seductive and destructive as a siren call."[17] On the day the treaty was signed (September 17), the entire West Bank and Gaza Strip were put under strict curfew; widespread demonstrations in protest ensued nevertheless.

The NGC proposed the establishment of an independent state of Palestine that would coexist alongside Israel, a more decisive step toward reconciliation with Israel than the PLO's official position. As Salim Tamari pointed out, "This fact is extremely important: the formation of the National Guidance Committee—militant, pro-PLO and popular, and at the same time willing to make territorial compromises with the state of Israel, with the aim of co-existence between the Israeli state and a future Palestinian state—[became] the subject of the most ferocious attack by the Likud [government]."[18] Israelis, especially those from the Likud Party, believed the NGC posed a real threat to their own plans to incorporate the occupied territories into "Greater Israel." Accordingly, the Israeli occupation army carried out mass arrests of grassroots activists and organizers, deported two elected mayors, and banned the NGC.[19]

Beginning in 1978, the main party of the PLO (Fateh) and Jordan formed a "joint committee" in coordination with the people of the West Bank and the Gaza Strip and instituted a "steadfastness fund" channeled up to $100–150 million annually to the occupied territories from various donor Arab states in the form of direct money transfers, medical supplies, educational hardware, communication technology, and qualified personnel. The committee's expressed aim was to organize and build civil institutions at

the grassroots level. The national Palestinian movement in the occupied territories was divided into two ideological camps: A leftist group was composed of the PFLP, the DFLP, the Palestine Communist Party (PCP), and
progressives from within Fateh; the other group was made up of conservative and dominant elements of Fateh and the Muslim Brotherhood. The
two groups expressed their conflict most importantly over the expenditure
of the steadfastness fund. "The conservative forces tend[ed] to organize resistance along the lines of traditional institutions, such as municipal councils, professional unions, women's organizations, notables. The left . . .
trie[d] either to build new organizations or to radicalize the rank and file of
existing organizations."[20] Although these conflicts did not debilitate the resistance movement—indeed, it may be argued that they led to greater
politicization and mobilization of the Palestinians under occupation—they
did have two major effects. The first was the increasing political influence
of the Palestinians of the occupied territories (known as those of *al-dakhel*)
and those in the diaspora (those of *al-kharej*). The second was the emergence of tension between the inside and outside wings of the national
movement. With the intifada, this division became all the more important.

Economic Subordination of the Occupied Territories: Policies and Practices

On the economic front, in the post–1967 war period Israel's previously
staggering economy boomed because of an enormous influx of financial
and military transfers, mainly from the United States. This upward structural shift reoriented Jewish labor toward higher-paying technical service
sectors and created a demand for low-skilled and cheap labor, especially in
construction and agriculture, a demand filled by Palestinians from the
newly conquered territories.[21] The Israeli Central Bureau of Statistics
recorded a steady increase of Palestinian daily labor migration into Israel
from 1968 (especially after 1970) until the intifada, in terms of absolute
numbers and percentage of the population. These figures exclude undocumented labor, which is generally estimated to be as high as 50 percent in the
construction sector and roughly 45 percent of the total Palestinian workforce in Israel (estimated numbers vary by year and season).[22]

Part of the explanation for the high rates of undocumented labor is that
Palestinian employment opportunities are strictly regulated by several
mechanisms tied to Israeli economic and political considerations. Palestinians must apply for a work permit, gained only after they obtain security
clearance from the Israeli occupation forces, and present proof of potential

employment by an Israeli. These permits must be renewed periodically for a fee and are limited to employment in what Israel deems "nonstrategic" sectors.[23] Very often, Israeli employers prefer to hire illegal workers in order to avoid paying benefits to Israelis who have trade union protection.

Although data are sparse, several studies show that after 1970, Palestinian women increasingly entered the workforce as migrant laborers in Israel and in the occupied territories. They represented at least 5–10 percent of the total workforce. Most of them are unmarried or widowed women who want to supplement their families' incomes, not to achieve independent status (although independence may be an unintended outcome). On the whole, Palestinians, with no effective means to prevent exploitation, constitute a "reserve army of labor in the Israeli economy."[24] Moreover, women make up the "most exploited segment . . . an 'invisible' proletariat."[25]

The possibility of gaining membership and benefits in the Histadrut, Israel's largest trade union federation, is slim for Palestinians, primarily because of a historical preference to protect and privilege Jewish labor. Moreover, not only are Palestinians limited to lower-wage jobs, but they also earn fewer benefits and lower wages than Jewish Israeli workers in comparable positions.[26]

Efforts to organize workers into Palestinian labor unions have consistently been labeled subversive, "terrorist" activity by the military authorities. Before 1967 thirteen of the twenty-four Palestinian unions were located in Jerusalem. After the annexation of Jerusalem, Israel particularly targeted Palestinian unions in the "reunification of the city under Israeli rule."[27] Efforts were made to co-opt workers into the Histadrut, against which the PNF successfully organized. Consequently, after a stringent crackdown in 1969, the Palestinian unionizing center shifted to Nablus.

As Israel continued to try to break up Palestinian unions, they became informal and hidden. Restrictions on printing and distributing union material, public meetings, recruiting and registering new members, and establishing new unions—as well as other nationalist organizations—compelled activists to circumvent the authorities in order to reach the masses. They accomplished this directly and indirectly by two means: encouraging democratic participation within the union structure, which enlarged the pool of potential leaders, and organizing unions by trade, geographic location, and political affiliation. Although decentralization and dispersion weakened the numerical strength of a particular group, they allowed for tighter coordination and for members to more easily elude the authorities. Unions provided their members primarily social rather than economic protection and services. They were particularly successful in administering health care services and medicine at minimum cost to members and their families. Unions also tried to provide legal aid and counsel, education, and recreational facilities.

Voluntary work committees (the first founded in 1972) and student federations (at the secondary and higher educational levels) organized projects that fused nationalistic ideology with localized social activity. Guided by a small core of leaders, as few as twenty or as many as thousands of participants would join together at a particular location and engage in tree planting, harvesting, road building, or cleanup efforts in villages or refugee camps.

The Islamic movement, embodied in the Muslim Brotherhood, initially focused less on resisting the Israeli occupation and more on countering secular tendencies prevailing throughout the West Bank and the Gaza Strip.[28] Because the group's central ideology was not jihad or active opposition to the Israelis, but the total Islamization of Palestinian society, the Israelis allowed (even encouraged) it to proliferate. The Muslim Brotherhood established libraries, religious and nursery schools, and sports and social clubs with funding from Muslims worldwide, but particularly in the Persian Gulf states. It distributed *zakat* (alms to the poor, one of the five pillars of Islam) to thousands in the Gaza Strip and the West Bank. Between 1967 and 1987, "the number of mosques in the West Bank rose from 400 to 750, in the Gaza Strip from 200 to 600."[29] These became sites for the Muslim Brotherhood to do political work and recruit with little interference by the Israelis.

During the 1970s, especially after the 1979 Iranian revolution, an important division occurred within the Muslim Brotherhood. Two 1948 refugees from Gaza, Fathi al-Shiqaqi and 'Abd al-'Aziz 'Adud, formed the Islamic Jihad (al-Jihad al-Islami), which retained an emphasis on the formation of an Islamic state but by more militant means. Ideologically, the Islamic Jihad inverted the relationship between "the centrality of the Palestine issue and proper timing for liberating the country" advocated by the Muslim Brotherhood.[30] In other words, the Islamic Jihad believed that Islamization of Palestinians should come after the liberation of Palestine, not before. The Islamic Jihad did not gain wide political support, nor did it manage to sway many of the Muslim Brotherhood, whose popularity rested on the organization's ability to distribute social services through its institutions.

Settler Colonialism: Land, Water, and Labor

Under the right-wing Likud Party government, which controlled the Israeli parliament from 1977 to 1992, Israel aggressively pursued one objective: to

gain control of the occupied land and its resources without formally incorporating the Palestinian people into Israel as citizens of its parliamentary
democracy. This goal had three strategic prongs, supported more or less by
both the Israeli political right and political left: (1) to extend Israel's control
of the territories by establishing Jewish settlements with security and administrative links only to Israel (officially sanctioned in the Israeli Knesset
on March 6, 1980); (2) to restrict, control, and even de-develop the Palestinian economy and proletarianize its labor; and (3) to suppress resistance
movements by coercive methods, such as extended incarceration or deportation of leaders, censorship of the Palestinian press, and collective punishment. Together, all three tactics were intended to force Palestinian
migration or submission by narrowing the opportunities for political, economic, and social independence, and thereby creating a relationship of controlled dependency.

To a large extent, the Likud government was successful in its effort, as reflected in part by the increase in numbers and expenditures for settler activity. In terms of absolute numbers, in 1976 there were 3,176 Jewish settlers
in the West Bank, but by 1986 the number had climbed to 60,500, amid the
Palestinian population of 938,000 (including 125,000 in East Jerusalem).[31]
The majority of settlers were enticed by the generous state subsidies attached to the development projects.[32] A slim but vocal minority, aligned
politically with rightist coalitions, were ideologically driven to settle in the
occupied territories. These groups, such as Gush Emunin and Kach (named
after its slain leader, Meir Kahane, an ultraorthodox militant emigrant
from Brooklyn, New York), posed a mortal menace to the Palestinians living in close proximity.

On the eve of the intifada in 1987, 120 Jewish settlements of various
sizes and durability peppered the West Bank. For example, Ma'aleh Adumim, located on a large strip of land between Jerusalem and Jericho, could
be likened to Tel Aviv in terms of quality of construction, whereas settlements deeper in the West Bank tended to be constructed of flimsy, prefabri-
cated housing materials. In most cases, once a settlement was established,
large tracts of land surrounding the compound were closed off to Palestinians as a security measure. For state/public, private, and security purposes,
by 1992 approximately 55 percent of the total land area of the West Bank
and 30 percent of the Gaza Strip had been appropriated by the Israeli
government.[33]

Although prohibited under the fourth Geneva Convention, large transfers of revenue from the occupied territories to Israel became a permanent
feature of the occupation. There was a deliberate attempt to stifle and

curtail Palestinian development in order to bolster the Israeli economy. This strategy was bluntly summed up by Defense Minister Rabin in 1984: "There will be no development initiated by the Israeli government, and no permits will be given for expanding [Palestinian] industry and agriculture which may compete with the state of Israel."[34]

Already in 1984, Israeli products accounted for 90 percent of all imports into the West Bank and the Gaza Strip, or 11 percent of all Israeli exports.[35] Most of the exports to the Palestinian economy were substandard manufactured consumer goods. As Sheila Ryan stated, the Palestinian market became "a convenient dumping ground for shoddy Israeli industrial products which could not compete with the local manufactures of the industrialized countries of Europe and North America."[36]

At first, during the 1970s, these tactics had an uneven impact on the Palestinian class structure. This dependency relationship hit hardest the 844,000 Palestinians in the twenty-seven refugee camps, who often had no other source of employment except in Israel. This problem was most acute in the Gaza Strip. Its population density is nearly ten times that of the West Bank, and refugees from 1948 Palestine compose more than 66 percent of the total population, compared with 40 percent in the West Bank.[37] Of the total Palestinian labor force, approximately 51,300 (31 percent) from the West Bank and 53,900 (46.1 percent) from Gaza worked in Israel, mostly in low-paid industrial and construction sectors without social benefits or job security.[38] Within the West Bank and the Gaza Strip, the top-level governing powers are held by Israelis. The Civil Administration (CA), which was under the military area commanders and ceased to exist in 1994, was responsible for all economic matters regarding Palestinian life. A 1993 World Bank mission reported that "currently the CA has about 22,000 employees, of which approximately 95 percent are Palestinians. Most policy-making and senior administrative positions in the CA are, however, staffed by Israelis."[39]

The service sector dominated the Palestinian economy. It made up about 85 percent of gross domestic product (GDP) and employed 47.3 percent of the workforce.[40] Merchants, professionals, educators, wage workers, and others have been greatly disadvantaged by Israeli policies over time, and consequently the occupied territories have fallen below the average level of Arab regional development. Public infrastructure, such as roads, telephones, electricity, and hospitals, which facilitates the distribution of goods and services, is underdeveloped in the cities, villages, and camps alike.

Palestinian agricultural products cost more than Israeli farm products because Palestinian farmers are not permitted to purchase advanced machinery; they are also actually prohibited from growing and selling certain crops. For example, it is illegal for Palestinians to pick thyme, a popular herb used in preparing traditional Arabic dishes, because they would compete with the kibbutzim's monopoly on the product. A more potent example is the Gaza Strip's citrus production, which before 1967 employed 25 percent of the total workforce, took up 20 percent of the land area, and brought $150 a ton in Western European markets.[41] Joan Mandell traced the decline of this sector from 1967 to the mid-1980s. First, in 1968 Israel banned independent Palestinian export to European markets but continued to allow export to the Arab world in order to circumvent the Arab boycott of Israeli goods. In 1983 a person who wanted an "exit permit" to Jordan had to pay roughly $150; in comparison, the average price per ton of fruit had dropped to $60. "Fifteen to 20 percent of Gaza's citrus trees were felled in 1983 as a result of restricted markets, rising fuel and fertilizer costs and water restriction."[42] Nevertheless, the initiation of widespread use of mechanical irrigation systems, fertilizers, and other technical devices increased total crop output per *dunum* over the course of Israeli occupation of the West Bank and the Gaza Strip. Accompanying these changes, however, were the expropriation of arable land and the proletarianization of the rural and refugee labor force, which both reduced the percentage of the total population and the percentage of gross national product (GNP) of Palestinians in agriculture.

During the 1980s, water, shared unequally by Israelis and Palestinians, was capped at pre-1967 levels. Restrictions included access to surface water sources and wells. In the Gaza Strip, the imbalance was most severe: 750,000 Palestinians consumed on average 30 percent of the water, and the rest was allotted to 4,000 Israeli settlers. Gaza's water, used by Palestinians for agriculture and drinking, was contaminated by raw sewage that flowed through open sewers in the camps and by high saline levels from the inflow of seawater. The contaminated water was neither tested nor monitored regularly and was treated only with chlorine.[43] The settlers sink deeper wells into freshwater sources, also contributing to lower water tables in Palestinian wells. In the words of Sharif Elmusa, "On the whole, Israel, when it comes to the water sources of the area, acts like a great sponge."[44]

While the Israeli assault on the entire Palestinian economic infrastructure and resources has been heavy, Sara Roy argues that the Gaza Strip has undergone a process of "de-development."[45] This concept, adapted from the wider literature on dependency and modernization theories, is defined as the total *regression* of political institutions, social structures, and economic infrastructures necessary to facilitate economic growth and independence.

Moreover, this process is not spontaneous or due to internal constraints within a society. Rather, as in the case of the Gaza Strip, de-development is intentionally "shaped and advanced by a range of policies, themselves a reflection of the ideological imperatives of the Zionist movement," which seeks to dispossess Palestinians from their land. In Roy's analysis, the Gaza Strip constitutes a separate social, cultural, economic, and political entity from the West Bank. It is distinguished by a culture torn apart by the inescapable violence of everyday life, virtually complete economic dependence on Israel, and a chaotic political system based on competing political groups with incompatible ideologies and aims.

De-development keeps necessary infrastructural supports for economic sectors such as industry, agriculture, and private business from performing essential functions. For example, in 1981 Israel allowed one branch of the Bank of Palestine to open in the Gaza Strip, mainly to cash checks from earnings in Israel. As Roy noted, "One of the bank's greatest handicaps has been its inability to issue letters of credit. Thus, although it has been the only bank in an area of over 800,000 people, it has not been able to support local enterprises."[46] Local entrepreneurs are forced to turn for money to commercial banks outside the occupied territories, international donor agencies, moneychangers, or family and friends. None of these sources effectively strengthens the domestic savings or investment potential of the Gaza Strip, so any investment is a high-risk venture and, in turn, self-reliance is undermined.

The Palestinian economy, vulnerable to external shocks, was squeezed even tighter by the international recessionary period of the 1980s. Regional and local growth due to the sharp rise in oil prices prior to that period shriveled when oil revenues and the consequent demand for expatriate workers in the Persian Gulf fell dramatically. During the oil boom, between 1973 and 1982, the emigration from the occupied territories, mostly of skilled young men, averaged 17 per 1,000. After 1985 the Bank of Israel officially reported that the emigration rate had fallen to 3 per 1,000. This decline meant a serious drop in the standard of living supported by the extra revenue generated by work in the Gulf: "Remittances into Jordan, much of which were destined for the Occupied Territories, dropped from $1.5 billion in 1982 to $887 million in 1988."[47]

As the income from employment in the Gulf states and in the local economy narrowed, Palestinian youth in particular perceived and experienced the structural constraints of the Israeli occupation. Their individual and collective futures looked bleak. Families, villages, towns, and cities turned inward to meet the daily needs of their members for food production, health services, and job training. Local developmental projects organized (for the most part) separately by the four main PLO parties gave the participants a feeling of personal self-worth and infused them with national aspirations. Most significant, a sense of community, interdependence, and cooperation emerged during the structural economic crisis in the mid-1980s.

The (Almost) Forgotten People

The PLO was becoming an ineffective player on the Arab and international scene. The Israeli government objected to and the Reagan administration in the United States rejected the 1985 Hussein-Arafat initiative, which offered land for peace (based on UN Resolution 242) and a Jordanian-Palestinian confederation. Also in 1985 Israel bombed the PLO's headquarters in Tunis, killing more than seventy officials. One year later Jordan's government ordered the closing of all twenty-five PLO offices in Amman and deported its top leader in Amman, Khalil al-Wazir.[48]

The Palestinian leadership became increasingly marginalized in the wider political arena. The sense of stagnation, however, was offset by an important restructuring of the PLO from within the organization. After nearly five years of divisive fragmentation, the four principal constituents of the PLO regrouped at a PNC meeting in Algiers in April 1987. United, for the first time ever, in strategy and action were the popularly supported Palestine Communist Party, the Popular Front for the Liberation of Palestine, the Democratic Front for the Liberation of Palestine, and Fateh.

In the occupied territories, the factions that had once competed for popular support among the general population began to coordinate their efforts and resources. Ann Mosely Lesch described her firsthand experience of the impact of these changes:

> The effect of the rapprochement among the key groups was already evident by June 1987. When I visited the West Bank that month, I found that the social unionist organizations sponsored by the different movements were beginning to work together and that a common sense of purpose was beginning to emerge. The organizational basis for the intifada was, in fact, being established. Moreover, the Islamic movement began to participate alongside the nationalist groups, for the first time. . . . They construed the primary enemy as Israel, not their fellow Palestinians.[49]

These reinvigorated, determined activists found promise in grassroots models of resistance. They were particularly inspired by the effective strategies practiced by the Shi‘a and other organizations in southern Lebanon against the Israeli occupation (1983–1985). The key to their success had been collective mobilization, which could sustain and promote individual sacrifice for the collective good in the face of a common threat. A sort of moral determination combined with mass resistance on the part of the Shi‘a against the Israeli occupation hurt the occupiers and created deep political divisions in Israeli society. With the political will lost, Israel's military was compelled to withdraw from most of Lebanon—to the so-called security zone along the northern Israeli border.

The event that finally crystallized the realization that the Palestinian struggle had lost its prominence for Arab leadership occurred at the November 1987 Arab summit in Amman. Those who attended the summit declared that the Arab enemy was Iran, a thousand miles to the east. As noted above, in the general communiqué issued at the end of the summit, the Palestine question was, contrary to custom, relegated to the end, almost as an afterthought. Furthermore, Jordan proposed that the Arab states normalize relations with Egypt (ostracized since it signed the Camp David Accords and a peace treaty with Israel) in order to throw strategic weight on the side of Iraq in the Iraq-Iran war and to isolate Syria and Libya, supporters of Iran. In January 1988, for the first time since the 1979 signing of the Egyptian-Israeli peace treaty, Egypt attended the conference of the Islamic Organization (a league of Islamic states) in Kuwait. To Palestinians, these moves toward regional reconciliation with Egypt were sobering. In retrospect, they signified the end to Palestinian hopes for settling the conflict within the larger Arab-Islamic context. Self-reliance and the ideology of unification finally replaced dependence on the diplomacy of Arab leadership and the hoped-for reasonableness of the United States and Israel.

Surprise: The Intifada Erupts

The initial outbreak of the intifada—mass demonstrations, confrontations with soldiers, labor and merchant strikes—occurred unexpectedly while the PLO, the Israeli public, the Israeli army, and the world watched. The harsh response of the occupation forces and the daring displayed by the Palestinians are often explained by the lack of readiness of the military. It was, however, the strength of the masses mobilized for direct confrontation with their occupiers that overwhelmed the Israeli military, at least initially. Brutal actions by the Israeli army—beatings, teargassing, house demolitions, and point-blank shooting of lethal rubber bullets and live ammunition—were not uncommon and, as discussed above, had been on the rise over the

TABLE 7.1 Human Rights Violations, September 2000–January 2006

29/9/2000–15/1/2006	*Occupied Territories*	*Israel*
Palestinians killed by Israeli security forces	3,295	56
Palestinians killed by Israeli civilians	41	
Israeli civilians killed by Palestinians	228	455
Israeli security force personnel killed by Palestinians	225	84
Foreign citizens killed by Palestinians	15	32
Foreign citizens killed by Israeli security forces	10	–
Palestinians killed by Palestinians	168	–
Palestinian minors killed by Israeli security forces	669	1
Israeli minors killed by Palestinians	38	80
Palestinians killed during the course of a targeted killing	319	–
Palestinians who were the object of a targeted killing	204	–
Palestinians killed by Palestinians for suspected collaboration with Israel	112	–

SOURCE: Palestine Human Rights Information Center, *Human Rights Update 2* (June 1994): 1. www.btselem.org/English/statistics/casualties.asp.

prior years. Table 7.1 provides data on Israeli human rights violations of the Palestinian people under occupation from September 2000 to January 2006.

What distinguished the intifada from past resistance efforts was not the increasingly draconian Israeli measures but the level of inclusion of nearly all sectors of Palestinian society and the media's capturing the horrifying images of their everyday life and the heroic struggle of an unarmed population against a vicious army. In the beginning the intifada dramatically rearranged what had seemed to be the immutable power relationship between the Palestinians and Israel, built over the twenty years of occupation. This is not to say that the Israelis suddenly became passive or even victims of the stones thrown by Palestinians. Defense Minister Rabin deployed more than 10,000 troops in the Gaza area. In the West Bank, according to UN reports, the number of soldiers grew from 700 to 8,000 in response to the intifada.[50] In the first three months of the intifada, with license from their commanding officers, troops killed more than 100 Palestinian demonstrators and bystanders, wounded hundreds, and placed thousands under military detention (imprisonment for up to six months without trial, subject to indefinite renewal).[51] Over time the Israeli military deployed sophisticated "antiriot devices": night-vision equipment, television cameras in strategic locations, shielded jeeps, and stone-hurling machines.[52]

The Palestinians could have been overwhelmed by the Israeli military, but they mobilized efforts on the economic, political, and social fronts. Within one month, Al-Qiyada al-Wataniyya al-Muwahhada li-l Intifada (the Unified National Leadership of the Uprising, or UNLU), created by the five major political groups represented in the PLO, captured the spontaneous momentum of the people and began to channel it into coordinated action through the already established popular committees and the institutionalized charitable, professional, and volunteer organizations.

Parallel to the UNLU, and in coordination with it, the leaders of the mainstream Muslim Brotherhood organized a militant wing to join the uprising, drawing members from its younger members and those in the Islamic Jihad. Based in Gaza, Hamas made its presence known in its first leaflet, issued in January 1988. Hamas put forth its ideology, aim, and strategy in its charter on August 18, 1988. The main thrust of the text is guided by an ideology that attempts to "cleanse" Palestinian society of both secular and Zionist influences "toward raising the banner of Allah on every inch of Palestine."[53]

Article 27 of the charter states Hamas's position regarding the PLO in relation to the wider struggle (see Appendix 13 for the text of this key article). In this passage Hamas calls the PLO "the father, brother, relative or friend" of the Islamic resistance movement because, as Hamas asserts, "Our nation is one, plight is one, destiny is one, and our enemy is the same." It clearly establishes the point that the Islamists and the PLO share the same side of the battlefield, but the PLO will not "be [the nation's] soldiers" unless "the Palestine Liberation Organization adopts Islam as its system of life." Short of that, "the position of the Islamic Resistance Movement toward the Palestine Liberation Organization is the position of a son toward his father, and a brother toward his brother, and the relative toward his relative" but not his friend.[54] Hamas thus explicitly rejected direct confrontation with the PLO but implicitly positioned itself as an alternative, even a rival, to its leadership and social programs.

Women also began to articulate and demonstrate a wider role in the struggle than they had before the intifada. But as Bir Zeit University professor Islah Jad argues, "Women's role in the popular committees became an extension of what it traditionally had been in the society: teaching and rendering services" across the political spectrum.[55] There was, however, a rural-urban divide: Urban women's political activity and productive work had a greater progressive social content, whereas the rural women's roles were more constricted by the traditional division of labor (although it was one with a nationalist flavor). During the intifada, women carved out a significant and fresh presence in the public space. Yet the "woman question" became subsumed by the "nationalist question" in the sexually segregated mosques, cafés, and prisons, where political strategizing was done.[56]

Because participation was so high and from such a wide cross section of the population, the Israeli army targeted nearly everyone who participated in the intifada as a possible leader. The space in the existing prison facilities became inadequate to hold as many as nine or ten thousand Palestinians at a given time.[57] For mass arrests, involving all of the males in a village or camp who were fourteen to sixty years old and were suspected of "terrorism," the Israeli army turned local schools into impromptu detention and interrogation centers. For more lengthy detention, the army hastily built tent camps that were "often the scene of brutal treatment of detainees."[58] The most notorious of these were Ansar II and III in the Gaza area and the Naqab (Negev) Desert. Just as the Israeli army turned schools into jails, it is said that the prisoners turned the jails into schools of the intifada. Inside the overcrowded detention centers, prisoners banded together to exchange information about the events of the intifada, to maintain their familial and political connections with the outside, and to plan strategy for the future.

The intifada was triggered in the camps, but it soon spread to the main urban centers and the five hundred villages (many of them, especially in the north, isolated and remote). It was virtually impossible for the Israeli military to subdue all areas continuously or to isolate key individuals effectively. Instead, it dealt out collective punishment in order to quell resistance area by area.[59]

Economic Resistance

The UNLU's first *bayan* (communiqué from the leaders to the membership), issued one month after the intifada began, extolled the Palestinian people's struggle as a whole. A more important aspect of the *bayan* was that it horizontally linked vertically positioned class actors to the wider struggle, reconciling the immediate and long-term interests and sacrifices of each class with regard to Israel as the greatest economic and political enemy:

In the name of God, the merciful, the compassionate . . .

All Sectors of our heroic people in every location should abide by the calls for a general and comprehensive strike. . . .

Brother workers, your abidance by the strike by not going to work and to plants is real support for the glorious uprising, a sanctioning of the pure blood of our martyrs, a support for the call to liberate our prisoners, and an act that will keep our brother deportees in their homeland.

Brother businessmen and grocers, you must fully abide by the call for a comprehensive strike. . . . We will do our best to protect the interests of our honest businessmen against measures the Zionist occupation force may resort to using against you. We warn against the consequences of becoming involved with some of the occupation authorities' henchmen who will seek to make you open your businesses. We promise to punish such traitor businessmen in the not too distant future. Let us proceed united to forge victory.

Brother owners of taxi companies . . . we pin our hopes on you to support and make the comprehensive strike a success. . . .

Brother doctors and pharmacists, you must be on emergency status to offer assistance to those of kinfolk who are ill. . . .

Let us proceed united and loudly chant: Down with occupation; long live Palestine as a free and Arab country.[60]

With the economic sector mobilized, the UNLU pressed for a Palestinian withdrawal from the Israeli economy. First and most effective was a general boycott of Israeli products that were either unessential consumer goods (such as beer, cigarettes, and clothing) or had a Palestinian-made equivalent (such as soap, soft drinks, eggs, meat, and candy). Second, the strikes against Israeli employers, with an emphasis on construction in settlements, were observed by an estimated 40–60 percent of the migrant workforce.[61] Third was a general tax revolt against direct taxation and licensing, accompanied by the mass resignation of tax collectors. The most celebrated tax revolt was that of the town of Beit Sahur.[62] By the end of 1988, the total cost of the intifada to Israel in the loss of revenue from the territories, the increase in military spending, property damage, and the slowdown of tourism was estimated to be around $2–3 billion, equivalent to 4.5–5 percent of the Israeli GNP.[63]

But the initial impact of the intifada was overall more devastating to the Palestinian economy than to the Israeli economy. Strikes, curfews, and the high rate of imprisonment and wounding of wage earners meant a steep decline in real wages for entire families and villages. Where the military might have failed to suppress the uprising, the Israeli army began meting out economic punishment by sector—an extension of preintifada practices. In the West Bank cities, phone lines, electricity, and fuel supplies were often cut. Everywhere, from the start, merchants' shops were forced open during strike hours or welded shut if the merchants disobeyed the order. Another crude and widespread tactic Israel used against merchants was to wantonly destroy foodstuff and equipment: "In many cases in the West Bank documented by al-Haq [a Palestinian human rights organization], soldiers entered shops and spoiled the goods, mixing bleach with flour, trampling on bread, smashing eggs, breaking a refrigerator full of meat and upturning stalls."[64]

Prolonged curfews particularly disrupted agricultural production in the villages. Entire crops were lost because farmers were unable to spray, irrigate, or harvest their fields. Additional constraints were placed on village farmers to prevent them from processing and exporting their produce. There were prohibitions on products, such as quarry stone, sage, eggs, antiques, medicine, and gasoline, but none was as devastating to the local economy as the ban on olive oil, which represented approximately 14.5 percent of total agricultural production and roughly 5 percent (but as high as 12 percent in good years) of total West Bank GNP.[65] Obtaining a license to export permitted products and operate processing machines was contingent upon payment of taxes and fines.[66] And not just the individual applying for a permit or license but the applicant's entire family had to have a clear record.

Another economic coercive tactic used by the Israeli army to corner the participants of the intifada and undermine general support in Gaza was the reissuing of the *hawiyya*. Operation Plastic Card, launched on June 6, 1988, required all Gazans who worked in Israel to obtain a new, brightly colored identity card. To purchase this card (which cost about ten dollars), the applicants had to have clear records and had to have paid any taxes that they or their relatives owed. The UNLU immediately called for a boycott, and local activists attempted to confiscate and destroy as many of what the Israeli military called "honesty cards" as possible. Nevertheless, by the fall of 1988 the army had managed to win this battle and isolate some of the core activists.[67]

International Response

One main feature that set the intifada apart from previous resistance efforts was international material and ideological support. Demonstrations of solidarity, involving thousands of protestors, erupted throughout the world, in

West Germany, Italy, Canada, the United States, the Netherlands, and Japan. All Arab regimes, regardless of their reservations about the PLO or fears that the intifada could become a model of insurrection in their own states, were compelled to pledge moral and financial support to ensure the continuation of the Palestinian uprising.[68] It is partly for these reasons that the intifada continued well beyond its predicted demise.

Shortly after the intifada began, Jordan pledged to continue to pay the salaries of teachers and civil servants regardless of strikes, curfews, or resignations. The government also offered pensions to families of those who were disabled or killed in the intifada. As a symbolic gesture, "Iraq began paying pensions to the families of those killed in the intifada equivalent to the pensions given to the families of its own soldiers killed in the [Iran-Iraq] Gulf war."[69] Unofficial sources reported that the Gulf states of Saudi Arabia, Kuwait, Qatar, and the United Arab Emirates together pledged $118 million for the first year of the uprising.[70] The summit also reaffirmed its annual $150 million payment to the PLO.

In the United States, the world's greatest ideological and financial ally of Israel, the images of Israeli brutality stirred a general outcry from the public. Until then it had for the most part been ignorant of the Palestinians' condition under occupation, and it was shocked at the unprecedented intensity and severity of the conflict. Israel's image was marred by the repeated acts of brutality reported in the newspapers.

Opinion polls tapping into the US public's attitudes toward the Israel-Palestinian conflict showed a general decline in support of the Israelis. A 1988 Gallup survey, confirmed by numerous other polls, found that about 30 percent of Americans "view Israel less favorably" than before the intifada. Surveys also revealed a sharp difference between public opinion and US government policies. A substantial majority of Americans (70 percent) became weary of the US funding of Israel. Once again, Gallup surveys found that 41 percent thought that US aid to Israel should be decreased, and 19 percent believed that it should be stopped completely. Moreover, 22 percent indicated that their negative opinion had been influenced by Israel's handling of the intifada.[71]

Israelis' public opinion was almost the opposite that of the Americans. Surveys showed 69 percent of Israelis favored taking a "tougher stand" in quelling (what was then labeled as) "the disturbances," 23 percent believed the level of response was appropriate, and only 7 percent thought it should be softened.[72] These attitudes were reflected in the Knesset, where, even before the intifada, calls for a "transfer" solution (an Israeli code word for the expulsion of the Palestinian population from the occupied territories) to the conflict over the West Bank and the Gaza Strip had been made by right-of-center political figures. In a speech to Israeli settlers on April 1, 1988, Prime Minister Shamir compared Palestinians to "grasshoppers" who could be crushed. To emphasize this point, the minister of industry and trade and former defense minister, Ariel Sharon, moved with his family into the Muslim quarter of Jerusalem's Old City.[73]

Consequences of the Intifada

Within this politically charged context, the intifada in less than a year not only upset the power relations inside Israel and also outside, tied to the occupation, but began to reorder them. On July 31, 1988, in a historic televised speech, King Hussein reversed four decades of the Hashemites' ruling policy regarding Jordan's administrative responsibility for the West Bank and its claim to represent the Palestinians of the West Bank as a legitimate substitute for the PLO. The king severed these links without consulting the PLO beforehand. L. Andoni speculated that the king hoped to catch the PLO off guard in order to demonstrate the organization's inability to "handle the responsibility it had always sought."[74] The Jordanian government immediately followed through on its new position: The next day it began to disentangle itself by revoking the Jordanian citizenship of West Bank Palestinians (reducing it to two-year travel documentation).

Four months later, as noted in the previous chapter, the PNC held its nineteenth session in Algiers (November 12–15, 1988) in order to make concrete its new position in view of these rapid and profound political changes. This historic session brought forth the Declaration of Independence of Palestine (text in Appendix 9), with Jerusalem as its capital. No less significant was Arafat's address to the forty-third session of the United Nations General Assembly in Geneva, on December 13, 1988,[75] where he formally and unequivocally recognized Israel's right to exist, denounced terrorism, and accepted territorial concessions. His speech reiterated the main points of the resolution passed at the PNC session.[76]

Palestinians inside the occupied territories celebrated their "national independence day" in widespread support of the PNC statement. The resolutions, however, drove a deeper wedge between Hamas and the UNLU. The Islamists issued an appeal to the PNC in Algeria that restated their position: "We condemn all the attitudes calling for ending the *jihad* and struggle, and for establishing peace with the murderers, and the attitudes which call for acceptance of the Jewish entity on any part of our land."[77] Nonetheless, the majority of Palestinians perceived that opening dialogue between the

United States and their sole and legitimate representatives, the PLO, as indeed "an achievement of the intifada" (UNLU *bayan* 31). It was a welcome political victory, as Palestinians were being hurt badly by the economic struggle against Israeli occupation.

The political optimism among all Palestinians that the intifada would produce a political solution—a negotiated settlement with Israel—to end the occupation, with the United States as the mediator, never materialized. Supported by the United States, Israel remained intransigent, offering its own version of a peace agreement: Palestinian autonomy over civilian affairs, but not the land or resources. Such a proposal resembled the provisions of the Camp David Accords and did not include the PLO or an independent Palestinian state in the end. The US and Israeli obstruction of any peace except on their own terms (demeaning to Palestinians through the denial of Palestinian national rights) undermined the Palestinian diplomatic initiative.[78] The Israeli-US counterproposal outraged the Palestinians under occupation and in the diaspora, all of whom overwhelmingly rejected it, as did the PLO. Thus the parties reached another deadlock.

Conclusion

The First Intifada was a historic culmination of all previous efforts by the Palestinian people to resist dispossession and the suppression of their national identity. It constituted the fourth major national effort in defense of the Palestinians' homeland against Zionism's and Israel's efforts to dispossess them completely and Judaize the country in the twentieth century. The first effort had been the 1936–1939 revolt against the authorities of the British mandate, the second was the 1947–1948 armed resistance to the partitioning of Palestine, and the third was the founding of the revolutionary PLO between 1964 and 1968. Unlike these previous endeavors, the intifada was strongly unified. It joined together the young and the old, men and women, urban dwellers and villagers, both Palestinian Muslims and Palestinian Christians, the poor and the rich, and all political currents, to form a genuine grassroots movement representing the latest strong expression of the collective Palestinian will.[79] It erupted twenty years after the start of the occupation and forty years after the United Nations vote to partition Palestine.

The intifada did not occur in a sociopolitical vacuum; it was the culmination of a resistance that had taken different forms in response to Israeli actions. Israel had practiced four major forms of subjugation to turn the occupied territories into Israeli colonies and to make them thoroughly Jewish rather than Palestinian. As detailed above, these forms of subjugation were political repression, economic exploitation, institutional destruction, and ideological and cultural suppression, combined with the establishment of privileged Israeli settlements on the Israeli-occupied Palestinian land. These processes had sown the seeds of the destruction of Israel's own policy. They generated discontent, blocked "legitimate" means of redressing grievances, denied Palestinian identity, and triggered innovative Palestinian strategies of resistance. The critical mechanisms that the Palestinian people created to counter centralized Israeli control and to decentralize empowerment were "popular sovereignties," which were self-reliant local committees, a blend of traditional and modern structures of sociopolitical organization, social service institutions, communication, and mobilization.

The intifada won international sympathy and support, but the PLO leadership, without credible international reach, failed to transform that sympathy into international solidarity for the Palestinian people and their cause. The intifada was not a mere political event; such a view locks it into a narrow calculation of immediate losses and gains. Instead, it should be seen as a total rejection of the Israeli occupation. The brilliant success of the intifada against Israeli repression, it is clear, not only galvanized the people under occupation but also reenergized the diaspora communities and healed the divisions within the PLO. Despite the new diplomatic initiative, including some major concessions by the PLO, the intifada was never able to overcome the obstructionism of Israel and the United States. Therefore the political impasse of the Palestinian-Israeli conflict remained. Palestinians had sacrificed too much—and perhaps had too great expectations—to accept a solution that fell short of restitution and independent statehood. Indeed as the intifada began to wane in 1990, Fateh and the PLO were floundering and suffering serious shock: the assassinations of two of their top three leaders (Khalil al-Wazir in 1988 and Salah Khalaf in 1990).

In 1990 Iraq's invasion of Kuwait and in 1991 the US-led allied Gulf War against Baghdad introduced a dramatic and strategically transformative dimension into the Middle East. The war quickly directed attention away from the ongoing intifada and realigned the regional balance of political power to the disadvantage of the Palestinians. Although the Gulf crisis overshadowed the intifada and the Palestine question and significantly reduced Arab support for them, it nevertheless gave the PLO leadership, under Arafat and his loyalists, a new window of opportunity to move the Palestinian issue once again onto the international political agenda. However, the ill-considered actions of Chairman Arafat—in actuality siding with Saddam Hussein of Iraq but rhetorically claiming otherwise[80]—isolated and delegitimized the PLO, and with it the Palestinian cause, not only in the international arena but also among a large number of Arab governments and people, especially the wealthy oil-exporting states and the politically influential ones such as Egypt and Syria. Thus, in the context of Israeli-US obstruction of a just peace in the Middle East, Arafat's incompetent and inept actions squandered the achievements of the intifada and set the stage for the precipitous decline of the PLO in the 1990s, making room for the start of both the inconclusive "peace process" initiated by the US government and the secret negotiations of the United States with the PLO and Israel that led to the Oslo Accords in 1993. These accords, signed by the PLO and Israel under US auspices, were a political earthquake in both the Arab region and the occupied territories. The terms and consequences of these accords, as discussed in the next chapter, will determine the destiny of Palestine and the Palestinians.

Notes

1. J. L. Abu-Lughod identified five categories of Palestinians and systematically discussed them in "Palestinians: Exiles at Home and Abroad," *Current Sociology* 36 (Summer 1988): 61–69.

2. *Facts and Figures About the Palestinians* (Washington, DC: Center for Policy Analysis on Palestine, 1993).

3. For example, an Israeli kibbutz, Beth-Alfa, supplied water cannons to the apartheid state of South Africa until 1987. This point raises the issue of why live ammunition and lethal rubber bullets were used against the Palestinian protesters. See J. Hunter, "Israel and South Africa: Sidestepping Sanctions," *Middle East International* (February 20, 1988): 16.

4. S. Roy, *The Gaza Strip: The Political Economy of De-Development* (Washington, DC: Institute for Palestine Studies, 1995).

5. This figure is an approximation based on demographic projections from census data collected by the British mandate in 1931, from 1967 Israeli census data, and from more recent sample surveys. See Abu-Lughod, "Palestinians," 69.

6. D. Peretz, *Intifada: The Palestinian Uprising* (Boulder, CO: Westview Press, 1990): 4.

7. See M. T. Dumper, "Jerusalem's Infrastructure: Is Annexation Irreversible?" *Journal of Palestine Studies* 22 (Spring 1993): 78–95. Dumper put the questions of demography and politics aside in this article and instead focused on the integrated water, electricity, and sewage systems of East and West Jerusalem. Admitting the political difficulty of dividing Jerusalem, he found "no overwhelming functional and technical obstacles to prevent" reversed annexation (p. 93).

8. For a detailed summary of this debate, see C. D. Smith, *Palestine and the Arab-Israeli Conflict* (New York: St. Martin's Press, 1988): 208–211.

9. T. Aruri, ed., *Occupation: Israel over Palestine,* 2nd ed. (Belmont, MA: Association of Arab-American University Graduates, 1989): 8.

10. A. K. Wing, "Legitimacy and Coercion: Legal Traditions and Legal Rules During the Intifada," *Middle East Policy* 2 (1993): 87–103.

11. A brilliant study of the structure and application of the Israeli military law and court system in the occupied territories is L. Hajjar, "Authority, Resistance and the Law: A Study of the Israeli Military Courts in the Occupied Territories," Ph.D. dissertation, American University, 1995.

12. Antonio Gramsci, *Selections from the Prison Notebooks,* translated by Geoffrey N. Smith and Quintin Hoare (New York: International Publishers, 1971).

13. S. K. Farsoun and J. M. Landis, "Structures of Resistance and the 'War of Position': A Case Study of the Palestinian Uprising," *Arab Studies Quarterly* 11 (Fall 1989): 59–86.

14. See S. R. Dajani, *Eyes Without Country: Searching for a Palestinian Strategy of Liberation* (Philadelphia: Temple University Press, 1994).

15. L. Hajjar, M. Rabbani, and J. Beinin, "Palestine and the Arab-Israeli Conflict for Beginners," in Z. Lockman and J. Beinin, eds., *Intifada: The Palestinian Uprising Against Israeli Occupation* (Boston: South End Press, 1989): 109.

16. N. H. Aruri, "Dialectics of Dispossession," in N. H. Aruri, ed., *Occupation: Israel over Palestine,* 2nd ed. (Belmont, MA: Association of Arab-American University Graduates, 1989).

17. Ibid., vi.

18. S. Tamari, "The Palestinian Demand for Independence Cannot Be Postponed Indefinitely," *MERIP Reports* 100–101 (October-December 1981): 34.

19. J. R. Hiltermann, *Behind the Intifada: Labor and Women's Movements in the Occupied Territories* (Princeton: Princeton University Press, 1991): 48.

20. Tamari, "Palestinian Demand," 30. Cited in Hiltermann, *Behind the Intifada,* 48.

21. Hiltermann, *Behind the Intifada,* 17–18.

22. M. K. Shadid, "Israeli Policy Toward Economic Development in the West Bank and Gaza," in G. T. Abed, ed., *The Palestinian Economy: Studies in Development Under Prolonged Occupation* (London: Routledge, 1988): 127.

23. Hiltermann, *Behind the Intifada,* 21.

24. Ibid., 25.

25. Ibid., 30.

26. This observation is derived from an extensive study on Palestinian-Israeli income and employment differences. The fifth major finding was that "not only have noncitizen Arabs been segregated to lower-status occupations, but their income has been considerably lower than that paid to other [Israeli] incumbents in these occupations"; M. Semyonov and N. L. Epstein, *Hewers of Wood and Drawers of Water: Noncitizen Arabs in the Israeli Labor Market,* Report 13 (New York: Cornell International Industrial and Labor Relations, 1987): 115.

27. Ibid., 62.

28. The discussion of the Palestinian Islamic movement is based on Z. Abu-Amr, "Hamas: A Historical and Political Background," *Journal of Palestine Studies* 22 (Summer 1993): 5–19.

29. Ibid., 8.

30. Ibid., 9.

31. M. Benvenisti, *1987 Report: Demographic, Economic, Legal, Social, and Political Developments in the West Bank* (Boulder, CO: Westview Press, 1987): 55.

32. According to Benvenisti, industrial enterprises and facilities for tourism "established across the green line receive a grant of 30 percent and loans at a real interest rate of 0.5 percent, or if dollar linked at 6 percent. These enterprises are also entitled to a grant for land development, structures and equipment, and a 5 percent rebate on financial charges." For housing, "the aid consists of a mortgage (11.5 percent) unlinked to the cost of living index, a linked but interest free loan (65.5 percent) and a linked loan bearing 6 percent interest (11.5 percent). Moreover, the price of an apartment is also subsidized in that the cost of the land is only 5 percent its actual value, and the infrastructure is provided to the settlement free of charge. Thus one can purchase an apartment only 30–45 minutes from Jerusalem for a cash payment of $2,000"; M. Benvenisti, with Z. Abu-Zayed and D. Rubinstein, *The West Bank Handbook: A Political Lexicon* (Boulder, CO: Westview Press, 1986): 111.

33. S. Tamari, professor of sociology at Bir Zeit University in the West Bank, makes this important point about the confiscation of Palestinian land: "There is an extra-territorial definition of public land in Israel so that it belongs to the Jews in totality and not to the Israel Jews in the State of Israel. Israeli citizens who are non-Jews have no access to this land, but Jews who are not Israeli do have access"; "What the Uprising Means," in Lockman and Beinin, *Intifada,* 130.

34. Ibid., 25.

35. In 1983 total Israeli exports to the West Bank and the Gaza Strip amounted to $680.5 million, whereas Israel exported to the United States $1,329.2 million, about twice as much. See Y. A. Sayigh, "Dispossession and Pauperization: The Palestinian Economy Under Occupation," in Abed, *Palestinian Economy,* 260. By 1986 total Israeli exports to the Palestinians grew to $780 million; Tamari, "What the Uprising Means," 129.

36. S. Ryan, "The West Bank and Gaza: Political Consequences of the Intifada," *Middle East Report* 74 (January 1979): 3.

37. Economic Intelligence Unit, *Israel/The Occupied Territories, 1993–1994* (London: Economic Intelligence Unit, 1994): 43.

38. The figures are for 1984 as reported in the *Statistical Abstract of Israel 1984,* No. 35 (Jerusalem: Central Bureau of Statistics, 1984), Tables XXVII/19 and XXVII/20: 762 and 763. This may be an underestimate because of the unaccounted-for, undocumented, and illegal employment.

39. Ibid., viii.

40. Compare the dominance of the service sector to others: Agriculture accounts for roughly 30 percent of GDP, industry about 8 percent, and construction approximately 12 percent; ibid., viii.

41. J. Mandell, "Gaza: Israel's Soweto," *Middle East Report* 136–137 (October-December 1985): 12.

42. Ibid.

43. United Nations Conference on Trade and Development, "Prospects for Sustained Development of the Palestinian Economy in the West Bank and Gaza Strip," UNCTAD/DSD/SEU/2 (Geneva: September 27, 1993): 29.

44. S. S. Elmusa, *The Water Issue and the Palestinian-Israeli Conflict* (Washington, DC: Center for Policy Analysis on Palestine, 1993): 7.

45. Roy, *Gaza Strip*.

46. Ibid., 272.

47. S. K. Farsoun and J. M. Landis, "The Sociology of an Uprising: The Roots of the Intifada," in J. R. Nassar and R. Heacock, eds., *Intifada: Palestine at the Crossroads* (New York: Praeger, 1990): 24.

48. He was later assassinated at his home in Tunis on April 16, 1988, and buried in Damascus, Syria. The *Washington Post* (April 21, 1988) reported that the operation was planned by the Mossad (the Israeli secret intelligence service) after being approved by the Israeli cabinet.

49. A. M. Lesch, *The Palestinian Uprising—Causes and Consequences,* UFSI Report 1 (Washington, DC: Universities Field Staff International, 1988–1989): 4.

50. Further, "annual reserve duty for men was increased from the normal 30 days to 62 days. (In contrast, at the height of the fighting in Lebanon, reserve duty extended for 45 days.)"; ibid., 9.

51. P. Johnson and L. O'Brien with J. R. Hiltermann, "The West Bank Rises Up," in Lockman and Beinin, *Intifada,* 29.

52. B. E. Trainor, "Israelis vs. Palestinians: Tactics Are Refined," *New York Times* (March 30, 1989): A9.

53. "Charter of the Islamic Resistance Movement (Hamas) of Palestine," *Journal of Palestine Studies* 22 (Summer 1993): 130–131.

54. Ibid.

55. I. Jad, "From Salons to the Popular Committees: Palestinian Women 1919–1989," in Nassar and Heacock, *Intifada,* 135.

56. Ibid.

57. Al-Haq, *Punishing a Nation: Israeli Human Rights Violations During the Palestinian Uprising, December 1987–December 1988* (Boston: South End Press, 1989): 346.

58. Ibid., 348.

59. Peretz, *Intifada,* 67.

60. All references to the texts of communiqués are from Lockman and Beinin, *Intifada,* Appendix II, 327–394.

61. This figure does not account for casual day laborers or illegal migrant workers.

62. See the study of the town of Beit Sahur by M. J. Nojeim, *Planting Olive Trees: Palestinian Non-Violent Resistance,* Ph.D. dissertation, American University, 1993.

63. Figures are extrapolated from Peretz, *Intifada,* 77, 150.

64. Al-Haq, *Punishing a Nation,* 388.

65. Ibid., 406–407.

66. Ibid., 405.

67. Hiltermann, *Behind the Intifada,* 185.

68. L. Andoni, "Solid Arab Backing," *Middle East International* (February 6, 1988): 7.

69. M. Jansen, "The Funds Which Help the Intifada," *Middle East International* (June 24, 1988): 6.

70. Ibid.

71. F. Moughrabi, *American Public Opinion and the Palestine Question,* Occasional Paper 4 (Washington, DC: International Center for Research and Public Policy, 1986): 248.

72. J. Kifner, "Arrests of Palestinians Approach 1,000," *New York Times* (December 26, 1987): A7.

73. "Home for Sharon amid Arabs," *New York Times* (December 17, 1987): A14.

74. Ibid., 170.

75. Arafat was denied a visa to enter the United States in order to address the United Nations at its headquarters in New York City on the grounds that he belonged to a "terrorist organization." On December 1, 1988, the United Nations General Assembly voted 151–2, with one abstention by Britain, to condemn the United States for violating a 1947 headquarters agreement that requires the United States not to obstruct persons with legitimate business at the United Nations.

76. Z. Abu-Amr, "The Politics of the Intifada," in M. C. Hudson, ed., *The Palestinians: New Directions* (Washington, DC: Center for Contemporary Arab Studies, Georgetown University, 1990): 5; omissions not in the original. For a full reproduction of the document produced at the November 1988 PNC meeting, see *Journal of Palestine Studies* 17 (Winter 1989).

77. As cited by Abu-Amr, "Politics of the Intifada," 9.

78. N. Aruri, *The Obstruction of Peace: The U.S., Israel and the Palestinians* (Monroe, ME: Common Courage Press, 1995); see also N. Chomsky, *World Orders: Old and New* (New York: Columbia University Press, 1994).

79. Farsoun and Landis, "Structures of Resistance," 60.

80. For a more complex interpretation of the behavior of the PLO in the Gulf crisis, see N. G. Finkelstein, *The Rise and Fall of Palestine* (Minneapolis: University of Minnesota Press, 1996), Ch. 4 and the epilogue.

8

The PLO-Israel Oslo Accords

Structure and Dynamics

The "peace process" on which the PLO and Palestinian leaders from the occupied territories embarked in 1991 in Madrid was a turning point in Palestinian history. After almost two years of frustrating and fruitless public negotiations between Israel and the Palestinian delegation from the occupied territories, top secret PLO-Israeli negotiations cultivated by the Norwegian government suddenly produced an accord. In late August 1993, Israel and the PLO announced agreement on a "set of principles" to resolve the hundred-year-old conflict between the two peoples. Initialed in Oslo, the Declaration of Principles on Interim Self-Government Arrangements (called the Oslo Accords because it also includes documents of mutual recognition between Israel and the PLO) was signed in September 1993 on the lawn of the White House.

How will the Declaration of Principles and the subsequent Cairo, Paris, and Oslo II Accords serve the cause of Palestine and the Palestinians? Specifically, will the accords lead to self-determination and an independent state for the Palestinian people? Or will the final outcome be the "technical resolution" of the Palestine question,[1] which in effect means the historic dissolution of the Palestinians as a people and the emergence of the diaspora communities as second-class minorities? Analysis of the accords and their implications for an independent future for Palestine and the Palestinians as a people is the subject of this chapter.

The Road to the Oslo Accords

The PLO's decline and isolation, the escalating cost of the intifada for Israel, and the US hegemony in the world (because of the end of the Soviet

Union) and the Middle East (through the victory over Iraq in 1991) were the circumstances behind the Madrid peace conference and the Oslo Accords. What finally pushed the PLO toward the accords were the "bridging measures" proposed by the administration of US president Bill Clinton, an attempt to resolve the impasse in the Washington peace talks (the negotiating formula following the Madrid conference). In June 1993, after ten rounds of futile Palestinian-Israeli negotiations, the Clinton administration prepared a proposal it labeled "Declaration of Principles," the first use of that phrase before the Oslo Accords. The proposal contained three elements that were unprecedented even in US diplomacy.

In effect, the US proposal reconceptualized the legal status of the West Bank and the Gaza Strip as *disputed* rather than *occupied* territories; second, it made no reference to the long-standing formula (embodied in UN Security Council Resolutions 242 and 338) of exchanging land for peace in order to resolve the Arab-Israeli conflict and made no mention of Israeli military withdrawal from the territories; third, it proposed that matters relating to Palestinian sovereignty were outside the scope of the negotiations for the interim agreement. Accordingly, issues of land and water, Israeli settlements, and Jerusalem were deferred for a number of years. The proposal was significant as well in that it contained no mention of the rights of the 1948 and 1967 Palestinian refugees. In turn, because the issues of land and the nature of the authority over the land were to be dealt with separately and in the future, negotiations concerning the interim period would be limited to authority over the *people* and *not* the *territory*. Hence the Palestinians of the West Bank and the Gaza Strip were reduced in this US proposal to "inhabitants" of those territories with only some civil but no national political rights. Both the Palestinian negotiating delegation and the PLO leadership were shocked and alarmed by this new and sharply biased formulation, itself a substantial departure from the conventional and long-standing US policy and from the guarantees (to the Palestinian delegation) of the George H. W. Bush administration.[2] With a broker (the United States) that seemed more Israeli than the Israelis, the impasse became all the more inescapable, and the PLO, without informing the Washington Palestinian negotiating team, opted for direct secret negotiations with Israel, where the terms could not possibly be worse.

The Declaration of Principles thus ushered in the current phase of the Palestinian-Israeli struggle. It is a dramatic turning point in the contemporary history of the Middle East. It was the breakthrough, on Israeli terms, for the political settlement not only of the Palestinian-Israeli conflict but also of the Arab-Israeli confrontation. Because of its terms, however, and because of what it ignored of Palestinian rights and what it committed the PLO to do, the Oslo Accords plunged the Palestinian people and their political institutions into the most serious and profound moral, cultural, identity, and political crisis. Most Palestinians agreed with Edward Said that "it was a betrayal of our history and our people."[3] Palestinians everywhere—inside and outside the occupied territories—were divided over the legitimacy, meaning, and consequences of the Oslo Accords.

The Oslo Declaration of Principles

After the 1991 Gulf War, it became clear to the United States, Israel, and the pro-Western Arab states that a new Middle Eastern order would not be possible without resolution of the Palestine question. The US imperative for control of the oil, the markets, and the strategic areas in the region dictated such a resolution.[4] For Israel, resolution of the Palestine problem would solve simultaneously both its domestic dilemma (the cost of the intifada) and its regional dilemma (by ending its political and economic isolation). Political settlement of the Palestinian question would also allow the Israeli economy to move in new and more favorable directions. As an Israeli analyst stated:

> For twenty years the occupied territories provided a partial substitute for the international market and a clandestine outlet to the Arab world. But the economic benefits of occupation—cheap and reliable labor supply and a captive market—were sharply reduced by the intifada. The costs of the occupation to the Israeli economy have come to overshadow its benefits. For these reasons, settling the conflict—meaning, in effect, decolonization of the occupied territories through accommodation with the PLO—became an economic necessity for Israel.[5]

And yet, despite these strategic, political, and moral incentives and the more sympathetic international view of the Palestinians, Arafat, isolated and weakened as he and the PLO were, signed a controversial agreement that has jeopardized the destiny of the Palestinians as a people and their hopes for independent nationhood. The Oslo agreement was a surprise to everyone except the dozen or so Palestinian, Israeli, and Norwegian officials directly involved in the negotiations. Not even Israel's superpower mentor and ally, the United States, was aware of the negotiations or the content of the agreement. On the Palestinian side, reportedly only four, including Arafat, knew of the negotiations and of the content of the accords when they were initialed.

Arguments in Support of the Declaration

Chairman Arafat and the faction of the PLO that supported him claimed that the Oslo Accords represented the best deal they could manage under the unfortunate circumstances[6] (which, of course, were in large measure of their own making). They typically answered their critics not with explanations but with a question that they considered to be the definitive comeback: "What is the alternative?" Further, they added that these "bad" Oslo Accords nevertheless would allow the Palestinians a toehold in their own homeland from which to carry on the struggle for self-determination, and that it would thus put the Palestinians in a much better position to achieve statehood.[7] Finally, Arab proponents of the agreement said that any new reality was better than the old status quo.

Among Palestinian intellectuals and activists, the best case for the declaration was made by Walid Khalidi, a Palestinian professor at Harvard University's Center for International Affairs. Khalidi listed the declaration's accomplishments for the Palestinians: (1) recognition of the PLO by Israel; (2) recognition of the PLO by the United States; (3) establishment of the principle of Israeli withdrawal from occupied Palestinian land; (4) establishment of the principle of more than municipal elections—a central Palestinian authority, emerging from general elections, that would have legislative powers and a strong police force; (5) establishment of the principle of a timetable for accomplishing the above; (6) establishment of the principle of the transfer of powers to the Palestinian authority; and (7) establishment of the provision of funds by world powers.

In combination, according to Khalidi, these Israeli "concessions" created "new conditions and thus provide new opportunities provided we [Palestinians] know how to exploit them." Khalidi thus rejected opposing the declaration on the grounds that "bringing it down would bring about a [Palestinian] fratricidal bloodbath." Similarly, forcing Arafat out would play into Israel's already strong hands: "It would remove the symbol linking Palestinians inside Palestine with those in the diaspora. It would also initiate a [destructive] struggle for succession." Thus the only course of action open to Palestinians was to support Arafat and the negotiated framework. "A sovereign Palestinian state in the 1967 frontiers with East Jerusalem as its capital," according to Khalidi, "is potentially realizable from the womb of Oslo." Khalidi did not elaborate on how to realize sovereignty, nor did he explain the contradiction in his assessment that such a "Zionist composition," as he called the agreement, could lead to a sovereign Palestinian state, the idea of which is internationally supported except by "two states: Israel and the United States." But therein lies the dilemma.[8]

Arguments Critical of the Declaration

Criticism by Palestinians, Arabs, and others of the various accords, of Arafat's handling of Palestinian affairs, of Israel's posture and actions, and of the role of the US and European governments are numerous. To begin with, the Declaration of Principles was signed by Arafat without public debate or approval and ratification by the PLO. By signing the agreement, Arafat squandered the efforts of a century of Palestinian struggle and sacrifice for national political rights—rights that had been repeatedly confirmed by international law and codified in numerous United Nations resolutions and by many other international forums.

In the White House signing ceremony in 1993, Arafat pronounced words that had all the flair of a rental agreement, words that made no mention of the extent of his people's suffering and loss. The Palestinians saw themselves characterized before the world as its now repentant assailants, and the thousands killed by Israel's bombing of refugee camps, hospitals, and schools in Lebanon; its expulsion of 800,000 people in 1948 (whose descendants now number about 5 million, many of them stateless refugees); Israel's conquest of the Palestinians' land and property; Israel's destruction of more than four hundred Palestinian villages; its invasion of Lebanon; and the ravages of twenty-six years of brutal military occupation were reduced to the status of terrorism and violence to be renounced retrospectively or dropped from reference entirely. In return for exactly what?[9]

Basically, in return for recognition of the PLO (and Chairman Arafat himself) as representative of the Palestinians, but not of the fundamental Palestinian rights.[10] Thus Arafat did resolve the problem of his own diminished leadership and that of the financially strapped and sinking PLO, which his faction controlled. As a result, Arafat, long vilified as an evil terrorist by the US and Israeli media and politicians, was suddenly catapulted to center stage on the international scene, labeled a peacemaker by his former detractors, given extensive access to the media, and was given an enthusiastic reception at the White House and by the US Congress.

What are those Palestinian rights that are threatened by the agreement? They include the internationally codified basic rights of self-determination and independent sovereign statehood, repatriation or compensation for both the 1948 and 1967 refugees, the restitution of the land and resources illegally confiscated in the West Bank and the Gaza Strip, and reparations for the people of Palestine. If the Palestinians are accorded these rights by Israel, the issues of borders and (East) Jerusalem would no longer be matters for negotiation because the frontiers of Israel and the 1967 occupied territories are clear. What would remain to be negotiated would be the modalities of Israeli withdrawal; the restoration of Palestinian land; Israel's payment of compensation and reparations for resource and land confiscation (for 1948 Palestine and the long occupation of the West Bank and Gaza); elimination of the illegal Israeli settlements; Israeli legal culpability for violations of individual human, civil, and property rights; and finally, establishment of security arrangements for both sides.

Instead of using international law and UN resolutions as the legal framework for negotiations, Arafat obviated the internationally codified Palestinian rights and turned them into mere negotiating positions. Although the reference in the declaration to UN Security Council Resolutions 242 and 338 (the land-for-peace formula) is important, the document ignores many other UN resolutions. It disregards, for example, UN General Assembly Resolution 194, which confirms the collective right of either return of Palestinian refugees to their homeland or compensation. The accord provides for the return of some individual refugees from the 1967 war, whom it refers to as "displaced persons," but not for the return of the 1948 refugees, who remain an item for the "final status" negotiations.[11] It should be clear, then, that the declaration excludes from its provisions the Palestinian refugees, nearly *two-thirds* (at the time, about 4.5 million) of all Palestinians who are outside the occupied territories.

All UN Security Council resolutions on Jerusalem are also ignored in the agreement.[12] The status of Jerusalem is placed on the agenda for future negotiations. Also excluded are resolutions on illegal Israeli settlements in the occupied territories.[13] The transfer of population of the occupying power and settlement in conquered territories under occupation contravenes not only UN resolutions but also provisions of the fourth Geneva Convention on war and occupation. By disregarding these internationally recognized standards and by consenting to the continuing presence of all Israeli settlements in the West Bank and the Gaza Strip—presumably pending final negotiations—the PLO under Arafat validated and legitimized the illegal settlements and provided Israel with a legal claim to the land.

As much as disregarding international law and United Nations resolutions jeopardizes Palestinian rights, the grossest blunder committed by

Arafat's PLO in the accords was its failure at the outset to extract from Israel an explicit recognition that the Palestinians are a people with the right to self-determination and that Israel is an *occupying power* in the Palestinian territories. Such a recognition would have meant that the accords would be nothing less than a declaration of principles governing negotiations over the methods and timing of Israeli withdrawal from the occupied territories, the transfer of power to the PLO, the establishment of an independent sovereign Palestine, and the restitution of the rights of the refugees.

Until the Oslo Accords were signed, the international consensus supported the idea of a complete Israeli withdrawal from the occupied West Bank and Gaza Strip and the right of the Palestinians to establish an independent state in the evacuated areas. Article 31 of the Oslo II Accords[14] states: "Neither party shall be deemed, by virtue of having entered into this agreement, to have renounced or waived any of its existing rights, claims, or positions." But as Norman Finkelstein argued, "Seemingly balanced, this provision actually signals a most crucial concession by the Palestinians. In effect, the PLO grants legitimacy to Israel's pretense of possessing 'existing rights' in the West Bank and Gaza. . . . The broadly affirmed title of Palestinians to the occupied territories is now put on a par with the broadly denied title of Israel to them."[15] The PLO, then, consented to negotiate with Israel as a claimant to the land—as the Clinton administration had proposed earlier—rather than as the occupier that it is.[16] In other words, after having recognized the existence of Israel and ceding to it the great majority of historical Palestine, the PLO accepted the idea that the remaining Palestinian land (the West Bank and the Gaza Strip) is disputed, not occupied, territory and therefore negotiable.

Whereas Israel totally ignored the internationally codified rights of the Palestinians, including an independent state, the PLO recognized the legitimate (not merely de facto) existence of the state of Israel. Arafat was also forced to renounce PLO violence and terrorism, and he promised to amend the PLO charter. In return, not one word in the accords obligates Israel to end its violence against the Palestinians in the occupied territories or its attacks on refugee camps in Lebanon and elsewhere or formally and officially to renounce its ambition to appropriate the land and resources of the West Bank and Gaza.

Last, the PLO leadership botched its negotiating strategy. The PLO consented to postpone "consideration" of the most pivotal and central issues—the refugees, Jerusalem, settlements, borders, sovereignty—until the so-called final status negotiations, three years after signing the first implementation agreement in 1994. Instead of achieving a single comprehensive agreement with Israel to be implemented in stages, it agreed to negotiate in stages and thus fragment further the implementation process. In the context of increasing Israeli strength and a commensurate decline in the Palestinian position, this strategy further disadvantaged the Palestinian people. In all agreements Israel has de facto veto power over issues of Palestinian sovereignty, internal affairs, and economics, whereas the Palestinian side has neither reciprocal rights, an equivalent veto, nor even the capacity to seek external binding arbitration.

Agreements on the Interim Period

The five-year limited autonomy provision embodied in the Declaration of Principles transferred specific and limited spheres (Article 6.2 of the Oslo II Accord) to the Palestinian authority (education and culture, health, social welfare, direct taxation, and tourism). It permitted the establishment of a Palestinian police force and an elected council (the Palestinian Interim Self-Governing Authority, or PISGA), whose size, powers, and responsibilities were negotiated in the third implementation agreement extending limited, autonomous self-rule to the West Bank in September 1995. Further, it allowed the creation of a group of specific economic authorities (electric, water, land, seaport, a monetary authority, and a Palestinian development bank). In addition, some joint economic actions on a regional basis are set out in other protocols of economic cooperation (the Paris protocol, signed April 29, 1994, and the two Cairo Accords, signed May 4 and August 29, 1994).

The first of the Cairo Accords, formally called Agreement on the Gaza Strip and Jericho Area, launched the five-year interim period. Israel withdrew from 62 percent of the Gaza Strip and from the small district of Jericho, a total area of only about 1 percent of historical Palestine (see Maps 8.1 and 8.2). But the agreement allows the Israeli army to move freely in the autonomous areas and to maintain military installations and zones there. Thus, although the Israeli military would presumably be "withdrawn" from Gaza and Jericho first, it would simply be redeployed in the rest of the West Bank "outside populated areas." Further, the Cairo agreements provided Israel's military administration exclusive authority in "legislation, adjudication, policy execution, in addition to conferring responsibility for the exercise of these powers in conformity with the norms of international law." In short, the Gaza Strip and the West Bank were to remain under the authority of the Israeli military occupation regime.

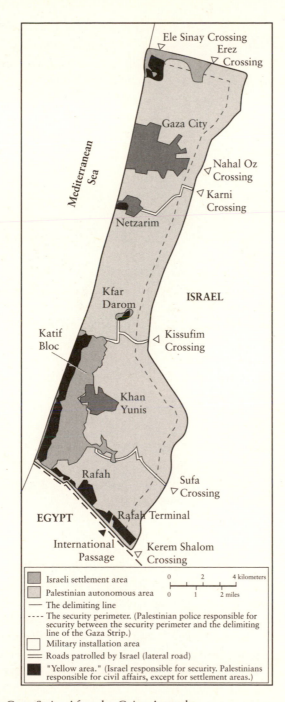

MAP 8.1   The Gaza Strip, After the Cairo Accords

SOURCE: *Settlements and Peace: The Problem of Jewish Colonization in Palestine* (Washington, DC: Center for Policy Analysis on Palestine, 1995): 16.

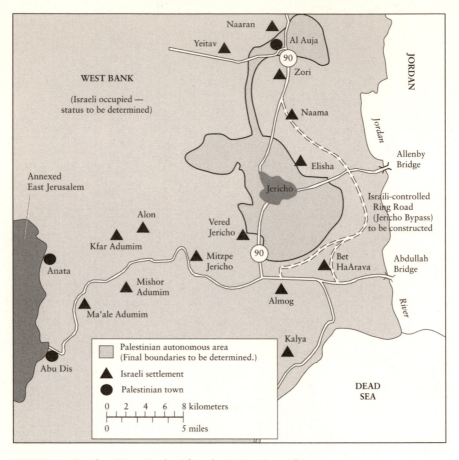

MAP 8.2   Jericho, West Bank, After the Cairo Accords
SOURCE: *Settlements and Peace: The Problem of Jewish Colonization in Palestine* (Washington, DC: Center for Policy Analysis on Palestine, 1995): 15.

It is remarkable that Arafat and the PLO consented to negotiate with Israel over purely internal Palestinian matters (the structure, size, powers, and responsibilities of the Palestinian Legislative Council, or PLC, and the executive authority), thus allowing Israel at the very least to influence, if not control, internal Palestinian affairs. Israel and its military occupation government, not the Palestinian people, are then the legitimate source of the limited-autonomy authority of the Palestinian Authority. The interim PA has no sovereignty over Palestinian territory—except over certain social and economic aspects of the Palestinian people's lives—and no basis to establish such sovereignty in the future, as all its laws and activities are circumscribed and must be approved by Israel, pending "final status" negotiations. This lack of authority is ensured not only by the legal provisions and constraints noted above but also by the liaison, review, and other joint committees established by the Declaration of Principles to govern all the powers of the PA. These committees are supposed to manage through consensus all security, economic, and administrative issues and to address differences in views between Israel and the PA. In effect, however, they provide Israel with veto power over all Palestinian decisions.

The Oslo II Accords

The second-phase agreement, formally entitled the Israeli-Palestinian Interim Agreement on the West Bank and Gaza (labeled Oslo II by some and Taba by others), initialed on September 24, 1995, in Taba, Egypt, and signed in Washington, D.C., four days later, incorporated the Cairo and Paris agreements, superseded them, and reaffirmed the same themes and structures worked out between the two sides in the earlier implementation agreements. The Oslo II agreement comprises over four hundred pages setting forth the structure of future relations between Israel and the PLO and the Palestinians of the occupied territories, including security arrangements, legal matters, economic relations, elections and the structure and powers of the Palestinian governing body and Legislative Council (which supersedes the current PA), the transfer of powers of civil affairs, the release of Palestinian prisoners, and Israeli-Palestinian cooperation.

Oslo II divides the West Bank into three zones. The first, or Area A—3 percent of the total area—is made up of the disconnected municipal areas of six Palestinian cities. Israeli troops there were to be redeployed over a period of not longer than six months to just beyond the near suburbs, or in a ring around the cities roughly one to two kilometers out. The second zone, or Area B—approximately 27 percent of the West Bank—covers the populated areas of about 450 villages and towns in the rural districts (where two-thirds of the West Bank Palestinians live). There the Israeli military and Palestinian police will "share" authority in joint patrols, the Palestinians overseeing civil affairs and maintaining public order inside the villages and the Israeli military having "overall security authority," including the right to intervene in those villages. The third, or Area C, incorporates existing and future Israeli military installations, settlements, and unpopulated (state land) areas—the rural land outside the towns, which makes up 70–73 percent of the land of the West Bank; this will remain under Israeli control. Israel was to redeploy its military from Area C (except from those Israeli military and other installations and settlements mentioned in the agreement) over eighteen months in six-month intervals and yield only civil affairs to the new Palestinian Legislative Council. To date, it has not.

In all, the PA gained limited civil autonomy over less than 4 percent of the area of historical Palestine. Israel redeployed its forces from five of the major cities by January 1996. The newly elected right-wing Likud government of Binyamin Netanyahu at first stonewalled on implementing the redeployment agreement and, after the violent upheaval in September 1996 over the opening of the archaeological tunnel under Al-Haram al-Sharif, was intent on renegotiating the terms of withdrawal. After long-delayed and crisis-ridden negotiations, the Netanyahu government agreed to a redeployment of Israeli troops from Hebron, which was carried out on January 16, 1997. This action left the Israeli army in exclusive control of about 20 percent of the city (the heart of the old city and the whole eastern sector), where 400–450 Jewish settlers and more than 20,000 Palestinians resided. Although the Palestinian officials defended the Hebron agreement, others criticized it not only for legitimizing the division of Hebron but also for legitimizing the existing Israeli settlement at the city's core.

The Netanyahu government failed to redeploy Israeli troops from Area B, as stipulated in Oslo II. But the Hebron agreement included a new accord on Israeli redeployment from Areas B and C. The agreement did not, however, formally specify the location and extent of the territorial redeployment Israel was expected to initiate. In March 1997 Netanyahu's government offered to withdraw from 9 percent of the rural areas in Area B (amounting to only 2 percent of land not in Palestinian hands), but Arafat's PA rejected the proposal as insulting.

As in the Gaza Strip, the Israeli civil administration will be dissolved and the military administration will be "withdrawn" but will retain ultimate authority.[17] Chapter 3, Article 17, Section 4.a of the Oslo II agreement specifically states that "Israel, through its military government, has the authority over areas that are not under the territorial jurisdiction of the Council, powers and responsibilities not transferred to the Council and Israelis." Thus, "although no longer physically present, Israeli administration remains very much in evidence within the PA areas as well. Birth certificates, identity cards, driver licenses, applications of various sorts, even Palestinian passports, must all be registered with and approved by the military government in order to attain official status."[18] The Israeli military forces will *not* leave the West Bank. Indeed, Israel will establish sixty-two *new* military bases there. It will retain control of entrances and exits to the cities and all the roads of the West Bank. Any Palestinian town or city can be sealed and any village can be reentered at will by Israel.[19] All commercial traffic between the autonomy areas is controlled by Israel. Israeli settlers will travel on superhighways that will bypass Palestinian cities, towns, and villages and on all other roads, while Palestinians will be allowed to use only existing old roads and will have to stop frequently for security checks on all highways.

As Map 8.3 shows, Oslo II created a disconnected patchwork of zones of control and overlapping jurisdictions that violates the integrity not only of the West Bank but also the West Bank in relation to the Gaza Strip. And this arrangement violates Article 4 of the original Oslo Declaration of Principles, which declared the West Bank and the Gaza Strip a "single territorial unit, whose integrity will be preserved during the interim period." This patchwork of control is what some Palestinian commentators (including Hanan 'Ashrawi, the former spokeswoman of the Palestinian delegation to the Washington talks) called the "Swiss cheese" or "leopard spots" model of Israeli domination: The holes in the Swiss cheese or the spots on the leopard are the Palestinian-controlled areas, and the rest of the piece or body is dominated by Israel. As a result, Israeli action on the ground created "disabling discontinuity," as Said once called it, between the main Palestinian cities and subregions and thus undermined (if not completely eliminated) the foundation of a contiguous Palestinian patrimony.

Oslo II marked the final transformation of Israel's belligerent occupation of the Palestinian territories into legitimate rule, with the official partnership of Arafat's PLO: "Oslo has allowed for the full rehabilitation of Israel. No longer condemned as an occupying power, Israel rather stands beyond reproach as a full-fledged peacemaker."[20] Israel achieved what it had set out to do since at least the signing of the Camp David Accords with Egypt in 1978: It won limited functional civil autonomy for the Palestinians of the occupied territories and a legalized tight grip on the land, resources, economy, and security of the areas.

The Legislative Council

The Oslo Accords provided for Palestinian elections of a council to govern the West Bank and the Gaza Strip, as well as a separate but simultaneous election of the head, or *ra'ees* (the Arabic term was used in the document in order to sidestep the controversy of calling the head of the authority *president,* as the PLO wanted, or *chairman,* as Israel demanded), of the executive authority after the completion of Israeli redeployment from the six

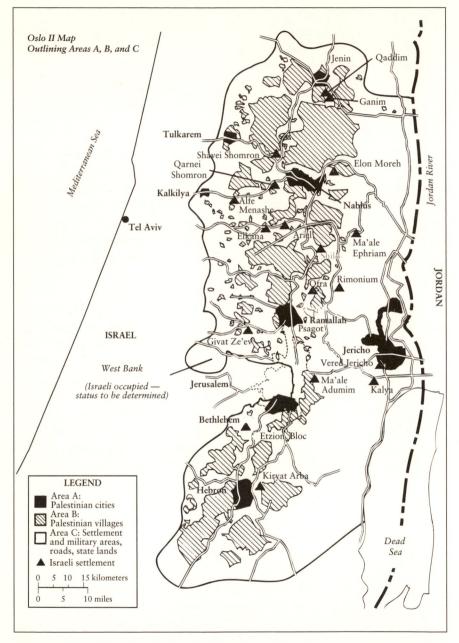

MAP 8.3 The West Bank, After the Oslo II Accords

SOURCE: *Report on Israeli Settlement in the Occupied Territories* 5, 6 (November 1995); 5.

Palestinian population centers. The council, according to the agreement, was to have eighty-two (a final figure of eighty-eight was accepted by Israel) representatives. Candidates for the council have to be approved by Israel; those "who commit or advocate racism" and "those who pursue the implementation of their aims by unlawful or non-democratic means" will be rejected.[21] A Palestinian living in Jerusalem cannot be a candidate unless he or she has a valid address in an area under the territorial jurisdiction of the PA.

The council is to have legislative powers over only the civil aspects of Palestinian life specifically authorized by Israel. Its legislative and executive powers are to be restricted to those areas and are subject to review and final approval by the Israeli authorities. The council will have the right to establish courts, also as specified and authorized by Israel. But the Palestinian Authority may not conduct independent foreign relations (except in economic aid agreements with donor countries and in cultural, scientific, and educational arrangements), control the Palestinian borders with Jordan or Egypt in addition to Israel, or control the air space or the electromagnetic spectrum for radio, television, and military communications (except for the bands authorized by Israel).[22] Israel is to retain control of natural resources in the West Bank and the Gaza Strip, especially land and water.

Most of the important decisions affecting Palestinian life in the West Bank and the Gaza Strip will be subject to a Joint Civil Affairs Coordination and Cooperation Committee, whose members represent the PA and Israel, and which, along with a large number of subcommittees, will operate by consensus and thus control Palestinian decisions.[23] Although this arrangement may seem fair, consensus gives Israel an effective veto power over all aspects of Palestinian life, including such important issues as water use, planning and zoning of land, custody of abandoned land, control of archaeological and religious sites, and the electric power grid.[24]

The Cairo and Oslo II Accords explicitly absolve Israel of any legal liability during its long (since 1967), brutal occupation of the Palestinian territories. Chapter 3, Article 20, Section 1.a of Oslo II states:

> The transfer of power and responsibilities from the Israeli military government and its civil administration to the Council, as detailed in Annex III, includes all related rights, liabilities and obligations arising with regard to acts or omissions which occurred prior to such transfer. Israel will cease to bear any financial responsibility regarding such acts or omissions and the Council will bear all financial responsibility for these and for its own functioning.

Describing the terms of the provision that transfers the financial liability to the PLO/PA, Naseer Aruri noted, "These provisions are tantamount to a blanket amnesty granted to the perpetrator by the victim, even prior to a peace agreement and while the victim has no assurance that his legal subordination can be altered under this agreement."[25]

Economic Control

The best illustration of continuing Israeli control and subordination of the Palestinian territories of the West Bank and the Gaza Strip is the economic provisions of the Declaration of Principles and the subsequent protocols and accords. These agreements cover trade, taxes, banking, labor, insurance, tourism, and so on, delineating the specific, limited spheres of autonomous Palestinian decisionmaking and the rules and conditions governing the future relationship between Israel and the autonomous Palestinian areas.[26] Specifically, the Paris protocols establish an Israeli-Palestinian customs union, demanded by Israel in order to sustain the level of its import tariffs, trade standards, import-licensing regulations, and protected industries. The various accords keep open Palestinian markets to Israel but restrict (through quotas and other measures) Palestinian exports to Israel's markets. In none of these protocols is there any equity or reciprocity in trade or economic relations between the two entities. Israel thus dictated the terms of all the agreements.

Nonetheless, George Abed, a Palestinian economist and a former official of the International Monetary Fund (IMF), currently the PA's chief of the Monetary Authority, was cautiously optimistic about the Paris Accords, which were subsidiaries of the Oslo Accords that dealt with financial arrangements. Especially in three economic areas, the accords grant elements of sovereignty "more favorable to the Palestinians than one would have expected from a careful reading of the [Declaration of Principles]."[27] Abed identified the following positive terms: endorsement of the principle of free trade between Israel and the territories, the PA's right to define its own tariff and import policy concerning a large number of commodities, and the PA's right to establish its own monetary authority, including the powers to license and regulate banks and manage financial reserves.

Despite such a positive interpretation of the economic agreements, most observers note that through all the provisions, Israel set both the framework and the constraints on the growth and development of the Palestinian economy for the duration of the interim period and in the future, as well as Israeli-Palestinian-Arab economic relations beyond the interim period. The clear consequence of these circumscribing agreements is to keep the Palestinian economy "completely within Israel's economic orbit . . . in a tight economic embrace,"[28] subordinate and dependent, its markets captive and open to Israeli goods and its labor cheap, unorganized, controlled, and exploitable by the more powerful and state-supported economy of Israel.

Israel gained, through these protocols, structures of controls that would reproduce the predatory colonial economic relations with the Palestinian territories in both the interim period and beyond. The agreement reached on water use should suffice as an example. Although Israel granted the Palestinians a small increment in water to meet immediate domestic use, water allocation is governed by "existing quantities of utilization" (Oslo II Accord, Annex III, Appendix I, Article 40). Average annual quantities give Israelis 80 percent and Palestinians 20 percent of their own West Bank water, a per capital allotment four times greater for the Israeli settlers (375,000 at that time) than for the Palestinians (more than 2 million).

Israel thus divested itself of the burden and cost of the social welfare institutions and of the expense and function of a policing government in the territories but retained control of the Palestinian economy and matters directly related to economic development and growth. In other words, Israel retained the capacity to exploit the natural resources and the labor of the territories, obstruct their independent economic development and expansion, restrict the mobility of their goods, and direct the structure of their investments. And besides all this control, Israel has also retained the right to use punitive economic measures against the autonomous Palestinian territories. Accordingly, sustained Palestinian economic growth and development under continuing Israeli dominion are nearly impossible.

Some Israeli intellectuals have described the "peace process" and the Israeli-Palestinian economic accords as "that of the old familiar transition known as 'decolonization.'"[29] As Yoav Peled remarked, "The outcome of decolonization has usually been neo-colonialism—that is, continued domination by the former rulers through mostly economic rather than mostly political means."[30] But in the case of the occupied West Bank and Gaza Strip, the Israelis, with the collaboration of the PLO, have set up a legitimized structure of domination over the Palestinian territories based on both economic *and* political means. Instead of decolonization, Israel has repackaged and extended old-fashioned predatory colonialism over the West Bank and the Gaza Strip. It has excluded from all arrangements the diaspora Palestinians except for the well-capitalized expatriate bourgeoisie, which is also being encouraged by Arafat's PA to invest in the territories and in joint ventures in the border areas.

Other Israeli intellectuals are, we believe, more accurate in their assessment of the accords. M. Benvenisti, former deputy mayor of Jerusalem and a long-term analyst of Israeli colonization of the West Bank whose works have been published in a series of research reports, noted, "A perusal of hundreds of the Agreement's pages can leave no doubt who is the winner and the loser in this deal. By seeing through all the lofty phraseology, all the deliberate disinformation, hundreds of pettifogging sections, sub-sections, appendices and protocols, one can recognize that Israeli victory was absolute and Palestinian defeat abject."[31] Indeed an American scholar of the Arab and Palestinian-Israeli conflicts systematically compared the structure and terms of the Oslo Accords to the documents that created the Bantustans of South Africa and concluded "that Oslo is a veritable carbon copy of the Transkei (Bantustan) constitution."[32] Benvenisti drew the same conclusion: "It goes without saying that 'cooperation' based on the current power relationship is no more than permanent Israeli domination in disguise, and the Palestinian self-rule is merely a euphemism for Bantustanization."[33]

The West Bank and the Gaza Strip are resource-poor territories, and any hope for developing these areas and solving the enormous economic and social problems of the people there depends largely on the skills of the people and of its political leadership, the active economic and institutional support of the world community, and independence from Israel's suffocating embrace. It is unfortunate that except for the skills of the people, none of the other conditions is present.

Under the auspices of the PLO, Yusif Sayigh, a Palestinian economist and planner, headed a team that produced a comprehensive and ambitious plan for the development of an independent national Palestinian economy, the Palestinian Development Programme (PDP). The team included not only the "normal" objectives of development, such as the creation of (a vast number) of employment opportunities, extensive housing, improvement and expansion of the economic and social infrastructure, and the satisfaction of basic human needs, but also measures for the correction of distortions, dislocations, imbalances, and bottlenecks of the current (occupied) economy.[34] The PDP's point of departure was the development of the economic capacity to satisfy the internal demand for basic human needs in contrast to the currently more fashionable economic emphasis on open markets, deregulation, privatization, foreign investment, and export orientation.[35] Under this development plan, the role of the future Palestinian government in overcoming the Israeli-instituted economic deformities would be central.

Neither the assumptions of the PDP nor its proposals were promoted by the PLO or considered by Israel, the international donors, the World Bank, or the IMF. Indeed, the World Bank[36] and privately produced[37] development plans all support the basic thrust of the Israel-PLO Paris Accords, stress continued Palestinian economic linkage (and therefore dependence on and subordination) to Israel, stress open markets and export orientation,[38] and encourage ties to Israel-centered regional projects—policies that are not conducive to independent socioeconomic development and growth. The Paris Accords—with the active support of the Western powers and international institutions (the IMF, the World Bank, and the Paris Club)—envision nothing more than a subordinate, exploitable, and dependent Palestinian economy, at best an Israeli colonial possession, at worst a Palestinian Bantustan.

The Politics of Implementation: Contradictions on the Ground

Since 1993 Israel and the PLO have negotiated several major agreements of implementation—the Paris Accords, the two Cairo Accords, and Oslo II. All the negotiations were problematic, tortuous, long, and bitter. As a result, the implementation of the agreements was repeatedly delayed much beyond the time specified in the Declaration of Principles. The establishment of the PA in Gaza and Jericho was delayed nine months beyond the "withdrawal" date—actually the redeployment—of Israeli military forces. Similarly, the redeployment from populated centers (except Jerusalem and Hebron) in the West Bank and the election of the governing Palestinian Legislative Council (PLC) were also postponed for over a year. The redeployments from the six West Bank cities, however, were swiftly carried out by Israel in December, just before the rescheduled date (January 1996) of the PLC elections in a transparent effort to boost Arafat's political popularity. This political objective was accomplished, as will be seen in a later section.

The disagreements between the PLO/PA and Israel derived from their differing conceptions of and aspirations for the resolution of the conflict and for the final, permanent status of the occupied territories. Israel's narrow, security-driven interpretation of the agreements as well as its bad-faith actions also came into play. The PLO/PA wanted to establish in the interim period the measures and conditions on the ground for eventual sovereign statehood, but Israel acts to prohibit that eventuality. The differing interpretations of the Declaration of Principles led to bitter arguments between the two parties, but the dismally uneven balance of power between them typically produced disadvantageous and humiliating protocols and accords for the Palestinians, agreements that have cast grave doubts on the possibility of extracting a sovereign Palestinian state out of, to use Khalidi's words again, "the womb of Oslo."

The PLO/PA repeatedly demonstrated, I believe, its incapacity for extricating from the Israelis a just and dignified solution to the Palestine question. This conclusion is all the more justified by the developments on the ground. Although the declaration specifies that neither party should do anything on the ground to prejudice the outcome of the "final status" negotiations, Israel continued to confiscate land and populate settlements, especially in and around East Jerusalem. According to former prime minister Netanyahu, under the Labor government of 1992–1996 the number of Israeli settlers in the occupied territories grew from 96,000 to 145,000.[39]

Since the signing of the Oslo Accords, Israel's violations of the human rights of Palestinians in the West Bank have continued. They have included administrative arrests; ill treatment and torture of detainees; extrajudicial killings by undercover military units (death squads), especially in the Gaza Strip; house demolitions; more severe restrictions of movement (than even before); and varied forms of collective punishment.[40] Also, during the first three years of Oslo, Israel closed the borders between the West Bank and the Gaza Strip and Israel to Palestinian workers at least six times, ostensibly for security reasons.[41]

Each closure reduced the number of Palestinian workers allowed to seek employment in Israel. Indeed, before the intifada, 180,000 Palestinian workers (including 80,000 from Gaza) were employed in Israel. After the 1991 Gulf War, the number declined to 100,000 workers. Following the signing of the declaration, the repeated closures of the borders reduced the number further—to a total of 45,000, with 16,000 from Gaza in 1995. This policy of reducing Palestinian labor employed in Israel and replacing it with foreign guest workers (by October 1994, Israel had imported around 59,000 foreign workers from eastern Europe and Southeast Asia), what Rabin called "separation" of the two populations, is considered justified by security concerns. According to the Israeli peace bloc, however, "separation is the exact Hebrew translation for the South African term Apartheid."[42]

In the mid-1990s, when the Oslo Accords were adopted, unemployment in the Gaza Strip reached 50 percent and in the West Bank around 35 percent,[43] and much higher (at least 60 percent and 40 percent, respectively) in 1996 because of nearly total border closure. The figure has continued to rise to the present. The repeated and increasingly longer closure of the Israeli borders to Palestinian goods and labor, the lack of or delay in investment by international donors, and the reluctance of private diaspora Palestinian and Arab capital to enter the unstable environment of the autonomous areas—all have led to dramatic economic downturn since the Oslo Accords were signed.

Only a minuscule amount of the $2.4 billion promised by international donors over a five-year period trickled into the autonomous territories in the first year: less than $60 million of the $570 million pledged for that year. The Palestinian Authority spent the bulk on salaries, especially of the police and the security forces, and not on development projects. International aid has not arrived either in the requisite and promised amounts or in investment in projects that would directly benefit the people of the autonomous and occupied territories. Such failure is typically blamed on both the donors and the PLO/PA. Arafat was reportedly unwilling (and perhaps unable) to establish a financial agency infused with sufficient transparency and accountability to satisfy the demands of the donors and managers (the World Bank and the IMF) of the aid funds. All this has fostered confusion and reluctance on the part of donors.

The dilemma of proletarianized, jobless Palestinians is not limited to the individuals themselves; it also affects their large families and the whole of society. Long used and exploited by Israel during the occupation, Palestinian workers became both a political and a security liability for Israel following the 1991 Gulf War. This fact coincided with the process of liberalization and privatization of Israel's evolving economy, which was developing different labor needs. Accordingly, after that war Israel embarked on a new policy, intensified and rationalized since the various accords were signed. It hoped that the new strategy would solve the two dilemmas simultaneously: replacing cheap Palestinian workers inside Israel with foreign guest workers and enlarging the productive base, especially of the Gaza Strip, in order to "restore [Palestinian] consumption capacity without encouraging competitive development."[44]

Israel began to facilitate the development of "industrial parks" in the northern border area of the Gaza Strip modeled on the maquiladora parks of northern Mexico. Since then, but even more since the signing of the Declaration of Principles, "Israel has been quietly building 'pockets of infrastructure' adjacent to the territories. Capital will be invested by joint Israeli, Palestinian and foreign ventures, but tied to the main contractors in Israel and directed to labor-intensive industries such as food-processing, textiles and furniture-making."[45] The main attraction for such investments is the large mass of available and un-unionized Palestinian labor in Gaza, which can be paid far lower wages than Israeli workers, receives few or no benefits, and can be used or discarded as the Israeli market demands.

These maquiladora-type factories and the absence of serious economic investment on the ground in the autonomous territories are far from the development plans of both Yusif Sayigh and the World Bank. Without immediate, rapid, deliberate, and systematic action by the PA to break the crippling shackles constraining West Bank and the Gaza Strip economic development, the Palestinian territories are doomed to the status of being fragmented Bantustans for Israel, at least for the short and medium terms.

The Palestinian Authority: Structure and Dynamics

In 1995, a year after his triumphant entry into Gaza, Arafat was a diminished leader, a "faded icon [who] is asked what he has done lately."[46] What Arafat did was to build a power base, an authoritarian regime composed of an extensive bureaucracy, security courts, and competing and overlapping security apparatuses and a police force, all under his individual control. The police force alone numbered over 19,000 by the end of the first year in the Gaza Strip, whereas only 6,000 teachers were employed for a population of nearly 1 million. The police force reached 30,000 members when the PA authority was extended into the six cities of the West Bank in late 1995.[47] Although more than twenty-five ministries were created, power was extraordinarily centralized in the hands of Arafat, who had tight control of all decisions, large and small. He was executive administrator, patron, legislator, and judge all in one. Despite the election of the Palestine Legislative Council in January 1996, the Arafat regime made no credible attempt to establish a basic modern system of governance: separated and accountable executive, legislative, and judicial institutions.

Arafat's autocratic style was supported by a chaotic legal structure composed of contradictory, inconsistent, and incomplete statutes and orders left over from Ottoman and Egyptian rule of the Gaza Strip, Jordanian rule of the West Bank, and the Israeli military occupation. In the absence of a clear regulatory and legal environment and an established rule of law, the Palestinian people have been at the mercy and whim of those in charge. As a result, corruption, malfeasance, and arbitrariness were widespread in the unrationalized institutions of the PA.[48] This is hardly an environment conducive to political stability (except perhaps through heavy-handed repression), to mobilization of the essential expatriate private Palestinian capital and expert talent, or to the provision of aid by international donors.

The evolving character of the increasingly autocratic PA regime depends on two factors. The first is the nature of the powers of the Palestine Legislative Council and of the electoral system that Israel and the PLO/PA have agreed to, and the second is the attitude and action of the Palestinian people subject to that regime. Of great significance to democracy in the Palestinian territories are the jurisdiction and powers of the PLC and its relationship to the executive authority. It has already been pointed out that the PLC's powers are severely circumscribed. It is clear from the Oslo II agreement (and the Palestinian constitution proposal inspired by the Arafat regime) that the head of the executive authority is simultaneously the head of the council, so there is little separation of political powers. Arafat, as the elected president of the executive authority, was allowed to create a strong internal security system that acted as an enforcer. Externally dependent on the sponsor of the Oslo Accords (the United States) and also on the Europeans, an authoritarian regime emerged in the West Bank and the Gaza Strip.

Democracy is not merely a process but also a political culture where the rule of law prevails and a climate of public confidence and trust in the political process and the leaders exists. Thomas Melia delineated four general indicators of the political climate that are conducive to meaningful elections and democracy: the separation of the state and the military; the degree of political openness and tolerance of opposition to the state; the status and rights of women; and the integrity of public institutions.[49] These public institutions should operate independently of the state but lend credibility and legitimacy to state action and policy because they diffuse political power throughout society and stabilize the political process. We believe another factor, not identified by Melia, is a politically conscious and active constituency that perceives the political process as fair, clean (uncorrupt), and rational.

In all these indicators, the Arafat regime was dismally deficient. The regime did not separate the state from the military (police). It combined the Palestinian civil, political, and military societies into one—a sure formula for authoritarianism. It was not open and tolerated neither opposition nor a free press, and it intimidated and suppressed critics. Indeed it had tried to co-opt and control, if not eliminate, all opposition, both secular and Islamic. Arafat's regime established parties and movements in the autonomous areas as cosmetic opposition that not only paralleled and delegitimized the actual opposition groups but also confused the public. The regime's security courts were secretive, violated Palestinian human rights, and created a climate of fear, not of tolerance and the rule of law.

Further, a number of Palestinian women's groups expressed their grievances concerning the authority's shortcomings on women's issues.

Accordingly, after decades of struggle and an intense and exhausting intifada, the Palestinian people inside the occupied territories (and in the diaspora) have become alienated and cynical about the conduct of Palestinian politics and the leadership. It is quite clear that the PA under Arafat had shown greater interest in state building and monopoly of the public political, economic, and social institutions than in establishing democratic, transparent, and accountable public agencies subject to the rule of law and guaranteeing an independent civil society. The Palestinian nongovernmental organizations (NGOs), which, as seen earlier, played such a pivotal role in the intifada, had been starved financially and manipulated by Arafat's PA regime.[50] In all the above, Arafat was supported not only by the extensive security apparatus but also by his political faction, the repatriated and local Fateh operatives, who were anxious to reap the rewards (in jobs, positions, contracts, etc.) of loyalty to Arafat and the Oslo Accords.

Generally speaking, three important and powerful social classes—the landlords, the mercantile capitalists, and the national and emergent comprador bourgeoisie—have not typically been enamored of democracy unless it served their interests and was under their control. In the West Bank and the Gaza Strip, Arafat had ingratiated himself with these important and economically powerful social groups, and they became supportive of his regime. Many old and new PA cabinet appointees, for example, are members of the families and clans belonging to these elite social classes.[51] There seemed to be an emergent ruling class, an alliance of local elites with Arafat's security officers, especially the police forces and the senior PA administrators. This alliance was much more interested in order, stability, and business deals than it is in democracy and the rule of law. Such a ruling social configuration is essentially antidemocratic.

The Legislative Council Elections

The significant thing about the Palestinian Legislative Council elections on January 20, 1996, is that they were held at all and without serious interference by Israel or the PA. The tacit coalition of opposition groups (Hamas, the PFLP, the DFLP, and other lesser groups) deliberately boycotted the elections, a form of protest of and opposition to the Arafat regime and the terms of the Declaration of Principles. These groups fielded no official candidates. And yet, despite calls from all these opposition groups to all Palestinians in the West Bank and the Gaza Strip to boycott the elections, official results certified that 86 percent of the Gaza Strip and 68 percent of the West Bank electorate went to the polls, an impressive turnout that showed the degree of political mobilization of the Palestinians. Although charges and allegations of fraud and vote rigging were made by several candidates and observers,[52] overall the elections were judged fair and clean.

In a parallel election, Arafat, running for the post of president of the Palestinian Authority, won by 87.1 percent of the vote against the only opponent, West Bank social activist and political leader Samiha Khalil. The structure and dynamics of the campaign (including control of the media and the press) guaranteed an Arafat victory. Nonetheless, the result of the presidential election was a personal vindication of Arafat. It showed that despite all the criticism and bitter denouncements, Arafat was still the symbol of Palestinian nationalism, at least for the majority of the West Bank and the Gaza Strip Palestinians.

As everyone expected, the PLC emerged from the election campaign with a strong majority in support of Arafat. Fifty of the eighty-eight seats were won by Fateh or Fateh-supported candidates; one was won by the Fida Party, a pro-Arafat and a pro-Oslo splinter group from the DFLP; and the remaining thirty-seven by independents. Other parties that ran candidates, especially the PPP, won no seats at all.

In short, the majority of the candidates who won election to the PLC were Arafat clients and loyalists and pro-Oslo people. And thus, "The election campaign . . . ended with a deepening feeling of emerging ruling elite, whose economic interests were tied with Israel."[53] After its election, PLC took several important steps toward internal organization. It elected a speaker, adopted certain standing orders, formed committees, and elected committee officers. However, the legal standing of the council's work and the physical surroundings in which it operated were not auspicious: Israel challenges council members' immunity to arrest, arresting them when it pleases, and the facility in which the council meets is totally inadequate. Council members and committees have no staffs and therefore have no assistance in drafting or reviewing legislation. The council also has no independent resource base or research unit. Its hope to act as an independent branch of the Palestinian government, to practice oversight of the Palestinian Authority, and to control the PA budget were constantly challenged and rejected by both Israel and Arafat, the head of the executive branch of the PA. Lacking a budget to run its own affairs, the council seeks the assistance of the Palestinian NGOs in its efforts to conduct its formal business. Power is not shared in the PA; it (and the purse strings) is in the hands of the *ra'ee*s.

Irrespective of the election results, reports of popular attitudes toward the regime indicated a reemergent political culture long asserted and valued by the Palestinian national liberation movement and the intifada. Palestinians, long under oppressive occupation, had built up a social structure made up of a network of autonomous social service organizations both as an alternative to the unresponsive and deliberately negligent Israeli authorities and as a means to mobilize opposition to the occupation. This rich experience and the political culture associated with it are bound to reemerge at some juncture, renewed and vigorous, but henceforth possibly in opposition to the Arafat regime's autocracy as well as Israeli repression.

Arafat probably won a legislature that would act in support of his pro-Oslo policies or at least serve as a rubber stamp for his regime; this backing, along with his control of the purse and the absence of a basic law or constitution, undoubtedly reinforced his authoritarian rule. Nonetheless, I believe that in the long run the process of elections—even under such dubious conditions—will eventually plant the seeds of democracy, which will become the legitimate mechanism for effecting change in both leaders and policy. Although this may happen for the Palestinians in the West Bank and the Gaza Strip, it will not change the disenfranchisement of the diaspora communities.

The 1996 election of a legislative council in the West Bank and the Gaza Strip neither created a legitimate independent body that could regulate the lives and affairs of the Palestinians still in their homeland under nominal autonomy nor produced a mechanism for effecting a just and lasting solution to the Palestine problem. If anything, it set up a dualistic structure of Palestinian representation and complicated the relationship between those in the homeland and those in the diaspora. The election of the Palestine Legislative Council may have affirmed and contributed further to the fragmentation of the Palestinian people and their destiny and thus to the political crisis that enveloped them as a result of the Oslo Accords.

"Final Status" Negotiations and Likud Israel

"Final status" negotiations over the occupied territories between Israel and the PLO/PA formally opened on schedule in early May 1996 in the Egyptian resort of Taba and adjourned quickly until after the Israeli elections of May 29, 1996. The pro forma meeting was largely ceremonial and accomplished little beyond being on schedule and showing the continuing interest of the two parties in carrying on the "peace process" in accordance with the Oslo Accords. This meeting took place during an extremely charged political environment in Israel itself, involving Israel and the PA on one side and Hamas and the Islamic movement on the other.

In Israel a right-wing Jewish religious militant, Yigal Amir, assassinated Prime Minister Yitzhak Rabin on November 4, 1995, and plunged the country into a short-term political crisis. Foreign Minister Shimon Peres took over the position of prime minister and promised to continue along the path of Rabin. However, despite the agreements and security cooperation between Israel and the PLO/PA, Israel kept up its underground war against Hamas and the Islamic Jihad. Israel's security forces, for example, assassinated Fathi al-Shiqaqi, the top Jihad political leader, in Malta. In the course of such attacks and retaliations, Hamas in February–March 1996 launched a series of suicide bombings inside Israel. The civilian death toll was high (fifty-eight dead and more than two hundred wounded), and the political reaction, both in Israel and internationally, was extremely strong. Accordingly, the Peres government called on Arafat to "crack down" heavily on Hamas and its supporters and itself initiated measures to prohibit entry of Palestinians from the territories to work in Israel.

Arafat's PA security forces arrested nearly a thousand Palestinians suspected of links to Hamas. Although Arafat received kudos from Peres and US president Clinton for his suppression of the Islamic militants, Israel proceeded to impose the tightest closure of the territories in its twenty-nine years of occupation. Not only were Palestinians prohibited from entering Israel, but the Israeli army imposed what the Israelis called "internal closure" on the autonomous population centers of the West Bank and the Gaza Strip: For nearly two weeks following the March 4, 1996, suicide attack in Tel Aviv, the Peres government placed the 1.3 million Palestinians of the West Bank under wholesale curfew, with all movement between the "autonomous" towns and villages completely prohibited.

The swift Israeli military closure and control of the autonomous Palestinian population—an action that would have provoked, at the very least, extensive civil unrest and popular resistance during the intifada—elicited no armed or popular resistance on the part of the Palestinians. But this closure occurred in coordination with the Palestinian security forces, which basically stepped aside as the Israelis swept through. The only centers the Israelis did not enter—but closed off tightly—were the six "autonomous" cities of the West Bank. There and in the Gaza areas, the PA itself imposed a heavy security mantle. In the wake of these events, Palestinian support for the PA plummeted.

And so has the pendulum of antipathy toward the "peace process" also swung in Israel. After the suicide bombings in early 1996, the public mood increasingly favored the hard-line right-wing political coalition (Likud and religious parties). The propeace sentiment that had surged and become politically powerful in Israel after the assassination of Prime Minister Rabin had waned and nearly disappeared by the May 29, 1996, elections. As a result, Netanyahu, the rightist leader of the Likud Party, was elected prime minister over Peres of the Labor Party, the principal architect of the accords with the PLO.

The victory of Netanyahu and the Likud-led coalition in Israel introduced a potentially problematic political situation not only in the Palestinian context but also throughout the Middle East, not least because of his campaign and postelection victory rhetoric. Netanyahu's five "nos" (no to a Palestinian state, no to a Palestinian East Jerusalem, no to withdrawal from Hebron as scheduled, no to an end of Israeli settlement in the occupied territories, and no to withdrawal from the Golan Heights in return for a peace treaty with Syria) were a direct rejection of the terms of negotiations largely based on UN Security Council Resolutions 242 and 338 (the land-for-peace formula), the Madrid Middle East peace conference, the Oslo Accords, and the "peace process." Netanyahu's recidivist reinterpretation of the terms of the "peace process" from "land for peace" to "peace for peace" or "peace with security" was "for those who with minimal knowledge of Israeli political semantics, . . . an unmistakable euphemism for retaining the occupied Arab land, including much of the West Bank, the Golan Heights and, of course, East Jerusalem."[54] This posture by the new Israeli leader and the rightist cabinet he assembled cast serious doubt on the potential for resumption of the "peace process," especially the "final status" negotiations, between Israel and the PLO/PA.[55]

Palestinian Public Opinion

Twelve years after the signing of the Declaration of Principles, and eleven years after the establishment of the PA in the Gaza Strip and the Jericho area, Palestinian political discourse shifted focus. The emphasis went from an exclusive concern with the declaration, and its shortcomings, legitimacy, and meaning for the Palestinian people, to a political debate centered more on three broad areas: the content of the subsequent agreements, the process and the results of the implementation of those agreements, and the performance in office of Arafat and the PA.

The gist of the debate was that the agreements on implementation of the declaration and the results on the ground tended to confirm the position of those who were initially skeptical, critical, or opposed to the agreement.[56]

The subsequent agreements were humiliating; the resultant arrangements and the treatment of Palestinians by the Israelis clearly unmasked Israel's bad faith in negotiations and its lack of desire for a historic resolution of the conflict and reconciliation with its victims: The process was carried out in the manner, style, and tone of a victor dictating terms to the vanquished. Palestinian negotiators were negotiating under the assumption that Israel was an occupying power engaged in transferring eventual sovereignty to them, whereas Israel was dealing with Palestinian "empowerment," at best, as an internal civil rights issue without any rationale for sovereignty—hence the repeated disagreements, delays, and breakdowns and the feelings of discouragement, frustration, and even rancor on the part of the negotiators and the Palestinian public.

Such feelings were reinforced by other actions taken by the Israelis after the signing of the Oslo Accords. In summary, they included continuing land confiscation, expansion of settlements, and persisting draconian security measures and violations of Palestinian human rights. For example, after the initial release of about 5,000 out of 11,000 Palestinian political prisoners, Israel administratively detained 2,000 more after the signing of the Declaration of Principles, bringing the 1995 total to 6,000–7,000. Barely a week after Oslo II was signed, Israel held up the promised release of all women prisoners.

In the new Palestinian political discourse, the performance of the PA came under extensive criticism by opponents and supporters alike. Such criticism of the whole regime typically derived from Arafat's autocratic style. Critics pointed to the improvised and chaotic manner in which the PA assumed power; established the economic and financial authorities to receive and manage aid from international donors (who were still skeptical of these authorities and commissions); and created the governing, legal, and social service institutions, as well as its failure to build a political culture of tolerance and respect for the rule of law, human rights, and democracy.

The manner of appointments to the PA also came under criticism because its basis was favoritism, loyalty to Arafat, and nepotism. As a result, power flowed to Fateh loyalists, Arafat's political faction and power base, and local economic and social elites. Such appointments, critics believed, were counter to the efficiency and effectiveness of the PA institutions and to rational and accountable institution building in general, practices so desperately needed to make the transition to self-rule and eventual statehood. The highly centralized, personalized, and indeed arbitrary manner of decisionmaking by Arafat and his loyal and dependent lieutenants was encouraged by the absence in the PA of any mechanisms of oversight or checks and balances on its power and therefore by its lack of accountability. The official oversight institutions of the PLO had been deliberately marginalized by Arafat and therefore became nonfunctioning. Furthermore, a minority in the elected Palestine Legislative Council had shown the will to be critical and ask for accountability and oversight but had not been able to institutionalize that important role.

The security forces of the PA, which received a hero's welcome upon their entry into the Gaza Strip in 1994, afterward lost much respect and became suspect to many Gazans and other Palestinians. In the years after the establishment of the PA, Arafat set up several (the reported number is nine) secret service security agencies, all of which competed with one another in the service of Arafat's regime and to intimidate his opponents. The Palestinian security forces were accused of human rights violations, political repression, and abuse of power.[57] They suppressed political dissent and opposition to the occupation, not only by independent secular critics in the press and elsewhere (for example, Edward Said's books have been confiscated from West Bank bookstores and their sale prohibited everywhere) but also by Hamas and Al-Jihad al-Islami, particularly after the acts of violence they perpetrated against Israeli military and civilian targets. Clashes between Palestinian security forces and Hamas supporters led to thirteen fatalities and scores of casualties in a major confrontation in November 1994. "At the heart of relations between the PNA [Palestinian National Authority, a synonym for the Palestinian Authority] and the opposition lies an essential contradiction: The authority is bound . . . to provide security and not to endanger the Israeli presence, while the opposition insists on its legitimate right to combat the remaining forms of occupation and resist the continued existence of Israeli settlements."[58]

The PA regime and the Palestinian security forces were typically viewed by Palestinians inside the territories and in the diaspora as little more than Israel's enforcers and as collaborators with the Israeli occupation authorities.[59] The initial euphoria upon Arafat's return faded rapidly and reached a low point after the November 1994 clashes between the regime's security forces and Hamas activists and supporters. These clashes and the continuing conflict with the Islamic and other secular nationalist groups derived not only from Arafat's security commitment to Israel but also from the regime's efforts to establish exclusive authority over the West Bank cities and the Gaza Strip. The intra-Palestinian power struggle in the Gaza Strip coincided with Israeli and US pressure on Arafat to control, if not eliminate, violent resistance to Israeli occupation.

Instead of establishing a "national authority," as a 1974 PNC resolution specified, to mobilize the Palestinians to carry on the struggle to end the occupation, Arafat's regime sought to end the resistance and act as Israel's enforcer/protector in the autonomous and occupied territories. Thus the Palestinian political division over the Declaration of Principles quickly emerged in the Gaza Strip between Arafat's PA regime on one side and Hamas and al-Jihad al-Islami (which together opposed the Oslo Accords and which reportedly commanded 20–40 percent of popular support) on the other. In the years since the Oslo Accords were signed, this conflict has created political tension and instability in the autonomous areas, as did the severe economic crisis and autocracy of Arafat himself. This conflict intensified to a climax in early 1996 in the wake of the February–March Islamic suicide bombings inside Israel. Arafat's swift repression (roundup and incarceration of suspected Islamic activists) earned him praise from Israel and the United States but failed to solve both the social and the political dilemmas he faced, which became more problematic with the election of a right-wing (Likud) government in Israel in May 1996. The PA conflict with Hamas and the other Islamic groups had pushed many activists underground.

The secular opposition became fragmented and ineffective, as were the reportedly large "silent majority" of discontented, passive, and politically alienated people. Yet the public was decidedly happy with the process of ending the oppressive Israeli occupation, even though the result of the flawed peace process did not favor Palestinian independence. Little, if any, celebration accompanied or followed the signing of the Oslo II agreement, despite the promise of Israeli military "withdrawal" from the six major cities of the West Bank and the end of direct Israeli intervention in everyday Palestinian life. But there was jubilation in the six cities when the Israeli military finally withdrew from them in late 1995, one month before the Palestinian elections. The West Bank and the Gaza Strip reactions to Oslo II were characterized by journalists as full of anger and frozen rage over the lack of achievement, mixed with resignation to the defeat. Given Israel's overwhelming power, many felt that there was no alternative. In the diaspora, Palestinian outrage at and animosity toward the dismal agreement were aggravated by political impotence. The statement of a Fateh leader in Hebron perhaps sums up the widespread sentiment: "The settlers in Hebron live in five buildings. . . . With this agreement, they get a district. What we get is the occupation."[60] The Oslo Accords have become less the path to independence, a better life, and dignity for the Palestinians of the occupied territories and more the core of the contemporary Palestinian dilemma, especially with the victory of the Israeli right-wing coalition in the 1996 and 2001 elections.

Notes

1. See N. G. Finkelstein, "Whither the 'Peace Process'?" paper presented at Georgetown and American Universities, Washington, DC, April 24 and 25, 1996, p. 21.

2. N. Aruri, *The Obstruction of Peace: The U.S., Israel and the Palestinians* (Monroe, ME: Common Courage Press, 1995): 193–218; see also H. Ashrawi, *This Side of Peace* (New York: Simon and Schuster, 1995).

3. E. Said, *The Politics of Dispossession: The Struggle for Palestinian Self-Determination, 1969–1994* (New York: Pantheon, 1994): xxxii.

4. S. K. Farsoun, "Palestine and America's Imperial Imperative," *Middle East International* (August 7, 1992): 16–17.

5. See Y. Peled, "From Zionism to Capitalism," *Middle East Report* 194–195 (May-June–July-August 1995): 13; see also S. Cohen, "Justice in Transition," *Middle East Report* 194–195 (May-June–July-August 1995): 2–5.

6. In a speech at the Jabalya refugee camp in the Gaza Strip upon his return to Palestinian soil in accordance with the Oslo agreements, Arafat said, "I know many of you here think Oslo is a bad agreement. It is a bad agreement. But it's the best we can get in the worst situation." Quotation in G. Usher, *Palestine in Crisis: The Struggle for Peace and Political Independence* (London: Pluto Press, 1995): 1.

7. These kinds of arguments were typically used by black African leaders who consented to the creation of Bantustans in South Africa's apartheid system. See Finkelstein, "Whither the 'Peace Process'?" 16–17, 19–20.

8. This conclusion of no alternative but to support the declaration was also reached by another prominent Arab intellectual, Samir Amin. Although Amin criticized the accords extensively, stating that "the Declaration of Principles was no more than a plan for establishing a Bantustan in the former Israeli occupied territories," he concluded: "History informs us that agreements evolve and are subject to interpretation, and that their contents depend on developments in the balance of power. The Declaration of Principles is no exception. Therefore I urge that we concentrate our struggle on a sincere, sober and serious implementation of the agreement which would force the Israelis to make necessary concessions"; S. Amin, "After Gaza and Jericho: The New Palestinian-Middle Eastern Problem," *Beirut Review* 8 (Fall 1994): 115.

9. Said, *Politics of Dispossession*, xxxvii.

10. See B. Dajani, "The September 1993 Israeli-PLO Documents: A Textual Analysis," *Journal of Palestine Studies* 23 (Spring 1994): 5–23.

11. Several tens of thousands of Palestinians did return to Gaza and Jericho, largely as part of Arafat's PA regime security forces and bureaucracy. A few of those deported by Israel during the occupation (such as Hanna Nasir, president of Bir Zeit University, and Abdul-Jawad Saleh, former mayor of the town of El-Bireh) were allowed to return to the West Bank.

12. These include UN Security Council Resolutions 252, 267, 271, 298, 476, and 474. Explicit reference to Jerusalem is also frequently made in resolutions affirming the illegality of Israeli settlements in the occupied territories.

13. See UN Security Council Resolutions 446 and 452.

14. Israel, Ministry of Foreign Affairs, *Israeli-Palestinian Interim Agreement on the West Bank and Gaza Strip*, September 28, 1995, accessible on the Internet through the Israeli Information Service Gopher, ask@israel-info.gov.il.

15. Finkelstein, "Whither the 'Peace Process'?" 2.

16. See C. Maksoud, "Peace Process or Puppet Show?" *Foreign Policy* 100 (Fall 1995): 117–124.

17. Chapter 1, Article I, Section 5 of the agreement.

18. M. Rabbani, "Palestinian Authority, Israeli Rule: From Transitional to Permanent Arrangement," *Middle East Report* 201 (October-December 1996): 5.

19. E. W. Said, "The Mirage of Peace," *The Nation* (October 16, 1995): 413.

20. Ibid.

21. Annex II, Article III, Section 2. As Said noted, "No parallel proscription on the Israeli side" exists that prohibits Israeli racists from being Knesset members; "Mirage of Peace," 414.

22. See Annex II, "Protocol Concerning Elections," of the Oslo II agreement, 75–92.

23. See Annex III, "Protocol Concerning Civil Affairs"; Annex V, "Protocol on Economic Relations"; and Annex VI, "Protocol Concerning Israeli-Palestinian Programs," of the Oslo II agreement.

24. See the text of the agreement's annexes.

25. N. H. Aruri, "Early Empowerment: The Burden Not the Responsibility," *Journal of Palestine Studies* 24 (Winter 1995): 37. The reference is to Article 9.1.a–b of the August 24, 1994, agreement, also known as "early empowerment," which is discussed fully in Dr. Aruri's essay.

26. S. Elmusa and M. El-Jaafari, "Power and Trade: The Israeli-Palestinian Economic Protocol," *Journal of Palestine Studies* 24 (Winter 1995): 14–32.

27. G. Abed, "Developing the Palestinian Economy," *Journal of Palestine Studies* 23 (Summer 1994): 41–51.

28. R. Owen, "Establishing a Viable Palestinian Economy," *Beirut Review* 8 (Fall 1994): 48–49.

29. Cohen, "Justice in Transition," 4. See also Peled, "From Zionism to Capitalism," 14.

30. Peled, "From Zionism to Capitalism," 14.

31. M. Benvenisti, "An Agreement of Surrender," *Ha'aretz* (May 12, 1994).

32. Finkelstein, "Whither the 'Peace Process'?" 15.

33. M. Benvenisti, *Intimate Enemies: Jews and Arabs in a Shared Land* (Berkeley: University of California Press, 1995): 232.

34. Ibid., 23–24.

35. See a summary of the Palestinian debate on this issue in Usher, *Palestine in Crisis*, 36–40.

36. World Bank, *Developing the Occupied Territories: An Investment in Peace*, 7 vols. (Washington, DC: World Bank, 1993).

37. Institute for Social and Economic Policy in the Middle East, John F. Kennedy School of Government, Harvard University, *Securing Peace in the Middle East: Project on Economic Transition* (Cambridge: Harvard University Press, 1993).

38. See W. Freedmen, "An Export Promotion Scheme for Palestine," *Graduate Review* 1 (1994): 34–45.

39. D. Neff, "Netanyahu Gets the Royal Treatment in Washington," *Middle East International* (July 19, 1996): 5.

40. B'Tselem (Israeli Information Center for Human Rights in the Occupied Territories), September and November 1994 reports. Can be found online at: www. Btselem.org. See also Human Rights Watch/Middle East, *Torture and Ill-Treatment: Israel's Interrogation of Palestinians from the Occupied Territories* (New York: Human Rights Watch, 1994).

41. The closures occurred especially after the suicide bombings and other attacks inside Israel and in the occupied territories.

42. See their statement in *Ha'aretz* (February 2, 1995). Cited in G. Usher, "Palestinian Trade Unions and the Struggle for Independence," *Middle East Report* 194–195 (May-June–July-August 1995): 21.

43. G. Abed, "The Political Economy of Development in the West Bank and Gaza Strip," paper delivered at the Workshop on Strategic Visions for the Middle East and North Africa, Economic Research Forum, Gammarth, Tunisia, June 9–11, 1995, p. 7.

44. E. Murphy, "Stacking the Deck: The Economics of the Israel-PLO Accords," *Middle East Report* 194–195 (May-June–July-August 1995): 36.

45. Usher, "Palestinian Trade Unions," 21.

46. J. Greenberg, "Faded Icon Is Asked What's He Done Lately," *New York Times* (June 30, 1995): A1.

47. G. Usher, "The Politics of Internal Security in Palestine," *Middle East International* (March 1, 1996): 15.

48. Abed, "Political Economy."

49. T. Melia, "Elections in Emerging Democracies," in *Palestinian Elections* (Washington, DC: Center for Policy Analysis on Palestine, 1995): 12–17.

50. "A Story of Manipulation, Containing the Palestinian NGOs," *Issues: Perspectives on Middle East and World Affairs* 5 (June 1996): 2–3, 14.

51. R. Brynen, "The Dynamics of Palestinian Elite Formation," *Journal of Palestine Studies* 24 (Spring 1995): 31–43.

52. K. M. Amaryeh, "Allegations of Vote-Rigging," *Middle East International* (February 2, 1996): 4.

53. L. Andoni, "A New Era," *Middle East International* (February 2, 1996): 4.

54. K. M. Amayreh, "Why Netanyahu Is Bad News for the Peace Process," *Middle East International* (July 19, 1996): 16.

55. See especially D. Neff, "Netanyahu Gets"; M. Jansen, "The Peace of the Sword"; G. Usher, "The Demand for 'Reciprocity'"; L. Andoni, "Dismay in Gaza"; K. M. Amayreh, "More Settlements Planned" and "Why Netanyahu," all in *Middle East International* (July 19, 1996).

56. The discussion in the next two paragraphs is based on Z. Abu-Amr, "Report from Palestine," *Journal of Palestine Studies* 24 (Winter 1995): 40–47.

57. See Amnesty International, *Trial at Midnight: Secret, Summary, Unfair Trials in Gaza* (London: Amnesty International, 1995); Amnesty International, *Human Rights in the Gaza Strip and Jericho Under Palestinian Self-Rule* 6 (September 1994). See also Gaza Center for Rights and Law (Affiliate of the International Commission of Jurists, Geneva), *Monthly Report* (May 1994 and June-July 1994); B. Gellman, "Palestinian Secret Force Wields Power in West Bank, Force Accused of 'Gross' Rights Violations," *Washington Post* (August 28, 1995): A1, A18; and G. Usher, "Elections Under Scrutiny," *Middle East International* (February 16, 1996): 7.

58. Usher, "Elections Under Scrutiny," 43.

59. See E. Said, "Symbols Versus Substance: A Year After the Declaration of Principles," *Journal of Palestine Studies* 24 (Winter 1995): 61.

60. G. Usher, "The Taba Agreement—Peace or Defeat?" *Middle East International* (October 6, 1995): 4.

9

The Structural Flaws of Oslo and Camp David II, and the Second Intifada

The factors that allowed the reproduction and intensification of the occupation and its worsening consequences have remained more or less unchanged since the first years of the Oslo process. Deteriorating conditions were bound to produce another upheaval, another intifada—the Al-Aqsa Intifada—against the brutal Israeli occupation, under the complicit rule of the Palestinian Authority. This chapter analyzes the deteriorated conditions in an effort to explain the political explosion that the Al-Aqsa, or Second, Intifada of 2000 was a response to.

Closures and Their Consequences

After the Oslo Accords, the Palestinian enclaves under the Palestinian Authority in the West Bank and the Gaza Strip continued to reflect "severe economic decline, social regression and political repression."[1] In sharp contrast to the ebullient economic scenarios that were projected, especially by the Palestinian leadership, early in the course of the peace process—and despite much assistance from the international donor community—the standard of living has continued to fall as a consequence of massive unemployment and rising poverty levels. Indeed, the de-development that has characterized the economic and social regression of the long years of occupation by Israel has not only not ended but has actually *accelerated* as a result of the Israeli policies in the occupied territories after the Oslo agreements.

With the advent of Oslo in 1993, the Palestinian economy was shocked by two developments: the decline of Palestinian labor demand in Israel and the loss of income sent to their families by Palestinian laborers working in the oil-producing countries of the Persian Gulf, because of the closing of those Gulf markets to Palestinian labor. Thus, at the initiation of the Oslo process, the Palestinian economy in agriculture and industry was weak, and its infrastructural services (electricity, communications, and water) were dependent on and controlled by Israel, even as the Palestinian population was growing rapidly and the potential labor force was increasing dramatically.

In the post-Oslo period, de-development has accelerated significantly as a result of newly instituted Israeli policies, especially closure, which has created economic fragmentation of the West Bank and the Gaza Strip. In the wake of the Oslo Accords Israel erected a border (with the Palestinian-administered areas) and established a system of permits (to work in Israel) that considerably restricted the mobility of Palestinian workers and goods and raised the cost of producing and shipping Palestinian goods substantially. Between 1992 and 1996 the number of work permits issued by Israel declined. As a result the number of Palestinians employed in Israel dropped from an annual average of 116,000 workers in 1992 to 28,100 in 1996.[2] Accordingly, earnings from employment in Israel plummeted dramatically, from an estimated 25 percent of Palestinian GNP in 1992 to 8 percent in 1996.[3]

Palestinian employment in Israel has been most severely affected by closures, which suppress physical movement as well as economic exchange among Palestinian enclaves. A UN study shows that the number of comprehensive closure days increased from 26 in 1993 to 121 days in 1996. Closures, which are a collective punishment that is illegal in international law, have been devastating to the Palestinians economically. In the spring of 1996 the combined average unemployment rate for the West Bank and the Gaza Strip was 28.4 percent.[4] However, various surveys of the Palestinian Central Bureau of Statistics (PCBS) indicate that about 20 percent of the labor force is normally unemployed, a rate that suddenly jumps to at least 30 percent (or higher) during closure, significantly higher in Gaza.[5] In addition, the context is high population growth and commensurately high potential labor force growth.

According to the PCBS, population growth has been high throughout the period of Oslo. Annual population growth rates for the period 1998–2003 were estimated by the PCBS at 4.4 percent for the West Bank and 5.0 percent for Gaza, with an overall percentage increase of 4.6 for the two regions combined.[6] These rates are among the highest, if not actually the highest, rates on record in the world. The increase in the size of the potential labor force was 5.7 percent in 1998 and 1999.[7] These are astoundingly high rates of population and labor force growth for an economy that has been deteriorating for more than a decade and is virtually collapsing as a result of the Israeli-imposed siege and economic strangulation during the Al-Aqsa Intifada.

The closures, which have affected employment rates and patterns, have also had serious effects on the incomes of Palestinians since 1993, the year when the first Oslo agreement led to the initiation of the Israeli policies. Real wage rates declined dramatically, 38 percent between 1992 and 1994 and an additional 15 percent between 1995 and 1997.[8] This deterioration in real wages is compounded by an inflation rate that is typically around 5 percent per year.

The most telling consequence of closures is the rise in the level of poverty, defined as an income of about $2 per day and $650 annually per person per year. According to a World Bank report, poverty affected nearly one in every four Palestinians in 1998.[9] This level of poverty is extremely high by regional standards.

The overall Palestinian poverty level, according to both the World Bank and the Palestinian National Commission on Poverty Alleviation, masks significant differences between the West Bank and the Gaza Strip and even within the Gaza Strip itself. Throughout the pre-Oslo occupation period and since Oslo, the ratio of poverty in the Gaza Strip has been far higher than in the West Bank. In 1998, for example, the ratio of poor families living in the Gaza Strip was 37 percent, compared to 15 percent in the West Bank.[10] In Rafah and southern Gaza, where poverty levels are the highest, two out of three poor families live in abject poverty, unable to meet the basic needs of food, housing, and clothing.

Compounding the dilemma for the Palestinian poor is how rudimentary and ineffective is the public safety net that is presumed to be in place. According to the World Bank report, "The formal safety net reached (only) about 30 percent of the poor in 1998, but did not raise a large proportion of them out of poverty. Substantial resources are being depleted since over half of the beneficiary households are non-poor."[11] If this statement is true, such practices show either inefficiency in delivery of aid to the poor or corruption or both. Two major social welfare programs have been established by the Palestinian Authority: an income support program of the Ministry of Social Affairs (MOSA) and a public works program. However, "the traditionally targeted groups for MOSA assistance represent a small percentage of the total poor. . . . Some 85 percent of the poor are not among these traditionally targeted groups."[12] The public works program, coordinated by the Palestine Economic Council for Development and Reconstruction (PECDAR), consists of labor-intensive community development projects that include the building of roads, schools, clinics, and water works; sanitation; and other such activity in poor communities. This public works program has apparently helped the poorer areas during closure days. In addition to the official PA poverty alleviation programs, there are numerous private or nongovernmental organizations (NGOs) that extend aid to the poor. It is estimated that about five hundred NGOs provide some kind of help to the poor. Al-Zakat Committees, perhaps one of the largest such NGOs, extended $9 million of cash assistance to 27,585 families in 1996.[13] In any case, the majority of the Palestinian poor (even during the better economic times of 1998, compared to the previous five years of Oslo) have not been helped and have been sinking into despair.

The World Bank study estimates that the minimum amount of assistance needed to raise poor Palestinian families to the poverty line would be 3.9 percent of Palestinian GDP in the occupied territories, but with the current low level of efficiency of the Palestinian economy, the amount would have to be 9 percent, about $390 million per year. Most relevant to alleviating poverty would be a vibrant and growing independent domestic economy—especially an export-oriented private sector—that does not depend on Israel for employment or as an export conduit. But that kind of economy is unlikely, given the tight economic constraints that Israel has thrown around the Palestinian enclaves.

In one sense, the worst aspect of comprehensive closure is the partitioning of the Gaza Strip from the West Bank. For years under Israeli occupation prior to the Oslo agreements, there was relatively free movement of people, goods, and services between the two Palestinian regions. Since the Oslo agreements, however, the ties between the two regions have steadily been eroded. Other than high Palestinian officials, a very small number of ordinary persons (maybe a few hundred per year) are able to move between the two regions. Gaza's 1997 agricultural produce sales to the West Bank dropped to one-third of what they were in 1993. Closure caused a spectacular deterioration in Gaza's agricultural exports as a result of closure with a consequent severe impact on Gazan standards of living. Gaza, which had once exported citrus fruit to Israel, now actually imports citrus fruit from Israel.

In short, instead of an integrated and unified economy that embraces the West Bank and the Gaza Strip, two separate enclaves have emerged. Furthermore, the West Bank itself has been fragmented into several enclaves, especially as transportation routes between the southern and northern areas of the West Bank that pass through the Jerusalem district have been disrupted or closed altogether. In fact, the total, including internal, closure that has been imposed during the Al-Aqsa Intifada has divided the Palestinian territories into 120 minienclaves or population islands, causing social and economic strangulation. Repeated closure and economic squeeze over the years have caused the disintegration of the Palestinian whole into relatively isolated parts and have created in them social and economic introversion and insularity—a key feature of de-development.

The Strategic Dilemmas of the Palestinian Economy and Society

As the frequency of closure declined during 1998–1999, the Palestinian economy and society began to recover from the deterioration of the first five years of the Oslo process, only to be brought to the point of collapse by the total closures imposed during the Second Intifada. Both the Palestinian Ministry of Finance (MOF) and the IMF estimated real GDP and real GNP growth at 7 and 8 percent, respectively, for 1998. One of the key reasons was the increased flow of Palestinian labor to Israel and to Jewish settlements and industrial zones.

Domestic employment grew by 8.1 percent in 1998 and 7.8 percent in 1999, jobs that were largely generated by the private sector. This growth contrasted sharply with the employment growth in the first period of the Oslo process, which was principally in the public sector, especially in the Palestinian Authority bureaucracy and its security agencies, both of which have come to number over 90,000 employees. In the private sector the sources of employment growth have remained more or less the same: construction, services, and agriculture. Construction remained the dominant employer, accounting for 56 percent of all employment in 1999. However, in trade with Israel in the same period, there was a real decline in the total value of Palestinian exports coupled with a real increase in the value of imports from Israel.

Although some improvement in the Palestinian economy occurred in a two-year period (1995–1996) during the Oslo process, it still suffered from structural weaknesses and liabilities that crippled the economic development of the Palestinian territories. The most important liabilities were a weakened, skewed, and dependent economy that was the legacy of a long occupation. The structural weaknesses included the asymmetric market relations with Israel, regulatory restrictions imposed by Israel even on investments, Israeli restrictions on access to natural resources, institutional underdevelopment, and huge infrastructural needs, such as free transportation, electricity, telecommunications, water, sanitation, and a legal framework conducive to investment. Of course, all this was severely compounded by territorial fragmentation and isolation.

The most important structural assets, on the other hand, also according to the World Bank study on Palestinian development under adversity, are social capital, the people and their culture, the money capital and the international networks of the Palestinian diaspora, and possibly international sympathy.[14] But all of the potential is unrealizable unless the occupation ends and a new state of Palestine is freed from the suffocating economic embrace of Israel.[15] The reality is that the short period of recovery came to a dead halt as the Al-Aqsa Intifada exploded and Israel imposed more devastating closures, a strangling siege, and a fragmentation that resulted in the sharp reversal of all the improvements of 1998–1999 and a far worse deterioration in a few months than had occurred in the first five years of the Oslo process. The Palestinian economy continued to deteriorate sharply under the impact of the Israeli reoccupation of Palestinian cities during the spring of 2002 and the subsequent construction of the so-called separation wall.

The UN Conference on Trade and Development (UNCTAD) issued a report in August 2005 warning that "years of economic retrenchment on top of almost four decades of occupation have increased poverty, reduced and distorted production, and heightened dependence on Israel. Prescriptions for Palestinian economic recovery must take into account the Israeli occupation, protracted conflict since 2000, and the imperatives created by the upcoming unilateral Israeli withdrawal from Gaza."[16] Citing the occupation as the principal source of de-development and economic turmoil, the UNCTAD report states:

> The Palestinian trade deficit grew faster than domestic production—from $1.8 billion in 2001 to $2.6 billion in 2004, representing 65% of GDP—with two thirds of this deficit arising from the chronic imbalance in trade with Israel. To pay for this deficit over the past four years, the Palestinian economy effectively channeled to Israel the equivalent of all aid received from the international community to provide relief during the ongoing crisis, plus the equivalent of half the remittances of Palestinian workers in Israel.[17]

The continued construction by Israel of the Apartheid Wall, known euphemistically as the Separation Fence, and the consolidation of Israeli settlements on Palestinian land will further eat away at the productive capacity of the West Bank and Gaza, threatening the people's livelihood and very survival. The confiscation of much of the Palestinian fertile lands has severely damaged the agricultural sector. By mid-2004, total agricultural land loss in the West Bank and Gaza was around 260 square kilometers, representing 15 percent of Palestine's cultivated area in 2003.

In short, as the World Bank analysts stated, "The Palestinian economy is on a knife's edge between take-off and collapse."[18] Recovery will depend on the resolution of the political questions: the end of occupation and the emergence of an independent and sovereign Palestine.

The Road to the Camp David Summit, 2000

The international context since the mid-1990s has been dominated and defined by US diplomatic, political, economic, and military power. At that same time, the United States has also consolidated its influence, if not hegemony, over the Middle East in general and the Arab world in particular. The US dual containment of Iraq and Iran and US sanctions against Libya have been legitimized by UN resolutions that the United States initiated and that the European powers (and Japan) and the principal Arab states acceded to. The United States has used this hegemony over the pivotal Arab states (especially Egypt, Jordan, and Saudi Arabia) and their leaders to pressure the Palestinian Authority to concede further procedural and substantive concessions to the successive agreements that derived from the Oslo process. This pressure reached a high point in the Hebron City Accord, the Wye River negotiations, and the Sharm El-Sheikh negotiations. All of these agreements were the result of Israeli intransigence and have been little more than efforts by Israel to renegotiate the terms of the Oslo II Accord, which have already been agreed to and signed.

The Oslo Accords presumed a phased transference of Israel's direct rule over the West Bank and the Gaza Strip to the Palestinian Authority, to be followed in five years (in 1998) by final status negotiations on the central issues: settlements, water, borders, Jerusalem, and the refugees. After the first redeployment of its military forces from Gaza and Jericho, Israel would presumably undertake three additional redeployments during the five-year interim period. Although the actual text of none of the agreements specifies the amount of territory to be given up by Israel, the Palestinian leadership and other supporters of the Oslo agreements typically assumed that the redeployments would entail all the areas captured in 1967 except for the Jewish settlements, the Israeli military bases, and, importantly,

Jerusalem. The second redeployment, scheduled to take place during Netanyahu's Likud government, was not implemented, had to be renegotiated, was contentious, and was quite tiny in area. Palestinian disappointment was high. And although the United States and the PA convinced themselves that a Labor government would be more forthcoming, Labor's prime minister Ehud Barak never executed the third redeployment and insisted on beginning final status negotiations without implementation of the already signed agreements.

The Israeli governments that followed Rabin's tenure (under the leadership of Netanyahu and Barak) were thus either reluctant or unwilling to implement the provisions of accords already reached with the PA. Compared to both Rabin and his interim successor Shimon Peres, Netanyahu was brash, aggressive, and abrasive. Yet the key difference was his apparent determination to undermine the Oslo process, with which he had disagreed before his election to office. Through aggressive measures—his intensified Jewish settlement drive, his opening of an archeological tunnel under the edge of the al-Haram al-Sharif, and his refusal to implement further redeployment of Israeli troops—Netanyahu alarmed not only the Palestinian Authority but also the Arab "Oslo party," the United States, the European Union and the international donor community, and the international economic organizations, all of whom had developed a vested interest in the "peace process."

The crisis that followed the tunnel opening, a mini but bloody intifada, involved Palestinian police who joined the demonstrators in responding to Israeli attacks. The crisis, along with Netanyahu's policies and his confrontational style, precipitated a US dilemma. President Clinton, who rarely, if ever, criticized Israel, stated that all was not well with the "peace process." More remarkably, an unprecedented op-ed statement in the *New York Times* collectively authored by former Secretaries of State Cyrus Vance, James Baker, and Lawrence Eagleburger and former National Security Advisor Zbigniew Brzezinski accused Netanyahu of undermining Israel's own security, as well as US interests.[19] Netanyahu's antics brought considerable US pressure to keep the "peace process" going. He was forced to negotiate the Hebron agreement and the redeployment, but he did so on his terms, as he did in the Wye River memorandum. In the final analysis, Israel's views usually prevailed in those agreements, typically with US support.

Netanyahu lost the 1999 Israeli elections to the supposed "peace candidate," Ehud Barak, who also would not implement the third prescribed redeployment in accordance with Oslo II. He pushed for moving directly into the final status negotiations without implementation of the terms of the previously agreed-on accords. The Clinton administration had progressively increased its involvement in the peace process through the high profile of the president himself in the Wye River and the Sharm El-Sheikh negotiations.

The Camp David Summit, 2000

In the last year of his administration, in July 2000, President Clinton and Prime Minister Barak forced the PA to accede to a premature (as Arafat insisted) trilateral (Israeli, Palestinian, and American) summit at Camp David, the US presidential retreat.[20] President Clinton led and orchestrated the summit himself, in order to get Israel and the Palestinian Authority to conclude a final agreement on the final status issues of the Palestine question.

Contrary to the official US-Israeli version and much of what was reported in the Western media, claiming that substantial agreement had been reached on all final status issues except Jerusalem, Akram Hanieh, a member of the Palestinian delegation, indicated that the sides remained far apart not only on Jerusalem but also on all other issues, especially on the question of the refugees. Hanieh contended that the timing and content of the summit were based on a flawed Israeli-US assumption that "the Palestinian leadership needed an achievement such as statehood and would be willing to pay a high price for it. They also assumed that the Palestinians did not enjoy enough Arab support to withstand pressure."[21]

The Israeli-US assumptions and the pro-Israel US role translated into several significant developments according to Hanieh. The basis of the Madrid conference and the Oslo process—that is, UN Security Council Resolution 242, which stipulates the exchange of conquered land for peace—was simply ignored by the United States in the Camp David negotiations. Neither the US nor the Israeli side made reference to, much less anchored their proposals in, this or any other UN resolution, or in international law. In addition, every proposal that was presented by the US mediators to the Palestinian side already had Israeli clearance. On practically every issue—especially on Jerusalem and the refugees—the US team simply adopted and argued for the Israeli position. This view is bluntly corroborated by Aaron David Miller, a senior negotiator on the Clinton team at Camp David and an Orthodox Jew. Miller publicly revealed that rather than serve as a true mediator in peace negotiations, successive US administrations, including Clinton's, have acted as "Israel's attorney."[22] Writing on the *Washington*

Post op-ed page in May 2005, Miller stated that Clinton and his team followed Israel's lead "without critically examining what that would mean for our own interests, for those on the Arab side and for the overall success of the negotiations."[23] The Clinton team's practice of running everything past Israel first "stripped our policy of the independence and flexibility required for serious peacemaking. Far too often ... our departure point was not what was needed to reach an agreement acceptable to both sides but what would pass with only one—Israel. The result was utter failure."[24]

In its "generous offer" to the PA with regard to land, borders, and security, Israel effectively sought to consolidate and legitimize the gains it had made in the 1967 war. It sought to maintain military bases and to annex civilian colonial settlements in several areas, especially along the Jordan River and in the huge settlement blocs around the northern, eastern, and southern sides of the city of Jerusalem and in the north and south of the West Bank. However, the "greatest failure" of the summit, according to Hanieh, was over the issue of the Palestinian refugees. Israelis denied completely any responsibility, moral or otherwise, for the Palestinian Nakbah, including the expulsion, killing, and massacring of innocent civilians and the expropriation of Palestinian property. In addition, they refused to be responsible for compensation to the Palestinian refugees and argued that an international fund should be established that would compensate the Palestinian refugees and also the Jews who had left Arab countries in the 1950s. Furthermore, no reference was made in the report to reparations to the Palestinian people.

On Jerusalem, the Israelis insisted on retaining sovereignty over al-Haram al-Sharif but offered to allow the PA custodial rights, or "custodial sovereignty" as they termed it.[25] It appears that although the American and Israeli rhetoric was about an open Jerusalem, the actual proposals divided and fragmented the city into an intertwined labyrinth of territorial and functional sovereignties. This was the Israeli proposal on Jerusalem and was almost word for word the proposal that Clinton presented to Arafat as the American "compromise." It was not accepted by the Palestinian team.

During the summit, Clinton attempted to enroll some Arab leaders via telephone diplomacy to pressure Arafat directly at Camp David, an effort that failed and appears to have infuriated the already frustrated Clinton. On December 30, 2000, the Palestinian Authority published and distributed its response to the proposal presented orally by Clinton during the Washington talks held earlier that month, after the Camp David summit. The response states that the US proposal failed to satisfy the conditions required for a permanent peace. As it stood, the US proposal would (1) divide a Palestinian state into three cantons connected and divided by Jewish-only and Arab-only roads and jeopardize the Palestinian state's viability; (2) divide Palestinian Jerusalem into a number of unconnected islands separate from each other and from the rest of Palestine; and (3) force Palestinians to surrender the right of return of Palestinian refugees. The US proposal seemed to the Palestinians to respond to Israeli demands while neglecting the basic Palestinian need: a viable state.[26]

Although the Palestinian leadership was at a very distinct negotiating disadvantage in all the negotiating cycles, and especially at the Camp David summit, it refused to accede to the unacceptable terms that Israel and the United States offered as a final status agreement at that summit. To the credit of the Palestinian Authority, it refused to accept the so-called generous peace offer, which was not only far below the minimum aspirations and the internationally guaranteed rights of the Palestinian people, and which contravened, as well, existing international law and UN resolutions, but that also would have extended and legitimized Israeli settler colonialism and occupation.

Camp David: Testing the Viability of Oslo

At least ten agreements had been concluded between Israel and the Palestinians between September 1993 and July 2000. Almost every one of them had been proclaimed a step forward on the road toward peace, and some were celebrated with pomp and pageantry. That record of diplomatic "success," however, was interrupted at Camp David, where the mother of all agreements was being anxiously awaited. Unlike the previous agreements, which dealt solely with issues designated as interim subjects, this one was to encompass the intractable issues deferred for "final status" negotiations; hence Camp David became the ultimate test of Oslo.

The July 25 collapse of the summit at Camp David signified a major diplomatic fiasco, despite the earlier "successes," if not *because* of them; the reason was that they were agreements to reach an agreement. It is not uncommon for negotiators to observe certain red lines. Clinton's principal red line was to refrain from faulting Israel under any circumstances. Instead, he placed the blame for failure squarely on Arafat, thus forfeiting even the pretense of impartiality.[27] Arafat's red lines had dwindled over the years and had become almost extinct, and yet, he had resolved not to go down in history as the one who gave Jerusalem away. Barak's red lines, on the other hand, were repeated for the umpteenth time on his way to Camp David. He told his constituents, "Separation—we here and they there; no return to the 1967 borders; Jerusalem united under our sovereignty; no foreign army west of the River Jordan; most settlers under Israeli sovereignty in the final status arrangement; Israel will not recognize any moral or legal responsibility for the (Palestinian) refugee problem."[28]

Such red lines had indeed sealed the fate of the summit. The Washington referee could engage in arm-twisting only vis-à-vis Arafat. When Arafat balked, he earned the reputation of the spoiler who had turned down a "generous" offer and tarnished the reputation and prestige of the US presidency.

Arafat was obviously facing his moment of truth at Camp David. It was one thing to talk about the amount of land ceded to his authority and the extent of that authority during the interim phase; it was quite another to deal with the intractable issues that had been deferred since 1993, which constituted the heart of the Palestine question. But when those issues were finally placed on the table, it became clear that in exchange for having accepted Israel on 78 percent of their national patrimony, the Palestinians would be allowed to have a borderless, nonsovereign, and fragmented Palestinian "state" in only 61 percent of the remaining 22 percent of Palestine. Israel's "compromise" on Jerusalem consisted of placing under Palestinian "administrative control" less than 15 percent of the sixty-four square kilometers it had annexed from the West Bank after 1967. On the issue of the refugees, Israel's "pragmatic" solution would have referred to UN Resolution 194, which called for repatriation, compensation, and restitution, but it would not have in any way obligated Israel to implement these actions, as the United Nations had directed in 1948, when it made Israel's admission to the world organization conditional on this implementation. Israel would have simply taken back less than 100,000 out of approximately 5 million refugees under a family reunification plan and on a case-by-case basis over a long period of time.

Was the Collapse of Camp David a Failure of Oslo?

The failure at Camp David was largely due to certain structural defects in the Declaration of Principles (DOP). First, there had been almost no transitions between the interim issues and the vexing final status issues. Hardly anything that was accomplished between 1993 and July 2000 could have been used to pave the way and bridge the gaps. Instead, the central feature of Clinton's methodology of conflict resolution was arm-twisting, as if a lasting peace would result from salesmanship and coercion.

Second, the structural flaws of Oslo were related to segmentation and deferral. For the Palestinians, segmenting the negotiations by issues, population categories, regions, towns and villages, and stages of negotiations remained one of the biggest obstacles to peace. Had the issue of land and settlements not been deferred during Oslo's "interim phase," for example, the question of settlement security would not have become a barrier to redeployment. Had the deferral pattern not been set, matters relating to self-governance and the resumption of negotiations would not have been treated as probationary. Could such a self-defeating process have been meant to result in real implementation?

For the United States and Israel, a Camp David agreement was the natural last step in a series of capitulations and concessions extracted from Arafat, beginning with the open-ended Oslo agreements. Clinton was counting on his creative diplomacy to produce one more agreement, even in the face of great skepticism at the time he summoned the parties to Camp David. This time, however, the "creative diplomacy" that had produced the earlier agreements by deferring the substantive issues had run its course. Having resisted Clinton's usual browbeating this time, Arafat spoiled the party and surprised his host by failing to sign off on a final surrender.

The failure at Camp David exposed Oslo as a forged agreement, and the mediator as a collaborator. President Clinton, who opened the summit by calling for a "principled compromise," somehow missed the reality that negotiations for a stable peace and ultimate reconciliation must be guided by principles—not merely principles designed to reflect the existing political realities, but principles that reflect the concerns of both parties and the requirements of international law. In conclusion, a principled compromise could not be brokered without the sponsorship of the international community and the force of the UN resolutions.

The George W. Bush Administration

Enter George W. Bush and the Republican Party. Although many of the Arab, and some international, media and politicians hailed the election victory of George W. Bush in November 2000 as heralding a constructive change in the Middle East policy of the United States, it is now clear that the fundamental nature of US policy toward the region has remained unchanged.[29] Carefully articulated views by administration officials and by Bush and Prime Minister Ariel Sharon themselves indicated that the United States and Israel faced what together they perceive as identical global and regional threats (e.g., international, especially Islamic, terrorism) that required increased collaboration between the two countries. In the speeches and statements the Bush administration officials made on the occasion of Sharon's first visit to Washington as prime minister in March 2001, they routinely articulated the standard political rhetoric of US policy regarding the state of Israel. Secretary of State Colin Powell, for example, shortly after his confirmation, gave the politically obligatory speech before the American Israel Public Affairs Committee (AIPAC), the most important pro-Israel lobby in Washington, in which he reaffirmed the resolute commitment of the United States to a strategic alliance with Israel and to the special US relationship with that country. He also reaffirmed the long-standing US commitment to aid Israel in maintaining a military edge over all the Arab states.

What was new early in the Bush administration policy was the downgrading of the "peace process" and a reduction of the high-profile involvement of senior US officials. In pointed statements by both Bush and Powell they specifically reduced the US role from "honest broker" (the rhetoric of the Clinton administration) to "facilitator for peace negotiations." But the Bush administration did not even want to engage in facilitating negotiations unless the "violence and terrorism" of the Al-Aqsa Intifada was reduced or ended altogether. It is clear that there was no real change in US policy toward the Palestine question and the Palestinians by the Bush administration. Most indicative is the reception by the Bush administration of the Mitchell Report.

George Mitchell, a former US senator, headed a commission to investigate the causes of "violence" in the Al-Aqsa Intifada, a commission that was demanded by the Palestinian side and agreed to by Israel in the Sharm El-Sheikh accord. The report stressed the importance of an end to violence, and it also called for a "freeze on settlements" in the occupied territories. The report is flawed and biased toward Israel in a number of ways. "It makes a spurious equivalence between the state violence of an occupying power and the improvised resistance of a people under occupation."[30] And remarkably, the report describes terrorism as exclusively Palestinian.[31] Nevertheless, the PA was desperate enough for a diplomatic initiative so that it accepted the Mitchell Report wholeheartedly, without comment or reservations. Whereas the PA accepted the report and adopted the recommendations without any reservations, Israel placed conditions on accepting the report by rejecting the settlement freeze clause. Perhaps in part because of Israeli objections, the Bush administration accepted the Mitchell report but was vague on support of the clause specifying the "freezing of settlements." Thus the situation early in the Bush II era was not auspicious for the Palestinians.

Powell's Missed Opportunity

A speech by Colin Powell at the University of Louisville on November 11, 2001, was a missed opportunity to move toward a negotiated settlement. Although Powell's speech failed to offer a remedy for the diplomatic absurdity of Oslo, it nevertheless claimed to offer a vision, to issue a presumed call for action, a diagnosis and prerequisites for resuming negotiations as well as the tools needed to proceed. The vision enunciated by Powell in the Kentucky speech was that of two viable states with recognized borders, one of which, Palestine, would be required to recognize Israel as a Jewish state and promise to exist alongside it and not "instead of it."

A review of recent diplomatic history reveals that what was somewhat new in Powell's vision was the use of the term *viable* to describe an independent Palestinian state. President Carter had fallen short of that description when, at Camp David, he countered Menachem Begin's dictum of "autonomy for the people but not for the land" with "full autonomy" (but not independence) for the Palestinians. However, the prospect of a "viable" and truly contiguous state with "recognized borders" seemed remote, as Sharon's agenda favored the establishment of disconnected Palestinian enclaves.

Powell's requirements also included "end the occupation," stop all violence, whether by vigilantes, irregulars, or uniformed soldiers, and "trade land for peace," in accordance with UN Resolutions 242 and 338. He added another significant phrase: "Recapture the spirit of Madrid," and work toward a comprehensive settlement.

The reemergence of the terms *occupation* and *Madrid* could have been important had the administration been willing to pay the political cost of implementation. First, the term *occupation* had been earlier totally excised from the Oslo lexicon. Mr. Powell's wish that Israel "must be willing to end its occupation," therefore, represented an interesting verbal twist from previous positions, but the declared intent came to naught.

The second interesting term in Powell's speech was *Madrid,* the venue for Arab-Israeli negotiations that, unlike Oslo, had called for a comprehensive peace between Israel and the Arab states, and that had something of an international-multilateral character (although largely symbolic), instead of the strictly bilateral Palestinian-Israeli negotiations under Washington's auspices. However, Powell's diagnosis seemed to skip Oslo; it went right from Madrid to the intifada, as if the intifada had occurred in a vacuum. The conditions that had created the intifada—namely, seven years of futile negotiations that had been used by Israel as a diplomatic strategy to swallow more Palestinian land and preempt a contiguous Palestinian state—seemed to have no impact on Powell's diagnosis. By implication, the uprising was seen as a form of wanton violence having nothing to do with legitimate resistance to a brutal military occupation.

With regard to Jewish settlement activity, however, Powell's call on Israel to stop did represent a departure from his previous position in a May 21, 2001, press conference, when he advocated "freezing" settlements as a "confidence-building measure" but rejected any link between a Palestinian cease-fire and an Israeli freezing. In the Kentucky speech, Powell said that settlement activity "preempts and prejudges" the outcome of negotiations and "cripples the chances for peace and security."

Finally, Powell asserted that the tools were in place to relaunch negotiations. But first, Arafat, not only Hamas and Jihad, was to cease all suicide bombings, round up activists to convince Israel and the United States of his good faith, and "dismantle the terror infrastructure." Arafat was also expected to collect all "illegally held firearms." In return, Powell would ask Israel to ease the economic blockade and to lift the siege, thus conveying a message to the Palestinians that "ceasing the violence" would pay. However, in general, Israeli violence, which amounted to state terrorism and dwarfed the largely sporadic and responsive Palestinian violence, did not seem to be a principal issue in that sequence.

In sum, although the Powell speech resurrected long-forgotten phrases conducive to a principled compromise, it nevertheless left unanswered many questions relating to borders, Jerusalem, refugees, and water—issues that the Bush administration has rarely addressed up to the present.

Between Powell's Kentucky speech in November 2001 and his April 2002 visit to the region in the aftermath of the Israeli all-out attack on West Bank cities and refugee camps, all the ideas presented in that speech had become practically outmoded. The speech became a forgotten casualty of the suicide bombing in Haifa and Jerusalem on December 1, 2001.[32] Described by the Israeli media and publicists as Israel's own "Twin Towers" attack (with twenty-six deaths and more than a hundred injured), the event was seized upon as a rallying cry for an all-out assault on Yasser Arafat, a convenient symbol of the Palestinian national movement. The suicide bombing had become a catalyst for avoiding any serious moves toward negotiations and a diplomatic settlement, in accord with Sharon's designs.

Not only did the suicide bombing play right into the hands of General Sharon, who would immediately declare Arafat Israel's Osama bin Laden and the PA its Taliban, but it would also ensure George W. Bush's seeing Israel as conducting its own "war against terrorism." No longer would the

Bush administration be satisfied with the standard condemnation of Palestinian "violence," now upgraded to "terrorism," while asking for Israeli restraint. Under the Bush administration, the United States would not even go through the motions of asking for Israeli restraint. It would simply grant Israel a green light for a major retaliation against Hamas's own retaliation, without qualifications regarding appropriate targets or real culpability.

Much of the Palestinian infrastructure was subsequently demolished when Israel launched military action known as Operation Defensive Shield on March 29, 2002, with an incursion into Ramallah, followed by entry into Tulkarm and Qalqilya on April 1, Bethlehem on April 2, and Jenin and Nablus on April 3. By April 3, six of the largest cities in the West Bank, and their surrounding towns, villages, and refugee camps, had been reoccupied.[33] The military attacks occurred in areas heavily populated by civilians, and in many cases heavy weaponry was used, causing the populations of the cities severe hardships. Although the Israeli forces announced the official end of the operation on April 21, its consequences lasted for much longer.

Washington had in fact given Israel tacit support in thwarting a UN mission of inquiry under the auspices of the Security Council.[34] However, the UN General Assembly adopted a resolution on August 5, demanding an immediate end to military incursions and all acts of violence, terror, provocation, incitement, and destruction in Israel and the occupied Palestinian territories. The US isolation in the international community was starkly revealed in the voting on that resolution, which passed by a vote of 114 in favor to 4 against (Micronesia, Israel, Marshall Islands, and the United States), with 11 abstentions.

Not surprisingly, President Bush adopted Sharon's position that a satisfactory "reform" of the Palestine Authority, together with the creation of administrative and security institutions, must precede political talks. By the time Sharon completed his fifth and sixth visits to Washington in June 2002, during which he was described by Bush as a "man of peace," and as "my teacher," not a speck of the Powell Kentucky speech remained relevant.[35]

The Bush Speech of June 24, 2002

A June 24, 2002, speech by George W. Bush marked a departure from the Clinton era's policy in that it effectively endorsed Sharon's abrogation of the Oslo process. For the first time since 1993, when the DOP was signed at the White House, the US government turned its back publicly on the mere idea of the two sides returning to negotiation. The bulk of the speech was instead devoted to articulating commands and conditions and issuing warnings to abandon "terror," addressed to the Palestinians but rarely to Israelis: "Today, Palestinian authorities are encouraging, not opposing terrorism. . . . This is unacceptable. And the United States will not support the establishment of a Palestinian state until its leaders engage in a sustained fight against the terrorists and dismantle their infrastructure."[36]

President Bush asked the Israelis to "restore freedom of movement"— but only after (Palestinian) "violence subsides"—and to withdraw to "positions held prior to September 28, 2000," and to stop "settlement activity." Bush's remarks about the occupation were limited to the friendly advice that it "threatens Israel's identity and democracy." Bush's substantive orders and threats were reserved for those "who are not with us"—Palestinians and their "terrorist" allies. Even US client states in the Arab world, which qualified with reservations for "being with us," were told to establish "full normalization of relations" with Israel, ignoring the rebuffed Arab League's expressed willingness to recognize Israel in exchange for terminating the occupation, as stated in the Beirut summit of April 2002.

Bush's speech called on the Palestinians to change their leaders, to "build a practicing democracy," to acquire "new political and economic institutions based on democracy [and a] market economy," to adopt a new constitution that "separates the powers of government," to conduct "multiparty local elections by the end of the year," to establish a "truly independent judiciary," to streamline the security system, and, of course, to stop "terrorism."[37] Only after the Palestinians met such a long list of unattainable demands would they be eligible to return to negotiations that could optimally offer them a "provisional" state.

A provisional state is a concept that lacks a proper definition and has no meaning in either politics or international law. A provisional state is likely to be just the state that Sharon supports: a collection of disconnected eight cantons in the West bank, separated from Israel by the Apartheid Wall, and from each other by Israeli checkpoints and bypass roads for Jews only.

The European press was almost unanimous in its cool reception of the Bush speech. George Bush was unable to sell his speech to his allies who were attending the G-8 meeting in Canada on the very next day. Almost every one of those leaders felt a need to distance himself from Bush's position by commenting on the right of the Palestinians to name their own leaders. Moreover, after Bush's speech, the Danish government, which held the rotating presidency of the European Union (EU) at the time, expressed worries that the "United States has effectively abandoned the Mideast peace process."[38]

In the final analysis, the Bush speech contained so many loopholes and so much gridlock that it enabled Sharon to try his favorite tactic: doing nothing diplomatically as he proceeds to establish more "facts on the ground"—more settlers (430,000 in 2005) and settlements (116 in 2005), more checkpoints, more isolation of the Palestinians, more destruction of their civilian and public infrastructure, more killing and maiming, and more fragmentation through the Apartheid Wall. In 2003, a new peace plan, the Road Map to Peace, was placed on the table, but like its predecessors, it has already fallen off the table, as will be seen in chapter 12.

Dynamics in Israeli Society and Politics

Ever since the victory of the Likud Party coalition in the 1977 elections, Israel has been shifting demographically and politically to the religious and nationalist right. Indeed, Rabin's (and Labor's) election victory in 1992 notwithstanding, the shift to the right includes many in Labor's own leadership, such as Barak. This rightward shift has defined the political discourse and actions that have characterized Israel since 1977.

Central to this discourse are the colonial settlements and the destiny of the settlers in the occupied territories. Accordingly, throughout the Oslo period, Israel not only did not stop building colonial settlements, moving settlers into the occupied territories, and developing the infrastructure to sustain them but actually accelerated the process.[39] Since the first Oslo Accord was signed, the settler population in the settlements in east Jerusalem, the West Bank, and the Gaza Strip has *doubled* to approximately half a million settlers by 1999, according to the authoritative *Report on Israeli Settlement in the Occupied Territories*. In regard to Jerusalem, in 1967 Israel extended its law and jurisdiction to 17,600 acres of Palestinian land in and around East Jerusalem, which became an enlarged municipality of seventy square kilometers.

The Oslo Accords actually facilitated rather than constrained the building and consolidation of settlements in the occupied territories. In the negotiations leading up to the Oslo Accords in 1993, the agreements were made possible by Arafat's agreeing to drop from the Palestinian agenda the existing settlements as well as the demand for a freeze on any additional settlements. Settlement expansion during the Oslo process is predicated not only on the understanding with Arafat and the PA, but also on the understandings that Israel had extracted from the United States in separate assurances and commitments. From the administrations of Jimmy Carter through the

Ronald Reagan, Bush I, and Clinton administrations, and in the Bush II administration, the United States has consistently vacillated on or conceded to Israel's determination to continue the settlement drive.

The prospects for contiguous Palestinian sovereignty in the occupied territories have been undermined by the Israeli settlements. Thus, the growing Jewish population; the expanding settlement communities; the creation and expansion of bypass roads; the development of settlement-based agricultural, industrial, and commercial enterprises; and the military presence that "protects" the settlements—all have become central factors in sabotaging the Palestinian hope for an independent contiguous sovereign state. Settlements are the principal strategic mechanism for the Israeli-imposed Bantustanization and enclavization of the occupied territories.

As the social, economic, and political impact of the Israeli settlements and occupation forces on the daily life of the Palestinians in the occupied territories has substantially worsened, and the humiliations have intensified, the level of popular frustration with the Oslo process has also become more intense. Thus, given the political vacuum of the impasse that followed the failed Camp David summit, and given the provocative actions of the Israeli government (especially the visit of Ariel Sharon to the al-Haram Al-Sharif), the deeply frustrated and humiliated Palestinian people in the occupied territories seemed to take the political initiative into their own hands and exploded on September 28, 2000, in a second rising—Al-Aqsa Intifada.

Al-Aqsa Intifada

In one sense the Al-Aqsa Intifada was a continuation of the intifada of 1987 that was interrupted and aborted by the Oslo Accords and the so-called peace process. The triumphant arrival of Arafat and the majority of the PLO and Fateh cadres in Gaza in 1994 to establish the Palestinian Authority initially promised relief from the Israeli occupation as well as economic growth and the seeming possibility of a resolution of the Palestinian-Israeli conflict through the creation of an independent sovereign Palestinian state, with the repatriation and restitution of the Palestinian refugees. With the establishment of the Palestinian Authority in the West Bank and the Gaza Strip, the Palestinian people witnessed the introduction of a new Palestinian political organization that was responsible for civilian rule over the populated centers. The PA created an overlap with the PLO and the Palestine National Council, both of which had represented, until the first Oslo Accord, the Palestinian political, ideological, and organizational consensus.

This organizational duality of the Palestinian movement, as well as the commitment to Israel and the United States to amend the PLO Charter, constituted Arafat's major challenges. He set about solving them in his traditional way. Slowly and systematically he suppressed, isolated, marginalized, and eliminated all opposition to the Oslo agreement and to his regime. He was aided in large measure by the dawning of new realities in the West Bank and the Gaza Strip, in the region, and internationally, the reality of political, diplomatic, and economic support and formal recognition extended to the Palestinian Authority, in addition to the nationalist legacy that he and the PLO carried.

But the Palestinian Authority's performance, specifically its inability to address the worsening daily living of the Palestinians under its authority, charges against it of corruption and favoritism, and its failure to advance the cause of ending the occupation, led to extensive discontent and disillusionment with Arafat's leadership and his PA regime among most segments of the Palestinian people. More specifically, the physical movement of Palestinians in their own society and territories became, under the Oslo agreements, more restricted than ever before, and Palestinian discontent and frustration was therefore increased. Although Gaza and the West Bank were declared one territory, movement between them almost came to a halt except for certain Palestinian Authority VIPs. The much-delayed "safe passage" between the Gaza Strip and the West Bank that was finally opened in 1999 turned out to be just as restricted as all the other highways, and the passes or permits required by the Israeli occupation forces choked off the use of this passage. Similarly, the Palestinian population centers became separated from each other and from the land surrounding them by Israeli checkpoints, settlements, and bypass roads built for exclusively Jewish use. Only within the municipal borders of Palestinian towns and cities are the people outside direct Israeli rule. It was therefore no surprise that in the context of the political vacuum of the failed summit and the difficult if not desperate daily situation, the Palestinians in the West Bank and the Gaza Strip took matters into their own hands and exploded in the Second Intifada.

The Two Intifadas Compared

The political contexts of the two intifadas were profoundly different. The First Intifada occurred during a time of Palestinian political despair, disorientation, and impasse following the Israeli invasion of Lebanon, the siege of Beirut, the Sabra and Shatila massacres, and the expulsion and dispersal of the PLO and its armed forces from Beirut. The PLO became diplomatically isolated, financially strapped, and politically floundering in faraway Tunis. Furthermore, the Arab summit in Amman shortly before the intifada erupted failed the Palestinians miserably. In the occupied territories, the Israeli occupation forces were in complete and tight control, and Jewish settlement activity was intensifying. Daily life was becoming untenable for most Palestinians and unbearable for many under the humiliation and abuse of the settlers and the Israeli army.

The uprising that erupted in 1987 was a long time in the making. It had gestated in resistance to and confrontation with the occupation since 1967. During that time the Palestinian people built an indigenous and vibrant civil society and a network of NGOs that served the important social and material needs of the population. Over the years the social mobilization of Palestinian society turned slowly but inexorably into sociopolitical mobilization that needed only a spark to explode into a popular uprising throughout the occupied territories. Indeed, the traditional forms of organization, such as family, *hamula*, mosque and church, village and town—all supported and aided the modern secular organizations, the NGOs, and the underground collective leadership that directed the intifada.

The Second or Al-Aqsa Intifada also erupted against the background of a political impasse, the failed international summit at Camp David, but in a different economic, social, and political context. The dire socioeconomic situation during the Oslo process period (1993–2000) has been outlined above. Politically, a Palestinian Authority comprising principally PLO returnees, an enlarged bureaucracy, a relatively sizable police, security agencies, and a known centralized leadership were in place, although the Palestinian Authority was limited to principal and disconnected population centers encircled by Israeli settlements and bypass roads, as well as the Israeli occupation forces.[40] Most significantly, however, instead of a mass-based civil uprising like the First Intifada, the Al-Aqsa uprising was more like an armed insurrection based in a minority of the population, with the majority sympathetic and supportive spectators. Although made frustrated and angry by the failure of the Oslo promise and the increasing depredations of the occupiers and the settlers, the Palestinian population in the West Bank and the Gaza Strip is politically demobilized and even apathetic.[41] Indeed, the traditional social organizations of family, *hamula*, and village that were integrated into and supportive of the more secular First Intifada were less involved in the Second Intifada.

The NGOs and the civil society organizations that launched and sustained the First Intifada have, since Oslo, been professionalized, have changed their programmatic emphasis (to development, democracy, and governance issues in general), and have had many of their functions taken over by the official agencies of the PA and/or corrupted by the bureaucrats of the PA and international donor agencies that support the Oslo process. To be sure, not all the NGOs have suffered this destiny, but the critical mass of the varied NGOs and their mass base that existed in the First Intifada were absent in the Second Intifada. The demise of the "popular sovereignties"[42] of the First Intifada was the direct result of the Oslo agreements and PA rule. In the West Bank and the Gaza Strip, the PLO/PA combined civil and political society into one all-compassing movement.[43] But in contrast to the Palestinian movement in Lebanon, "the function of this overall strategy under the PA has not been mobilization but control and cooptation, and with it the dilution of the rule of law and democratically elected institutions."[44]

Another crucial difference between the two intifadas is "the geography of the confrontation."[45] The First Intifada was an uprising of an unarmed civilian population confronting the Israeli occupation forces in the center of the Palestinian cities and towns. Its tactics of civil disobedience and economic and social self-reliance were not only innovative but also effective and received considerable positive support overseas. In the Second Intifada, instead of a mass civilian uprising, limited armed clashes typically occurred on the fringes of the autonomous Palestinian cities and towns, and at road junctures, Israeli military checkpoints, and the approaches to settlements. In contrast to the civilian character of the First Intifada, the Second Intifada was more militarized with frequent stone throwing and armed clashes. The presence of over forty thousand lightly armed Palestinian policemen and security forces (mandated by Oslo) and, more important, the armed factions of Fateh—the *Tanzim*—gave the Second Intifada the character of an armed insurrection and rationalized, as well, Israel's use of excessive, savage force.[46] The armed clashes in the Second Intifada were between the Israeli occupation forces and the armed settlers and, on the Palestinian side, principally the loosely organized and locally commanded irregular Tanzim factions (occasionally joined by the Preventive Security Force of the PA).

Interestingly, although Hamas emerged in the First Intifada as a major sociopolitical force, the religious dimension of that intifada was muted. In the Second Intifada, on the other hand, the religious dimension had a major mobilizing and symbolic role, especially because the Al-Aqsa or al-Haram al-Sharif confrontation was the principal trigger of the uprising.[47] This religious saliency diminished and subsumed the role of the nationalist and secular movement.

Finally, in regard to communication and mobilization, the media role in the Second Intifada was distinctive and pronounced. Satellite-based coverage of the intifada for the Arab world galvanized Arab popular public opinion as never before, mobilizing it in various Arab states and forcing those states to act politically and diplomatically, individually and through the Arab League, in support of Palestinian demands.

Conclusion

Besides the seemingly inexorable process of Israeli colonial settlement in the occupied territories, there are new Palestinian facts developing. The Palestinian population in historical Palestine, including the segments in Israel, the Gaza Strip, and the West Bank, is likely to exceed that of the Israeli Jews by 2010 and will become once again the majority in their own historical homeland. Second, the Palestinians now are intensely aware of the Israeli tactics designed to force them to abandon their land. As many of the social and political leaders have repeatedly indicated, they are determined to stay on the land or die resisting expulsion or "transfer" as the Israelis wish. And finally, the internationally legitimized presence of the PA, with its police force and varied institutions in the autonomous areas, cannot be easily or legitimately eliminated. Given these facts and the political impasse, if not deadlock, of the "peace process" and the powerful forces arrayed against the Palestinians, the political reality dawning on many of the intellectuals is that the three segments of the Palestinian population (in Israel, in the occupied territories, and in diaspora) will find that their goals (for equality, for self-determination, and for return and compensation) are unlikely to be achieved by the present methods, especially in the short and medium terms.

Notes

1. S. Roy, "De-Development Revisited: Palestinian Economy and Society Since Oslo," *Journal of Palestine Studies* 28 (Spring 1999): 64. This part depends largely on Sara Roy's study.

2. Ibid., 5.

3. Ibid.

4. Ibid., Figure 1, p. 2.

5. Reported in ibid., 4.

6. World Bank, *MENA Region, Poverty in the West Bank and Gaza* (January 2001): Section 2.22.

7. UNSCO, 15.

8. Figures from UNSCO, cited by Roy, "De-Development Revisited," 76.

9. World Bank, *MENA Region*, 6.

10. Ibid., 7.

11. Ibid., 39

12. Ibid., 48.

13. Ibid., 44.

14. Diwan and Shaban, 8–11.

15. L. Farsakh, "Economic Feasibility of a Palestinian State in the West Bank and Gaza Strip: Is It Possible Without National Sovereignty and Geographic Unity," *Journal of Palestinian Studies* 44 (Spring 2000): 44–61.

16. See press release online at http://www.unctad.org/Templates/Webflyer.asp?docID=6169&intItemID=2068&lang=1, or full report at http://www.unctad.org/en/docs/td52d2_en.pdf.

17. Ibid.

18. Ibid., 33.

19. *New York Times*. September 26, 1996.

20. See H. Ashrawi, "Barak's Political Exports: Used Goods to Arafat and a Snub to Clinton," *Miftah,* available at www.miftah.org. See also R. Malley, "Fictions About the Failure at Camp David," *New York Times* (July 8, 2001).

21. Malley, "Fictions," 76.

22. See Kathleen Christison, "Anatomy of a Frame-Up: Camp David Redux," *Counterpunch* (August 15, 2005). On line at http://www.counterpunch.org/christison08152005.html.

23. Ibid.

24. Ibid; for a similar view, see also Clayton Swisher, *The Truth About Camp David: The Untold Story About the Collapse of the Middle East Peace Process* (New York: Thunder's Mouth Press/Nations Books, 2004).

25. Confirmed by Malley, "Fictions."

26. "Remarks and Questions from the Palestinian Negotiating Team Regarding the United States' Proposal," *Report on Israeli Settlement in the Occupied Territories* 11 (January-February 2001): 9–12.

27. "Clinton Blames Arafat for Peace Talks Failure," *World Net Daily* (June 21, 2004). Available online at http://www.worldnetdaily.com/news/article.asp?ARTICLE_ID=39066.

28. *Yediot Ahoronot* (July 11, 2000).

29. This section is based on N. Aruri and S. Farsoun, "Bush and the Palestinians," *Middle East International* 648 (April 20, 2001): 20–22.

30. G. Usher, "Raising the Military Stakes," *Middle East International* 650 (May 18, 2001): 4. See also the comments of E. W. Said, "Sharpening the Axe," at www.MSANews.org.

31. Ibid.

32. The full text can be read in the *Guardian* (London) of November 20, 2001. Also available online at http://www.guardian.co.uk/print/0,3858,4302866-103552,00.html.

33. See *Report on the Military Operation by the UN Secretary-General: Tenth Emergency Special Session*, Agenda Item 5, Illegal Israeli Actions in Occupied East Jerusalem and the Rest of the Occupied Palestinian Territory, Report of the Secretary-General Prepared Pursuant to General Assembly Resolution ES-10/10. This report was requested by the General Assembly in May (Resolution ES-10/10, adopted on May 7, 2002), after the disbanding of the team that the Secretary-General, supported by the Security Council (Resolution 1405 of April 19, 2002), had proposed to send to Jenin to establish the facts at the site.

34. The UN Secretary-General felt that he had been forced to disband the fact-finding mission organized in response to Security Council Resolution 1405, dated April 19, 2002. On August 1, 2002, the Secretary-General released a report prepared pursuant to General Assembly Resolution ES-10/10. Summing it up, the *Guardian* wrote: "In Jenin and elsewhere last spring, as in Gaza last week, Israel exceeded the limits of its legal right to self-defence. It placed itself in prima facie breach of the fourth Geneva convention and the international covenant on civil and political rights. Specifically, after an ambush on April 9 in Jenin that killed 13 soldiers, it resorted to random, vengeful acts of terror involving civilians. As we said last April, the destruction wrought in Jenin looked and smelled like a crime. On the basis of the UN's findings, it still does"; "Truth-Seeking in Jenin: Israel Is Still Wanted for Questioning," *Guardian* (London) (August 2, 2002).

35. For a detailed description of these visits and the changing US diplomatic posture under George W. Bush, see Naseer Aruri, *Dishonest Broker: The US Role in Israel and Palestine* (Cambridge, MA: South End Press, 2003): Ch. 11.

36. See speech online at www.usembassy-israel.org.il/.

37. Aruri, *Dishonest Broker*, 206–208.

38. www.haaretzdaily.com 6/28/2002.

39. *Report on Israeli Settlement in the Occupied Territories*, Vol. 9 (Washington, DC: Foundation of Middle East Peace, May-June 1999): 4.

40. R. Hammami and S. Tamari, "Anatomy of Another Rebellion" (a manuscript sent to Naseer Aruri by Salim Tamari on 5/7/06).

41. See N. Picadou, "Between National Liberation and State Building: A New Intifada, a New Strategy," *Le Monde Diplomatique*, English Edition online (March 2001): 1–5. See also Hammami and Tamari, for comparisons between the two intifadas.

42. S. Farsoun and J. Landis, "Structures of Resistance and the 'War of Position': A Case Study of the Palestinian Uprising," *Arab Studies Quarterly* 11 (Fall 1989): 59–86.

43. G. Giacaman, "In the Throes of Oslo: Palestinian Society, Civil Society and the Future," in G. Giacaman and D. J. Lonning, eds., *After Oslo, New Realities, Old Problems* (London: Pluto Press, 1998), cited in R. Hammami and S. Tamari, 18–19.

44. Hammami and Tamari, 19.

45. Ibid., 1.

46. Ibid., 12. See also Commission on Human Rights, Economic and Social Council, United Nations, "Question of the Violation of Human Rights in the Occupied Arab Territories, including Palestine," E/CN.4/2002/121, March 16, 2001.

47. Ibid.

10

Palestinian Refugees and Their Right of Return

The question of the Palestinian refugees has not been central in what came to be known from 1969 to 2006 as the Middle East Peace Process, under American auspices, which have merely succeeded in perpetuating the 1967 occupation while keeping the 1948 issues off-limits. This has been a peace process largely driven by geopolitics rather than by international law. The use of international law, represented by countless United Nations resolutions and other instruments, might possibly have neutralized one of the major stumbling blocks (the imbalance of power) that has retarded the pursuit of a political settlement in Israel/Palestine. Not only is there no military solution to the Arab-Israeli conflict, but a political solution, which is rather remote at present, will not be lasting if it emanates purely from geopolitics.

Since the inception of this problem in 1948, when Israel was established on 78 percent of what used to be Palestine, the question of refugee rights, among other components of the Palestine question (borders, sovereignty, water, Jewish settlements, mutual recognition) has continued to bedevil the international community, and particularly the permanent members of the UN Security Council. Numerous proposals for a settlement have emanated primarily from Washington since the June 1967 Arab-Israeli war, but all of them, from the Rogers Plan of 1969 all the way up to the Oslo Accords of September 1993, have ended in total failure.[1] Almost every single US plan since the 1950s has removed the refugee component of the Palestine question to the sidelines. The Oslo Accords, signed at the White House on September 13, 1993, designated the refugees as a "final status" issue to be left until the very end of the negotiations.[2]

This chapter demonstrates how the primacy assigned to geopolitics, as well as the efforts of various governments in the region and outside, have not only resulted in the marginalization of Palestinian rights, particularly refugee rights, but also have eroded the earlier consensus built around General Assembly Resolution 194(III), adopted on December 11, 1948.[3] Paragraph 11 of the resolution deals with the refugees by stating that the General Assembly:

> Resolves that the refugees wishing to return to their homes and live at peace with their neighbors should be permitted to do so at the earliest practicable date, and that compensation should be paid for the property of those choosing not to return and for the loss of or damage to property which, under principles of international law or in equity, should be made good by the Governments or authorities responsible.[4]

This resolution was voted upon every single year beginning in 1948, but although it was reaffirmed annually until 1993, the year of the Oslo agreement, it was never implemented. The late British philosopher Bertrand Russell sent a message to the International Conference of Parliamentarians in Cairo in February 1970, stating the following about the Palestinian refugees' right of return:

> The tragedy of the people of Palestine is that their country was "given" by a foreign power to another people for the creation of a new state. The result was that many hundreds of thousands of innocent people were made permanently homeless. With every new conflict their numbers increased. How much longer is the world willing to endure this spectacle of wanton cruelty? It is abundantly clear that the refugees have every right to the homeland from which they were driven, and the denial of this right is at the heart of the continuing conflict. No people anywhere in the world would accept being expelled en masse from their country; how can anyone require the people of Palestine to accept a punishment which nobody else would tolerate? A permanent just settlement of the refugees in their homeland is an essential ingredient of any genuine settlement in the Middle East.[5]

The right of return, as defined in Resolution 194, became a rallying cry for grassroots organizing throughout the 1990s and especially after the failure of the Camp David meeting in 2000, which was, in effect, a failure of Oslo in July 2000.[6] An international solidarity movement, which had been working on behalf of the Palestinian cause since the early 1970s, and which had to step aside after the "historic handshake" of Arafat and Rabin in September 1993, came back after the failure of Oslo in 2000, hoping to succeed where governments had failed in ameliorating the plight of the Palestinians, particularly the refugees. This chapter traces the developments that led to the present situation, where the fulfillment of the right of return seems more remote than ever, and where local and international civil society are now assuming a more active role in the struggle for refugee rights.

A Historical Overview

In 1948, about 800,000 Palestinians, constituting 83 percent of the Palestinian population, became refugees.[7] An additional 320,000 Palestinians became refugees as a result of the 1967 war.[8] There are today 5 million refugees, of whom 3.7 million are registered with the United Nations Relief and Works Agency, and 1.3 million are unregistered refugees.[9] Since the 1948 Palestinian Catastrophe (al-Nakbah)[10] and its creation of the Palestinian refugee crisis, the issues of return, compensation, and restitution have taken a backseat to discussions surrounding the overall question of Palestinian statehood.

During most of the past five decades, the issue of refugees has been marginalized, even though Israel's admission to the United Nations was made contingent on its compliance with UN General Assembly Resolution 194 of December 1948. General Assembly Resolution 273 of May 11, 1949, made Israel's admission conditional on Israel's unambiguous commitment to "unreservedly" respect UN resolutions pertaining to the Arab-Israeli conflict, including Resolution 194.[11]

Israel was admitted to the United Nations without complying with its obligations to the Palestinian refugees, and the refugee crisis continues. General Assembly Resolution 194 has been ritualistically reaffirmed numerous times,[12] and Israel's noncompliance has impelled the General Assembly to adopt other resolutions calling on Israel to meet its obligations to the refugees. For example, Resolution 3236 of November 22, 1974, upheld the "inalienable right of the Palestinians to return to their homes and property from which they have been displaced and uprooted."[13] And in 1997, Resolution 52/62 reaffirmed that the "Palestine Arab refugees are entitled to their property and to the income derived there from, in conformity with the principles of justice and equity."[14]

With the emergence of the Palestine Liberation Organization and the resumption of armed struggle during the 1960s, the issue of the refugees, rather than becoming the central human dimension of the revolutionaries' struggle to reverse the Nakbah, was relegated to a humanitarian, charitable issue better left to organizations such as UNRWA. The Palestinian national movement declared its objective in 1968 as the creation of a single democratic secular state in all of Palestine, in which Muslims, Christians, and Jews would be equal before the law. In that setting, the Palestinian national movement assumed that the refugees would exercise their right of return and would be accommodated in the future unitary state.

The 1967 war exacerbated the refugee crisis by creating a new generation of refugees. At the same time, the refugee crisis completely disappeared from the PLO agenda. The overarching objective of the PLO became global recognition of its status as sole legitimate representative of the Palestine people.[15] The PLO perceived the plight of the refugees as a distraction from the "important" issues. True, the refugees remained a humanitarian concern, but only to showcase the "social" institutions that the PLO had built in Lebanon during the 1970s, an infrastructure of a state-in-waiting.[16] Yet from the perspective of national rights, the refugee question continued to lack any political content and force.[17]

After 1972, as the armed struggle gave way further to a new form of diplomatic work, the refugee question became dormant. The arrangements formulated in Arab summit conferences in Algiers, Rabat, and Cairo during the mid-1970s encouraged the PLO to promote itself with a program of "self-determination" in a mini-Palestinian state in the West Bank and Gaza, which constituted less than 22 percent of pre-1948 Palestine. In return for supporting the "new" PLO, with such watered-down objectives, the Arab governments demanded an unwritten quid pro quo. The PLO would drastically scale down its guerrilla operations and cease its rhetoric about a democratic secular state in all of historical Palestine. In return, not only would the PLO be "rewarded" with Arab diplomatic support in far-flung countries, but the Arab governments would also increase economic assistance to the organization.

For the following two decades, this unwritten agreement, and the search for a "two-state solution," would consume the combined energies of the Palestinians and the Arab states. The PLO quest for international recognition, both as the sole legitimate representative of the Palestinian people and as a solid bargaining partner for the creation of a ministate, claimed the largest portion of Arab states' and Palestinians' energies. As a result, refugee rights and interests suffered. And although the PLO achieved its goal of becoming the focal point of the Palestine question, ironically it became in 1993 the first Arab party to sign an agreement that effectively deferred the internationally recognized refugee rights.[18] More drastically, it agreed in the meetings in 2000 at Camp David not to insist on the right of return.

The joint Arab-Palestinian pursuit of the two-state solution was never taken seriously by the United States and Israel, yet it was exploited by them repeatedly in their own attempts to marginalize the refugee issue and remove it from the active diplomatic agenda. The United States has assumed the role of chief arbiter, if not sole peacemaker, in the Middle East since 1972.[19] All other would-be conciliators, including the United Nations, have been held at bay. Indeed, the Arab-Israeli conflict is one of the very few that has effectively been removed from the international arena of conflict resolution.

An Overview of US Policy Toward the Refugee Question

The Palestine policy of the United States in the 1940s can be described as inconsistent, if not altogether incoherent, vacillating between acknowledging self-determination for the Palestinians and, alternatively, justifying its denial by colonial-settler Jews and a Palestinian Jewish minority. Until 1947, the US State Department had acknowledged the Palestinians' rights to self-determination. But the US government lobbied strongly for the UN partition plan,[20] which denied that right by proposing the establishment of a Jewish state in 55 percent of Palestine and an Arab state in 43.5 percent,[21] although the Jews constituted less than one-third of the population and owned no more than 6 percent of the total land. In 1948, the United States began to float the idea of replacing the partition plan with a UN trusteeship under Chapter XII of the UN Charter. When the partition plan failed to materialize, and the Zionist militias prevailed over the Palestinian resistance and the Arab fighters who came haphazardly to their defense, US policy began to shift toward support of a Jordanian takeover of the 22 percent of Palestine that was not under Israeli control. Jordan was also encouraged to absorb most of the refugees who were the victims of Zionist ethnic cleansing in 1948.

At the same time, the United States took an active part in drafting General Assembly Resolution 194 of December 11, 1948, stating that those "refugees wishing to return to their homes and live in peace with their neighbors should be permitted to do so at the earliest practicable date."[22] That resolution, which also called for compensation and restitution, established the United Nations Conciliation Commission on Palestine (UNCCP)[23] to help in economic rehabilitation, and to provide legal protection.

Israel, however, proceeded to make its own rules even though its admission to the United Nations was linked to its own compliance with UN resolutions, particularly Resolution 194. Israel decreed that a comprehensive settlement in the region—that is, one that ends with a peace treaty based on the status quo—must precede any discussion of the refugee question. The US administration of President Harry S Truman set a precedent by accommodating that position, thus allowing Israel to set the pace in Middle East policy. Despite expressing some misgivings about Israel's handling of the refugees, Truman approved an Israeli plan to repatriate about 100,000 on the basis of family reunification. The Truman administration also attempted to settle about 100,000 Palestinian refugees in Iraq. Resettlement of the refugees in other Arab countries became effectively an American policy goal and remains so to the present, despite an annual pro forma endorsement of Resolution 194 at the General Assembly.[24] In late March 1949, the Truman administration announced that the refugee problem was "a likely channel for Soviet exploitation" that could jeopardize the "stabilization of the Near East," which was "a major objective of American foreign policy."[25] Yet the administration failed to insist that Israel comply with the UN resolution, not only for the sake of legality, but also for the sake of US strategic interests.

By the time Lyndon B. Johnson inherited the presidency, the refugee question had been downgraded in US policy planning, which veered much closer to the Israeli position of resettling the refugees in Arab countries. In fact, the Israeli position of "resettlement" was incorporated into the platform of the Democratic Party on which Johnson was elected in 1964. The important new reality affecting US policy on the refugee question was the Arab-Israeli war of June 1967 and the new issues created by that war. The defeat of Arab armies in only six days elevated the role of Palestinian resistance to new heights and shifted the focus away from the refugee issue, now deemed a charitable, humanitarian matter that paled next to the issue of PLO recognition.

After the June 1967 War, any proposals emanating from Washington would address the refugee question in a merely ritualistic manner. That approach relegated the whole Palestine issue to the sidelines, superseded by the attempt to find an acceptable Arab-Israeli formula based on land for peace. Consequently, the Palestinian right of return was subordinated to minimizing the chances of a wider conflict with global ramifications.

A new chapter in the marginalization of the Palestinians right of return was opened under US president Jimmy Carter, who began his reassessment of Middle East policy with a specific reference to the Palestinian people who "suffered so much and who were in need of a home."[26] Carter's proposed "self-governing authority," together with Egypt, Israel, and Jordan, was empowered to decide on the modalities for admission of persons *displaced* from the West Bank and Gaza in 1967. As for the 1948 refugees, the Camp David plan merely called for a "just solution," with no mention of what that might entail.[27] The Palestinian dimension of Carter's Middle East policy was abandoned in favor of a separate peace between Israel and Egypt.

Although the PLO legitimately controlled representation of the Palestinian people for over ten years and struggled for national self-determination with the support of a global consensus and UN General Assembly resolutions, US president Ronald Reagan considered Palestine a problem of *mere* refugees, that is, a humanitarian problem rather than the national political issue of self-determination. He also considered the PLO a terrorist organization, enrolled in the service of the "evil empire" (i.e., the USSR).[28]

From the outset of his administration, Reagan exempted Israel from responsibility for the plight of the refugees, placing most of the burden of redress on Jordan in accordance with the ideology espoused by revisionist Zionists. This ideology assumed that a Palestinian state already existed in Jordan, even though in 1947 the United Nations had divided Palestine, west of the River Jordan, into a Palestinian Arab state and a Jewish state.[29] According to revisionist Zionist thinking, the former Palestine mandate given to Britain by the League of Nations after World War I included all the area lying to the east of the River Jordan (now Jordan).

Reagan made only one reference to the question of refugees in his 1982 plan: "The departure of the Palestinians from Beirut dramatizes more than ever the homelessness of the Palestinian people. Palestinians feel strongly that their cause is more than a question of refugees. I agree."[30] Despite that agreement, Reagan later ordered his UN ambassador to reject a General Assembly resolution condemning the perpetrators of the massacres of Sabra and Shatila, and resolving that the Palestinian people should be enabled to return to their homes and property, in accordance with previous UN resolutions. The United States was joined in this rejection by one other state: Israel.

With the advent of the George H. W. Bush administration, all attention was focused on Iraq and subsequently on the Madrid Conference of October 1991, with much of the emphasis placed on an Israeli-Palestinian deal based on Carter's 1978 Camp David notion of Palestinian autonomy. On March 3, 1990, George H. W. Bush and his secretary of state, James Baker, threatened Israel that an agreement providing Israel with a $10-billion loan guarantee would be jeopardized if Israel continued to build settlements in and around Jerusalem. Israel and its US supporters were incensed by the implication that Washington considered Jerusalem occupied territory. George Mitchell, then the US Senate majority leader, led a campaign in the Senate against the Bush administration. Bush finally gave in.[31] The issue of refugees remained dormant during the senior Bush's presidency.

President Bill Clinton continued Bush's policy of benign neglect of the refugee issue but went further than any previous president in embracing Israel's conditions overall on the question of Palestine. For example, a State Department white paper dated June 30, 1993, entitled "Declaration of Principles" implied that the United States now considered the West Bank and Gaza "disputed" rather than occupied territories.[32] When Clinton presided at the Oslo signing, on September 13, 1993, it became clear that the refugee issue had, in fact, been relegated to a "final status" issue, not to be considered until after five years of a "transition" period.[33] By the summit meeting at Camp David in July 2000, the most that refugees could realistically hope for was limited and regulated repatriation to the Palestinian entity, but not to their homes and certainly not to property in present-day Israel.[34] The latter, if available at all, would have been open only to token numbers and strictly in accord with what Israel designated "family reunification." Ehud Barak's "generosity" on the refugee issue at Camp David 2000 extended to allowing four thousand refugees each year to enter what is now Israel within the framework of what he called "family reunions," not the "right of return": "We cannot allow even one refugee back on the basis of the 'right of return' . . . and we cannot accept historical responsibility for the creation of the problem."[35]

Palestinian Civil Society and the Refugees

Despite the exceedingly numerous meetings between Palestinian and Israeli negotiators during the seven years since the signing of the Oslo Accords, input by the five million Palestinian refugees had never been sought. When the right of return began to resurface as a top item on the Palestinian people's agenda around 1999–2000, the role of the Palestinian Authority was minimal. In fact, the issue was placed on the public agenda not by the Palestinian Authority or the PLO, but by various segments of Palestinian civil society.[36] In particular, grassroots organizations, new and old alike, seized the initiative by restoring the right of return to a central place in the discourse about Palestine.[37]

For example, on September 16, 2000, two demonstrations attended by several thousand activists were held simultaneously in Washington, DC, and London to promote the right of return. During the same period, similar demonstrations, most of which coincided with the eighteenth anniversary of the 1982 massacres at the Sabra and Shatila refugee camps in Lebanon, were also staged in the Lebanese refugee camps, and in Palestine. Numerous conferences, workshops, and rallies have been held in and outside the region since 2000, bringing together community leaders, activists, and scholars to discuss various strategies for reviving the right of return. Numerous gatherings, mass rallies, symposia, and public protests have been repeated in various cities and refugee camps in the region and around the world. Their leaders have vowed to continue such nongovernmental actions until the right of return is dealt with fairly and legally in any future settlement. The whole endeavor seems like a public reminder that the failure of the governments and the United Nations to produce any justice for the refugees has made it incumbent on civil society to step in on behalf of the Palestinian refugees.

Another civil society project aiming to empower the refugees by enabling them to make choices and raise issues about how they would participate in decisions that impact their lives and future is known as Civic Structures for the Palestinian Refugee Camps and Exile Communities (CIVITAS).[38]

This eighteen-month project, which was supported by the EU, was based on the premise that it is the refugees themselves who are the best experts on what their needs are, not outside experts. The needs and priorities of the refugee camps and exile communities were established from four questions on civic structures and processes discussed by refugees, as communities. These questions were disseminated to all communities between November 2004 and February 2005 and were then debated between March and May 2005 in a series of public meetings and workshops. The questions directed to the Palestinian refugee community were: (1) What structures and channels of communication would help you communicate with various public policy bodies? (2) What civic structures and mechanisms do you, as a refugee community, now use to communicate with these various bodies? (3) What are the civic, legal, social, economic, and political issues that you would like to raise with these bodies? And finally, (4) as a community, what are your most urgent needs and priorities while you are refugees?[39] The polling on these questions was done through delegates and local partners, associations and institutions, and other means, such as email, websites, and ordinary mail. This program was a voluntary exercise, run by the communities for the communities themselves, and included all strands of Palestinian political and civic society.

Israel and the Refugee Question

If there were ever the slightest hope that the refugees could possibly attain even a modicum of their internationally recognized rights within the context of the Oslo framework, such hopes have been absolutely dashed. Under the unwritten rules of the "peace process," now defunct as a result of the September 2000 Palestinian intifada, Ariel Sharon's inflexibility, and US president George W. Bush's scant attention to Middle East diplomacy, it would be considered a sign of intransigence if Palestinian president Mahmoud Abbas, or any of his negotiators, were to bring up the right of return, Resolutions 194, or the November 29, 1947, UN partition resolution.[40]

For Israelis across the ideological spectrum, including members of the so-called peace camp, the return of refugees constitutes a clear and present danger, a real demographic threat to an exclusively Jewish state. Since Israelis insist that their state remain exclusively Jewish, juridically and otherwise, such a position, although illegal and immoral, is consistent with the Zionist framework of the state. The Palestinian refugees' right of return to their previous homes and property now in Israel is not only absent from the public Israeli agenda and from the consciousness of the Israeli Jewish public but also opposed by Israel's peace movement. For example, thirty-three prominent members of the Israeli Jewish peace movement addressed a message to the "Palestinian Leadership" in a front-page advertisement in the Israeli daily *Ha'aretz,* saying in part:

> We recognize the true and urgent need to resolve the problem of the 1948 refugees, and we recognize the part of the State of Israel, also, in the creation of the problem. The refugees will have the right to return to their homeland, Palestine, and settle there. But, we want to clarify that we shall never be able to agree to the return of the refugees to within the borders of Israel, for the meaning of such a return would be the elimination of the State of Israel.[41]

One of the signatories, the noted writer Amos Oz, wrote an article in the *New York Times,* "Let Palestinians Govern Palestinians—Now," in which he praised Barak's government for offering to let the Palestinians govern themselves, while describing the Palestinian Authority as the real "obstacle for peace" because it had raised the issue of the right of return: "Implementing the Palestinian 'right of return' would amount to abolishing the Jewish people's right to self-determination. It would eventually make the Jewish people no more than an ethnic minority in the country, just as fundamentalist Islam would have it." [42]

The Israeli public seems united in its rejection of international law as it pertains to the rights of the Palestinian refugees. Thus, of all the issues to be addressed in Oslo's final round of negotiations labeled by the parties as "final status negotiations"—borders, Jerusalem, settlements, water, refugees—the question of the refugees is certainly the most difficult.

From the point of view of the Palestinians, the conflict with Israel emerged in 1948, when Jewish/Israeli forces conquered more than three-quarters of Palestine (78 percent) and expelled 80 percent of the Palestinian population of the territory under its control or caused them to flee. The Palestinian demand for repatriation includes return to their villages and towns inside what is now Israel. In most instances, they will not be able to return to their homes and towns as Israel has razed them. After the conquest of the rest of Palestine (the West Bank and Gaza) in 1967, Israel initiated a policy and practice of building Jewish colonial settlements on the territories occupied in 1967. Thus, over the years, Palestine has been reformed and reshaped little by little. Even if Palestinians return, they are not returning to the homeland of their expectations. Instead, Palestinian refugees would return to a homeland defined by those who originally displaced them.

Since 1967, Israel's approach to the "peace process" (before Sharon assumed power in 2001) was partially based on the notion that the conflict began in 1967 and not in 1948. Paradoxically, the 1967 borders, known as "the green line," have continually been eroded by the insatiable appetite of successive Israeli governments for settlements. That ever-elusive "green line" has, in effect, ceased to exist. In 2006, the conflict is being viewed in Israel as having started in October 2000, when the intifada is presumed to have shattered the status quo. Not only is the refugee issue absent from the table, but more refugees will be created as a result of Israel's Apartheid Wall, which is separating Palestinian communities from each other and from their land.[43]

Current Attempts to Liquidate
the Right of Return

The right of return has been one of the major stumbling blocks to a political settlement based on mutual recognition and self-determination for both

Palestinians and Israelis. Renewed attempts to continue that process by the Sharon government and Washington, with the implicit support of Arab and European governments anxious for an implementation of the so-called Road Map to Peace, have entered a new and serious phase in 2003. Emboldened by the US occupation of Iraq and the prospects of a new US strategic hegemony in the region and beyond, the Bush-Sharon axis seemed poised to deliver a knockout punch to any Palestinian insistence that refugee rights be an integral part of a peace settlement in Palestine.

The attempts to dilute and undermine the right of return have recently enlisted supporters in the compliant circles of the Palestinian leadership as well as key community activists in Palestine and elsewhere. Israeli and US insistence in 2003 on linking any return to the negotiations table to a Palestinian agreement to appoint an "empowered" prime minister who would "dismantle the terrorist infrastructure," a euphemism for Palestinian resistance, is based on an expectation that the right of return, among other basic components designated as final status issues, would be surrendered for the sake of a settlement. In fact, that surrender was one of fourteen reservations delineated by Sharon's cabinet as a condition for accepting the Road Map.

Another attempt to undermine the case of refugees is an unofficial agreement with an international-sounding designation—called the Geneva Accord perhaps because it was financed by Switzerland. It surfaced during October 2003, at the time of a crippling impasse, with Sharon having a free hand to kill and maim Palestinians, destroy homes and farms, and build his wall, all in the name of fighting terror. This agreement, which had the blessings of Labor Party luminaries, such as Amram Mitzna, Avraham Burg, and author Amos Oz, as well as the implicit approval of Yasser Arafat and the younger Fatah leadership, planned to do away completely and unequivocally with the right of return, giving Israel the prerogative of admitting whatever number of the refugees it deemed tolerable. Moreover, the Palestinians would have had to recognize Israel as a Jewish state and concede the major settlement blocs surrounding Jerusalem (Ma'aleh Adumim, Givat Zeev, and the Etzion Bloc)—all that in return for some sort of authority over Islam's Jerusalem holy places. Nevertheless, the agreement incurred the wrath of Sharon, who accused the Israeli sponsors of being unauthorized agents who were sacrificing Israel's security.[44]

The latest attempt to undermine the refugees' right of return came from UNRWA under its new leadership after the removal of its longtime head, Peter Hansen, under pressure by the Bush administration. A statement attributed by Reuters to Karen Koning Abu-Zayd, Commissioner General–

UNRWA, and published in the *Washington Post,* stated that "few Palestinian refugees want to return to [their] lands lost in 1948 war of Israel's creation" and "any solution of this issue must be acceptable to both sides [i.e., including Israel]."[45] However, the Right of Return Congress, a refugee advocacy group, issued a rebuttal of this position on August 10, 2005, asserting the following:

UNRWA has no independent position on the refugees other than that of the UN General Assembly which created UNRWA and to which UNRWA reports. The UNGA [UN General Assembly], in its well-known resolution 194, has affirmed the Right of Return over 130 times and designated it as "Inalienable Right." Generally, the same position has been affirmed by the Treaty-Based UN Committees, the regional conventions on human rights and practically all human rights NGOs. The question of whether some refugees choose to return or not is irrelevant. The Inalienable Right has no statute of limitation. It is neither conditional nor a subject of political bargaining or speculation. . . . The Right of Return has been exercised, with the support of the international community, in Kosovo, Bosnia, East Timor, Rwanda, Guatemala and many other places. It is not exercised yet in Palestine because major Western powers sided with Israel against the rights of the Palestinians under international law. Israel refused to accept the Right of Return since 1948 because it ethnically cleansed Palestine to build Israel on its ruins. Israel therefore is not, must not be a party to any solution "acceptable to both sides." Israel must abide by international law or be subject to penalties as applied elsewhere.[46]

The current president of the PA, Mahmoud Abbas, had attached his name to the agreement (the Beilin-Abu-Mazen agreement), which relinquished the right of return in 1994. More recently, in July 2005, Abbas startled his audience when he announced that it was agreeable to have certain Arab governments grant citizenship to the Palestinian refugees in the host countries. Justifying Abbas's bold announcement, the director general of the PLO Refugees Affairs Department, Saji Salameh, said the following as reported by the Ramallah-based publication *Palestine Report*:

It is only natural that Abu Mazen [Mahmoud Abbas] would pose the problem of the Palestinians in the diaspora in the context of his tour of various Arab countries including Syria, Lebanon and Jordan. He brought up a number of issues exclusive to the situation of refugees so of course this included labor, travel and residency rights. They also spoke about the issue of citizenship. In this context, Abu Mazen expressed his concerns about refugees in the diaspora

and even those in the homeland, stressing on their adherence to the right of return to their homes and the rejection of being resettled, which would ulti-
mately end the refugee problem. On this premise, Abu Mazen declared that
there was nothing to prevent the Arab countries from taking a sovereign decision to offer citizenship to refugees to anyone who wants. This of course is
with the guarantee that such a measure would in no way impinge on the legal
right of refugees to return, to restitution and to compensation.[47] (Italics
added.)

The right-of-return movement was almost overwhelmingly unimpressed.
A typical rebuttal of Abbas's audacious proposition was an editorial in the
London-based monthly magazine *al-Awda*:

The call by the PA President Mahmoud Abbas urging Arab governments to
grant naturalization to Arab refugees living within their domains has dangerous implications for the right of return. . . . If the rationale for this call is easing life conditions for these refugees, why did he not emphasize that concern
insisting instead on the right of naturalization?[48]

These conglomerations of groups, individuals, and parties have the potential to constitute an oppositional movement if they choose to unify their
ranks and establish a coherent political movement. After all, their raison
d'être (the right of return) no longer occupies a prominent place on the PA's
active agenda, because they know that Israel and the United States would
consider a hostile act any insistence by the PA on this fundamental right.

The New Meaning of the Right of Return

Despite all attempts to undermine the rights of refugees, a growing tendency on the part of international civil society and the United Nations itself
to vigorously reassert these rights has been causing great discomfort to
many governments, including that of the United States, which seems unable
to reconcile its declared principles with its geopolitical commitments. Condoleezza Rice, for example, took a tour of Sudanese refugee camps in July
2005 and expressed unambiguous sympathy and deep compassion for the
refugees, citing their right to be repatriated, but refrained from visiting a
single Palestinian refugee camp upon continuing her trip to Palestine and
Israel.

The current prime example of progress on the part of the United Nations
and international civil society is the adoption by the UN of a sweeping se-

ries of principles on August 11, 2005, that urge governments everywhere to ensure that all refugees and persons displaced due to conflict and natural disasters are entitled to return to, recover, and reside in their original homes, lands, and properties.[49] The pathbreaking new global standards were prepared by the United Nation's Special Rapporteur on Housing and Property Restitution, Paulo Sergio Pinheiro of Brazil, and are now known as the Pinheiro Principles. Pinheiro summarized the essence of his principles in the following words:

> The best solution to the plight of millions of refugees and displaced persons around the world is to ensure they attain the right to return freely to their countries and to have restored to them housing and property of which they were deprived during the course of displacement, or to be compensated for any property that cannot be restored to them. It is the most desired, sustainable, and dignified solution to displacement.[50]

A press release issued by the Geneva-based Centre on Housing Rights and Evictions (COHRE), an independent human rights organization, stated that

> Millions of refugees and displaced persons—Palestinians, Sudanese, Croatian and Kosovar Serbs, Bhutanese, Burmese and others—continue to be prevented from returning to their former homes and lands. Many countries responsible for displacing persons from their homes have adopted laws seeking to confiscate the homes, land and properties of refugees and displaced persons. The Pinheiro Principles firmly declare such laws as unlawful, and urge all States which have adopted such laws to repeal them.[51]

According to the Pinheiro Principles, the right of return itself acquires a new and expanded meaning, which includes the right to housing, land, and property restitution, encompassing not merely returning to one's country, but also to one's original home, should one wish.[52] Scott Leckie, the executive director of COHRE, elaborated on this new meaning thus:

> Housing and property restitution is an essential element of reconstruction and recovery in post-conflict situations. It is a primary means of reversing "ethnic cleansing" and vital to securing a war-torn nation's future stability. The plight of refugees and IDPs (internally displaced persons) such as the six million Palestinian refugees, and millions of other displaced persons in Sudan, Sri Lanka, the Balkans and elsewhere, clearly indicates that the prospects for

workable peace agreements are highly unlikely until the restitution question is properly addressed. . . . The dispossession of Palestinian homes, lands and properties remains at the heart of the longstanding conflict which today seems no closer to being resolved. More than half of the original Palestinian population has been displaced from Palestine, and some six million Palestinian refugees need to achieve residential justice through the exercise of their legal rights to housing, land and property restitution. Any peace agreement between the Israelis and Palestinians will not be feasible until Israel acknowledges the right of Palestinians to return to and re-possess their homes which are now controlled by Israel.[53]

The Pinheiro Principles are truly a landmark development in international human rights and humanitarian law and standards, particularly insofar as they relate to refugee rights and the entire question of international protection:

These guidelines are crucial. Firstly, they make clear that no amount of interference by a state deprives individuals of their right to be protected from displacement. Secondly, the guidelines insist that in the event of being arbitrarily deprived of their housing, land or property, they are entitled to restitution and/or compensation. Thirdly, they are entitled to have their claim of restitution/compensation considered by an independent body. The guidelines also provide that governments are required to consult with and ensure there is adequate participation of people who may be affected by displacement. Most importantly of all, the guidelines reaffirm the principle of non-discrimination, that everyone has the same rights to be protected, irrespective of race, religion or "other status."

Conclusion

The omission from Oslo's Declaration of Principles of the refugee question within the meaning of UN General Assembly Resolution 194 is the single most serious impediment to genuine redress of the refugees' grievances. It follows countless efforts by Israel and the United States throughout the past half century to utilize the peace process and other means for keeping the issue off the agenda.

The creation of refugees in 1948 was intended to ensure a permanent Jewish majority in the Jewish state. Today, more than a half century later, the overwhelming majority of Israelis consider the return of those refugees a mortal danger, a demographic threat to Israel. Therefore, no change has occurred in the Zionist movement's reliance on ethnic cleansing as an instrument to ensure that all of Palestine is its own domain, clean of non-Jews. Accordingly, the indigenous Palestinians can be tolerated only as a scattered minority living in enclaves under overall Jewish control. It was no accident that the Israeli architects of Oslo bestowed on Israel the control of "external security," a euphemism for sovereignty. Nor was it a coincidence that the Palestinian Authority's Legislative Council and the PA's executive were granted neither judicial nor legislative powers that could someday enable the Palestinians to enact a law of return of their own.

The question of return has been marginalized also by the fact that it has already been regarded by the DOP as a regional matter affecting *all* refugees, including Jews who left property in Arab countries. That is why both Camp David I (1978) and the DOP (1993) called for the establishment of a committee consisting of Israel, Jordan, Egypt, and the Palestinian Council (Oslo's name for the Palestinian Legislative Council) to settle that problem, with Israel retaining an effective veto.

We are now at a crucial juncture. The present caretaker government, led by Sharon's successor, Ehud Olmert, regards the 1948 war as not having enabled Israel to reach its goal of conquering *all* of Palestine. Like its predecessor government, which had been engaged in completing that 1948 phase since 2000, its pronouncements regarding borders, settlements, and annexation of the Jordan Valley are likely to lead in a similar direction—hence the campaign since 2000 to destroy the infrastructure of the Palestinian Authority and the institutions of civil society, together with the confiscation and destruction of Palestinian resources and property that might be in the way of the Zionist scheme of completion.

To thwart these attempts, calls have been made by Palestinian and international civil society as well as right-of-return activists to convene a representative Palestinian body, comprising all sectors—from the refugee camps of Lebanon, Jordan, and Syria; from the West Bank and Gaza; from Israel proper; and from the United States, Australia, and elsewhere—to reaffirm the refugees' rights under a single banner. This representative Palestinian body would reestablish the right of a reconstituted PLO to resolve the refugee question with Israel. Such a body, not the PA's negotiators nor any other would-be interlocutors, would decide which rights the Palestinians would affirm and which, if any, they would relinquish. Such an enterprise is regarded by these activists as capable of initiating the process of redress, one that could give a voice to the voiceless.

Notes

1. For a discussion of these plans, see Naseer Aruri, *The Obstruction of Peace: The U.S., Israel and the Palestinians* (Monroe, ME: Common Courage Press, 1995); and Naseer Aruri, *Dishonest Broker: The U.S. Role in Israel and Palestine* (Cambridge, MA: South End Press, 2003).

2. For a discussion of the Oslo Accords, see Yossi Beilin, *Touching Peace: From the Oslo Accords to a Final Agreement* (London: Weidenfeld and Nicolson, 1999); Edward W. Said, *The End of the Peace Process: Oslo and After* (New York: Pantheon Books, 2000); and Geoffrey R. Watson, *The Oslo Accords: International Law and the Israeli-Palestinian Peace Agreements* (Oxford/New York: Oxford University Press, 2000).

3. UN General Assembly Resolution 194, UN Document A/810, at 21 (1948).

4. See partial text in Naseer Aruri, ed., *Occupation: Israel over Palestine,* 2nd ed. (Belmont, MA: Association of Arab-American University Graduates, 1989): 94–95.

5. *New York Times* (February 23, 1970).

6. See Aruri, *Dishonest Broker,* Ch. 10.

7. For figures, causes, consequences, and other details of the 1948 exodus, see Benny Morris, *The Birth of the Palestinian Refugee Problem, 1947–1949* (Cambridge: Cambridge University Press, 1987); see also Michael Palumbo, *The Palestinian Catastrophe: The* 1948 *Expulsion of a People from Their Homeland* (London: Quartet Books, 1987); Ilan Pappé, *The Making of the Arab-Israeli Conflict, 1947–51* (New York: Macmillan/St Anthony's Press, 1992); and Simha Flapan, *The Birth of Israel: Myths and Realities* (New York: Pantheon, 1987).

8. Harris estimated that the West Bank lost 250,000 of its inhabitants, and the Gaza Strip lost 70,000; William Harris, *Taking Root: Israeli Settlement in the West Bank, the Golan and Gaza-Sinai 1967–1980* (Chichester, UK: Research Studies Press, 1980).

9. For details about the refugees, their villages, those registered with the United Nations Relief and Work Agency, and those unregistered, see Salman H. Abu-Sitta, *The Palestinian Nakba 1948: The Register of Depopulated Localities in Palestine (with Accompanying Map, "Palestine 1948 50 Years After Al Nakba: The Towns and Villages Depopulated by the Zionist Invasion of 1948")* (London: Palestine Return Centre, 2000); see also the UNRWA home page at http://www.un.org/unrwa.

10. Also called the cataclysm; the events of that year included the mass deportation of Palestinians from their homes, massacres of civilians, and the leveling of hundreds of Palestinian villages. See generally Palumbo, *The Palestinian Catastrophe.*

UN General Assembly Resolution 194 (III), UN Document A/810 at 21 (1948); see also W. Thomas Mallison and Sally V. Mallison, *An International Law Analysis of the Major United Nations Resolutions Concerning the Palestine Question* (New York: United Nations, 1979).

11. UN General Assembly Resolution 273, UN Document A/RES/273 (III) (1949).

12. See Aruri, *Occupation,* 94–95.

13. UN General Assembly Resolution 3236, UN XXIX 13th Session, at 1(b)2 (1974). See also Aruri, *Occupation,* 95–96.

14. UN General Assembly Resolution 52/62, UN Document A/RES/52/62, at Section 1 (1997). For further information on restitution, see Atif Kubursi, "Valuing Palestinian Losses in Today's Dollars," in Naseer Aruri, ed., *Palestinian Refugees and Their Right of Return* (London: Pluto Press, 2001): 217–251. See also Susan Akram, "Reinterpreting Palestinian Refugee Rights Under International Law," in Aruri, *Palestinian Refugees,* 165–194.

15. For example, the Arab states' meeting at summit conferences in Algiers in 1972 and Rabat, Morocco, in 1974 recognized the PLO as the sole legitimate representative of the Palestinian people. By the end of the 1970s, the PLO was recognized as such by most members of the nonaligned movement in the United Nations and the communist bloc.

16. See Cheryl Rubenberg, *The Palestine Liberation Organization: Its Institutional Infrastructure.* Belmont, MA: Institute for Arab Studies, 1983.

17. See Aruri, *Palestinian Refugees,* which describes the marginalization of the refugee issues in PLO-Arab dealings.

18. See "Declaration of Principles on Interim Self-Government Arrangements," September 13, 1993, signed by Israel and the PLO, available at http://www.us-israel.org/jsource/peace/dop.html.

19. See Aruri, *Dishonest Broker,* especially Chs. 2 and 3.

20. UN General Assembly Resolution 181(II), UN GAOR, at 131–132, UN Document A/310 (1947).

21. Ibid.

22. UN General Assembly Resolution 194(III), UN GAOR, at 24, UN Document A/810 (1948).

23. See Akram, "Reinterpreting Palestinian Refugee." Resolution 194 established the Conciliation Commission for Palestine, composed of three member states: France, Turkey, and the United States. The commission was given broad authority to carry out the functions previously entrusted to the UN Mediator, Count Folk Bernadote, who was assassinated by the Jewish Stern Gang. See also W. Thomas Mallison and Sally V. Mallison, *The Palestinian Problem in International Law and World Order* (London: Longman, 1986): 177–179.

24. Luke T. Lee, "The Right to Compensation and Countries of Asylum," *American Journal of International Law* 80 (1986): 532, 535.

25. Fred Lawson, "The Truman Administration and the Palestinians," *Arab Studies Quarterly* 12 (Winter-Spring 1990): 1–2.

26. For discussion of the contents of Carter's 1972 speech regarding reassessment of Middle East policy, see the Interview with Carter at http://www.gwu.edu/~nsarchiv/coldwar/interviews/episode–18/carter1.html.

27. See Camp David Agreements, September 17, 1978, Egypt-Israel-U.S., 17 I.L.M. 1466 (signing "A Framework for Peace in the Middle East"), available at http://www.israel-mfa.gov.il/mfa/go.asp?MFAH0f1z0.

28. See George Schultz, "Terrorism and the Modern World," *Terrorism* (1985): 431–447; and Yoav Tadmor, "The Palestinian Refugees of 1948: The Right to Compensation and Return," *Temple International and Comparative Law Journal* 8 (1994): 403–434. For a comparison of the Sandinistas, the PLO, and the Libyans, see Gerald Boyd, "Reagan Presses Hard for Contra Aid," *New York Times* (June 7, 1986).

29. The founder of Revisionist Zionism, Ze'ev Jabotinsky, wrote an article in 1923 titled "The Iron Wall," in which he said that Zionism should endeavor to bring about a Jewish state in the whole land of Israel (meaning Jordan and Palestine), regardless of the Arab response. See Flapan, *Birth of Israel,* 117.

30. The full text of the Reagan plan is available at http://www.us-israel.org/ jsource/Peace/reaganplan.html. The departure of PLO military and civilian personnel from Lebanon in the fall of 1982 was arranged by US ambassador Philip Habib after the Israeli invasion of June 1982. The United States worked out an agreement between Israel and the PLO whereby the besieged Arafat forces were given safe exit and US guarantees of the safety of their dependents left behind. Nevertheless, Israel's right-wing Lebanese allies entered the Palestinian refugee camps of Sabra and Shatila on September 16, 17, and 18 and committed a massacre under Israel's watchful eyes. The largely civilian victims numbered between twenty-five hundred and three thousand. Defense Minister Ariel Sharon was accused of 'indirect responsibility' by his own country's Kahan Commission, which was organized to investigate the massacres committed while Israel was occupying Lebanon.

31. For details of the controversy, see Aruri, *Obstruction of Peace,* 273–275, 326–329; and Aruri, *Dishonest Broker.*

32. This "Declaration of Principles" should not be confused with the DOP, which refers to the Oslo Accords signed in the White House Rose Garden on September 13, 1993, by Israeli prime minister Yitzhak Rabin and Palestinian leader Yasser Arafat. For a discussion of the State Department DOP, see Aruri, *Dishonest Broker,* Ch. 6.

33. For more details on Oslo and the refugee issue, see ibid., Chs. 6 and 10.

34. For details on Camp David and the issue of refugees, see ibid., 172–177.

35. For relevant details about this issue, see Benny Morris, *The Birth of the Palestinian Refugee Problem, Revisited* (Cambridge: Cambridge University Press, 2002).

36. Among these organizations is the BADIL Resource Center for Palestinian Residency and Refugee Rights in Bethlehem, at http://www.badil.org; A'idun ("We Will Return") in Lebanon and Syria; SHAML, the Palestinian Diaspora and Refugee Centre in Jerusalem, at http://www.shaml.org/; and Al-Awda (the Return) in the United States, at http://www.al-awda.org (accessed March 22, 2003).

37. http://www.nuff.ox.ac.uk/projects/Civitas/about_keyquestions.aspx.

38. Ibid.

39. Ibid.

40. See "Bush and Sharon: Defining the Path," Ch. 11 in Aruri, *Dishonest Broker.*

41. *Ha'aretz* (January 2, 2001).

42. Amos Oz, "Let Palestinians Govern Palestinians—Now," *New York Times* (January 6, 2001): A13.

43. See www.stopthewall.org.

44. See the Israeli Text and Context of the Geneva Accord (by Shiko Behar and Michael Warschawski) at http://www.merip.org/mero/mero112403.html.

45. *Washington Post* (August 9, 2005).

46. A Statement from the Right of Return Congress (info@rorcongress.com) was emailed to a mailing list on August 10, 2005.

47. http://www.palestinereport.org on July 13, 2005. See also Rym Ghazal, "Abbas Calls for Citizenship for Palestinian Refugees," *Daily Star* (Beirut) (July 12, 2005).

48. "Abbas's Call for Naturalization of the Refugees: Is It Really Meant to Ease Their Suffering?" (in Arabic), editorial in *Al-Awda,* London, Issue 164, August 2005.

49. http://www.indybay.org/news/2005/08/1759069.php.

50. Ibid. A text of the Pinheiro Principles is posted at http://www.al-awdacal.org/alert-pinheiro.html.

51. COHRE press release, August 2005.

52. http://www.indybay.org/news/2005/08/1759069.php.

53. Ibid. *See also* Jeff Handmaker and Adri Nieuwhof, "Compensation If You Are Displaced, Unless You Are Palestinian," *Electronic Intifada* (August 15, 2005), posted at http://electronicintifada.net/v2/printer4086.shtml.

11

Jerusalem

A whole mythology has been forged to convince the world that Jerusalem is the nerve center of the Jewish universe and Israel's most important national symbol. The late prime minister of Israel Yitzhak Rabin, who conquered the city in 1967 from the Jordanians, wanted to commemorate the earlier conquest of the city by David from the Jebusites. Although scholars are not certain when David's conquest took place, year-long "Jerusalem 3000" celebrations were formally opened in September 1995, thus declaring 1996 an anniversary year, to celebrate Jewish "continuity" and to assert authenticity.

The Jerusalem festival was tantamount to a declaration that the city, which was described by K. A. Creswell as one of the most perfectly preserved examples of medieval Islamic cities, belongs to the Jews.[1] The festival was designed to promote the erroneous view that Jerusalem had always been the capital of the Jews since its presumed creation by David three thousand years ago, except for periods during which Jews were overpowered by invaders and expelled, only to come back and reclaim their patrimony. This time Israel's leaders vowed that the dialectic had reached a climax and that the Jews were finally here to stay in their "eternal capital."

Historical Background

Jerusalem, known to Jews as the City of David, is in fact not three thousand years old but five thousand years old. Excavations carried out on Mount Ophel have revealed an Early Bronze Age settlement about 2600 BCE and a Middle Bronze Age town surrounded by a massive wall about 1800 BCE.[2] Archaeological evidence suggests that Jerusalem began as a small nine-acre settlement, whose holy character was not unique.

The oldest name of the city was Urusalem, which refers to a Canaanite-Amorite god. The Jebusites, an extraction of the Canaanites, inhabited the city during the Late Bronze Age around 1400 BCE, when it was known as Jebus. The city was conquered, not founded, around 1000 BCE by David, a descendant of Abraham. In AD 135, Hadrian expelled the Jews from Jerusalem into the Diaspora, after a revolt had erupted in AD 132. The emperor Hadrian ordered the building of the new city of Aelia Capitolina upon the ruins of Jerusalem in 135. Jerusalem became a Roman colony for the next two centuries, and a period of Christian ascendancy over the city extended from 324 to 638.[3]

The conversion to Christianity in 325 of the emperor Constantine brought the first great buildings of Christian importance, such as his basilica of the Church of the Resurrection or the Holy Sepulchre on the site of Jesus' burial. Constantine is also known for the building of Constantinople as capital of the eastern part of the Roman Empire—the Byzantine Empire—which survived nearly a thousand years after the fall of the western part of the empire in 476.

Under Constantine and his successors, Jerusalem achieved a renewed prominence and became a center of pilgrimage, where foreign visitors came in considerable numbers. Constantine continued Hadrian's policy of not allowing Jews to live in Jerusalem except for an annual pilgrimage to the Western Wall of the Temple to lament its destruction.

The Byzantine Empire was challenged by Chosroes, the leader of the Sassanid Persian Empire, who invaded Syria, took Damascus in 613, and marched toward Jerusalem in 614. Assisted by the Jewish population in the countryside seeking revenge for their suffering under Rome and Byzantium, the Persians entered the city and demolished everything in sight, even the tomb of Christ. They slaughtered numerous citizens, sold many Christians as slaves, and left the Jews in control of the city. The Persians later expelled the Jews and allowed the destroyed churches to be restored. By 629 the Persians were in disarray and Byzantine rule was restored.

The Arab/Islamic Period

While the Roman and Persian armies were confronting each other, a new challenge was mounted against both from Arabia. The prophet Muhammad had sent military contingents, which were initially defeated, but five years later the Arabs reached the outskirts of Gaza, advanced to twenty miles southwest of Jerusalem, and defeated the Roman army at the decisive battle of Yarmouk in AD 636, causing it to retreat from Syria. Jerusalem had been besieged by the Arabs since 637, and in the following year, the third caliph, Omar Ibn al-Khatab, received a message from the patriarch of Jerusalem, Sophronius, that he would surrender the city but to the caliph alone.[4] Sophronius was terribly haunted by memories of only twenty-two years earlier, when the Persians had wreaked havoc on the city, and he realized that the situation was desperate. By surrendering to the caliph himself, the patriarch was hoping to guarantee the survival of the city and its population. It was indeed the first time that the city had been spared destruction by a conqueror. Omar, a tolerant, modest, and devout person, set an example for his followers when he declined the patriarch's invitation to pray with him in the Church of the Holy Sepulchre in order not to encourage his followers to turn the church into a mosque later. Moreover, the terms of surrender revealed a rare magnanimity, whereby the safety, property, and churches of the vanquished were guaranteed in return for the payment of a tax known in Arabic as Jizyah.

The Jews—barred by the Byzantines from Jerusalem for all but one day a year—were allowed to live and worship in the city. The Israeli historian Zev Vilnay expressed it this way:

> Whenever Jerusalem came under the rule of Christians, Jews were not allowed to stay or live in it. Those Jews who happened to come to the city during their (the Christian) rule were either killed or expelled. On the other hand, whenever the Muslims occupied the city they used to call the Jews in, allow them to live inside the city . . . and they lived in peace.[5]

> [Omar] had set one of the highest standards for rule in Jerusalem in that he respected the rights of Jews and Christians to live in the city and practice their faiths. Following his example, Muslim rule sustained the most notable period of co-existence among the three faiths in Jerusalem from 638 AD—1039 AD.[6]

Jerusalem had already been venerated by Muslims almost from the inception of Islam. A year before the *hijra* from Mecca to Medina (AD 621), it was revealed that the prophet's nocturnal journey, *Isra,* was from Mecca (al-Masjed al-Haram) to al-Masjed al-Aqsa, or the Haram, the Noble Sanctuary in Jerusalem. Jerusalem's special place in Islam was also bolstered by the caliph Omar's short visit. He went to the Haram area, which the Christians had neglected, cleared the ground by the rock, and prayed at a spot where the Mosque of Omar later was constructed. The fourth caliph, Uthman, inaugurated the Silwan Spring as *Waqf* (a religious endowment), in this case water for public use by all. It was the first of the Muslim endowments for Jerusalem (Bayt al-Maqdis) throughout the ages.[7]

The historic and religious significance of Jerusalem for Muslims and Arabs had grown steadily under the Umayad Dynasty, which ruled from 661 to 675 and had spread Islam's domain to North Africa and Spain. The caliph Muawiya said from the pulpit of the mosque in Jerusalem: "The area between the two walls of this Mosque is dearer to God than the rest of the earth."[8] Moreover, two of the Umayad caliphs were inaugurated in Jerusalem. The Dome of the Rock was built by the Umayad caliph Abd al-Malik Ibn Marwan in 691–692 as a shrine meant to rival Mecca.

Around the end of the seventh century, Arabic replaced Greek as the official language in the city, and the Arabic dinar replaced Byzantium's coinage. Veneration for the city grew widely during the Abbasid period (750–969). The major contribution of the Abbasids was the restoration and rebuilding of the Aqsa Mosque by Caliph Abu-Jafar al-Mansour. The Dome of the Rock was also repaired by Caliph al-Mamoun, who, like other Abbasid caliphs, visited the city. The Abbasid Dynasty reached its zenith under Haroun al-Rashid, who established good relations with Western Christendom. However, the close of the tenth century witnessed a general decline among both Christian and Muslim powers. The Abbasids lost power in 969 to descendants of the caliph Ali and the prophet Muhammad's daughter, Fatima. Calling themselves the Fatimids, the new rulers captured Jerusalem in 966 and set up an oppressive regime, which was succeeded by the Seljuk Turks (1071–1096).

Jerusalem Under the Crusades

As the Seljuk and Fatimid Empires fragmented, the call to arms was being sounded in Europe, which had not forgotten the Arab conquest of Spain and the defeat of Byzantium by the Turks. Stories about Muslim persecution of Christians in Jerusalem and alarms sounded about danger to the holy places were used to rally support for the Crusades. In 1099, the crusaders defeated the Fatimids and conquered Jerusalem, interrupting four and a half centuries of Arab-Muslim rule. It was a temporary situation, however: The sanctity of Jerusalem made it a symbol of *Jihad* against the invaders, and the brutality of the conquerors confirmed the resolve of Muslims and Arabs to obtain redress.

The conquest by the crusaders was a sharp contrast to Omar's conquest four and a half centuries earlier. William of Tyre wrote about the massacre that on July 15, 1099, after a month's siege, the city was subjected to one of the greatest massacres in its tragic history. . . . The carnage lasted two days and threatened even the Christians living in the city. Members of the small Jewish community were burned in their synagogue. More than 70,000 Muslim and Jewish civilians were put to the sword. . . . It was impossible to see without horror that mass of dead. . . . Even the sight of the victors, covered in blood, was an object of terror.[9]

It was William of Tyre who expressed great fears that a single Muslim prince would reunite the realms of Syria and Egypt and abolish the very name Christian.[10]

Islamic Restoration and Loss Again

That prince was to emerge in the person of Salah al-Din al-Ayyubi (Saladin), who defeated the Franks in the famous battle of Hittin on July 4, 1187, and recaptured Jerusalem for the Muslims three months later. His treatment of Jerusalem represented a sharp contrast to that of its crusader captors in 1099. He treated the civilian population well and offered safe passage. He allowed Christian pilgrims to enter Jerusalem in his treaty with King Richard I (the Lion-hearted) of England in 1191. He restored the Church of the Holy Sepulchre to the Eastern Orthodox Church, and in keeping with the caliph Omar's tradition, he allowed the Jews to return to Palestine and gave them freedom of worship.[11] The Spanish-Jewish poet Yehuda al-Harizi is quoted by Asali as expressing the following significance of Salah al-Din's recovery of Jerusalem for Jews:

> God aroused the spirit of the prince of the Israelites (Salah al-Din), a prudent and courageous man, who came with his entire army, besieged Jerusalem, took it and had it proclaimed throughout the country that he would receive and accept the entire race of Ephraim (the Jews), wherever they came from. . . . We now live here in the shadow of peace.[12]

Salah al-Din was intent on fortifying Jerusalem and restoring its Arab-Muslim character. Fear of the crusaders' return prompted him to undertake a more predominant Islamization of the city than had the caliph Omar. He thus built numerous religious, educational, and cultural institutions and foundations and made the city accessible to the three religious communities.

By 1219 the Mongols under Genghis Khan had devastated much of the Islamic world and were stopped at last, in 1517, by the armies of the

Mamelukes (who ruled the Islamic empire from 1247 to 1517). For the next two hundred years, Mameluke sultans did much reconstruction and decoration of the Haram area and accelerated the building of schools and foundations. By 1517, both Jerusalem and Cairo had fallen to the Ottoman Turks, who continued to renovate the Muslim holy places. Sultan Suleyman the Magnificent left a lasting imprint on Jerusalem by completely rebuilding its walls between 1537 and 1541. That trend of reconstruction continued until the end of Ottoman rule in 1917, when Jerusalem fell to the British. Thus, Muslim rule over Jerusalem and Palestine lasted thirteen centuries, except for the brief Christian interregnum. By contrast, the Jews lived in the city as a small minority between the seventh century AD and the mid nineteenth century.

According to the late A. K. Asali, during the 5,000 years of Jerusalem's history, Jews lived in the city perhaps 1,135 years as a majority, during which they ruled the city for only about 600 years.[13] Until 1850, they constituted less than 4 percent of the total population of Palestine, which was approximately 350,000.[14] In 1882, Jewish immigration to Palestine began to mount under the impetus of the Zionist movement, which emerged as a response to European anti-Semitism. According to Alexander Schölch, the number of Jews in Jerusalem was 2,000 in 1800, had increased to 17,000 by 1880, and had more than doubled to 34,400 in 1922.

Jerusalem Under the British Mandate

In 1922, the entire area of Palestine was placed under a League of Nations mandate, which was administered by Britain until 1948. During the mandate period, tensions rose between Arabs and Jews after the Zionist movement embarked upon making Palestine a national home for the Jewish people and stepped up a campaign of mass immigration. Since the people of Palestine were overwhelmingly Muslim and Christian Arabs, the mandate assumed full responsibility for "preserving existing rights" in the holy places. After a serious outbreak of violence over the Western Wall (Wailing Wall) in the area of the Haram al-Sharif, an international commission was appointed under Article 14 of the mandate to investigate the claims of the two parties in Jerusalem. On the fundamental question of religious rights, the commission resolved:

> To the Muslims belong the sole ownership and the sole proprietary right to the Western Wall, seeing fit that it forms an integral part of the Haram-esh-Sharif

area. . . . To the Muslims there also belongs the ownership of the pavement in front of the Moghrabi (Moroccan) Quarter opposite the Wall.[15]

This division was made law on June 8, 1931, and remained in effect until the end of the British mandate.

After the Palestinian rebellion of 1937–1939 against Jewish colonization and British repression, a British royal commission proposed the partition of Palestine into an Arab state and a Jewish state, with a Jerusalem-Bethlehem enclave encompassing the holy places to be endowed with international status.

The United Nations and Jerusalem, 1947–1949

Partition and internationalization were proposed again by the United Nations after Britain declared its inability to resolve the Palestine conflict in 1947. The UN Special Committee on Palestine, appointed by the General Assembly to present proposals for settlement, estimated that there were about 100,000 Jews (many of whom were recent immigrants) and 105,000 Arabs in Jerusalem.[16] The committee unanimously recommended that "the sacred character of the Holy Places shall be preserved" and that "existing rights" also be preserved. It also recommended the partition of Palestine and the internationalization of Jerusalem, which were accepted by the General Assembly in its Resolution 181 II on November 29, 1947.[17] A demilitarized Jerusalem was envisaged as *corpus separatum* under the aegis of the UN Trusteeship Council, to be ruled by a governor and a legislative council elected by residents of the city on the basis of universal suffrage irrespective of nationality. The principle of upholding "existing rights" in the holy places was also maintained in the partition resolution. (See Map 11.1.)

It is important to note that Jerusalem acquired a legal status both as a city and as a district in the mid nineteenth century. When the British assumed power following the Ottomans' defeat, they began to tamper with the city's municipal borders in order to tilt the demographic balance in favor of the Jewish community. Such gerrymandering ensured that many new Jewish neighborhoods would be incorporated into the city and that adjacent Arab villages remained outside the municipal boundaries. Palestinian geographer Khalil Toufakji described the tampering by the British mandate authorities this way: "The Western boundaries (abutting Jewish neighborhoods) were made to stretch for several Kilometers, while the Southern and Eastern boundaries, abutting Arab areas, were stretched by only several meters."[18]

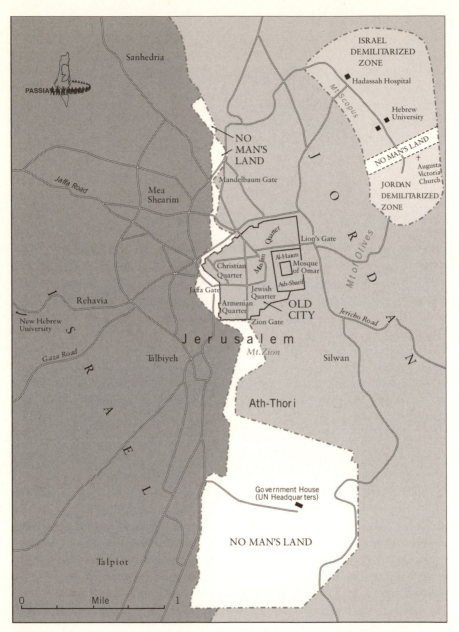

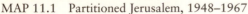

MAP 11.1   Partitioned Jerusalem, 1948–1967

SOURCE: H. M. Sachar, *A History of Israel* (Knopf, 1979). Reprinted with permission of PASSIA (Palestinian Academic Society for the Study of International Affairs, www.passia.org).

Map 11.2 shows what looks like a hook, which illustrates the demographic engineering. Thus, the Arab communities of Al-Tour, Abu, Tour, Ras, al-Amoud, Shoufat, Lifta, Deir Yasin, Ein Karem, al-Maliha, Beit Safafa, Silwan, and Al-'ezariya, which were close to the city, were excluded, but the Jewish communities to the west, comprising Bet Hakerem, Beit Vegan, and Qiryat Moshe, make up the strange "hook."[19]

The conflict in Palestine—which erupted after the Zionist militia expelled more than half a million Palestinians from the would-be Jewish state (according to the partition resolution) between November 1947 and April 1948, while Britain was still in charge of law and order—ruled out a diplomatic settlement. Neither the partition of Palestine nor the internationalization of Jerusalem was implemented.

In actuality the fate of Palestine and that of Jerusalem were determined by force of arms. After the Zionist forces had decisively defeated the Arab armies, the United Nations arranged for negotiated truce agreements, which were reached on November 16, 1948, and on April 3, 1949. Israeli control had expanded deep into the proposed Arab state and into the western part of Jerusalem, which included the Arab neighborhoods of Qatamon, Baqa'a, and Talbiya. The truce agreements resulted in a de facto division of the city between Jordan, whose forces were in the eastern part, and Israel in the west (see Map 11.3), but the United Nations continued to press for internationalization, in accordance with Resolution 181 II.

The Transformation of Jerusalem

The city of Jerusalem, which had become, in a way, the capital of Palestine during the nineteenth century, and whose importance for about three thousand years derived less from commerce, communications, or defense than from its religious and political character, was in danger of losing that character in the mid twentieth century. A continuous Muslim-Arab rule had prevailed for nearly thirteen centuries, from 637 until 1917. Subsequently, three decades of British rule paved the way for a transformation of the city and the country. By the end of that rule, a systematic attempt to dwarf its Muslim-Arab character and to make it a predominantly Jewish metropolis had proceeded with extraordinary vigor and enormous hype. Whereas the city's multireligious character had been preserved throughout the thirteen centuries of Muslim-Arab rule, the campaign by Israel and the Zionist movement has been geared toward a Jewish ascendancy and an erosion of Christian and Muslim influence. To that end, the tampering with Jerusalem

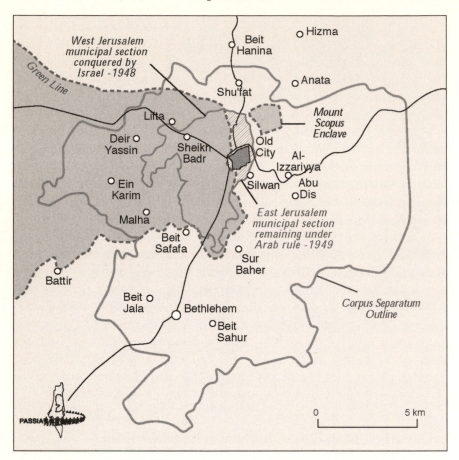

MAP 11.2   Jerusalem and the *Corpus Separatum* Proposed in 1947

SOURCE: Reprinted with permission of PASSIA (Palestinian Academic Society for the Study of International Affairs, www.passia.org).

at the level of boundaries, demography, culture, and history has been an ongoing process since 1948.

East and West Jerusalem, 1948–1967

With Jordanian and Israeli forces occupying East and West Jerusalem, respectively, in 1948, the city of Jerusalem began to assume a dual character. The policies of both states were directed toward integrating each occupied section into the respective state. Both took their own separate steps to ex-

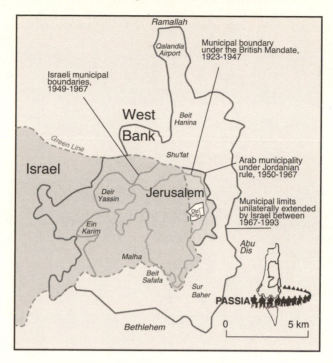

MAP 11.3   Jerusalem Municipal Boundaries, 1947–2000
SOURCE: Reprinted with permission of PASSIA (Palestinian Academic Society for the Study of International Affairs, www.passia.org).

tend their own jurisdiction to the portions they occupied, in the face of international disapproval. Jordan established a municipal council in December 1948 and expanded the borders of the municipality to include the Arab villages and neighborhoods of Silwan, Aqabat al-Suwana, Ard al-Samar, Ras al-Amoud, and Southern Shoufat. The only Jewish sectors of Jerusalem lost to Jordan in 1948 were Mount Scoupus, the Jewish Quarter, and the Western (Wailing) Wall inside the old city.

Israel, on the other hand, extended its jurisdiction to nine Arab villages and neighborhoods, which together made up the bulk of what has become known as West Jerusalem and has commonly been considered Israeli since 1948. In fact, as Map 11.3 shows, the predominantly Jewish section of West Jerusalem was only a slice of what became known as Israeli West Jerusalem. The Arab villages annexed to "West Jerusalem" were Lifta, Deir Yasin, Ein Karem, and Al-Maliha. The urban centers annexed to West Jerusalem were Talbiya, Al-Qatamoun, upper and lower Baqa'a, Mamila,

334

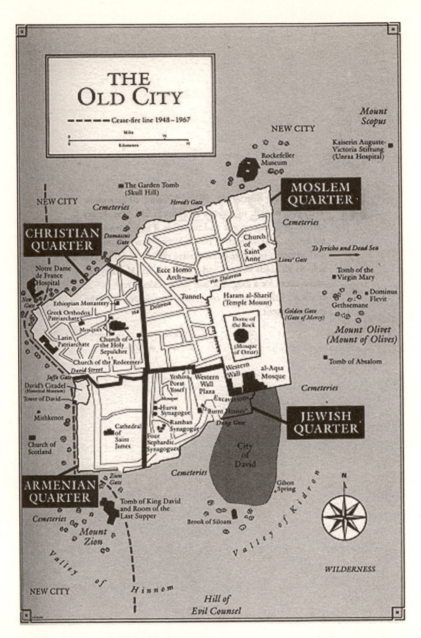

MAP 11.4   Jerusalem: The Old City

SOURCE: *Jerusalem: City of Mirrors* (London: Weidenfeld and Nicolson, 1989).
Reprinted with permission of PASSIA (Palestinian Academic Society for the Study
of International Affairs, www.passia.org).

and the Abu-Tour-Musrara quarter. Over thirty thousand of the inhabitants of the Arab villages and urban centers around Jerusalem were driven out by force or fled the outbreak of violence, several months before two thousand Jews were forced out of the Jewish quarter in the Old City by the Jordanians.[20] The residence of the Israeli president stands today on Palestinian-owned land in Talbiya. The nearby Muslim cemetery of Mamila was converted to the Israeli Independence Park with lawns, playgrounds, and restrooms.

According to British mandate statistics, the Jerusalem subdistrict contained slightly over a quarter of a million inhabitants, of whom 59.6 percent were Arabs and 40.4 percent were Jews. After the armistice of 1949, the land of new West Jerusalem was 40 percent owned by Arabs and 26 percent owned by Jews; the rest was public land and religious property.[21] This Arab-owned land, like other land throughout Palestine, was transferred by the government of Israel to the Israel Land Authority (Keren Keyemet) and to the Jewish National Fund (JNF), whose charter prohibits the transfer of JNF land to any non-Jews. Thus, the intent was to make the seizure of land irrevocable and the redefinition of Jerusalem permanent.

Israel moved on to consolidate its control of the large tracts of land annexed in 1948–1949 when Israel's Parliament (Knesset) proclaimed Jerusalem the capital of Israel on January 23, 1950. Israeli ministries were also moved to the newly demarcated city in 1951. Following that, Jordan moved to formalize its control of the West Bank and East Jerusalem, though with the declared promise that the move would not prejudice the final outcome of the Palestine question.

As the division began to assume a permanent character, the political, psychological, religious, and cultural barriers were also consolidated. By the 1950s Jerusalem had become two very different cities, one Arab, the other European. Meanwhile the UN efforts to keep internationalization alive were fading, and yet, most countries maintained embassies and diplomatic legations in Tel Aviv in deference to the UN-mandated status.

The Land Grab Post-1967 and the Legal Facade

Having consolidated its control of West Jerusalem after 1948, Israel used its 1967 conquest as an opportunity to extend its jurisdiction to Jordanian-ruled East Jerusalem, and to enlarge the boundaries yet another time to add numerous new Arab villages and neighborhoods. During thirty-eight years of a second ongoing occupation (from 1967 to 2006), a significant portion of the West Bank was expropriated and incorporated into a newly created greater Jerusalem. The Israeli chief of staff, General Moshe Dayan, declared his government's intentions soon after he conquered the Old City on June 7, 1967: "The Israeli Defense Forces have liberated Jerusalem. We have reunited the torn city, the capital of Israel. We have returned to this most sacred shrine, never to part from it again."[22]

Shortly after that, the physical barriers between East and West Jerusalem were removed. The Moghrabi section of the Old City was totally razed to accommodate a new plaza in front of the Western Wall. That activity was followed by mass expulsions from the Moghrabi Quarter and the Jewish Quarter of the Old City in order to facilitate archaeological excavations and to construct new buildings for Jews only. Today, the Jewish Quarter stands at four times its original size.

General Dayan's declaration was formalized by the Israeli Parliament three weeks after the fall of Jerusalem. Defying UN resolutions on Jerusalem and the entire Palestine question, the Israeli Knesset adopted three legislative acts on June 27, 28, and 29, 1967, extending Israeli law to the occupied eastern sector of the city and enlarging the municipal boundaries of "united" Jerusalem.[23] The Israeli occupation forces seized all property, furniture, records, and equipment belonging to the Jerusalem Arab Municipality and to the Jordanian government. They abolished Jordanian law in the city and brought all government departments and courts under their control, making the Arab population of Jerusalem Israeli subjects. All of these forcible changes, which amounted to annexation, were described euphemistically as "unification," while the dissolution of the Arab municipality was declared an "integration of services."

The enlargement of the city and the new land seizure were guided by a strategy of colonizing the land while minimizing the number of Palestinians in the expanded boundaries. To bolster the Zionist dictum of acquiring the land without the people, the occupation authorities carried out a general census of the entire occupied territory, including Jerusalem, on July 25, 1967. All residents who were away working, visiting relatives, or touring were considered absentees and thus were denied their right to reside in the city. That criterion was also applied to the citizens who either had fled the fighting or were persuaded to board the Israeli buses waiting to take them eastward to the Allenby Bridge. As a result, an estimated 100,000 people lost their international right to belong to Jerusalem.

The reaction of the United Nations to Israel's 1967 unilateral measures was swift and unequivocal in declaring them illegal. On July 4, 1967, the UN General Assembly adopted Resolution 2253, calling upon Israel to "rescind all measures already taken [and] to desist forthwith from taking any actions which would alter the status of Jerusalem."[24] Ten days later the General Assembly adopted Resolution 2254 (ES-V) deploring Israel's failure to abide by the previous resolution but, most important, emphasizing that the "status of Jerusalem" would not be affected by Israel's unilateral annexation.

The Security Council also adopted Resolution 252 in 1968 declaring invalid the measures taken by Israel to change the status of Jerusalem. As far as the United Nations was concerned, the legal status of Jerusalem was the one governed by General Assembly Resolution 181-II of November 29, 1947, which called for the partition of Palestine into a Jewish state and an Arab state, and for the establishment of the City of Jerusalem "as a *corpus separatum* under a special international regime [which] shall be administered by the United Nations."[25] This resolution, together with 194 of December 11, 1948, continues to constitute international legality with regard to the city, and no subsequent resolution was ever adopted altering that status. In fact, that status was also confirmed by the Security Council in Resolution 267 of July 3, 1969; Resolution 271 of September 15, 1969; and Resolution 298 of September 25, 1971. In each of these resolutions, the Security Council deplored the failure by Israel to abide by previous UN resolutions calling for the rescinding of all measures of annexation and alteration of the "status" of Jerusalem.

Before the extension of Israeli law to the occupied Arab sector, the Knesset had proclaimed the city Israel's capital on January 23, 1950, and had made the annexation official on July 30, 1980. In doing so, Israel was ignoring Security Council Resolution 242 of 1967, which called on Israel to withdraw to the lines of June 4, 1967.

The Israeli argument, however, has been based on a denial of the existence of the Palestinian people and the fatuous assertion that no other state can produce a legal claim to Palestine equal to that of Israel.[26] Israeli jurists pressed the argument that the Jordanian occupation of the city in 1948 was an act of aggression and hence illegal, and that by accepting the "illegal" act, the Palestinians relinquished their right to establish a Palestinian state under UN General Assembly Resolution 181-II. Moreover, they maintained that Jordan "again" committed aggression in June 1967 and lost Jerusalem, which had been accorded a special status under Resolution 181-II. That resolution, therefore, was "overtaken by events."[27]

This polemical thesis is at the core of the continuing colonization of the occupied territories, including Jerusalem, because Israel does not view them as occupied. It was the basis for the Israeli measures that altered the status of Jerusalem, which themselves were the prelude to the de facto annexation of the West Bank. On December 17, 1967, for example, Israel dropped the term *West Bank* from official usage and adopted the biblical name Judea and Samaria. To reconfirm that change, Israel introduced another measure on February 19, 1968, according to which the occupied territory was no longer referred to as "enemy territory."[28] The position of the United Nations, however, remains that Jerusalem is occupied territory in accordance with Security Council Resolution 242, and that the Geneva Convention applies to it. But the Israeli measures exemplify Israel's ability and willingness to manipulate the law in pursuit of strategic political objectives. They also reflect its tenacity in defying the world community and international public opinion. Gradually but persistently, Israel was able, over a quarter of a century, to sway the US position toward its own.

Colonization and Judaization: Greater Jerusalem in Formation

The colonial settler nature of the Zionist movement is illustrated nowhere better than in Jerusalem and its vicinity. The process of dispossession, displacement, dismemberment, disenfranchisement, and dispersal, which was savagely applied to the Palestinians in 1948, was reenacted systematically after 1967. In Jerusalem and its surroundings, the objective was to create a huge Jewish metropolis that would disrupt the territorial continuity of the West Bank and preempt any sovereign existence of the Palestinians there. To that end, ethnic cleansing has become the official policy of the state of Israel in Jerusalem and its vicinity.

The territorial and demographic facts thus created would render all UN resolutions on Jerusalem practically irrelevant. The colonization and Judaization of the area would preclude any return to the status quo ante, as mandated by Resolution 242. That fait accompli, much more than any dubious historical claim, accounts for the real reasons behind the stand that the fate of an "eternal capital" is not a negotiable item. It is not the religious and emotional attachment that makes Jerusalem so sacred for the predominantly secular Israeli society; it is the religiopolitical imperative and the *raison d'état,* which emanates from the colonial settler nature of the Zionist ethos.

To operationalize that imperative, Israel mobilized varied resources and utilized legal gimmickry that would first facilitate the passing of Arab land into Jewish ownership and then make it off-limits to Arabs. Expropriation for "public purpose" and for "defense purposes" served the exclusive interests of the Jewish public and helped build Jewish settlements in contravention of international law.[29] The second (post-1967) phase of the colonization of the area in and around Jerusalem began with the land seizure of January 1968 in the Shaykh Jarrah Arab neighborhood of East Jerusalem. Privately owned land there was seized, and the new Jewish residential colonies of French Hill, Ma'alot Dafna, Ramat Eshkol, and Mount Scopus stand today on that land. The next rash of colonization took place in 1970, erecting a belt around East Jerusalem by building Ramot Alon, Rekhes Shoufat, East Talpiot, Gilo, Atarot, Gei Ben Hinom, Jaffa Gate, and Ramat Rahel. The belt starts from northeast Jerusalem at Neve Yaacov to the west in Ramot, then southeast to Gilo. A string of settlements connects West Jerusalem with the Hebrew University and commands the important road that connects Jerusalem with Ramallah.

A third wave of colonization, which started in 1980 and is still going on, involves the expropriation of vast tracts of land belonging to the villages of Beit Hanina and Shoufat to build the settlements of Pisgat Ze'ev and Pisgat Omer. (See Map 11.5.)

In the course of more than half a century of its existence as a state, Israel has thus been able to depopulate large areas of West and East Jerusalem during two wars, and to expand the city to nearly three times its former size. Land conquest and population control went hand in hand as part of a systematic Israeli policy, implemented largely during "peaceful" times under the guise of urban renewal, residency rules, modern zoning, housing policy, and fulfillment of the need for natural growth along with protection of the environment. The net result of thoroughgoing Judaization and corresponding de-Arabization is being accomplished not only by the force of arms, but also by the force of "law." A plethora of legal subterfuges is being enforced to allow ethnic cleansing, the robbing of property, denial of the right to build on one's own property, and demolition of what has been built "illegally." In addition, "security" regulations, which have been utilized to deny the Palestinians access to the city and its expanded zones, most of which were acquired through legal facade, are intended to perpetuate Israel's colonial rule over Jerusalem and all of Palestine. These measures are not about security, they are about conquest and ethnic cleansing.

Quiet Deportation:
Confiscation of the Jerusalem Residency Card

Central among Israel's laws that achieve a high degree of ethnic purity in Palestine and that allow the acquiring of land without the indigenous population is the Law of Entry into Israel (1952), which was amended in 1974.

MAP 11.5   Arab East Jerusalem Within "Greater" Jerusalem
SOURCE: Reprinted with permission of PASSIA (Palestinian Academic Society for the Study of International Affairs, www.passia.org). Planned settlements and settlements under construction have not been included (e.g., Har Homa).

Regulation 11 of the 1952 law states that "if a permanent resident lives outside of Israel for more than seven years, becomes a permanent resident of another country or applies for citizenship in another country, s/he is liable to lose his/her status as a permanent resident of Israel." The 1952 law became the basis for achieving a bureaucratic eviction by cancellation of the residency rights of Jerusalem's indigenous population. The regulation is thus "legal" and nonviolent inasmuch as it is carried out by bureaucrats in Jerusalem and at various foreign embassies in various countries abroad, away from media scrutiny. Unlike the confiscation of new land to build a settlement, there is neither an announcement, nor bulldozers, nor armed police and intransigent settlers clashing with dispossessed Palestinian owners appearing on television screens and newspaper front pages.

The 1974 amendment was meant to enable the Israeli government to enforce the 1952 law by revoking the Jerusalem residency of Palestinians who resided outside Israel for seven years or acquired citizenship or residency status in another country. Meanwhile, Israel continued to issue reentry visas—valid for one to two years—to Palestinian residents of Jerusalem living abroad, who were thus made to believe that such renewal would protect their residency right. Not so, ruled Israel, and starting in 1982, Jerusalem hospitals were ordered not to register children whose fathers were not Jerusalem residents. In 1988, the Israeli high court ruled in a landmark decision that Palestinian/American peace activist Mubarak Awad must be deported because Jerusalem had ceased to be the "center of his life." A legal precedent had thus been set and was applied in the cases of all Jerusalem female residents applying for residency status for their spouses.

Starting in 1994, those females had to meet the "center of life" criterion, but in the following year, all Jerusalemites living "abroad" had to satisfy the same criteria. A key term here is "abroad," which covered all Jerusalemites living a few miles away in the West Bank.

As if the "center of life" doctrine were not a sufficient instrument to thin out the Arab population of Jerusalem, beginning in 1966 Israel ordered the confiscation of Jerusalem identification cards from those holding foreign passports under the rule against "dual nationality." Of course, that rule does not apply to Israeli Jews such as Jonathan Pollard, the American Jewish spy convicted of espionage for Israel in the United States. Nor does it apply to the Miami bingo mogul and real estate tycoon Dr. Irving Moscovitz, who bought stolen property in the Arab neighborhood of Jerusalem known as Ras al-Amoud and rented it to three "families" from the notorious fundamentalist group Atarot Cohanim Yeshiva, in order to build a settlement in 1997. The injunction against "dual nationality" is indiscriminately applied to Arabs but not to Jews, on the pretext that the Arabs of Jerusalem are not Israeli citizens but "permanent residents of Israel," according to Israeli law. Since 1996, thousands of Palestinians have lost their residency rights through the Israeli authorities' large-scale confiscation of their identification cards, and thousands more are in jeopardy of losing their cards in the future.[30]

The Apartheid Wall Around Jerusalem

A so-called Separation Fence stretches 64 kilometers around Greater Jerusalem, and it annexes 336 square kilometers of territory in the West Bank joining three settlement blocs to the city: Giv'at Ze'ev in the north, Ma'aleh Adumim in the east, and Gush Etzion in the south. Concurrently, in East Jerusalem, five new Jewish settlements, designated as neighborhoods, are planned, whose main purpose is expanding Israeli control while placing a barrier between Palestinian cities and neighborhoods to the south of Jerusalem and those to the north.[31] (See Map 11.6.)

According to the Israeli human rights organization, B'Tselem, current Israeli planning calls for the wall to encircle East Jerusalem and disconnect it from the rest of the West Bank.[32] The overriding principle in setting the route in the Jerusalem area is to run it along the city's municipal border. In 1967, Israel absorbed into Jerusalem substantial parts of the West Bank, a total of some 70,000 *dunum*s (17,500 acres). About a quarter million Palestinians now live in these annexed areas, within the municipal boundaries, and most of them will be isolated from the West Bank when the wall is completed.

The towns of Ramallah and Bethlehem and surrounding villages, situated not far from Jerusalem's border, and home to hundreds of thousands of Palestinians, have strong ties to Jerusalem. These ties are particularly close for residents of communities situated east of the city: a-Ram, Dahiyat al-Barid, Hizma, 'Anata, al-'Eizariya, Abu Dis, Sawahreh a-Sharqiya, and a-Sheikh Sa'ad (hereafter called the suburbs).[33] The suburbs, with a population in excess of 100,000, are contiguous with the built-up area of neighborhoods inside Jerusalem. Until recently, the city's border had had an inconsequential effect on the daily lives of the residents on both sides of the border. Residents of the suburbs who carry Palestinian identity cards officially need permits to enter East Jerusalem, but many routinely enter without a permit. Running the wall along the municipal border completely ignores the "fabric of life" that has evolved over the years and threatens to destroy it altogether:

- In light of the housing shortage in East Jerusalem, over the years tens of thousands of residents of East Jerusalem have moved to the suburbs. They still hold Israeli identity cards and receive many services in the city.

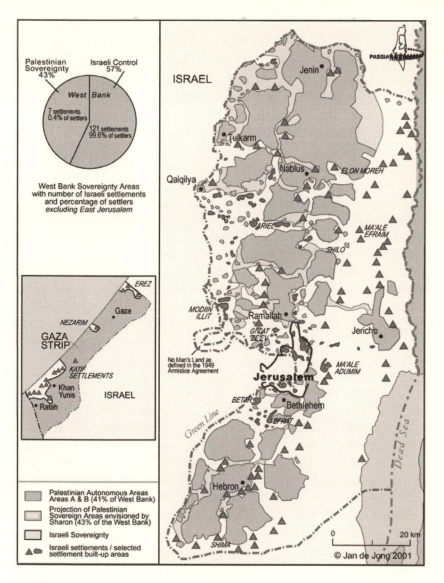

MAP 11.6   Palestinian Sovereign Areas According to the Sharon Proposal,
2001

SOURCE: Reprinted with permission of PASSIA (Palestinian Academic Society for the
Study of International Affairs, www.passia.org).

- Thousands of children living in the suburbs study in schools in East Jerusalem, and many children living in Jerusalem study in schools outside the city.
- The suburbs do not have a single hospital. Most of the residents use hospitals and clinics in East Jerusalem.
- A large proportion of the workforce in the suburbs is employed in Jerusalem, East and West. Shops, businesses, and factories in the suburbs rely on customers coming from Jerusalem. Many businesses have closed since construction of the wall began.

Israel contends that gates in the wall will enable residents to cross from one side to the other and to maintain the existing fabric of life. However, experience regarding the operation of the gates in the northern West Bank section of the wall raises grave doubts about the gates' providing a workable solution: Crossing through the gates requires a permit, and many persons wanting to cross are listed as "prevented" for varied reasons; most of the gates are open only a few hours a day, far fewer than are needed to meet the residents' needs; and residents must often wait a long time at the gates, sometimes because the gates do not open on time, and sometimes because of long lines.

Israeli officials state on every occasion that two considerations were instrumental in the choice of the route: maintaining security and obstructing Palestinian life as little as possible. However, using the municipal border as the primary basis for determining the route is inconsistent with these two considerations. On the one hand, the route leaves more than 200,000 Palestinians, who identify with the struggle of their people, on the "Israeli" side of the wall; on the other hand, the route separates Palestinians and curtails the existing fabric of life on both sides of the wall.

The decision to run the barrier along the municipal border, along with the weak arguments given to explain that decision, lead to the conclusion that the primary consideration was political: the unwillingness of the government to pay the political price for choosing a route that would contradict the myth that "unified Jerusalem is the eternal capital of Israel."

The latest Israeli plan to expropriate Palestinian land on a massive scale is to make the separation wall surround the Ma'aleh Adumim settlement and a dozen adjoining settlements to the east of occupied Jerusalem.[34] This plan, approved on August 25, 2005, by the Israeli high court, aims to cut off 1,800 *dunum*s (450 acres) of Palestinian lands from the towns of Abu Dis, Anata, al 'Eizariya, and At Tur in order to expand the Ma'aleh Adumim settlement, adding about thirty-five additional residential units, ten hotels and restaurants, an industrial zone, and an Israeli police station.

This plan is expected to accomplish the following objectives:

- Adjoin Ma'aleh Adumim to "Greater Jerusalem," making the apartheid wall the real "border" instead of the 1967 border.
- Divide the West Bank into two disconnected parts, thereby forfeiting the option of an independent Palestinian state in final status negotiations when and if they are held.
- Turn the more than seven thousand Palestinian bedouin families who have grazed here for centuries into homeless people.
- Deny access of the Palestinians to the city, which constitutes a commercial, cultural, medical, and spiritual center.
- Cut the ancient road between Jericho and Jerusalem and ghettoize several Palestinian villages and suburbs, such as al-Za'im and al-'Eizariya.
- Make travel between the northern West Bank and the southern West Bank extremely difficult if not impossible, and sever the link between East Jerusalem, which the international community recognizes as the capital of the future Palestinian state, and the rest of the West Bank.

Nevertheless, the matter of extending Ma'aleh Adumim eastward through what is known in Israel as the E-1 area to create contiguity with Jerusalem had become a political issue between Ariel Sharon and his Likud archrival Binyamin Netanyahu during the summer and fall of 2005. The latter accuses Sharon of not doing enough in the aftermath of the Gaza pullout in August 2005 to adjoin Ma'aleh Adumim to Jerusalem. Sharon's vice premier, Ehud Olmert, insisted that the E-1 area would be built up: "I can tell you that the American administration knows without a doubt that Ma'aleh Adumim is an inseparable part of the State of Israel. . . . There is no chance that we'll be able to give this up."[35]

The *Jerusalem Post* reported on September 2, 2005, that according to sources close to Sharon, he intended to redraw Israel's borders to annex all the main settlement areas, including Ma'aleh Adumim, as sovereign territory and to mark out a frontier with an emasculated Palestinian state along the route of the West Bank barrier now being built. The article added that if Sharon's vision were realized, tens of smaller settlements in the West Bank would have to go. But the large colonies, housing 90 percent of the

400,000 Jews in the occupied territories, would be annexed to Israel.[36] This, in fact, is the likely scenario in view of US president George W. Bush's April 2004 declaration that these settlements are "facts on the ground."

Notes

1. Abdullah Schleifer, *The Fall of Jerusalem* (New York: Monthly Review Press, 1972): 2.

2. Alistaire Duncan, *The Noble Sanctuary: Portrait of a Holy Place in Arab Jerusalem* (London: Middle East Archive, 1972): 12.

3. John Wilkinson, "Jerusalem Under Rome and Byzantium, 63 B.C.–637 A.D." in J. K. Asali, ed., *Jerusalem in History* (London: Scorpion, 1989): 75.

4. Ibid., 102–103.

5. Quoted in Dan Almaghore, "Jerusalem: Daughter of All Generations," *Yediot Ahoronot* (January 29, 1993).

6. From a lecture by Karen Armstrong at the Center for Policy Analysis on Palestine, Washington, DC, June 4, 1997, in *CPAP Newsletter* 5 (July-August 1997): 5.

7. Abdul-Aziz Duri, "Jerusalem in the Early Islamic Period," in Asali, *Jerusalem*, 108.

8. Duncan, *The Noble Sanctuary*, 49–50.

9. Mustafa A. Hiyari, "Crusader Jerusalem 1099–1187 A.D.," in Asali, *Jerusalem*, 165.

10. Ibid.

11. Steven Runciman, *History of the Crusades* (Cambridge: Cambridge University Press, 1952): 467.

12. A. K. Asali, "Jerusalem in History," *Arab Studies Quarterly* 16 (Fall 1994).

13. Ibid.

14. Ibid., quoting A. Schölch, *Palestine in Transformation, 1856–1882: Studies in Social, Economic and Political Development,* translated by W. C. Young and M. C. Gerrity (Washington, DC: Institute for Palestine Studies, 1993).

15. *The Status of Jerusalem* (New York: United Nations, 1979): 3.

16. United Nations, *Official Records of the General Assembly, Second Session, Supplement No. 11,* Vol. 1 (Document A/364, UNSCOP Report): 54.

17. For a discussion of the partition resolution, see Chapter 4.

18. Khalil Toufakji, "The Judaization of East Jerusalem: Facts and Figures," presented to the UN General Assembly (September 1995), posted on pnet@banumusa.csl.uiuc.edu.

19. Michael Dumper, "Jerusalem's Final Status: What Will Be Left to Negotiate?" *The Link,* Vol. 26 (New York: Americans for Middle East Understanding, July-August 1995): 3.

20. Edward Said, "Projecting Jerusalem," *Journal of Palestine Studies* 25 (Autumn 1995): 7.

21. Henry Cattan, *The Palestine Question* (London: Croom Helm, 1988): 253.

22. *Facts on File* 27 (June 7, 1967).

23. See Ibrahim Dakkak, "The Transformation of Jerusalem: Juridical Status and Physical Change," in Naseer Aruri, ed., *Occupation: Israel over Palestine,* 2nd ed.

(Belmont, MA: Association of Arab-American University Graduates Press, 1989): 139–171.

24. *The Status of Jerusalem* (New York: United Nations, 1979): 17–18; prepared for and under the guidance of the Committee on the Exercise of the Inalienable Rights of the Palestinian People.

25. Ibid.

26. The late Israeli prime minister Golda Meir, who was born in Russia and grew up in the United States, summed up this position thus: "There is no such thing as a Palestinian. . . . It was not as though there was a Palestinian people in Palestine considering itself as a Palestinian people and we came and threw them out and took their country away from them. They did not exist." *London Sunday Times* (June 15, 1969).

27. See "Testimony of Yehuda Zvi Blum," *Hearings Before the Subcommittee on Immigration and Naturalization of the Committee on the Judiciary,* U.S. Senate, Ninety-fifth Congress, October 17 and 18, 1977 (Washington, DC: Government Printing Office, 1978): 25–26, 35. A number of scholars argued that the Israeli thesis is a rationalization of unilateral acts undertaken illegally and not a bona fide legal judgment. See, for example, Seth Tillman, "The West Bank Hearings," *Journal of Palestine Studies* (Winter 1979): 21, 27; see also "Testimony of W. T. Mallison," in *Hearings Before the Subcommittee on Immigration and Naturalization,* 46–56; Henry Cattan, "The Status of Jerusalem," *Journal of Palestine Studies* (Spring 1981); Kathleen Kenyon, *Digging Up Jerusalem* (London: Ernest Benn, 1974); and M. A. Amiry, *Jerusalem: Arab Origin and Heritage* (London: Longmans, 1978).

28. See Raja Shehadeh, *The West Bank and the Rule of Law* (New York: International Commission of Jurists and Law in the Service of Man, 1980).

29. Many of the statistics on land seizure were compiled from data in the following sources: Geoffrey Aronson, *Settlements and the Israel-Palestinian Negotiations: An Overview* (Washington, DC: Institute for Palestine Studies, 1996): 17–26; Ibrahim Matar, "To Whom Does Jerusalem Belong?" in *Jerusalem* (Washington, DC: Center for Policy Analysis on Palestine, 1993): 7–17; and Toufakji, "The Judaization of East Jerusalem."

30. *Report on Israeli Settlement in the Occupied Territories* 7 (September-October 1997): 8.

31. Yariv Oppenheimer, "The Settlements Are Still Winning," *Ha'aretz* (August 28, 2005).

32. Much of the information in this section is based on a report by B'Tselem and can be found online at: http://www.btselem.org/English/Separation_Barrier/Jerusalem.asp.

33. Ibid.

34. Department of Arab and International Relations (DAIR), Ramallah; press release on Ma'aleh Adumim (August 29, 2005) can be found online at dair@palnet.com.

35. Jonathan Lis, "Vice PM: Ma'aleh Adumim Is an Inseparable Part of Israel," *Ha'aretz* (September 1, 2005).

36. Ibid.

12

From Camp David to the Road Map

The "Disengagement" from the Peace Process

The Road Map in Historical Perspective

The failure at Camp David in 2000 was followed by two years of American diplomatic reticence. By 2003, however, the European Union, together with the Russian Federation and the United Nations, had convinced the United States to cosponsor a new "peace" plan, which became known as the Road Map to Peace. Both the Oslo Accords and the Road Map were distinguished by built-in tendencies toward deliberate ambiguity, which hampers real diplomatic activity and impedes progress. These tendencies have had an adverse effect on the Palestinian negotiating position, which has had to grant increasing concessions under relentless Israeli and US pressure. These concessions began to reach new heights during the diplomatic quagmire of Oslo, but even newer heights were reached as George W. Bush began to align his position with that of the right-wing Likud Party after the horrendous crimes of September 11. The Road Map, with a token of international sponsorship, was actually grounded in the June 24, 2002, speech[1] by Bush II, which embraced Ariel Sharon's perspective and agenda.[2] By contrast, the unconditional Palestinian embrace of the Road Map reflected power inequality. In sum, the Road Map was the perfect instrument to enable Sharon to prolong the never-ending stalemate, consistent with the well-established

Israeli strategy of opting for unilateral interim settlements and the never-ending pretense of negotiations, of which Oslo is the best example. The aftermath of Oslo has seen a modified Israeli strategy in which unilateralism (Bush's favorite approach) has replaced the bilateral contact of the Clinton era. Meanwhile, Israel would continue to declare the Palestinian leadership recalcitrant and irrelevant, not deserving to sit at the table before ending "terror," and thereby would ensure a continuous freeze of the "peace process."

The Road Map:
A Peace Plan or Another Palliative?

Unlike for the September 13, 1993, Declaration of Principles (DOP), there was no Rose Garden ceremony or historic handshake. Absent also were the Oslo euphoria and the hasty declarations of victory for US diplomacy after twenty-six years of a crippling impasse. The Road Map was handed to an "empowered" Palestinian prime minister on April 30, 2003, by one of the sponsors, the EU, while the US ambassador (representing the lone superpower) released the text to Israel, as if to signal a significant hierarchical order.

Unlike the Oslo DOP, which had been drawn up by Israel's Foreign Office lawyers but sponsored by the United States, the Road Map originated in a seemingly international document sponsored by the United States, the European Union, Russia, and the United Nations. Why did Sharon and his superrightist colleagues, who rejected Oslo, seem undisturbed by a document that is presumed to entail a more "generous" offer to the Palestinians? The answer has to do with the linguistic structure and the built-in gridlock, which invite conflicting interpretations meant to benefit the stronger party. A major flaw in the Road Map is the absence of mutuality, reciprocity, and sequentialism, in favor of conditionality. The language is so vague and nonconstraining that Israel's obligation would not ever take effect until the Palestinians declared and established a unilateral "cease-fire," hoping to evoke a positive reaction from Israel. Sharon would simply sit still, and indeed he did for more than three years, waiting for the Palestinians to fulfill their obligations to his own satisfaction. In the absence of international monitors, he alone makes such determinations, even though the Palestinian cease-fire is expected from the Palestinians' *opposition,* while Israel's decision—if and when it comes—would be governmental.

The Road Map delineates three phases with dates and duties as well as a connection between goals and results. Thus, Phase I, which was supposed to end in May 2003, would have seen the end of the Second Intifada and the resumption of security cooperation between Palestinians and Israelis. The premise of this plan is that the nearly forty-year-old impasse is not caused by an abnormal and illegal occupation but by the Palestinian resistance to that occupation. Progress was thus linked to ending the intifada and all acts of resistance rather than ending the occupation or reversing decades of colonial impoverishment of land, resources, and institutions.

Indeed, the threshold of the requirements of Palestinians was raised so high that not only would the first Palestinian prime minister, Mahmoud Abbas (whose appointment was consistent with Washington's desires, and who at that time lacked domestic legitimacy), not have been able to reach it, but even the late Arafat himself, a symbol of Palestinian nationalism, would have flunked the test. This is an asymmetrical plan, whose reciprocity is so lopsided as to render it unworkable. If Israel, the regional superpower, had been unable to suppress the intifada for more than five years, how could the decimated PA forces, led by an untested prime minister, widely regarded as an American-Israeli choice, have completed that task? The Palestinians' role at best would only earn them the status of quislings and potential promoters of civil war.

Phase II was to have begun in June 2003 and to have ended in December 2003, during which time "efforts are focused on the option of creating an independent Palestinian state with provisional borders and attributes of sovereignty." The Palestinian leadership was obligated to act "decisively against terror" and demonstrate its willingness and ability to "build a practicing democracy." This phase was to start after Palestinian elections were held, and to end with the possible creation of an independent Palestinian state with "provisional"[3] borders in 2003.

The important question is this: Where and how was that state to be established? How could it be viable if it was not contiguous? The West Bank is already fractured into three Bantustans, and each one of those Bantustans has been fragmented into some sixty to seventy enclaves separated by Jewish settlements, infrastructure, and checkpoints. Moreover, the Apartheid Wall currently under construction in the West Bank and around metropolitan Jerusalem is already separating Palestinians from their agricultural land, schools, hospitals, relatives, neighbors, jobs, and other centers of life.

Moreover, the phrase "provisional borders" is not a known concept in international law. Either the state has borders that it controls, in which case it is independent, or it does not have them or control them, in which case it is a dependency. Oslo's concept of "external security," which was assigned to Israel, came to mean that Israel had control over the so-called self-rule areas' space and borders. Post-Oslo Israel will not settle for anything less. At best, this Palestinian "state" with "attributes of sovereignty" will not be independent, nor will it exceed 50–60 percent of the West Bank, commensurate with Sharon's configurations in his plan of 1981. The new phrase "attributes of sovereignty" is just the latest fiction that extends earlier ploys, such as "shared sovereignty," "sort of sovereignty," and "dual sovereignty."

In the third phase, Israeli-Palestinian negotiations would have begun with the assistance of an international conference aiming at a "permanent status agreement, including borders, Jerusalem, refugees, and settlements," thus ending the Israel-Palestinian conflict in 2005. That has not occurred. Phase III also included an "agreed, just, fair, and realistic solution to the refugee issue, and a negotiated resolution on the status of Jerusalem that takes into account the political and religious concerns of both sides, and protects the religious interests of Jews, Christians, and Muslims worldwide, and fulfills the vision of two states, Israel and sovereign, independent, democratic and viable Palestine, living side by side in peace and security."[4]

Again, as in Oslo, the "final status" issues would be negotiated outside the international consensus and without an international framework. UN Resolutions 242, 338, and 1397 would not be adequate, since Israel had already declared the inapplicability of 242 to the West Bank. Additionally, none of these resolutions included Palestinian fundamental rights enshrined in countless UN resolutions. Hence, the "realistic solution to the refugee issue" called for in the Road Map would not be based on UN Resolution 194, Article 13 of the Universal Declaration of Human Rights, or the Covenant on Civil and Political Rights. In fact, Sharon told Army Radio on the fifty-fifth anniversary of Israel's establishment that Palestinian renunciation of the right of return "is something Israel insists on and sees it as a condition for continuing the process."

Nor did the "negotiated resolution on the status of Jerusalem" include UN Resolution 194 (internationalization) or Resolution 2253 of July 4, 1967, calling upon Israel to "rescind all measures taken [and] to desist forthwith from taking any action which would alter the status of Jerusalem." Given that these final status issues are the core of the Palestine question, their resolution outside the international framework is likely to be at least as intractable and contentious as the previous attempts at Camp David.

Contradictory Encounters at the Rose Garden: Bush, Abbas, and Sharon

Not only did George W. Bush dismantle what remained of the international framework for settling the Palestine-Israel conflict, but he also endorsed Sharon's abrogation of the Oslo process, which Clinton's United States considered the centerpiece of its Middle East diplomacy. Bush had outlined his own prerequisites for peace, most of which parroted Sharon's: Change Palestinian leaders, end violence and dismantle the infrastructure of terror, build a practicing democracy, and acquire new institutions based on transparency, a multiparty system, free elections, and a market economy. In return, the Palestinians might be reinvited to a table that might be given the descriptor *negotiation*.

The warm welcome Bush extended to the new Palestinian prime minister, Mahmoud Abbas, in July 2003 was a mere diplomatic nicety devoid of real substance. Every compliment showered on Abbas by Bush was coupled with a reminder that Abbas was "committed to a complete end to violence and terrorism" or was related to Abbas's recognition that terror is "a dangerous obstacle to the achievement of a Palestinian state." Bush even promised to reward the "moderate" Abbas with a $20-million direct grant to the Palestine Authority and announced the establishment of a joint US-Palestinian Palestine Economic Development Group. His secretaries of commerce and treasury were to be dispatched to the area in the fall to help "build a solid economic foundation for a free and sovereign Palestinian state." Not surprisingly, that promise was never fulfilled.

Undoubtedly, such praise stood in stark contrast to the contemptuous manner in which Washington has been addressing or referring to Palestinian leaders since the failed Camp David summit in July 2000. The important thing, however, is that Abbas's mission (he expected Bush to persuade Israel to move on the Road Map) had not succeeded, and there were no grounds for his delegation's expressed optimism. Abbas's presentation conveyed the message that "the occupation that started in 1967" must end, and that a "just and agreed solution to the refugee question on the basis of UN Resolution 194" must be effected, as the Road Map requires. Abbas's more immediate concerns, however, were issues relating to prisoners, settlements, Arafat's captivity, and the need to avoid a Palestinian civil war by opting for a cease-fire instead of dismantling Hamas and the Islamic Jihad. On the question of the so-called separation wall, Bush was initially forthcoming, even acknowledging that a problem might exist between Israel and the United States: "I think the wall is a problem and I discussed this with Ariel Sharon. It is very difficult to develop confidence between the Palestinians and the Israelis . . . with a wall snaking through the West Bank."[5]

That opinion, however, did not last for even a week. When Bush greeted Sharon at the White House, Sharon's argument, which went unchallenged by Bush, was that the wall was a "security fence," not a wall, and it was tied to the issue of terror, which in turn had an impact on the peace process. By contrast to the businesslike manner in which he had treated Abbas, Bush was clearly unequivocal in endorsing Sharon's demand that dismantling Hamas and the Islamic Jihad was a prerequisite to the pursuit of peace in accordance with the Road Map. He even announced, during his joint appearance with Sharon on July 29, 2003, that Abbas himself had committed himself to dismantling the resistance forces: "And the positive news is that Prime Minister Abbas made a public declaration that we would work together to dismantle terrorist organizations, . . . to cut off money to terrorist organizations, to prevent the few from damaging the aspirations of the many."[6] Given Abbas's concern about avoiding a Palestinian civil war, it was remarkable that he did not even respond to Bush's statement.

As for the settlements, Sharon pledged to dismantle the so-called unauthorized settlement outposts, as if the more than two hundred "authorized" settlements built since the 1970s were legal. In his joint press conference with Sharon, Bush unquestionably accepted the Israeli argument anchored in the notion of Palestinian "terrorism." After showering praise on Sharon and reminding his audience that Sharon's eighth visit was indicative of a deep and abiding friendship, he declared that the "fundamental obstacle to peace is terrorism," not the occupation, which has vanished altogether from the Washington vocabulary.

The sum result of these two competing visits was that the threshold of requirements for Abbas had again become even higher. Performance became solely a Palestinian responsibility, and resistance was relabeled as terror, thus replacing occupation as the essence of the problem. Abbas went home empty-handed, despite all the cosmetics, and Sharon would brag to his ultrarightist supporters that concessions were not in the lexicon, as he continued to impress his friend "George," who had earlier called him a "man of peace" and "my teacher." If the June 24 speech by Bush represented a unilateral substitute for international legitimacy, Abbas's acquiescence in Bush's White House remarks represented an implicit Palestinian approval and bestowed a measure of legitimacy on a perspective that has been for decades in conflict with Palestinian aspirations, the global consensus, and international law.

The Assassination of Ahmad Yassin and the Threat to Peace

The assassination of Shaykh Ahmad Yassin, the political and spiritual leader of the Islamic resistance movement Hamas, on March 22, 2004, represented an escalation in Israel's ongoing US-tolerated policy of daily incursions, house demolition, economic strangulation, killings of civilians, and other forms of collective punishment calculated to block any initiatives for a political settlement consistent with the global consensus.

Why is peace a threat to Sharon, and why kill Yassin? There is an international consensus on the notion that peace requires a political resolution in which Israel terminates the occupation, accepts responsibility for the expulsion of the 1948 and 1967 refugees, and accepts an internationally agreed-upon boundary separating two states living side by side in mutual respect and peaceful coexistence.

These assumptions of a diplomatic settlement have been untenable for Ariel Sharon, who has been engaged during his tenure as prime minister in implementing his 1981 plan to annex half the West Bank and restrict the Palestinians to limited autonomy in fragmented entities, in order to ensure that the area between the Jordan River and the Mediterranean Sea will never accommodate more than a single sovereign state: Israel.[7] Akiva Eldar, the political columnist for the Israeli newspaper *Ha'aretz,* offered the following interpretation of Sharon's reference to a "Palestinian state" in his recycled 1981 plan:

> Sharon's decision to pronounce the words "Palestinian state" was greeted in Israel and the world with great excitement; it even helped pave the way for the Labor Party to join Sharon's first government. So joyful was the response that the public failed to notice that, beyond the headlines, it was hard to find in the details of Sharon's plan any resemblance to the standard definition of a "state." Few, for example, bothered to search the globe for a sovereign state all of whose land links to the outside world was controlled by another state. (Sharon insists that even under a final status accord, Israel will control all border transit points of the Palestinian "state.") The proof that nothing has really changed in Sharon's mind is provided by the course of the separation barrier and the continuous expansion of the settlements in the three areas that the prime minister seeks to annex to Israel. And even a meager Palestinian state would only be permitted by Sharon to emerge after 15, 20 or even 50 years of interim arrangements.[8]

For Sharon, the danger of peace emanates from a perceived demographic threat. By the year 2006, Palestinian Arabs living under Israeli control will become a majority between the Jordan and the Mediterranean for the first time since 1948. Short of giving the Palestinians equal rights in one state, Israel is left with three options: acquiescing in the establishment of a separate sovereign Palestinian state, expelling much of the Palestinian population, or keeping them confined in apartheid-style cantons, enjoying what Sharon calls "transportation contiguity,"[9] but deprived of territorial contiguity, which in essence is Sharon's plan of 1981.

Which brings us to the second question: Why Yassin? When Hamas was established in 1987 at the start of the First Intifada, Israel at first saw the organization as a useful counterweight to the secular nationalism of the PLO. But under Yassin's leadership Hamas quickly dispelled such illusions. Yassin acquired a reputation as a pragmatist willing to settle on the basis of a two-state solution. For Palestinians, he emerged as a national leader, whose influence cut across ideological and sectarian lines, particularly when he called publicly for a number of cease-fires in exchange for Israeli military withdrawals. With the late Arafat sidelined and bruised by corruption charges and the dishonorable legacy of Oslo, Yassin, for many, began to fill the leadership vacuum. Hamas's network of charitable organizations, known for honesty and transparency, gave him a legitimacy based on taking care of people's social and economic needs as much as their spiritual ones. Such credentials marked him for elimination by Sharon, who considered any form of political settlement based on two states a mortal danger for the Zionist movement.

Assassinating Yassin was consistent with Sharon's regional strategy of fighting "terror," which he sold to George W. Bush and the 2004 Democratic US presidential candidate, John Kerry, both of whom endorsed Israel's right to assassinate Palestinian civilians under the guise of self-defense. No sooner had his air force set its US-supplied missiles on Yassin than Sharon bragged that "we got our Bin Laden." Such distortion of the Palestine-Israel conflict is aimed at ill-informed public opinion in the United States, which is being fed a steady diet of "Islamic terror." In that confused atmosphere, Sharon hopes to keep a simple conflict about ending a military occupation away not only from the global agenda, but even from that of his strategic ally, where electoral concerns supersede genuine commitments to peace.

This point calls into question whether a peace process can be conducted not only by a reluctant peacemaker, but also by the strategic ally, bank-roller, and arms supplier of one of the protagonists? One wonders if the time will ever come when the world community decides to exercise its obligations to provide protection for civilians under occupation, and to start along the path to an international conference and an equitable settlement.

What is really interesting about this whole issue is that the failure of the peace process was, in fact, a success—not only for the Likud in Israel, but also for its US counterpart coalition of neoconservatives and Christian Zionists. A sign of US satisfaction with the stalemate that reinforces the status quo came in July 2004 when the Palestine Authority offered to hold elections as early as January 2005. The attempt to meet a long-standing US demand was rebuffed by Secretary of State Colin Powell, who said, "Although the United States supports the principle of elections, such elections have to be well thought out, well prepared, and consistent with what's going on with respect to the Road Map."[10] But of course such an election would have been won by Yasser Arafat, and that was the real reason that Washington opposed them while he was alive but turned around abruptly soon after his death. In fact, after Arafat's death in November 2004, the Palestinians in the West Bank and Gaza were allowed to have their elections, and again, Washington's favorite candidate, Mahmoud Abbas, became their president.

Such obstructionism is not even subtle in Washington, which keeps on adding rules and new conditions that seem designed almost to ensure a continuous diplomatic paralysis. Given such a strategy, the desired stalemate has been ensured. Paradoxically, a stalemate begins to look like diplomatic progress.

The Gaza Disengagement, 2005

Sharon's unilateral plan known as the Gaza disengagement was implemented during six days in mid-August 2005 amid a media frenzy involving some nine hundred journalists covering what was described as a "historic event."[11] The evacuation of Israeli settlers and the razing of their former settlements were widely touted as Israel's first ceding back to Palestinians territory it had seized in 1967. Among the television viewers throughout the world were the 950,000 refugees from the 1948 exodus, out of the 1.3 million living in the Gaza Strip. Israeli writer Roni Ben Efrat commented poignantly on the contrast between their eviction in 1948 and the "eviction" of the Jewish settlers:

> The thing that most astonished me during the six days of disengagement was the almost complete absence of any reference, on TV or in print, to the "disaster of

others." For there had been another uprooting, of another people, in this land 57 years ago—only with certain differences, among them the lack of round-the-clock TV coverage. Here in the August heat of 2005 we were treated to scenes of heartbreak and grief. But what about *that* heartbreak, *that* grief—when you weren't about to be compensated with an average of $450,000 per family, when you weren't being moved to an air-conditioned hotel, when you weren't being provided with food and schools and health care, when no one was apologizing? Wouldn't some pundit make the point? Here we had a pale example. Take away the cameras, make the tears real, and multiply them by a million.[12]

Jonathan Steele of the London *Guardian* described the coverage of the tender evacuation of Jewish settlers from their homes in the settlements of the Gaza strip and contrasted it with the noncoverage of the expulsion of Palestinians from Rafah in the Gaza Strip during the previous year:

Contrast the world's overwhelming coverage, especially on television, of the departure of Israeli settlers from Gaza with the minimal reporting of larger and more brutal evictions in previous months. There was no "sensitivity training" for Israeli troops, no buses to drive the expellees away, no generous deadlines to get ready, no compensation packages for their homes, and no promise of government-subsidized alternative housing when the bulldozers went into Rafah. . . . As many as 13,350 Palestinians were made homeless in the Gaza Strip in the first 10 months of last year by Israel's giant armor-plated Caterpillar bulldozers—a total that easily exceeds the 8,500 leaving Israeli settlements this week. In Rafah alone, according to figures from the UN relief agency UNRWA, the rate of house demolitions rose from 15 per month in 2002 to 77 per month between January and October 2004.[13]

Another one of these rare media voices, Charley Reese, struck a similar tone:

As I watched the extensive, plainly sympathetic coverage of Jewish settlers being evicted from their Gaza homes, I couldn't help but take note once again of the striking double standard applied by American news media as well as the U.S. government. I cannot recall any sympathetic coverage of Palestinians being evicted from their homes. No interviews with weeping mothers or fathers. No discussions of whether the evictions were right or wrong. This is obviously a deliberate policy on the part of America's television networks, for after all, they had [numerous] opportunities to report on Palestinian evictions since September 2000.[14]

In addition, US consumers of the mass media have rarely heard about Israel's ongoing expansion of the "buffer zone" between Egypt and Gaza, a border Israel will continue to control despite the "disengagement." Already several hundred homes inhabited by Palestinian families, mostly refugees from 1948, have been razed to the ground in Rafah, displacing thousands. After the next phase of expansion, Human Rights Watch estimated that hundreds, if not thousands, of Palestinian homes will be destroyed, and tens of thousands more in the Gaza Strip will be displaced.

According to Israeli journalist Amira Hass, during 2000–2005 alone, Israel killed 1,719 Palestinians in Gaza, two-thirds of them unarmed, including 379 children and 96 women; injured 9,000 Gaza residents; destroyed 2,704 homes; partially destroyed 2,187 more houses; and devastated over 60,000 acres of agricultural land.[15] Such gruesome statistics, which are published in the Israeli media, somehow rarely make it to the US mass media.

Gaza, which very few Israelis view as worth hanging on to, has always been a costly venture for the Israeli government because the eight thousand Jewish settlers in the territory, who constituted a virtual contingent of human shields, needed a whole division and several battalions to protect them. The Gaza burden was recognized many years ago by the late Israeli prime minister Yitzhak Rabin, when he said in September 1993:

I prefer the Palestinians to cope with the problem of enforcing order in the Gaza [Strip]. The Palestinians will be better at it than we were because they will allow no appeals to the Supreme Court and will prevent the [Israeli] Association for civil rights from criticizing the conditions there by denying it access to the area. They will rule there by their own methods, freeing—and this is most important—the Israeli army soldiers from having to do what they will do.[16]

Sharon's "disengagement" plan, which was implemented in mid-August 2005, owes its "legitimacy" to an exchange of statements, a Bush letter of assurance, and a subsequent joint press conference between US president George W. Bush and Israeli prime minister Ariel Sharon on April 14, 2004. That entire package was subsequently likened by Palestinians and their supporters to the Balfour Declaration of 1917 in terms of the documents' potential impact on the future course of the Israel-Palestine conflict.[17] What Bush embraced is a unilateral plan by Sharon, whose stated aim is to relinquish some control over Gaza in order to ease Israel's demographic/security problem there, but not to terminate the occupation.

In fact, early in 2005, the International Committee of the Red Cross, the guardian of international humanitarian law, sent the Israeli government a confidential position paper making it clear that the removal of the Israeli troops and settlers from Gaza would not end the occupation. The paper stated: "Israel will retain significant control over the Gaza Strip, which will enable it to exercise key elements of authority. Thus . . . it seems at this stage the Gaza Strip will remain occupied for the purposes of international humanitarian law."[18] This view was corroborated by the UN report submitted to the General Assembly in September 2005 by John Dugard, Special Rapporteur of the Commission on Human Rights. It says:

Although uncertainty surrounds the full extent and consequences of Israel's withdrawal from Gaza, it seems clear that Gaza will remain occupied territory subject to the provisions of the Geneva Convention relative to the Protection of Civilians in Time of War, of 12 August 1949 (Fourth Geneva Convention) as a result of Israel's continued control of the borders of Gaza. The withdrawal of Jewish settlers from Gaza will result in the decolonization of Palestinian territory but not result in the end of occupation.[19]

The report plays down the significance of the redeployment and alludes to the quid pro quo, which many observers and commentators have referred to:

During the past year, Israel's decision to withdraw Jewish settlers and troops from Gaza has attracted the attention of the international community. This focus of attention on Gaza has allowed Israel to continue with the construction of the wall in Palestinian territory, the expansion of settlements and the de-Palestinianization of Jerusalem with virtually no criticism.[20]

Professor Richard Falk concluded an article on "disengagement" this way:

This disengagement represents a dangerous step backward in the struggle to find a just peace for these two peoples based on sovereign equality, respect for international law and fair solutions to the status of Jerusalem and the claims of Palestinian refugees. The sooner these core issues are addressed, the better the prospects for avoiding new cycles of violence, extremism and despair, especially on the Palestinian side. Sadly, the Gaza disengagement makes such clarity even less likely than it was during the dismal decades of Israeli settlement and brutal administrative control.[21]

Moreover, Israel's "disengagement" from the Gaza Strip does not meet even the minimum expectations articulated publicly by the United States. Secretary of State Condoleezza Rice stated that "when the Israelis withdraw from Gaza it cannot be sealed or [an] isolated area, with the Palestinian people closed in after that withdrawal. We are committed to connectivity between Gaza and the West Bank, and we are committed to openness and freedom of movement for the Palestinian people."[22]

However, under Sharon's "disengagement" plan, which Bush endorsed as superseding all others,[23] Gaza would be exchanged de facto for the West Bank, which Israel regards as the real economic and strategic prize. Sharon has put into effect a redeployment from an unwanted, overpopulated, and poverty-stricken swath of land in return for US acquiescence in a "long-term interim" arrangement that would consolidate and make permanent Israel's control over the West Bank.[24]

Dror Etkes, director of the Israeli organization Settlement Watch, described the exchange thus: "It's a trade off: the Gaza Strip for the settlement blocks; the Gaza Strip for Palestinian land; the Gaza Strip for unilaterally imposing borders. . . . They don't know how long they've got. That's why they're building like maniacs.[25]

In fact, more settlers will go to the West Bank than those who evacuated Gaza, and consequently more settlements were built during 2005 in the West Bank. About four thousand homes were under construction in October 2005 in Israel's West Bank colonies, with thousands more homes approved in the Ariel and Ma'aleh Adumim blocks that penetrate deep into the occupied territories. The total number of settlers rose again in 2005, with an estimated 14,000 moving to the West Bank, compared with 8,500 forced to leave Gaza.[26]

The deal smacks of the dismantlement of the Sinai settlement of Yamit in 1978 and the withdrawal from Sinai and Sharm El-Sheikh, in exchange for peace with Egypt, which enabled the Israelis to invade Lebanon and deal a crippling blow to the Palestinian national movement in 1982. From Sharon's vantage point, the "disengagement" deal provides him with strategic gains without his having to go into negotiations with the Palestinians, which would inevitably require some concessions. Moreover, getting rid of the 1.3 million Palestinians under its direct jurisdiction would ease Israel's demographic nightmare.

Israeli professor Baruch Kimmerling described Sharon's motives behind the Gaza "disengagement" thus:

Sharon's reasoning is that in exchange for dismantling all of the Jewish settlements in the Gaza Strip and the four isolated small settlements in the West Bank, he will retain all of the major settlement blocs in the West Bank. These contain approximately 300,000 settlers and 700 kilometers of roads for the exclusive use of settlers. More importantly, Sharon will gain the political and moral ability to impose such an exchange presenting himself as a peace-maker.[27]

And yet, Sharon makes no effort to conceal the fact that he has no intention of promoting any discussion of Israel's eastern frontier, or even of being a part of any debate about the fate of the West Bank for some time to come. The Israeli veteran journalist, Akiva Eldar explained it thus:

Everyone has forgotten that the disengagement plan was, and still is, a unilateral move aimed at shortening Israel's lines of defense on its southern border and subtracting 1.3 million Arabs from the demographic balance. Sharon himself once again is reiterating that he has no intention in the foreseeable future of opening the much more complex and important debate on Israel's eastern border, about the fate of 97 percent of the country's settlers and Jerusalem.[28]

Although this fact is seldom stated publicly in the US media, it was revealed openly by Dov Weissglas, Ariel Sharon's senior aide, in an interview with *Ha'aretz*, in which he stated, "The disengagement is actually formaldehyde. It supplies the amount of formaldehyde that's necessary so that there will not be a political process with the Palestinians."[29] Indeed, no Israeli government is now expected in the foreseeable future to repeat what has been portrayed as a severe national trauma. The precedent of unilateralism also gives Israel a free hand to decide the future of the Palestinians without Palestinian participation.

Israeli peace activist Michael Warschawski adds, "The reasons for the evacuation of a few thousands settlers from the Gaza Strip are to help in creating a 'Gazastan,' part of the 1981 Sharon plan of 'cantonization' of the occupied territories."[30]

In fact, throughout 2004–2005, far from the eyes of Israeli society and the rest of the world, construction continued in the isolated settlements, in the settlement blocs, and in East Jerusalem. Of the existing 101 outposts, 51 were established during the Sharon government. Yariv Oppenheimer, the secretary-general of the Israeli organization Peace Now, wrote in *Ha'aretz* that the Sharon government is still building in the occupied territories at a greater rate than it is evacuating:

In recent months, construction projects have continued in 40 outposts and in 33 of them building along with permanent settlement has begun. The Israeli government has committed itself, not just on a single occasion, in public and in writing, to acting against the outposts in the territories and to dismantling them after the implementation of the Disengagement plan. The requirement to evacuate them appears in the Road Map plan and is a part of the U.S. government's agenda.[31]

Shifts in US Policy Under Bush

By maintaining deliberate silence on the 1967 borders during his April 14, 2004, meeting with Sharon, US president George W. Bush, in effect, recognized a permanent Israeli occupation of the 22 percent of Palestine that Israel did not conquer in 1948. Bush described Israel's West Bank settlements as "facts on the ground," thus exempting Israel, as the occupying power, from withdrawal under Resolution 242.

Bush's move in 2004–2005 undercut much of US diplomatic work over the past thirty-eight years, thus creating a dramatic shift in US policy. Since 1948, American policy on the issue of occupation has always had two faces, declared and undeclared. Although it has always tried, however disingenuously, to masquerade as being in accord with international legality on issues such as Jerusalem, the refugees, the occupation, and Israeli settlements, Washington's declared policy has come to deviate ever further from the international consensus. Now, even the pretension of conformity with international legitimacy has been abandoned by President George W. Bush, notwithstanding his hollow reference to an independent Palestinian state.

Although the policy on refugees has remained vague and cautious since the mid-1990s, Bush's new declaration restricts the Palestinian right of return even to the truncated and isolated cantons fenced in between Israeli highways, settlements, and checkpoints. In endorsing Israel's refusal to consider allowing Palestinian refugees to return to their homes in Israel, Bush endorses the racially motivated demographic imperative that Israel must retain its "Jewish character" regardless of the rights of the indigenous Palestinian people.

On the issue of settlements, which international law has long considered illegal, US policy now for the first time accepts permanency, and hence legality, as "firmly rooted facts on the ground." On March 27, 2005, Sharon was hardly subtle about this duplicity. He said, "We can't expect to receive explicit American agreement to build freely in the settlements." The large blocs of settlement "will remain in Israel's hands and will fall within the fence, and we made this position clear to the Americans. This is our position, even if they express reservations."[32]

The United States and Israel are, in effect, trying to determine the fate of the Palestinians in bilateral agreements reached between them behind closed doors. Palestinian leaders are not usually present when the future of their people is being decided by the self-designated catalyst for peace and the occupier of their land. The Palestinian leadership has been bypassed entirely both from the US-Israeli negotiations at the end of 2003 on Sharon's so-called disengagement plan and from the meetings leading up to the April 14, 2004, press conference. Incidentally, these negotiations were led, on the American side, by Elliot Abrams, a neoconservative who was convicted (and pardoned by Bush) for having lied to Congress during the Iran-Contra affair in the 1980s.

The assassination of Palestinian political leader Abd al-Aziz Rantisi by Israel, only four days after the Sharon-Bush meeting, was seen in many parts of the world as a legitimization of state terrorism by the United States. Even Britain, the closest ally of the United States over Iraq, condemned Israel's assassination policy as unacceptable and illegal. By granting Sharon a blank check, George W. Bush, acting as partner and accomplice, has forfeited whatever claims the United States has to playing the role of mediator.

Again, the United States adhered to what has become accepted practice over the past few decades. Israel provides the framework for a plan, just as it did at Camp David in 1978 and in 1993 in Oslo, and the United States provides the endorsement. Not only did Sharon sell Bush a recycled version of his 1981 plan to keep at least 50 percent of the West Bank, relegating the Palestinians to three fragmented entities (Jenin and Nablus in the north, Ramallah in the center, and Hebron and Bethlehem in the south), but he also sought to guarantee US acceptance based on the prevailing strategic realities in the region and the domestic political realities at home. Bogged down in an increasingly bloody war in Iraq, which was urged by Sharon and his Washington allies in the first place, Bush felt he could ill afford to say no to the Israeli leader, who implicitly linked stability in his country to the success of his "separation" plan.

In another blatant departure from existing US policy, Oslo's designation of "final status" was summarily dismissed as Bush proceeded to preempt and foreclose on the issues falling under that heading. A frequently used phrase in the United States cautioning against "prejudging" a final settlement evaporated like dust, with Bush's instincts seemingly fixated on his electoral prospects and his "war on terror." In conceding final status issues such as boundaries, refugees, settlements, and Jerusalem, Bush seemed either ignorant of or oblivious to what his predecessors had put on the negotiating table at Camp David I, Camp David II, the Clinton parameters (December 2000), and Taba. The proposals posited then that Israeli territorial acquisitions that accommodated Israeli settlers would entail a swap, whereby Israel was under obligation to cede "comparable" land to the Palestinian Authority. Bush's generous offer takes no account of such reciprocal arrangements, bestowing upon Israel land that is neither his nor Sharon's to bestow.

The Future

With the reelection of George W. Bush in 2004, there are new administrations in Washington, Tel Aviv, and Ramallah. And yet, Republicans and neoconservatives remain in power in Washington, Sharon has co-opted the Labor Party into a coalition that would execute his own plans and strategy, and Fateh remained in power in the occupied territories in the aftermath of Arafat's death, until it was ejected by Hamas's victory in the January 25, 2006, legislative elections.

Although there are some changes in the short-term objectives of the three actors, their long-term objectives remain largely unaltered. Israel is eager to stop the resistance and end the intifada, which saps its resources and energies and tarnishes its reputation, but not at the expense of giving up its long-term goal of scuttling Palestinian independence. The Palestinians are desperately in need of a deal that would ease restrictions on the movement of goods, people, and labor and would thus improve the dire economic conditions under which they live. The Bush administration is eager to cash in on the Palestinian January 2005 presidntial elections in an attempt to reconvene a stalled "peace process" and repair its sagging prestige, debilitated by diplomatic failure in Palestine and a military-political failure in Iraq. Therefore, the three actors' common denominator in the short run is to decrease the level of the violence and restore a modicum of normality in a turbulent environment.

The long-term picture is quite distinct for the three actors, who cling tenaciously to objectives that remain fixed despite cosmetics and a choice of trappings. Washington is keenly aware that any possible chance of a successful exit strategy in Iraq, and for US-Israeli plans to shape the future of the Greater Middle East, depends on their ability to create a stable environment for the Israeli colonial project, which has been hiding behind the "peace process." The latest cover-up of this project consists of Sharon's "disengagement" plan, the emasculated "Road Map," and to some extent, the January 2005 Palestinian elections. The Zionist project, on the other hand, which has Washington's support, precludes the existence of more than a single sovereignty in the area lying between the Jordan River and the Mediterranean Sea. US policy is not likely to stray beyond the parameters of this strategic position. Meanwhile, President Abbas's long-term goal remains what it has been since the mid-1970s: a viable, independent Palestinian state in the West Bank and Gaza and a solution for the refugee problem on the basis of international law. Whether or not he will acquiesce in the Bantustanization of the West Bank and Gaza remains to be seen.

At the operational and tactical levels, there are no indications that Bush's new national security apparatus will push for structural adjustments in Israeli conditions and demands from the new Palestinian leadership. Meanwhile, Israel's conditions and terms are likely to continue to focus on what Palestinians are expected to do for the sake of a settlement, rather than on whether Israel would be willing to end the occupation, to dismantle settlements, to seek a decent compromise on Jerusalem, to stop building the wall, and to negotiate the rights of refugees on the basis of international law.

There are simply no incentives for the United States to lean on Israel at present. Meanwhile, the Bush foreign policy team includes people like David Wurmser, a hard-line Likudist neoconservative and Middle East adviser to the Office of the Vice President, and John Negroponte, Director of National Intelligence, who are steeped in the politics of "terrorism," as well as Elliot Abrams, who continues to hold the main spot on the National Security Council and who will not be inclined to drift away from Sharon's parameters. The replacement of the weak secretary of state Colin Powell by Condoleezza Rice, who is sympathetic to Christian Zionism, does not augur well for the only really possible solution: an imposed settlement, on which the United States would have to pressure Israel.

A viable independent and contiguous Palestinian state has no place on Bush's real agenda, although it will be central in the rhetorical aspects of US policy. Moreover, Bush has recently postponed the target date for its implementation from 2005 to 2009. Meanwhile, Sharon's "disengagement" plan was described by confidant Dov Weisglass as a device to freeze the "peace process." According to Weissglas, "The significance of the disengagement plan is the freezing of the peace process. And when you freeze that process, you prevent the establishment of a Palestinian state, and you prevent a discussion on the refugees, the borders and Jerusalem. Effectively, this whole package called the Palestinian state, with all that it entails, has been removed indefinitely from our agenda."[33] In his speech at the annual Herzliya Conference (December 2004), Sharon put it unequivocally thus: "The understandings between the U.S. President and me protect Israel's most essential interests: first and foremost, not demanding a return to the '67 borders; allowing Israel to permanently keep large settlement blocs which have high Israeli populations; and the total refusal of allowing Palestinian refugees to return to Israel."[34] In an interview with Israel Radio on July 22, 2005, Foreign Minister Silvan Shalom said the current US administration represents a departure from the stance of previous US administrations, which ever since 1967 have resolutely opposed the settlement project. Shalom said that "recent statements made by the Bush administration for the first time express an acknowledgement by an American president that permanent borders will be determined according to facts on the ground, i.e. established settlement blocs."[35]

Conclusion

At present, the so-called disengagement plan of Ariel Sharon has been declared the only game in town. It will not terminate the occupation, despite the removal of the twenty-one Israeli settlements, but it will selectively invoke the Road Map even after Sharon's unilateral pronouncement of the death of that map. Israeli forces will continue to control the Israeli points of entry and exit, including the air space, the sea, and the land, and will also continue to patrol the entire Gaza Strip, which will become a vast concentration camp for 1.3 million Palestinians, most of whom are refugees. Gaza will serve as a model for a political settlement in the West Bank, where contiguity has been ruled out by the so-called separation wall, which is rapidly consolidating most of the settlement blocs and rendering the West Bank a fragmented area suitable for Palestinian enclaves.[36] The so-called disengagement plan, together with the wall, is intended to fulfill a fundamental Zionist objective: to get the land without the people.

What is unfolding on the Israeli side is a post-Oslo strategy of sequential unilateralism. Having redeployed his forces from the Gaza Strip, Sharon, who received high marks from the international community, has placed the ball in the Palestinian court. His Machiavellian game requires the Palestinians to "reciprocate": to demonstrate their ability to rule Gaza and face up to Hamas's challenge by maintaining total calm, leading, in effect, to the termination of the intifada. Of course, Sharon would invoke the second phase of the Road Map and wait for the Palestinians to implement his requirements before moving next to divide the West Bank along the lines demarcated unilaterally and illegally by the Apartheid Wall. The Palestinians, who will be hard-pressed to rebuff such a move, would be told to declare their "independent state with provisional borders," again in accordance with the Road Map. All of this, of course, is expected to be carried out unilaterally, not bilaterally, with Israel in control. It will be Sharon's version of a final settlement and Bush's delivery of his long-promised Palestinian state, away from Oslo, away from bilateralism, away from final status negotiations, and away from an international parley to fulfill the requirements of international law. In fact, Sharon's senior strategy adviser, Eyal Arad, said on September 28, 2005, that if the diplomatic deadlock with the Palestinians continues, Israel may consider turning unilateral disengagement into *government policy,* including the annexation of West Bank territory and withdrawal to what the Jewish state would set as its permanent border: "If we see that the standstill continues—despite the fact that is a standstill in a diplomatic situation which is 'easy on Israel'— there may be room to consider turning disengagement into a strategy," a move that has already been taken by Sharon's successor, Ehud Olmert.[37]

Such a pessimistic assessment of the prospects for peace must, nevertheless, be seen against the background of a genuine transformation in the global balance. The Bush doctrine of preventive wars has already broadened the gulf between the United States and Israel, on the one hand, and, on the other, much of the rest of the world, which clings to the rule of law and the peaceful resolution of international disputes. The July 9, 2004, release of an advisory opinion on the legal consequences of Israel's Apartheid Wall by the International Court of Justice (ICJ) is a stark reminder of this cultural-political divide.[38] The 14–1 vote against Israel in the world court on most legal issues recalls the numerous Security Council vetoes cast by the United States to shield Israel from international legal scrutiny.[39] The result of such callous obstruction of justice, however, is likely to be further international isolation for the United States and Israel, which could spawn international action to compel Israeli compliance with international law in accordance with the ICJ's ruling, similar to what happened in Namibia in the 1980s, and in East Timor in the 1990s. The ICJ ruling invoked Article 1 of the 1949 Geneva Convention stating that aid or assistance to Israel is unlawful, thus providing an opportunity to question US aid to Israel, which constitutes Israel's lifeline.

This was a landmark ruling going beyond the wall to rule that the occupation itself is illegal, that settlements are illegal, and that the 1949 cease-fire lines and the 1967 lines cannot be unilaterally changed. The ICJ ruled that Israel must stop building this illegal wall, compensate all those who were harmed by the wall, and abolish the legislation that authorized the construction.[40] It called on the international community to take concrete steps to "insure compliance"; thus all the "High Contracting Parties" to the 1949 Geneva Convention are obligated to ensure compliance. The ruling further expected the United Nations, and especially the General Assembly and the Security Council, to consider what further action is required to bring about an end to the illegal situation resulting from the wall.

David Clark, a former British Labor government adviser, decried the unilateralism of Bush and Sharon, for whom "politics can only ever be the continuation of war by other means," and emphasized the need for an accord that would break the monopoly of US diplomacy, which has so far proven destructive to the peace process:

> Israel's territorial acquisitiveness—its desire to hold on to what it is not entitled to in either morality or law—has now been officially sanctioned by the United States. In defiance of UN resolutions, and even his own road map, George Bush has pre-empted a final status agreement by accepting that Israel can hold on to its West Bank settlements and refuse the right of return to Palestinian refugees. . . . It must be understood that there can be no possibility of real peace without justice. . . . And if a just and workable settlement is to become possible, it will be necessary for others to combine and act self-consciously as a strategic counterbalance to American influence in the region. The most obvious vehicle for this would be the European Union's common foreign policy, but there are many other countries that could form part of a powerful international coalition.[41]

Notes

1. See N. H. Aruri, *Dishonest Broker: The U.S. Role in Israel and Palestine* (Cambridge, MA: South End Press, 2003): 206–210.

2. See "A Performance-Based Road Map to a Permanent Two-State Solution to the Israeli-Palestinian Conflict," Washington, DC, US Department of State: Office of the Spokesman, April 30, 2004. http://www.state.gov/r/pa/prs/ps/2003/20062pf.htm.

3. The quotations are from the full text of the Road Map, from the BBC News of April 30, 2003. It is available at http://news.bbc.co.uk/2/hi/middle_east/2989/783.stm. For a discussion of the Road Map, see Graham Usher, "Road to Nowhere," *Al-Ahram Weekly* (June 9, 2002).

4. From the full text of the Road Map.

5. From remarks by President Bush and Prime Minister Abbas in the White House Rose Garden, July 25, 2003. The text is available at http://www.Whitehouse.gov/news/releases/2003/07/print/20030725-6.html.

6. "President Discusses Middle East Peace with Prime Minister Sharon," The White House, July 2003. Available at http://www.whitehouse.gov/news/releases/2003/07/20030729–2.html.

7. See Nizar Sakhnini, "Village Leagues," Toronto, December 28, 1999. Available at http://www.al-bushra.org/palestine/nizar.htm.

8. Akiva Eldar, "Sharon's Palestinian 'state'—in the Eyes of the Beholder," *Daily Star* (Beirut, Lebanon) (June 21, 2004). Available at http://dailystar.com.lb/article.asp?edition_id=10&categ_id=5&article_id=5453.

9. Ibid.

10. Ori Nir, "White House Cool to Palestinian Proposal to Hold General Elections," *Forward* (July 2, 2005). Available at http://www.forward.com/main/article.php?ref=nir20040701258.

11. For a cogent analysis of the disengagement plan in the broader context of Sharon's long-term strategy, see Gary Sussman, "Ariel Sharon and the Jordan Option," *Merip* (March 2005). Available online at http://www.kibush.co.il/downloads/13.3.2005%20Gary%20Sussman%20Ariel%20Sharon%20and%20the%20Jordan%20Option.doc.

12. Roni Ben Efrat, "Angles on Disengagement, 1: The Hype," *Challenge Magazine* 93 (September-October 2005); see also "Heartless Disengagement," *Ha'aretz* (August 18, 2005). See also "Israel to Seek $2.2 Billion from U.S. for Gaza Pullout," *Washington Post* (July 12, 2005): A16.

13. Jonathan Steele, "The Settlers' Retreat Was the Theatre of the Cynical," *Guardian* (London), August 19, 2005.

14. Charley Reese, "Gaza Evacuation Should Be Americans' Last Straw," available online at http://www.antiwar.com/reese/?articleid=7022. See also the following account, which appeared in the Israeli newspaper *Ha'aretz:* "The way the media made it look, you would think that the Israeli settlers in Gaza were dragged from their homes and sent penniless into exile. . . . The settlers have a knack for acting like hapless victims. . . . Many shoved their children in front of the cameras wearing yellow Stars of David because, they claimed, this was "another Holocaust." . . . For months they have refused to talk to government officials who were attempting to arrange a compensation agreement with them. And what a deal they got in the end! Their houses were valued at $1,000 per square meter. They got compensation for every year of residence in Gaza, a six-month vacation, two years of free rent and a pension for anyone above 55. . . . The average evacuated family will get $450,000. Those who lived there almost rent-free for two years will receive $150,000. . . . In the meantime, the poor of Israel continue to be neglected by the state and the Palestinians go on enduring the nightmare of Israel's brutal and unjust occupation"; excerpted from Nehemia Strasler, "Don't Let the Settlers Fool You," *Ha'aretz* (August 23, 2005).

15. Amira Hass, "The Remaining 99.5 Percent," *Ha'aretz* (August 24, 2005), available at http://www.haaretz.com/hasen/spages/616309.html.

16. *Yediot Aharonot* (September 7, 1993), quoted in N. H. Aruri, *The Obstruction of Peace: The U.S., Israel and the Palestinians* (Monroe, ME: Common Courage Press, 1995): 210.

17. See "President Bush Commends Israeli Prime Minister Sharon's Plan: Remarks by the President and Israeli Prime Minister Ariel Sharon in Press Availability. The Cross Hall." Available at http://www.whitehouse.gov/news/releases/2004/04/print/20040414–4.ht.

18. Paul McCann, "The World's Largest Prison Camp: Gaza." Posted at http://blog.gophercentral.com/modules.php?name=News&new_topic=42. For more information about the Israeli and PA positions on Disengagement, see Palestinian Technical Team on Israel's Evacuation, "Israel's Unilateral Disengagement: Future of the Gaza Strip," September 1, 2005. Received by email from Diana Butto (diana@ardna.ps) on September 5, 2005.

19. http://www.americantaskforce.org/unreport.pdf.

20. Ibid.

21. Richard Falk, "Gaza Illusions," *The Nation* (September 12, 2005). Available online at http://www.thenation.com/docprint.mhtml?i=20050912&s=falk.

22. "Remarks Following Meeting with President Mahmoud Abbas," Secretary Condoleezza Rice, Jerusalem, July 23, 2005, Available online at http://www.state.gov/secretary/rm/2005/49973.htm.

23. The Bush letter declares that "the United States will do its utmost to prevent any attempt by anyone to impose any other plan."

24. Population density in the Jabalya Refugee Camp in Gaza is seventy-four thousand per square kilometer, compared with twenty-five thousand in Manhattan. See Sara Roy, "Praying with Their Eyes Closed: Reflections on the Disengagement from Gaza," *Journal of Palestine Studies* 136 (Summer 2005).

25. Chris McGreal, "Israel Redraws the Road Map," *The Guardian* (London) (October 18, 2005).

26. Ibid.

27. Baruch Kimmerling, "The Pullout of Gaza: Its Real Meaning," August 19, 2005. Available online at http://www.dissidentvoice.org/Aug05/Kimmerling0819.htm.

28. Akiva Eldar, "An Insufficient Remedy," *Ha'aretz* (August 29, 2005).

29. "Interview with Dov Weissglas," *Ha'aretz* (October 6, 2004).

30. Email from: ye_harel@netvision.net.il, July 25, 2005, to: alef@list.haifa.ac.il.

31. Yariv Oppenheimer, "The Settlements Are Still Winning," *Ha'aretz* (August 28, 2005).

32. Aluf Benn, "PM: Israel Will retain Settlement Blocs," *Ha'aretz* (March 28, 2005). Available online at http://www.haaretzdaily.com/hasen/spages/557472.html.

33. *Ha'aretz* (October 6, 2004).

34. http://www.israelpr.com/sharonspeech1006.html.

35. Ibid.

36. http://www.gush-shalom.org/thewall/index.html.

37. http://www.haaretzdaily.com/hasen/spages/630325.html.

38. The full text of the ICJ opinion can be found on the website of Electronic Intifada: http://electronicIntifada.net, http://electronicIntifada.net/downloads/pdf/icj20040709.pdf. See also the following articles about the ICJ's advisory opinion: Baruch Kimmerling, "The ICJ Ruling and Israel's Fence," *Boston Globe* (July 10, 2004); also available online at http://www.boston.com/news/globe/editorial_

opinion/oped/articles/2004/07/10/the_icj_ruling_and_israels_fence/; George Bisharat, "A Non-Violent Victory in Israel," *San Diego Union Tribune* (July 12, 2004); and Susan Akram and John Quigley, *The International Court of Justice Advisory Opinion on the Legality of Israel's Wall in the Occupied Palestinian Territories: Legal Analysis and Potential Consequence* (Washington, DC: Palestine Center, September 2004).

39. The UN General Assembly, the European Union, the Gulf Cooperation Council, and the Arab League have all called for the wall to come down and have criticized it as a "land grab." The UN Security Council voted on a draft resolution urging Israel to halt construction of the wall, which the United States vetoed. In November 2003, the UN General Assembly adopted Resolution ES 10/13, which demanded that Israel stop construction of its "security fence" in the occupied Palestinian territories, including in and around East Jerusalem, in violation of the 1949 Armistice Line. On July 9, 2004, the ICJ ruled that Israel was in violation of international humanitarian law, and that the wall violates the right of Palestinians to self-determination, the right of worship, the right to property, and the rights of the child. This ruling (Advisory Opinion) was made in response to a December 2003 General Assembly Resolution (ES10/14) requesting the ICJ to issue an Advisory Opinion on the legal consequences of an occupation force's constructing an extensive complex of fences and walls inside an occupied territory. See the fact sheet by Lyndi Borne and Liam Stack, "Israel's Wall in the Occupied Palestinian Territories" (Washington, DC: Palestine Center, September 2004).

40. It has been estimated that about 875,600 Palestinians, 38 percent of the West Bank population, have been harmed by the wall. The construction has so far uprooted 102,320 olive and citrus trees, 75 acres of greenhouses, and 19 miles of irrigation piping. In addition, about 20,000 Palestinians will be living in closed zones, such as Dab'a and Wadi Rasha, among other towns and villages where the residents will need permits to live in their homes and work on their land, plus certificates showing land registration, inheritance, and proof that they are still alive. Once these zones are completed, the number of Palestinians living in them will go up to 402,000, and they will find themselves living next to 300,000 Israeli settlers who do not need permits; PENGON, "Stop the Wall in Palestine: Facts, Testimonies, Analysis, and Call to Action," *Jerusalem*, June 2003, p. 25. Available online at www.btselem.org.

41. David Clark, "For Sharon, Gaza Was Just the Latest Act of a Long War: The US Backing of the Pullout Has Loaded the Dice in Israel's Favour," *The Guardian* (London) (August 22, 2005).

13

Whither the Palestinians?

Five Phases of Conflict

The Palestinian-Israeli conflict passed through five distinct phases.

The First Phase: To 1948

The first phase of the Palestinian-Israeli conflict emerged with the process of Zionist settler colonialism, which started in the late nineteenth century and intensified greatly after World War I during the British mandate (1921–1948). Palestinian resistance to European Jewish colonization, settlement, immigration, and the British mandate was best symbolized by the great Palestinian revolt of 1936–1939 against British authorities and then again by the internal (Palestinian–Jewish/Israeli) war of 1947–1948. This phase ended with the destruction and dismemberment of Palestine and the dispossession and dispersal of its people.

The Second Phase: 1948–1967

In the second phase, the Palestinian-Israeli conflict was "Arabized" into the Arab-Israeli state conflict, which culminated in the 1967 war and in the swift defeat of the armies of the nationalist Arab states that had promised to liberate Palestine. The 1967 defeat plunged Arab nationalism into a political-ideological crisis: a no-war–no-peace situation with Israel, a compromise with the conservative monarchical regimes of the oil-rich Arabian Peninsula, and accommodation with the Western powers protecting them and Israel. Thus the "Arabization" of the Palestinian-Israeli conflict failed to liberate Palestine or to resolve the Palestine question. It did, however, lead to the emergence of a radical, Palestinian-controlled PLO. The radical

Palestinians promised not only the liberation of Palestine but also social revolution through people's armed struggle. But they were quickly crushed by Jordan in 1970–1971.

In the October 1973 war against Israel, Egypt and Syria fell back on conventional military means in an attempt to correct the strategic imbalance between Israel and the nationalist Arab states. This campaign was only partially successful. Thereafter, the Arab states, with the support of the Soviet Union, became willing to negotiate a political settlement, but Israel and its Western supporters remained intransigent.[1] The latter also rejected the PLO as the representative of the Palestinian people, consistently portraying it as a terrorist organization dedicated to Israel's destruction. During this phase Israel and the West dismissed PLO peace proposals out of hand. As Edward W. Said noted, "None of the Palestinian positions taken since the 1970s—on a two-state solution, on mutual recognition, on the imperatives for peaceful negotiations—has ever been reported [in the West] with requisite care or accuracy."[2]

Instead of seeking peace according to the internationally acknowledged formula of land for peace, Israel embarked on a program of colonizing and absorbing the West Bank and the Gaza Strip, the remaining parts of historically Arab Palestine. The possibility of a comprehensive political settlement and a just peace was effectively ruled out with the 1979 Egyptian-Israeli peace treaty, which not only removed Egypt, the strongest Arab country, from the Arab-Israeli conflict but altered significantly the strategic balance between Israel and the other Arab states.

The strategic imbalance began to invite aggressive Israeli expansionism in the West Bank, Gaza, and the Golan Heights and military adventurism focused on Lebanon. Israel not only intervened in internal Lebanese affairs but also sought to destroy the PLO, which was headquartered there.[3] These efforts culminated in the 1982 Israeli invasion of Lebanon, the siege of Beirut, and the negotiated exit of the PLO and its military forces from the city. During this period Israel also formally annexed "greater" Jerusalem (East Jerusalem and an area extended around the city in the West Bank) and the Golan Heights and significantly intensified its colonization and settlement of the West Bank and the Gaza Strip.

Also during the 1980s, the decline in oil revenues; the sharp rise of Arab state indebtedness; the profound economic, social, and political-ideological transformation of the eastern Arab world (especially the surge of political Islam); and the Iraq-Iran war—all diverted Arab attention from the Palestine question and hastened the eclipse of the PLO (which had shifted its base to Tunis). Arab state disengagement from the Arab-Israeli conflict reflected the erosion of popular public Arab support for the cause of Palestine. This change in the political culture of the Arab peoples—perhaps commensurate with the demise of Arab nationalism—increasingly isolated the Palestinians and the PLO.

The Third Phase: 1987–1992

These same eventualities exacerbated the horrendous conditions of Palestinians under occupation in the West Bank and the Gaza Strip. Within a month of the Arab summit meeting in 1987, however, a spectacular intifada marked the third major phase of the Palestinian-Israeli struggle. The First Intifada (1987–1992) allowed the Palestinian people, including the PLO, to regain self-confidence, to galvanize the far-flung diaspora communities into renewed political activism, and to reassert Palestinian rights before a rapt international audience. In a dramatic sense the intifada re-Palestinized the conflict that had so long been Arabized. As important, it exposed the limits of Israeli power and the arrogance, brutality, and racism of the Israeli occupation.

The First Intifada not only revitalized the Palestinian question on the international and regional levels but also tipped the balance of power locally, inside Israel and the occupied territories. The intifada raised the issue of the political, economic, and social cost of the occupation for Israel. As a result, the Likud government participated in the Madrid peace conference in 1991, and Labor won the 1992 Israeli elections on the peace platform of a negotiated settlement with the Arab states and the Palestinians.

In 1991 Israel unleashed a new type of counterinsurgency, what it called a "security offensive," against the intifada. The intifada began to wane because of the massive and unrelenting measures by Israel, the Israeli and Western financial and economic blockade, and the loss of Arab financial and political support. This increasingly untenable situation for the Palestinians in the occupied territories, in combination with the failure of the PLO to relieve if not end the occupation, led to the rise, especially in Gaza, of Hamas and the more extremist al-Jihad al-Islami,[4] which began to challenge the legitimacy and leadership of the PLO and Arafat.

The Fourth Phase: 1992–2000

Arab economic and political support of the Palestinians never returned to the level of the 1970s, despite the popularity of the intifada and the end of the Iraq-Iran war in 1988. The PLO under Arafat's direction established closer relations with militarily strong Iraq. But in the 1991 Gulf War the US-led military alliance destroyed Iraq's forces and the country's infrastructure, devastated its economy, and turned the politically weak oil-exporting states of the Arabian Peninsula into US protectorates. The PLO policy of opposition to US military intervention in the Iraq-Kuwait crisis prompted the Arab oil states to end their support for Arafat, the PLO, and Palestinian social service institutions.

The cessation of aid from the oil-exporting Gulf States precipitated the disintegration of all PLO institutions. As thousands of functionaries were laid off, the social, welfare, and educational services to the Palestinian refugees were suspended. The Arab governments and many of their citizens quickly turned hostile to the Palestinians. Indeed the large Palestinian communities in Kuwait (about 350,000–400,000 people) and to a smaller extent in other Gulf States were expelled; only a fraction (25,000–50,000), who had lived in Kuwait since the 1950s, were allowed to remain. Palestinian activism in the post–Gulf War period in the Gulf States was constrained, and the PLO was thus profoundly isolated and weakened as never before in its history.[5]

On the diplomatic front, the two documents signed by Israel and the PLO on September 13, 1993, had created a fundamental change in the political terrain on which the struggle for a political settlement had begun a quarter of a century earlier. The Declaration of Principles and the Mutual Recognition statements, signed in an atmosphere of exuberance and euphoria, were broadly greeted as the long-awaited turning point in the Arab-Israeli conflict that would usher in a new epoch and declare a breakthrough. The reluctant handshake between Yasser Arafat and Yitzhak Rabin was seen through the hyped media coverage as a sign of a new dawn, the start of a new chapter that would enunciate a historic change and would convert a perpetual conflict to a new peaceful coexistence. Peace, however, proved elusive, and the negotiations that had begun in the spring of 1997 remained at a virtual standstill until 2000. Each party claimed that the other had failed to meet commitments under the agreements. Of course, by 2001, the entire Oslo process had been disavowed by Ariel Sharon. Periodic revisions of these agreements have become virtually routine since the process began. Each suspension led to a resumption, which in turn produced a new and more complex agreement. The result was a multiplication of the problems and inevitable new conflicts over interpretation.

The strategic imperatives for a negotiated settlement, largely on US terms and under US auspices, were created by the effective collapse of the Soviet Union and the destruction of Iraq. The Soviet Union was transformed from chief diplomatic backer and arms supplier to the Arab states to Russia, a US appendage in the "peace process." Iraq was reduced from the champion of strategic balance with Israel to an impotent nation preoccupied with the preservation of its sovereignty and territorial integrity. Thus, with deterrence having suddenly vanished at the global and regional levels, the United States was left without any serious opposition for the first time since Gamal Abdul-Nasser.

For the United States, this was the first "opportunity" to reshape the strategic landscape of the Middle East without the countervailing influence of the Soviet Union and in the absence of a single Arab power that professed responsibility for mutual deterrence vis-à-vis Israel. The Madrid conference (1991) was more in tune with Israel's bilateral (later to become unilateral) approach and rather far from the concept of a multilateral international conference with supervisory powers. For Israel, this was the first time since the peace treaty with Egypt in 1979 that a number of Arab states seemed ready to conclude peace with it outside the context of an international peace conference and in direct bilateral negotiations, which Israel had long insisted on. The Gulf War of 1991 had effectively demolished the official Arab consensus on Palestine, eroded Arab solidarity, and exposed regime insecurity in the Persian Gulf–Arabian Peninsula region. The Palestinians were left to fend for themselves, ending reluctantly at the 2000 summit at Camp David, for whose failure they were unreasonably held responsible.

The Fifth Phase, 2000–2005

The marginalization of the Palestinians during the previous phase is still going on and was in fact exacerbated by the advent of the extreme right wing in the politics of both Israel and the United States. A special relationship has been forged between the teams of Ariel Sharon and George W. Bush, supplementing the existing institutional relationship between the two countries, which goes back to the early 1970s. Bush and Sharon share an almost indistinguishable worldview based on the need to launch "antiterrorist" wars to dismantle oppositional structures, organized resistance elements, and anti-Western forces. This relationship culminated in the US invasion of Iraq in the spring of 2003 at the behest of Israel, in order to facilitate a settlement of the Arab-Israeli conflict on terms wholly agreeable to General Sharon. The United States has not only been fighting its own war of hegemony, but unlike in 1991, it has also been fighting Israel's war.

When the president's father invaded Iraq in 1991, his strategy did include crippling the capacity of Iraq plus destroying its infrastructure in pursuit of two goals: one American and the other Israeli. The American goal was to prevent Saddam Hussein from setting the pace in the Gulf in terms of the rate of oil production, pricing, and marketing. Bush I wanted to establish that such a highly strategic endeavor could never be conceded to an ambitious third-world leader and must remain entrusted to the United States after the demise of the Soviet Union. As for the Israeli objective, Bush I wanted to convince Tel Aviv that a crippled Iraq could not possibly threaten Israel; hence the time had come to head to the negotiating table to reach a long-overdue political settlement based on a watered-down version of the two-state solution.

Between Bush I and Bush II, however, Clinton and later the neoconservatives were able to steer Washington in totally different directions. Clinton had fallen prey to the Israeli Oslo trap—a diplomatic facade that enabled Israel to foreclose on a territorial settlement based on the two-state option. Then entered the neocons, who were enabled by September 11, 2001, to launch the "war on terror" against Afghanistan and Iraq and extend a version of it to Palestine and from there possibly to Syria, Lebanon, and maybe Iran. It was this victory of the neoconservatives and Christian Zionists in the United States that became instrumental in transforming the Palestine question from a nationalist struggle for self-determination to a war of terror against the Jewish state and US interests. The invasion of Iraq, which was vigorously promoted by Israel and its US allies, has sent most Arab regimes scurrying to protect their very existence, leaving the Palestinians to face unachievable US-Israeli demands for "reform," ending the resistance, and surrendering internationally guaranteed basic rights. In the aftermath of Arafat's passing, today's Palestinian leadership seems willing to meet Israel and the United States far more than "halfway."

During this phase, the Palestinians in the occupied territories lost their entire public and civilian infrastructure when Sharon's forces were unleashed against Palestinian cities and refugee camps in the spring of 2002. The Palestinian leadership was demonized and branded terrorist and an unqualified partner for peace negotiations. Arafat himself, whose organization had enjoyed greater international recognition than had the state of Israel during the late 1960s, the 1970s, and the 1980s, was held captive in his own Ramallah headquarters, having to beg for Israeli permission to secure visits by foreign dignitaries, to conduct visits of his own domain, or travel abroad for medical treatment. His first and last visit abroad was his one-way trip to a Paris hospital in November 2004. Since 2000, the

PLO/PA has been rendered helpless, having launched the Second Intifada and failed. The combination of Israeli determination to use whatever force necessary plus the shifting regional and global environment has robbed the Palestinians of whatever assets they built during the days of the revolution and the subsequent days of diplomacy bolstered by Arab resources.

The Palestinian Political Crisis

The sudden, unexpected agreement between Israel and the PLO and the signing of the Declaration of Principles by Arafat in 1993 plunged the PLO and the whole Palestinian people into a momentous political crisis. The shock and stunned disbelief that greeted announcement of the Oslo Accords quickly turned into four diversified reactions. It thus created new political fault lines related less to ideological considerations than to issues of substance and process.[6]

The first reaction was enthusiastic support from those who believed that the agreements were a historic breakthrough that would lead to Israeli military withdrawal from the occupied territories and Palestinian self-determination by the end of the interim period. The Palestinians who reacted this way were small in number: those in the PLO bureaucracy; most of the PLO functionaries and diplomats; and most of Arafat's supporters, allies, clients, and dependents.

The second tendency was conditional approval: Some Palestinians saw in the agreement essential progress, although they viewed it as far from satisfactory. Adherents of this view included important elements of the Palestine People's Party and wide sectors, perhaps a plurality, of the Palestinian people in the West Bank and the Gaza Strip. This group was most interested in ridding the occupied territories of the repressive Israeli troops and finding some socioeconomic relief and normality in the promised economic aid.

The third response, by those who had long supported peaceful resolution of the Israeli-Palestinian conflict, was to see the accord as thoroughly flawed and potentially fatal for Palestinian national aspirations and survival as a people. The adherents of this view were outraged at the enormous concessions of Palestinian rights that Arafat had made without consultation, public debate, or legitimate formal approval. Above all, this constituency was afraid that the Declaration of Principles, which disregarded international law and UN resolutions on Palestine, undermined the internationally recognized and codified rights of the Palestinian people.

Finally, the "rejectionists" saw the accords as high treason, capitulation to the enemy, and a violation of the Palestinian national consensus and principles of the national covenant or PLO charter and PNC resolutions. They believed the agreements would never lead to independence and statehood. This group included Hamas and al-Jihad al-Islami on the right and the PFLP, the DFLP, and a score of other minor parties on the left. This view also had significant support both inside the occupied territories and in the diaspora, especially in the refugee camps.

In 1994 Arafat returned to Gaza to set up the Palestinian Authority in accordance with the terms of the Oslo Accords. The jubilation of the Gaza people upon his entry was genuine, as they expressed the joy of freedom from harsh Israeli control. Through a large police force (agreed to in the accords), Arafat set about imposing order and his authority on a restive population, a chaotic situation, and the active resistance to the continuing Israeli occupation. Against his opponents, especially Hamas, Arafat utilized his tried-and-true political tactics of negotiation to build a consensus and, failing that, cooptation, infiltration, and force. These tactics failed to resolve the disappointment and discontent of the great majority of the Palestinians with the accords, Arafat, and the PLO. The political lines and divisions were drawn, and the crisis persisted.

The Institutional Crisis: The Representation Dilemma

The accords between the PLO and Israel triggered not only a political crisis but also an institutional one. It raised the question of the representativeness, legitimacy, and credibility of the PLO, its institutions, and its leadership. With the creation of the Palestinian Authority, with limited civil and police powers over the population centers of the West Bank and the Gaza Strip, the relationship between the PLO and the PA became an issue. Just as confounding for all Palestinians was the election of a Legislative Council in the autonomy areas in January 1996, which raised questions of institutional legitimacy and representativeness and of the council's relationship to the existing PNC. The PA and the council, legitimate as they may have been in the eyes of the West Bank and the Gaza Strip Palestinians (and much of the rest of the world), in no way could speak for or represent the diaspora communities. Although the Legislative Council may have become the institution that articulated the will and aspirations of 1.3 million voters in the West Bank and the Gaza Strip, who represented the 6 million diaspora Palestinians? Indeed, which institution was to authorize and ratify the "final status" agreements? Compounding this dilemma was the behavior of Arafat, who continued to hold on to the supreme official powers of both institutions: the PLO and the PA.

The 1996 PNC meeting in Gaza effectively eliminated the existing but moribund PLO Executive Committee, which was anchored in the long-held national consensus and composed of representatives of the major *feda'iyyin* groups and political parties and some independents. Arafat replaced it with a new Executive Committee made up of his allies and loyalists, a rubber-stamp group. In the context of the disarray of the opposition, Arafat reasserted his authority over the long-established and legitimate institution of the Palestinian diaspora. The PLO, its Executive Committee, and its legislative council, the PNC, became controlled institutions of the Arafat regime, the PA. Shortly after these developments, the PFLP, itself in disarray, formally withdrew from the PLO. The diaspora was without a collective or organized voice, perhaps for the first time since 1948.

The Disorganized Opposition

After the initial shock of the Oslo Accords and the installation of the PA, the secular leftist opposition began a more pragmatic approach to the new political realities. It sought to strengthen the West Bank and Gaza Strip institutions and to work for their democratization. However, dissension in relations between the "internal" (West Bank and Gaza) cadres and "external" (diaspora) leadership emerged. Within the diaspora communities, the leftists and nationalists carried on business as usual, despite the alarm in their rhetoric about the threatened destiny of the cause.

The only serious opposition to both the Declaration of Principles and the PA regime is Hamas and al-Jihad al-Islami, which are particularly strong in the Gaza Strip. The specific objectives of the secularists and Hamas differed substantially. Whereas the former wanted to reform and revive the PLO and its institutions and to eliminate the Arafat leadership, the latter has been ambivalent standing under the PLO umbrella, until its victory in the legislative election of January 2006. The Hamas attacks against the occupation troops and Israeli civilians inside Israel have been branded by most of the international media and those controlled by the PA regime as terrorist actions against peace. The Hamas power base in the Gaza Strip is quite strong and represents, after the years of PA rule, a continuing challenge to the regime's authority and legitimacy. But despite the political and violent confrontations in Gaza, the PA-Hamas conflict has settled into mutual accommodation. Although Hamas is the only serious threat to the PLO-Israeli arrangements, it remains to be seen whether its impact has stopped or modified the march of events.

Palestinian Opposition in Relation to the Abbas Regime and Sharon

The current PA-Israel inactive diplomacy under Abbas and Sharon's successors seems to rest on the assumption that Hamas must be neutralized. Sharon's demands that Abbas demolish "the infrastructure of terror" as a precondition for negotiations are clearly a euphemism for disarming and destroying Hamas and a tactic for forestalling serious negotiations. And yet, the current PA under Abbas lacks the reputation and Palestinian consensus to be a truly representative body that can reach an effective diplomatic settlement with a hard-line Israeli government. As was revealed in the municipal elections in May 2005, Hamas enjoys more popularity than Fateh not only in the Gaza Strip but also in the West Bank, as was demonstrated in the January 25, 2006, legislative elections. It has no reason to yield its power entirely to a corrupt and disorganized PA seen as incapable of gaining any concessions from Sharon. In the wake of Abbas's cancellation of legislative elections in the summer of 2005 in order to forestall a Hamas success, the prospects seemed dim for either an equitable political settlement or a stable and representative Palestinian polity in the West Bank and Gaza. Now that Hamas has crushed Fateh in the 2006 elections, the prospects for an early renewal of the suspended negotiations with Israel will be a distant dream, despite the wide expectation that Hamas would be willing to leave diplomacy to President Abbas in his capacity as head of the PLO, which signed the Oslo Accords.

In an interview with a local Gaza news agency, Mahmoud al-Zahar, a senior Hamas official in the Gaza Strip, said Hamas was not willing "to serve as a fig leaf" for PA control of Gaza following the Israeli disengagement of August 2005. Hamas, he said, would not give up its weapons and was liable to continue bombarding Israel with mortars and rockets from Gaza after the disengagement "in order to liberate the West Bank and Jerusalem."[7] And yet, after January 2006, Zahar said on an Arab television program on February 12, 2006, that "America is not our enemy, and she holds the key to peace in the Middle East."[8] Moreover, the Hamas leader in Damascus, Khaled Mish'al, declared at the same time that Hamas will respect all agreements signed by the Palestinian Authority.[9]

Even before the legislative elections, senior Hamas officials moved quickly to try to moderate the fears of civil war that Zahar's earlier interview aroused among the Palestinian public. Sheikh Hassan Yusif, a senior Hamas leader from Ramallah, for instance, published a statement saying that Zahar "exaggerated in describing [Hamas's] differences of opinion with the Palestinian Authority and Abu Mazen."[10] The agreement to hold legislative elections in 2006 has already made Yusuf's perspective on the issue the more plausible. It is the perspective that is more likely to prevail with Hamas now at the helm. Hamas in power is expected to demonstrate the healthy measure of realism compatible with the constraints of power.

Despite the display of such moderation on the part of central sections of Hamas, however, Sharon persisted between 2001 and 2005 in equating his long-standing demand for the eradication of the "infrastructure of terror" with barring Hamas from the ballot box in the legislative elections, but these elections were held on January 25, 2006, and Hamas scored a decisive victory. Seeking to appease his far-right constituency ahead of crucial internal Likud Party elections slated for the first week of October 2005, Sharon escalated his rhetoric against Hamas, with new demands that would result in the disenfranchisement of this group, which has steadily become an essential political player in the Palestinian arena. From New York, where he spoke before the UN General Assembly in September 2005, Sharon warned that Israel would prevent the organization of the elections if the PA failed to meet two conditions: disarming Hamas and getting it to abandon its anti-Zionist ideology.[11] "We will make every effort not to help the Palestinians. I don't think they can have elections without our help," Sharon said. The Israeli premier threatened to maintain roadblocks throughout the West Bank, making it difficult for Palestinians, voters and candidates alike, to move around.[12] Remi Kanazi, founder of the political website "poeticInjustice.net," explained the strategy this way: "Sharon is trying to politically de-legitimize Hamas by keeping it out of the elections, while demonizing Abu Mazen for not cracking down on 'terror' and using the excuse of having 'no partner for peace' as a ploy to further expand settlements, the Apartheid Wall, and to impose greater restrictions on Palestinian life in the West Bank, and East Jerusalem."[13] Sharon's successor, Ehud Olmert, has done just that.

Not only did Sharon escalate his rhetoric about Hamas, but he also ordered aerial attacks on the Gaza Strip six weeks after the evacuations of the settlements there in accordance with the so-called disengagement (September 22 and 23, 2005). These aerial attacks killed four Palestinians; injured many civilians, including children; and destroyed civilian infrastructure, including a school.[14] At the same time, a massive Israeli arrest campaign rounded up some two hundred key Palestinian figures running in the third round of municipal elections, scheduled for October 2005 in 105 local councils in the West Bank, as well as in the fourth round scheduled for December 2005. Several of those arrested were planning to run on Hamas's ticket for the Palestinian Legislative Council elections on January 25. Most prominent was Sheikh Hassan Yusif, the leader of the moderate wing of Hamas in the West Bank, and his two sons, as well as Mohammad Ghazal, a Hamas leader in the Nablus area.[15] In early October 2005 Israeli soldiers also arrested dozens of Islamist political activists, including a number of municipal council officials and Hakim Shalalda, the elected mayor of Sair in the Hebron district.[16] Among the arrested were also fifteen Islamist activists in al-Shuyukh, also in the Hebron district, and the seven elected members of the municipal council of the village of Shuqba in the northern West Bank, all of them banished to the Katziot detention camp in the Negev desert. Most of the detainees were given five to six months of "administrative detention," meaning they will be incarcerated without charge or trial for political reasons. At present, there are nine thousand to ten thousand Palestinian detainees in Israeli prisons.[17]

Palestinian political commentator Hani Masri described the Israeli strategy this way:

> Israel realizes that genuine democracy empowers the Palestinian people, and a strong Palestinian people are the last thing Israel would want to see. . . . Fateh would lose in the eyes of the Palestinian public if it participated in the next elections, irrespective of Hamas's participation. . . . Then two things would happen. First, the elections would be, more or less, a one horse race; and, second, Fateh would be viewed by a majority of Palestinians as conniving with Israel against Hamas and carrying out Israel's agenda.[18]

Masri added:

> Israel would be responsible for sabotaging the Palestinian elections. . . . The PA should cancel the polls and throw the ball in the court of the international community. . . . Everybody knows that without Hamas there will be no genuine elections. Similarly, we all realize that a Fateh-dominated parliament would perpetuate the status quo and deepen the crisis facing the entire Palestinian political system.[19]

The arrest of leaders of the moderate Hamas wing who were encouraging participation in the electoral process has increased Hamas's popularity and in turn weakened the Palestinian Authority, leading to the decisive victory of Hamas but leaving the Palestinian political system without a vital center. Thus the Palestinian political spectrum in the aftermath of Arafat's demise lacks a stable, dominant center and has a perplexed periphery and a confounded opposition. The late Edward W. Said described that spectrum in 1995 as consisting of "quite a large group of silent and disappointed Palestinians, a second group of PA loyalists, a third group waiting around to see if things will get better for them and, lastly, a group opposing the process and the PA who can't seem to get together."[20] This remains largely true today, except for Hamas's stunning victory.

Popular Disillusionment

The disaffected Palestinian majority has become disillusioned, demoralized, politically paralyzed, and unable to mount any significant action to change conditions in the occupied territories or internationally. This situation reflects the deepening crisis in the Palestinian national movement. This crisis has also produced widespread political cynicism and depoliticization and, among some, desperation and profound hopelessness. In the hapless slums of Gaza, many angry young men have volunteered for suicide missions against the Israelis. Many (including former Fateh militants) have rallied to the cause of Hamas not out of religious conviction as true believers but because Hamas has emerged as the only group to resist the truly unjust and disappointing turn of events. The Second Intifada of 2000 and Israel's harsh measures to subdue it produced the Al-Aqsa brigades under Fateh leadership, which have been mounting suicide missions of their own.

And yet in their bleak social, economic, and political situation, the Palestinian people have made efforts not only to redefine the nature of Palestinian national identity and consciousness but also to address emergent social issues. The slim hope of renewal among Palestinian progressives derives from the new contradictions that have arisen over the shape and structure of Palestinian society. "We are at a stage where the old Palestinian movement is dying, and a new movement is not created yet," said Mustafa Barghouti, who challenged Mahmoud Abbas for the Palestinian presidency in the presidential elections of January 2005, and who heads a "third-way" group called the Palestinian National Initiative, or *al-Mubadara* in Arabic.[21]

Expressive of this third-way movement are two political efforts in the West Bank and the Gaza Strip: the "democratic building movement" led by Haidar Abdul-Shafi and the Third Force led by a coalition of independents and certain party activists (from the PPP, PFLP, DFLP, and others).[22] Both movements see the Palestinian political terrain as monopolized by the PA on one side and the Islamists on the other. Both movements also believe that the majority of the Palestinian public—the proverbial silent majority— tends to be secular, democratic, supportive of the idea of Palestinian sovereignty, and unhappy with Arafat's unprincipled concessions to Israel and his role as Israel's enforcer. The movements are confident that this silent majority, including a multiplicity of NGOs, the intellectuals, the unions, women's groups, and other economic and cultural organizations in cities, villages, and refugee camps, will be responsive to the proposed alternative: a broad movement that would break the political monopoly of the PA regime and the religious opposition.[23] By the turn of the century, however, the third-way seed had failed to produce a plant.

Most of these social service and cultural organizations were the popular groups that mobilized the Palestinian people against Israeli occupation during the intifada. At that time they were morally, politically, and financially supported by legitimate PLO and Arab and international donors. Currently, however, they are constrained, undermined, and financially starved by Israel, the PA/PLO, and the formerly generous Arab and international donors.[24]

The varied efforts of intellectual activists and leftist politicians to produce a third-force coalition, under way since 1994, have not had enough unity or coherence to produce a genuine mass-based movement. In early 2006, their combined efforts generated two separate groupings, which, despite a unity of purpose and ideological affinity, remain torn by personal differences and narrowly construed interests. In fact, during the January 25, 2006, elections for the PLC, in which Hamas scored a smashing victory over Fateh (74 seats to 56 seats), the smaller secular leftist groups, which perceived themselves as a third force, could muster only 7 seats in the 132-seat council. The first grouping, called the Palestinian National Initiative (al-Mubadara), established on June 17, 2002, is rooted in the Communist Party and other nationalist secular factions. It is highly critical of the PA and its domestic as well as its foreign policy.[25] The second group, the Palestinian Democratic Coalition (al-Tajammu al-Democrati al-Filastini, or PDC), was formed on September 2, 2003, under a leadership whose roots are also in the Communist Party and other secular, nationalist/leftist groups. In fact, there is hardly any difference between the two contending coalitions' perspectives on the so-called third way. In an interview with the Hebrew publication *Mahsom,* Dr. Mustafa Barghouthi, the leader of the Initiative, offered the following rationale for the existence of that movement:

For the Israelis, the Palestinian people as a whole are divided between supporters of Fatah and supporters of Hamas, but everyone forgets—I hope not on
purpose—that there is a large third camp, made up of almost half of the Palestinian people. This camp participated in the presidential elections and received
more than 30 percent of the votes. And I represent this camp, which demands
clean politics, free of corruption, nepotism, and the pursuit of narrow personal
interests.[26]

In another speech in Bahrain (June 23, 2005) Barghouthi asserted that
the majority of Palestinians in the West Bank and Gaza prefer the third way
to the two major competing groups. He put it succinctly thus: "Over 50 per
cent do not want to have to choose between the existing authority or
Hamas fundamentalists. They want a third alternative—a true democratic
alternative."[27]

The second group hoping to lead the third force, the Palestinian Democratic Coalition (PDC), articulated the reasons for its existence in almost
identical terms, underlining

the need within the Palestinian political arena for filling the political vacuum
created by the hegemony of two main extremes on the country's political scene:
on the one hand, the mainstream pole, which is dominant in the Palestinian National Authority with all its components, and on the other, the religious political trend. Absent from the lead of the current Palestinian political movement is
the trend that has always represented a large and broad democratic Palestinian
public, whose various factions, organizations, social, democratic and union institutions have been, for the last fifty years, a main pillar in the Palestinian national struggle, and who has played a decisive role in leading and directing this
struggle towards achieving the national and liberation goals, with the aim of
bringing the day closer when full independence and freedom are achieved
within the framework of a national independent state, under the leadership of
the PLO as the sole legitimate representative of the Palestinian people.[28]

With regard to the so-called peace process, both movements—the PDC
and al-Mubadara—adhere to the two-state solution, and both are critical
of Sharon's so-called disengagement plan. Both were critical of Oslo, but
both participated in the January 2005 presidential elections held under the
terms of Oslo and the so-called peace process. Both are critical of the PA's
proclivity for making rapid concessions. In that regard, al-Mubadara's
Barghouthi said the following:

The PA accepted Israel's rules of the game there as well and fell into the trap that Sharon set for it, that works against the interests of both sides, against the two-state solution. Sharon replaced the road map with his own plan and succeeded in drawing in the Palestinian Authority, the US, Europe, and the entire international community—they all were drawn into a plan that turns Gaza into a big prison and inflicts a death blow on the establishment of an independent Palestinian state. . . . The independent Palestinian state is the solution, since we will not leave our land.[29]

Opposition in the Diaspora

Among the diaspora Palestinians, little in the form of opposition to the PA's policies existed beyond passive antagonism, disaffection, anger, and rhetoric. Diaspora Palestinians are politically rudderless and isolated in the different and disconnected communities. The demise of the PLO institutions all but eliminated the transnational connectedness of the refugee and other diaspora communities. Independent groups have attempted to start initiatives to organize the diaspora communities and give them a political voice. The most promising is an independent ad hoc grouping of Palestinian intellectuals and others from the United States, Jordan, Lebanon, Syria, and Egypt who have called for a gathering of diaspora Palestinians, the Conference of "Return" and Self-Determination, to reassert internationally recognized and codified Palestinian diaspora rights and to voice their interests and concerns.

Despite the exceedingly numerous meetings held between Palestinian and Israeli negotiators since the signing of the Oslo Accords, the input of the community of five to six million Palestinian refugees has never been sought. When the right of return began to resurface as a top item on the Palestinian people's agenda around 1999–2000, the role of the Palestine Authority was minimal. In fact, the right of return was placed on the public agenda not by the PA or by the PLO, but by various segments of Palestinian and global civil society.

The right of return, as defined in UN Resolution 194, became a rallying cry for grassroots organizing throughout the 1990s and especially after the failure of the Camp David meeting, which was, in effect, a failure of Oslo in July 2000.[30] An international solidarity movement, which had been working on behalf of the Palestinian cause since the early 1970s, and which had to step aside after the "historic handshake" of Arafat and Rabin in September 1993, came back after the failure of Oslo in 2000, hoping to succeed where governments had failed in ameliorating the plight of the Palestinians, particularly the refugees.

A major scholarly and political conference was organized by the Boston-based Trans-Arab Research Institute in April 2000 on the campus of Boston University School of Law. It was attended by more than a thousand people, some of whom met after the conference and established a refugees' advocacy group known throughout the world now as al-Awda (the Return).[31] Numerous conferences, workshops, and rallies were also held in and outside the Middle East between 2000 and 2005, bringing together community leaders, activists, and scholars to discuss various strategies for reviving the right of return.

The Call for Sanctions, Boycott, and Divestment: 2005

About 170 Palestinian civil society organizations representing the three integral parts of ten million Palestinians—Palestinian refugees, Palestinians under occupation, and Palestinian citizens of Israel—have issued a call for boycott, divestment, and sanctions until certain objectives are realized. The call was originally issued on the first anniversary of the advisory opinion by the International Court of Justice on Israel's wall under construction on occupied Palestinian land (July 9, 2005). It states, in part:

> We, representatives of Palestinian civil society, call upon international civil society organizations and people of conscience all over the world to impose broad boycotts and implement divestment initiatives against Israel similar to those applied to South Africa in the apartheid era. We appeal to you to pressure your respective states to impose embargoes and sanctions against Israel. We also invite conscientious Israelis to support this Call, for the sake of justice and genuine peace.[32]

The call states further that the nonviolent punitive measures should be maintained until Israel meets its obligation to recognize the Palestinian people's inalienable right to self-determination and fully complies with the precepts of international law by:

- Ending its occupation and colonization of all Arab lands and dismantling the Wall;
- Recognizing the fundamental rights of the Arab-Palestinian citizens of Israel to full equality; and

- Respecting, protecting and promoting the rights of Palestinian refugees to return to their homes and properties as stipulated in UN resolution 194.[33]

The call for boycotts, divestment, and sanctions is critical in the struggle of the Palestinians for several reasons:

- It sets out a Palestinian agenda for struggle—ending the occupation, and asserting the right of return and equal rights of Palestinians in Israel—in a way that a significant and diverse number of Palestinians can relate to.
- It is the closest thing the Palestinians as a people have as a national agenda—something that has been increasingly fragmented since Oslo.
- It is crucial for the Palestinians to have a clear national agenda as a guide, given the growing physical fragmentation not just in exile but now within the West Bank, where the majority of people do not interact across the eleven different enclaves in which they're trapped.

Palestinians desperately need a proactive agenda to counteract the political passivity, not to say complicity, of the Palestinian leadership and political parties.

The conglomeration of groups, individuals, NGOs, and parties constituting Palestinian society has the potential to create an oppositional movement if they choose to unify and to establish a coherent political movement. After all, their raison d'être (the right of return) no longer occupies a prominent place on the PA's active agenda, which knows that Israel and the United States would regard any PA insistence on this fundamental right as hostile. The concession by Abbas giving up the right of return could itself line up a huge opposition against Abbas should the right-of-return movement, as well as the fragmented third way, choose to seek greater unity.

Palestinian Destiny

The Palestinian people now face a number of serious historic challenges whose resolution will determine their destiny as a people and the fate of their country. These challenges are of two types: immediate dilemmas and longer-term predicaments. In the political sphere, the immediate dilemmas include finding a credible, rational, and legitimate political process for decisionmaking that will involve and satisfy most political groups and viewpoints, including the new ruling party Hamas and the radicals, as well as the mass of the "silent majority" in both the occupied territories and the diaspora. Central to the Palestinian political dilemma is the restructuring of the relationship between the PLO and the PA, in which the PA exists as the agency of self-rule in the West Bank and the Gaza Strip, while a reinvigorated, legitimate, and functioning PLO (or successor organization) and its institutions reemerge as the political framework and representative of *all* Palestinians, not just those in the occupied territories.

In the economic sphere, the dilemmas include planning development and investment in order to generate needed jobs; creating a legal and rational regulatory environment for the orderly conduct of economic and financial activity; and building the physical infrastructure. Above all, the Palestinians' leadership must describe a vision of the future society—humane, free, democratic, socially just, and based on the rule of law—that would inspire the people to translate that vision into specific political, economic, social, and legal institutions and practice. However, even assuming unprecedented goodwill and cooperation on the part of the Israelis, these are tremendously demanding challenges for the Palestinian people and the ineffectual or incapable PLO/PA, previously under Arafat and then under Mahmoud Abbas. Now that Hamas has replaced Fateh, which had been in power twelve years, the Palestinian Arabs will have to grapple with two principal challenges. The first is the possibility that funds from the European Union and United States will be interrupted unless Hamas meets humiliating conditions: amending its charter, which considers Palestine the territory lying between the Mediterranean Sea and the Jordan River, and recognizing Israel's right to exist. The fact that Hamas entered the electoral process in January 2006 is a major concession in itself, given that the PLC is an institution created by Oslo. Of course, the PA under Hamas could expect funding from the Arab states, but these states are not free to act without US approval, so that the Palestinians and Hamas would still have to make concessions.

The second challenge facing the Palestinians under Hamas could emerge if Hamas decides to translate its conservative social agenda into law. Palestinian society is highly secular and nationalistic and thus would be repelled by the injection of religion into politics and the legal system. It should be kept in mind, however, that the Palestinian majority that voted Hamas into office was not endorsing the Hamas social agenda; it was voting against the ruling party, Fateh, because of its corrupt governance, cronyism, and inability to deliver an independent Palestinian state.

The Gaza-based psychiatrist and activist Eyad al-Sarraj explained the situation this way:

> Palestine was hit with a powerful political tsunami which has the promise of dramatically changing the Middle East and beyond. This is the first time ever that an Islamic movement rises to power in the Arab world and in very peaceful and clean democratic elections. The religion contribution to victory was not more than 15%, the rest was a beating vote against the authorities and Fatah for their dismal record on all fronts and a defiant call against the Israeli occupation and American policies.[34]

After Arafat

Despite his largely ineffectual leadership, Arafat accomplished the extraordinary feat of injecting Palestine into the global public mind, but he was also a victim of US and Israeli rejectionist policies. He has been demonized and branded an unqualified partner for peace. By rights, his death should rob Israel and the Bush administration of the "no-partner" mantra that has long served to freeze the so-called peace process and block any serious advance toward peace. And yet, his death will not provide the often-stated cliché about the new opportunity for peace. After his Arafat card was taken away, Sharon immediately fell back on the terrorism excuse. The new leader, Mahmoud Abbas, who has already renounced armed action as a means of resisting the Israeli occupation, will have to contend with a reformulated Sharon alibi that will ensure diplomatic paralysis. Meanwhile, Hamas had agreed to a cease-fire with Israel in January 2005 and has continued to adhere to it. The cease-fire is part of Abbas's strategy of integrating Hamas into the Palestinian political system. Not only did that strategy succeed, but Hamas was able to topple Abbas's party and replace it at the helm.

Sharon, who was stricken by a series of strokes in January 2006 and lies in a coma, had been granted two commitments, in the aftermath of Arafat's death, from Bush and British prime minister Tony Blair, to maintain the status quo by keeping the so-called peace process scrupulously frozen. The significance of the disengagement plan is the freezing of the peace process. And yet, Abbas stated after his June 2005 visit to Washington that he had succeeded in swaying the US side to his position, a rather boastful, as well as groundless, claim:

> We succeeded, particularly during our visit to the United States, in obtaining the support of the US Administration for our position: (1) that the evacuation

of the Gaza Strip is part of a larger plan that will lead to the end of Israel's military occupation that began in 1967 and (2) it is unacceptable that the evacuation of the Gaza Strip be at the expense of the continued occupation and colonization of Jerusalem and the West Bank.[35]

Bush's proclaimed intention to spend "political capital" for the purpose of Palestinian statehood was rendered superfluous by his endorsement of Sharon's long-term interim phase (from 2005 to 2009). Additionally, Blair's visit to Ramallah in December 2004 produced the idea of an international conference that was held in March 2005, which Israel chose not attend, and in which final status issues were kept off the agenda. Indeed, as expected, the Palestinians were lectured again on how to stop "terrorism"—that is, armed resistance to the occupation—and how to pursue "democratic" governance. In fact, the so-called opportunity for peace in Palestine has never existed since the demise of Arafat.

In Arafat's absence, we cannot underestimate Israel's propensity to foment disorder and instigate chaos in the occupied territories in order to support its spurious claims that Palestinians cannot govern themselves, though, in fact, the Palestinians in the occupied territories have already demonstrated political maturity by ensuring a smooth transition from Arafat to Abbas in December 2004–January 2005 and then by holding successful legislative elections in January 2006 that were regarded widely throughout the world as fair, orderly, and democratic.

Arafat's absence from the scene will undoubtedly be felt by all sectors of Palestinian society, including his most ardent critics. It is not to be forgotten that the PLO, which he chaired throughout his adult life, remains the anchor of nearly six million dispersed Palestinians. And yet, the Palestinians in the West Bank and Gaza seem to be putting their eggs in Abbas's basket, whose own eggs are placed in rather empty US and Israeli baskets in the groundless hope that a measure of normality will eventually be restored. As Hamas transforms itself into a political party that has already made a decent showing in the municipal elections of May 2005 and won the January 2006 legislative elections, a possible alteration of the political landscape seems imminent. Fateh's hegemony in Palestinian political life is being undermined for the first time since 1965. Arafat's aloof successor, who lacks a base in Fateh and elsewhere, is not likely to reenergize a crumbling political organization, whose disparate groups are reluctant to take orders from the new chief, and whose crushing defeat in 2006 is likely to keep it paralyzed for years to come, unless it agrees to Hamas's request for a coalition government. At present, the Bush administration is trying to sabotage such a prospect in order to punish the Palestinians for having elected Hamas, a task that Olmert has already embarked upon.

Even in death, Arafat continued to epitomize the Palestinian tragedy: He had a funeral in stages, including a state funeral in Cairo, shielded from the masses, followed by a presumed "transitional" burial in the West Bank (prior to being buried, as he wished, in Jerusalem). This progression ironically recalls the infamous Oslo modality for dividing issues into an "interim phase" and a "final status." The remark by the Israeli Minister of Justice, Yosef Lapid, that "Jerusalem is a city where Jews bury their kings. It's not a city where we want to bury an Arab terrorist, a mass murderer," captures the essence of this conflict: The settler is deemed a native, the actual terrorist is deemed a king, and the actual mass murderer is deemed a man of peace.

Arafat's death reminded the world of the injustices and sufferings of his people. Whereas millions of European Jewish settlers enjoy full rights in Arafat's homeland, his right to be buried in the land of his birth was denied. Meanwhile, even in his absence, the issues that defined the conflict throughout most of his career have not changed. Unfortunately, but not surprisingly, the Middle East remains in turmoil largely due to the unenlightened policy the United States has pursued in the region. The Bush administration's embrace of the extremist agenda of the Sharon regime, as well as its military misadventures in Iraq, have only added to the turmoil in the region.

Needless to say, the right of the Palestinian people to establish an independent state in the West Bank and the Gaza Strip with East Jerusalem as its capital, the dismantling of all Israeli settlements on occupied Arab territories, and the confinement of Israel to its pre-1967 borders remain the key to peace in the Middle East—a fact that the United States has refused to confront since the beginning of the so-called peace process in 1969.

Long-Term Challenges

The longer-term challenges facing the Palestinians are even more daunting. They can be grouped into several categories:

- Determining the future status of the Palestinian diaspora communities, which comprise about 55–60 percent of the Palestinian people (the most important challenge in human terms).
- Rebuilding the integrity of the Palestinians as a people who must now construct and maintain a new transnational political and cultural identity, reconnecting and organizing the separated and iso-

lated diaspora communities, which have already been transformed by widely varied circumstances, experiences, and social histories.
- Redefining the relationship between Palestinians in the homeland and those in the diaspora.
- Redefining and remolding the character, structure, and goals of their transnational political organization.
- Planning for long-range economic development.
- Consolidating democracy and the rule of law in a socially just society.

Like many other critics before us, we believe that a careful reading of the Declaration of Principles, its annexes, and the derivative Cairo, Paris, and Oslo II Accords indicates clearly that they provide for only a limited Palestinian administration—for a fraction of the Palestinian people on a fraction of its land—and do not envision the building of an independent Palestinian state. Because these agreements envision neither political nor economic independence for the Palestinian territories, such independence is not possible through the current "peace process." We therefore believe that because of the imbalance of power between the politically weak Palestinian Authority and a strong Israel, the Declaration of Principles will *not* lead to Palestinian self-determination and independent statehood nor to the restoration of or compensation for the internationally codified rights of the Palestinian diaspora.

What, then, would be the character of the emergent Palestinian entity? Gone are the days of struggle for the revolutionary liberation of Palestine, during which the Palestinian intellectual and political leaders had the luxury of imagining a liberated, progressive, democratic, and socially just future Palestine. That dream and that option are now destroyed as much by the erstwhile Palestinian leadership of the PLO as by the enemies of Palestine and the Palestinian people—Israeli, American, European, and Arab. We believe that the so-called peace process, and specifically the implementation of the Oslo-inspired agreements, will create in the occupied territories—with the consent of the PA—a permanent reality of fragmented, subjugated, exploited, miniature Palestinian cantons under Israeli-style apartheid. Israel has already established this form of colonialism, in which it has invested enormous resources, economic interests, and political capital, and for which it has garnered international, Arab, and official PLO/PA support. Little, if any, evidence suggests that Israel will, in the "final status" negotiations, abandon such a privileged, profitable, and controlled colonial structure and grant independent Palestinian statehood or repatriation of the diaspora.[36] At best, Israel may in the future allow the PA to *call* this colonized, politically and economically controlled entity a "state" and grant it cosmetic symbols of statehood—a flag, a token army and perhaps a navy, an airline, and foreign missions—but this so-called state will be effectively devoid of sovereignty, freedom, self-determination, and dignity. It will be a client state, a dependent state, a symbolic state that will not satisfy the needs and aspirations of the Palestinian people.[37] Sharon's current plan, espoused now by his successor, Ehud Olmert, is still his 1981 plan, which envisaged the absorption of 58 percent of the West Bank, the rest of which will become an assortment of disconnected and fragmented Palestinian Bantustans in a reconfigured occupation. Sharon's successors in his newly established political party, Kadima, are not expected to deviate from the basic principles and the general precepts of Sharon's policies, despite the touting of Kadima as a "centrist" party.[38] There will be no compromising when it comes to the issue of total Israeli sovereignty in the area lying between the Jordan River and the Mediterranean Sea. Sharon's successors in Kadima might even extend their "generosity" to giving up 75 percent of the West Bank as long as they are able to annex 90 percent of the many West Bank–Jerusalem settlements, described by George Bush as "facts on the ground." In that case, the Jordan option might be resurrected by those who were once proponents of the slogan "Jordan is Palestine."

If in this analysis of the emergent Palestinian entity no direct mention is made of the Palestinians of the diaspora, it is because they have not only been disenfranchised by the PA but also been largely abandoned to their own destiny by their leaders and the international community.

In the accords that may emerge from the final status negotiations, if they resume, the best that can be expected is that a small symbolic group of Palestinian refugees may be allowed to exercise their right of return, while the majority will be given symbolic compensation and "naturalized"—a process labeled *tawtin* in Arabic—as residents in some other Arab country. There they will become second-class citizens (if they are lucky) or subjugated, disadvantaged, and exploitable minorities (if they are not). They could well become another group of *bedoon*s (literally, "without," as they are a Kuwaiti community of the undocumented), like those who are official Kuwaiti residents but who have no citizenship and few or no civil rights. Any reparations, symbolic or otherwise, from Israel are likely be folded into international aid and paid directly to the PLO/PA. The political result of the *tawtin* in Arab and other countries of the Palestinian diaspora communities will be "Armenianization," not the Kurdistanization in several neighboring states, as some intellectuals have suggested. For, except in Jordan, the Palestinian exiles will not have the critical population and geographic mass, as the Kurds have in Turkey and Iraq, that would give them some political leverage in their host countries. Instead, I believe, they are more likely to become fearful minorities, as the Armenian refugee communities were in the countries they took refuge in after World War I.

In debates taking place inside the occupied territories among some Palestinian intellectuals about the future of the occupied Palestinian territories, two possible scenarios are being proposed: the Bantustan plan or the binational option. The first scenario (the Bantustan plan) is that of two peoples (Israeli and Palestinian) living under *one*—Israeli—sovereignty. Under this plan the Palestinians of the West Bank and the Gaza Strip would—unlike the so-called Israeli Arabs (the Palestinian citizens of Israel)—have only civil autonomy, but like them, they would become controlled, economically disadvantaged residents of greater Israel. They could commute to work in lesser Israeli jobs but return at night to townshiplike communities of their own. Even the right-wing Likud is not averse to this possible outcome.

In the binational option, Israel-Palestine would presumably become a democratic and not just a Jewish state, where the two ethnic nationalities would retain their cultural identity and eventually coexist in harmony in an integrated economy and single sovereignty. This option seems unlikely to us in the short run, much as it may superficially resemble the "secular democratic state" imagined by the Palestinian revolutionaries of the 1960s. It may, however, emerge in the long run, as the only viable alternative to perpetual conflict.

Since about 1993, Israel and the United States have pursued policies that have dealt a crippling blow to the two-state solution, while continuing to pay lip service to the concept of an independent Palestinian state. One wonders whether they failed to realize that those policies have unwittingly paved the way to a binational solution and a single pluralistic state for Arabs and Jews in what the former call historical Palestine and the latter call Eretz Israel. The Oslo process sealed the fate of Palestinian statehood, ironically leaving the vision of a single state for two equal communities as the only dignified solution.

On the Palestinian side, the late Edward Said emerged as one of the key champions of the idea of a single state. He wrote the following in 1997: "The lives of Israelis and Palestinians are hopelessly intertwined. There is no way to separate them. You can have fantasy and denial, or put people in ghettos. But in reality there is a common history. So we have to find a way to live together."[39] In an interview with David Barsamian, Said again endorsed secular binationalism, not only as a desirable outcome but also as a necessary reality: "It is unlikely that a place like Israel—which is surrounded on all sides by Arab states—is going to be able to maintain what, in effect, is a system of apartheid for Palestinians."[40]

Other Palestinian intellectuals in the occupied territories, inside Israel, and in exile, including Nadim Rouhana, Adel Ghanem, Azmi Bishara, and Adel Samara, joined the call for a single state. Azmi Bishara, an Arab member of the Israeli Knesset, considers Israel a de facto binational state, although without equality for one of the two nationalities: the Arab one. For Bishara, the struggle for equality and group rights is inextricably linked to the struggle for democratic binationalism: "Individual equality in Israel cannot be achieved without having group rights. It is impossible for the Arabs in Israel to fuse with Jewish Israelis into a single nation as happened in France and the US, because this invalidates the essence of Israel's structure."[41]

Other Palestinian intellectuals like Nadim Rouhana perceived the connection between Oslo's failure and the eventuality of a single binational state in all of historical Palestine:

> The failure of the Oslo process to yield a viable Palestinian state could lead to the convergence of interests of all segments of the Palestinian people in calling for a unitary state in Palestine. Indeed the most likely response to the fading hopes for a Palestinian state will be not the acceptance of a Bantustan system of government in the West Bank, but the development of a mainstream political program that redefines the Israeli-Palestinian conflict from one over territory and sovereignty to a conflict over power sharing and equality of Palestinian and Jew in historic Palestine in the form of a binational or secular state—the same issue that the Palestinians in Israel are struggling for.[42]

On the Israeli side, Meron Benvenisti, a former deputy mayor of Jerusalem, made the link between Sharon's "disengagement plan" and Bush's declarations, on the one hand, and an eventual binational state, on the other:

> And Ariel Sharon—crowned by victory and convinced that he has unveiled a daring new initiative which will foil all schemes—will be surprised to discover that in Washington he was pushed into embracing an accelerated process of founding the State of Israel as a bi-national state based on Apartheid. . . . The Bantustan plan is now in swing; and the scenario which Sharon so badly wanted to avoid will unfold.[43]

Israeli academic and the son of Holocaust survivors Haim Bresheeth views the single state as the only solution now that Israel has made sure that the two-state solution is off the agenda:

> What [Noam] Chomsky is suggesting [the two-state solution] is too little, too late. Not because Palestine rejected this solution, but because Israel did. The Palestinians are not turkeys, and will not vote for Christmas, and the idea that they can be forced into the 16 ghettoes is ludicrous. But so also is the idea that Israel will go back to the 1967 borders willingly. The international community bears full responsibility for failing to act when it could. While it is not clear when such an advanced [binational] solution of Jews and Arabs living together may materialize, it seems that it is the only one left, as Israel has made damned sure no other solution is allowed even half a chance. The question seems to be: Must we have a bloody showdown, massacres and ethnic cleansing before it emerges? That is a question international society can ill-afford to ignore.[44]

Another Israeli, Daniel Gavron, who has been a Zionist for most of his life, wrote that the only solution that could preserve the Jewish state—partition into two states, Israel and Palestine—is no longer tenable. If Israeli Jews now wish to secure their long-term future in the region, he explained, they must agree to abdicate Jewish sovereignty and move swiftly, while the balance of power still tilts in their favor, to a multiethnic democracy:

> After 55 years of Jewish sovereignty, the time has come to dissolve the Jewish state and establish, in its place, a single Israeli-Palestinian state. . . . Having reached the conclusion that the territory between the Mediterranean and the Jordan River must be shared, but cannot be sensibly partitioned . . . we are left with only one alternative: Israeli-Palestinian coexistence in one nation.[45]

Haifa University's historian Ilan Pappé sees no alternative to the secular democratic state in all of pre-1948 Palestine: "In the short term, what people want to do is separate. But it never delivers the goods. All that separation has delivered is more violence. . . . I don't think even a bi-national state is the last phase. I think it is a democratic, secular state."[46]

For the Palestinians, a single binational state is not a new idea, having been as their first choice for liberation after the 1967 occupation, when they called for a democratic secular state. That idea, however, which was linked to armed struggle, was summarily dismissed before it had even been debated, in order to accommodate the Arab states' preference for a diplomatic struggle.

Unlike the South Africans, who also espoused armed struggle but continued to cling to the goal of a unified state, the Palestinian leadership dropped the unitary approach and embraced a two-state solution. In retrospect, this might have been a most harmful decision. That goal of a separate, independent existence remained intact even when the Palestinian struggle *inside* the occupied territories finally shifted toward the political dimension during the 1970s and right through the intifada of the 1980s and early 1990s, which focused on empowerment and socioeconomic progress. Thus, while Palestinian civil society *inside* the occupied territories focused on civil disobedience, trying to make the occupation not only undesirable but impractical, the PLO leadership *outside* put all its eggs in the Arab diplomatic basket, which is the US basket that brought disaster to the Palestinian cause. That was the beginning of the end of the two-state solution, perhaps leaving the unitary approach as the only alternative to apartheid. The South African veteran journalist Allister Sparks recently recommended the South African model as the ideal and practical way out of the Palestinian-Israeli conflict:

> To appreciate what an exceptional achievement this has been, imagine this model for the Israeli-Palestinian conflict. I don't mean the two-state solution of the Oslo accords or the Bush administration's so-called "roadmap," for those are segregationist, apartheid solutions (like those used in divided Cyprus and the ethnically segregated former Yugoslavia). No, a South African solution in the Middle East would consolidate Israel, the Gaza Strip and the West Bank into one country ruled by an elected majority, which soon would be Palestinian. The Jewish people would live as a minority group, albeit an economically dominant one. If that strikes anyone as improbable, then let it be the measure of judging South Africa's achievement—one that has turned this country, so recently the racist polecat of the world, into a paradigm for a world ravened by racial, ethnic and religious strife.[47]

Any realistic alternative to Oslo and the Sharon-Bush understanding must guarantee the removal of constraints inflicted on the Palestinians in three spheres: those under the 1967 occupation, the Palestinians in Israel proper, and those of the diaspora. That guarantee would require a determined, systematic, and protracted struggle, combining the three segments of the Palestinian people with Israeli Jews who wish to be neither master of another people, nor privileged in an apartheid system, nor colonial settlers denying the existence of the indigenous natives of the land, nor wishing those natives' disappearance.

The goal of the struggle would have to be equal protection under the law in any such unified state: the illegality of any discrimination by the law, the end of segregation, and its social, economic, and legal removal. Equality for every single human being in Palestine-Israel would be the goal of the new struggle. This kind of struggle may sound unrealistic, and the goal idealistic or utopian, but it certainly is not less realistic than Oslo's open-ended formula, which has already been relegated to the dustbin of history. The process that began in Oslo, now stuck at the Road Map and derailed by Sharon's disengagement plan, can reach nowhere because the current fundamental nature of the Israeli state precludes any equal coexistence with the Palestinian people.

In the final analysis, the Palestinians ask whether Israel, as a regional superpower, can actually prosper as an isolated Western outpost in the region. And although any move toward cooperation, let alone integration, seems unthinkable at present, Israel's dilemma will persist as long as its exclusionist stance continues to undermine the purported moralistic principles upon which this state was established. The question of whether Zionism is a movement of national plundering or a movement of a persecuted people, acting on a human ethic, and seeking compromise and peace would have to be broached openly and unapologetically.

Only when this kind of critique is broadened beyond the academy to include the mainstream and penetrate the consciousness of the average Jewish Israeli will the so-called peace process begin to assume truly peaceful dimensions. Only when the Palestinians decide to rediscover their democratic secular framework of the 1960s and transform it from a slogan to a viable program that can be publicly debated and adapted to present realities will the hope for a real peace be rekindled. No matter by what name we refer to this entity—a binational state, a federal system, a cantonal arrangement on the Swiss model—the common denominators would still be equal rights, equal citizenship, plurality, and coexistence.

Alternative Solutions

Confederation with Jordan

Another scenario being debated is more oriented to the short term. The Palestinian elections may, perhaps after several rounds, eventually produce an increasingly autonomous Palestinian Council—independent from both Israel and the Arafat-type regime—that will establish a new model of intra-Palestinian politics and will draw the West Bank and the Gaza Strip away from Israel's octopus-like grip toward a confederation with Jordan, or a Jordanian-Israeli condominium. Of course, this option is the old Jordanian option long preferred by earlier Israeli governments and US administrations. Jordanian dominion over the occupied territories is indeed possible in the medium to long run, especially as the PA is unable to cope with the domestic dilemmas of the West Bank and the Gaza Strip and squanders much of the foreign aid upon which it so desperately depends. Its record of diplomacy, economic policy and practice, and programs of social service to its people do not augur well for the future. It may therefore waste all of its political and economic capital and succumb to either Jordanian control or dual Jordanian-Israeli condominium. Should this happen, the economically subordinated Palestinian territories are likely to remain poor and exploitable areas of a confederation.

Fragmented Bantustans

More likely in our judgment is a Palestinian future of fragmented cantons in parts of the original homeland, with the people enjoying fewer political and civil rights than the Palestinians of Israel or those of Jordan. This fragmentation is likely to be coupled with the Armenianization of the diaspora communities. If this occurs, it will be a tragic outcome for a people that has struggled and sacrificed so much for so long. To rephrase a famous statement made by Prime Minister Winston Churchill at the conclusion of the Battle of Britain, never have so many sacrificed so much for so little. The short and the medium terms are unbelievably bleak for Palestine and the Palestinians.

However, despite the capitulation of the PA and the imposition of a new Israeli order over Palestine, the Palestinians, who have consistently rejected defeat and shown themselves to be resilient, will continue the struggle in other forms in the emergent Middle Eastern realities. The Palestinians' destiny, in the final analysis, is in their own hands. They may need a third intifada, now not only against the repackaged Israeli occupation but also against the PA, "because not only are we [Palestinians] still fighting the Israeli occupation, but in fact we are fighting an enforcer of the occupation—namely the PLO—which has the distinction of being the first national liberation movement in history to keep an occupying power in place."[48]

In our judgment, it would be a mistake to assume that once established, the new Palestinian order under Israeli dominion would remain unchanged. The region as well as the world is in profound transformation. The global, regional, and local balances of power may well shift to give the Palestinians new and different opportunities to pursue their struggle for an equitable, just, and lasting peace with the Israelis. Finally, we believe that the failure to establish a just peace through which the Palestinian people will restore their inalienable rights will lead to the unraveling of the Declaration of Principles and its derivative agreements and to future conflict in the Middle East. It is not the end of Palestinian history.

Notes

1. See N. Aruri, *The Obstruction of Peace: The U.S., Israel and the Palestinians* (Monroe, ME: Common Courage Press, 1995). See also N. Chomsky, *World Orders: Old and New* (New York: Columbia University Press, 1994), and N. G. Finkelstein, *Image and Reality of the Israel-Palestine Conflict* (London: Verso, 1995).

2. E. W. Said, *The Politics of Dispossession: The Struggle for Palestinian Self-Determination, 1969–1994* (New York: Pantheon, 1994): xxvi. See a study of earlier Israeli rejectionism in E. Berger, *Peace for Palestine: First Lost Opportunity* (Gainesville: University Press of Florida, 1993).

3. The Israeli attack on the PLO was largely to blunt its "peace offensive." See the analysis of Finkelstein, *Image and Reality*, especially Ch. 6.

4. Z. Abu-Amr, *Islamic Fundamentalism in the West Bank and Gaza* (Bloomington: Indiana University Press, 1994).

5. Former secretary of state Henry Kissinger reported that when he met Arafat, he asked him "why the Israelis should trust him." "Because the Saudis have cut us off," he replied, "the Jordanians are trying to weaken us and the Syrians are seeking to dominate us"; H. Kissinger, "Retooling the Process for Peace," *Washington Post* (July 1, 1996).

6. M. Rabbani, "'Gaza-Jericho First': The Palestinian Debate," *Middle East International* (September 24, 1993): 16–17.

7. Arnon Regular, *Ha'aretz* correspondent; http://www.haaretzdaily.com/hasen/spages/596871.html.

8. Eyad al-Sarraj, "On Hamas Victory," sent to the author by email on February 12, 2006, heba@gcmhp.net.

9. Ibid.

10. Arnon Regular, *Ha'aretz*.

11. Khaled Amayreh, "Sharon's Democratic Nightmare," *Al-Ahram Weekly* 761 (September 22–28, 2005).

12. Ibid.

13. Remi Kanazi, "Shattering Democracy: Sharon's Plan for Palestine," *Media Monitor Networm* (September 28, 2005). Available online at http://usa.mediamonitors.net/content/view/full/19841.

14. http://www.palestinemonitor.org/nueva_web/updates_news/updates/4_assassinate, d_israel.htm.

15. Ibid.

16. Khalid Amayreh, "Israel Accused of Skewing Elections," Aljazeera.net, October 3, 2005.

17. Ibid.

18. Ibid.

19. Ibid.

20. E. W. Said, "Symbols Versus Substance: A Year After the Declaration of Principles," *Journal of Palestine Studies* 24 (Winter 1995): 61.

21. Cited in D. Connell, "Palestine on the Edge, Crisis in the National Movement," *Middle East Report* 194–195 (May-June–July-August 1995): 7.

22. "Founding Declaration of the Palestinian Democratic Building Movement" was distributed at a talk by Abdul-Shafi at the Center for Policy Analysis on Palestine, Washington, DC, June 1995. An unofficial statement of the Third Force was distributed by fax in July 1995.

23. N. H. Aruri, "The Serious Challenges Facing Palestinian Society," *Middle East International* (August 25, 1995): 17. See also T. Aruri, "Some Features of Palestinian Political Life and Its Future," paper presented at a workshop, Muwaten Institute, Jerusalem, August 8, 1995, and T. Aruri, "Some Expected Political Consequences from Establishing an Elected Palestinian Council," paper presented at a workshop of the Palestinian People's Party, August 18, 1995.

24. "A Story of Manipulation, Containing the Palestinian NGOs," *Issues: Perspectives on Middle East and World Affairs* 5 (June 1996): 2–3, 14.

25. http://www.almubadara.org.

26. *Mahsom* (June 28, 2005). Also available online at http://www.mahsom.com/article.php?id=1147. Translated from the Hebrew by Daniel Breslau.

27. http://www.almubadara.org/news/23_06_2003en.htm.

28. Statement issued by the Palestinian Democratic Coalition, Ramallah, September 2, 2003.

29. *Mahsom* (June 28, 2005); see Note 24.

30. See Naseer Aruri, *Dishonest Broker* (Cambridge, MA: South End Press, 2003), Chapter 10, Note 2.

31. The proceedings of the conference were published in book form: Naseer Aruri (ed.), *Palestinian Refugees: The Right of Return* (London: Pluto Press, 2001).

32. Text online at http://www.badil.org/Publications/Press/2005/press390–05.htm.

33. Ibid.

34. Al-Sarraj, "On Hamas Victory."

35. A speech by Palestinian president Mahmoud Abbas to the Palestinian people on July 16, 2005, online at http://www.americantaskforce.org/abbas_speech.htm.

36. See the Likud-Labor agreement on permanent status: G. Aronson, "The Beilin-Eitan Agreement on Permanent Status and Its True Antecedents," *Report on Israeli Settlement in the Occupied Territories* 7 (March-April 1997): 1, 7; see also Gary Sussman, "Ariel Sharon and the Jordan Option," *Merip* (March 2005), online at http://www.kibush.co.il/downloads/13.3.2005%20Gary%20Sussman%20Ariel%20Sharon%20and%20the%20Jordan%20Option.doc.

37. See the compelling analogy to the creation of Transkei in apartheid South Africa made by N. G. Finkelstein, "Whither the 'Peace Process'?" unpublished paper presented at Georgetown and American Universities, Washington, DC, April 24 and 25, 1996, pp. 14–17.

38. Following the November 2005 elections of the Israeli Labor Party, in which the Moroccan-born labor unionist leader Amir Peretz was elected, Sharon departed from his Likud Party and established Kadima. In anticipation of the March 2006 general elections, his intentions were to engineer a three-way competition: Peretz as the candidate of the "left," Netanyahu leading the right, and himself in the "center."

39. "A Single State in Palestine," *Christian Science Monitor* (May 27, 1997).

40. David Barsamian, "Edward W. Said," *The Progressive* (April 1999): 35.

41. Azmi Bishara (Interview), "Equal Rights for Arabs in the Jewish State: A Goal Unrealizable," MERIP Press, Washington Information, Note 12, December 14, 1999.

42. Nadim Rouhana, "The Test of Equal Citizenship," *Harvard International Review* 20 (1998): 78.

43. Meron Benvinisti, "Founding a Bi-National State," *Ha'aretz* (April 22, 2004).

44. Haim Bresheeth, "Two States, Too Little, Too Late," *Al-Ahram Weekly* (March 14, 2004). Available online at http://weekly.ahram.org.eg/2004/681/op61.htm.

45. Peter Hirschberg, "One State Awakening," *Ha'aretz* (December 12, 2003). Available online at http://www.haaretz.com/hasen/spages/370673.html.

46. http://www.washingtonpost.com/wp-dyn/articles/A36478–2004Jul8.html.

47. Allister Sparks, "What South Africa Can Teach the Middle East," *Washington Post* (April 18, 2004): B2. Available online at http://www.washingtonpost.com/wp-dyn/articles/A19462–2004Apr17.html.

48. Said, "Symbols Versus Substance," 62.

APPENDIX 1

UN Security Council Resolution 242, November 22, 1967

The Security Council,

Expressing its continuing concern with the grave situation in the Middle East;

Emphasizing the inadmissibility of the acquisition of territory by war and the need to work for a just and lasting peace in which every State in the area can live in security;

Emphasizing further that all Member states in their acceptance of the Charter of the United Nations have undertaken a commitment to act in accordance with Article 2 of the Charter;

1. Affirms that the fulfillment of Charter principles requires the establishment of a just and lasting peace in the Middle East which should include the application of both the following principles:

(i) Withdrawal of Israeli armed forces from territories occupied in the recent conflict;

(ii) Termination of all claims or states of belligerency and respect for and acknowledgment of the sovereignty, territorial integrity and political independence of every State in the area and their right to live in peace within secure and recognized boundaries free from threats or acts of force;

2. Affirms further the necessity

a) for guaranteeing freedom of navigation through international waterways in the area;

b) for achieving a just settlement of the refugee problem;

   c) for guaranteeing the territorial inviolability and political independence of every State in the area, through measures including the establishment of demilitarized zones;

3. Requests the Secretary-General to designate a Special Representative to proceed to the Middle East to establish and maintain contacts with the States concerned in order to promote agreement and assist efforts to achieve a peaceful and accepted settlement in accordance with the provisions and principles in this resolution;

4. Requests the Secretary-General to report to the Security Council on the progress of the efforts of the Special Representative as soon as possible.

APPENDIX 2

The Balfour Declaration

November 2, 1917

Dear Lord Rothschild,

I have much pleasure in conveying to you, on behalf of His Majesty's Government, the following declaration of sympathy with Jewish Zionist aspirations which has been submitted to and approved by the Cabinet.

"His Majesty's Government view with favour the establishment in Palestine of a national home for the Jewish people, and will use their best endeavours to facilitate the achievement of this object, it being clearly understood that nothing shall be done which may prejudice the civil and religious rights of existing non-Jewish communities in Palestine, or in any other country."

I should be grateful if you would bring the declaration to the knowledge of the Zionist Federation.

Yours sincerely,
Arthur James Balfour

APPENDIX 3

McMahon-Hussein Correspondence, 1915–1916

Ten letters passed between Sir Henry McMahon, British high commissioner in Cairo, and Sharif Hussein of Mecca from July 1915 to March 1916. Hussein offered Arab help in the war against the Turks if Britain would support the principle of an independent Arab state. The most important letter is that of October 24, 1915, from McMahon to Hussein, from which the following is excerpted:

> I regret that you should have received from my last letter the impression that I regarded the question of limits and boundaries with coldness and hesitation; such was not the case, but it appeared to me that the time had not yet come when that question could be discussed in a conclusive manner. I have realized, however, from your last letter that you regard this question as one of vital and urgent importance. I have, therefore, lost no time in informing the Government of Great Britain of the contents of your letter, and it is with great pleasure that I communicate to you on their behalf the following statement, which I am confident you will receive with satisfaction.
>
> The two districts of Mersina and Alexandretta and portions of Syria lying to the west of the districts of Damascus, Homs, Hama and Aleppo cannot be said to be purely Arab, and should be excluded from the limits demanded.
>
> With the above modifications, and without prejudice to our existing treaties with Arab chiefs, we accept those limits.
>
> As for those regions lying within those frontiers wherein Great Britain is free to act without detriment to the interest of her ally, France, I am empowered in the name of the Government of Great Britain to give the following assurances and make the following reply to your letter:

(1) Subject to the above modifications, Great Britain is prepared to recognize and support the independence of the Arabs in all the regions within the limits demanded by the Sherif of Mecca.

(2) Great Britain will guarantee the Holy Places against all external aggression and will recognize their inviolability.

(3) When the situation admits, Great Britain will give to the Arabs her advice and will assist them to establish what may appear to be the most suitable forms of government in those various territories.

(4) On the other hand, it is understood that the Arabs have decided to seek the advice and guidance of Great Britain only, and that such European advisers and officials as may be required for the formation of a sound form of administration will be British.

(5) With regard to the vilayets of Baghdad and Basra, the Arabs will recognize that the established position and interests of Great Britain necessitate special administrative arrangements in order to secure these territories from foreign aggression, to promote the welfare of the local populations and to safeguard our mutual economic interests.

I am convinced that this declaration will assure you beyond all possible doubt of the sympathy of Great Britain towards the aspirations of her friends the Arabs and will result in a firm and lasting alliance, the immediate results of which will be the expulsion of the Turks from the Arab countries and the freeing of the Arab peoples from the Turkish yoke, which for so many years has pressed heavily upon them. . . .

APPENDIX 4

Excerpts from the Report of the King-Crane Commission, August 18, 1919

Perhaps for fear of being confronted by recommendations from their own delegates that might conflict with official policy, both Britain and France declined to nominate members to a commission the Allies created to inform them of the wishes of the Arabs in Palestine. President Wilson appointed two Americans, Henry King and Charles Crane, whose subsequent findings were suppressed and kept secret for three years. Their report was not published until 1922.

If the strict terms of the Balfour Statement are adhered to—favoring "the establishment in Palestine of a national home for the Jewish people, it being clearly understood that nothing shall be done which may prejudice the civil and religious rights of existing non-Jewish communities in Palestine"—it can hardly be doubted that the extreme Zionist program must be greatly modified. For "a national home for the Jewish people" is not equivalent to making Palestine into a Jewish State; nor can the erection of such a Jewish State be accomplished without the gravest trespass upon "civil and religious rights of existing non-Jewish communities in Palestine." The fact came out repeatedly in the Commission's conference with Jewish representatives, that the Zionists looked forward to a practically complete dispossession of the present non-Jewish inhabitants of Palestine, by various forms of purchase.

In his address of July 4, 1918, President Wilson laid down the following principle as one of the four great "ends for which the associated people of the world were fighting": "The settlement of every question, whether of territory, of sovereignty, of economic arrangement, or of political relationship upon the basis of the free acceptance of that settlement by the people immediately concerned, and not upon the basis of the material interest or advantage of any other nation or people which may desire a different settlement for the sake of its own exterior influence or mastery." If these principles are to rule, and so the wishes of Palestine's population are to be decisive as to what is to be done with Palestine—nearly nine-tenths of the whole—are emphatically against the entire Zionist program. The tables show that there was no one thing upon which the population of Palestine were more agreed than upon this. To subject a people so minded to unlimited Jewish immigration, and to steady financial and social pressure to surrender the land, would be a gross violation of the principle just quoted, and of the people's rights, though it kept within the forms of law.

No British officer consulted by the Commissioners believed that the Zionist program could be carried out except by the force of arms. That of itself is evidence of a strong sense of the injustice of the Zionist program, on the part of the non-Jewish populations of Palestine and Syria. Decisions, requiring armies to carry out, are sometimes necessary, but they are surely not gratuitously to be taken in the interests of a serious injustice. For the initial claim, often submitted by Zionist representatives, that they have a "right" to Palestine, based on an occupation of two thousand years ago, can hardly be seriously considered.

APPENDIX 5

UN General Assembly Resolution 181 on the Future Government of Palestine, November 29, 1947 (The Partition Plan)

The General Assembly,

Having met in special session at the request of the mandatory Power to constitute and instruct a special committee to prepare for the consideration of the question of the future government of Palestine at the second regular session;

Having constituted a Special Committee and instructed it to investigate all questions and issues relevant to the problem of Palestine, and to prepare proposals for the solution of the problem, and

Having received and examined the report of the Special Committee (document A/364) including a number of unanimous recommendations and a plan of partition with economic union approved by the majority of a Special Committee;

Considers that the present situation in Palestine is one which is likely to impair the general welfare and friendly relations among nations;

Takes note of the declaration by the mandatory Power that it plans to complete its evacuation of Palestine by 1 August 1948;

Recommends to the United Kingdom, as the mandatory Power for Palestine, and to all other Members of the United Nations the adoption and implementation, with regard to the future government of Palestine, of the Plan of Partition with Economic Union set out below;

Request that:

a) The Security Council take the necessary measures as provided for in the plan for its implementation;

b) The Security Council consider, if circumstances during the transitional period require such consideration, whether the situation in Palestine constitutes a threat to the peace. If it decides that such a threat exists, and in order to maintain international peace and security, the Security Council should supplement the authorization of the General Assembly by taking measures, under Articles 39 and 41 of the Charter, to empower the United Nations Commission, as provided in this resolution, to exercise in Palestine the functions which are assigned to it by this resolution;

c) The Security Council determine as a threat to the peace, breach of the peace or act of aggression, in accordance with Article 39 of the Charter, any attempt to alter by force the settlement envisaged by this resolution;

d) The Trusteeship Council be informed of the responsibilities envisaged for it in this plan;

Calls upon the inhabitants of Palestine to take such steps as may be necessary on their part to put this plan into effect;

Appeals to all Governments and all peoples to refrain from taking any action which might hamper or delay the carrying out of these recommendations, and;

Authorizes the Secretary-General to reimburse travel and subsistence expenses of the members of the commission referred to in Part I, Section B, paragraph 1 below, on such basis and in such form as he may determine most appropriate in the circumstances, and to provide the commission with the necessary staff to assist in carrying out the functions assigned to the Commission by the General Assembly.

Authorizes the Secretary-General to draw from the Working Capital Fund a sum not to exceed $2,000,000 for the purposes set forth in the last paragraph of the resolution on the future government of Palestine.

At its hundred and twenty-eighth plenary meeting on 29 November 1947 the General Assembly, in accordance with the terms of the above resolution, elected the following members of the United Nations Commission on Palestine:

Bolivia, Czechoslovakia, Denmark, Panama and Philippines.

APPENDIX 6

UN General Assembly
Resolution 194, December 11, 1948
(The Right of Return)

The General Assembly,

Having considered further the situation in Palestine,

1. Expresses its deep appreciation of the progress achieved through the good offices of the late United Nations Mediator in promoting a peaceful adjustment of the future situation of Palestine, for which cause he sacrificed his life; and extends its thanks to the acting Mediator and his staff for their continued efforts and devotion to duty in Palestine;

2. Establishes a Conciliation Commission consisting of three States members of the United Nations which shall have the following functions:

a) To assume, in so far as it considers necessary in existing circumstances, the functions given to the United Nations Mediator on Palestine by resolution 186 (S-2) of the General Assembly of 14 May 1948;

b) To carry out the specific functions and directives given to it by the present resolution and such additional functions and directives as may be given to it by the General Assembly or by the Security Council;

c) To undertake, upon the request of the Security Council, any of the functions now assigned to the United Nations Mediator on Palestine or to the United Nations Truce Commission by resolutions of the Security Council; upon such request to the Conciliation Commission by the Security Council with respect to all the remaining functions of the United Nations Mediator on Palestine under Security Council resolutions, the office of the Mediator shall be terminated;

3. Decides that a Committee of the Assembly, consisting of China, France, the Union of Soviet Socialist Republics, the United Kingdom and the United States of America, shall present before the end of the first part of the present session of the General Assembly, for the approval of the Assembly, a proposal concerning the names of the three States which will constitute the Conciliation Commission;

4. Requests the Commission to begin its functions at once, with a view to the establishment of contact between the parties themselves and the Commission at the earliest possible date;

5. Calls upon the Governments and authorities concerned to extend the scope of the negotiations provided for in the Security Council's resolution of 16 November 1948 and to seek agreement by negotiations conducted either with the Conciliation Commission or directly, with a view to the final settlement of all questions outstanding between them;

6. Instructs the Conciliation Commission to take steps to assist the Governments and authorities concerned to achieve a final settlement of all questions outstanding between them;

7. Resolves that the Holy Places—including Nazareth—religious buildings and sites in Palestine should be protected and free access to them assured, in accordance with existing right and historical practices; that arrangements to this end should be under effective United Nations supervision, that the fourth regular session of the General Assembly in its detailed proposals for a permanent international regime for the territory of Jerusalem, should include recommendations concerning the Holy Places in that territory; that with regard to the Holy Places in the rest of Palestine the commission should call upon the political authorities of the areas concerned to give appropriate formal guarantees as to protection of the Holy Places and access to them; and that these undertakings should be presented to the General Assembly for approval;

8. Resolves that, in view of its association with three world religions the Jerusalem area, including the present municipality of Jerusalem plus the surrounding villages and towns, the most eastern of which shall be Abu Dis; the most southern, Bethlehem; the most western, Ein Karim (including also the built-up area of Motsa); and the most northern, Shu'fat, should be accorded special and separate treatment from the rest of Palestine and should be placed under effective United Nations control;

Requests the Security Council to take further steps to ensure the demilitarization of Jerusalem at the earliest possible date;

Instructs the Commission to present to the fourth regular session of the General Assembly detailed proposals for a permanent international regime for the Jerusalem area which will provide for the maximum local autonomy for distinctive groups consistent with the special international status of the Jerusalem area;

The Conciliation Commission is authorized to appoint a United Nations representative, who shall co-operate with the local authorities with respect to the interim administration of the Jerusalem area;

9. Resolves that, pending agreement on more detailed arrangements among the Governments and authorities concerned, the freest possible access to Jerusalem by road, rail or air should be accorded to all inhabitants of Palestine;

10. Instructs the Conciliation Commission to seek arrangements among the Governments and authorities concerned which will facilitate the economic development of the area, including arrangements for access to ports and airfields and the use of transportation and communication facilities;

11. Resolves that the refugees wishing to return to their homes and live at peace with their neighbors should be permitted to do so at the earliest practical date, and that compensation should be paid for the property of those choosing not to return and for loss of or damage to property which, under principles of international law or in equity, should be made good by the Governments or authorities responsible;

Instructs the Conciliation Commission to facilitate the repatriation, resettlement and economic and social rehabilitation of the refugees and the payment of compensation and to maintain close relations with the director of the United Nations Relief for Palestine Refugees and, through him, with the appropriate organs and agencies of the United Nations;

12. Authorizes the Conciliation Commission to appoint such subsidiary bodies and to employ such technical experts acting under its authority, as it may find necessary for the effective discharge of its functions and responsibilities under the present resolution;

The Conciliation Commission will have its official headquarters at Jerusalem. The Authorities will be responsible for taking all measures necessary to ensure the security of the Commission. The Secretary-General will provide a limited number of guards for the protection of the staff and premises of the Commission;

13. Instructs the Conciliation Commission to render progress reports periodically to the Secretary-General for transmission to the Security Council and to the Members of the United Nations;

14. Calls upon all Governments and authorities concerned to cooperate with the Conciliation Commission and to take all possible steps to assist in the implementation of the present resolution;

15. Requests the Secretary-General to provide the necessary staff and facilities and to make appropriate arrangements to provide the necessary funds required in carrying out the terms of the present resolution.

APPENDIX 7

UN General Assembly Resolution 3236, November 22, 1974

The General Assembly,

Having considered the Question of Palestine,

Having heard the statement of the Palestine Liberation Organization, the representative of the Palestinian people,

Having also heard other statements made during the debate,

Deeply concerned that no just solution to the problem of Palestine has yet been achieved and recognizing the problem of Palestine continues to endanger international peace and security,

Recognizing that the Palestinian people is entitled to self-determination in accordance with the Charter of the United Nations,

Expressing its grave concern that the Palestinian people has been prevented from enjoying its inalienable rights, in particular its right to self-determination,

Guided by the purposes and principles of the Charter,

Recalling its relevant resolutions which affirm the right of the Palestinian people to self-determination,

1. Reaffirms the inalienable rights of the Palestinian people in Palestine, including:

    a) The right to self-determination without external interference;

    b) The right to national independence and sovereignty;

2. Reaffirms also the inalienable right of the Palestinians to return to their homes and property from which they have been displaced and uprooted, and calls for their return;

3. Emphasizes that full respect for and the realization of these inalienable rights of the Palestinian people are indispensable for the solution of the Question of Palestine;

4. Recognizes that the Palestinian people is a principal party in the establishment of a just and durable peace in the Middle East;

5. Further recognizes the right of the Palestinian people to regain its rights by all means in accordance with the purposes and principles of the Charter of the United Nations;

6. Appeals to all States and international organizations to extend their support to the Palestinian people in its struggle to restore its rights, in accordance with the Charter;

7. Requests the Secretary-General to establish contacts with the Palestine Liberation Organization on all matters concerning the Question of Palestine;

8. Requests the Secretary-General to report to the General Assembly at its thirtieth session on the implementation of the present Resolution;

9. Decides to include the item "Question of Palestine" in the provisional agenda of its thirtieth session.

APPENDIX 8

UN Security Council Resolution 338,
October 22, 1973

The Security Council,

1. Calls upon all participants to the present fighting to cease all firing and terminate all military activity immediately, no later than 12 hours after the moment of the adoption of this decision, in the positions they now occupy;

2. Calls upon the parties concerned to start immediately after the cease-fire the implementation of Security Council Resolution 242 (1967) in all of its parts;

3. Decides that, immediately and concurrently with the cease-fire, negotiations start between the parties concerned under appropriate auspices aimed at establishing a just and durable peace in the Middle East.

APPENDIX 9

Excerpts from the Declaration of Palestinian Independence, November 15, 1988

Despite the historical injustice inflicted on the Palestinian Arab people resulting in their dispersion and depriving them of their right to self-determination, following upon UN General Assembly Resolution 181 (1947), which partitioned Palestine into two states, one Arab, one Jewish, yet it is this resolution that still provides those conditions of international legitimacy that ensure the right of the Palestinian Arab people to sovereignty. . . .

. . . Whereas the Palestinian people reaffirms most definitively its inalienable rights in the Land of it patrimony:

Now by virtue of natural, historic and legal rights, and the sacrifices of successive generations who gave of themselves in defence of the freedom and independence of their homeland;

In pursuance of Resolutions adopted by Arab Summit Conferences and relying on the authority bestowed by international legitimacy as embodied in the resolutions of the United Nations Organization since 1947;

And in exercise of the Palestinian Arab people of its rights to self-determination, political independence, and sovereignty over its territory;

The Palestine National Council, in the name of God, and in the name of the Palestinian Arab people; hereby proclaims the establishment of the State of Palestine on our Palestinian territory with its capital Holy Jerusalem (Al-Quds Ash-Sharif).

The state of Palestine is the state of Palestinians wherever they may be. The state is for them to enjoy in it their collective national and cultural identity, theirs to pursue in it a complete equality of rights. In it will be safeguarded their political and religious convictions and their human dignity by means of a parliamentary democratic system of governance, itself based on freedom of expression and the freedom to form parties. The rights of minorities will duly be respected by the majority, as minorities must abide by decisions of the majority. Governance will be based on principles of social justice, equality and non-discrimination in public rights of men or women, on grounds of race, religion, colour or sex under the aegis of a constitution which ensures the rule of law and independent judiciary. Thus shall these principles allow no departure from Palestine's age-old spiritual and civilizational heritage of tolerance and religious coexistence.

The State of Palestine is an Arab state, an integral and indivisible part of the Arab nation, at one with that nation in heritage and civilization, with it also in its aspiration for liberation, progress, democracy and unity. The State of Palestine affirms its obligation to abide by the Charter of the League of Arab States, whereby the coordination of the Arab states with each other shall be strengthened. It calls upon Arab compatriots to consolidate and enhance the emergence in reality of our state, to mobilize potential, and to intensify efforts whose goal is to end Israeli occupation.

The State of Palestine proclaims its commitment to the principles and purposes of the United Nations, and to the Universal Declaration of Human Rights. It proclaims its commitment as well to the principles and policies of the Non-Aligned Movement. . . .

. . . The State of Palestine herewith declares that it believes in the settlement of regional and international disputes by peaceful means, in accordance with the UN Charter and resolutions. Without prejudice to its natural right to defend its territorial integrity and independence, it therefore rejects the threat or use of force, violence and terrorism against its territorial integrity or political independence, as it also rejects their use against the territorial integrity of other states. . . .

APPENDIX 10

The Stockholm Statement,
December 7, 1988

The text of the joint PLO–American Jewish delegation statement, presented by Swedish foreign minister Stern Anderson:

The Palestinian National Council [PNC] met in Algiers from November 12 to 15, 1988, and announced the declaration of independence which proclaimed the state of Palestine and issued a political statement.

The following explanation was given by the representatives of the PLO of certain important points in the Palestinian declaration of independence and the political statement adopted by the PNC in Algiers.

Affirming the principle incorporated in those UN resolutions which call for a two-state solution of Israel and Palestine, the PNC:

1. Agreed to enter into peace negotiations at an international conference under the auspices of the UN with the participation of the permanent members of the Security Council and the PLO as the sole legitimate representative of the Palestinian people, on equal footing with the other parties to the conflict; such an international conference is to be held on the basis of UN resolutions 242 and 338 and the right of the Palestinian people of self-determination, without external interference, as provided in the UN Charter, including the right to an independent state, which conference should resolve the Palestinian problem in all aspects;

2. Established the independent state of Palestine and accepted the existence of Israel as a state in the region;

3. Declared its rejection and condemnation of terrorism in all its forms, including state terrorism;

4. Called for a solution to the Palestinian refugee problem in accordance with international law and practices and relevant UN resolutions (including right of return or compensation).

The American personalities strongly supported and applauded the Palestinian declaration of independence and the political statement adopted in Algiers, and felt there was no further impediment to a direct dialogue between the United States Government and the PLO.

APPENDIX 11

The Palestinian Peace Initiative, December 13, 1988: Excerpts from the Speech by Yasser Arafat to the UN General Assembly in Geneva

In my capacity as Chairman of the PLO Executive Committee, presently assuming the functions of the provisional government of the State of Palestine, I therefore present the following Palestinian peace initiative:

First: That a serious effort be made to convene, under the supervision of the Secretary General of the United Nations, the preparatory Committee of the international conference for peace in the Middle East . . . to pave the way for the convening of the international conference, which commands universal support except from the government of Israel.

Second: . . . That actions be undertaken to place our occupied Palestinian land under temporary United Nations supervision, and that international forces be deployed there to protect our people and, at the same time, to supervise the withdrawal of the Israeli forces from our country.

Third: The PLO will seek a comprehensive settlement among the parties concerned in the Arab-Israeli conflict, including the State of Palestine, Israel and other neighbors, within the framework of the international conference for peace in the Middle East on the basis of Resolutions 242 and 338 and so as to guarantee equality and the balance of interests, especially our people's rights to live in freedom, national independence, and respect the right to exist in peace and security for all.

If these principles are endorsed at the international conference, we will have come a long way toward a just settlement, and this will enable us to reach agreement on all security and peace arrangements. . . .

I come to you in the name of my people, offering my hand so that we can make true peace, peace based on justice.

I ask the leaders of Israel to come here under the sponsorship of the United Nations so that, together, we can forge that peace. . . .

And here, I would address myself specifically to the Israeli people in all their parties and forces, and especially to the advocates of democracy and peace among them. I say to them: "Come let us make peace. Cast away fear and intimidation. Leave behind the spectre of the wars that have raged continuously for the past 40 years."

APPENDIX 12

UN Security Council Resolution 298 on Jerusalem, September 25, 1971

The Security Council,

Recalling its resolutions 252 (1968) of 21 May 1968, and 267 (1969) of 3 July 1969, and the earlier General Assembly resolution 2253 (RS-V) and 2254 (RS-V) of 4 and 14 July 1967, concerning measures and actions by Israel designed to change the status of the Israeli-occupied section of Jerusalem,

Having considered the letter of the Permanent Representative of Jordan on this situation in Jerusalem and the reports of the Secretary-General, and having heard the statements of the parties concerned in the questions,

Recalling the principle that acquisition of territory by military conquest is inadmissible,

Noting with concern the non-compliance of Israel with the above-mentioned resolutions,

Noting with concern also that since the adoption of the above-mentioned resolutions Israel has taken further measures designed to change the status and character of the occupied section of Jerusalem;

1. Reaffirms its resolution 252 (1968) and 267 (1969);

2. Deplores the failure of Israel to respect the previous resolutions adopted by the United Nations concerning measures and actions by Israel purporting to affect the status of the City of Jerusalem;

3. Confirms in the clearest possible terms that all legislative and administrative actions taken by Israel to change the status of the City of Jerusalem, including expropriation of land and properties, transfer of populations and legislation aimed at the incorporation of the occupied section, are totally invalid and cannot change the status;

4. Urgently calls upon Israel to rescind all previous measures and actions and to take no further steps in the occupied section of Jerusalem which may purport to

change the status of the City, or which would prejudice the rights of the inhabitants and the interests of the international community, or a just and lasting peace;

5. Requests the Secretary-General, in consultation with the President of the Security Council and using such instrumentalities as he may choose, including a representative or a mission, to report to the Council as appropriate and in any event within 60 days on the implementation of the present resolution.

APPENDIX 13

Article 27 of the Charter of the Islamic Resistance Movement (Hamas): [On the] Palestine Liberation Organization

Article 27

The Palestine Liberation Organization is closest of the close to the Islamic Resistance Movement, in that it is the father, the brother, the relative, or friend; and does the Muslim offend his father, brother, relative, or friend? Our nation is one, plight is one, destiny is one, and our enemy is the same, being affected by the situation that surrounded the formation of the organization (PLO) and the chaotic ideologies that overwhelm the Arab world due to the ideological invasion that befell the Arab world since the defeat of the Crusades and the ongoing consolidation of orientalism, missionary work, and imperialism. The organization (PLO) adopted the idea of a secular state, and as such we considered it.

Secularist ideology is in total contradiction to religious ideologies, and it is upon ideology that positions, actions, and decisions are made. From here, with our respect for the Palestine Liberation Organization and what it might become, and not understanding its role in the Arab-Israeli struggle, we cannot exchange the current status and future of Islam in Palestine to adopt the secular ideology because the Islamic nature of the Palestinian issue is part and parcel of our din (ideology and way of life) and whosoever neglects part of his din is surely lost.

And who turns away from the religion of Abraham but such as debase their souls with folly?

Sura 2: Baqara: 130

When the Palestine Liberation Organization adopts Islam as its system of life, we will be its soldiers and the firewood of its fire, which will burn the enemies. Until this happens, and we ask Allah that it be soon, the position of the Islamic Resistance Movement toward the Palestine Liberation Organization is the position of a son toward his father, and the brother toward his brother, and the relative toward his relative. He will be hurt if a thorn pricks him; he supports him in confronting the enemy and wishes guidance from him.

Your brother, your brother he who has no brother is like one going to battle without weapons.

And know that your cousin is like your wings; and does the falcon fly without wings?

Glossary

Ahl al-Kitab. "People of the Book" (the Bible). A reference to Christians and Jews.

Aliyah. Moving to Israel, expected of "diaspora" Jews.

Amir. A prince or powerful local ruler.

Aqsa intifada, al-. The Uprising of the al-Aqsa Mosque, or the Noble Sanctuary in Jerusalem.

Aradi Sultaniyya. Sultanic lands or state land during the Ottoman era.

'Ard, al-. The honor of the women in a family.

Ard, al-. The land.

Ard al-Muqaddasah, al-. The Holy Land.

Arz-i Filistin. Turkish for "land of Palestine."

Ashraf. The Islamic Arab "nobility," descendants of the Prophet Muhammad or his early companions.

Awda, al-. The Return, a term used widely in reference to the right of the refugees to return to their homes and property.

A'yan. Political and economic notables.

Ba'ath Party. An Arab nationalist political movement and party that sought unity of the Arab world and the liberation of Palestine.

Balad, al-. The National Democratic Assembly, a democratic, progressive national Palestinian party.

Balfour Declaration. The declaration by the imperial British government in 1917 of its support for the establishment in Palestine of a national home for the Jewish people.

Barrakiyat. Refugee camp dwellings made up of corrugated iron, tin, wood, or other materials.

Bayan (pl. *bayanat*). Communiqué issued by the leaders of the intifada to direct the followers' action.

Bayt al-Maqdis. The Holy Abode, the city of Jerusalem.

Corpus separatum. Literally, separate entity: the international status (independent from the Arab and Jewish states in Palestine) that Jerusalem and Bethlehem would come under according to the 1947 UN partition plan for Palestine.

Corvée labor. Forced labor.

Dakhel, al-. Inside; a reference to the area inside historical Palestine where the Palestinians are still resident.

Declaration of Principles. The Israel-PLO agreements to resolve the conflict between them. Also called the *Oslo Accords* of 1993.

Dibs. Molasses made from carob.

Dunum. Approximately one-quarter of an acre of land.

Durra. Maize.

Fallah (pl. *fallahin*). Peasant. Also transliterated as *fellah*.

Fard (Turkish *ferde*). Individual. Also used to denote a capitation tax.

Fasa'il. Guerrilla bands of the 1936–1939 Palestinian Arab revolt against the British. Also used to describe the various guerrilla groups that made up the PLO.

Fateh. Conquest or opening; a reverse acronym for the Palestine National Liberation Movement (often transliterated as *Fatah, al-Fatah,* or *Fath*). One of the earliest, largest, and dominant political guerrilla groups constituting the PLO. It was led by Yasser Arafat from 1968 to his death in 2004.

Feda'iyyin. Self-sacrificers (also transliterated as *fedayeen*); the name Palestinians give to guerrilla fighters or groups.

Fida Party. A small DFLP splinter group that supports the Oslo Accords.

Ghor. The rift valley of the Jordan River.

Ghourba, al-. Estrangement; a term used by Palestinians to refer to their diaspora.

Green Line. The lines separating Israel proper from the West Bank, which prevailed until June 5, 1967. They were demarcated in 1949 on the island of Rhodes.

Haganah. The official Jewish forces during the mandate period in Palestine.

Hajj. The pilgrimage to Mecca. Also a title for one who has performed the hajj.

Hamas. Literally, "zeal" or "enthusiasm"; an Arabic acronym for the Islamic Resistance Movement, based largely in the Gaza Strip.

Hamula. Patrilineal lineage or clan.

Hanafi. One of the four schools of Islamic jurisprudence.

Harakat al-Muqawama al-Filastiniyya. Palestinian Resistance Movement.

Harakat al-Tahrir al-Islami. Islamic Liberation Movement, whose acronym is *Hamas*.

Harakat al-Tahrir al-Watani al-Filastini. Palestine National Liberation Movement.

Haram al-Sharif, al-. The Noble Sanctuary (or Temple Mount) in Jerusalem, where the two holy Islamic mosques of al-Aqsa and the Dome of the Rock are located.

Hatt-i Humayun. Turkish for "Imperial Rescript," a second reform decree in the nineteenth century.

Hatt-i Sherif of Gulhane. The first royal edict of Ottoman reform, issued in 1839.

Hawakir (sing. *hakourah*). Small plots of productive land.

Hawiyya. Identity card.

Hijazi. A person who hails from Hijaz, modern Saudi Arabia.

Hijra. The emigration of the Prophet Muhammad and his followers from Mecca to Medina, marking the beginning of the Islamic calendar.

Histadrut. Jewish labor federation established in 1920 in Palestine.

Hovevei Zion. Lovers of Zion, a Zionist movement.

Hukoumat 'Umoum Filastin. The All-Palestine Government, declared by the Mufti of Jerusalem, Haj Amin Husseini, in 1984.

Ikhwan al-Muslimin, al-. The Muslim Brotherhood, a political Islamic movement.

Innana 'ai'doun (or *Innana raji'oun*). Arabic for "We shall return," the phrase that became the slogan expressing diaspora Palestinians' desire to return home to Palestine.

Intifada. The Palestinian uprising against Israeli occupation of the West Bank and the Gaza Strip.

Irgun Z'vai Leumi. A Jewish Zionist underground terrorist organization during the 1940s led by Menachem Begin, later (1977–1982) prime minister of Israel.

Isra. The Necturion Journey, in which, according to Islamic legend, Muhammad ascended to heaven, visited Jerusalem, and returned to Mecca in the same night.

Istiqlal Party. The Arab independence party during the British mandate period..

Jaysh al-Inqath. Army of Salvation, an Arab volunteer force that fought the Jewish Zionist militias in the 1947–1948 Jewish-Palestinian war.

Jihad. Struggle; often interpreted as armed struggle in defense of Islam or Islamic society and institutions.

Jihad al-Islami, al-. Islamic Jihad, a radical Islamic political movement anchored largely in the Gaza Strip.

Jihad al-Muqaddas, al-. Holy Struggle, a volunteer force in the Jewish-Palestinian war of 1947–1948.

Kaffiyya. The traditional Arab checkered headdress, worn by the youthful activists and militants of the intifada.

Karameh, al-. The name of the refugee camp and village in East Jordan in which an Israeli military force fought a pitched battle against Palestinian guerrillas in 1968. The battle marked a turning point in the political rise and surfacing (from clandestine status) of the Palestinian guerrilla *(feda'iyyin)* movement. In Arabic, *karameh* means "dignity."

Karmel, al-. Mount Carmel, near the city of Haifa; also the name of a Palestinian newspaper during the period of the British mandate.

Keren Hayesod. The Palestine Foundation Fund.

Keren Kayemeth Leisrael. The Jewish National Fund.

Kha'in. Traitor (in Arabic).

Khalil, al-. Hebron.

Khan. Turkish for an inn for travelers and their animals. Also a Turkish honorific.

Kharej, al-. Outside; a reference to any area outside Palestine where refugees live.

Kibbutz. A Jewish cooperative agricultural settlement in Palestine.

Kiles. One *kile* equals 36 liters.

Knesset. The Israeli parliament.

Lohamei Herut Yisrael (Lehi). A Jewish Zionist underground terrorist organization during the 1940s. Also known as the Stern Gang after its founder, Abraham Stern.

Ma'arakat al-massir. The battle of destiny against Israel.

Madaniyyin (sing. *madani*). Urbanites or city-dwellers.

Maghreb. The Arab west, or North Africa.

Majlis (pl. *majalis*). Local or village council.

Manfa, al-. Exile; a reference to the Palestinian diaspora.

Maqam. A sacred sanctuary, usually the tomb of a *wali*, or popular saint.

Mashreq. The Arab east, or Arab Asia and Egypt.

Masjed al-Aqsa, al-. Al-Aqsa mosque on al-Haram al-Sharif in Jerusalem.

Metayer. Tenant farmer.

Millet. Religious sect; taxed collectively by the Ottomans.

Miri. State land owned by the amir (the ruler).

Mubadara, al-. Arabic for the Palestinian National Initiative.

Muhajjarin. Displaced persons, a reference to camp-dwellers who sought shelter in other secure camps or settlements during the Lebanese civil war.

Muharram. One of the months in the Islamic calendar. Also the name of a decree issued by Ottoman authorities in the nineteenth century that consolidated European financial control over the Ottoman Empire.

Mukhtar. Village selectman or mayor, a representative of the Turkish authorities.

Mulk (also transliterated as *milk*). Private property.

Muqata'aji. Feudal lord and tax farmer.

Muqawama al-Filastiniyya, al-. Resistance; Arabic name for the Palestinian Resistance Movement, sometimes shortened to *al-Muqawama*.

Musha'a. Communal land in Palestine during the nineteenth century and the first half of the twentieth century.

Mutasariffiyya. An administrative subdistrict during the Ottoman period.

Nabi Musa. The Prophet Moses, a popular *wali*, or saint, recognized throughout Palestine.

Nabi Saleh. The Prophet Saleh, a popular *wali*, or saint, recognized throughout Palestine.

Nahiya. During the Ottoman period, a small administrative subdistrict composed of several villages.

Nakbah, al-. Catastrophe or disaster; the term that Palestinians use to refer to the destruction of their society in 1948.

Naqib. Elected leader of the *ashraf* "nobility" in urban nineteenth-century Palestine.

Oqqas. One *oqqa* equals 1.28 kilograms.

Oslo Accords of 1993. The agreements, officially labeled the Declaration of Principles, negotiated between Israel and the PLO in secret meetings in Oslo in 1993.

Palestinian Authority. The transitional governing authority created for Palestinian Arab self-governance by the Oslo Accords of September 1993.

People of the Book. The book referred to is the Bible. An Islamic reference to Christians and Jews.

Qadi. Court judge.

Qa'id. Leader; specifically, leader of a guerrilla band of the 1936–1939 Palestinian Arab revolt against the British.

Qays. One of the lineage-based traditional political factions in Palestine and the Arab east.

Qilli. An alkaline powder, a raw material crucial in the production of soap.

Qiyada al-Wataniyya al-Muwahhada li-1 Intifada, al-. Unified National Leadership of the Uprising (UNLU).

Qubbat al-Sakhra. The holy mosque of the Dome of the Rock.

Quds, al-. Literally, "the Holy," the city of Jerusalem.

Ra'ees. Head, the title that the Israel-PLO accords settled on for Yasser Arafat. Arafat and the Palestinian negotiators wanted to use the title *president,* and the Israelis wanted him to use the title *chairman.*

Rakah. The Communist Party of Israel, with Jewish and Arab membership.

Sabr. Cactus bush that has become a national symbol for the West Bank and Gaza Strip Palestinians under occupation. The term also means "patience," "perseverance."

Salam. Nineteenth-century Arabic term for futures purchase (not to be confused with current usage, in which the term means "peace").

Sanjak. An administrative subdistrict of an Ottoman governorate.

Sha'ab al-Filastini, al-. The Palestinian people.

Sha'abi. Poor residential areas or slums.

Shari'a. Islamic law.

Shaykh. Tribal leader, religious cleric, or dignitary.

Shi'a. One of the two great sects of Islam. The Shi'a are the partisans of Ali, cousin and son-in-law of the Prophet Muhammad.

Souq. The traditional Arab market (bazaar).

Sultan. King or sovereign.

Sumoud. Perseverance.

Sunni. The largest and dominant orthodox sect of Islam.

Tabu (Turkish *tapu*). Land registration law.

Tanzim. The armed factions of Fateh.

Tanzimat. The administrative and economic reforms within the Ottoman Empire during the middle of the nineteenth century.

Tawtin. Naturalization and settlement of Palestinian refugees in the Arab host countries.

'Ulama. Islamic theologians.

Umma. Nation or community.

'Urf. Customary law.

Waqf (pl. *awaqf*). Tax-free religious endowment.

Watan. Homeland.

Wilaya. Governorate.

Wujaha. Political and economic notables.

Yaman. One of the lineage-based factional political divisions that cut across the whole country of Palestine and the region.

Yishuv. The Jewish settler-immigrant community in Palestine.

Zakat. Islamic obligation of almsgiving.

Selected Bibliography

Books and Dissertations

Abboushi, W. *The Unmaking of Palestine* (Brattleboro, VT: Amana Books, 1990).

Abcarius, M. F. *Palestine Through the Fog of Propaganda* (London: Hutchinson, 1946).

Abed, G. T., ed. *The Palestinian Economy: Studies in Development Under Prolonged Occupation* (London: Routledge, 1988).

Abu, Iyad, with Eric Rouleau. *My Home, My Land* (New York: Times Books, 1981).

Abu-Amr, Z. *Islamic Fundamentalism in the West Bank and Gaza* (Bloomington: Indiana University Press, 1994).

Abu El-Haj, N. "Excavating the Land, Creating the Homeland: Archaeology, the State and the Making of History in Modern Jewish Nationalism." Ph.D. dissertation, Duke University, 1995.

Abu-Ghazaleh, A. *Arab Cultural Nationalism in Palestine* (Beirut: Institute for Palestine Studies, 1973).

Abu-Lughod, I., ed. *The Transformation of Palestine* (Evanston, IL: Northwestern University Press, 1971).

'Allush, N. *Arab Resistance in Palestine (1917–1948)* (in Arabic) (Beirut: Dar al-Tali'a, 1975).

Amin, S. *The Arab World Today* (London: Zed, 1978).

Anderson, B. *Imagined Communities: Reflections on the Origin and Spread of Nationalism* (New York: Verso, 1991).

Anidjar, Gil. *The Jew, the Arab: A History of the Enemy* (Stanford: Stanford University Press, 2003).

Antonius, G. *The Arab Awakening: The Story of the Arab National Movement* (New York: Capricorn Books, 1965).

'Arif, 'A. al-. *History of Gaza* (in Arabic) (al-Quds: Matba'at Dar al-Aytam al-Islamiyya, 1943).

Aronson, G. *Creating Facts: Israel, Palestinians and the West Bank* (Washington, DC: Institute for Palestine Studies, 1987).

Aruri, N. H. *Dishonest Broker: The U.S. Role in Israel and Palestine* (Cambridge, MA: South End Press, 2003).

_____. *Jordan: A Study in Political Development, 1921–1965* (The Hague: Nijhoff, 1972).

_____. *The Obstruction of Peace: The U.S., Israel and the Palestinians* (Monroe, ME: Common Courage Press, 1995).

_____, ed. *Occupation: Israel over Palestine*, 2nd ed. (Belmont, MA: Association of Arab-American University Graduates, 1989).

_____. *Palestinian Refugees: The Right of Return* (London: Pluto Press, 2001).

_____, ed. *Palestinian Resistance to the Israeli Occupation* (Wilmette, IL: Medina University Press, 1970).

Ashrawi, H. *This Side of Peace* (New York: Simon and Schuster, 1995).

Awad, A. *Introduction to the Modern History of Palestine, 1831–1914* (in Arabic) (Beirut: Arab Institution for Studies and Publishing, 1983).

Ayyoub, S. M. *The Class Structure of Palestinians in Lebanon* (in Arabic) (Beirut: Beirut Arab University, 1978).

Badran, N. *Education and Modernization in Palestinian Arab Society* (in Arabic) (Beirut: PLO Research Center, 1978).

Barghouthi, O., and K. Tawtah. *History of Palestine* (in Arabic) (Jerusalem, 1923).

Benvenisti, M. *Intimate Enemies: Jews and Arabs in a Shared Land* (Berkeley: University of California Press, 1995).

_____. *1986 Report: Demographic, Economic, Legal, Social, and Political Developments in the West Bank* (Boulder, CO: Westview Press, 1986).

_____. *1987 Report: Demographic, Economic, Legal, Social, and Political Developments in the West Bank* (Boulder, CO: Westview Press, 1987).

_____, with Z. Abu-Zayed and D. Rubinstein. *The West Bank Handbook: A Political Lexicon* (Boulder, CO: Westview Press, 1986).

Ben-Yehuda, Hemda, and Samuel Sandler. *The Arab-Israeli Conflict Transformed: Fifty Years of Interstate and Ethnic Crises* (Albany: State University of New York Press, 2002).

Berger, E. *Peace for Palestine: First Lost Opportunity* (Gainesville: University Press of Florida, 1993).

Bernstein, Deborah S. *Constructing Boundaries: Jewish and Arab Workers in Mandatory Palestine* (Albany: State University of New York Press, 2000).

Bethell, N. *The Palestine Triangle: The Struggle Between the British, the Jews and the Arabs, 1935–48* (London: Andre Deutsch, 1979).

Binder, Leonard. *Ethnic Conflict and International Politics in the Middle East* (Gainesville: University of Florida Press, 1999).

Bishara, Marwan. *Palestine/Israel: Peace or Apartheid? Prospects for Resolving the Conflict* (London: Zed Books, 2002).

Blight, Alexander, ed. *The Israeli Palestinians: An Arab Minority in the Jewish State* (London: Frank Cass, 2003).

Bornstein, Avram S. *Crossing the Green Line Between the West Bank and Israel* (Philadelphia: University of Pennsylvania Press, 2001).

Bowersock, G. W. *Roman Arabia* (Cambridge, MA: Harvard University Press, 1983).

Bowker, Robert. *Palestinian Refugees: Mythology, Identity, and the Search for Peace* (Boulder, CO: Lynne Rienner, 2003).

Boyle, Francis A. *Palestine, Palestinians, and International Law* (Atlanta, GA: Clarity Press, Inc., 2003).

Brand, L. A. *Palestinians in the Arab World* (New York: Columbia University Press, 1988).

Bromley, S. *American Hegemony and World Oil* (University Park: Pennsylvania State University Press, 1991).

Brown, Nathan. *Palestinian Politics After the Oslo Accords: Resuming Arab Palestine* (Berkeley: University of California Press, 2003).

Brynen, R., ed. *Echoes of the Intifada: Regional Repercussions of the Palestinian-Israeli Conflict* (Boulder, CO: Westview Press, 1991).

_____. *Sanctuary and Survival: The PLO in Lebanon* (Boulder, CO: Westview Press, 1990).

_____. *A Very Political Economy: Peacebuilding and Foreign Aid in the West Bank and Gaza* (Washington, DC: United States Institute of Peace, 2000).

Budeiri, M. *The Palestine Communist Party, 1919–1948* (London: Ithaca Press, 1979).

Buheiry, M., ed. *Intellectual Life in the Arab East: 1890–1939* (Beirut: American University of Beirut Press, 1981).

Bunzl, John, ed. *Islam, Judaism, and the Political Role of Religions in the Middle East* (Gainesville: University Press of Florida, 1994).

Carey, Roane. *The New Intifada: Resisting Israel's Apartheid* (London: Verso Press, 2001).

Carnoy, M. *The State and Political Theory* (Princeton, NJ: Princeton University Press, 1984).

Chomsky, N. *Deterring Democracy* (New York: Vintage, 1992).

_____. *The Fateful Triangle: The United States, Israel and the Palestinians* (Boston: South End Press, 1983).

_____. *World Orders: Old and New* (New York: Columbia University Press, 1994).

Cobban, H. *The Palestinian Liberation Organization: People, Power and Politics* (Cambridge: Cambridge University Press, 1984).

Cohen, A. *Economic Life in Ottoman Jerusalem* (Cambridge: Cambridge University Press, 1989).

_____. *Palestine in the 18th Century* (Jerusalem: Magnes Press, 1973).

_____, and G. Baer, eds. *Egypt and Palestine—A Millennium of Association (868–1948)* (New York: St. Martin's Press, 1984).

_____, and B. L. Lewis. *Population and Revenue in the Towns of Palestine in the Sixteenth Century* (Princeton, NJ: Princeton University Press, 1978).

Cooley, J. K. *Green March, Black September: The Story of the Palestinian Arabs* (London: Frank Cass, 1973).

Dajani, S. R. *Eyes Without Country: Searching for a Palestinian Strategy of Liberation* (Philadelphia: Temple University Press, 1994).

Davidson, Lawrence. *America's Palestine: Popular and Official Perceptions from Balfour to Israeli Statehood* (Gainesville: University Press of Florida, 2001).

Dieckhoff, Alain. *The Invention of a Nation: Zionist Thought and the Making of Modern Israel* (New York: Columbia University Press, 2003).

Dodd, P., and H. Barakat. *River Without Bridges: A Study of the Exodus of the 1967 Palestinian Arab Refugees* (Beirut: Institute for Palestine Studies, 1969).

Doumani, B. B. "Merchants, Socioeconomic Change and the State in Ottoman Palestine: The Nablus Region, 1800–1860." Ph.D. dissertation, Georgetown University, 1990.

_____. *Rediscovering Palestine: Merchants and Peasants in Jabal Nablus, 1700–1900* (Berkeley: University of California Press, 1995).

Dumper, Michael. *The Politics of Sacred Space: The Old City of Jerusalem in the Middle East Conflict* (Boulder, CO, and London: Lynne Rienner, 2002).

Ellis, Marc H. *Israel and Palestine: Out of the Ashes—The Search for Jewish Identity in the Twenty-first Century* (Sterling, VA: Pluto Press, 2002).

Enderlin, Charles. *Shattered Dreams: The Failure of the Peace Process in the Middle East, 1995–2002* (New York: Other Press, 2002).

Esco Foundation for Palestine. *Palestine: A Study of Jewish, Arab, and British Policies,* Vols. 1 and 2 (New Haven, CT: Yale University Press, 1947).

Finkelstein, N. G. *Image and Reality of the Israel-Palestine Conflict* (London: Verso, 1995).

_____. *The Rise and Fall of Palestine* (Minneapolis: University of Minnesota Press, 1996).

Finn, J. *Stirring Times,* 2 vols. (London: C. Kegan Paul, 1978).

Flapan, S. *The Birth of Israel: Myths and Realities* (New York: Pantheon, 1987).

Frischwasser-Ra'anan, H. *The Frontiers of a Nation: A Re-examination of the Forces Which Created the Palestine Mandate and Determined Its Territorial Shape* (London: Batchworth Press, 1955).

Ghabra, S. *The Palestinians in Kuwait: The Family and Politics of Survival* (Boulder, CO: Westview Press, 1987).

Gibb, H. A. R., trans. *The Damascus Chronicle of the Crusades* (London: Luzac, 1932).

_____, and H. Bowen. *Islamic Society and the West,* Vols. 1 and 2 (Oxford: Oxford University Press, 1950, 1957).

Gilbar, G. G., ed. *Ottoman Palestine, 1800–1914: Studies in Economic and Social History* (Leiden: E. J. Brill, 1990).

Glubb, J. B. *A Soldier with the Arabs* (London: Hodder & Stoughton, 1957).

Graham-Brown, S. *Education, Repression and Liberation: Palestinians* (London: World University Service UK, 1984).

Gramsci, A. *Selections from Prison Notebooks* (New York: International Publishers, 1971).

Granott, A. *The Land System in Palestine,* translated by M. Sinion (London: Eyre and Spottiswoode, 1952).

Gresh, A. *The PLO: The Struggle Within* (London: Zed, 1985).

Habiby, E. *The Secret Life of Saeed, the Ill-fated Pessoptimist: A Palestinian Who Became a Citizen of Israel,* translated by S. K. Jayyussi and T. Le Gassick (New York: Vantage, 1982).

Hadawi, S. *Palestinian Rights and Losses in 1948: A Comprehensive Study* (London: Saqi Books, 1988).

Haddad, Simon. *The Palestinian Impasse in Lebanon: The Politics of Refugee Integration* (Brighton, UK, and Portland, OR: Sussex Academic Press, 2003).

Hagopian, E., ed. *Amal and the Palestinians: Understanding the Battle of the Camps* (Belmont, MA: Association of Arab-American University Graduates, 1985).

Haim, S. G., ed. *Arab Nationalism: An Anthology* (Berkeley: University of California Press, 1964).

Halevy, N., and R. Klinov-Malul. *The Economic Development of Israel* (New York: Praeger, 1968).

Haq, al-. *Punishing a Nation: Israeli Human Rights Violations During the Palestinian Uprising, December 1987–December 1988* (Boston: South End Press, 1989).

Harkabi, Y. *Fedayeen Action and Arab Strategy* (London: Institute for Strategic Studies, 1968).

Hass, Amira. *Reporting from Ramallah: An Israeli Journalist in an Occupied Land* (Cambridge: MIT Press, 2003).

Heiberg, M., and G. Ovensen. *Palestinian Society in Gaza, West Bank and Arab Jerusalem: A Survey of Living Conditions,* FAFO Report 151 (Oslo: FAFO, 1993).

Heyd, U. *Ottoman Documents on Palestine 1552–1615* (Oxford: Oxford University Press, 1960).

Hiltermann, J. R. *Behind the Intifada: Labor and Women's Movements in the Occupied Territories* (Princeton, NJ: Princeton University Press, 1991).

Himadeh, S. B., ed. *Economic Organization of Palestine* (Beirut: American University of Beirut, 1938).

Hirst, D. *The Gun and the Olive Branch* (London: Futura, 1977).

Hitti, P. K. *History of Syria* (London: Macmillan, 1957).

Hourani, A. *Arabic Thought in the Liberal Age: 1798–1939* (Oxford: Oxford University Press, 1970).

_____. *A History of the Arab Peoples* (Cambridge, MA: Harvard University Press, 1991).

_____. *A Vision of History* (Beirut: American University of Beirut, 1961).

_____, P. Khoury, and M. C. Wilson, eds. *The Modern Middle East: A Reader* (London: I. B. Tauris, 1993).

Hudson, M. C. *Arab Politics* (New Haven, CT: Yale University Press, 1989).

_____, ed. *The Palestinians: New Directions* (Washington, DC: Center for Contemporary Arab Studies, Georgetown University, 1990).

Hurewitz, J. C. *The Struggle for Palestine* (New York: W. W. Norton, 1950).

Husseini, M. Y. al-. *Socioeconomic Development in Arab Palestine* (in Arabic) (Jaffa: al-Taher Bros., 1946).

Hyamson, A. M. *Palestine Under the Mandate, 1920–1948* (Westport, CT: Greenwood Press, 1950).

Institute for Social and Economic Policy in the Middle East, John F. Kennedy School of Government, Harvard University. *Securing Peace in the Middle East: Project on Economic Transition* (Cambridge, MA: Harvard University Press, 1993).

Issawi, C., ed. *The Economic History of the Middle East, 1800–1914* (Chicago: University of Chicago Press, 1966).

Kanafani, G. *Men in the Sun,* translated by H. Kilpatrick (Washington, DC: Three Continents Press, 1991).

Karmi, Ghada. *In Search of Fatima: A Palestinian Story* (New York: Verso, 2002).

Kazziha, W. *Palestine in the Arab Dilemma* (New York: Barnes and Noble, 1979).

_____. *Revolutionary Transformation in the Arab World: Habash and His Comrades from Nationalism to Marxism* (London: Charles Knight, 1975).

Kerr, M. H. *The Arab Cold War* (New York: Oxford University Press, 1971).

Khalaf, I. *Politics in Palestine* (Albany: State University of New York Press, 1991).

Khalaf, S., and P. Kongstad. *Hamra of Beirut: A Case of Rapid Urbanization* (Leiden: E. J. Brill, 1973).

Khalidi, R. *Under Siege: PLO Decision-Making in the 1982 War* (New York: Columbia University Press, 1986).

_____, and C. Mansour, eds. *Palestine and the Gulf* (Beirut: Institute for Palestine Studies, 1982).

Khalidi, T., ed. *Land Tenure and Social Transformation in the Middle East* (Beirut: American University of Beirut, 1984).

Khalidi, W., ed. *All That Remains: The Palestinian Villages Occupied and Depopulated by Israel in 1948* (Washington, DC: Institute for Palestine Studies, 1992).

_____. *Before Their Diaspora: A Photographic History of the Palestinians, 1876–1948* (Washington, DC: Institute for Palestine Studies, 1984).

_____. *From Haven to Conquest: Readings in Zionism and the Palestine Problem Until 1948* (Beirut: Institute for Palestine Studies, 1971).

Khouri, E. *Palestinian Statistics* (Beirut: PLO Research Center, 1979).

Khouri, F. J. *The Arab Israeli Dilemma,* 3rd ed. (Syracuse, NY: Syracuse University Press, 1985).

Khoury, Y. *Arab Press in Palestine: 1876–1948* (in Arabic) (Beirut: Institute for Palestine Studies, 1976).

Kidron, Peretz, ed. *Refusenik! Israel's Soldiers of Conscience* (London: Zed Books, 2004).

Kimmerling, Baruch. *Politicide: Ariel Sharon's War Against the Palestinians* (New York: Verso, 2003).

_____. *Zionism and Territory* (Berkeley: Institute of International Studies, University of California, 1983).

Kimmerling, Baruch, and Joel S. Migdal. *The Palestinian People: A History* (Cambridge, MA: Harvard University Press, 2003).

_____. *Palestinians: The Making of a People* (New York: Free Press, 1993).

Klauss, Dorothée. *Palestinian Refugees in Lebanon—Where to Belong?* (Berlin: Laus Schwarz Verlag, 2003).

Krogh, P. F., and M. C. McDavid, eds. *Palestinians Under Occupation: Prospects for the Future* (Washington, DC: Center for Contemporary Arab Studies, Georgetown University, 1989).

Künzig, Andrea. *Visions: Palestine* (Heidelberg, Germany: Kehrer Verlag, 2004).

Kurd Ali, M. *The Book of al-Sham's Ways* (in Arabic) (Damascus: Maktabat al-Nuri, 1983).

Kushner, D., ed. *Palestine in the Late Ottoman Period: Political, Social and Economic Transformation* (Jerusalem: Yad Izhak Ben Zvi, 1986).

Laskier, Michael. *Israel and the Maghreb: From Statehood to Oslo* (Gainesville: University Press of Florida, 2004).

Lehn, W., and U. Davis. *The Jewish National Fund* (London: Kegan Paul International, 1988).

Le Strange, G. *Palestine Under the Moslems* (London: A. P. Watt, 1890).

Lewis, B. L. *The Middle East and the West* (Bloomington: Indiana University Press, 1964).

Lockman, Z., and J. Beinin, eds. *Intifada: The Palestinian Uprising Against Israeli Occupation* (Boston: South End Press, 1989).

Luciani, G., ed. *The Arab State* (Berkeley: University of California Press, 1990).

Lustick, I. S., ed. *The Conflict with Israel in Arab Politics and Society* (New York: Garland, 1994).

_____. *From Wars Toward Peace in the Arab-Israeli Conflict 1969–1993* (New York: Garland, 1994).

Lutsky, V. *Modern History of the Arab Countries* (Moscow: Progress House, 1971).

Mallison, W. T., and S. V. Mallison. *The Palestine Problem in International Law and World Order* (New York: Longman, 1986).

Mandel, N. *The Arabs and Zionism Before World War I* (Berkeley: University of California Press, 1976).

Ma'oz, M. *Ottoman Reform in Syria and Palestine, 1840–1861: The Impact of the Tanzimat on Politics and Society* (Oxford: Oxford University Press, 1968).

_____, ed. *Studies on Palestine During the Ottoman Period* (Jerusalem: Magnes Press, 1975).

_____, and Sari Nusseibeh. *Jerusalem: Points of Friction—And Beyond* (The Hague: Kluwer Law International, 2000).

Masalha, Nur. *Imperial Israel and the Palestinians: The Politics of Expansion* (London: Pluto Press, 2000).

_____. *A Land Without a People: Israel, Transfer and the Palestinians* (London: Faber and Faber, 1997).

_____. *The Politics of Denial: Israel and the Palestinian Refugee Problem* (London and Sterling, VA: Pluto Press, 2003).

Mattar, P. *The Mufti of Jerusalem* (New York: Columbia University Press, 1992).

Migdal, J. S., ed. *Palestinian Society and Politics* (Princeton, NJ: Princeton University Press, 1980).

Miller, Y. N. *Government and Society in Rural Palestine, 1920–1948* (Austin: University of Texas Press, 1985).

Morris, B. *The Birth of the Palestine Refugee Problem, 1947–1949* (Cambridge: Cambridge University Press, 1987).

_____. *1948 and After* (New York: Oxford University Press, 1990).

Muslih, M. Y. *The Origins of Palestinian Nationalism* (New York: Columbia University Press, 1988).

Naff, T., and R. Owen, eds. *Studies in Eighteenth Century Islamic History* (Carbondale: Southern Illinois University Press, 1977).

Nakhleh, N., and E. Zureik, eds. *The Sociology of the Palestinians* (London: Croom Helm, 1980).

Nassar, J. R. *The Palestine Liberation Organization* (New York: Praeger, 1991).

_____, and R. Heacock, eds. *Intifada: Palestine at the Crossroads* (New York: Praeger, 1990).

Nathan, R. A., O. Gass, and D. Creamer. *Palestine: Problem and Promise* (Washington, DC: Middle East Institute, 1946).

Nazzal, N. *The Palestinian Exodus from Galilee* (Beirut: Institute for Palestine Studies, 1978).

Nimr, I. al-. *History of Jabal Nablus and al-Balqa* (in Arabic) (Nablus: n.p., 1937; reprinted 1961).

Norton, A. R. *Amal and the Shi'a: Struggle for the Soul of Lebanon* (Austin: University of Texas Press, 1987).

_____, and M. H. Greenberg, eds. *The International Relations of the Palestine Liberation Organization* (Carbondale: Southern Illinois University Press, 1989).

O'Mahony, Anthony. *Palestinian Christians: Religion, Politics and Society in the Holy Land* (London: Melisende, 1999).

Ovensen, G. *Responding to Change, Trends in Palestinian Household Economy,* FAFO Report 166 (Oslo: FAFO, 1994).

Owen, R. *The Middle East in the World Economy, 1800–1914* (London: Methuen, 1981).

_____, ed. *Studies in the Economic History of Palestine in the Nineteenth and Twentieth Centuries* (Carbondale: Southern Illinois University Press, 1982).

Palumbo, M. *The Palestinian Catastrophe: The 1948 Expulsion of a People from Their Homeland* (London: Quartet Books, 1987).

Peretz, D. *Intifada: The Palestinian Uprising* (Boulder, CO: Westview Press, 1990).

_____. *Israel and the Palestinian Arabs* (Washington, DC: Middle East Institute, 1958).

Peteet, J. *Gender in Crisis: Women and the Palestinian Resistance Movement* (New York: Columbia University Press, 1991).

Petran, T. *The Struggle over Lebanon* (New York: Monthly Review Press, 1987).

Polk, W. E., and R. L. Chambers, eds. *Beginnings of Modernization in the Middle East* (Chicago: University of Chicago Press, 1968).

Porath, Y. *The Emergence of the Palestinian Arab National Movement, 1918–1929* (London: Frank Cass, 1974).

_____. *The Palestinian Arab National Movement, from Riots to Rebellion* (London: Frank Cass, 1977).

Quandt, W. B., F. Jabber, and A. M. Lesch. *The Politics of Palestinian Nationalism* (Berkeley: University of California Press, 1973).

Qubain, F. *Crisis in Lebanon* (Washington, DC: Middle East Institute, 1961).

Qumsiyeh, Mazin B. *Sharing the Land of Canaan: Human Rights and the Israeli-Palestinian Struggle* (London: Pluto Press; Ann Arbor: University of Michigan Press, 2004).

Ramini, A. al-. *Nablus in the Nineteenth Century* (in Arabic) (Amman: Dar al-Sha'ab, 1979).

Rayyes, R. N. el-, and D. Nahhas. *Guerrillas for Palestine: A Study of the Palestinian Commando Organizations* (Beirut: An-Nahar Press, 1974).

Rouhana, Nadim N. *Palestinian Citizens in an Ethnic Jewish State: Identities in Conflict* (New Haven, CT: Yale University Press, 1997).

Roy, S. *The Gaza Strip: The Political Economy of De-development* (Washington, DC: Institute for Palestine Studies, 1995).

Rubenberg, C. *The Palestine Liberation Organization: Its Institutional Infrastructure* (Belmont, MA: Institute for Arab Studies, 1983).

Rubin, B. *Revolution Until Victory? The Politics and History of the PLO* (Cambridge, MA: Harvard University Press, 1994).

_____. *The Transformation of Palestinian Politics: From Revolution to State-Building* (Cambridge, MA: Harvard University Press, 1999).

Runciman, S. *History of the Crusades* (Cambridge: Cambridge University Press, 1952).

Rustum, A. J. *The Royal Archives of Egypt and the Disturbances in Palestine, 1834* (Beirut: American University of Beirut, 1938).

Said, E. W., with photographs by Jean Mohr. *After the Last Sky* (London: Faber and Faber, 1986).

_____. *Orientalism* (New York: Pantheon, 1978).

_____. *Peace and Its Discontents: Essays on Palestine in the Middle East Peace Process* (New York: Vintage, 1995).

_____. *The Politics of Dispossession: The Struggle for Palestinian Self-Determination, 1969–1994* (New York: Pantheon, 1994).

_____. *The Question of Palestine* (New York: Vintage, 1980).

_____, and C. Hitchens, eds. *Blaming the Victims* (London: Verso, 1988).

Samara, Adel. *Epidemic of Globalization: Ventures in World Order, Arab Nation and Zionism* (Glendale, CA: Palestine Research and Publishing Foundation, 2001).

Sayigh, R. *Palestinians: From Peasants to Revolutionaries* (London: Zed, 1979).

_____. *Too Many Enemies: The Palestinian Experience in Lebanon* (London: Zed, 1994).

Schölch, A. *Palestine in Transformation, 1856–1882: Studies in Social, Economic and Political Development*, translated by W. C. Young and M. C. Gerrity (Washington, DC: Institute for Palestine Studies, 1993).

Segal, Rafi, and Eyal Wezman. *A Civilian Occupation: The Politics of Israeli Architecture* (London: Verso, 2003).

Seikaly, M. *Haifa: Transformation of an Arab Society, 1918–1939* (London: I. B. Tauris, 1995).

Semyonov, M., and N. L. Epstein. *Hewers of Wood and Drawers of Water: Noncitizen Arabs in the Israeli Labor Market*, Report 13 (New York: Cornell International Industrial and Labor Relations, 1987).

Shafir, G. *Land, Labor and the Origins of Israeli-Palestinian Conflict, 1882–1914* (Cambridge: Cambridge University Press, 1989).

Sharabi, H. *Arab Intellectuals and the West: The Formative Years, 1875–1914* (Baltimore: Johns Hopkins University Press, 1970).

_____. *Governments and Politics of the Middle East in the Twentieth Century* (Princeton, NJ: Van Nostrand, 1962).

Shehadeh, Raja. *When the Birds Stopped Singing: Life in Ramallah Under Siege* (South Royalton, VT: Steerforth Press, 2003).

Shipler, D. *Arab and Jew: Wounded Spirits in a Promised Land* (New York: Penguin, 1987).

Shlaim, A. *Collusion Across the Jordan: King Abdullah, the Zionist Movement, and the Partition of Palestine* (New York: Columbia University Press, 1988).

_____. *The Politics of Partition: King Abdullah, the Zionists and Palestine, 1921–1951* (New York: Columbia University Press, 1990).

Smith, B. J. *The Roots of Separatism in Palestine, British Economic Policy, 1920–1929* (Syracuse, NY: Syracuse University Press, 1993).

Smith, C. D. *Palestine and the Arab-Israeli Conflict* (New York: St. Martin's Press, 1988).

Smith, P. A. *Palestine and the Palestinians, 1876–1983* (New York: St. Martin's Press, 1984).

Stein, K. W. *The Land Question in Palestine* (Chapel Hill: University of North Carolina Press, 1984).

Stoyanovsky, J. *The Mandate for Palestine: A Contribution to the Theory and Practice of International Mandates* (Westport, CT: Hyperion Press, 1976).

Swedenburg, T. R. *Memories of Revolt: The 1936–1939 Rebellion and the Palestinian National Past* (Minneapolis: University of Minnesota Press, 1995).

Szerezewski, R. *Essays on the Structure of the Jewish Economy in Palestine and Israel* (Jerusalem: Maurice Falk Institute, 1968).

Tibawi, A. L. *Arab Education in Mandatory Palestine: A Study of Three Decades of British Administration* (London: Luzac, 1956).

Turki, F. *The Disinherited, Journal of a Palestinian Exile* (New York: Monthly Review Press, 1972).

Usher, G. *Palestine in Crisis: The Struggle for Peace and Political Independence* (London: Pluto Press, 1995).

Vital, D. *The Origins of Zionism* (Oxford: Oxford University Press, 1975).

Wallach, J., and J. Wallach. *The New Palestinians: The Emerging Generation of Leaders* (Rocklin, CA: Prima Publishers, 1992).

Warriner, D. *Land and Poverty in the Middle East* (London: Royal Institute of International Affairs, 1948).

Wasserstein, Bernard. *Divided Jerusalem: The Struggle for the Holy City* (New Haven, CT: Yale University Press, 2001).

Wolfsfeld, Gadi. *Media and the Path to Peace* (Cambridge and New York: Cambridge University Press, 2004).

Wolkenson, Benjamin W. *Arab Employment in Israel: The Quest for Equal Employment Opportunity* (Westport, CT: Greenwood Press, 1999).

Zureik, E. *The Palestinians in Israel: A Study in Internal Colonialism* (London: Routledge & Kegan Paul, 1979).

Documents and Reports

Amnesty International. *Human Rights in the Gaza Strip and Jericho Under Palestinian Self-Rule* 6, 10 (September 1994).

_____. *Trial at Midnight: Secret, Summary, Unfair Trials in Gaza* (London: Amnesty International, 1995).

Anglo-American Committee of Inquiry. *A Survey of Palestine,* Vol. 1 (1945–1946; reprint, Washington, DC: Institute for Palestine Studies, 1991).

Barron, J. B. *Palestine: Report and General Abstracts of the Census of 1922* (Jerusalem: Government of Palestine, 1923).

B'Tselem (Israeli Information Center for Human Rights in the Occupied Territories). September and November 1994 reports.

Center for Palestine Research and Studies, Nablus (West Bank). "Palestinian Public Opinion Poll III," September 1995.

Economic Intelligence Unit. *Israel/The Occupied Territories, 1993–94* (London: Economic Intelligence Unit, 1994).

Elmusa, S. S. *The Water Issue and the Palestinian-Israeli Conflict* (Washington, DC: Center for Policy Analysis on Palestine, 1993).

Facts and Figures About the Palestinians (Washington, DC: Center for Policy Analysis on Palestine, 1993).

Foundation for Middle East Peace. *Report on Israeli Settlement in the Occupied Territories* 5, 5 (September 1995).

Gaza Center for Rights and Law (Affiliate of the International Commission of Jurists, Geneva). *Monthly Report,* May 1994; June/July 1994.

Hope Simpson, John. *Palestine, Report on Immigration, Land Settlement and Development* [Hope Simpson Report] (London: His Majesty's Stationery Office, 1930).

Human Rights Watch/Middle East. *Torture and Ill-Treatment: Israel's Interrogation of Palestinians from the Occupied Territories* (New York: Human Rights Watch, 1994).

Israel, Ministry of Foreign Affairs. *Israeli-Palestinian Interim Agreement on the West Bank and Gaza Strip,* September 28, 1995. Accessible on the Internet through the Israel Information Service Gopher, ask@israel-info.gov.il.

Kossaifi, G. F. *The Palestinian Refugees and the Right of Return* (Washington, DC: Center for Policy Analysis on Palestine, 1996).

Kubursi, A. *Palestinian Losses in 1948: The Quest for Precision* (Washington, DC: Center for Policy Analysis on Palestine, 1996).

Lesch, A. M. "The Palestinian Uprising—Causes and Consequences," UFSI Report 1 (Washington, DC: Universities Field Staff International, 1988–1989).

Palestine Human Rights Information Center, Jerusalem/Washington. *The Washington Report on Middle East Affairs* 13, 1 (June 1994).

Sayigh, Y. *Programme for Development of the Palestinian National Economy for the Years 1994–2000, Executive Summary* (Tunis: PLO, 1993).

Statistical Abstract of Palestine, 1944–1945 (Jerusalem: Government of Palestine, 1946).

United Nations. *The Origins and Evolution of the Palestine Problem, 1917–1988* (New York: United Nations, 1990).

_____. *Report of the Commissioner-General of the UNRWA in the Near East, 1 July 1992–30 June 1993* (New York: United Nations, 1994).

United Nations Commission for Western Asia. *Statistical Abstract of the Study on the Economic and Social Situation and Potential of the Palestinian Arab People in the Region of Western Asia* (New York: United Nations, 1983).

United Nations Conference on Trade and Development. "The Palestinian Financial Sector Under Israeli Occupation," UNCTAD/ST/SEU/3, Geneva, July 8, 1987.

_____. "Prospects for Sustained Development of the Palestinian Economy in the West Bank and Gaza Strip," UNCTAD/DSD/SEU/2, Geneva, September 27, 1993.

Uteibi, Y. J. el-, and M. Amous. "Jordanian Returnees Profile." Photocopy, Returnees Compensation Center, the Hashemite Charity Organization, Geneva, 1993.

World Bank. *Developing the Occupied Territories: An Investment in Peace,* 7 vols. (Washington, DC: World Bank, 1993).

Journal Articles, Conference Papers, and Other Sources

Abed, G. T. "Developing the Palestinian Economy." *Journal of Palestine Studies* 23, 4 (Summer 1994): 41–51.

_____. "The Political Economy of Development in the West Bank and Gaza Strip." Paper delivered at the Workshop on Strategic Visions for the Middle East and North Africa, Economic Research Forum, Gammarth, Tunisia, June 9–11, 1995.

Abu-Amr, Z. "Hamas: A Historical and Political Background." *Journal of Palestine Studies* 22, 4 (Summer 1993): 5–19.

_____. "Report from Palestine." *Journal of Palestine Studies* 24, 2 (Winter 1995): 40–47.

Abu-Khalil, A. "The Palestinian-Shi'ite War in Lebanon." *Third World Affairs* (1988): 77–89.

Abu-Lughod, I. "Educating a Community in Exile: The Palestinian Experience." *Journal of Palestine Studies* 2, 3 (Spring 1973).

Abu-Lughod, J. L. "The Demographic Transformation of Palestine: Relevance for Planning Palestine Open University," in *Palestine Open University Feasibility Study,* Part 2 (Paris: UNESCO, 1980): i–xxii, 1–91.

_____. "Palestinians: Exiles at Home and Abroad." *Current Sociology* 36 (Summer 1988): 61–69.

Amin, S. "After Gaza and Jericho: The New Palestinian-Middle Eastern Problem." *Beirut Review* 8 (Fall 1994): 113–120.

Aronson, G. "'Final Status' to Preserve Settlements." *Report on Israeli Settlement in the Occupied Territories* 5, 3 (May 1995).

_____. "Historic Israeli-PLO Accord Leaves Settlements Intact." *Report on Israeli Settlement in the Occupied Territories* 4, 4 (July 1994).

Aruri, N. H. "Early Empowerment: The Burden not the Responsibility." *Journal of Palestine Studies* 24, 2 (Winter 1995): 33–39.

_____, and J. J. Carroll. "A New Palestinian Charter." *Journal of Palestine Studies* 23, 4 (Summer 1994): 5–17.

Aruri, T. "Some Expected Political Consequences from Establishing an Elected Palestinian Council." Paper presented at a workshop of the Palestinian People's Party, August 18, 1995.

_____. "Some Features of Palestinian Political Life and Its Future." Paper presented at a workshop, Muwaten Institute, Jerusalem, August 8, 1995.

Asad, T. "Anthropological Texts and Ideological Problems: An Analysis of Cohen on Arab Border Villages in Israel." *Review of Middle East Studies* 1 (1975): 1–40.

Badran, N. "The Means of Survival: Education and the Palestinian Community, 1948–67." *Journal of Palestine Studies* 9, 4 (Summer 1980): 44–74.

———. "The Palestinian Countryside Before World War I" (in Arabic). *Palestine Affairs* 7 (March 1972).

Barkan, O. L. "The Price Revolution of the Sixteenth Century: A Turning Point in the Economic History of the Near East." *International Journal of Middle East Studies* 6 (January 1975): 3–28.

Ben-Arieh, Y. "The Growth of Jerusalem in the Nineteenth Century." *Annals of the Association of American Geographers* 65 (1975).

Bishara, A. "Only Two Alternatives Remain: The Bantustan Plan or the Bi-National Option." *News from Within* 11, 7 (July 1995): 14–17.

Bowersock, G. W. "Palestine: Ancient History and Modern Politics." *Journal of Palestine Studies* 14, 4 (Summer 1985): 49–57.

Brynen, R. "The Dynamics of Palestinian Elite Formation." *Journal of Palestine Studies* 24, 3 (Spring 1995): 31–43.

Buheiry, M. "The Agricultural Exports of Southern Palestine, 1885–1914." *Journal of Palestine Studies* 10, 4 (Summer 1981): 61–81.

Caradon, Lord. "The Palestinians: Their Place in the Middle East." Paper presented at the annual conference of the Middle East Institute, Washington, DC, September 30–October 1, 1977.

Childers, E. "The Other Exodus." *Spectator* (May 12, 1961).

Cockburn, A. "Why Say No?" *Nation* (October 4, 1993): 342–343.

Cohen, S. "Justice in Transition." *Middle East Report* 194/195 (May-June/July-August 1995): 2–5.

Connell, D. "Palestine on the Edge, Crisis in the National Movement." *Middle East Report* 194/195 (May-June/July-August 1995): 6–9.

Dabdoub, L. "Palestinian Public Opinion Polls on the Peace Process." *Palestine-Israel: Journal of Politics, Economics and Culture* 5 (Winter 1995): 60–63.

Dajani, B. "The September 1993 Israeli-PLO Documents: A Textual Analysis." *Journal of Palestine Studies* 23, 3 (Spring 1994): 5–23.

Dehter, A. "How Expensive Are West Bank Settlements?" *The West Bank Data Project* (Jerusalem: Jerusalem Post, 1987): 3.

Diwan, I., and M. Walton. "Palestine Between Israel and Jordan: The Economics of an Uneasy Triangle." *Beirut Review* 8 (Fall 1994): 21–43.

Doumani, B. B. "The Political Economy of Population Counts in Ottoman Palestine: Nablus Circa 1850." *International Journal of Middle East Studies* 26, 1 (February 1994): 1–17.

Drake, L. "Between the Lines: A Textual Analysis of the Gaza-Jericho Agreement." *Arab Studies Quarterly* 16, 4 (Fall 1994): 1–36.

Dumper, M. T. "Jerusalem's Infrastructure: Is Annexation Irreversible?" *Journal of Palestine Studies* 22, 3 (Spring 1993): 78–95.

Elmusa, S., and M. El-Jaafari. "Power and Trade: The Israeli-Palestinian Economic Protocol." *Journal of Palestine Studies* 24, 2 (Winter 1995): 14–32.

Erakat, S. "Preparation for Elections," in *Palestinian Elections* (Washington, DC: Center for Policy Analysis on Palestine, 1995).

Farsoun, S. K. "Oil, State and Social Structure in the Middle East." *Arab Studies Quarterly* 10, 2 (Spring 1988): 155–175.

———, and W. Carroll. "The Civil War in Lebanon: Sect, Class, and Imperialism." *Monthly Review* 28, 2 (June 1976): 12–37.

———, and J. M. Landis. "Structures of Resistance and the 'War of Position': A Case Study of the Palestinian Uprising." *Arab Studies Quarterly* 11, 4 (Fall 1989): 59–86.

———, and R. B. Wingerter. "The Palestinians in Lebanon." *School of Advanced International Studies Review* 3 (Winter 1981/1982): 93–106.

_____, and C. Zacharia. "Class, Economic Change and Democratization in the Arab World," in R. Brynen, B. Korany, and P. Noble, eds., *Political Liberalization and Democratization in the Arab World,* Vol. 1 (Boulder, CO: Lynne Rienner, 1995).

Finkelstein, N. G. "Whither the 'Peace Process'?" Paper presented at Georgetown and American Universities, Washington, DC, April 24 and 25, 1996.

Freedmen, W. "An Export Promotion Scheme for Palestine." *Graduate Review* 1, 6 (American University, 1994): 34–45.

Gerber, H. "Modernization in Nineteenth Century Palestine: The Role of Foreign Trade." *Middle Eastern Studies* 18 (July 1982): 250–264.

Halevi, N. "The Political Economy of Absorptive Capacity: Growth and Cycles in Jewish Palestine Under the British Mandate." *Middle Eastern Studies* 19 (October 1983): 456–469.

Hijjawi, S. "The Palestinians in Lebanon" (in Arabic). *Journal of the Center for Palestinian Studies* (Baghdad) 22 (May-June 1977).

Hoexter, M. "The Role of Qays and Yaman Factions in Local Political Divisions: Jabal Nablus Compared with the Judean Hills in the First Half of the Nineteenth Century." *Asian and African Studies* 9 (Fall 1973): 249–311.

Hout, B. N. al-. "The Palestinian Political Elite During the Mandate Period." *Journal of Palestine Studies* 9, 1 (Autumn 1979): 85–111.

Hudson, M. C. "The Palestinian Arab Resistance Movement: Its Significance in the Middle East Crisis." *Middle East Journal* 23, 3 (Summer 1969).

Jabber, F. "The Arab Regimes and the Palestinian Revolution." *Journal of Palestine Studies* 2, 2 (Winter 1973): 79–101.

Jenin, J. "Economic Wedlock: Israel to Keep Upper Hand. Breaking the Siege," *Newsletter of the Middle East Justice Network* 6, 2 (June-July 1994).

Khalidi, A. "The Palestinians: Current Dilemmas, Future Challenges." *Journal of Palestine Studies* 24, 2 (Winter 1995): 5–13.

Khalidi, R. "A Palestinian View of the Accord with Israel." *Current History* 93, 580 (February 1994): 62–66.

_____. "The Role of the Press in the Early Arab Reaction to Zionism." *Peuples Méditerranéens/Mediterranean Peoples* (July-September 1982).

Khalidi, T. "Palestinian Historiography: 1900–1948." *Journal of Palestine Studies* 10, 3 (Spring 1981): 59–76.

Khalidi, W. "Plan Dalet: The Zionist Masterplan for the Conquest of Palestine, 1948." *Middle East Forum* (November 1961): 22–28.

Kimmerling, B. "Sociology, Ideology and Nation Building: The Palestinians in Israeli Sociology." *American Sociological Review* 57 (August 1992): 446–460.

Maksoud, C. "Peace Process or Puppet Show?" *Foreign Policy* 100 (Fall 1995): 117–124.

Mandell, J. "Gaza: Israel's Soweto." *Middle East Report* 136/137 (October-December 1985): 7–19, 58.

McTague, J. J., Jr. "The British Military Administration in Palestine, 1917–1920." *Journal of Palestine Studies* 7, 3 (Spring 1978): 55–76.

Metzer, J. "Economic Structure and National Goals—The Jewish National Home in Interwar Palestine." *Journal of Economic History* 38 (March 1978): 101–119.

_____. "Fiscal Incidence and Resource Transfer Between Jews and Arabs in Mandatory Palestine." *Research in Economic History* 7 (1982): 87–132.

Moughrabi, F. "American Public Opinion and the Palestine Question," Occasional Paper 4 (Washington, DC: International Center for Research and Public Policy, 1986).

Murphy, E. "Stacking the Deck: The Economics of the Israel-PLO Accords." *Middle East Report* 194/195 (May-June/July-August 1995): 35–38.

Nakhleh, K. "Anthropological and Sociological Studies on the Arabs in Israel: A Critique." *Journal of Palestine Studies* 6, 4 (Summer 1977): 41–70.

Ogram, P. "Settlement Expansion." *Middle East Report* 194/195 (May-June/July-August 1995): 17.

Owen, R. "Establishing a Viable Palestinian Economy." *Beirut Review* 8 (Fall 1994): 45–57.

Peled, Y. "From Zionism to Capitalism." *Middle East Report* 194/195 (May-June/July-August 1995): 13–17.

Rabbani, M. "Palestinian Authority, Israeli Rule: From Transitional to Permanent Arrangement." *Middle East Report* 201 (October-December 1996): 2–6.

Reilly, J. "The Peasantry of Late Ottoman Palestine." *Journal of Palestine Studies* 10, 4 (Summer 1981): 82–97.

Rishmawi, M. "The Actions of the Palestinian Authority Under the Gaza/Jericho Agreements." *The Palestine National Authority: A Critical Appraisal* (Washington, DC: Center for Policy Analysis on Palestine, 1995).

Ryan, S. "The West Bank and Gaza: Political Consequences of the Intifada." *Middle East Report* 74 (January 1979): 3–8.

Said, E. W. "The Mirage of Peace." *Nation* (October 16, 1995): 413–420.

_____. "Symbols Versus Substance: A Year After the Declaration of Principles." *Journal of Palestine Studies* 24, 2 (Winter 1995): 60–72.

Schölch, A. "Britain in Palestine, 1838–1882: The Roots of the Balfour Policy." *Journal of Palestine Studies* 22, 1 (Autumn 1992).

Sharif, M. al-. "A Contribution to the Study of the Process of the Emergence of the Arab Labor Movement in Palestine" (in Arabic). *Samed al-Iqtisadi* 26 (July 1980).

_____, and N. Badran. "Emergence and Evolution of the Palestinian Working Class" (in Arabic). *Samed al-Iqtisadi* 27 (April 1981).

Shlaim, A. "The Founding of Israel." *Commentary* 89 (February 1990).

Singer, J. "The Declaration of Principles on Interim Self-Government Arrangements, Some Legal Aspects." *Justice* (February 1994): 4–13.

Tamari, S. "The Palestinian Demand for Independence Cannot Be Postponed Indefinitely," *Middle East Report and Information Project Reports* 100–101 (October-December 1981): 28–35.

Teveth, S. "Charging Israel with Original Sin." *Commentary* 88 (September 1989): 24–33.

_____. "The Palestine Arab Refugee Problem and Its Origins." *Middle Eastern Studies* 26 (April 1990): 214–249.

Tuma, E. H. "The Peace Negotiations, Economic Cooperation and Stability in the Middle East." *Beirut Review* 8 (Fall 1994): 3–20.

Usher, G. "Closures, Cantons and the Palestinian Covenant." *Middle East Report* 199 (April-June 1996): 33–37.

_____. "Palestinian Trade Unions and the Struggle for Independence." *Middle East Report* 194/195 (May-June/July-August, 1995): 20–24.

Wenger, M. "The Money Tree: US Aid to Israel." *Middle East Report* 164/165 (May-August 1990): 12–13.

Wing, A. K. "Legitimacy and Coercion: Legal Traditions and Legal Rules During the Intifada." *Middle East Policy* 2, 2 (1993): 87–103.

Zacharia, C. E. "Public Opinions of West Bank and Gaza Strip Palestinians Toward Participation in Elections" (Washington, DC: American University, Department of Sociology, 1995).

Zahlan, A. B., and E. Hagopian. "Palestine's Arab Population." *Journal of Palestine Studies* 3, 4 (Summer 1974): 32–73.

_____, and R. S. Zahlan. "The Palestinian Future: Education and Manpower." *Journal of Palestine Studies* 6, 4 (Summer 1977): 103–112.

Zureik, E. "Toward a Sociology of the Palestinians." *Journal of Palestine Studies* 7, 4 (Summer 1977): 3–16.

Index